Chinese Intellectual Property and Technology Laws

Chinese Intellectual Property and Technology Laws

Edited by

Rohan Kariyawasam

BSc, MA, Fulbright Cert (Harvard), Solicitor, FRSA, Professor of Law, Cardiff Law School, Cardiff University, UK and Visiting Professor, Peking Law School, Peking University (2010)

Edward Elgar

Cheltenham, UK • Northampton, MA, USA

Published by
Edward Elgar Publishing Limited
The Lypiatts
15 Lansdown Road
Cheltenham
Glos GL50 2JA
UK

Edward Elgar Publishing, Inc.
William Pratt House
9 Dewey Court
Northampton
Massachusetts 01060
USA

A catalogue record for this book
is available from the British Library

Library of Congress Control Number: 2011925744

MIX
Paper from
responsible sources
FSC® C018575

ISBN 978 1 84980 008 2 (cased)

Typeset by Servis Filmsetting Ltd, Stockport, Cheshire
Printed and bound by MPG Books Group, UK

Contents

Contributors

Jiang Zhipei, former Chief Justice of the IPR Tribunal of the Supreme People's Court. As one of the most distinguished experts in the area of intellectual property law, Dr. Jiang served as Commissioner of the Trial Committee and Chief Justice of the Third Civil Tribunal (Intellectual Property Right Tribunal) of the Supreme People's Court. He has retired recently from these posts. Dr. Jiang is the Vice President of the IPR Association of China Law Society, Deputy Managing Director of China Copyright Association and Vice President of AIPPI's China Branch. He is also the Executive Director of the China Intellectual Property Society and the China Science and Technology Law Academy, and the Director of the China Judge Academy. Dr. Jiang is an adjunct professor at China Renmin University, Beijing Foreign Studies University, National Judges College, China University of Political Science and Law, Wuhan University, and Huazhong University of Science and Technology, and a research fellow at China Renmin University's Commercial Law Research Foundation. He participated in the writing and editing of *The Intellectual Property Litigation; Internet and Electronic Business Law*; and *Application and Judicial Interpretation of Intellectual Property Law*, among others. In 1999, he founded the www.chinaiprlaw.cn website. Dr. Jiang received his Ph.D. degree in commercial law from China Renmin University.

Guo He is Professor of Law at Renmin Law School, Academic Supervisor for LL.D. Candidates, Assistant to the Dean, RUC Law School, Director, Intellectual Property Research Institute, RUC Law School, and Chief Curator, RUC Law Library. His appointments include Standing Council Member, Intellectual Property Law Research Association, China Law Society, Council Member, China Intellectual Property Society (CIPS), Council Member, Copyright Society of China (CSC), Panel Member, Domain Name Dispute Resolution Center, China International Economic and Trade Arbitration Commission (CIETAC), Council Member, National Technical Committee 463 on Product Defect and Safety Administration of Standardization Administration of China, Member, Inter-Ministerial Conference Office, National Promotion of Enterprises Usage of Genuine

Software Initiative, Member, Expert Committee, China Chamber of Commerce for Import and Export of Machinery and Electronic Products (CCCME).

Li Zuming is Associate Professor at the China University of Political Science and Law (Beijing) and Associate Director of the Institute of Intellectual Property Law. He is a member of the Expert Group for the State Intellectual Property Strategy and an expert of the Examination Group for Geographical Indications of General Administration of Quality Supervision, Inspection and Quarantine of the People's Republic of China. He also works as an advisory expert on China's public health policy for the Ministry of Health of the People's Republic of China and as a member of the Expert Group for Commercial Secrets of State Administration for Industry and Commerce, the Expert Committee of the China Trademark Association and the Council of the Intellectual Property Law Research Society. He is an Attorney of Law in China.

Li Yufeng is a Professor of Law and Director of the Intellectual Property Research Institute of the Southwest University of Political Science and Law (SWUPL), majoring in copyright law and trademark law. He is an arbitrator at Chongqing Arbitration Commission and a Director of the Intellectual Property Research Association of China Legal Society. He is also a member of the Expert Group of the Chongqing First Intermediate Court and a member of the Expert Group of the IPR Judicial Theory Committee of the Supreme People's Court of China.

Hu Kaizhong is a Professor at Zhongnan University of Economics and Law and is also a part-time researcher at the Intellectual Property Research Institute of Shanghai, and Director General of the Korea-China Intellectual Property Association of Korea. Professor Hu has published more than ten books, including a study on the hypothesis of rights, a comparative study on intellectual property, research on intangible property (composite work), research on basic questions of IPR (composite work) etc. and more than 50 academic articles in the *Study in Law and Business*, *Chinese Journal of Law*, *Science of Law* and other core journals.

Liu Xiaohai is Professor of Law at the Intellectual Property Institute and Chair Professor for the Bayer IP Foundation, at Tongji University. He graduated from Renmin University of China with a Bachelor of Law degree in 1983, and became a lecturer in the law department of Fudan University in Shanghai before going to Germany for further study, where he received his LL.M. in 1992 and a Doctorate in Law from Hamburg University in 1999. From 1996 to 1998 he studied at the Max Planck Institute for Intellectual Property Law in Munich.

Michael Pendleton is Professor of Intellectual Property Law at the Chinese University of Hong Kong. He is the leading academic authority on Hong Kong intellectual property law. He has researched, taught, and practised Hong Kong intellectual property law for more than 25 years and is one of the leading authorities on Chinese intellectual property law. His frequent co-author is the late Professor Zheng Chengsi, IP Institute, China Academy of Social Sciences, Beijing. Michael Pendleton graduated from Sydney University Faculty of Law in 1976 where he then taught for three years. He was appointed a member of the Copyright Law Review Committee (CLRC) by the Prime Minister of Australia in 2000 and again in 2003. He has held appointments on the Law Reform Commission of Hong Kong, Sub Committee on Privacy by Breach of Confidence Actions, and the Law Reform Commission of Hong Kong, Sub Committee on Copyright. He practised as a consultant solicitor for Blake Dawson Waldron, Deacons, Australia and Baker & Mckenzie, Hong Kong. He is the author of a treatise and nine books published by major international publishers and over 100 chapters, articles and papers on intellectual property.

Liu Chuntian is Professor of Law, Academic Supervisor for LL.D. Candidates, and Executive Director of the Intellectual Property Teaching and Research Center, Renmin Law School. He is also Executive Director of the Research Center for Civil and Commercial Law (Key Research Institute of Ministry of Education), Renmin Law School.

Zhang Ping holds a Ph.D. and is Professor at the Peking University Law School and Administrative Vice President, School of Intellectual Property Law, Peking University. She has been an active researcher on the frontiers of intellectual property since 1991 and has undertaken several key research projects for the Chinese government and multinationals. She has also served as the Secretary General of the Intellectual Property Association of Chinese Universities since 1998, Director of the Science and Technology Law Center of Peking University since 2008, Director of the Internet Law Center of Peking University Law School since 2005, and an expert arbitrator on the Asian Domain Name Dispute Resolution Center (ADNDRC) and the Beijing Arbitration Commission. She is a qualified patent agent and lawyer in the PRC besides being the editor-in-chief of several internet and IPR law journals.

Meng Zhaoping is Assistant Professor at Peking University Law School. He was a coordinator of the Peking University Law School *Yahoo* Internet Law Centre.

Cong Lixian is Professor at the law school of Beijing Foreign Studies University (BFSU) and is also a research fellow of the Center for Studies of Intellectual Property Rights at Zhongnan University of Economics and Law (CSIPR). He received his doctorate from the Institute of International Law at Wuhan University. Professor Cong is the director of the China Society of Private International Law (CSPIL). In recent years, Professor Cong has published more than 600,000 characters of legal research results and his research has won honors and rewards at provincial and ministerial level, and at the military level (colonel-level). Professor Cong has published dozens of academic papers in the core academic journals in China, such as *Law Review*, *China publishing Journal*, *Social Science Journal* and other publications, and more than ten books. Professor Cong has presided over or participated in more than ten national, provincial and ministerial research projects. His independent research project, 'A Study on Intellectual Property Protection of Chinese Traditional Superiority Domain,' won special funding from the First China Postdoctoral Science Foundation.

Huang Young is Professor of Economic Law at the University of International Business & Economics (Beijing) and Chairman of the Competition Law Centre (UIBE). He obtained his LL.B. from the Peking University of China and both an LL.M. and a Ph.D. from the University of International Business and Economics (UIBE). He also has the role of Dean of the Faculty of Economic Law. In February 2005, he was nominated as a member of the experts committee for the legislation of the Anti Monopoly Law (AML) by the Legal Affairs Office of the State Council. In July 2009, he was again chosen by the Legislative Affairs Commission of the National People's Congress as one of the legal experts for the AML legislation. He is legal consul to the Supreme People's Procuratorate for civil and administrative affairs, special supervisor to Beijing People's Procuratorate, arbitrator of the China International Economic and Trade Arbitration Commission (CIETAC), arbitrator of the Beijing Arbitration Commission, legal consul on insurance law for the China Insurance Regulatory Commission (CIRC), standing director of the Economic Law Research Academy of the China Law Science Association, and a member of the academic commission of the Jianhua Research Institute of the Renmin University.

Zhang Zhe obtained two Master's degrees in Law, respectively from Peking University (as J.M.) and from the University of Oxford (as Magister Juris). Currently, he is completing his Ph.D. in Law at the University of International Business and Economics, Beijing, China.

Xu Shiying is Professor of Law at the East China University of Political Science and Law (ECUPL) and Director of the Research Institute of Competition Law of ECUPL, People's Republic of China. She obtained her Bachelor of Economics at Shanghai University of Finance and Economics; she holds a Ph.D in Management Science from the Central South University Business School and has been a Visiting Scholar at the School of Law, Boston College, USA, 1990, a Senior Visiting Scholar at the School of Law, University of Tokyo, 1995, and a Visiting Professor at the University of Seoul, Korea, 2006. Professor Xu is the Executive Director, China Economic Law Studies Association (CELSA), Director, China WTO Study Association, a member of the Expert Group of Trade and Competition Policy, Commerce of the State Council of the PRC, and a Consultant Expert of the Commerce Commission of the municipal government of Shanghai, and arbitrator, Shanghai Arbitration Commission of China. She has written and contributed to over ten published monographs and textbooks.

Kong Qingjiang is the Dean of the Faculty of Law and Professor of International Economic Law at Zhejiang Gongshang University (Hangzhou). He has published over 20 articles in English in leading journals and has authored three books in English, including *China and the World Trade Organization: A Legal Perspective*. He was the winner of the prestigious Qian Duansheng Legal Scholarship Prize in 2007 and in 2008, and the An Zijie International Trade Scholarship Prize in 2004.

Jack Chang is the Senior IP Counsel of the General Electric Company for Asia, based in Shanghai, and the Chairman of the Quality Brands Protection Committee (QBPC), which was founded in March 2000 by 28 multinational brand owners and has now grown to an organization of 152 members dedicated to enhancing IP protection in China via the co-operational approach. Before joining GE in March 2006, Mr. Chang had worked for Johnson & Johnson since 1989 as an in-house legal counsel in Taiwan and was relocated to China in 1998. Mr. Chang was one of the QBPC founding members and served as the QBPC Legal Committee Chair in 2001, Vice Chair of the QBPC in 2002 and has been Chairman of the QBPC since 2003. He also chairs the Intellectual Property Sub-committee of AmCham Shanghai and is a guest researcher of the IP Center of East China University of Political Science & Law in Shanghai.

Helen Hui (assistant editor) works at the Confucius Institute, Cardiff University. Prior to coming to Cardiff, she was a senior consultant with the US management consultancy, APCO, in Beijing. Helen has worked as a consultant for HusonBay Consulting in Beijing and for the United Nation's International Labour Organization, Beijing. She holds a BA from Yan'an University and an LL.B. from Tsinghua University.

Rohan Kariyawasam (editor) is Professor of Commercial Law, Cardiff University. Prior to Cardiff, he was Director of the Program in Information Technology, E-Commerce & Media Law at the University of Essex. He qualified as a Solicitor with DentonWildeSapte (Denton Hall), working in their media, intellectual property, and communications law practice and then worked in private practice as a consultant for several law firms, including Field Fisher Waterhouse LLP and Clifford Chance LLP. In industry, he has worked in brand management with Unilever in the UK and as the Asia-Pacific Product Manager in Hong Kong and Malaysia for Northern Business Information, a strategic business technology research consultancy and subsidiary of McGraw-Hill Publishing. His career began as a telecommunications engineer at Marconi Underwater Systems. Rohan studied at Harvard Law School as a Berkman Fellow, at the University of Kent at Canterbury, the College of Law in London, and the Centre for Commercial Law Studies at Queen Mary University of London. In 2001, he was awarded a Fulbright Scholarship to Harvard. In 2006, he was elected a Fellow of the Royal Society of Arts (RSA). He has completed research projects for the ESRC, AHRC/AHRB, the World Bank, the Department for International Development, the Office of Communications (previously OFTEL in the UK), the European Commission, the Commonwealth Telecommunications Office, and Harvard Law School. He is the founding trustee to the Rahula Trust (http://www.rahula-trust.org), a UK registered charity, which provides sponsorship to poor, academically gifted children in the developing world. His research interests include the intersection of the law of intellectual property, technology, development, and world trade. In 2011, he was awarded a MC Fellowship by the British Academy to research the neutrality of the internet ('net neutrality') and electronic privacy.

Foreword

Jiang Zhipei

For over twenty years, I have been involved with trial work for Intellectual Property Rights (IPR) disputes and have witnessed over this time an important period in the development of IPRs in China. My experience indicates a very strong demand for the effective protection of IP worldwide. Although the modern IPR system in China started quite late, China spent three decades completing the modernization of its IPR system, whilst many Western countries achieved the same over two to three hundred years. In this respect, China's achievement has attracted worldwide attention.

The development of China's IPR system draws on the useful experience of other countries' IPR development. However, due to its own national conditions and the overall impact of its legal structures, the development of Chinese IPR law still retains many Chinese characteristics. In the process of global economic and trade integration, the differences between Western legal systems and China's systems and other interests have gained prominence, and this collision has at times created conflict that may lead to misunderstanding and friction. There is a real need therefore to understand and appreciate these differences objectively and accurately in order to maintain the legitimate rights and interests of all.

Using legal means to protect the interests of all parties, we need to have a full understanding of the rights of IP owners, specific remedies for infringement, and a country's legislative and judicial practice. In 2007, I met with the US chief IP Counsel of a major multinational at China's Supreme People's Court, and briefed him that China had been dealing with approximately 15,000 civil IPR cases a year, of which 95% were Chinese domestic litigation cases between Chinese companies and individuals, with less than 5% representing litigation between foreign and Chinese companies. The Chief Counsel was very surprised by this news because he thought the majority of IPR infringement cases in China would be cases with the foreign company as plaintiff suing Chinese companies. He kept asking: 'the figure of 95% of domestic cases is very hard to believe. Do these cases cover all aspects including patent, trademark and copyright?

Are Chinese companies willing to pay so much attention to self-developed patents?' I answered his question in detail and explained to him that the legal documents of these cases could be found on the relevant websites. He strongly recommended that the Chinese Government should make greater efforts to advertise its IPR development to the outside world in order to generate greater understanding of China's legislative instruments and judicial system on the protection of IPRs.

It has become very necessary to widely communicate to the outside world the great improvements and effort legislators have made in improving the IP system in China. China has a unique IPR protection system that involves both administrative and judicial protection. In this two-track protection system, judicial protection is dominant. With reform of the judicial system, IPR judicial protection will play an increasingly important role, assisted by administrative protection, which is better at dealing with infringements and is more efficient at preventing counterfeiting, piracy and other forms of infringement. Significantly, China's IPR administrative and judicial protection systems are not in conflict, but instead cooperate and complement each other.

In recent years, new issues are arising with the use of IP on the internet. Copyright in digital content has attracted a great deal of discussion. The obligation of internet service providers and the determination of their infringements are contentious issues, and this has generated much debate. In my view, an inappropriate response to this problem could cause further infringement, harm the rights' owner's interests or even harm the development of the internet information industry and the public right of access to information. According to Article 3 of Interpretations of the Supreme People's Court on Several Issues Concerning the Application of Law in the Trial of Cases Involving Copyright Disputes over Computer Networks (2000, amended in 2003 and 2006), 'In case an Internet Service Provider is involved in any other person's act of infringement on copyright through the network, or abets any other person to commit or assists any other person in committing an act of copyright infringement the people's court shall subject the Internet Service Provider and other doers or persons directly committing the infringing act to contributory infringement liabilities according to the provisions of Article 130 of the General Principles of the Civil Law'. This removes the concerns of the IP rights owner, as long as the internet service provider making the infringement is at fault; no matter whether the ISP is simply providing the hardware used to access content or provides the content directly, the ISP will have to bear civil liability. By contrast, if the ISP complies with the law, the ISP will enjoy the principle of being a 'safe harbor' and will be exempt from liability. Chinese judges have already tried to handle P2P (peer-to-peer) cases under the principle of 'joint liability' under China's civil law principles. As a result, China's laws and judicial practice of IPR protection in the electronic environment is attempting a unique and new way of dealing with online infringement. Because China is a statute law country, the judge always acts 'according to the law' in seeking the best way to resolve disputes under the existing legal framework, and by issuing judicial interpretations to constantly update the law. Also, the precedents of the Supreme People's Court plays an increasingly important guiding role, by making abstract legal norms become 'flesh and blood' and actively demonstrating the integrity of Chinese IP law. Therefore, for internet IP disputes, foreign readers should not only know the basic legal provisions, but must also pay attention to China's latest judicial precedents.

Multilateralism and globalization of trade has brought more opportunities to the Chinese economy, while a variety of competitive disputes have inevitably followed. The handling of unfair competition cases has always been a part of China's IPR protection system, including trade secrets, business names and well-known product names, packaging and get-up etc. In 2008, in order to balance the relationship between market players who enjoy monopoly positions and smaller undertakings, China adopted the Anti-Monopoly law of the People's Republic of China. In our Anti-Monopoly Law, we specially provide for regulating IP monopolistic behavior. Disputes arising under this law are heard by Chinese IP tribunals, because of the close relationship between IP rights and monopolies. All of this demonstrates that the increasingly complex and expanding scope of the Chinese IP system will require further progressive development.

The concept and awareness of IP in China has become increasingly popular, and many foreign companies are gaining better access to China's IP legislation and enforcement information. At the same time, it is important to introduce China's IPR legal protection system and law enforcement practices accurately in English, so that foreign friends who come to China for investment and cooperation have a better understanding of Chinese law. This book, *Chinese Intellectual Property and Technology Laws*, will play an important role as a bridge in introducing China's IP and technology laws to the world from an objective and practical viewpoint, with an accurate and comprehensive discussion of modern Chinese law. The book not only describes general copyright, patent, and trademark law, but also covers unfair competition, trade secrets, anti-monopoly law regarding IPR rights, and the role of IPRs in China's trade laws. The book not only describes traditional areas of IPR, but also the protection of IP in the electronic environment, including a discussion of information technology, computer software, telecommunications and e-commerce laws. This kind of panoramic view of China's IPR legislative environment is very rare and precious, and it is even more commendable that many of the book's contributors are some of China's leading IP legal experts and academics with a deep understanding of Chinese IP law, with their own unique insights on statute and case analysis, and who can help readers gain a comprehensive grasp of the IP legal framework and the model of IP protection in China. This book shows the world a unique legal perspective and the capability of in-depth insight, which has extremely far-reaching significance for the world in understanding Chinese IP as well as various other aspects of Chinese technology, trade and competition law.

Dr *Jiang Zhipei* (蒋志培), Former Chief Justice of the IPR Tribunal, PRC Supreme People's Court, Professor of Law

Table of Cases

Li Fangping v Beijing Branch of CNC (unreported at time of writing) **307–8, 314**
Linda Chih Ling Koo v Lam Tai Hing (1991–1992) 23 IPR 607 **202, 219**
Lion Laboratories v Evans [1984] 2 All ER 417 **224, 225**
Malone v Commissioner of Police [1979] Ch 344 **217**
Marion White v Frances [1972] 1 WLR 1423 **212**
Merchandising Corp of America v Harpbond [1983] FSR 32 (CA) **176**
Merrell Dow Pharmaceuticals Ltd v NH Norton & Co Ltd [1995] RPC 233 at p 241 (CA), upholding Aldous J at [1994] RPC 1 **195**
Metix v Maughan [1997] FSR 718 **176**
MGA Entertainment Inc v Yokon International Ltd & Ors, HCA No 4380 of 2003 'Excello' Trade Mark [1972] HKDCLR 67 **168–9**
Microsoft computer software infringement, filed in Shanghai Municipality Pudong New District People's Court 2008 **384**
Microsoft Corp (The Computing Technology Industry Association Inc and Others Intervening) v Commission of the European Communities (Software & Information Industry Association and Others, Intervening), Case T-201/04, [2007] 5CMLR 11, September 2007 **328**
Min Yue No 1, Guangdong Dongguan Intermediate People's Court criminal judgment (December 2009) **385**
Mitsubishi Rayon's acquisition of Lucite, MOFCOM Notice (2009) No 28 **306**
Morrison v Moat (1851) 9 Hare 241 **210, 221**
Naomi Campbell v Mirror Newspapers [2002] 2 All ER 120 **204**
Newspaper Licensing Agency Ltd v Marks & Spencer Plc [2001] Ch 257, [2000] 3 WLR 1256, [2001] RPC 5 (p 76) (CA) **185**
Nicrotherm v Percy [1957] RPC 207 **205**
Nordenfelt v Maxim Nordenfelt [1894] AC 535 **213–14**
Northern Office Microcomputers (Pty) Ltd v Rosenstein [1982] FSR 124 **208**
Nova Productions Ltd v Mazooma Games Ltd [2006] RPC 14 **179**
Novello & Co Ltd v Keith Prowse Music Publishing Co Ltd [2005] RPC 23 **180**
Novex Electronics Co Ltd v Wave-Sonic Electronics Ltd [1980] HKC 708 **176**
Ocular Sciences Ltd & Anor v Aspect Vision Care & Ors [1997] RPC 289 **182**
Oriental Press Group Ltd v Apple Daily Ltd [1997] 2 HKC 515 (CA); [1998] 4 HKC 131 (CFA) **176**
Oswald, Hickson, Collier & Co v Carter-Ruck, English Court of Appeal, 20 January 1982, unreported **215**

Table of national acts, regulations, notices and measures

Table of international conventions and treaties

1. Introduction

Rohan Kariyawasam[1]

This book is the first of its kind to introduce Chinese intellectual property (IP) and technology laws in a single volume in English. Its unique perspective for a book covering intellectual property law is that it also includes chapters on competition and trade law, and provides as full a spectrum as possible of Chinese legislation which impacts on the regulation of telecommunications, information technology and electronic commerce.

The first eight chapters focus on intellectual property. The remaining chapters look at the regulation of technology, competition and trade. The aim of the book is to introduce readers to the rich mix of Chinese IP and technology laws currently undergoing rapid reform and to discuss appropriate case law where relevant.

China is quickly moving from 'made in China' to 'created in China' and with this change comes an incredible rate of change of amendments to IP and other laws that impact on the delivery of content over the Internet. Added to this process of change is China's unique system of law that has origins in Confucian thought, but with overtones of Japanese and German influence in China's more recent history. There exists a complex mix of administrative, civil and criminal law. The country's unique 'one country, two systems' approach, which provides a differentiated autonomy in China's special administrative regions of Hong Kong, Macau and Tibet, also gives its law making processes a special 'Chinese Flavour'. This is particularly the case in the telecommunications sector. The current Telecommunications Regulations 2000 ('Regulations'), for example, are not laws, but *administrative* regulations. The impact of this distinction lies in the hierarchy of legislative instruments used in Chinese legal practice. So for example, the National People's Congress (NPC) is the highest authority and has responsibility for any amendments to the Chinese Constitution. Both the NPC and its Standing Committee are responsible for the enactment and amendment of laws. The State Council is the government of the People's Republic of China under the authority

---

1 Professor of Law, Cardiff Law School, Cardiff University.

of Articles 85–98 of the Chinese Constitution (1982).[2] Under Article 85 of the Constitution, the State Council is the highest organ of state power, and of state administration. The State Council consists of the Premiers, Vice-Premiers, State Councillors, Ministers in charge of ministries, Ministers in charge of commissions, the Auditor-General and the Secretary-General. Under Article 86, the State Council has a term of office of five years.

The State Council formulates administrative regulations according to the Constitution and laws. The State Council will often enact administrative regulations, including ordinances, measures, provisions, rules and decisions, with a formal law (through the NPC) generally following afterwards. Local law/regulations are enacted by local people's congresses: departmental regulations are enacted by the separate ministries (e.g., MIIT, MOFCOM etc.) and which fall under the jurisdiction of the State Council. Therefore, the general hierarchy of laws in China is the Constitution; NPC Laws; State Council Administrative regulations; local laws/regulations and departmental regulations. If there is any conflict between local laws/regulations and departmental regulations, the State Council will decide which law/regulation/measure etc., will apply.[3]

The Chinese judiciary, or system of courts, is also hierarchical. In several sections of this book, particularly the IP sections, there are references to both courts and procuratorates. Articles 123–135 of the Constitution govern the judicial system of the PRC, and consist of the people's courts, the Supreme People's Court, the people's procuratorates, the Supreme People's Procuratorate, military procuratorates and other special people's procuratorates. At the top is the Supreme People's Court (SPC), the Higher People's Courts, the Intermediate People's Courts, and then the Basic People's Courts at the lowest level. Article 129 Constitution refers to the people's procuratorates as 'state organs for legal supervision'. The Supreme People's Procuratorate reports to the NPC and its Standing Committee and is the highest prosecutorial agency in China,

---

[2] An English version of the Chinese Constitution (adopted by the fifth National People's Congress on 4 December 1982 and revised 1988, 1993, 1999, and 2004) can be viewed at: http://english.people.com.cn/constitution/constitution.html, accessed November 2010.

[3] For a more detailed treatment of Chinese civil, administrative and criminal law (in English), including the court system, please see: Bin Liang, *The Changing Chinese Legal System, 1978 – Present*, London: Routledge, 2007; Daniel C. K. Chow, *The Legal System of the People's Republic of China in a Nutshell*, St Paul, Minn.: West, 2003; Donald C. Clarke, *China's Legal System: New Developments, New Challenges,* Cambridge: Cambridge University Press, 2008. Also, for a complete discussion of these issues (in Chinese) see: http://www.sypf.com/fzxw/pfcz01/074.htm, accessed November 2010.

exercising and supervising prosecutorial authority at all state and local levels. Procuratorates investigate cases brought by public security agencies to decide if a suspect should be arrested or not, and whether a case should be prosecuted. Procuratorates are *not* courts, but they support the work of the courts (similar perhaps to the UK's Crown Prosecution Service). They institute and support public prosecutions in criminal cases.[4]

It is also highly significant that the NPC has the power to withdraw departmental or local administrative laws, regulations, measures etc., that contravene laws already issued by the NPC. This power of the NPC illustrates well the internal dynamics of China's legislative structure – it is one primarily of subordination, unification and supervision, and quite unlike the internal dynamics of Western structures, which tend more to represent a relationship of restraint and legislative balance between the legislature, judiciary and executive.[5] Further, no Chinese administrative or local law, measure, regulation, rule or ordinance is allowed to contravene the state Constitution and state law. Though with some exceptions, some laws and regulations of the autonomous regions may differ from the Constitution and state law, [6] although in the drafting of such laws, regional legislative institutions must abide by the Constitution, the Law of Self-government in Minority Autonomous Regions (1984, amended 2001) and the Legislation Law of the People's Republic of China (2000), and report to the NPC's Standing Committee for prior approval.[7] The great variety of legislative instruments is seen in several of the chapters that follow, but particularly in patents, copyright, and telecommunications.

The IP chapters of the book start with a discussion of patents by Professor Guo He (Renmin University) in Chapter 2. Professor He writes on the new Patent Law (2008) ('New Patent Law'), which amongst its major amendments introduces new provisions on employee remuneration for patent inventions. Recently, the Chinese Supreme People's Court ('SPC') has issued regulations on the implementation of the Patent Law 2008, which include the Interpretation on the Application of Law

---

[4] For an overview see, *LawInfoChina*, a brief introduction (in English) at: http://www.lawinfochina.com/Legal/index.asp, accessed November 2010.

[5] See China's current legislation and structure (in English) at: http://www.china.org.cn/english/kuaixun/76212.htm, accessed November 2010.

[6] There are five autonomous regions in China: the Tibetans in Tibet, the Zhuangs in Guangxi, the Uyghurs in Xinjiang, the Mongols in Inner Mongolia, and the Huis in Ningxia. See Wikipedia at: http://en.wikipedia.org/wiki/Autonomous_regions_of_the_People's_Republic_of_China, accessed November 2010.

[7] China's current legislation and structure (English) at: http://www.china.org.cn/english/kuaixun/76212.htm, accessed November 2010.

concerning Several Issues in Handling Patent Infringement Disputes ('Interpretation Rules', effective January 2010) and also revision of the Rules for Implementation of the Patent Law of PRC ('Implementation Rules', effective 1 February 2010). The Interpretation Rules cover guidelines for the calculation of damages (particularly damages in relation to gains from infringement of the rights of the patent holder) and also rules on indirect infringement that are not covered in the New Patent Law. For indirect infringement, the use of a patented product as a component in the manufacture of another product, as well as the sale of manufactured products, is considered as indirect infringement. However, the rules introduce an exception for industrial designs, in that the manufacture of another product using an industrial design product as a component will not be considered as an infringement if the use is limited to the technical function of the product only. As regards the Implementation Rules, new provisions are included on service patents. The previous patent law did make provision for employees of Chinese state owned enterprises, but no detailed rules were given for companies other than state owned enterprises. The new Implementing Rules extend the provision given to employees of State Owned Enterprises to all types of company. Also, the New Patent Law introduces a disclosure obligation for the application of patents based on genetic resources. The Implementation Rules clarify further some terms included in the New Patent Law as regards genetic material. For example, at Article 26 Implementation Rules both 'genetic resources' and 'invention relying on genetic resource' are defined, but no definitions are given for 'direct source' and 'original source' as yet. Finally, the New Patent Law also provides guidance on the granting of compulsory licenses in China. Under the New Patent Law, the patent authority can grant compulsory licenses where a patent holder fails to exploit or fully exploit his patent without any justified reason within three years of the patent grant date or four years of the patent application date, or where the patent right holder has been exploiting the patent rights in a monopolistic manner. The Implementation Rules clarify that failing to exploit a patent could happen in the event that the patent rights holder's (or its licensee's) methods or scale of exploiting the patent cannot fulfill the need for the patented product in China.

In China, design right falls within the patent law (unlike the UK, for example, where both registered and unregistered design rights are separate from patent rights). Article 11 of the New Patent Law provides that 'after the grant of the patent right for a design, no entity or individual may, without the authorization of the patentee, exploit the patent, that is, make, offering for sell, sell or import the product incorporating its or his patented design, for production or business purposes'. This provision seems to leave out the stocking and exporting of products, which might leave open the potential for dealing in counterfeit designs.

Finally, the New Patent Law provides the patent authority with the right to grant Chinese companies the license to manufacture patented medicine and/or export the medicines to countries or regions with whom China has already concluded relevant international treaties. This new provision on compulsory licensing is likely to give the Chinese government extra bargaining power when negotiating the scope of monopoly patent rights with patent holders.

Associate Professor Li Zuming (China University of Political Science and Law) discusses the current Chinese Trademarks Act 2001 (as revised) in Chapter 3. China's trademark law was adopted on 23 August, 1982, and has been revised twice, in 1993 and 2001. The latest amendment on 27 October 2001 includes 64 articles stipulating the basic protection of a trademark, the definition of a registered trademark, the definition of rights, holders, and the content of rights as well as penalty provisions. Work on the third revision began in 2004. The State Administration for Industry and Commerce of the PRC (SAIC) issued a proposal for the third revision of the trademark law on 20 June 2009 (updated 2010), which at the time of writing, is still under review by the National People's Congress (NPC). It is anticipated that the third revision of the Trademark Act will take effect within the next two years. Under the current trademark law, a trademark registration may be filed for any visible mark including a word, sign, letter, number, 3D (three-dimensional) mark, color combination, or any combination of the elements mentioned above, that distinguish the commodities of the natural person, legal person or other organization from those of others. A sound, smell or an animation cannot compose a registered trademark. However, the third revision of the Trademark Law is likely to extend the concept of a 'brand', which means that non-traditional trademarks such as sound, smell and color labels might also be accepted. The new draft also looks to improve the prospects for foreign brands, which are not currently 'famous' brands, for example, to protect such brands from registrations in bad faith.

As regards well-known marks, in April 2009, the SPC issued the Interpretation on Certain Issues Concerning the Application of Law in the Trial of Civil Dispute Cases Involving Protection of Well-Known Trademarks (Fa Shi [2009] No. 3 ('Interpretation')). This follows earlier guidance from the SPC on well-known marks, such as the overlap of trademarks with domain names in Interpretation of the Supreme People's Court on Several Issues Concerning the Application of Law to the Trial of Civil Dispute Cases Involving Computer Network Domain Names (promulgated 24 July 2001) and Interpretation of the Supreme People's

Court on Certain Issues Concerning the Application of Law in the Trial of Civil Cases Involving Trademark Disputes (16 October 2002). The 2001 revision of the Trademark Law allows for a well-known mark to be protected through both administrative procedures and judicial procedures. Administrative procedures govern organs of the state whereas judicial procedures are processed through China's court system. The function of the 2009 Interpretation is to set out more clearly the conditions for the protection of well-known marks in China. Article 1 Interpretation defines a well-known trademark as a mark that is 'well-known to the relevant public in China'. The Article does not refer to 'market reputation', but includes market reputation as one of the factors to be considered in Article 5(1)(5) of the Interpretation as to what constitutes a well-known mark. The knowledge of the public will therefore be important in determining whether a mark is well-known in China and the level of this knowledge will relate not only to the distinctiveness of the mark, but also to 'classes and ways of use of goods designated by the trademark, such as sales regions and sales methods'.[8]

As regards the conflict between well-known marks and registration of *domain names* identical to the mark, in earlier guidance (listed above), the SPC made clear that if such a conflict arises, the courts could have power to determine whether a mark was well-known or not. However, Article 3 of the 2009 Interpretation now strengthens the hand of rights owners of well-known marks in that if the mark has already garnered a certain amount of 'fame', the courts may be more willing to accept that a defendant's registration and use of a similar or identical domain name will be sufficient to mislead the relevant public, leading to a potential ruling of trademark infringement and unfair competition (without the formal need for the plaintiff to prove that the mark is 'well-known').[9] The third revision of the trademark law might include a restriction on the power to object, which will hopefully speed up the registration process, but how the objection process might be limited is still unclear at the time of writing.

Further improvements are also likely both with the level of compen-

---

[8] See comments by Kong Xianjun (Vice Chief Judge of IP Division, SPC) and Xia Junli (Presiding Judge, IP Division, SPC) in 'Understanding and Application of the Interpretation on Certain Issues Concerning the Application of Law in the Trial of Civil Disputes Involving Protection of Well Known Trademarks', *China Intellectual Property*, HurryMedia, May–June 2009, 5–6 (30), 89.

[9] See the unofficial English version of the 2009 Interpretation available at: http://www.procedurallaw.cn/english/law/200905/t20090508_217007.html, accessed September 2010.

sation for infringement (increases are likely) as well as a requirement for the trademark authority to complete the examination of an application within 12 months from the filing date (although whether the latter is likely to make it into the final law is also uncertain given the current number of trademark applications to the Trademark Office (TMO) of the Chinese State Administration for Industry and Commerce (SAIC), and the backlog in pending cases). Also included might be greater powers for the local administrations for industry and commerce (Administration of Industry and Commerce (AIC)) which might lead to greater administrative efficiency, but with a corresponding loss of potential legal certainty.

As with patents and trademarks, copyright in China has also been the focus of intense discussion. In the last two years, China has had to deal with two World Trade Organization (WTO) cases: (1) *China – measures affecting the protection and enforcement of intellectual property rights*, 26 January 2009 ('*China – IP*', Panel report adopted 20 March 2009);[10] and (2) *China – measures affecting trading rights and distribution services of certain publications and audiovisual entertainment products* ('*China – Audiovisual*', Appellate Body report, 21 December 2009).[11] Both cases required China to make amendments to its laws, and both concern the issue of copyright to some extent. In summary, *China – IP* concerned an application by the US to the WTO's Dispute Settlement Body (DSB) that China's IP law and practice, specifically: (1) the denial of copyright protection of censored works in China; (2) the disposal by donation and auction of seized counterfeit goods; and (3) the unavailability of criminal sanctions for piracy and counterfeiting of copyright and trademark rights below certain thresholds, all fell foul of China's accession commitments under the Agreement on Trade-Related Aspects of Intellectual Property (TRIPS). As regards (1), the US claim was founded on the allegation that Article 4 China's Copyright Law 2001 was inconsistent with Article 9.1 TRIPS that incorporates Articles 5(1) and 5(2) Berne Convention (1971).[12] As to (2), the US claimed that China's system for disposal of

---

[10] *China – measures affecting the protection and enforcement of intellectual property rights*, WT/DS362/R, 26 January 2009.

[11] *China – measures affecting trading rights and distribution services for certain publications and audiovisual entertainment products*, WT/DS363/AB/R, AB-2009-3, 21 December 2009.

[12] Paragraphs 2.4 Panel Report (China-IP): 'The United States claims that China is acting inconsistently with its obligations under the TRIPS Agreement by denying the protection of its Copyright Law to creative works of authorship (and, to the extent Article 4 of the Copyright Law applies to them, sound recordings

seized counterfeit goods violated Articles 46 and 59 of the TRIPS, which require that counterfeit goods do not re-enter trade channels.[13] At the time of the case, China had an agreement with the Red Cross to ensure no commercial use of donated goods and for the removal of trademarks prior to auction, for example.[14] For the final claim (3), the US challenged China's absence of criminal penalties for trademark infringement below particular quantitative and qualitative thresholds. In other words, the US was challenging China's threshold levels set for criminal penalties for IP infringement as well as the factors used to establish these thresholds, arguing that Article 61 TRIPS imposed a positive obligation on China to implement domestic criminal law penalties for 'willful trademark counterfeiting or copyright piracy on a commercial scale'. [15] The US was largely successful in the first and second claims, which required China to amend its copyright law (which it did in 2010), and to abandon its current system of auctions for disposal of seized counterfeit goods. However, on the third claim, the panel argued that the US had not submitted sufficient evidence that was accurate enough to prove piracy levels on a commercial level in

---

and performances) that have not been authorized for, or are otherwise prohibited from, publication or distribution within China.' See also 3.1(c) Panel Report, WT/DS362/R, 26 January 2009.

[13] Paragraph 7.197 Panel Report: 'The United States claims that the competent Chinese authorities lack the scope of authority to order the destruction or disposal of infringing goods required by Article 59 of the TRIPS Agreement. The measures at issue create a "compulsory scheme" so that the Chinese customs authorities cannot exercise their discretion to destroy the goods and must give priority to disposal options that allow infringing goods to enter the channels of commerce or otherwise cause harm to the right holder'. China's response is in paragraph 7.198: 'China responds that its Customs authorities possess the authority to order both disposal and destruction of infringing goods in accordance with Article 59 of the TRIPS Agreement. *Donation to social welfare bodies* and *sale to the right holder* constitute disposal outside the channels of commerce in such a way as to avoid harm to the right holder. Article 59 must be read in conjunction with Article 1.1 of the TRIPS Agreement. Chinese law sets forth criteria that reflect an official preference for the use of disposition methods besides destruction but Customs has the discretion to determine whether the criteria are met and therefore which disposition method is appropriate. China Customs chose to destroy 58 per cent of the total value of infringing goods between 2005 and 2007 which proves that the putative hierarchy of disposition options does not hinder Customs' ability to order *destruction* of infringing goods . . .' (emphasis added).

[14] Paragraph 7.303 Panel Report.

[15] Paragraph 2.2 Panel Report: 'The United States claims that China has not provided for criminal procedures and penalties to be applied in cases of wilful trademark counterfeiting or copyright piracy on a commercial scale that fail to meet certain thresholds . . . [Chinese measures identified omitted].'

China and sufficient to challenge the threshold levels China had set for criminal penalties for IP infringement. [16]

In *China – Audiovisual*, the US bought a claim to the DSB arguing that some Chinese measures (specifically Articles 5 and 7 of the Chinese Audiovisual Products Regulation 2001) limited the right to import audiovisual entertainment products and some publications to Chinese state-designated and wholly or partially state-owned companies (in effect, imposing a discriminatory *right to trade* on foreign imports of these products).[17] Following a panel report largely upholding the US claims, the Chinese appealed to the Appellate Body of the DSB. In a report of the Appellate Body (AB) issued in December 2009,[18] the AB recommended that the DSB request that China bring into conformity the measures found to be inconsistent with its Accession Protocol, its Accession working party report, the GATS, and the GATT 1994. The Appellate Body upheld several of the panel's findings, and in particular, upheld the panel's findings that Chinese measures preventing foreign-invested companies from engaging in 'the wholesale of imported reading materials, the exclusive sale of books, periodicals and newspapers, and the master wholesale and wholesale of electronic publications' were inconsistent with China's national treatment commitments under Article XVII of the General Agreement on Trade in Services (GATS).[19] The Appellate Body also found that 'China's measures limiting the distribution of audiovisual materials to joint ventures with Chinese majority ownership' were inconsistent with China's commitments under the GATS.[20]

---

[16] Paragraph 7.628 Panel Report: 'The Panel has reviewed the press articles and notes that none of them are corroborated, nor do they refer to events or statements that would not require corroboration. Whilst the publications are reputable, most of these particular articles are brief and are quoted either for general statements or random pieces of information. Most are anecdotal in tone, some repeating casual remarks about prices of fake goods, anonymous statements or speculation.' Also in paragraph 7.629: '. . . For the reasons set out above, the Panel does not ascribe any weight to the evidence in the press articles and finds that, even if it did, the information that these press articles contain is inadequate to demonstrate what is typical or usual in China for the purposes of the relevant treaty obligation.'

[17] Paragraph 2.3 Panel Report (*China – Audiovisual*) WT/DS363/R, 12th August 2009.

[18] *China – measures affecting trading rights and distribution services for certain publications and audiovisual entertainment products*, WT/DS363/AB/R, AB-2009-3, 21 December 2009 ('AB Report').

[19] Paragraph 8 AB Report (WT/DS363/AB/R) citing the earlier panel's wording.

[20] Paragraph 414 AB Report.

An important issue was whether China could invoke the 'public morals' defense under Article XX(a) GATT to restrict imports (the first time that the defense had been run in a GATT case: the US attempted a similar defense in *US – Gambling*[21] under Article XIV GATS[22]). The AB in *China – Audiovisual* found that the panel had erred in failing to recognize that the Chinese state plan requirement in Article 42 of the Publications Regulation was 'apt to make a material contribution to the protection of public morals',[23] but that China had nevertheless failed to prove that its measures for the import of foreign audiovisual products were 'necessary'[24] for the protection of public morals in China as required by Article XX(a) GATT.[25]

A further important issue determined in *China-Audiovisual* was the

---

[21] Appellate Body Report, *United States – Measures Affecting the Cross-Border Supply of Gambling and Betting Services*, WT/DS285/R (20 April 2005) (hereafter *US – Gambling* (AB).

[22] Article XIV(a), The General Agreement on Trade in Services' 'public morals' exception states: 'Provided that such measures do not "constitute a means of arbitrary or unjustifiable discrimination between countries . . . or a disguised restriction on trade in services" GATS allows the "adoption or enforcement by any Member of measures: (a) necessary to protect public morals or to maintain public order."' General Agreement on Trade in Services, 15 April 1994, WTO Agreement, Annex 1B 33 ILM 1168 (1994) (hereafter GATS).

[23] Paragraph 415(b)(iii) AB Report: '. . . finds that the Panel erred, in paragraph 7.836 of the Panel Report, in finding that the State plan requirement in Article 42 of the Publications Regulation is apt to make a material contribution to the protection of public morals and that, in the absence of a reasonably available alternative, it can be characterized as "necessary" to protect public morals in China.'

[24] The 'necessity test' involves a process of 'weighing and balancing' the objectives of the challenged measure, with its trade restrictive aspects on commerce. At paragraph 240 AB Report, the Appellate Body refers to the AB's report in the *US – Gambling* case cited above to explain the meaning of necessity: 'In US – Gambling, for example, the Appellate Body addressed, in the context of Article XIV(a) of the GATS, the proper means of assessing "necessity" through a process of "weighing and balancing" a number of factors. The Appellate Body explained that the process begins with an assessment of the relative importance of the interests or values furthered by the challenged measure. A panel should then turn to the other factors that are to be weighed and balanced, which will in most cases include: (i) the contribution of the measure to the realization of the ends pursued by it; and (ii) the restrictive effect of the measure on international commerce. Additional factors may be relevant in specific cases. Once a panel has identified the factors to be weighed and balanced, a comparison of the challenged measure and possible alternatives should be undertaken, and the results considered in the light of the importance of the objective pursued.'

[25] Paragraph 415(e) AB Report.

classification of 'sound recording distribution services'. China argued that electronic sound recording distribution services were *not* covered by China's schedule of commitments. However, both the panel and AB found that sound recording distribution services in sector 2.D of China's GATS Schedule extended to the distribution of sound recordings in non-physical form through electronic means and upheld the panel's conclusion (in paragraph 8.2.3(b)(i) of the Panel Report) that the provisions of China's measures prohibiting foreign-invested entities from engaging in the distribution of sound recordings in electronic form were inconsistent with Article XVII of the GATS. This is an important finding and further strengthens the precedent established in the earlier WTO case of *US – Gambling* that online products are equivalent to their physical counterparts, and that the WTO is able to extend the commitments made by a member to include intangible products delivered over the internet.

Both cases have significant implications for China and demonstrate a common thread running from the issue of piracy of copyrighted works in *China – IP* to market access commitments for foreign content material in *China – Audiovisual*. It could be argued that the strict censorship laws on foreign content in China have contributed to the rise in potential piracy of foreign content. There is a danger, however, that the international trading community, particularly the developing nations, could perceive the judgment by the AB in *China – Audiovisual* as indicative of a threat to national sovereignty, and also that the US's challenge to China's interpretation of the necessity test under the Article XX(a) 'public morals' GATT defence, could be further perceived as an expression of cultural dominance by the US in exporting audiovisual products overseas.[26]

Professor Li Yufeng (Southwest University of Political Science and Law) discusses China's copyright laws in Chapter 4. Although copyright can be traced back in China to the Han Dynasty (206 BC–220 AD), it became codified only in the latter Qing period and after the Opium Wars (1840–42 onwards) with the establishment of the Great Qing Copyright Law of 1910.[27] The current copyright system embodies a three level legislative hierarchy. The first level comprises the laws adopted by the NPC and its Standing Committee, such as the General Principle of Civil Code

---

[26] For a more detailed discussion of the implications of *China – Audiovisual*, see Elenor Mangin, 'Market Access in China – Publications and Audiovisual Materials: A Moral Victory with a Silver Lining', *Berkeley Technology Law Journal*, 25 (1), 2010.

[27] Xue Hong and Zheng Chengsi, *Chinese Intellectual Property Law in the 21st Century*, HongKong: Sweet & Maxwell Asia, 2002, p. 30.

1986 (GPCC) and the Copyright Law 2001 (CL). The second level consists of regulations, administrative measures and orders endorsed by the State Council: Regulations for the Implementation of the Copyright Law 2002 (CLIR); Regulations for the Protection of Computer Software 2001 (CSPR); Regulations for the Protection of the Right of Communication through Information Network 2006 (RCPR), and Regulations for the Collective Management of Copyrights 2005 (RCMC), and Interim Measures for Video and Television Broadcasting and Sound Recording Products 2010.

In February 2010, China adopted the second revision of its copyright law, the Copyright Law of the People's Republic of China (revised 2010) and coming into effect in April 2010.[28] The major changes include dropping Article 4(1) Copyright Law 2001, and introducing a new Article 26 on the pledging of copyright.[29] The prior Article 4(1) was a controversial provision that created some uncertainty as to whether foreign films and other audiovisual material that had not obtained approval under China's censorship regulations enjoyed copyright under the CL 2001. As a result of a challenge by the US and a decision by the WTO's Appellate Body in December 2009 (discussed above in *China – IP*), Article 4(1) was dropped from the CL (revised 2010).[30]

The CL (revised 2010), however, has still failed to list the right of rental for *performers*, which runs foul of the WIPO Performances and Phonograms Treaty 1996 (WPPT).[31] The WPPT was binding on China from 9 June 2007.

Also, Chapter 4 makes clear that the term 'broadcasting' in China actually refers to two different types of dissemination: broadcasting in a wireless form, and cable casting in a wire form. The mainstream view held by NCAC officials and SPC judges is that 'broadcasting' in China refers to broadcasting in a wireless form and retransmission of the wireless-

---

[28] The Decision of the Standing Committee of the National People's Congress on Revision of the Copyright Law of the People's Republic of China, adopted at the 13th meeting of the Standing Committee of the 11th National People's Congress of the People's Republic of China on 26 February 2010 and coming into force on 1 April 2010.

[29] Article 26 CL (revised 2010): 'In case of pledge of copyright, the pledger and the pledgee shall go through registration of the pledge with the copyright administration under the State Council.'

[30] *China – measures affecting trading rights and distribution services for certain publications and audiovisual entertainment products*, WTO Appellate Body Decision WT/DS363/AB/R, December 2009.

[31] See WPPT, Articles 9 and 15.

broadcasted programs using wired means.[32] In other words, it does not cover direct cable casting.

This narrow definition, which reflects the intention of the legislators, is not consistent with requirements of the WCT and WPPT. This will naturally cause conflict between Chinese law harmonization and international conventions. In addition, the definition may to some extent be outdated given that cable and webcasting services are developing so rapidly and will soon overtake wireless broadcasting and (potentially) dominate the Chinese market. As a consequence, the wireless-based definition of 'broadcasting' in the current CL may subject all the cable broadcasters and webcasters to a lacuna in protection.

Chapter 5 on unfair competition by Professor Hu Kaizhong (Zhongnan University of Economics and Law) discusses China's Anti-Unfair Competition Law 1993 (AUCL). Article 2 of the AUCL defines unfair competition as '. . . activities made by business operators who damage the others' legal rights and interests, disturb the order of social economy and violate the provisions of this Law'. This provision is the legal standard for judging any act of unfair competition in China. The chapter provides a wide range of examples of unfair competition, an area of law that China is seeking to revise (along with the trademark law). Also mentioned is the relationship between the AUCL and China's Anti Monopoly Law (discussed further below).

One important aspect of the AUCL are the provisions on counterfeit trade. There has been much discussion of China and the trade in counterfeit goods. Article 5 AUCL focuses on counterfeit trade as a form of unfair competition. Counterfeiting of goods is provided in Article 5 and includes confusion of commodity and the false marking of goods. Business operators who breach Article 5 and cause damage to infringed business operators will bear the liability for compensating for damage. The amount of this compensation will be equivalent to the profit made by the infringer during the period of infringement (if it proves difficult to measure the amount of damage done). Also, the infringer will be required to compensate for the reasonable costs to the infringed party to investigate the unfair competition acts of the infringer. The infringed party can sue the infringer in the People's Court when its legal interests and rights are damaged due to unfair competition. Meanwhile, if the business operator imitates the

32 CL (revised 2010), Article 11 defines the 'right of broadcasting' as: '. . . the right to publicly broadcast or disseminate works by wireless means, to disseminate broadcast works to the public by wired dissemination or rebroadcast, and to disseminate broadcast works to the public by audio amplifier or other similar instruments for transmission of signs, sounds or images'.

other's registered trademark, uses the other enterprise's name or personal name without permission, forges or fakes the mark of certificate, the mark of famous or high quality products, fakes the original place of production, makes a fake or creates misunderstanding over the description or quality of products, the infringer will be punished in accordance with the provisions of the Trademark Law of the PRC and the Product Quality Law of the PRC.[33]

There is pressure on China to improve its provisions on counterfeit trade. The recent WTO *China – IP* case mentioned above highlights (particularly US) concerns over the limited availability of criminal sanctions for piracy and the absence of criminal penalties for infringements below particular quantitative and qualitative thresholds (claims that the WTO did not uphold). Furthermore, the Anti Counterfeit Trade Agreement (ACTA) being pursued plurilaterally by the US, including Japan and the EU amongst others, has now reached an advanced stage with, at the time of writing, a draft of the treaty available in the public domain. The ACTA treaty is likely to include stringent provisions on digital rights management and anti-circumvention.[34]

It is clear that the AUCL is now in need of revision. Chapter 5 highlights several ways in which the current law can be amended. Discussion of the AUCL continues in Chapter 6 by Professor Liu Xiaohai (Tongji University), with Professor Liu expanding the discussion of unfair competition to include the overlap between trade secrets and other IP rights, such as copyright and the law of trademark, and then going on to discuss the licensing of know-how and confidentiality in Chinese employment contracts. Under Chinese law, the relationship between trade secrets and patents is (before the patent application becomes public) anything related to the patent application. Patents and trade secrets coexist in the technical solutions set out in the patent. The termination of the patent would not prevent the trade secret from continuing to exist in the patented technical solution. As regards the relationship between trade secrets and copyright, under Chinese law, copyright work can be protected as a trade secret as long as it has not been partially or fully disclosed. For example, if the confidential part of the source code of computer software has not been disclosed, it may still be protected as a trade secret.[35] Chapter 6 includes

---

[33] See Chapter 3 on Trademarks.

[34] See, for example, Chapter 2 (Section 4) ACTA available at: https://www.ige.ch/en/legal-info/legal-areas/counterfeiting-piracy/acta.html, accessed September 2010.

[35] See Article 12 of the Measures for the Registration of Computer Software Copyright (2002).

extensive discussion of licensing of know-how and technology transfer and technology development contracts under Chinese law. Also covered are the conditions that can be imposed on employees to guarantee trade secrets and restraint of trade provisions.

Chapter 7 by Professor Michael Pendleton (Chinese University of Hong Kong) discusses the IP framework in China's Special Administrative Region (SAR) of Hong Kong. Much of China's entire legal system was created in the early 1980s, the Trademark Law in 1982 for example. However, Hong Kong has as long a history and immersion in intellectual property as many countries of Western Europe or the United States, mainly due to the UK's influence over the period of colonization. For at least a century, Hong Kong's laws have been heavily biased in favor of the rights holder in order to attract foreign capital. Hong Kong was the first member of the WTO to seek TRIPS compliance for its intellectual property laws and is a member of the WTO independently of China, and in its own right as the only non-sovereign member state of the WTO. As we see in Chapter 7, Hong Kong has a strong regime to enforce and protect intellectual property, and quite distinct from mainland China. For example, civil remedies include the ex parte Anton Piller order, Mareva and interlocutory injunctions. For over half a century, the criminal enforcement regime has been a pioneer, instigating criminal enforcement of copyright from the 1960s. In a recent case, *Chan Nai Ming v Hong Kong SAR*, a man was jailed for uploading a genuine VCD to a peer-to-peer (P2P) server.[36] He was held to have distributed an infringing copy, i.e. the copy of the genuine VCD he made on his PC to facilitate uploading.[37]

In *Chan Nai Ming*, the defendant was charged with, inter alia, attempting to distribute infringing copies of three copyright films contrary to the original section 118(1)(f) (now section 118(1)(g)) Copyright Ordinance. The distribution was by means of the peer-to-peer system BitTorrent, and the defendant was the 'seeder' who created the seed files for others to download. The defendant was sentenced to three months' imprisonment on each charge, the sentences to run concurrently. The case went all the way to the Court of Final Appeal and the decision and sentence were upheld.

In Hong Kong as regards anti-circumvention of technological measures for copyright protection, copyright owners commonly employ technological measures to prevent or restrict unauthorized access to, or copying of,

---

[36] [2005] 4 HKLRD 142; [2007] 1 HKLRD 95 (CFI); [2007] 2 HKLRD 489 (CFA). The reasons for sentence were given separately on 7 November 2005 (TMCC No. 1268 of 2005).

[37] *HKSAR v Chan Nai Ming* [2007] 1 HKLRD 95.

copyright works in electronic form that are issued or made available to the public.[38] Chapter 7 makes clear that the HK Copyright Ordinance has already provided civil liability for the circumvention of such measures.[39] To further combat such circumvention, the civil liability provisions have been expanded, and new criminal sanctions introduced following the 2007 amendments.[40] Chapter 7 discusses the full range of IP rights available, including a broad discussion of design rights and confidential information.

Chapter 8 on copyright protection in the electronic environment by Professor Liu Chuntian (Renmin University) is a discussion about China's evolving IP framework for dealing with network technology issues. The chapter introduces some of the problems facing regulators in dealing with designing legal frameworks to cope with new technology. The challenge for China is to move from a system where currently the state has interests in being (both) a market player and a regulator to where, in the next three decades, private enterprise will take the lead in innovation and design, and the state will need to take a more supportive role. The chapter makes clear that China is still in a state of transition: there are examples of innovation and development that are on par with the best international practice, but there are also many parts of China that remain undeveloped. A mature understanding of IP throughout the country is lacking. The chapter argues that China needs to find a way to harmonize private monopoly IP rights with its civil law system. Also guidance from the SPC will be necessary in assisting the lower courts to rule effectively on technology disputes. The chapter makes reference to several lower court decisions on copyright infringement involving P2P networks and the internet. In this way, Chapter 9 functions as a 'bridging chapter', bringing together the more traditional aspects of regulation of IP in terms of black-letter law with a broader discussion of the underlining policy issues that regulators need to bear in mind when designing new legal frameworks for IP in dealing with the internet. In taking as a central theme the use of the network to disseminate intangible products, the chapter also acts as a bridge to the next two chapters that discuss the regulation of information technology and electronic commerce.

Chapter 9 by Professors Zhang Ping and Meng Zhaoping (Peking University Law School) discusses the regulation of information

---

38 See the consultation document issued by the Commerce & Industry Branch, 'Review of Certain Provisions of Copyright Ordinance', (December 2004), paragraph 6.1.

39 Copyright Ordinance, s 273, as enacted.

40 Copyright Ordinance, s 273A to s 273C, inserted by virtue of the Copyright (Amendment) Ordinance 2007, s 69. See also the exceptions in s 273D to s 273F.

technology, computer software and e-commerce (Chapter 10 extends the discussion of e-commerce – discussed further below). In Chapter 9, the authors look at the aspects of Chinese civil law that underpin the regulation of technology. They cover the aspects of the Patent Law (2008) that look at the patenting of business processes and technical inventions and regulations looking at computer security and database protection. Under Chinese law, databases can also be protected. A database comprises of data and a system for managing the data. Also, the system management software may be eligible for patent protection. For example, the invention 'System and method for executing search in a relational database' was granted a patent in China on 14 January 2009.[41]

The development of e-commerce has generated a large number of business method-related inventions. As early as 1996, CitiBank filed business method applications with the Chinese State Intellectual Property Office (SIPO) and was granted patents.[42] The essential issue lies in the patentability of computer software. It should be noted that pure business methods are *not* patentable under the Patent Law 2008 (New Patent Law). There is extensive discussion of the protection of computer software under copyright laws in Chapter 9, but owing to the special features of computer software, whether other aspects of software that have not been defined by the law, such as character databases, menu and user interfaces, are protected by copyright law is, at the time of writing, still under discussion in China.

Chapter 10 by Professor Cong Lixian (Beijing Foreign Studies University, and Research Fellow of Zhongnan University of Economics and Law) extends the discussion of e-commerce introduced in Chapter 9. There is a more extensive discussion of domain name registration and the relationship between domain names and trademarks under Chinese law. Also discussed is the issue of privacy. China does not at present have any specific laws on the protection of privacy. The chapter discusses one of the many 'human flesh cases' that has resulted in some guidelines from the SPC on privacy in China.

As mentioned above, counterfeit trade has been a central issue for the Quad countries (US, Japan, Canada and the European Union) in their relationship with China. Chapter 10 discusses some aspects of counterfeit trade involving the two local search and auction portals *E-Bay* and *Alibaba*. The chapter goes on to discuss differences in the regulation of e-commerce at a provincial level, taking three main areas as examples:

---

[41] Patent Application No. 200610064263.4; Issuance No. 100452047C.

[42] For instance, patent application No. 92113147.X was granted on 18 December 2002.

Guangdong (one of China's most successful Special Economic Zones), Shanghai (often seen as the commercial capital of China) and Beijing (the political capital).

The next two chapters, Chapter 11 by Professor Huang Young and Dr Zhang Zhe (both of the University of International Business and Economics) and Chapter 12 by Professor Xu Shiying (East China University of Political Science and Law) focus on the application of anti-monopoly law in China. An effective competition framework is important in markets characterized by network externalities where operators with market power can leverage their dominance from downstream markets into several upstream markets. China introduced a new Anti-Monopoly Law (AML) in 2008.

The AML targets three main monopoly behaviors: monopoly agreements; the abuse of market dominance; and the concentration of undertakings. Several draft rules providing further guidance as to the AML's implementation were published in January 2011 (following a period of public consultation from the publication of draft rules in May 2010), such as the Rules of Administrative Authority for Industry and Commerce on Prohibition of Abuse of Dominant Market Position ('Dominance Rules') and coming into effect on 1 February 2011.[43]

Article 17 AML defines market dominance as a 'market position where an undertaking is capable of controlling price, quantity or other trading terms within a relevant market, or deterring or affecting other undertakings' ability to enter into a relevant market'. The Dominance Rules are important in that they define more clearly (than the AML) the types of behavior by a dominant undertaking that may be classed as unlawful abuse (for example, the imposition of unreasonable restrictions on payment terms, delivery terms or the manner of service provision). Also, guidance is given on possible defenses to abuse of dominance allegations by undertakings. Article 8 Dominance Rules defines the factors that the Administration for Industry and Commerce (AIC) will consider when looking at valid justifications for abusive dominant behavior. The consultation period for the draft rules ended in June 2010. The Dominance Rules came into effect on 1 February 2011. Regulations on *procedural provisions* with regard to abuse of dominance, monopoly agreements, and

---

[43] Also published on the Anti Monopoly and Anti Unfair Competition Bureau of the State Administration for Industry and Commerce website are the Rules on Monopoly Agreements (2010) and Rules on Prohibition of Abuse of Administrative Powers to Eliminate and Restrict Competition (2010) both coming into effect on 1 February 2011. See Chapters 11 and 15.

abuse of administrative powers are already published by SAIC in June 2009.

In Chapter 11, Professor Huang Young and Dr. Zhang Zhe write about the AML, describing in detail its background history and implementation. Professor Huang was one of the early drafters of the AML. The chapter looks at the regulatory framework for the enforcement of the AML in China at both state and provincial level and reviews the areas of the AML that are still in need of clarification. Interestingly, in conformity with the theory of 'one country, two systems' proposed by Mr. Deng Xiaoping, the Chinese leader in the 1980s, Hong Kong and Macau are able to maintain their separate legal systems so long as they are not in contradiction with the Basic Law of the Hong Kong Special Administrative Region and the Basic Law of the Macau Special Administrative Region. In this sense, the Chinese AML is *not* applicable in Hong Kong or Macau. In fact, on 6 May 2008, the local government of Hong Kong launched a second public consultation on its own competition law. However, the attempt encountered a major setback when on 27 February, in the House Committee of the Legislative Council, the administration confirmed that the competition law would be postponed due to 'technical issues'. On the other hand, as provided by Article 2 of the Chinese AML, the exclusion of Hong Kong, Macau and Taiwan does not prevent the enforcement authorities from investigating any anti-competitive activities with an impact on the Chinese domestic market. Chapter 11 also looks at the overlap of the AML with other Chinese laws impacting on anti-competitive practices, such as Articles VII (commodities entering markets) and XV (bid rigging) of the AUCL.

Chapter 12 by Professor Xu Shiying (East China University of Political Science & Law) discusses the relationship between IPRs and the AML in greater detail. Article 55 AML is concerned with the potential abuse of a dominant position by an undertaking in exercising monopoly IPR rights. The Chinese government has no problem with a monopoly exercising its IPR, but is concerned (as with other developed competition regimes, such as in the US and EU) with the *abuse* of monopoly IPRs. For this reason, Article 55 reads: 'This law is not applicable to conducts by undertakings to implement their intellectual property rights in accordance with relevant IP laws and administrative regulations; however, this law is applicable to the conduct by undertakings to eliminate or restrict market competition by abusing intellectual property rights'.

At the time of writing, the Enforcement Bureau for Anti Monopoly and Anti Improper Competition of SAIC is expected to publish guidelines on the abuse of IPRs under the AML. For example, unlike in the EU with the EC regulation on technology transfer agreements (EC 772/2004), and other exemptions (for example on vertical agreements: Reg 2790/99 and R&D agreements: 2659/2000), at the time of writing, no similar guidance in China exists. As such, new guidelines on the interface of competition law and IP are much anticipated, as multinationals based in China are understandably fearful that Article 55 AML could be used against them when protecting their IPRs (for example, refusing to license a patent or copyright, as might be the case in the computer software sector).

Already, following litigation in the EU, the US, Japan and Korea, Microsoft is facing a legal challenge in China on the potential abuse of a dominant position arising from its use of IPRs. The allegation against Microsoft is that it is using its dominant market position to manipulate software prices in China, and has breached Articles 6, 17 and 19 of the AML, which prohibit abuse of market dominance. However, under Chapter 2, Article 15 of the AML, a competent anti-monopoly authority can approve exemptions from Articles 13 and 14 if certain monopoly agreements among operators are beneficial (for example, in improving technology or research and developing new products; upgrading product quality and improving operational efficiency and enhancing competitiveness of small and medium sized entities etc.). Microsoft may attempt to invoke the Article 15 exemptions by arguing that its business operations in China are beneficial to improving technology or research and developing new products (Article 15(i)). However, any exemption is subject to the approval of a competent anti-monopoly authority and it is still unclear which specific agency (MOFCOM, NDRC or SAIC) is the relevant 'competent anti-monopoly authority' for the purposes of Article 15(i).

Also, the leading Intelligent Messaging operator in China, *Tencent*, with its refusal to interconnect its QQ platform (similar to Microsoft's MSN network) with other competitors gave rise to a legal challenge in the courts which Tencent eventually won. The *Tencent* case is discussed in Chapters 8 and 12.

Chapter 13 moves to the arena of international trade and specifically the use of IPRs in China's negotiations with other WTO member states and its implementation of the TRIPS Agreement. Professor Kong Qingjiang (Zhejiang Gongshang University) discusses the Doha Round and China's unique position in the round as both a trading giant, but also a developing country, and therefore having the potential to mediate between different interest groups, both developed and developing countries. What is clear is that with China surpassing Japan in terms of purchasing power parity as the second largest economy in the world (soon to be followed by India in the next year or so), China and India are destined to play even more significant roles in the WTO in the years ahead. In terms of IP, both nations, together with Brazil, Cuba, the Dominican Republic, Ecuador, Pakistan, Thailand, Venezuela, Zambia and Zimbabwe, submitted a communication to the Council on TRIPS, stressing the need to modify the TRIPS Agreement and arguing that it contained no provisions to prevent biopiracy (illegal access and use) or ensure prior informed consent and the fair and equitable sharing of benefits. The communication proposed several conditions for the acquisition of patent rights related to biological materials of traditional knowledge, including requirements for patent applicants to disclose the source of origin of the biological resource and associated traditional knowledge and evidence of prior informed consent and benefit-sharing.[44]

Also, against the backdrop that the Quad countries of the USA, Japan, Canada and the EU have been pushing for TRIPS-plus provisions in several bilateral and free trade agreements, China too is now adopting a similar position on the use of regional trade agreements to secure specific IPR provisions with its own bilateral and regional trading partners.[45]

China has also had to deal with two WTO DSB cases (*China – IP* and *China – Audiovisual*) mentioned above, the former case leading to an amendment to China's copyright laws. Also, to further implement WTO commitments post-Doha, China has implemented the Doha Declaration on Public Health in its patent laws with the third amendment to the Patent Law (Patent Law 2008 discussed above), providing for a more definitive statutory basis to compel compulsory licenses, and also new rules that restrict the general scope of compulsory licensing while making it more feasible and likely for compulsory licenses to be granted in the area of pharmaceuticals[46] and semiconductor technology.[47] As such, in the event of a public health crisis, such as SARS or bird flu, the Chinese government is likely to grant a compulsory license to manufacture and export the required patented drugs.

---

44 IP/C/W/356.

45 At the time of writing, China and Peru are preparing for the negotiation of a free trade agreement. From the Joint Feasibility Report released by the Ministry of Foreign Trade and Tourism of Peru and the Ministry of Commerce of the People's Republic of China, both parties agreed that '[a]ccording to the characteristics of bilateral trade between China and Peru, the intellectual property protection can be fulfilled under the frame of TRIPS'. They seemed not to go beyond the minimum requirements of the TRIPS Agreement. Available at http://www.mincetur.gob.pe/newweb/Portals/0/Peru-China%20JFS%20Final.pdf, accessed July 2010.

46 Article 50 of the Patent Law (2008).

47 Article 52 of the Patent Law (2008).

Also discussed in Chapter 13 is the relationship between the New Patent Law 2008 and the AML. The New Patent Law stipulates that compulsory licensing may be granted to remove or reduce the negative effects of competition due to monopoly acts caused by the patentee exploiting the patent.[48] In other words, the issuance of a compulsory license is now a remedy for patent misuse in China.

Unlike many of the previous chapters in this book that focus purely on the content of the law with regard to IP and technology, Chapter 14 (the QBPC chapter) written by the Quality Brands Protection Committee (QBPC) chair, and Senior IP Counsel to GE China, Mr. Jack Chang, takes as its central focus the view of multinationals present in China and the challenges faced when protecting their IP under the evolving Chinese legislative framework. The chapter looks at the early formation of the Quality Brands Protection Committee, a coalition of foreign multinationals that came together with the aim of working with the Chinese government to improve IP protection in China. The chapter offers a unique perspective on QBPC's achievements and case law work over the several years since its early formation in 1998. Also, the chapter sets out some practical recommendations going forward as China continues to amend its legislative framework for IP protection and enforcement. The chapter provides a practical insight into the protection of IP and detailed legal provisions that illustrate the difficulties faced by brand owners in protecting their well-known labels from the threat of counterfeit trade.

Chapter 15 on telecommunications and the internet, written by the editor, Professor Rohan Kariyawasam (Cardiff University), brings together a discussion of telecommunications infrastructure with regulation of content in a converged environment. Discussion focuses on China's Telecommunications Regulations 2000 and their relevance to trade on the internet and new regulations from the Ministry of Industry and Information Technology, and State Administration of Radio, Film and Television on new electronic services, such as mobile TV and IPTV. At the time of writing, the Chinese legislature, the Financial and Economic Committee of the National People's Congress (NPC), has submitted the latest draft of the new planned telecommunications law (rumored to be called the 'Communications Law' when finally implemented to reflect the converged telecoms, broadcasting and internet networks in China) to the State Council. The new draft telecoms law was initially proposed as far back as 1980 to replace the current Telecommunications Regulations, but was delayed mainly due to difficulties on reaching an agreement between

[48] Article 48 of the Patent Law (2008).

industry players. Although the State Council is currently revising the draft law, this is not the first time that the draft law has been reviewed in this way. In 2005, a draft of the telecoms law was also received by the State Council, but the draft never reached the highest organ of the Chinese legislature, the NPC, for final approval. The discussion of the current new draft law in Chapter 15 therefore can only be seen as cursory, although the Chinese government is said to be committed to the idea of finalizing the law as quickly as possible to give legislative effect to the convergence of telecommunications, the internet, and cable networks and to give greater certainty to investors. The current draft law is now on the NPC's Standing Committee legislative planning timetable and in the State Council's legislative work plan.

The focus of network infrastructure regulation in Chapter 15 is on aspects of the digital network that looks to deliver new content services, such as IPTV (TV over internet networks) and mobile TV, where there is an overlap between infrastructure regulation and content regulation (viz. broadcasting). The chapter discusses the current Telecommunications Regulations 2000 with a focus on licensing, and particularly the Ministry of Industry and Information Technology's (MIIT's) recent Measures on the Administration of Licensing for Telecommunication Services Business (effective 10 April 2009), [49] and interconnection, and clarifying the status of the Telecommunications Regulations within the complex hierarchy of laws, regulations, measures, rules and notices within China. Also reviewed is the regulation of internet infrastructure, and converged audiovisual services delivered over internet networks, and new measures introduced on network security in 2009. The chapter also looks briefly at Next Generation Networks.

A significant issue for China is the involvement and investment of foreign operators in the telecoms sector. Chapter 15 looks at the complex regulatory environment for foreign telecommunication enterprises in China under the Provisions for the Administration of Foreign-Investment Telecommunications Enterprises (Revised), State Council Decree No. 534 (promulgated and effective 10 September 2008) ('FITE Rules'), and the interplay of the Anti-Monopoly Law with the Telecommunications Regulations, including the 2010 Dominance Rules published by the State Administration for Industry and Commerce (SAIC), discussed above, before concluding with a brief discussion of the new draft Telecommunications Law.

---

[49] This replaced the older Measures on the Administration of Licensing for Telecommunication Services Business (1 January 2002).

Finally, it should be noted that this book aims to provide an *introduction* to the major IP and technology laws impacting on the delivery of electronic content over the Internet. The main purpose is to introduce the relevant laws to a foreign readership in a single work in English. Furthermore, as indicated by this introduction, Chinese law is very complex, with a mix of civil, administrative and criminal provisions. A detailed treatment of the relationship between these different systems is beyond the scope of this book, but individual authors do touch on this mix throughout.[50]

---

[50] For a more detailed treatment of Chinese civil, administrative and criminal law (in English), including the court system, please see: Bin Liang, *The Changing Chinese Legal System, 1978 – Present*, London: Routledge, 2007; Daniel C. K. Chow, *The Legal System of the People's Republic of China in a Nutshell*, St Paul, Minn.: West, 2003; Donald C. Clarke, *China's Legal System: New Developments, New Challenges,* Cambridge: Cambridge University Press, 2008. Also, see China's Judicial System at: http://www.olemiss.edu/courses/pol324/chnjudic.htm, accessed November 2010: and a slightly dated research guide, but still useful at: http://www.llrx.com/features/prc.htm#family, accessed November 2010. For a more detailed treatment (in Chinese), please see: *Research Report on the Socialist Legal System with Chinese Characteristics*, editors Zhu Jingwen and Han Dayuan, China Renmin University Press, March 2010; *An Overview of the Chinese Legal System*, Gao Qicai and Luo Xu, Tsinghua University Press, October 2005; and *Internationalization and Localization: The Formation of the Modern Chinese Legal System*, Cao Quanlai, Peking University Press, April 2005.

2. Patents

Guo He[1]

2.1. THE DEVELOPMENT OF CHINESE PATENT LAW

In the late 1970s, China started to plan for the establishment of a patent system. In 1980, the State Council approved the founding of the China Patent Office and began drafting a new patent law. At the same time, China was undergoing changes in its approach to the economy and an intense debate ensued on whether China should promote 'capitalism' through the patent system or pursue 'socialism' and whether or not capitalism or socialism could harm or benefit the Chinese economy. The debate shifted back and forth, but in October and November 1980, a symposium for patent issues and a workshop on patent law were held respectively. The prevailing opinions arising from these meetings were that the patent system was a technical system with legal overtones which could be utilized by a socialist state, and that establishing a patent system in China would benefit the country. However, even though the 11th draft of the patent law was delivered to the State Council for opinion in March 1981, there were still major objections to the law being passed. Drafting of the new patent law stagnated for more than a year. In 1982, the legislative procedure was again restarted, and in August 1983, the draft patent law was approved by a meeting of the State Council and delivered to the National People's Congress for consideration the following September. On 12 March 1984, the Chinese Patent Law was finally adopted at the fourth session of the Standing Committee of the Sixth National People's Congress. The China Patent Law was publicized on 20 March 1984 and entered into force on 1 April 1985. This was the first time that a patent law had been implemented throughout China.[2] Countries worldwide welcomed the implementation

[1] Professor of Law, Renmin University.

[2] In 1944, the Republic of China issued the first patent law of China, and the law entered into force in 1949. But in 1949, the government of Kuomintang was in full retreat to Taiwan and was incapable of considering the patent law. Therefore,

of the China Patent Law, and even more importantly, the law gained the support of numerous domestic inventors. On 1 April 1985, which was the first date of the implementation of the patent law, the number of filings reached 3,455.

There are three kinds of patents regulated by the China Patent Law: inventions, utility models and industrial designs.[3] The first to file system is used.[4] For a patent for an invention, the early publication and delayed examination system is adopted[5] and the priority system under the Paris Convention is used.[6] The China Patent Law allows for foreign nationals to receive the benefit of National Treatment when applying for patents.[7] In 1992, eight years after the China Patent Law was issued, and pursuant to a bilateral agreement between China and the US, with the experience already accumulated through the implementation of the patent law, China introduced its first amendment to the patent law. The amendment involved the following aspects.[8] First, extending the protection range of the patent law: beverages, food, flavorings and drugs, as well as substances obtained by means of chemical methods, which the patent law of 1984 did not expressly protect,[9] were now protected by the patent law. Second, strengthening the force of a patent right: the right of importation was added in the contents of the patent right; the force of a process patent could extend to its product.[10] Third, lengthening the term of protection: the term of protection for patents for inventions was extended from 15 years to 20 years; the term of protection for patent for a utility model and design was extended to 10 years.[11] Fourth, introducing a domestic priority system:[12] The introduction of a priority system ensured that a first applicant in China could have equivalent standing to an applicant filing

---

the patent law never, in fact, came into effect in mainland China. After taking power, the government of the Communist Party released Regulations for the Protection of the Right of Invention and Patent Right, but the number of invention and patent rights awarded amounted to less than ten before the Regulations were abolished.

[3] See Article 2, Patent Law (1984).

[4] See Article 9, Patent Law (1984).

[5] See Article 34 and Article 35, Patent Law (1984).

[6] See Article 29, Patent Law (1984).

[7] See Article 18, Patent Law (1984).

[8] See the Decision Regarding the Revision of the Patent Law of the People's Republic o China, adopted at the 27th Session of the Standing Committee of the Seventh National People's Congress on 4 September 1992.

[9] See Section 4 and Section 5, Article 25, Patent Law (1984).

[10] See Article 11, Patent Law (1993).

[11] See Article 45, Patent Law (1993).

[12] See Section 2, Article 29, Patent Law (1993).

a first application in a foreign country. Fifth, abolishing the objection system in the examination and replacing it with a revocation system after grant: the effect of this was to shorten the time for examination. With these amendments, the Chinese patent system was brought onto an almost equal footing with that of most developed countries.

In 2000, to conform with the minimum requirements in the agreements and regulations made in the course of China's accession to the World Trade Organization (WTO) and related international treaties, China once again made substantial amendments to its patent law. The amendments related to the following aspects.[13] First, there was further strengthening of the force of patent rights. In the patent law of 2000, 'offering to sell' was also included in the protection scope of the patent right.[14] Under such a provision, even if infringing products were not sold directly for profit, the act of offering to sell the patented product or a product obtained directly by way of the patented process would also constitute infringement. Second, the system of examination of patents now came under full judicial supervision.[15] All kinds of administrative examinations of patents would now fall under the judicial supervision of the people's court. The amendments directly reflect the principle of the rule of law and were made to conform with Article 62 of the Agreement on Trade-Related Aspects of Intellectual Property (TRIPS). According to Article 62, any administrative decision made in relation to the acquirement and maintenance of IPR, as well as related procedures, is subject to judicial review or quasi-judicial review. Before the adoption of TRIPS into Chinese law, under the patent laws of 1992 or 1984, only disputes regarding the application, invalidation, revocation or objection of patents for invention could be heard by the local courts; as for disputes regarding the application, invalidation, revocation or objection of patents for utility models and designs, the decision made by the Board of Reexamination of Patent would be final.[16] Third came the adding of conservative measures in litigation in order that the interests of patentees could be sufficiently protected. For some infringement acts, so long as the rights owner or the interested person had evidence to prove that such an infringing act, if not checked or prevented in a timely manner, could cause irreparable harm, the court

---

[13] See the Decision Regarding the Revision of the Patent Law of the People's Republic of China, adopted at the 17th Session of the Standing Committee of the Ninth National People's Congress on 25 August 2000.

[14] See Article 11, Patent Law (2000).

[15] See Section 2, Article 41, Patent Law (2000).

[16] See Sections 2 and 3, Article 49, Patent Law (1984); Sections 2 and 3, Article 43, Patent Law (1993).

could, according to the party's request, adopt measures for ordering the suspension of the relevant acts and the preservation of property.[17] This kind of system is similar to the provisional injunction in UK and US laws. Fourth, the cancellation of revocation procedures of patent rights was added in the earlier amendment to simplify the procedure and to bring it within the invalidation procedure. With these amendments, the Chinese patent law was now fully in line with the requirements of the WTO's TRIPS agreement, raising Chinese law on the protection of patents to an international standard.

With the further development of the domestic economy and technology in China, new requirements were being demanded of the patent law. In 2005, preparations for the third amendment of the patent law started. Compared with the first two amendments, the motivation for the third amendment was different. The impetus for the early amendments came from outside, whilst the need for the third amendment originated from within China, that is to say, the majority of the third amendment was to meet the needs of the development of the domestic economy and technology originating in China. Before the third amendment was formulated, the relevant State Intellectual Property Office (SIPO) entrusted a 40-strong group of domestic experts and scholars with the task of researching the relevant issues that would form the basis of amendments to the patent law. The Patent Law (draft) was completed on the advice of this expert group and was open to public consultation and comment. In many respects, this open mode public consultation reflected the great advances China had made in structuring its legislative framework for intellectual property.

On 27 December 2008, the Standing Committee of the National People's Congress of China adopted the Decision Regarding the Amendment of the Patent Law of the People's Republic of China. The Decision bought about several amendments to the Chinese Patent Law, including: first, enhancing the requirements of granting a patent, changing the original mixed novelty standard to an absolute novelty standard;[18] adjusting the requirement for granting a patent for a design;[19] adding requirements with respect to the validity of acquiring genetic resources and disclosure of source for the inventions and creations depending on the genetic resource.[20] Second, provisions concerning foreign-related patent agencies were abolished. Any Chinese patent agency established under Chinese law could now deal

---

17 Article 61, Patent Law (2000).
18 See Section 2, Article 22, Patent Law (2008).
19 See Article 23, Patent Law (2008).
20 See Section 5, Article 5 and Section 5, Article 26, Patent Law (2008).

with foreign-related patent cases.[21] Prior to the implementation of this decision, only those patent agencies recognized by the government could handle foreign-related cases. Third, the scope for adjusting the provisions on compulsory licenses was enlargened. The provisions on compulsory license resulting from having not exploited or having not sufficiently exploited were added.[22] Compulsory licenses in relation to public health[23] and semiconductor technologies[24] were to be expressly stipulated. Fourth, provisions similar to the *Bolar exception* in the USA[25] were incorporated, specifically the limitation of patent rights relating to the administrative examination and approval procedure for drugs and medical instruments.[26] Fifth, provisions regarding parallel importation were added. Under this provision, parallel importation would now become completely legal in China.[27] Sixth, the amount of statutory damage to be awarded for infringement of patent rights was clearly set out.[28] Seventh, the clause of prior art as a defence to limit improper legal action was added.[29] Moreover, amendments were also made with respect to the issues of the preservation of evidence,[30] ban before action[31] and exercise of joint patents.[32]

Eight years passed from the adoption of the patent law in 1984 to the first amendment of the law in 1992. Another eight years passed from the first amendment of the patent law to its second amendment in 2000. The third amendment of the patent law was completed in 2008 (coming into effect on 1 October 2009).[33] That each amendment should come every

---

[21] See Section 1, Article 19, Patent Law (2008).
[22] See Article 48, Patent Law (2008).
[23] See Article 50, Patent Law (2008).
[24] See Article 52, Patent Law (2008).
[25] *Roche Product, Inc v Bolar Pharmaceutical Co*, 733 F. 2d 858 (Fed. Cir. 1984).
[26] See Section 5, Article 69, Patent Law (2008). The provision is 'for the purpose of providing the information needed for the administrative approval, manufacture, use, import of a drug or medical apparatus, and exclusively for such manufacture any import of a patented drug or patented medical apparatus', will not be classed as infringing acts.
[27] See Section 1, Article 69, Patent Law (2008). In this provision, the right of importation is exhaustion, which causes that parallel importation is legal in China now.
[28] See Section 2, Article 65, Patent Law (2008).
[29] See Article 62, Patent Law (2008).
[30] See Article 67, Patent Law (2008).
[31] See Article 66, Patent Law (2008).
[32] See Article 15, Patent Law (2008).
[33] The Implementing Regulations for the Third amendment of the Patent Law and the new Patent Examination Guidelines (2010) came into force together on 1 February 2010. The Implementing Regulations 2010 replace the Implementing

eight years is a total coincidence. But over the three eight-year periods, the Chinese economy has continued to develop to dizzying heights. It is believed that, following its third amendment, the patent law will continue to assist China in developing its economy and help to form a more creative state.

2.2. THE OWNERSHIP OF A PATENT

An inventor means any person who, during the course of accomplishing the invention or creation, makes a creative contribution to the solution of an invention or creation and its embodiment. Any person who only puts forward a problem to be solved by the invention and who does not provide concrete ideas on how to solve the problem, or who only brings forward some general opinions, or who takes part in other auxiliary functions (such as typewriting, drawing, etc.), or who is responsible only for organizing work, or who offers facilities for making use of material and technical means, will not be considered an inventor under the law.[34] Generally, the right to the invention or creation belongs to the inventor, that is to say, the inventor has the right to apply for a patent with regard to the invention or creation accomplished by him or her. After the application is approved, the applicant is known as the 'patentee'.

Joint invention When an invention is accomplished through the cooperation of two or more persons, the invention is called a joint invention. The right to the invention will be jointly owned by the joint inventors. The co-owner's consensus will be obtained before applying for a patent with regard to the joint invention. Article 15 of the Chinese Patent Law (2008) states that: 'If there is any agreement between the joint owners of the right to apply for a patent or a patent right regarding the exercise of the relevant right, the agreement shall be followed. If there is no such agreement, any of the joint owners may exploit the patent independently or license others to exploit the patent by means of ordinary license. In the case of licensing others to exploit the patent, royalties charged shall be distributed among the joint owners.'

Service invention The employee's invention referred to in the patent laws of Western countries is called a service invention under the China

---

Regulations 2001. The Patent Examination Guidelines (2010) revise the Patent Examination Guidelines (2006).

[34] See Article 13, Implementing Regulations of the Patent Law of China (2010).

Patent Law. Section 1, Article 6 of the China Patent Law provides: 'An invention-creation, made by a person in execution of the tasks of the entity to which he belongs, or made by him mainly by using the material and technical means of the entity is a service invention-creation. For a service invention-creation, the right to apply for a patent belongs to the entity. After the application is approved, the entity shall be the patentee.' Thus it is clear that there are two kinds of service invention under the China Patent Law: the first is made by a person in execution of the tasks of the entity for which he works; the second is made by him mainly by using the material means of the entity. According to the provisions of Article 12 of Implementing Regulations of the Patent Law(2010), the invention made by a person 'in execution of the tasks of the entity to which he belongs' shall include at least any invention made: (1) in the course of performing his own duty; (2) in execution of any task, other than his own duty, which was entrusted to him by the entity to which he belongs; (3) within one year after the retirement, transfer from the entity to which he originally belongs or the labor and personnel relationship being terminated, where the invention-creation relates to his own duty or the other task entrusted to him by the entity to which he previously belonged. 'Material and technical means of the entity' mean the entity's money, equipment, spare parts, raw materials or technical materials, which are not disclosed to the public. Although the right to apply for a patent for the service invention belongs to the entity, the entity shall award to the inventor or creator of a service invention a corresponding reward.

Commissioned invention This is an invention made by another person under a contract. Ownership of the invention will be in accordance with the provisions of the contract. Where the contract is not clear or there is no such agreement on the ownership, the provisions of the law will apply to favor the party who accomplishes the invention, namely that the patentee's rights shall be owned by the party who made the invention.[35]

2.3. TYPE OF PATENT

Patents can, based on different classification methods, be divided into patents for inventions, patents for utility models, patents for designs, patent for plants, supplementary patents, importation patents, etc. As mentioned

---

[35] See Article 8, Patent Law (2008).

earlier, Chinese patent law allows for three main types of patents: patents for inventions, patents for utility models and patents for designs.

2.3.1. Invention

As specified above, an 'Invention' means any new technical solution relating to a product, a process or their improvement.[36] An invention will have the following features: first, creation or innovation will be included in the invention, namely the invention must be unprecedented compared to any prior art, and have a definite progress and technical difficulty. Second, the invention must be made by utilizing any rules of natural science. From the point of view of the patent law, a solution without utilizing the rule of natural science will not be referred to as 'invention', and should not be protected by patent law. Technologies are the various techniques and production skills, as well as the relevant productive tools, materials and equipment. Third, the invention must be a concrete technical solution to a problem. So called 'concrete' means that the invention can be exploited and will have a definite technological effect and be repeatable. The duration of a patent right for an invention will be 20 years, under the China Patent Law.[37]

2.3.2. Utility Model

The patent for a utility model is another form of protection for a technical solution under the China Patent Law. For developing countries, this type of protection is of particular significance. Annually, there are a great number of applications for patents in China, most of which are for utility models. A utility model means any new technical solution relating to the shape, the structure, or their combination in a product, which is fit for practical use.[38] Both utility models and inventions are forms of technical solutions. However, there are still differences between the two as follows: (1) the scope of protection is different. The subject matter when applying for a patent for a utility model will be only those products with a fixed form or structure; while the subject matter when applying for a patent for an invention can be a product as well as a process. (2) The requirement for the inventiveness of patents for utility models is less strict than that of patents for inventions so that many small inventions with lower

---

[36] See Section 2, Article 2 of China Patent Law (2008).
[37] See Article 42 of China Patent Law (2008).
[38] See Section 3, Article 2 of China Patent Law (2008).

levels of technical difficulty are more suitable as applications for utility model patents. (3) The examination procedure for utility model patents is simpler and faster than that for invention patents. The level of protection for utility model patents is correspondingly lower because of the less strict requirements for the grant of a utility model patent. For instance, the duration of a utility model patent is ten years, shorter than that for the patent of an invention, which is twenty years.

2.3.3. Design

Design means any new design of the shape, pattern, colour, or their combination, of a product, which creates an aesthetic feeling and is fit for industrial application.[39] The characteristics of a design are: (1) The design must depend on a product. Any design dissociated from the concrete product may, at best, be deemed as a kind of work of art, which can be protected under copyright law but not protected as a design under the patent law. (2) Shape, pattern and color of a product are the elements of design, with a view towards aesthetic feeling, without pursuit of practical functions. Contrast this with an invention or a utility model which are both technical solutions that must have definite practical functions and can be used for solving specific technical problems. This is the distinguishing difference under Chinese law between a design and invention or utility model. Many Western countries, for example, have a specific design right separate from patent rights. (3) The design must be fit for industrial application, namely the design must be capable of being reproduced on a large scale by means of industry. The current Chinese Patent Law provides that the duration of a patent for design shall be ten years.[40]

2.4. THE PATENT PROCESS

2.4.1. Application for a Patent

A patent comes into being after the application and examination stages. The following outlines the procedure for applying for a patent for an invention and a patent for a utility model in China. First, a written request for patent is submitted to the patent office. The request is a standard form, printed specially by the administrative organization of national

---

39 See Section 4, Article 2 of China Patent Law (2008).
40 See Article 42 of China Patent Law (2008).

patents (SIPO), which applicants must complete in the prescribed format.[41] Second, the applicant needs to state its claims. The claim is also made in written form and states specifically the extent of the patent protection asked for in terms of the invention-creation.[42] After the application for the patent is approved, the claim will then become the written document, which defines concretely the extent of the patent right.[43] Third, the applicant needs to submit a detailed description of the patent.[44] The description will need to reflect the whole technical solution in a sufficiently clear and complete manner. Besides the above application documents, a qualified application for a patent for invention or a patent for a utility model must have at least an abstract of the description, and the application for a utility model must include drawings.[45]

As regards design patents, two application documents are required: (1) a request for the design. The content of the request is similar to that of a patent for invention; (2) drawings or photographs.[46] The drawings or photographs will generally be the best format for describing the design, and should reveal features of the design clearly, distinctly and objectively. In the application for a patent for a design, drawing or photographs perform the same function as the 'claims' in the application for a patent for an invention or a patent for a utility model.[47]

Various additional application documents may be submitted at filing, on the request of applicants, such as a statement of early publication of the invention, a request for a substantive examination, a power of attorney, a declaration of change of bibliographic data, a request for reduction or postponement of payment of fees, a brief description of the design, etc. Whether or not these documents need to be submitted will depend on the applicant's requirements.

2.4.2. The Examination System of the Chinese Patent

After receiving the application for patent for invention, the Chinese Patent Office will complete a preliminary examination. The content of the preliminary examination includes whether or not the application for a patent for invention meets the formal requirements of the patent law, such

---

41 See Section 2, Article 26, Patent Law (2008).
42 See Section 4, Article 26, Patent Law (2008).
43 See Section 1, Article 59, Patent Law (2008).
44 See Section 1 and Section 3, Article 26, Patent Law (2008).
45 See Section 3, Article 26, Patent Law (2008).
46 See Sections 1 and 2, Article 27, Patent Law (2008).
47 See Section 2, Article 59, Patent Law (2008).

as whether the composition of the patent application is eligible or not, whether the categories of the documents are complete or not, whether the number of copies of the documents is sufficient or not. Applications which meet the requirements will be published after the expiration of 18 months from the date of filing. The applicant may request the Patent Office to proceed to examine the application as to its substance at any time within three years from the date of filing. The Patent Office will, upon a request for examination as to substance, proceed to examine the application as to its substance. The content of the substantive examination includes the examination of novelty, inventiveness and usefulness. For applications that meet these requirements, a patent right will be granted and all of the documents about the patent will be opened, and related information published in the national gazette.

The examination procedure for a patent for a utility model and a patent for a design is by contrast simpler. After receiving an application, the Patent Office will proceed with a preliminary examination. The content of the preliminary examination is very similar to the procedure for 'invention applications' described above. If, following the preliminary examination, there is no cause for rejection of the application, the Patent Office will directly make a decision to grant the patent right for a utility model or a design patent without further substantive examination and will announce it.[48]

Where an application is rejected, the applicant may, within three months from the date of receipt of the notification of the decision of the Patent Office rejecting the application, request the Patent Re-examination Board to make a re-examination.[49] The Patent Re-examination Board will examine the reasons for re-examination and notify the party concerned as to the conclusion of the re-examination. Where an applicant for a patent for invention is not satisfied with the re-examination decision of the Patent Re-examination Board, the applicant may, within three months from the date of receipt of the notification, institute administrative proceedings in the people's court, with the Patent Re-examination Board as defendant.[50]

Where any party considers that the grant of the patent right by the Patent Office is not in conformity with the relevant provisions of the patent law, such party may request the Patent Re-examination Board to invalidate the patent.[51] The Patent Re-examination Board will, after re-examination of the request to invalidate the patent, make a decision to

[48] See Article 40, Patent Law (2008).
[49] See Section 1, Article 41, Patent Law (2008).
[50] See Section 2, Article 41, Patent Law (2008).
[51] See Article 45, Patent Law (2008).

uphold the patent right or a decision to invalidate the patent right. A party who is not satisfied with the decision made by the Patent Re-examination Board may institute legal proceedings in the people's court.[52]

2.4.3. Requirements for Grant of Patent Right

There are two kinds of requirement provided in the Chinese Patent Law, namely passive and active requirements respectively.

2.4.3.1. Passive requirements

First, no patent right shall be granted for any invention-creation that is contrary to the laws of the State or social morality. If the purpose, effect and function etc., of any invention-creation is contrary to the laws, or the constitution and application of any invention-creation is possibly detrimental to the public interest, no patent right shall be granted.[53] Here, 'detrimental to the public interest' means that the exploitation or use of an invention may cause detriment to the public or to society or may disrupt the good order of the State and the society,[54] for example, the use of an invention may seriously pollute the environment, or seriously waste energy or resources, disrupt ecological balance, or impair the public health. Section 2, Article 5 of the Patent Law also provides: 'No patent right shall be granted for any invention-creation which is completed on the basis of genetic resources of which the acquisition or use breaches the stipulations of related laws and regulations'. This provision was added to the patent law in 2008 in accordance with the Convention on Biological Diversity (CBD), as China is a signatory to the CBD.

Second, no patent right shall be granted for scientific discoveries.[55] Scientific discoveries per se are not inventions defined under the patent law.

Third, no patent right shall be granted for rules and methods for mental activities.[56] Rules and methods for mental activities are rules and methods governing people's thinking, expression, judgment and memorization, rather than technical solutions or designs, and do not constitute an invention defined under the patent law. For example, computer languages, computing rules, computer programs per se, method and system of managing

52 See Section 2, Article 46, Patent Law (2008).

53 See Section 1, Article 5, Patent Law (2008).

54 State Intellectual Property Office, Guidelines for Patent Examination 2006, p. 112.

55 See Item 1, Section 1, Article 25, Patent Law (2008).

56 See Item 2, Section 1, Article 25 of China Patent Law (2008).

organization, production, commercial activities, etc. shall not be granted a patent right.[57]

Fourth, no patent right shall be granted for methods for the diagnosis or treatment of diseases.[58] Methods for the diagnosis or for the treatment of diseases have a direct effect on people's well-being and health. To allow the patenting of such techniques could harm the general development of solutions to public health issues.

Fifth, no patent right shall be granted for animal and plant varieties.[59] In the current Chinese Patent Law, no patent right shall be granted for animal and plant varieties but patent rights can be granted for processes used in producing animal and plant varieties.[60] On the other hand, according to the Regulations of Protection of New Plant Varieties of China (1997), any variety listed in the catalog of protection[61] may be protected in accordance with the provisions of the Regulations. Because China is a signatory of Act 1978 of the International Convention for the Protection of New Varieties of Plants (UPOV Act 1978), rather than that of UPOV Act 1991, the government of China can issue catalogues which cover the scope of protection.

Sixth, no patent right shall be granted for substances obtained by means of nuclear transformation.[62]

Seventh, no patent right shall be granted for two-dimensional designs of images, colors, or combinations of the two, which mainly serve as indicators.[63]

2.4.3.2. Active requirements

The first active requirement is the need for *novelty*. In China, the frame of reference used to judge novelty is *prior art*. Prior art means any technology known to the public before the date of filing of the patent application in China or abroad.[64] If the content of the technology when applying for

---

57 See Chapter 9 (Information Technology, Computers and Computer Software) where this subject is further discussed.

58 See Item 3, Section 1, Article 25 of China Patent Law (2008).

59 See Item 4, Section 1, Article 25 of China Patent Law (2008).

60 See Section 2, Article 25 of China Patent Law (2008).

61 The catalogues of protection on new varieties of plant are issued by Ministry of Agriculture and State Forestry Administration, of China. The web sites are www.cnpvp.cn and www.cnpvp.net, on which the catalogues are published.

62 See Item 5, Section 1, Article 25 of China Patent Law (2008).

63 See Item 6, Section 1, Article 25 of China Patent Law (2008). Contrast this with trademarks potentially being possible for 3D shapes (and smells and flashing marks) under the planned third amendment to the trademark law. See Chapter 3.

64 See Section 5, Article 22 of China Patent Law (2008).

a patent differs from that for the prior art, the technology has novelty. Article 22 of the Chinese Patent Law provides: 'Novelty means that the invention or utility model shall neither belong to the prior art, nor has any entity or individual previously filed before the date of filing with the patent administrative department under the State Council an application on an identical invention or utility model which was recorded in patent application documents or other gazetted patent documents published after the said date of filing'. For example, a claim for patent application is 'a core of a motor rotor made of Nd-Fe-B permanent magnet alloy having a tetragonal crystal structure and a main phase of Nd2Fe14B intermetallic compound'. If the prior art contains 'a core of a motor rotor made of Nd-Fe-B magnet', the novelty of the application is lost, because a person skilled in the art knows that 'Nd-Fe-B magnet' covers 'Nd-Fe-B permanent magnet' and the 'Nd-Fe-B permanent magnet' means the Nd-Fe-B permanent magnet alloy having a tetragonal crystal structure and a main phase of Nd2Fe14B intermetallic compound.[65]

For a design patent, the novelty standard provided in the patent law is less than that required for a patent for invention and a patent for a utility model. Article 23 of the Chinese Patent Law provides: 'Any design for which a patent right may be granted must not belong to a prior design; nor has any entity or individual previously filed before the date of filing with the patent administration department under the State Council an application on an identical design which was published in patent documents published after the said date of filing'. Here prior design means any design known to the public before the date of filing. Furthermore, 'The design for which a patent right may be granted must be substantially different from prior designs or a combination of the features of prior designs',[66] 'must not be in conflict with any prior legal rights of any other person',[67] and must not be 'the design serving as identification to the pattern and color or their combinations of the plane presswork'.[68]

There are some exceptions provided for under the Chinese Patent Law that will not allow for a loss of novelty. For example, any invention-creation for which a patent is applied shall not lose its novelty if, within six months before the filing date of the application, one of the following events has occurred:[69] (1) it was exhibited for the first time at an interna-

---

65 The State Intellectual Property Office, *Guidelines for Patent Examination (2006)*, p. 149, Intellectual Property Publishing House (Beijing), 2006.
66 See Section 2, Article 23 of China Patent Law (2008).
67 See Section 3, Article 23 of China Patent Law (2008).
68 See Section 4, Article 23 of China Patent Law (2008).
69 See Article 24 of China Patent Law (2008).

tional exhibition sponsored or recognized by the Chinese government; (2) it was made public for the first time at a prescribed academic or technical conference; or (3) it was disclosed by any person without the consent of the applicant. For these three cases, although novelty is not lost, the applicant cannot exclude a third party's application for the patent of the same invention, if a third party files a patent application with regard to the same invention in advance.

The second active requirement is the need for *inventiveness*. After an invention passes the examination stage of novelty, the Patent Office will further examine whether or not the invention has inventiveness. Inventiveness is also called 'non-obviousness' or 'creative step' in some other countries. Inventiveness under the Chinese Patent Law is defined as: 'compared with the prior art the invention has prominent and substantive distinguishing features and represents a marked improvement, or the utility model possesses substantive distinguishing features and represents an improvement'.[70] Here, 'substantive distinguishing features' of the invention means the invention has, compared with the prior art, essential distinguishing features, and these distinguishing features are technical. If the person skilled in the art can obtain the invention just by logical analysis, inference or limited experimentation on the basis of the prior art, the invention has no substantive distinguishing feature. For example,[71] the claimed invention concerns a building component made of aluminium, and the purpose of the claimed invention is to reduce the weight of the building component. A reference document discloses a building component with the same structure and points out that it is made of lightweight material, but does not mention it is made of aluminium. Another reference document discloses that aluminium is one kind of lightweight material and can be used as a building component. In this situation, the claimed invention is obvious and fails to have substantive distinguishing features.

'Improvement' means that the level of the invention, compared with the prior art, must be higher, or can produce an advantageous rather than retrograde, technical effect. For example, the invention has overcome the defects in the existing technology, or has provided a different technical solution to solve a certain technical problem, or represents a certain new trend in technical development. In detail, the invention may produce the following circumstances: quality improved, output increased, energy saving, environmental pollution prevented or controlled, etc.

---

70 See Section 3, Article 22 of China Patent Law (2008).

71 State Intellectual Property Office, *The Guidelines for Examination (2006)*, p. 164, Intellectual Property Publishing House (Beijing), 2006.

The third active requirement is *usefulness*.[72] The examination and judgment of usefulness is simpler in the substantive examination procedure of a patent. Usefulness means that the invention or utility model can be made or used and can create positive results. That means a product shall be able to be made industrially and solve a technical problem, or a process shall be able to be used industrially and solve a technical problem. Only when a patent application for a product or process satisfies such requirement can it be granted a patent right. Novelty and inventiveness are requirements for the grant of patent, but usefulness not only is a requirement, but represents also the *purpose* of the invention.

2.5. CONTENT OF PATENT RIGHT

2.5.1. Rights of Patentee

Patent rights can be divided into two parts in form, namely that the patentee may carry out certain actions and that patentee may prohibit others from carrying out certain actions. Under patent law, rights holders enjoy a form of monopoly right in prohibiting third parties from exploiting the patented technology. There are different scopes of prohibition provided in the Chinese Patent Law. For a patent for an invention and a patent for a utility model, according to the Chinese Patent Law, no entity or individual may, without the authorization of the patentee, exploit the patent, that is, make, use, offer to sell, sell or import the patented product, or use the patented process, or use, offer to sell, sell or import the product directly obtained by the patented process, for production or business purposes.[73] After the grant of the patent right for a design, no entity or individual may, without the authorization of the patentee, exploit the design, namely make, offer to sell, sell, or import the design patented product for production or business purposes.[74] In this respect, the provisions of the China Patent Law are identical with internationally accepted standards.

2.5.2. Limitation of Patent Right

There are several limitations on a patent right. These limitations are in the public interest. The first limitation is a limit on the duration of the patent

72 See Section 4, Article 22 of China Patent Law (2008).
73 See Section 1, Article 11 of China Patent Law (2008).
74 See Section 2, Article 11 of China Patent Law (2008).

right. The current China Patent Law provides that the duration of the patent right for inventions shall be twenty years, counted from the date of filing; the duration of the patent right for utility models and the duration of the patent right for designs shall be ten years, counted from the date of filing.[75]

The second limitation is on the exercise of the patent right. First, after the sale of a patented product or products directly obtained by using the patented process, which was made by the patentee or an entity/individual authorized by the patentee, if any other person uses, offers to sell, sells or imports that product, then the original patent is exhausted.[76] The first instance of sale triggers the doctrine of exhaustion. Because the right of importation is introduced into the range of exhaustion of rights under the China Patent Law, the parallel importation of goods becomes legal in China. Second, before the date of filing the patent application, any person who has already made the identical product, using an identical process, or makes the necessary preparations for its making or using, may continue to make or use it within the original scope of the patent only.[77] The right of the person to conduct such an act of exploitation is referred to as rights derived from prior exploitation or right of prior use. Third, any foreign means of transport which temporarily passes through the territory, territorial waters or territorial airspace of China using the patent concerned for its own needs, in its devices and installations will not be deemed an infringement of a patent right.[78] This provision arises from the Paris Convention.[79] Fourth, any person using a patent concerned solely for the purposes of scientific research and experiments will not be classed as an infringing act.[80] Fifth, for the purpose of providing the information needed for the administrative approval, manufacture, use, import of a drug or medical apparatus, and exclusively for such manufacture any import of a patented drug or patented medical apparatus, will not be classed as infringing acts.[81] Moreover, for the acts of offering to sell, sale or use of the products infringing others' patent right without knowledge that such acts are infringing acts and provided that the legal source of the products can be determined, the party committing the acts will not bear liability for infringement.[82] This is called innocent infringement.

---

75 See Article 42 of China Patent Law (2008).
76 See Section 1, Article 69 of China Patent Law (2008).
77 See Section 2, Article 69 of China Patent Law (2008).
78 See Section 3, Article 69 of China Patent Law (2008).
79 See Article 5ter of Paris Convention for the Protection of Industrial Property.
80 See Section 4, Article 69 of China Patent Law (2008).
81 See Section 5, Article 69 of China Patent Law (2008).
82 See Article 70 of China Patent Law (2008).

There are some other limitations of patent right in the Chinese Patent Law, such as for compulsory licenses.[83] All of the provisions concerning compulsory licenses, however, derive from the Paris Convention and the TRIPS Agreement.

2.6. PROTECTION OF PATENT RIGHT

In the China Patent Law, the scope of protection for an invention patent or a utility model patent is determined on the basis of the patent claims. The description and the appended drawings may be used to interpret the claims. The scope of protection for a design patent is determined by the product's design shown in the relevant drawings or photographs. The brief statement of the patent will be used to interpret the design of the product shown in the drawings or photographs.[84] For example, in the final decision of the infringement case on the Chinese word inputting method of 'Five-stroke character', the panel of judges wrote: 'The first instance decision did not follow the principle for determination of patent infringement, did not define the scope of the patent according to the patent claims. . . . It only compared the characterizing portion of the independent claim as the 'main technical feature' to the accused product, and did not compare the preamble portion of the independent claim which concerned known technology. That enlarges the scope of the patent.'[85]

Where any infringement dispute involves an invention patent for a process for the manufacture of a new product, any entity or individual manufacturing the identical product will need to provide proof to show that the process used in the course of producing the product is different from the patented process.[86] According to the judgment of China's court, the standard of 'new product' is the same requirement as of novelty.[87]

During a patent infringement dispute, if the alleged infringer has evidence proving the technology used or the design belongs to the prior art or

---

[83] See Articles 48–58 of China Patent Law (2008).

[84] See Article 59 of China Patent Law (2008).

[85] *Beijing Wangma Computer Co v China Dongnan Technology Trade Co*, The Civil Judgment of Beijing Higher People's Court, [1994] Gao_Jing_Zhi_Zhong_Zi No. 30. See *Intellectual Property Study*, vol. 4, p. 327, China Fangzheng Publishing House (Beijing), 1998.

[86] See Section 1, Article 61 of China Patent Law (2008).

[87] Intellectual Property Tribunal of Beijing First Intermediate People's Court, *Review of Well-known IP Cases 5*, pp. 313–15, Intellectual Property Publishing House (Beijing), August 2008.

is a prior design, the production of the good will not be classed an infringing act.[88] All these provisions are found in the patent laws of other countries. There have been several cases involving the prior art defence in China in recent years;[89] however, few of them have been supported by the courts.[90]

There is, however, a special feature in the procedure for handling infringement cases under the China Patent Law. When an infringement of patent right occurs, the patentee may institute legal proceedings in the people's court, or request the administrative authority for patent affairs to handle the matter. The administrative authority for patent affairs handling the matter may take cognizance of whether the infringement is established or not and order the infringer to stop the infringing act immediately, but may not make a decision with respect to compensation for damages.[91]

When the court determines the damages to be awarded to compensate for infringement, the amount of compensation will be assessed on the basis of the loss actually suffered by the patentee, or the profits which the infringer has earned through the infringement if it is difficult to specify the loss. If it is difficult to determine the losses which the patentee has suffered or the profits which the infringer has earned, the amount may be assessed by reference to the appropriate multiple of the amount of the royalty fee for patent exploitation. The amount of damage shall include any reasonable costs incurred in stopping the patent infringement.[92] If it is difficult to determine the losses which the patentee has suffered, the profits which the infringer has earned, or the royalty fee for exploitation of the patent, the people's court may award damages of between 10,000 Yuan and 1,000,000 Yuan[93] depending on the type of patent right, the nature and gravity of the infringing act.

---

[88] See Articles 59, 61 and 62 of China Patent Law (2008).

[89] *Beijing Shute Architectural Science and Technology Co. et al v Shanghai Ronghe Enterprise Ltd*, The Civil Judgment of Beijing Higher People's Court, [2003] Gao_Min_Zhong_Zi No. 00159. See *Review of Well-known IP Cases 5*, p. 316, Intellectual Property Publishing House (Beijing), August 2008. *Shandong Joyoung Small Household Electric Appliances Co et al v Shanghai Shuaijia Electronic Science and Technology Co et al.*, The Civil Judgment of Shandong Higher People's Court, [2007] Lu_Minsan_Zhong_Zi No. 38. See *100 High-profile IP Cases in China (Case Briefs)*, p. 41, China Patent Agent (HK) Ltd, 2009.

[90] Intellectual Property Tribunal of Beijing First Intermediate People's Court, *Summarization of IP Cases*, p. 119, Intellectual Property Publishing House (Beijing), September 2008.

[91] See Article 60 of China Patent Law (2008).

[92] See Section 1, Article 65 of China Patent Law (2008).

[93] See Section 2, Article 69 of China Patent Law (2008). At the time of writing the amount of compensation available under the patent law is larger than the compensation provided in the China Copyright Law (2001) and China Trademark

Before filing a suit for infringement, if any patentee or interested party has evidence to prove that another person is infringing or will soon infringe its patent right and that if such infringing act is not checked or prevented from occurring in time, it is likely to cause irreparable harm, he or she may, before filing a suit, apply to the people's court for an order to stop the relevant acts. The applicant shall provide a bond for the above-mentioned motions; if the applicant does not provide a bond, the application for an injunction will be rejected. Upon receiving the request, the people's court will make a ruling within 48 hours, but where there are special circumstances that require extension, the court may extend the time limit. If a ruling is made to stop the related acts, this ruling will be enforced immediately. If the parties are not satisfied with the ruling, they can apply for a one-time review; the enforcement of the ruling will not be suspended during the course of a review. If the applicant does not file a lawsuit within 15 days after the people's court has issued an order to stop the related acts, the people's court shall withdraw the prior ruling. If the application is in error, the applicant shall compensate the opposite party for losses caused by stopping the relevant acts.[94] This system is similar to the provisional injunction in the laws of the UK and the US.

Besides the above provisional injunction system, an evidence preservation system has also been introduced into the Chinese Patent Law. Article 67 of the China Patent Law provides: 'In order to prevent infringing activities, under the circumstance that the evidence might be destroyed or later be difficult to obtain, the patentee or a related injured party may before filing a law suit apply to the people's court for evidence preservation. The people's court may order the applicant to provide a guarantee for the application of evidence preservation, and if no guarantee is provided by the applicant, reject the application. Upon accepting the request, the people's court shall make a ruling within 48 hours; if the court rules to preserve evidence, this ruling should be enforced immediately. If the applicant does not file a lawsuit within 15 days after the people's court issues an order to preserve evidence, the people's court shall withdraw the prior ruling.' In the China Copyright Law and Trademark Law, there are similar express provisions relating to injunction and evidence preservation measures,[95] which can be derived from the China Civil Procedure Law.[96]

Law (2001), where the maximum compensation is 500,000 Yuan. See Section 2, Article 48 of China Copyright Law (2001), and Section 2, Article 56 of China Trademark Law (2001).

[94] See Sections 1–5, Article 66 of China Patent Law (2008).

[95] See Articles 49 and 50 of China Copyright Law (2001), and Articles 57 and 58 of China Trademark Law (2001).

[96] See Articles 93–6, and Article 99 of China Civil Procedure Law (1991).

The period of limitation for filing a suit concerning the infringement of a patent right is two years, counted from the day on which the patentee or the interested parties became aware or should have become aware of the act of infringement. This is identical to the provision of the China General Principles of the Civil Law.[97]

After the third amendment, the China patent legislation has now reached an internationally accepted level of protection for patents. China has gained much experience in the execution of its patent law over a period of 20 years or more. This is an incremental approach to developing an effective legislative system for the protection of patents in China, but one that has actively gained rapid momentum. Of course, there are some aspects of the China Patent Law which should be improved in future years. For example, there are no provisions on the doctrine of equivalents, contributory infringement, partial design protection, etc. These may be dealt with in the next amendment.

97 See Article 135, China General Principles of the Civil Law (1986).

3. Trademarks

Li Zuming[1]

3.1. INTRODUCTION – WHAT ARE TRADEMARKS?

A trademark is a commercial mark that distinguishes a provider of commodities or services from others. Trademarks include registered trademarks and unregistered trademarks. Registered trademarks are those that have been approved and registered by the Trademark Office (TMO) of the Chinese State Administration for Industry and Commerce (SAIC). Trademark registrants have exclusive use of their trademarks and are protected by Chinese law. Unregistered trademarks are those commercial marks that have not been approved and registered by the Trademark Office, but are used as trademarks.[2]

In China, an application for trademark registration may be filed for any visible mark including a word, sign, letter, number, 3D (three-dimensional) mark, color combination, or a combination of the elements mentioned above, that distinguish the commodities of the natural person, legal person or other organization from those of others. A sound, smell or an animation cannot compose a registered trademark.[3]

According to the Trademark Law of the People's Republic of China of 22 February 1993 (as amended) to use a registered trademark, the trademark registrant must use '注册商标' (meaning a *registered trademark*) or a sign indicating the trademark is registered (the registration signs

[1] Associate Professor in Law at the China University of Political Science and Law and Associate Director of the Institute of Intellectual Property Law. I would like to express my sincere appreciation to Mr. Robert Yeargin for his valuable assistance with the English version of this chapter.

[2] Some unregistered trademarks, such as unregistered well-known marks and other unregistered trademarks with a certain influence can be protected by the Trademark Law, the Law of the People's Republic of China Against Unfair Competition and the Civil Law of the People's Republic of China in China. Detailed information can be found at 3.2.4.2.

[3] The draft of the third revision of the Trademark Law (2010) provides that sound, smell or animation (flashing marks) can be registered subject to the rules promulgated by the SAIC.

include the Chinese character '注' and 'R'). The revised trademark law of 27 October 2001 provides, however, that: 'A trademark registrant has the right to mark the words, "Registered trademark"', or 'a sign indicating that the trademark is registered' on its goods.

With respect to commodities that the state has designated as requiring the use of a registered trademark, an application for a trademark registration must be filed; the goods may not be sold on the market before registration is granted. After 15 September 2002 when the Implementing Regulations of the Trademark Law (fourth version) entered into force, applications for the registration of trademarks of cigarettes, cigars and packed cut tobacco had to be made and approved before the relevant goods could be marketed and sold in China.[4] Applications for the registration of trademarks of other commodities and services are optional.

3.2. OUTLINE OF RELEVANT LAWS AND REGULATIONS IMPACTING THE DOMESTIC CHINESE SECTOR

At present, the laws, regulations, judicial interpretations and rules relevant to trademarks include, but are not limited to, the following:

(1) General Principles of the Civil Law of the People's Republic of China (effective 1 January 1987);
(2) The Trademark Law of the People's Republic of China (adopted at the 24th meeting of the Standing Committee of the Fifth National People's Congress on 23 August 1982; amended for the first time 22 February 1993; amended for the second time 27 October 2001);
(3) Law of the People's Republic of China Anti-Unfair Competition (effective 1 December 1993);
(4) Criminal Law of the People's Republic of China (effective 1 October 1997, amended 1999, 2001, 2002, 2005, 2006, 2009);
(5) Civil Procedure Law of the People's Republic of China (effective 9 April 1991);
(6) Implementing Regulations of the Trademark Law of the People's Republic of China (promulgated 10 March 1983, revised 3 January

[4] Law of the People's Republic of China on Tobacco Monopoly, Article 20: applications must be made for the registration of trademarks of cigarettes, cigars and packed cut tobacco, which shall not be manufactured and marketed before the trademark is registered upon approval. The production and sale of tobacco products with counterfeit trademarks is forbidden.

1988, revised 15 July 1993, revised 23 April 1995 and revised again 3 August 2002);

(7) The Judicial Interpretations of the Supreme People's Court Concerning the Application of Laws in the Trial of Cases of Civil Disputes Arising from Trademarks (effective 16 October 2002);

(8) The Rules of the Supreme People's Court on Issues Concerned in the Trial of Cases of Civil Disputes over the Conflict between Registered Trademarks or Enterprise Names with Prior Right (effective 1 March 2008);

(9) The Judicial Interpretations of the Supreme People's Court on the Application of Laws for Protection of Well-Known Marks in the Trial of Trademark Infringement Civil Cases (effective 1 May 2009);

(10) The Judicial Interpretations of the Supreme People's Court Concerning the Application of Laws in the Trial of Cases of Civil Arising from Unfair Competition (effective 1 February 2007);

(11) The Judicial Interpretations of the Supreme People's Court on the Applicable Laws Concerning the Pre-trial Stop of the Acts Infringing the Rights for Exclusive Use of Registered Trademarks and the Conservation of Evidences (effective 22 January 2002);

(12) The Circular of the Supreme People's Court ('SPC') Providing Guidelines for Courts Exercising Jurisdiction over Cases Involving Patent and Trademark Rights Grants and Rights Determinations (effective 1 July 2009);

(13) The Judicial Interpretations of the Supreme People's Court Concerning the Application of Laws in the Trial of Cases of Civil arising from Well-known Mark Protection (effective 22 April 2009);

(14) The Judicial Interpretations of the Supreme People's Court and the Supreme People's Procuratorate Concerning the Application of Principles Regarding Infringement Intellectual Property Rights in Criminal Cases (1) (effective 22 December 2004), and The Judicial Interpretations of the Supreme People's Court and the Supreme People's Procuratorate Concerning the Application of Principles Regarding Infringement Intellectual Property Rights in Criminal Cases (2) (effective 5 April 2007);

(15) Regulations of PR China on the Protection of Intellectual Properties by the Customs (promulgated by the State Council on 2 December 2003 and effective 1 March 2004);

(16) The Trademark Office of the Administrative Department for Industry and Commerce under the State Council, which is in charge of trademark registration and administration throughout the country, has promulgated many administrative regulations concerning trademark registration and administration, such as Trademark

Review and Adjudication Rules, and Rule of Determination and Protection of Well-known Trademarks, amongst others.[5]

At the time of writing, the third revision of the Trademark Law of the People's Republic of China is still being revised after a period of open consultation.

3.2.1. Classification of Trademarks

Trademarks are divided as follows:

3.2.1.1. Commodity trademarks and service trademarks

Commodity Trademarks refer to the marks used to distinguish the providers of commodities. Service Trademarks refer to the marks used to distinguish the providers of services.

China has adopted the International Classification of Products and Services (under the Nice Agreement, eighth edition), which includes 34 classes of goods and 11 classes of services.

3.2.1.2. Certification marks and collective marks

Certification marks are marks controlled by organizations with supervisory power over certifications of particular commodities or services that are used by units or individuals to certify the origins, raw materials, manufacturing methods, quality or other specific characteristics of those commodities or services.[6]

Collective marks are marks that are registered in the name of groups, associations or other organizations and that are provided to the members of those organizations for business activity use to indicate the membership of the users in those organizations.[7]

3.2.1.3. Registered trademarks and unregistered trademarks

Registered trademarks are marks for which an applicant applies for registration to the Trademark Office of the Administrative Department for Industry and Commerce under the State Council. After examination and approval of the trademark registration, the Trademark Office issues the trademark registration certificate and publicly announces the trademark.

---

5 For a list of websites that display Chinese regulations on trademarks see the following: http://ipr.mofcom.gov.cn/index.shtml; http://www.saic.gov.cn/; http://www.nipso.cn/, http://sbj.saic.gov.cn/, http://www.ipr.gov.cn/cn/index.shtml.

6 Article 3(3) of The Trademark Law of the People's Republic of China.

7 Article 3(2) of The Trademark Law of the People's Republic of China.

Unregistered trademarks are those marks for which no application for registration has been made or which have not been registered by the Trademark Office.

Unregistered trademarks may be identical with or similar to other commercial marks such as packaging, or decorations, or goods name, or geographic indication, or special symbol, or business name. Experts therefore suggest that the Trademark Law should instead be called the 'Law of Commercial Marks'. In China, matters concerning unregistered trademarks can be dealt with in accordance with the Trademark Law, the Law of the People's Republic of China Against Unfair Competition 1993 and relevant judicial interpretations, administrative regulations and rules.

3.2.2. Registered Trademarks

3.2.2.1. General provisions

3.2.2.1.1. Application for trademark registration Any natural person, legal person or other organization that needs to acquire the right to the exclusive use of a trademark for the commodities it produces, manufactures, processes, selects or markets, or services it provides must file an application for commodity trademark registration with the Trademark Office.[8]

3.2.2.1.2. Examination of trademark registration The Trademark Office must, in accordance with the Trademark Law and regulations, examine applications for registration of trademarks. After conducting investigation and research, the Trademark Office will decide whether to approve or reject the application for trademark registration.[9]

When an application for trademark registration has been rejected and the trademark will not be publicly announced, the Trademark Office will notify the applicant in writing. The applicant may apply to the Trademark Review and Adjudication Board for a re-examination within 15 days from the day notification is received. The Trademark Review and Adjudication Board then has to make a decision and notify the applicant in writing of its decision.[10]

If a party does not agree with the decision of the Trademark Review and Adjudication Board, it may file an action in the people's court within 30 days of receipt of the notification.[11]

---

[8] Article 4 of The Trademark Law of the People's Republic of China.
[9] Article 27 of The Trademark Law of the People's Republic of China.
[10] Article 28 of The Trademark Law of the People's Republic of China.
[11] Article 32 of The Trademark Law of the People's Republic of China.

3.2.2.1.3. Preliminary examination and approval and announcement When an application has been made to register a trademark that is in conformity with the relevant provisions of the Trademark Law, the Trademark Office makes a preliminary examination and approval of that trademark and publicly announces it.

Any person may file an opposition to a trademark which has been given preliminary examination and approval within three months from the day it was publicly announced.[12] The grounds for opposition include infringement of Articles 10, 11, 12, 13, 15, 16 or 31 of The Trademark Law.

If an opposition is filed against a trademark, which has been given preliminary examination and approval and has been publicly announced, the Trademark Office hears the petitions of the person opposing the trademark and also the applicant. The Trademark Office, after further investigation and verification, will make a ruling. If a party disagrees with the decision, it may apply to the Trademark Review and Adjudication Board for a re-examination within 15 days from the day on which the notification of decision is received.[13] The Board will then make a ruling and notify both parties in writing.

If a party does not agree with the ruling of the Trademark Review and Adjudication Board, it may bring a suit before a people's court within 30 days from the day on which notification is received. The court shall notify the opposite party to the trademark re-examination proceedings to join the case as the third party.[14]

3.2.2.1.4. Grant registration If no opposition is filed before the period of public announcement expires, or there is a final ruling against an opposition, the Trademark Office will grant the registration, issue the trademark registration certificate, and publicly announce the trademark.

3.2.2.1.5. Principle of first application If two or more trademark registration applicants apply to register identical or similar trademarks for the same kind of commodities or similar commodities, the trademark whose registration was first applied for is given preliminary examination and approval and is publicly announced. If the applications are filed on the same day, the trademark which was first used is given preliminary examination and approval and is publicly announced, and the applications of the others are rejected and are not publicly announced.[15]

---

12 Article 30 of The Trademark Law of the People's Republic of China.
13 Article 33(1) of The Trademark Law of the People's Republic of China.
14 Article 33(2) of The Trademark Law of the People's Republic of China.
15 Article 29 of The Trademark Law of the People's Republic of China.

3.2.2.1.6. Principle of right of priority If an applicant applies to register the same trademark for commodities of the same class within six months from the day of filing the application for trademark registration of its trademark in a foreign country, it may enjoy the right of priority in accordance with the agreement concluded between that foreign country and China or the international treaty to which both countries are parties, or according to the principle of mutual acknowledgement of the right of priority.[16]

3.2.2.2. Absolute grounds for refusal[17]

According to the Trademark Law the following words or devices shall not be used as trademarks:[18]

(1) Those identical with or similar to the State name, national flag, national emblem, military flag, or decorations, of the People's Republic of China; and those identical with the names of particular venues where the Central State government organizations are located, or with the names or graphics of symbolic buildings or the Central State government organizations;
(2) Those identical with or similar to State names, national flags, national emblems or military flags of foreign countries, unless consent has been given by the relevant country's government;
(3) Those identical with or similar to names, flags or emblems or names, of international intergovernmental organizations, unless the organizations agree otherwise on the use or the use will not easily mislead the public;[19]
(4) Those identical with or similar to official signs and hallmarks indicating control and warranty, unless the use thereof is otherwise authorized;
(5) Those identical with or similar to the names or symbols of the Red Cross or the Red Crescent;
(6) Those having the nature of discrimination against any nationality;
(7) Those having the nature of exaggeration and fraud in advertising goods or services;
(8) Those detrimental to socialist morals or customs, or having other influences not condoned by the State (so called 'unhealthy influences').

Geographical names such as the administrative divisions at or above the county level and foreign geographical names well known to the public

---

[16] Article 24(1) of The Trademark Law of the People's Republic of China.

[17] In fact, the grounds for refusal are divided by researchers into absolute grounds and relative grounds. Generally, the absolute grounds can be used directly by the Trademark Office to refuse a trademark registration without any person filing an opposition to the trademark, and the relative grounds are used by a person to file an opposition. Any person may file an opposition to a trademark on relative grounds.

[18] Article 10 of The Trademark Law of the People's Republic of China.

[19] There is no definition of 'confusion' currently within China's trademark law. In practice, confusion will be that experienced by ordinary members of the public purchasing the relevant goods or services in question.

are not to be used as trademarks. Such geographical names as have second meanings or are elements of a collective mark or a certification mark are permitted as exclusive trademarks. Where a trademark using any of the above-mentioned geographical names has been approved and registered, it continues to be valid. For example, 'Qing Dao' is the name of Qing Dao City, but has been registered as a trademark on beer as it has been well-known for prior use.

The following signs shall not be registered as trademarks:

(1) Those which consist exclusively of generic names, designs or models of goods, in respect of which the trademark is used;
(2) Those which consist exclusively of signs or indications that have direct reference to the quality, main raw materials, function, intended purpose, weight, quantity or other characteristics of goods or services;
(3) Those which are devoid of any distinctive character.

Where trademarks under the preceding paragraphs have acquired distinctiveness through use and become easily distinguishable, they may be registered as trademarks.[20]

Further, in case of the application for trademark registration of three-dimensional (3D) marks, registration shall not be granted if the 3D figures are generated simply by the nature of the commodities, where the commodity figures are needed for technical effects, or the figures make the commodities gain substantial value.[21]

3.2.2.3. Relative grounds for refusal[22]

3.2.2.3.1. Infringing existing rights Anyone applying for trademark registration may not infringe the existing rights of others obtained by priority.[23]

Existing rights are those rights that are gained before the application for a registered trademark is filed. These rights include the right of a registered trademark, design patent, copyright, enterprise name, geographical indication, and so on.

---

20 Article 11 of The Trademark Law of the People's Republic of China.

21 Article 12 of The Trademark Law of the People's Republic of China.

22 As mentioned in footnote 17, the grounds for refusal are divided by researchers into absolute grounds and relative grounds. Generally, the absolute grounds can be used directly by the Trademark Office to refuse a trademark registration without any person filing an opposition to the trademark, and the relative grounds are used by persons to file an opposition. Any person may file an opposition to a trademark on relative grounds.

23 Article 31 of The Trademark Law of the People's Republic of China.

If a trademark contains the geographic mark of the commodities, but the commodities do not come from the region indicated by that mark, and thus mislead the public, the trademark shall not be registered and shall be prohibited from use. Those that have been registered in good faith, (i.e., without any form of deception) however, continue to be valid.[24]

3.2.2.3.2. Violating the principle of honesty and credibility

1. Anyone applying for trademark registration may not register by illicit means, a trademark which has been used but not registered by others, and which has become influential.[25]
2. If a trademark, for which an application for registration is filed, is the copy, imitation or translation of a well-known trademark of the same or similar commodity which has not been registered in China, misleads the public and leads to possible damage to the interests of the registrant of that well-known trademark, it shall not be registered and shall be prohibited from use.
3. If a trademark, for which an application is filed, is the copy, imitation or translation of a well-known trademark of a different or dissimilar commodity which has been registered in China, misleads the public and leads to possible damage to the interests of the registrant of that well-known trademark, it shall not be registered and shall be prohibited from use.[26]
4. If an agent or a representative registers the trademark of the principal or the represented in his/her own name without authorization, the trademark shall not be registered and shall be prohibited from use upon the opposition raised by the principal or the represented.[27]

3.2.2.3.3. Late application If an application has been made to register a trademark that is identical with or similar to another person's trademark which has already been given preliminary examination and approval for use on the same kind of commodities or similar commodities, the Trademark Office shall reject the current application and shall not publicly announce that trademark.[28]

---

[24] Article 16 of The Trademark Law of the People's Republic of China.

[25] Article 31 of The Trademark Law of the People's Republic of China.

[26] A 'well known' mark refers to a trademark that is widely known by the general public in China. In the consultations on the third revision of the TM law, 'well known' marks will be well known by the public and have a high reputation.

[27] Article 15 of The Trademark Law of the People's Republic of China.

[28] Article 29 of The Trademark Law of the People's Republic of China.

3.2.2.3.4. Reservation If a registered trademark is revoked or is not renewed after its period of validity expires, the Trademark Office shall not approve any application for the registration of a trademark identical with or similar to the said trademark within one year from the day of the revocation or cancellation.[29]

3.2.3. Surrender, Removal, Revocation, Modification and Rectification

3.2.3.1. Surrender

If a registrant needs to continue to use the registered trademark after the period of validity expires, an application for renewal of registration must be made within six months before the expiration. If the registrant fails to make such application within that period, an extension period of six months may be granted. If no application has been filed before the extension period expires, the registered trademark is cancelled.[30]

3.2.3.2. Removal

A trademark registrant may apply for the removal of the registered trademark from the Register. In such cases, the registrant shall send an Application for Trademark Removal and return the original Certificate of Trademark Registration to the Trademark Office.

Where the registrant of a trademark dies or ceases to exist and no formalities have been gone through for transfer of the registered trademark, any person is entitled at the expiration of one year from the date of the death or cessation to apply to the Trademark Office for the removal, from the Register, of the registered trademark.[31]

3.2.3.3. Revocation

If a registered trademark violates the provisions of Articles 10, 11 or 12 of Trademark Law, or the registration of the trademark has been obtained by deceitful or other illicit means, the Trademark Office may cancel that registered trademark on its own authority. Other units or individuals may request the Trademark Review and Adjudication Board to cancel that registered trademark.

If a registered trademark violates the provisions of Articles 13, 15, 16 or 31 of Trademark Law, the owner or the interested persons of a

---

[29] Article 46 of The Trademark Law of the People's Republic of China.

[30] Article 38 of The Trademark Law of the People's Republic of China.

[31] Article 47 of Implementing Regulations of the Trademark Law of the People's Republic of China.

trademark affected by that violation may, within five years from the day on which the violation trademark is registered, request the Trademark Review and Adjudication Board to revoke the registered trademark violating the law. The owner of a well-known trademark shall not be subject to the limit of five years to request the revocation of (bad-faith) registration.[32]

In disputes over registered trademarks, apart from the circumstances described in the two preceding paragraphs, an application may be filed with the Trademark Review and Adjudication Board for a ruling within five years from the day on which that disputed trademark was registered upon approval.[33]

If a registered trademark is used on crudely manufactured commodities that are passed off as being of high quality, thus deceiving consumers, the administrative departments for industry and commerce at various levels may, according to the circumstances, order rectification of the situation within a specified period and may, in addition, circulate a notice on the matter or impose a fine. The Trademark Office may also revoke the registered trademark.

3.2.3.4. Modification

When applying for modification of the name, address or other registration matters, the registrant shall file an Application for Modification with the Trademark Office. The Trademark Office shall, upon examination and approval, issue the trademark registrant with the relevant certificates, and make an announcement. Where the application is not approved, the Trademark Office shall notify the applicant in writing and explain the reason for refusal.[34]

3.2.3.5. Rectification

In the event of any of the following acts concerning the use of a registered trademark, the Trademark Office will order rectification of the situation within a specified period or will revoke the registered trademark:

(1) the registered trademark is altered without authorization from the Trademark Office;

---

[32] Article 41(2) of The Trademark Law of the People's Republic of China.

[33] Article 41(3) of The Trademark Law of the People's Republic of China.

[34] Article 24 of Implementing Regulations of the Trademark Law of the People's Republic of China.

(2) the registrant's name, address or any other registered matters concerning the registered trademark is changed without authorization from the Trademark Office;
(3) the registered trademark is assigned without authorization from the Trademark Office; and
(4) the registered trademark has not been used for three consecutive years.[35]

In the event of any of the following acts concerning the use of an unregistered trademark, the local administrative department for industry and commerce shall stop the use of the trademark, order rectification of the situation within a specified period and may, in addition, circulate a notice on the matter or impose a fine:

(1) the trademark is falsely represented as being a registered one;
(2) the trademark violates the provisions of Article 10 of the Trademark Law; or
(3) the trademark is used on crudely manufactured commodities that are passed off as being of high quality, thus deceiving consumers.[36]

3.2.4. Protection

3.2.4.1. Determination of infringement

3.2.4.1.1. Protection of registered trademark

1. The right to exclusive use of a registered trademark is limited to trademarks which have been approved for registration and to commodities on which the use of a trademark has been approved.
2. Any of the following acts is an infringement upon the right to the exclusive use of a registered trademark:

   (a) use of a trademark, which is identical with or similar to the registered trademark on the same kind of commodities or similar commodities without a license from the registrant of that trademark;
   (b) sale of the commodities that infringe upon the right to exclusive use of a registered trademark;

---

35 Article 44 of The Trademark Law of the People's Republic of China.
36 Article 48 of The Trademark Law of the People's Republic of China.

(c) forging or manufacture without authorization of the marks of a registered trademark of others, or selling the marks of a registered trademark forged or manufactured without authorization;
(d) replacement of a registered trademark with another trademark and putting the commodities with the changed trademark into the market without the consent of the registrant of that trademark; and
(e) other damage caused to the right to exclusive use of a registered trademark of another person.[37]

3. Any of the following acts are considered acts that cause damage to the right to exclusive use of a registered trademark of another person:

(a) use of any design which is identical with or similar to the registered trademark of another person on the same or similar goods, such as the designation or decoration of the goods, so as to mislead the public; or
(b) intentionally providing any other person with such facilities as storage, transportation, postal service, and concealment to aid the infringement of the exclusive right of another person to use a registered trademark.[38]

4. (a) Use of any word identical with or similar to the registered trademark of another person on the same or similar goods, such as the name of the enterprise, which misleads the public; or
(b) Use of a trademark which copies, imitates or translates, in whole or in core part a well-known trademark of others, which has been registered in China, on a different or dissimilar commodity, and misleads the public and leads to possible damage to the interests of the registrant of that well-known trademark.
(c) Use of a word, which is identical with or similar to the registered trademark of another person as a registered domain name, and use of this domain name in electronic commerce relevant to goods on which the registered trademark is used, thus misleading the public.[39]

---

[37] Article 52 of The Trademark Law of the People's Republic of China.

[38] Article 50 of Implementing Regulations of the Trademark Law of the People's Republic of China.

[39] Article 1 of Interpretations of the Supreme People's Court Concerning the Application of Laws in the Trial of Cases of Civil Disputes Arising from Trademarks (effective as of 16 October 2002).

5. If a trademark, for which an application is filed, of a different or dissimilar commodity is the copy, imitation or translation of a well-known trademark of others already registered in China, and misleads the public and leads to possible damage to the interests of the registrant of that well-known trademark, it shall not be registered and shall be prohibited from use.[40]
6. A person who uses a mark, copies, imitates or translates in whole or in core part a well-known trademark of others which has not been registered in China, as a trademark on an identical or similar commodity, thus misleading the public, bears the responsibility to stop infringement of other trademarks.[41]

3.2.4.1.2. Protection of unregistered trademarks

1. If a trademark, for which an application is filed of the same or similar commodity, copies, imitates or translates a well-known trademark of others which has not been registered in China, and misleads the public, it shall not be registered and shall be prohibited from use.[42]
2. If an agent or a representative registers the trademark of the principal or the represented in the agent's own name without authorization, the trademark shall not be registered and shall be prohibited from use upon the opposition raised by the principal or the represented.[43]
3. If a trademark is used for the first time on commodities displayed at any international exhibition sponsored or acknowledged by the Chinese government, the applicant for registration of that trademark may enjoy the right of priority for six months from the day on which the said commodities are displayed.[44]
4. If two or more trademark registration applicants apply for registration of identical or similar trademarks for the same kind of commodities or similar commodities, the trademark applicant received first shall be given preliminary examination and approval and shall be publicly announced. If the applications are filed on the same day, the trademark which was first used shall be given preliminary examination and approval and shall be publicly announced, and the other application shall be rejected and shall not be publicly announced.[45]

---

40 Article 13(2) of The Trademark Law of the People's Republic of China.
41 Article 13(1) of The Trademark Law of the People's Republic of China.
42 Article 13(1) of The Trademark Law of the People's Republic of China.
43 Article 15 of The Trademark Law of the People's Republic of China.
44 Article 25 of The Trademark Law of the People's Republic of China.
45 Article 29 of The Trademark Law of the People's Republic of China.

5. Applicants for trademark registration may not damage the existing rights of others obtained by priority. Anyone applying for trademark registration may not register by illicit means, a trademark which has been used but not registered by others, and which has become influential.[46]
6. The Unfair Competition Law provides that a business operator shall, in market transactions, follow the principles of equality, fairness, honesty and credibility and observe generally recognized business ethics.[47]
7. The following acts are considered unfair competition, which is prohibited:

   (a) use on a commodity without authorization of a unique name, packaging, or decoration of another's famous commodity, or using a name, package or decoration similar to that of another's famous commodity, thereby confusing the two and leading purchasers to mistake the former for the latter;[48] or
   (b) use without authorization of the name of another enterprise or person, thereby leading people to mistake their commodities for those of the said enterprise or person.[49]

Because an unregistered trademark may be identical with or similar to other commercial marks, such as the unique name of a commodity, or packaging, or decoration of a famous commodity, or the name of an enterprise or person, these regulations are also used to protect unregistered trademarks.

8. The principles of honesty and credibility which are set out in the General Principles of the Civil Law of the People's Republic of China also are used to protect unregistered trademarks.[50]

---

[46] Article 31 of The Trademark Law of the People's Republic of China.

[47] Article 2(1) of Law of the People's Republic of China Anti Unfair Competition.

[48] Article 5(2) of Law of the People's Republic of China Anti Unfair Competition.

[49] Article 5(3) of Law of the People's Republic of China Anti Unfair Competition.

[50] Article 4 of General Principles of the Civil Law of the People's Republic of China (effective as of 1 January 1987).

3.2.4.2. Administrative protection and judicial protection

It is the Chinese approach to protect trademarks with judicial measures in cooperation with administrative measures. Administrative protection, which is significant in China is discussed below.

3.2.4.2.1. Administrative protection In China, in the event that any of the acts listed in Article 52 of the Trademark Law[51] infringe upon the right to exclusive use of a registered trademark, and a dispute arises accordingly, the parties will have to negotiate to settle the dispute; if any party refuses to negotiate or the negotiation has failed, the registrant of that trademark or the interested persons may bring a suit before a people's court, and either may then request the administrative department for industry and commerce to handle the matter. If the administrative department for industry and commerce conclude that an infringement is valid, it may order an immediate stop to the infringement, and may confiscate or destroy the infringing commodities and the tools used for the manufacturing of infringing commodities and the forging of marks of the registered trademark, and may impose a fine in addition. If a party disagrees with this decision, it may bring a suit before a people's court within 15 days from the day of receiving the notification according to the Administrative Procedure Law of the People's Republic of China; if, at the expiration of such a period, the infringer has neither brought a lawsuit nor performed the decision after the period expires, the administrative department may apply to the people's court for compulsory enforcement of its order. The administrative department for industry and commerce handling the case may, upon the request of a party, conduct mediation over the amount of compensation for the infringement of the right to exclusive use of the trademark; if the mediation has failed, the party may bring a suit before a people's court according to the Civil Procedure Law of the People's Republic of China.[52]

---

[51] Article 52: Any of the following acts shall be an infringement upon the right to exclusive use of a registered trademark: (1) using a trademark which is identical with or similar to the registered trademark on the same kind of commodities or similar commodities without a license from the registrant of that trademark; (2) selling the commodities that infringe upon the right to exclusive use of a registered trademark; (3) forging, manufacturing without authorization the marks of a registered trademark of others, or selling the marks of a registered trademark forged or manufactured without authorization; (4) changing a registered trademark and putting the commodities with the changed trademark into the market without the consent of the registrant of that trademark; and (5) causing other damage to the right to exclusive use of a registered trademark of another person.

[52] Article 53 of The Trademark Law of the People's Republic of China.

The administrative department for industry and commerce shall have the right to investigate and punish the acts infringing upon the right to exclusive use of a registered trademark.[53]

The administrative departments for industry and commerce at the county level,[54] or above, may exercise the following powers when investigating and punishing the acts that are suspected of infringing upon the right to exclusive use of a registered trademark of others, based on the evidence for suspecting of illegal acts or reports made by other people:[55]

(1) inquiring of the parties concerned, investigating the information relating to the infringement of the right to exclusive use of a registered trademark of others;
(2) consulting and copying the contracts, vouchers, account books and other relevant materials relating to the infringing activities of the party;
(3) conducting on-the-spot examinations of the places where the party is suspected of having committed the acts infringing upon the right to exclusive use of a registered trademark of others; and
(4) examining the articles relating to the infringing activities; including sealing up or seizing the articles proved by evidence to have infringed upon the right to exclusive use of a registered trademark of others.

The parties shall assist and cooperate with the administrative departments for industry and commerce in exercising the powers prescribed in the preceding paragraph, and may not refuse or impede them.

'Customs protection of intellectual property rights' refers to the implementation of protection by customs of the exclusive rights to use a trademark, copyrights and the rights related thereto, and patent rights that are related to import and export goods and that are protected by PRC laws and administrative regulations.[56]

Where an owner of intellectual property rights discovers that goods

---

[53] Article 54 of The Trademark Law of the People's Republic of China.

[54] The general structural hierarchy in China (top down) is as follows: provincial level, prefecture level, county level, township level, and finally the village level. See Wikipedia.org.

[55] Article 55 of The Trademark Law of the People's Republic of China.

[56] Article 2 of the Regulations of PR China on the Protection of Intellectual Properties by the Customs (promulgated by the State Council on 2 December 2003 and effective as of 1 March 2004).

suspected of infringing upon rights are about to be imported or exported, he may submit an application for impoundment of goods suspected of infringing upon rights to the customs of the place where the goods are to enter or exit from China.[57]

Where impounded goods suspected of infringing upon rights are confirmed as having infringed upon intellectual property rights after investigation by customs, customs shall confiscate the goods.[58]

3.2.4.2.2. Judicial protection The owner of a trademark or an interested person with a trademark may bring a suit before a people's court while the trademark is infringed.

If a party refuses to accept a judgment of first instance by a local people's court, he shall have the right to file an appeal with the people's court at the next higher level within 15 days from the date on which the written judgment is served.[59]

If a party refuses to accept an order of first instance of a local people's court, he shall have the right to file an appeal with a people's court at the next higher level within ten days from the date on which the written order is served.[60]

In trying an appealed case against a judgment, the people's court shall make a final judgment within three months after the case was filed as one of second instance. Any extension of the term necessitated by special circumstances shall be subject to the approval of the president of the said court.[61]

The judgments and orders of a people's court of second instance shall be final.[62]

If the president of a people's court at any level finds some definite error in a legally effective judgment or order of his court and deems it necessary

---

[57] Article 12 of the Regulations of PR China on the Protection of Intellectual Properties by the Customs (promulgated by the State Council on 2 December 2003 and effective as of 1 March 2004).

[58] Article 27 of the Regulations of PR China on the Protection of Intellectual Properties by the Customs (promulgated by the State Council on 2 December 2003 and effective as of 1 March 2004).

[59] Article 147(1) of Civil Procedure Law of the People's Republic of China (adopted on 9 April 1991).

[60] Article 147(2) of Civil Procedure Law of the People's Republic of China (adopted on 9 April 1991).

[61] Article 159(1) of Civil Procedure Law of the People's Republic of China (adopted on 9 April 1991).

[62] Article 158 of Civil Procedure Law of the People's Republic of China (adopted on 9 April 1991).

to have the case retried, he shall refer it to the judicial committee for discussion and decision.[63]

If the Supreme People's Court finds some definite error in a legally effective judgment or order of a local people's court at any level, or if a people's court at a higher level finds some definite error in a legally effective judgment or order of a people's court at a lower level, it shall have the power to bring the case up for trial itself or direct the people's court at a lower level to conduct a retrial.[64]

If a party considers that a legally effective judgment or order has some error, he may apply to the people's court which originally tried the case or to a people's court at the next higher level for retrial; however, execution of the judgment or order shall not be suspended.[65]

When the people's procuratorate decides to lodge a protest against a judgment or order made by a people's court, it shall produce a written protest.[66]

The people's court shall, in retrying a case protested by the people's procuratorate, notify the people's procuratorate to send personnel to the court.[67]

3.2.4.3. Legal liability for infringement

The infringer will bear legal liability, such as civil liability, administrative liability or criminal liability. Each is discussed in the following sections.

3.2.4.3.1. Civil liability The main methods of bearing civil liability are:[68]

(1) cessation of infringements;
(2) compensation for losses;
(3) elimination of ill effects and rehabilitation of reputation; and
(4) extension of apology.

---

[63] Article 177(1) of Civil Procedure Law of the People's Republic of China (adopted on 9 April 1991).

[64] Article 177(2) of Civil Procedure Law of the People's Republic of China (adopted on 9 April 1991).

[65] Article 178 of Civil Procedure Law of the People's Republic of China (adopted on 9 April 1991).

[66] Article 187 of Civil Procedure Law of the People's Republic of China (adopted on 9 April 1991).

[67] Article 188 of Civil Procedure Law of the People's Republic of China (adopted on 9 April 1991).

[68] Article 134 of General Principles of the Civil Law of the People's Republic of China.

The above methods of bearing civil liability may be applied exclusively or concurrently. When hearing civil cases, a people's court, in addition to applying the above stipulations, may serve admonitions, order the offender to sign a pledge of repentance, and confiscate the property used in carrying out illegal activities and the illegal income obtained. It may also impose fines or detentions as stipulated by law.

3.2.4.3.2. Administrative liability If the administrative department for industry and commerce concludes that an infringement has been constituted, it may order an immediate stop of the infringement, and may confiscate or destroy the infringing commodities and the tools especially used for the manufacturing of infringing commodities and the forging of marks of the registered trademark, and may impose a fine in addition.[69]

3.2.4.3.3. Criminal liability Whoever uses a trademark identical with another person's registered trademark on the same kinds of goods without permission from the owner of the registered trademark shall, if the circumstances are serious, be sentenced to a fixed-term imprisonment of not more than three years of criminal detention, and concurrently or independently be sentenced to a fine. If the circumstances are especially serious, the offender shall be sentenced to a fixed-term of imprisonment of not less than three years and not more than seven years, and concurrently be sentenced to a fine.[70]

Whoever uses a trademark which is identical with a registered trademark on the same merchandise without the permission of the registered trademark owner shall, in any of the following circumstances, be deemed to have caused 'the serious consequences' as prescribed in Article 213 of the Criminal Law, and shall be sentenced to a fixed term of imprisonment of not more than three years of criminal detention for the crime of counterfeiting the registered trademark, and/or be given a pecuniary fine:[71]

(1) The amount from illegal business proceeds is no less than 50,000 Yuan or the amount of illegal proceeds is no less than 30,000 Yuan;
(2) He/it counterfeits two or more registered trademarks, with the amount of proceeds arising from illegal business operations to be no

69 Article 53 of The Trademark Law of the People's Republic of China.
70 Article 213 of The Criminal Law of the People's Republic of China (entered into force as of 1 October 1997).
71 Article 1(1) of Interpretation of the Supreme People's Court and the Supreme People's Procuratorate Concerning Some Issues on the Specific Application of Law for Handling Criminal Cases of Infringement upon Intellectual Property Rights (entered into force on 22 December 2004).

less than 30,000 Yuan or the amount of illegal proceeds to be no less than 20,000 Yuan;

(3) Other circumstances in which the consequences are serious.

In any of the following circumstances, he/it shall be deemed to have caused 'the particularly serious consequences' as prescribed in Article 213 of the Criminal Law, and shall be sentenced to a fixed term imprisonment of not less than three years but not more than seven years for the crime of counterfeiting a registered trademark, and be concurrently given a pecuniary fine:[72]

(1) The amount from illegal business operation is no less than 250,000 Yuan or the amount of illegal proceeds is no less than 150,000 Yuan;
(2) He/it counterfeits two or more registered trademarks, with amount of proceeds arising from illegal business operations to be no less than 150,000 Yuan or the amount of illegal proceeds to be no less than 100,000 Yuan;
(3) Other circumstances in which the consequences are particularly serious.

Whoever knowingly sells goods bearing counterfeited registered trademarks shall, if the sum obtained through sale is relatively huge, be sentenced to fixed-term imprisonment of not more than three years of criminal detention, and concurrently or independently be sentenced to a fine. If the sum obtained through sale is large, the offender shall be sentenced to fixed-term imprisonment of not less than three years and not more than seven years, and concurrently be sentenced to a fine.[73]

Whoever sells the merchandise under a counterfeited registered trademark when he/it clearly knows the fact, with the sales amount to be no less than 50,000 Yuan, shall be deemed that 'the amount is relatively large' as prescribed in Article 214 of the Criminal Law, and the offender shall be sentenced to a fixed-term of imprisonment for not more than three years of criminal detention for the crime of selling merchandise under a counterfeited registered trademark, and/or be sentenced to a pecuniary fine.[74]

---

[72] Article 1(2) of Interpretation of the Supreme People's Court and the Supreme People's Procuratorate Concerning Some Issues on the Specific Application of Law for Handling Criminal Cases of Infringement upon Intellectual Property Rights (entered into force on 22 December 2004).

[73] Article 214 of The Criminal Law of the People's Republic of China (entered into force as of 1 October 1997).

[74] Article 2(1) of Interpretation of the Supreme People's Court and the Supreme People's Procuratorate Concerning Some Issues on the Specific

If the sales amount is no less than 250,000 Yuan, it shall be deemed that 'the amount is large' as prescribed in Article 214 of the Criminal Law, and the offender shall be sentenced to a fixed-term of imprisonment of not less than three years but not more than seven years for the crime of selling merchandise under a counterfeited registered trademark, and be concurrently sentenced to a pecuniary fine.[75]

Whoever forges or makes without authorization representations of registered trademarks of another person or sells representations of registered trademarks which are forged or made without authorization shall, if the circumstances are serious, shall be sentenced to a fixed-term of imprisonment of not more than three years, criminal detention or public surveillance, and concurrently or independently be sentenced to a fine. If the circumstances are especially serious, the offender shall be sentenced to a fixed-term of imprisonment of not less than three years and not more than seven years, and concurrently be sentenced to a fine.[76]

Whoever forges or illegally produces the marks of another's registered trademark, or sells forged or illegally produces the marks of another's registered trademark shall, in any of the following circumstances, be deemed to have caused 'the serious consequences' as prescribed in Article 215 of the Criminal Law, and shall be sentenced to a fixed term of imprisonment of not more than three years of criminal detention or criminal custody for the crime of illegally making or selling illegally made marks of another's registered trademark, and/or be imposed upon a pecuniary fine:[77]

(1) having forged or illegally produced 20,000 pieces or more of any other's trademark or sold 20,000 pieces or more of the forged or illegally made trademark or where the amount of proceeds arising from illegal business operations is no less than 50,000 Yuan, or the amount of illegal proceeds is no less than 30,000 Yuan;
(2) having forged or illegally made 10,000 pieces or more of two or more

---

Application of Law for Handling Criminal Cases of Infringement upon Intellectual Property Rights (entered into force on 22 December 2004).

75 Article 2(2) of Interpretation of the Supreme People's Court and the Supreme People's Procuratorate Concerning Some Issues on the Specific Application of Law for Handling Criminal Cases of Infringement upon Intellectual Property Rights (entered into force on 22 December 2004).

76 Article 215 of The Criminal Law of the People's Republic of China (entered into force as of 1 October 1997).

77 Article 3(1) of Interpretation of the Supreme People's Court and the Supreme People's Procuratorate Concerning Some Issues on the Specific Application of Law for Handling Criminal Cases of Infringement upon Intellectual Property Rights (entered into force on 22 December 2004).

kinds of registered trademarks or having sold 10,000 pieces or more of two or more kinds of forged or illegally made registered trademarks or where the amount of proceeds arising from illegal business operation is no less than 30,000 Yuan, or the amount of illegal proceeds is no less than 20,000 Yuan;
(3) other circumstances in which the consequences are serious.

In any of the following circumstances, he/it shall be deemed to have caused 'the particularly serious consequences' as prescribed in Article 215 of the Criminal Law, and shall be sentenced to a fixed-term imprisonment of not less than three years but not more than seven years for the crime of illegally making or selling illegally made marks of another's registered trademark, and to have imposed a pecuniary fine:[78]

(1) having forged or illegally made 100,000 pieces or more of any other's registered trademarks or having sold 100,000 pieces or more of the forged or illegally made registered trademarks or where the amount of proceeds arising from illegal business operations is no less than 250,000 Yuan, or the amount of illegal proceeds is no less than 150,000 Yuan;
(2) having forged or illegally made 50,000 pieces or more of two or more kinds of registered trademarks or having sold 50,000 pieces or more of two or more kinds of forged or illegally made registered trademarks or where the amount of proceeds arising or the amount of proceeds arising from illegal business operations is no less than 150,000 Yuan, or the amount of illegal proceeds is no less than 100,000 Yuan;
(3) other circumstances in which the consequences are particularly serious.

3.3. PROBLEMS WITH DIFFERENCES OF INTERPRETATION AND ENFORCEMENT OF LAWS ACROSS CHINA

3.3.1. The Problem with the Distinctive Characteristics of Trademarks

The distinctive characteristic is one of the essential characteristics of a trademark. A trademark cannot be used to distinguish providers of goods

---

[78] Article 3(2) of Interpretation of the Supreme People's Court and the Supreme People's Procuratorate Concerning Some Issues on the Specific Application of Law for Handling Criminal Cases of Infringement upon Intellectual Property Rights (entered into force on 22 December 2004).

or services from others if the trademark lacks distinctive characteristics. In Chinese Trademark Law, the lack of a distinctive characteristic is an absolute reason to reject an application for a registered trademark. All countries with modern trademark statutes face similar difficulties in determining the distinctive characteristic of a trademark under the relevant law.

3.3.2. The Problem with the Similarity between two Trademarks

Interpretations of the Supreme People's Court Concerning the Application of Laws in the Trial of Cases of Civil Disputes Arising from Trademarks (effective October 16, 2002) provides:

> The similarity between two trademarks in Article 52 (1) of Trademark Law, refers to those similarities in character pattern, pronunciation, meanings of words, or color and composition of pictures, or combination of the elements, or three-dimensional (3D) mark or color combinations, that mislead the public to confuse providers of commodities or mislead the public to believe there is a special relationship between the goods on which the defendant's trademark is used and the goods on which the plaintiff registered trademark is used, in comparing the defendant's trademark with the plaintiff's trademark.

The following principles are observed in determining the similarity of trademarks:[79]

(1) to determine the similarity of trademarks a standard shall be used based on the common relevant public opinion or public perception of the marks concerned; and
(2) the comparison shall be made not only of the totality, but also of the main parts of the trademarks in question, and the comparison shall be done with the comparable matter isolated from other parts; and
(3) the distinctive characteristics of the protected trademark and the extent to which a protected trademark is known to the public will be taken into consideration in determining the similarity of trademarks.

Since there are few standards for determining the similarity of trademarks, differences in practice often produce different results. This problem is not unique to China.

---

[79] Article 10 of Interpretations of the Supreme People's Court Concerning the Application of Laws in the Trial of Cases of Civil Disputes Arising from Trademarks (effective 16 October 2002).

3.3.3. The Problem with the Determination of Well-known Trademarks

To determine the popularity of a trademark, a party concerned shall, in light of the concrete circumstances of the case, provide the following proofs to demonstrate that its trademark is already famous at the time of occurrence of the trademark right infringement or unfair competition:[80]

1. the market share, marketing regions, profits, taxes, etc. of the commodities using the trademark;
2. the duration for which the trademark has been continuously used;
3. the manner, duration, extent, money input, and geographical scope of publicity or promotion of the trademark;
4. records showing that the trademark has been protected as a famous trademark;
5. the market reputation of the trademark; and
6. other facts that can demonstrate that the trademark is famous.

The duration, scope, manner, etc., as described in the preceding paragraph regarding the use of the trademark, shall include information about the continuous use of the trademark prior to the examination and approval of its registration.[81]

The people's court shall, by taking into consideration other proof for determining the popularity of the trademark, objectively and thoroughly examine this proof, including the length of use of the trademark, industrial ranking, market investigation reports, market value assessment reports, and whether the mark has ever been certified as a famous trademark.[82]

There are few standards to determine the extent to which a trademark (including well-known trademarks) is known to the public, even though there is some guidance provided by the Law of Trademark, and Article 5 of Interpretations of the Supreme People's Court Concerning the Application of Laws in the Trial of Cases of Civil Disputes Arising from Protection of Well-known Trademarks (effective 1 May 2009).

---

[80] Article 5(1) of The Interpretations of the Supreme People's Court on Several Issues Concerning the Application of Law to the Trial of Cases of Civil Disputes over the Protection of Famous Trademarks (come into force as of 1 May 2009).

[81] Article 5(2) The Interpretations of the Supreme People's Court on Several Issues Concerning the Application of Law to the Trial of Cases of Civil Disputes over the Protection of Famous Trademarks (come into force as of 1 May 2009).

[82] Article 5(3) The Interpretations of the Supreme People's Court on Several Issues Concerning the Application of Law to the Trial of Cases of Civil Disputes over the Protection of Famous Trademarks (come into force as of 1 May 2009).

3.3.4. The Problem with Applying for Trademark Registration by Illicit Means a Trademark that has been Used, but Not Registered, by Others and has Become Influential

Anyone applying for trademark registration may not infringe the existing rights of others obtained by priority. Anyone applying for trademark registration may not register by illicit means a trademark which has been used, but not registered by others, and which has become influential.

This provision of the Trademark Law is a very important regulation for the protection of unregistered trademarks. However, determinations regarding 'illicit means' or 'whether a trademark has become influential' also present difficult factual questions. Further guidance is required as to how to interpret these terms from the Trademark Office, the courts and applicants.

3.3.5. The Problem with the Amount of Compensation for Infringement

Because intellectual property is intangible, it is very difficult to determine the amount of compensation due for infringing a trademark. The Trademark Law states:[83]

> The amount of compensation for infringing upon the right to exclusive use of a trademark shall be the proceeds obtained from the infringement during the period of infringement, or the losses suffered by the infringed due to the infringement that time, including the reasonable expenses paid by the infringed to stop the infringing acts.
>
> If it is difficult to determine the proceeds obtained from the infringement referred to in the preceding paragraph, or it is difficult to determine the losses suffered by the infringed due to the infringement, the people's court shall determine a compensation of up of 500,000 Yuan, according to the circumstances of the infringing acts.

In view of the complicated nature of this issue, the Supreme People's Court's Concerning the Application of Laws in the Trial of Cases of Civil Disputes Arising from Trademarks promulgated further implementing regulations:[84]

> The proceeds obtained from the infringement during the period of infringement at article 56(1) of the Trademark Law of the People's Republic of China, may

[83] Article 56 of The Trademark Law of the People's Republic of China.

[84] Articles 14, 15 and 16 of the Supreme People's Court Concerning the Application of Laws in the Trial of Cases of Civil Disputes Arising from Trademarks.

be determined by multiplying the amount of commodities sold (goods) by the unit profit of the infringed goods. If the unit profit of the infringed cannot be clearly determined, the unit profit of registered trademark goods shall be used instead of the unit profit of the infringed goods.

The losses suffered by the infringed due to the infringement may be calculated by multiplying the unit profit of registered trademark goods by the lost sales of goods due to the infringement or the number of infringing commodities sold.

When people's courts determine the amount of compensation, they shall take into consideration:

1) The characteristics, period and result of the acts of infringement;
2) The reputation of the trademark;
3) The amount of license fee of trademark;
4) The sort, time, and scope of the trademark license;
5) The reasonable expenses paid by the infringed to stop the infringing acts.

Even though there are further regulations about infringement in the Interpretations of the Supreme People's Court 'Concerning the Application of Laws in the Trial of Cases of Civil Disputes Arising from Trademarks', further guidance will be required from best practice around the world to help advise China's trademark enforcement authorities.

3.4. IMPACT OF INTERNATIONAL LAW (TREATIES, SUCH AS THE WORLD TRADE ORGANIZATION (WTO) OR MEMBERSHIP IN INTERNATIONAL CONVENTIONS) ON THE CHINESE DOMESTIC MARKET

As of 31 December 2008, there are six international treaties concerning trademarks that China has already signed:

1. The Convention Establishing the World Intellectual Property Organization (entered into force 3 June 1980);
2. Paris Convention for the Protection of Industrial Property (entered into force 3 June 1980);
3. Madrid Agreement for International Registration of Trade Marks (entered into force 4 October 1989);
4. Protocol Relating to the Madrid Agreement Concerning the International Registration of Marks (entered into force 1 December 1995);
5. Nice Agreement Concerning the International Classification of Goods

and Services for the Purposes of the Registration of Marks (entered into force 9 August 1994);
6. Agreement on Trade-Related Aspects of Intellectual Property Rights (entered 11 December 2001).

While China is pressing ahead with accession to international conventions concerning trademarks, it is at the same time strengthening its domestic trademark protection system. In order to enter the Agreement on the WTO's Trade Related Aspects of Intellectual Property Rights (TRIPs), China revised many articles of the Trademark Law to make them consistent with the TRIPs in 2001.

There were more changes made in the second amendment to the Trademark Law. To the original Trademark Law, 43 articles, 47 amendments and 22 (new) articles were added, making a total of 64 articles in the new Trademark Law. The fourth amendment of the Implementing Regulations of the Trademark Law was also a large undertaking, including 58 amendments and 22 new articles, producing a new total of 58 articles, up from 50 articles in the original law.

Significant amendments to the Trademark Law and the Implementing Regulations of the Trademark Law are the following:

1. new regulations to protect collective marks and certification marks;
2. clarification and definition of the regulations concerning protection of geographical indications;
3. natural persons now have the right to use a trademark. Therefore a user of trademarks under the new law may include natural persons, legal persons or other organizations. Under the old law, users of trademarks were limited to enterprises, institutions, or individual producers or traders;
4. increased elements such as 3D elements, which compose registered trademarks;
5. strengthened regulations concerning protection of well-known trademarks;
6. new regulations about the right of priority;
7. new regulations about judicial review;
8. strengthened trademark administration, and greater powers to combat trademark infringement;
9. clarification of regulations concerning the amount of compensation for trademark infringement;
10. new regulations about temporary measures to protect the right to exclusive use of a trademark before filing suit;

11. strengthened regulations for the supervision and administrative enforcement of a trademark.

At present, a *third* revision of the Trademark Law is being prepared which is discussed in the next section.

3.5. FUTURE LEGISLATION LIKELY TO IMPACT THE SECTOR

Eight years after the second revision of the Trademark Law, further revisions are needed because of changes in the market economy. At the time of writing, a third revision is anticipated. The main amendments of the third revision are expected to include:

(1) an increase in the type of marks that can be registered, including sound, smell, and animation (flashing marks);
(2) the third revision of the Trademark Law is expected to permit application for registration of the same trademark on commodities in different classes at one application of a trademark registration. The present Trademark Law requires that, if an applicant intends to apply for the registration of the same trademark on commodities in different classes, it must submit separate applications for registration in accordance with the classification of commodities;
(3) new regulations to permit application by electronic means;
(4) new regulations concerning retraction, for example, permitting an applicant to retract an application for trademark registration or other matters concerning a trademark before a decision is made by the Trademark Office;
(5) new regulations to improve protection of unregistered trademarks under Article 31 of the Trademark Law, to prohibit an application for trademark registration, which violates the principle of honesty and credibility;
(6) enlarging the scope of the right of exclusive use of a registered trademark by enumerating more acts which infringe the right of exclusive use;
(7) new regulations concerning Original Equipment/Entrusted Manufacture (OEM);
(8) more detailed regulations about civil compensation liability for infringing the right of exclusive use of a registered trademark, raising the limitations on compensation a court can determine.

3.6. CONCLUSION

From the Trademark Administrative Regulation effective 10 April 1963, to the Trademark Law of the People's Republic of China effective on 1 March 1983, to the first amendment to the Trademark Law in 1993, to the second amendment to the Trademark Law of the People's Republic of China in 2001, and the third amendment, which at the time of writing is still in progress, the trademark laws and regulations in China are gradually improving. Today, China has already established a greatly improved legal system composed of the General Principles of the Civil Law of the People's Republic of China, the Trademark Law of the People's Republic of China, the Law of the People's Republic of China Against Unfair Competition, the Criminal Law of the People's Republic of China, the Civil Procedure Law of the People's Republic of China, the Criminal Procedure Law of the People's Republic of China, the Anti-monopoly Law of the People's Republic of China, and relevant judicial interpretations, administrative regulations, administrative rules and international conventions and treaties. The protection of trademarks in China is provided by people's courts in cooperation with people's Procuratorates, the administrative departments for industry and commerce, departments of public security, customs department, administrative departments for agriculture, and intellectual property bureaus. The Chinese approach is to protect trademarks with judicial measures in cooperation with administrative measures, and this protection system has already made significant progress.

Following China's creation of a uniform trademark registration system in 1979, the number of trademark registration applications has continued to grow. In 1980, the Trademark Office received 26,000 applications. In 2010, the Trademark Office received 1,072,087 trademark registration applications.[85]

In 2010, the Trademark Office dealt with 16,142 territorial extension applications of Madrid International registration for trademarks filed by foreign companies via the International Bureau of WIPO (one trademark covering multiple classes), and the cumulative number reached 154,302, making China the first in the world for this type of application for six years in a row.[86]

---

85 China's Intellectual Property Protection in 2010, provided by State Intellectual Property Office of the People's Republic of China.

86 China's Intellectual Property Protection in 2010, provided by State Intellectual Property Office of the People's Republic of China.

The cumulative number of registered trademarks in China as of 2010 was 5,628,000.[87]

In 2010, administrations for industry and commerce (AICs) at all levels across China investigated 56,034 cases of trademark violations, 48,548 of which were for infringement and counterfeiting and 7,486 general violations. Ninety-one cases involved sales of fakes via the internet. A total of 11,524 foreign-related trademark cases were investigated and handled. AICs seized and removed 12,752,200 (value 1,405,610,000 yuan) sets of illegal trademark labels, and handled over 175 cases and 163 suspects to the judicial authorities for suspected criminal violations.[88]

In 2010, courts of law nationwide took 8,460 first-instance trademark civil cases, and 2,026 first-instance trademark administrative cases.[89]

The National Intellectual Property Strategy, drafted from 2005 to 2007 under the guidance of the central government, has been put into practice, so that trademark legislation, trademark enforcement and judicial protection are further improving. The following elements of China's Action Plan on IPR Protection 2010 concerning trademarks are currently being implemented:

(1) accelerated revision of the Trademark Law and further amendment of the Implementing Regulations of the Trademark Law;
(2) promote formulation of regulations on lawyer's practice in trademark agencies;
(3) Improve substantial result of the Special Compaign against IPR Infringement and the Production and Sale of Counterfeited and Forged Commodities; emphasize illegal behaviours of infringing foreign-related trademarks and well-known trademarks; practically constrain malicious registered trademarks; strictly investigate and punish illlegal printing of trademarks labels and trademark packaging designs of famous commodities;
(4) revision of the Ant.: Unfair Competition and undertake the drafting and research work of its implementation;
(5) promulgate Several Opinions of the Supreme People's Court on Piloting Trial of All Civil Administrative and Criminal IPR Cases Concentratively by IP Tribunals of some local People's Courts.

[87] China's Intellectual Property Protection in 2010, provided by State Intellectual Property Office of thc Pcople's Republic of China.

[88] China's Intellectual Property Protection in 2010, provided by State Intellectual Property Office of the People's Republic of China.

[89] China's Intellectual Property Protection in 2010, provided by State Intellectual Property Office of the People's Republic of China.

Although the legal system for the protection of trademarks in China does not have a long history, it has already made great progress. With changes in politics, economy, culture and international cooperation and communication, trademark laws and regulations in China are likely to continue to improve in the future.

4. Copyright protection in China

Li Yufeng[1]

4.1. CHINESE COPYRIGHT LAW AND THE IMPACT OF INTERNATIONAL LAW

'Concerns in China over unauthorized copying can be traced back to the copying of Chinese classics in the Han Dynasty (206 BC–220 AD).'[2] However, substantial effort was made to protect copyright in the late 1800s with the coming of the gunboat, opium and extraterritoriality.[3] Foreign countries and external pressures have played an important role in reforming the Chinese system of copyright. From the Opium War (1840–1842) onwards, the traditional Chinese order was destroyed, and the economy, politics and culture were in great disorder. In the words of Li Hongzhang,[4] 'China saw tremendous changes never before undertaken in the previous three thousand years'. To save the nation from subjugation and to ensure its survival, the latter Qing Dynasty began its reforms, one step of which was to build the Chinese modern legal system. The Western powers promised that they would give up exterritoriality in China when a stable legal system was created. The latter Qing initiated its law-making process to create stability, wealth and power. In this climate, the first copyright law, the Great Qing Copyright Law of 1910, was instituted with the help of foreign exporters. However, it didn't take root in China on account of decades of war, famine and revolution.[5]

---

[1] Ph.D. in Law, Professor at Southwest University of Political Science and Law in the People's Republic of China (dryufeng@hotmail.com). I owe thanks to Professor Kariyawasam, Jessie Qin, and Yun Xuan (formerly of IP Counsel GE China) who read the manuscript and clarified my analysis.

[2] Li Yufeng and W.C. Ng, 'Understanding the Great Qing Copyright Law of 1910', *The Journal of the Copyright Society of the USA*, 2009.

[3] P. Feng, *Intellectual Property in China*, Hongkong: Sweet & Maxwell Asia, 2002, p. 3.

[4] Li Hongzhang (1823–1901), a well-known diplomat of the latter Qing Dynasty.

[5] Supra note 3, p. 3.

In 1949, the People's Republic of China (PRC) was founded. As a result of the cold war, China dedicated itself to bridge a socialist legal system and imitated the former Soviet Union's copyright system. With the lack of a coherent and consistent policy, the interests of authors was limited to remuneration (*gaofei*). In 1979, in the wake of the so-called Great Proletarian Culture Revolution (*wenge*) that commenced in 1966, China implemented the policy of reform and began to restore the disturbed social order. In order to attract foreign investment, China concluded the Agreement on Cooperation in the Field of High Energy Physics and Agreement on Trade Relations with the USA. Article 6 of both agreements stated that China should protect American intellectual property rights (in China). The USA was reluctant to cooperate in any field where China could not establish an ambitious modern intellectual property system. Reformists in the post-Mao era were pragmatically inclined to yield to these external pressures. A second copyright system was introduced to China. In 1980, China entered into the Convention Establishing the World Intellectual Property Organization. The National Copyright Administration specifically regulating copyright was founded in July 1985. Regional copyright administrations were also created soon after. In 1986, 'as private property, the IPRs joined the newly established civil rights system under the General Principle of Civil Code 1986 (GPCC)'.[6] The Copyright Law of PRC was adopted by the National People's Congress (NPC) Standing Committee in 1990, effective on 1 June 1991. In the same year, the Copyright Law Implementation Rules were promulgated by the State Council. Given the gap between the Copyright Law of 1990 and international law with reference to copyright, China acceded respectively to the Berne Convention for the Protection of Literary and Artistic Works and the Universal Copyright Convention in 1992. And in the same year, *Provisions on the Implementation of the International Copyright Treaties* was promulgated.

Early in the 1990s, Deng Xiaoping formulated the blueprint for the socialist market economy for China, which forced China to keep pace with the world economy and international rules. Then GATT was reorganized into the WTO. In the mid-1990s, China was committed to gaining membership of the GATT and to accede to the WTO. Meanwhile, China faced many changes thrown up by the digital and Internet revolutions. Two important treaties, the WIPO Copyright Treaty (WCT) and WIPO Performances and Phonograms Treaty (WPPT), mainly regulating copyright relations over the Internet, were signed in 1996. In order to adapt

---

6 Supra note 2, p. 5. Also translated as China General Principles of the Civil Law.

itself to the development of the market economy and changes from the Internet, and to conform with the TRIPs, China felt obliged to revise its domestic copyright law. The first modification of Copyright Law 1990 was completed in 2001 and its Implementing Regulation in 2002. On 16 March 2007, the Fifth Session of the Tenth NPC accepted the Real Right Law of PRC, Article 223 of which provides that intellectual property can be used as the subject of a mortgage.

Given computer software's difference from other works of literature, art and social sciences, the State Council promulgated Regulations for the Protection of Computer Software (CSPR) in 1991, and amended it in 2001. Another significant national regulation is Regulations on the Customs Protection of Intellectual Property Rights (IPRCPR) adopted in 1995 and revised in 2003, which regulates importation and exportation with regard to intellectual property goods.

Unlike the first coming of copyright, the second coming reveals China's initiative. China's copyright system reform in the early 21st century partly aims to respond to the changes in the country's social economy. In its desire to ensure that copyright law was suitable to the modern market economy, the state had to be increasingly flexible even if some of the changes required, for example under TRIPS, were not as welcome. In 2008, China embraced the world by hosting the Olympic Games and demonstrated its economic and cultural strength. In particular, the State Council published its National Intellectual Property Strategy Outline on 5 June 2008 to improve China's capability in intellectual property creation, utilization, protection and administration, and help create innovation in China. Dependent on the establishment of an efficient intellectual property system, China was (and is) committed to becoming one of the leading countries in the world in terms of its creation of intellectual property. In February 2010, China adopted the second revision of its copyright law, the Copyright Law of the People's Republic of China (revised 2010) and coming into effect in April 2010.[7] The major changes include dropping Article 4(1) Copyright Law 2001, and introducing a new Article 26 on the pledging of copyright.[8] Article 4(1) is discussed further below. The article was a controversial pro-

[7] The Decision of the Standing Committee of the National People's Congress on Revision of the Copyright Law of the People's Republic of China, adopted at the 13th meeting of the Standing Committee of the 11th National People's Congress of the People's Republic of China on 26 February 2010 and coming into force on 1 April 2010.

[8] Article 26 CL (revised 2010): 'In case of pledge of copyright, the pledger and the pledgee shall go through registration of the pledge with the copyright administration under the State Council'.

vision that created some uncertainty as to whether foreign films and other audiovisual material that had not obtained approval under China's censorship regulations enjoyed copyright under the CL 2001. As a result of a challenge by the US and a decision by the WTO's Appellate Body in December 2009, Article 4(1) was dropped from the CL (revised 2010).[9]

4.2. SOURCES OF COPYRIGHT LAW

The current copyright system embodies a three level legislative hierarchy.[10] The first level consists of the laws adopted by the National People's Congress and its Standing Committee, such as the General Principle of Civil Code 1986 (GPCC) and the Copyright Law 2001 (CL). The second level comprises regulations, administrative measures and orders endorsed by the State Council: Regulations for the Implementation of the Copyright Law 2002 (CLIR); Regulations for the Protection of Computer Software 2001 (CSPR); Regulations for the Protection of the Right of Communication through Information Network 2006 (RCPR), and Regulations for the Collective Management of Copyrights 2005 (RCMC), and Interim Measures for the Payment of Remuneration for Audio Products Played by Radio and TV Stations 2010. Many of these are local regulations approved by provincial and municipal legislatures, and administration or administrative stipulations embraced by the ministries or departments under the State Council, which are only referred to in judicial activities, such as the Provisions of Shanghai Municipality on the Copyright Management approved in 2000.

It is also worth mentioning that the Interpretation of the Supreme People's Court Concerning the Application of Laws to the Trial of Civil Disputes of Copyright (CLJI, effective from 15 October 2002) and Interpretation of the Supreme People's Court Concerning the Application of Laws to the Trial of Copyright Cases involving the Disputes over Computer Network (CNJI, effective from 22 November 2000, and revised in 2003 and 2006 respectively) play an important role as guidance to courts at various levels, even though they are not an official source of legal resources under the *Legislation Law* (a constitutional document, effective

---

9 *China – Measures Affecting Trading Rights and Distribution Services for Certain Publications and Audiovisual Entertainment Products*, WTO Appellate Body Decision WT/DS363/AB/R, December 2009 (discussed more fully in the Introduction to this book).

10 Xue Hong and Zheng Chengsi, *Chinese Intellectual Property Law in the 21st Century*, Hong Kong: Sweet & Maxwell Asia, 2002, p. 30.

1 July 2000). As Xue and Zheng argue, 'the influence of judicial explanations on IPRs enforcement should by no means be overlooked'.[11] China, however, does not enjoy a precedent tradition unlike many common law jurisdictions where judge-made law is much more significant. However, lawyers usually refer to typical cases decided by Chinese courts at different levels and circulated by the Gazette of the Supreme People's Court when similar cases arise, even though they are not binding. Judges are always proud of their achievements when cases decided by them are published in the Gazette, which actually acts as an (informal) index that grades professional competence.

4.3. FRAMEWORK OF THE COPYRIGHT LAW

The existing copyright system enumerates copyright's qualification and substance, copyright work, originality, ownership of copyright, neighbouring rights, limitation on rights, infringements and legal liability.

4.3.1. What is Copyright?

The statutory Chinese term for 'copyright' is *zhuzuoquan*, which is retranslated from Japanese legal parlance. Japanese statutes were modeled on Germany, thus *zhuzuoquan* includes the concept of the Continental author's right.[12] When drafting the Copyright Law of 1990, fierce controversy was triggered in terms of choosing the terms: *zhuozuoquan* or *banquan* (copyright).[13] Therefore, as a compromise, Article 51 provides that the term *zhuzuoquan* (author's rights) is synonymous with the term *banquan* (copyright).

In a narrow sense, copyright refers to the author's rights in China, which is used to describe the area of intellectual property law that regulates the creation and use of a range of cultural goods.[14] Various rights are conferred on the owner of copyright, from the right to copy the work to

---

[11] Ibid.

[12] Supra note 2, p. 76.

[13] For further details, please see Wu Handong, 'Inquiry Into and Analysis of Zhuzuoquan & Copyright', *Modern Law Science*, No. 6 (1989); Liu Chuntian, 'Reflections on Zhuzuoquan Legislation in China', *China Legal Science*, No. 4 (1989); Zheng Chengsi, 'Works, Zhuzuowu & Copyright', *Intellectual Property*, No. 1 (1989).

[14] Lionel Bently and Brad Sherman, *Intellectual Property Law* (second edition), Oxford: Oxford University Press, 2004, p. 29.

the right to broadcast the work under the CL (as revised). From the beginning, copyright was composed of both moral rights and economic rights (property rights) in China, different in contrast to the Anglo-American legal system. The rights that Article 10 of the CL set out are as follows:

(1) the right of publication;
(2) the right of authorship;
(3) the right of alteration, that is, the right to alter or authorize others to alter one's work;
(4) the right of integrity;
(5) the right of reproduction;
(6) the right of distribution;
(7) the right of rental;
(8) the right of exhibition;
(9) the right of performance;
(10) the right of presentation;
(11) the right of broadcasting;
(12) the right of communication through information network;
(13) the right of cinematography;
(14) the right of adaption;
(15) the right of translation;
(16) the right of compilation;
(17) the rights to be enjoyed by the copyright owner.

Subparagraph (17) makes copyright an open field, which means some rights may be granted to owners of copyright even if it is not stipulated in the CL. Judge Posner argued that a right is an important interest presumptively protected against interference by others.[15] One case is *Wang Meng and others v Cenpok Telecommunication Technology Ltd* (1999),[16] in which Beijing Haidian District Court held that the plaintiffs enjoyed the exclusive right to exploit their works in any manner and that they should have the right to prohibit unauthorized uses of their copyrighted works. The transmission of works over the Internet is also a form of exploitation of work, just like publication or broadcasting. Thus, in *Wang Meng* the defendant was held to have infringed the plaintiffs' copyright by communicating the plaintiffs' copyrighted works on the Internet, even if the right

15 R.A. Posner, *The Problems of Jurisprudence*, Cambridge, MA: Harvard University Press, 1990, p. 331.

16 *Wang Meng and others v Cenpok Telecommunication Technology Ltd.*, Bejing Haidian District Court, 18 September 1999.

of communications by network was then not specified in the CL. This right was added to the CL on 27 October 2001.

Another example is *Edko Films Ltd v UUSee.com.*[17] In this case, the defendant (UUSee) webcasted a movie owned by the plaintiff (Edko) with a fixed schedule (basically it streamed the same movie on the Internet in a circle). The case is interesting in that the webcast did not literally infringe upon either the 'right to broadcast' that requires that the work must be communicated to the public via a wireless means first, or the 'right of communication through information network' that only regulates the interactive transmission of a work on an information network. Therefore, to hold the defendant liable for its illegitimate exploitation of the plaintiff's movie, the court cited Article 10(17) again as the legal ground.

In a broad sense, Chinese copyright covers neighboring rights, which is based upon the dissemination of the work rather than the creation of the work. Under the CL, neighboring rights consist of the rights of the typographical design of the book or the periodical, the rights of performers, the rights of producers of sound recordings or video recordings and the rights of radio stations or television stations.[18]

4.3.2. Copyrighted Works

A work (*zuopin*) is defined as a fruit of intellectual creation with originality in the literary, artistic or scientific domain, insofar as it can be reproduced in a tangible form.[19] The CL enumerates nine types of works for subsistence of copyright:

(1) written works;
(2) oral works;
(3) musical, dramatic, *quyi*,[20] choreographic and acrobatic works; (Acrobatic works were included in 2001. The purpose of the inclusion is to highlight characteristic Chinese works and to protect well-known Chinese acrobatics.[21])
(4) works of the fine arts and architecture;

---

17 *Edko Films Ltd v Beijing Shi Yue Network Technology Ltd.*, the Second People's Intermediate Court of Beijing, 21 September 2008.

18 See Chapter 4 of CL.

19 CLIR, Article 1.

20 *Quyi* works are those works created mainly for performance in a way involving recitation, singing, or both, such as cross-talk, clapper talk, ballad singing and story telling.

21 Supra note 2, p. 8.

(5) photographic works;
(6) cinematographic works and works created by a process analogous to cinematography;
(7) graphic works such as drawings of engineering design and product designs, maps and sketches, and model works;
(8) computer software (computer programs and their relevant files); and
(9) other works as provided for in laws and administrative regulations.

The list is not well-classified, nor in fact complete, but follows customary usage for the sake of easier implementation. The catch-all 'other works' provision presumably is meant to take care of any omissions. The changing world of works has to be examined in light of more specific administrative guidelines and judicial interpretation.[22] For example, Article 2(2) of Interpretations of the Supreme People's Court Concerning the Application of Laws to the Trial of Civil Disputes of Computer Network Copyright (2000) provides that rights formulated in Article 10 (defining personal and property rights) of CL are all applicable to digital works.

A work must satisfy four requirements to qualify for copyright protection. First, it must be a literary, artistic or scientific work. There is a boundary line between copyright protection and patent protection, as the latter only aims to meet people's utility demand. The boundary line may not be a clear-cut one as industrial design patents also require that the protected subject has a certain aesthetic characteristic. On the contrary, a copyright work will satisfy people's aesthetic requirements. Second, it is an expression of an idea. Copyright extends to the expression rather than the idea (concepts, procedure, fact, process, principle, system, and methods of operation or mathematical concepts as such) of a work. The reason why the CL does not protect ideas is to defend freedom of speech which is of significant value to any constitution. As McDonnell argues, the idea/expression dichotomy serves as a safety valve of tension between copyright law and freedom of speech.[23] However, the boundary of the idea/expression dichotomy is not always readily drawn. It has given rise to some enlightening cases.[24] The idea/expression dichotomy does not

22 Supra note 2, p. 59.

23 B. McDonnell, 'Freedom of Speech and Appellate and Summary Judgment Review in Copyright Cases', *Yale Law Journal*, 107 (1998).

24 Supra note 3, p. 60. See *Guangxi Radio and Television Guide v Guangxi Coal Miners Daily* (1994), in which Guangxi Liuzhou Intermediate Court held that a television program schedule *per se* is not copyrightable.

emerge in the CL of 2001 by virtue of its vagueness. In my opinion, the dichotomy is far too vague. Judges prefer to deem a subject as an idea whenever they think that it should not be shielded, and vice versa.[25] Third, a copyrightable work should be original. The CL does not define originality. The majority of scholars deem originality as 'creativity' in the CL. Originality differs from novelty[26] in the Patent Law, and it requires that a work should originate from its author rather than be copied from another work. But what does originality actually mean? Lawyers and commentators have no consensus of opinion. Wei holds that originality should be defined as 'independent creation and creativity'.[27] However, Feng and Feng interpret originality as a 'work of personality'.[28] Regretfully, judges seldom discuss originality directly in copyright disputes. The last but not least important requirement is that a work can be reproduced in a tangible form. Reproduction can be in a variety of forms, such as printing, photocopying, lithographing, making a sound recording or video recording, duplicating a recording, or duplicating a photographic work. Judges hold that the term 'reproduction' in this sense fails to cover the construction or manufacture of industrial products on the basis of drawings of engineering and product designs and descriptions thereof.[29] In *Shanghai Dbtel Industry Co., Ltd v Motorola (China) Electronics Ltd & Shanghai Bailian Group Co., Ltd* (2002),[30] the court concluded that the defendant's production activity of a printed circuit board according to drawings of a printed circuit board is not reproduction as stipulated in the CL. Fixation in a tangible medium is not a prerequisite for copyright protection. Hence, oral works, those expressed in the form of spoken language, such as impromptu speeches, lectures and court debates, qualify for copyright protection. The common objection to this approach is premised on the fact that, without fixation, it is often impossible to show evidence of

---

[25] Y.F. Li, 'Review on Idea/Expression Dichotomy in Copyright Law', *Peking University Law Review*, 8 (2007).

[26] 'Novelty' of patent law means that an identical invention or utility model has been publicly disclosed in the country or abroad before the date of filing.

[27] Wei Zhi, *On Intellectual Property*, China: Intellectual Property Press, 2002, p. 46.

[28] Feng Xiaoqing and Feng Ye, 'On Originality of Works under CL', *Journal of The East China University of Politics and Law*, No. 5 (1995).

[29] Supra note 2, p. 11.

[30] *Shanghai Dbtel Industry Co., Ltd v Motorola (China) Electronics Ltd & Shanghai Bailian Group Co., Ltd*, Shanghai Second Intermediate Court, 2002. For further analysis see Xu Chao, *Evaluation and Analysis on Complicated Problems of Copyright*, Hangzhou: Zhejiang Education Press, 2000, pp. 20–26.

copyright at all.[31] At the time of writing, case law is yet to be determined with regard to oral works in China.

4.3.3. Non-copyrighted and Banned Works

4.3.3.1. Government documents

Government documents are detailed as the 'laws and regulations, resolutions, decisions and orders of State organs, other documents of a legislative, administrative or judicial nature and their official translations'.[32] These documents may be original, and qualify entirely for copyright protection. The reason why they are excluded for copyright protection is that these documents represent the will of the state organs that make them, and that they must not be 'privatized'.[33] Furthermore, the use of these documents is linked with the public and national interest so that they should be made as fully accessible as possible.[34]

4.3.3.2. News on current affairs

News on current affairs means that mere facts or happenings conveyed through the media, such as newspapers, periodicals and radio and television programs, are not copyrightable.[35] The justification for this exclusion is that news on current affairs is just a simple and direct recording of objective events such as time, location, and happening, and into which it fails to mix the intellectual labor of the author. News on current affairs is limited to pure factual news. Obviously, events per se also do not qualify for copyright protection.

However, the distinction between news on current affairs and commentary on current affairs by journalists should be made clearly and correctly. The latter refers in particular to a written work that mirrors journalists' opinion with regard to objective events and meets the originality requirement, and is therefore copyrightable.

4.3.3.3. Calendars, numerical tables and forms of general use, and formulas

These subjects fall within the realm of ideas, or common information for public use. In this category, the term of 'numerical tables of general use'

---

31 Supra note 2, p. 60.

32 CL, Article 5(1).

33 Zhang Yumin, *Intellectual Property Law*, Beijing: Law Press, 2005, p. 94.

34 Wang Qian, *The Textbook on Intellectual Property Law*, Beijing: China Renmin University Press, 2007, p. 71.

35 CLIR, Article 5(1).

was originally the 'numerical table' in the CL of 1990. Some numerical tables in the special field are regarded as subjects of copyright protection. Thus, 'general use' was added to the MCL.

4.3.3.4. Banned works

Article 4(1) of the old CL 2001 was mentioned above. This article has now been dropped from the CL (revised 2010). The old Article 4(1) required that works, publication and dissemination of which were prohibited by law, should not be protected by Chinese copyright.[36] China exercises a press control policy. Under the Regulations on the Administration of Publication 2001 (PAR), all publication activities, including publication and printing of publications or the duplication and distribution thereof should be subject to government control for the sake of promoting the building of a socialist spiritual civilization and material civilization. 'It took some time to convince the concerned propaganda officials and cultural regulators that copyright would not cancel the existing regime of planning and censorship, and only the mode of control would have to change a little'.[37] This thinking reflects the unwholesome legacy of certain political factions holding the view that the creation, publication and dissemination of works must be policed to maintain a stable cultural order. The official reason as to why the CL did not protect banned works was as follows: first, China's laws have to adhere to the Four Cardinal Principles (*sixiang jiben yuanze*) of the Communist Party of China (CPC) as a socialist state. Works inciting to split the country and endanger sovereignty, and to undermine the solidarity of the nation, propagate obscenity, gambling, violence or to instigate crime, and others objecting to the basic principles determined in the Constitution run foul of socialism, and cannot claim copyright protection. Second, citizens, legal persons and other organizations should undertake civil activities in accordance with the spirit of the law; where there are no relevant provisions in the law, they shall accord with state policies under the General Principle of the Civil Code. This means that authors' intellectual creations shall be protected only if they observe Chinese laws, policies and social public moralities. Third, banned works do not raise the issue of protection, but concern legal liability. Article 105(1) of Criminal Law of PRC (2009 amended) lays down that a person who incites to subvert the state's political power or to overthrow

---

[36] Article 4 CL (revised 2010) now reads: 'Copyright owners, in exercising their copyright, shall not violate the Constitution or laws or infringe upon the public interests. The publication and dissemination of works shall be subject to the administration and supervision of the State.'

[37] Supra note 2, p. 64.

the socialist system by starting a rumor, slander or any other means shall be sentenced to a fixed term of imprisonment of not more than five years, criminal detention, public surveillance or deprivation of political rights; and the ringleaders or the persons whose crimes are severe shall be sentenced to a fixed term of imprisonment of not less than five years. In this regard, the CL will conflict with the Criminal Law where it offers copyright protection for illegal works. Lastly, Article 4 matched Article 17 of the Berne Convention for the Protection of Literary and Artistic Works.[38]

Under the PAR, the sanction applies to all materials. A book number or special permission from a competent administration is necessary if a writer wants to publish his work. All publications explicitly state the names and addresses of the author, publisher, typography/reproducer or distributor, the book number, serial number/publisher's code, the publication date, the publishing frequency and other relevant items,[39] the aim of which is to find the individual or unit (*danwei*) who should be responsible for the content.[40] A publisher's failure to obtain a publication number or special permission may result in the works concerned being banned, as well as confiscation of publications, illegal income and special instruments used in legal activities, and fines. Where the case is serious enough for criminal punishment, offenders will be investigated for criminal liability in accordance with the Criminal Law for illegal business operations.[41] Similarly, an editor also bears the responsibility for guaranteeing that the content included in publications conforms with the PAR.[42] However, the PAR is silent on the liability of authors.

What can be included under banned works? The following are listed by the PAR:

(1) those against the basic principles established in the Constitution;
(2) those endangering the unification, sovereignty and territorial integrity of the State;
(3) those which divulge secrets of the State, endanger national security or jeopardize the honor or benefits of the State;
(4) those which incite the national hatred or discrimination, undermine the solidarity of the nations, or infringe upon national customs and habits;

---

[38] Yao Hong (ed.), *Explanation of the Copyright Law of PRC*, Beijing: Populace Press, 2001, pp. 62–3.
[39] See PAR, Article 29.
[40] A unit is a factory, workplace, work entity etc.
[41] See PAR, Article 55.
[42] See PAR, Article 25.

(5) those which propagate evil cults or superstition;
(6) those which disturb the public order or destroy the public stability;
(7) those which propagate obscenity, gambling, violence or instigate crimes;
(8) those which insult or slander others, or infringe upon the lawful rights or interests of others;
(9) those which endanger public ethics or the fine national cultural traditions;
(10) other contents prohibited by laws, administrative regulations or provisions of the State.

Also Article 4(1) of the CL stated that in exercising copyright, no copyright owner could violate the Constitution or laws, and impair public interest. Here, as the legislature did not differentiate copyrightability per se from the exercising of copyright, it was not possible to distinguish between CL and press law or publication law. Copyrightability makes a work subject to originality, idea/expression dichotomy and so on. The exercising of copyright focuses on the effects that the content of a work has on the social order and public morality. In addition, Article 51(1) of the Berne Convention notes that copyright will be automatically created, and this is also incorporated into the TRIPS Agreement. Based on these factors, the United States filed complaints to the WTO that Article 4(1) of Copyright Law of the PRC conflicted with Article 9.1 of the TRIPS Agreement, incorporating Articles 5(1) and 5(2) of the Berne Convention (1971), as well as Article 14; Article 61, 1st and 2nd sentence; and Article 41.1 of the TRIPS Agreement. The dispute settlement panel of the WTO found that 'China is unable to explain why censorship interferes with copyright owners' rights to prevent third parties from exploiting prohibited works', and released a decision in favor of the United States in January 2009.[43]

As a consequence of the WTO's Appellate Body Decision in December 2009, China has now dropped Article 4(1) from the revised CL (2010). Some Chinese scholars argued, however, that Article 4(1) did not say that *all* works distributed in China that had *not* received administrative permits

[43] See 'WTO Decision On Adequacy of China's Intellectual Property Laws has Potentially Significant Consequences for Counterfeiting and Piracy Enforcement Standards Around World', http://www.sidley.com/files/News/e1723619-0fa8-42f3-957a-ba8fd2cd0a18/Presentation/NewsAttachment/a37414da-c742-4ff8-a2ea-869b42dd7fc0/International%20Trade%20&%20Intellectual%20Property%20Update%2029.01.09_revised_Layout%202.pdf, accessed July 2010. China appealed the panel decision. The Appellate Body released its decision in December 2009.

were not protectable under the CL. According to the SPC judges and NCAC officials, only those works whose content was *explicitly* banned by censorship standards were deprived of copyright protection. In other words, for those works that had not received their distribution permit for other reasons like importation quota, lengthy censorship procedures, or even simply that the rights holders had not submitted their works for approval, rights holders could still obtain protection under the CL, though in judicial practice the rights holder might receive much lower damages for unapproved works than those that had been approved, if the rights owner sued the infringer(s) in a Chinese court. However, from the industry perspective, the lower damages approach was also unjustified as it did not consider the rights holder's loss of expected revenue once the works had been permitted to be distributed on the Chinese market.

4.3.4. Ownership of Copyright

Copyright vests (in principle) in the author, unless the CL provides otherwise.[44] The author of a work is the natural person (citizen) who creates the work.[45] The term 'creation' refers to 'intellectual activities in which literary, artistic or scientific works are directly created'.[46]Any organizational activity, consultation, material support or other auxiliary services conducted or offered for another person's creation does not belong to intellectual activity, and may not be considered as a creation. So a person undertaking this activity is not an author.

Article 11(2) limits the author to natural persons. However, where a work is created under the auspices and according to the will of the legal person or other organizations that bears full responsibility for the work, such legal person or other organizations (legal entities) shall be deemed to be the author of the work.[47] This sort of work is named the work of a legal entity (*faren zuopin*).

4.3.4.1. Ownership of co-authored works

A work is described as co-authored if it is created jointly by two or more authors. The term co-authored work is used in a broad sense. It comprises not only the work that cannot be separated into individual parts and exploited separately but also those works that can be divided into

44 CL, Article 11(1).
45 CL, Article 11(2).
46 CLIR, Article 3.
47 CL, Article 11(3).

individual parts and used separately. The former is labelled as a work of 'joint authorship', and the latter as the work of 'compounded contribution'. Thus the ownership in co-authored works actually refers to two different types of ownership: joint ownership of the co-authored work as a whole and, where the co-authored work is a compound, each co-author's distinct ownership of the separable parts.[48]

4.3.4.2. Ownership of cinematographic works or the like

Cinematographic works or the like include cinematographic works and works created by a process analogous to cinematography, and signify works which are recorded on some material, consisting of a series of images, with or without accompanying sound and which can be projected with the aid of suitable devices or communicated by other means.[49]

Copyright in cinematographic works or the like shall be enjoyed by the producer of the work, while its scriptwriter, director, cameraman, lyricist and composer and other authors shall enjoy the right of authorship. The authors of a script, musical works and other works included in a cinematographic work or in a work created by a process analogous to cinematography and which can be exploited separately are entitled to exercise their copyright independently.[50]

4.3.4.3. Ownership of service works ('works for hire')

A 'service work' is a work created in the course of employment under Chinese Copyright Law, which refers to a work created by a natural person in the fulfillment of a task assigned to him by a legal person or other organization.[51] The term 'task' is not defined in the CL, but is mentioned at Article 16 and presumably means the duties the employee shall fulfill in the legal person or organization by which s/he is employed.[52] The copyright in the service work vests in principle in the author unless enunciated in the law, regulation or contract. The unit (*danwei*) enjoys a two-year priority of use of the service work within its scope of business or normal functions.

Pursuant to Article 16(2) of the CL, the author of a service work enjoys the right of authorship, while the unit enjoys the other rights included in the copyright under the particular circumstances. This kind of service work is labeled as a 'special service work' (*teshu zhiwu zuopin*) Special service works fall broadly into two categories: (a) the drawings of engi-

---

48 Supra note 3, p. 84.
49 CLIR, Article 15(1).
50 CL, Article 15(2).
51 CL, Article 16.
52 Ibid.

neering designs, product designs, maps, computer software and other works created in the course of employment, mainly with the material and technical resources[53] of a legal person or other organization and for which a legal person or other organization bears responsibility; or (2) works created in the course of employment, the copyright in which is, in accordance with laws, administrative regulations or contracts, enjoyed by the legal person or other organization.

4.3.4.4. Special clause

In addition, the CLJI specifies the ownership of copyright in special works with Chinese characteristics. In the light of Article 13 CLJI, the copyright in works (except works of a legal person), such as reports or speeches written by others but proofread and finalized by the persons delivering the reports or making the speeches themselves and published in the name of the latter, shall be owned by the persons giving the reports or making the speeches. The copyright owners may pay the person who does the writing appropriate remuneration.

Article 14 CLJI provides that in respect of an autobiographic work created by interested parties entering into an agreement, on the basis of the life experiences of a specific person, where the interested parties have an agreement on the ownership of the copyright, the agreement shall prevail. Where there is no agreement concluded between the two parties, copyright shall be owned by 'such specific persons whose experiences are utilized' (i.e. the person whose life is being written about). Where the person who does the writing or compiler has contributed to the creation of the work, the rights owner should pay them appropriate remuneration.

Under Articles 13 and 14, the position of leadership or the life experience of a specific person is the basis of copyright, which has triggered widespread criticism on account of inconsistency with the doctrine of copyright law.[54]

4.3.5. Neighbouring Rights

Neighboring rights include: the rights of the publishers; the rights over the typographical design of the book or the periodical; the rights of performers; the rights of producers of sound recordings or video recordings, and the

---

[53] The term 'material and technical resources' means the funds, equipment or materials purposely provided to natural person by the legal person or organization by which he is employed for the creation of a work. See CLIR, Article 11(2).

[54] Wang Qian, *Textbook on Intellectual Property Law*, Beijing: Renmin University of China Press, 2007, p. 195.

rights of radio stations or television stations. Without the author's creative activity in a work, there can be no 'neighboring' right (in a narrow sense). The owner of a neighboring right only spreads a work, rather than creates it. The textbook justification for such rights is that publishers, performers, producers of sound recordings or video recordings, or broadcasting organizations make investments in programmes, equipment, technique, time, and/or labor in disseminating works to the public, and they should therefore be rewarded. This argument, as an expression of gratitude to a disseminator from a legal perspective, seems to be fair, and conforms to general expectations.

The rights of the typographical design of a book or periodical should be enjoyed by a publisher, who shall have the right to permit another person to exploit, or prohibit such person from exploiting, the typographical design of the book or the periodical which the publisher publishes.[55]

The term of protection for such rights is ten years, expiring on 31 December of the tenth year after the first publication of the book or the periodical in which the typographical design is used.[56]

As for a performer, Article 38, Section 2 (Chapter IV) CL (revised 2010) sets out a list of the rights that can be enjoyed, including the right:

(1) to claim performance rights;
(2) to protect the image inherent in his/her performance from distortion;
(3) to authorize others to make live broadcasts and public transmission of its or his/her performance and to receive remuneration thereof;
(4) to authorize others to make sound recordings and video recordings, and to receive remuneration thereof;
(5) to authorize others to reproduce or distribute sound recordings and video recordings incorporating his/her performance, and to receive remuneration thereof; and
(6) to authorize others to communicate his/her performance to the public on an information network, and to receive remuneration thereof.

The CL (revised 2010) has still failed to list the right of rental for performers, as well as the right to remuneration from *broadcasting and communicating* publicly phonograms in which their performance is fixed, which runs foul of the WPPT.[57] The WPPT was binding on China from 9 June 2007 onward.

---

55 CL, Article 36(1).
56 CL, Article 36(2).
57 See WPPT, Articles 9 and 15.

The rights that a producer of sound recordings or video recordings shall have comprise those rights to authorize others to reproduce, distribute, rent and communicate to the public on an information network such sound recordings or video recordings and the right to obtain remuneration. Besides, a producer of video recordings shall enjoy the right to authorize a television station to broadcast his video recordings and to receive remuneration.[58] Such a right is not directly listed in articles concerning a producer of recordings or video recordings but implied in the article regarding a television station's obligation.[59] However, a producer of sound recordings cannot enjoy the right to receive remuneration from broadcasting and communicating his/her sound recording by another person, which (again) is not in accordance with Article 15(1) WPPT. And (again) the legislature in the CL (revised 2010) has not included this right in the copyright law.

The broadcasting organization refers generally to both radio and television stations. Under the Berne Convention and Rome Convention, the term 'broadcasting' is limited to disseminating works in a wireless means, and does not incorporate the dissemination of work in a wire form such as over cable networks. Japanese copyright law, by contrast, includes cable rights. However, the term 'broadcasting' in China actually refers to two different types of dissemination: broadcasting in a wireless form, and cable casting in a wire form. The mainstream view held by NCAC officials and SPC judges is that 'broadcasting' in China refers to broadcasting in a wireless form and retransmission of the wireless-broadcast programs in a wired means.[60] In other words, it does not cover direct cable casting. This narrow definition, which reflects the intention of the legislators, is not consistent with the requirements of the WCT and WPPT. This will naturally cause conflict between Chinese law harmonization and international conventions. In addition, it is obviously outdated given that cable and webcasting services are developing so rapidly that they will soon overtake wireless broadcasting and dominate the market. As a consequence, the wireless-based definition of 'broadcasting' may subject all the cable broadcasters and webcasters to a lacuna in protection and consequent loss of investment in production and licensing.

---

[58] CL, Article 45.

[59] CL, Article 45.

[60] CL (revised 2010), Article 11 defines the 'right of broadcasting' as: '. . . the right to publicly broadcast or disseminate works by wireless means, to disseminate broadcast works to the public by wired dissemination or rebroadcast, and to disseminate broadcast works to the public by audio amplifier or other similar instruments for transmission of signs, sounds or images'.

4.4. PROBLEMS WITH DIFFERENCES OF INTERPRETATION AND ENFORCEMENT OF LAWS ACROSS CHINA

The People's Republic of China (PRC) has been set on building a modern copyright system since 1979. After 30 years' of development, China has greatly improved its copyright laws and regulations, and has created an effective enforcement system, including copyright offices at different administrative levels. Nevertheless, from the industry perspective, the current copyright enforcement system is still far from being labeled 'efficient'. Generally, the copyright office has only a small team (200+ according to NCAC officials) responsible for all administrative actions throughout the country, and civil IPR courts are overwhelmed by copyright cases that are still growing at a double-digit rate each year, as existing civil remedies are not proving enough of a deterrent to new/repeat infringements. Criminal cases are also growing but it is still not easy to initiate a criminal investigation as this becomes extremely difficult with regard to Internet piracy, mainly due to difficult evidentiary requirements. However, despite these setbacks, the substantial effort made by China in establishing a modern system of copyright to keep pace with developed countries is becoming the focus of international attention. It has been argued that it took China only 30 years to develop a modern system of copyright compared with 300 years for some developed countries. However, Western countries have also criticized China's protection of copyright and particularly as regards *enforcement* of copyright.[61]

There are various reasons for this divergence. First, some stipulations of Chinese copyright law are inconsistent with international conventions (as seen above), particularly where foreign owners of copyright are not protected under Chinese law, or at least not fully protected. For example, under the International Copyright Treaties Implementing Rules (1992), foreigners' applied art, for example, will be protected for 25 years from the year the work is created. This provision contrasts with the protection of domestic works, where domestic works qualify as 'artistic' works,[62] and enjoy protection for 50 years after the death of the author if s/he is a

---

[61] Liu Ying and Yang Cheng, 'Enforcement is the Focus of Intellectual Property Protection in China: Special Visit by Mr. Thomas Pattloch, An Intellectual Property Official of EU Delegation to China', http://ip.people.com.cn/GB/136674/136696/8218948.html (visited 16 July 2009).

[62] See *Hu Sansan v Qiu Haisuo & the National Art Museum of China*, Beijing Second Intermediary Court, 2000; *Shanghai Luolai Hometextile Co. Ltd v Foshan Nanhai Fuli Fashion Co., Ltd*, Chengdu Intermediary Court, 2008.

natural person or after the first publication if the author is a legal person or other organization. The term of protection for foreign applied art is shorter than for Chinese works, which has potential implications for the violation of the national treatment principle under the TRIPS for foreign works.[63] Another example is that there are increasing disputes concerning foreign interests on the Internet. Some network service providers allow users to download digital foreign cinematography without authorization through the Internet. The owners of these cinematographic works have taken legal proceedings against the violation of copyright. Before the CL was revised in 2010 (and Article 4(1) was dropped as discussed above), some local courts had decided that such foreign content was not fully protected in China because these works did not receive censorship authorization of importation from the relevant departments in charge under Article 4(1) of the CL.[64]

Second, the vagueness of the legal term in Chinese copyright law makes the decisions of the courts contradictory. For example, the 'catch-all provision' has the manifold faces of Proteus. China shares the Continental tradition of natural law, which believes in human reason, holding that human beings can enact detailed law. Meanwhile, in order to take into account potential omissions missed by the law, the CL includes several 'catch-all provisions' that could fall foul of general principles of natural law. These include: the catch-all 'other works' provision in Article 3(9); the catch-all 'other rights' provision in Article 10(17) and the catch-all 'other infringements' in Article 47(11). These catch-all provisions give considerable flexibility to local courts and judges in exercising their right of discretion; conversely, such flexibility to exercise discretion also gives rise to the potential for making contradictory decisions. For example, in *Gao Liya v Chongqing Nanan District Sigongli Primary School* (2005),[65] the plaintiff handed in 48 notebooks (*jiaoanben*) with her teaching plans

---

[63] However, some scholars argue that this conflict no longer exists as the Copyright Law was amended in 2001, and it supersedes the 1992 implementing rules, therefore eliminating this difference.

[64] *Shuimunianhua Internet Café of Chongqing New-High Technology Industry and Development Zone v Guangzhou Zoke Culture Co., Ltd*, Chongqing Municipality High People's Court, 2009. However, at the time of writing, this decision or a relevant report of the case cannot be found on the Internet, so it is unclear how the local courts actually ruled in the dispute. As mentioned above, the mainstream view of the SPC judges and NCAC officials is that a work should not be deprived of copyright protection merely because it has yet to receive the required censorship approval.

[65] See *Gao Liya v Chongqing Nanan District Sigongli Primary School*, Chongqing First Intermediary Court, December 2005.

for pupils to the defendant, and had not made any copies of these teaching plans. The defendant only returned four notebooks to her, and the rest 'disappeared'. The plaintiff sued the defendant for infringement of copyright. The defendant pleaded that the plaintiff's teaching plans were not reproduced, published, translated and exploited in the other forms as set out in Article 10. What the defendant did was to dispense with the plaintiff's 44 notebooks, which is not the subject of copyright but that of ownership (*suoyouquan*): in this case, the notebooks possessed by the plaintiff were issued for the purpose of preparing lessons by the defendant, ownership of which could be enjoyed by the defendant. Based on the catch-all 'other infringements' provision, the court drew the conclusion that the defendant had infringed the plaintiff's copyright in the teaching plans notwithstanding the defendant having not reproduced, published or translated the teaching plans in question.[66] However, this decision has not been uniformly followed in China.

Third, to some extent, the allocation of enforcement resources to protect copyright is unreasonable and costly. Just as Stigler pointed out that government organs function in the interests of the state, and not in the public interest,[67]a badly defined administrative structure of authorities in enforcement sectors impels them to seek a variety of rents. An official from the Team of Economic Crime Investigation of Chongqing Municipal Public Security Bureau, who refused to be named, told me that as to the crime of copyright infringement, the Team of Public Order, the Team of Economic Crime Investigation and Criminal Investigation Team all have jurisdiction. Actually, when facing some cases that result in corruption, they choose to escape, and when they meet cases involving good money, they are inclined to snatch. The agency cost of government organs remains the permanent focus of politics. In addition, there exists local protectionism in China. The upper-level layers of government rate lower officials in terms of an economic index. Thus, if the defendant is a taxpayer with a high annual contribution to local taxes (*nashuidahu*) who creates many employment opportunities for the unemployed, the regional enforcement organs are reluctant to investigate and fix the defendant's liabilities for infringement.

---

[66] Also see *Gaolei v China Theatre Press*, Beijing Haidian District Court, 2004. Cf. *Wang Gengxin v Central Academy of Drama Theater*, Beijing Dongcheng District Court (2008). In this case, the court concluded that the defendant had lost mimeographed copy of the plaintiff's works, and infringed the ownership of the plaintiff under the Real Right Law (there was no discussion as to whether the plaintiff had another copy of the lost works).

[67] George J. Stigler, 'The Theory of Economic Regulation', *Bell Journal of Economics and Management Science*, 3 (1971).

The last but most important factor concerns Chinese legal thinking on copyright protection. After 30 years of reform and the gradual opening of markets, the Chinese understanding of rights has been tremendously strengthened. However, there is still a gap between the cognition of copyright protection in China and that of developed countries. Traditional Confucian ideology still remains in Chinese society. Authors prefer to have their works disseminated publicly than to claim copyright. Most Chinese authors have varying concepts of the meaning of 'originality'. The proverb 'all writings in the world are copies' (*tianxia wenzhang yidachao*) is not far from the Confucian analects – *I transmit rather than create; I believe in and love the Ancients*.[68] However, at the same time, the fruit of intellectual creation by others is not always respected. For example, 'pirated' books are believed to be different from stolen goods. The words of Kong Yiji, a well-known figure in Lu Xun's novel,[69] are particularly relevant in this context: 'to steal a book is an elegant offense'.[70] The increasing problems of plagiarism are but mirrors of such a thought. It is reported that a student, a Master of Statistics of a leading university in the northeast of China, copied the dissertation of another colleague almost in its entirety. The Academic Degrees Committee of the University rescinded his master's degree and withdrew the degree certificate on 27 May 2009.[71] The latest case is an incident of plagiarism involving the Vice-Chancellor of a major university in the southwest of China. The Vice-Chancellor's doctoral dissertation was revealed to be in part a copy of another's material.[72] These events have triggered widespread discussion related to academic regulation and copyright protection in China.

The content industry is very concerned with China's copyright enforcement system for a number of reasons:

1. Administrative enforcement is insufficient due to a lack of manpower and 'real teeth' to order the shutdown of operators involved in serious or repeated violations. Better and more efficient coordination

---

68 *The Analects of Confucius*, Book 7. See William P. Alford, *To Steal a Book is an Elegant Offense*, Stanford, CA: Stanford University Press, 1995, p. 9.

69 Lu Xun, *Self-Selected Works of Lu Xun*, Tianjin: Tianjin People's Press, 2005.

70 Supra note 68.

71 http://news.sina.com.cn/c/2009-05-25/032217881074.shtml (accessed 23 August 2010).

72 http://www.eol.cn/kaoyan_news_3989/20090716/t20090716_391512.shtml, accessed August 2010.

is needed among different agencies regulating different but highly connected media sectors, including the General Administration of Publication and Press, the National Copyright Administration, the Ministry of Culture, the State Administration of Radio, Film and TV, the Ministry of Industry and Information Technology, the Ministry of Public Security, etc.

2. Without deterrent damages, including punitive damages, powerful injunctions including preliminary injunctions, and enforcement of court orders, the civil remedies are giving advantages to infringers who use the courts as an institution to seek compulsory licenses from rights holders. Evidentiary bars are also too high for the plaintiffs to establish a case with the court and to prevail. For instance, notarization of documents for submission as evidence to court is almost a 'must-have' to prove infringement and nearly every piece of evidence obtained from overseas is required to be notarized and legalized through Chinese embassies or consular officials, which usually causes higher costs and delays for plaintiffs filing a case. The absence of real discovery proceedings also makes it very difficult for the rights holder to collect critical evidence in the possession of defendants.
3. The thresholds for criminal enforcement are in most cases a real obstacle because the police usually take the conviction standards as the bar for initiating an investigation. Therefore, to take or not to take a complaint and investigate is a totally arbitrary decision subject to the manpower, political will and workload of the local public security bureaus. There is also no uniform theory to prosecute copyright thefts as the local judiciary can forum-shop among Article 217 (Copyright Infringement), Article 218 (Sale of Infringing Copies) and Article 225 (Illegal Operation) in the criminal code. The fundamental problem lies in outdated criminal provisions (enacted in 1996 and never improved since, despite the fact that almost all Chinese IPR laws were amended around 2000–01). The new round of reform of specific IPR laws (for example, the New Patent Act 2008, and at the time of writing, planned revisions to the Trademark and Anti-Unfair Competition Acts covered elsewhere in this book) has begun, but the Criminal Code has yet to be amended. At present, criminal evidentiary rules are unnecessarily rigid. For instance, the evidence collected by administrative enforcement agencies are usually inadmissible to the police. Also, the political will to seriously punish copyright theft is still weak due to a lack of awareness of the significance of copyright protection for the economy and society, the low priority given to such crimes on the police's agenda, and an improper performance evaluation system for policemen, prosecutors and judges.

4.5. CONTINUING REFORM AND FUTURE LEGISLATION

4.5.1. Continuing Reform

A plethora of problems concerning enforcement of intellectual property (including copyright) troubles China's IP authorities. In a particular copyright case, for example, three sorts of procedure, including civil, administrative and criminal may all be initiated. Civil procedure is subject to an intellectual property tribunal, and administrative and criminal procedures are subject respectively to administrative tribunals and criminal tribunals. Inconsistent decisions often occur. In order to optimize the allocation of trial resources, to simplify relief procedure and to effectively protect the rights owners of intellectual property, China is attempting to create a trinity of judicial procedures (*sanshenheyi*) for intellectual property: civil, administrative or criminal cases concerning intellectual property are uniformly accepted by intellectual property tribunals in the relevant jurisdiction. This 'trinity' approach was initiated by the Shanghai Pudong District Court in 1996, and has now been extended to other regions.

However, improvements need to continue. The administrative system on copyright protection is still in need of reform. Administrative protection is an important enforcement system with a particular Chinese characteristic or 'flavor'.[73] 'Compared to judicial enforcement, administrative enforcement is quicker, more flexible and more effective.'[74] However, there exist a variety of problems with current administrative enforcement. According to the National Copyright Administration, the problems are as follows:[75]

(1) Administrative organs are not complete. Professional enforcement organs only extend to provinces and some important cities. Prefecture-level cities and regions (mostly) have no specialized administrative enforcement organs.
(2) Some non-administrative organs' lack of enforcement authority under the CL has caused them to act outside their areas of responsibility.

---

73 Administrative protection means that the National Copyright Administration and Copyright Administrations at the local level also have authority to attack piracy even if victims do not initiate litigation.

74 Supra note 6.

75 Supra note 54.

(3) Administrative enforcement measures should be strengthened to deal with the growing transmission of works over the Internet.
(4) Close scrutiny of Article 48 of CL reveals that impairing the public interest is the prerequisite for administrative enforcement. But the related laws fail to clarify the meaning of the term 'public interest'.
(5) At the time of writing, the related mediation and arbitral institutions for copyright disputes have not yet been created.
(6) Administrative enforcement is not effectively harmonized with judicial enforcement.

It is therefore necessary to continue to reform the administrative enforcement system. For example, enforcement subjects should be regulated in a unitary and uniform direction; law enforcement needs expanding; mediation mechanisms should be set up and facilitated.[76]

From an industry perspective, administrative enforcement can also be enhanced through increased manpower and resources; high penalties with real teeth to deter violations, especially the power to order the shutdown of illegal businesses; unification or at least better coordination of enforcement by different agencies, and clearer guidance and incentives for the administrative agencies to transfer cases to criminal investigation/prosecution where prima facie evidence may point to a possible crime.

4.5.2. Forthcoming Legislation

After years of development, the CL has now gone through its second revision. The National Copyright Administration initiated a program of investigation and research as to the effects of the CL in 2008. The survey revealed that some problems still exist.[77] Unfortunately, the CL (revised 2010) has not dealt effectively with many of these problems and the following need to be put on the agenda for future amendment:

(1) The provisions of the CL are inconsistent with the coexistence of multi-ownership in a socialist market economy. Under the CL, the copyright of a legal entity's work is enjoyed by the legal entity even if it is completed by an employee; other rights of copyright in the special service work vest in the legal entity, and the right of authorship vests in the author as a natural person. But the legal entity's work and the special service work overlap. Hence, it is suggested that

---

[76] Supra note 54.
[77] Ibid.

Article 11(3) should explicitly state that the legal entity shall acquire original copyright.[78]

Under Article 19 CL, property rights in copyright enjoyed by a natural person should be transferred in accordance with the provisions of the Law of Succession after his/her death and during the term of protection. Then, copyright in the absence of a successor or legatee will belong to the state, which is obviously not conducive to disseminating works. It is proposed that works in this case should enter into the public domain.[79]

(2) Several provisions need to be updated following China's ratification of the WCT and WPPT. Under Article 9 of the WPPT binding China from 2007, performers enjoy the exclusive right of authorizing the commercial rental to the public of the original and copies of their performances fixed in phonograms. Article 15(1) provides that performers and producers of phonograms shall enjoy the right to a single equitable remuneration for the direct or indirect use of phonograms published for commercial purposes for broadcasting or for any communication to the public. The CL (revised 2010) fails to list these rights. Under Article 10(12) CL, the right of communication through information networks only regulates communication of works in such a way that members of the public may access these works from a place and at a time individually chosen by them (on demand). But Article 8 of WCT includes *any* communication of works (both real time and on demand).

(3) Unjustified provisions and loopholes of the CL should be removed. The related provisions have proved to be elaborate after years of development. Such examples are ownership of copyright, ownership of cinematographic works or the like, limitation on copyright and collective management of copyright and so on. For instance, Article 19 of the CL provides that where the copyright in a work belongs to a citizen, the property rights in respect of the work shall, after his death, during the term of protection provided for in this Law, be transferred in accordance with the provisions of the Inheritance Law. But the CL is silent on who will own the rights if there is no successor.

(4) Problems with related regulations. Administrative regulations related to copyright protection in China include the CLIR, CSPR,

---

78 Currently Article 11(3) CL (revised 2010) states: 'Where a work is created according to the intention and under the supervision and responsibility of a legal entity or another organization, such legal entity or organization shall be the author of the work.'

79 Li Yufeng, *Copyright Law*, China: Xiamen University Press, 2007, p. 63.

Collective Management of Copyright Regulations (effective from 1 March 2005), and the Ordinance on the Protection of the Right to Network Dissemination of Information[80] (effective from 1 July 2007), the bringing into force of the draft Regulations for the Protection of Copyright in Works of Folk Literature and Art,[81] and the Interim Measures for the Payment of Remuneration for Audio Products Played by Radio and TV Stations.[82] These regulations not only raise law-making costs but also introduce overlap and contradictions. The regulations need to be tidied up and put in order to eliminate contradiction and regulatory cost.

(5) Copyright registration. Copyright will be automatically created, and not conditional on registration. However, copyright registration facilitates burden of proof. Failure to lay down this regime adds to the difficulties of copyright protection.[83]

(6) Interaction with other laws. Subject matter such as applied art is copyrightable, and it may enjoy trademark protection in the light of its distinctiveness, and a design patent, when it satisfies the relevant requirements of the New Patent Law, may also protect it. The overlap and conflict with other IP regimes are unavoidable. In addition, the boundary line with the PAR should also be properly examined.

(7) Anti-camcording: the taping or recording of a show or movie in the theatre should be made illegal and excluded from 'personal use' exceptions because camcording is one of the major sources of piracy.

(8) Civil remedies: the 'John Dow' theory should be incorporated to facilitate the filing of a case and application for a preliminary injunction against imminent but unsubstantiated infringements; the cap for statutory damages should be lifted and minimum standards stipulated; punitive damages should also be introduced into the law to punish and deter willful and/or repeated infringements.

Besides these further amendments to the CL (revised 2010) suggested above, the civil procedure law and correlated evidential rules should also

---

[80] Also translated as Regulations for the Protection of the Right of Communication through Information Network.

[81] The first draft of this regulation was completed in 1996 and the second draft was revised in 2002.

[82] The Order is issued by the State Council of the People's Republic of China (No. 566); it was promulgated in November 2009 and became effective in January 2010.

[83] Ibid.

be improved to make it easier for rights holders to file cases and compel evidence from defendants. The IPR provisions in the Criminal Code also need to be revised to bring them into line with the copyright law and international trends for criminal enforcement, in particular to make it easier to fight digital piracy.

4.6. CONCLUSION

The PRC has built its stable ambitious intellectual property framework after 30 years' of great effort. The two-track system (namely, administrative and judicial enforcement) of intellectual property laws enforcement has effectively protected the copyright of both domestic and foreign owners. A variety of measures and actions have been taken to remove the label of China as the 'counterfeiting capital of the world'. Now, after these considerable developments, the image of China is improving. Unlike the Great Qing Copyright Law of 1910, the second coming of a new copyright system has left China in considerably better circumstances. Challenges and opportunities still exist and there remain many problems, as this chapter has highlighted, concerning copyright protection (especially as regards enforcement), implying that both further modification of copyright law and the simultaneous cultivation of the legal consciousness of its citizens have been and will continue to be of decisive influence.

5. Unfair competition/trade secrets (1)

Hu Kaizhong[1]

The market economy as a competitive economy suggests that competition should be based on impartiality and honesty. However, some business operators of corporate concerns often infringe fair competition principles and try to use various kinds of unfair methods to damage others' legal rights and interests. Therefore, many countries around the world have brought into effect Anti-Unfair Competition Laws to deal with such methods. In recent years, a series of acts of unfair competition have emerged in the field of intellectual property in China, which has caused damage to consumers' welfare and business operators, and other undertakings competing in the same markets. As a consequence, China has felt an urgent need to amend current laws to protect the normal order of competition.

5.1. ACTS OF UNFAIR COMPETITION

The market economy is based on competition built on the relationship between commodity supply and demand, which in essence is an economy with free competition. The role of free competition can only be fully played in a 'perfect competition' market.[2] However, not all competition in daily life is the result of perfect competition. In practice, the realistic

1 Professor of Law, Zhongnan University of Economics and Law.

2 So-called perfect competition exists only in markets where (1) there are many small firms and consumers, and all the sellers are decision-makers on price; (2) all firms aim to maximize profits while all customers aim to maximize effectiveness; (3) all firms produce homogeneous goods; (4) there are no entry/exit barriers; (5) it is easy for all people (customers, competitors and possible investors) to fully access market information, including quantity, quality, price and demand for products; and (6) there is no need for any external agencies (this mainly refers to the involvement and intervention of the government) to decide on the producing and selling activities. See Ruan Fan-min, *EU Competition Law*, China: China University of Political Science and Law Publishing House (1998), pp. 51–2.

model of competition is one of 'effective competition', which means 'where one of the conditions of perfect competition is absent, the presence of others may lead to greater rather than less imperfection'.[3] In other words, we can pursue a market order with fair, sufficient and effective competition under certain market conditions, that is, a fair competitive order. A fair competitive order requires that all competitors abide by the principles of equality, impartiality, honesty and good faith and compete in accordance with market economy rules. Under this model, full business competition can prevent markets from being influenced by destructive political powers and dominant, large corporations and can also maximize the effectiveness of the market economy and promote the country's economy prosperity.

Unfair competition violates the fair competitive order. The market economy is a kind of competitive economy designed to allocate social and economic resources. Under this system, each market player aims to maximize its own profits and therefore it is inevitable that some methods of competition will breach fair competition rules (if any exist). These can be referred to as 'unfair competition activities'. In other words, unfair competition activities refer to activities carried out by business operators of undertakings which violate fair competition laws, damage the interests of competitors and customers and disturb the order of social competition through dishonest or unfair ways.

Because an act of unfair competition violates the fair competition principle and damages the interests of other business operators and customers, most advanced economies have enacted anti-unfair competition laws to prohibit unfair competition. Many countries have adopted international conventions into local law on the definition of an act of unfair competition. For example, Article 10 *bis* (2) of the Paris Convention for the Protection of Industrial Property provides that any act of competition contrary to honest practices in industrial or commercial matters constitutes an act of unfair competition. Article 50 of the Model Law for Developing Countries on Trademarks, Trade Names and Acts of Unfair Competition drafted by WIPO made almost the same provision on unfair competition. Article 1 of the Anti-Unfair Competition Law of Germany defines an act of unfair competition as 'an act of competition in violation of good faith'. As can be seen from the above, any act of competition which violates the principle of 'honesty' and 'impartiality' shall be called an act of unfair competition.

According to Article 2 of the Anti-Unfair Competition Law 1993 of the

---

[3] M.J. Clarke, 'Toward a Concept of Workable Competition', *American Economic Review*, 30, 1940, 241–56.

PRC, unfair competition acts, 'in this Law, means activities made by business operators who damage the others' legal rights and interests, disturb the order of social economy and violate the provisions of this Law'. This provision is the legal standard for judging any act of unfair competition in China. An act of unfair competition has several characteristics, including the following.

First, it occurs in the process of competition. The competition act regulated in the Anti-Unfair Competition Law is an act of economy competition, which takes place within a business operation or market transaction. In other words, if an act of competition takes place between governments or individuals, such as in a sports competition or competitive learning, it is not an act of market competition. Article 2 of the Anti-Unfair Competition Law of the PRC (AUCL) defines the subjects of unfair competition as 'business operators', which include legal persons, other organizations or individuals. This provision aims to distinguish unfair competition from civil torts. For example, the act of infringing the reputation of an enterprise is deemed as a tort if there is no competitive relationship between the infringer and infringed. A similar act would be classed as unfair competition only when it aims to defame or crowd out other competitors.[4]

Second, all business operators aim to compete. Unfair competition activities such as passing off other's registered trademarks, stealing others' business secrets and defaming competitors all aim to compete and would fall foul of the AUCL.

Third, an act of unfair competition violates the competitive principles of honesty, good faith and impartiality. As mentioned above, all market players need to abide by the principles of voluntariness, equality, impartiality, honesty and good faith, and also need to observe public commercial ethics in their business transactions. Any acts in violation of these principles are acts of unfair competition.

Fourth, an act of unfair competition disturbs the social and economic order. Unfair competition aims to crowd out competitors, and it will damage the interests of other competitors and customers, impede and destroy the normal market competitive order. The purpose of anti-unfair competition law is to encourage and protect fair competition, prohibit unfair competition, protect the legal rights and interests of busi-

---

[4] However, most German civil law scholars consider unfair competition to be a tort under Article 823.1 of the Civil Code of Germany. In their opinion, any manager has an absolute right over its business, which belongs to 'other rights' in accordance with Article 823.1 of the Civil Code of Germany. Therefore, any manager who is infringed by an act of unfair competition is entitled to bring an action for tort against the infringer.

ness operators and customers, and safeguard and promote the healthy development of the market economy.

5.2. TYPES OF UNFAIR COMPETITION

The AUCL is designed to regulate the competitive relationship between business operators in their business transactions. In a narrow sense, it only concerns how to regulate unfair competition acts. In a broad sense, it includes not only anti-unfair competition law, but also China's recently adopted Anti-Monopoly Law.[5] Due to the different political, economic and legal traditions of countries, the legislative frameworks of unfair competition will differ. To sum up, there are two general models for regulating unfair competition: the first is the separate legislative framework model, as in Germany and Japan, where anti-monopoly law and anti-unfair competition law are enacted separately; the second is the combined legislative model, as in the US, where anti-trust and anti-unfair competition are enacted within the same legislative framework. In countries that follow the separate legislative model, the anti-unfair competition law only covers certain acts of unfair competition while other competition acts are governed by the anti-monopoly law. However, the general trend is to integrate anti-unfair competition laws with relevant anti-monopoly laws.

China follows the separate legislative framework model. In February 1993, China enacted the Anti-Unfair Competition Law of the People's Republic of China, which came into effect on 1 December, 1993. This law mainly includes provisions on some unfair competition acts, such as the act of imitating another's registered trademark, infringement of business secrets, and some provisions on acts of restricting competition, such as crowding out of competitors. The AUCL attempts to reflect current business practice in commercial markets and the need to regulate market competition, although, as discussed below, the AUCL is in need of amendment. On 30 August, 2007, the Anti-Monopoly Law of the People's Republic of China was enacted and came into effect on 1 August, 2008. The Anti-Monopoly Law includes provisions mainly on monopoly agreements, abuse of a dominant position, the concentration of undertakings, and abuse of administrative powers to eliminate or restrict competition. As can be seen from the above, the Anti-Unfair Competition Law and the Anti-Monopoly Law differ in their scope.

---

5 See Chapters 11 and 12.

Article 10.2.3 of the Paris Convention for the Protection of Industrial Property provides for three main types of unfair competition, stating that

> the following in particular shall be prohibited: (i) all acts of such a nature as to create confusion by any means whatever with the establishment, the goods, or the industrial or commercial activities, of a competitor; (ii) false allegations in the course of trade of such a nature as to discredit the establishment, the goods, or the industrial or commercial activities, of a competitor; (iii) indications or allegations the use of which in the course of trade is liable to mislead the public as to the nature, the manufacturing process, the characteristics, the suitability for their purpose, or the quantity, of the goods.

Article 5–14 of the AUCL provides for the following unfair competition activities:

5.2.1. Counterfeiting of Goods

Counterfeiting of goods is provided for in Article 5 of the AUCL and includes confusion of commodity and the false marking of goods. Confusion of commodity refers to the act of using other competitors' business credit or the reputation of goods unfairly, with the result that customers are confused as to the source of the commodity. False marking refers to the act of marking the quality, reputation, origin or source of the commodity and other characteristics falsely, leading to misunderstandings regarding the commodity by other competitors or customers. The false marking provision is different from the confusion of commodity provision in that the former does not necessarily lead to confusion over the specific commodity, nor does it directly damage the interests of a particular competitor; however, it damages the overall interests of all other competitors in the same industry, and therefore damages the interests of all customers.

Articles 5.1–5.3 of the AUCL covers three specific activities of commodity confusion: (1) feigning others' registered trademark; (2) using the specific name, package, decoration of the famous or noted commodities, or using a similar name, package, decoration of the famous or noted commodities, which may confuse consumers in distinguishing the commodities from famous or noted commodities; (3) using the name of other enterprises or personal names with the aim of creating confusion between the relevant commodity and a competitor's commodity.

Article 5.4 of the AUCL covers the provision on false marking, which states: (1) to feign or pretend to be the certificate of attestation, mark of fame and high qualification; (2) to feign a certificate of origin regarding the place of production of the commodities; (3) to make a false statement on the quality of the commodities leading to misunderstanding by others.

Business operators who breach Article 5 and cause damage to the infringed business operators will bear liability for compensating for damage. The amount of compensation will be equivalent to the profit made by the infringer during the period of infringement if it proves difficult to measure the amount of damage done. Also, the infringer will be required to compensate the infringed party for the reasonable costs of investigating the unfair competition acts of the infringer. The infringed party can sue the infringer in the People's Court when its legal interests and rights are damaged due to unfair competition. Meanwhile, if the business operator imitates another's registered trademark, uses another enterprise's name or personal name without permission, forges or fakes the mark of certificate, the mark of famous or high quality products, fakes the original place of production, makes a fake or creates misunderstanding over the description or quality of products, the infringer will be punished in accordance with the provisions of the Trademark Law of the PRC and the Product Quality Law of the PRC.[6]

The supervision authority shall order the cessation of the illegal acts, confiscate illegal income, and also set fines of one to three times the illegal income and may revoke the business license in serious circumstances (for example, if the business operator uses the special name, package, decoration of famous or noted commodities or uses a similar name, package, decoration to that of famous or noted commodities and makes commodities that cause confusion with famous or noted commodities). If a business operator sells false or bad commodities and violates the criminal law, she shall be investigated in accordance with the criminal law.

5.2.2. False Propaganda

An act of false propaganda refers to the act by which a business operator uses an advertisement or other method to spread false information (the actual law uses the term 'propaganda') related to its commodity which makes customers misunderstand, and as a result, purchase the operator's commodities by mistake (Article 9 AUCL). The business operator who uses false propaganda will often use all kinds of advertising media to release false information, such as through newspapers, magazines, broadcasts, television, billboards, promotional merchandise columns, etc.; besides, s/he may use other forms of publicity, such as product information conferences, trade fairs, product brochures etc., to boost the goods and services.

The content of false propaganda includes the quality, composition,

---

[6] See Chapter 3 on Trademarks.

function, usage, producer, time of efficacy and origin of goods. In reality, the false propaganda of an enterprise mainly takes two forms: the first is to make a false statement about the goods, for instance, publicizing ordinary goods as famous brands; the second is to issue misleading publicity, for instance, making overstatements or exaggerating the goods in some way, leading customers to have false expectations about the goods or services, and then influencing their choice of goods or services to such an extent that they purchase the wrong goods or accept the wrong services.

The business operator who uses an advertisement or other methods to make a fake or misleading description, knowing it to be untrue (or who should be in a position to know that it is untrue), for any of its commodities will be liable for damages. The supervising authorities will order a stop to the illegal activities, and may issue fines of between 10,000 and 200,000 Yuan, depending on the circumstances. The supervisor can confiscate all illegal income and set fines in accordance with the law.

5.3. INFRINGEMENT OF BUSINESS SECRETS

A business secret is referred to as technological information or operational information that is not generally known to the public, and which is capable of bringing economic benefits to the owner of rights, has practical applicability and which the owner of rights has taken measures to keep secret. Technological information is referred to as some form of technological achievement that is concluded or found in the process of production and management, including designs, software programs, product formulations, production processes and methods. For instance, computer software is a variety of important technological information. The scope of business information is quite extensive, including all kinds of information used for business activities that can bring a competitive advantage to their legal owner (with the exception of technological information), such as management know-how, customer lists, sources of information, production and marketing strategies, information on bidding and tenders. According to Chinese law, to qualify for protection a business secret should meet four criteria: (a) not generally being known to the public; (b) be capable of bringing economic benefits to the owner of the rights; (c) have practical applicability; and (d) that the rights owner has taken measures to keep secret. According to Article 10 of the AUCL, an infringement of a business secret often includes the following:

(1) obtaining business secrets from the owners of rights by stealing, promises of gain, resorting to coercion or other improper means;

(2) disclosing, using, or allowing others to use business secrets belonging to the owners of such rights obtained by the means mentioned above;
(3) disclosing, using or allowing others to use business secrets that s/he has obtained by breaking an engagement or disregarding the requirement of the owners of the rights to maintain the business secrets in confidence.

Where a third party obtains, uses or discloses the business secrets of others when s/he obviously has or should have full awareness of the illegal acts mentioned in the preceding paragraph, s/he shall be deemed to have infringed the business secrets of others. The business operator who infringes business secrets will bear civil liabilities, including ceasing of the illegal act, removing obstacles, extending apologies for infringement, compensating for loss, and paying compensation for breach of contract (liquidated damages). According to Article 25 of the AUCL, the supervising authorities can order the cessation of the illegal acts and may impose a fine of not less than 10,000 Yuan but not more than 100,000 Yuan in light of the circumstances. If the infringement of the business secret is regarded as serious, the infringer will also bear civil liability.

The two cases discussed next illustrate the business secret protection in China. In *Gong Rengni and others violations of trade secrets* in 2006,[7] the Guangzhou Intermediate People's Court, Guang Dong Province, heard a typical criminal case involving the infringement of business secrets. The appeal court confirmed that the defendant Liyuanjin (Li), the ex Vice-General Manager of the plaintiff company, had disclosed the plaintiff company's business secrets by disregarding the requirement of the plaintiff company to maintain its business secrets in confidence and in breach of Li's contract. The other defendant 'Gong Rengui' (a cousin of Li), and also a previous employee recruited by Li from the plaintiff company, obtained through Li the plaintiff company's business secrets in full awareness that acquisition of such information was in breach of company confidentiality provisions. The acts of both defendants (the acquisition and disclosure of confidential information relating to die-cast machinery) led to a serious loss for the plaintiff company. On appeal, the appeal court denied the defendant's claim that the plaintiff's technological information (production processes) was in the public domain. The evidence that the defendants submitted, such as special invoices, related certificates and some other blueprints, could not prove that they had acquired the

[7] Guangzhou Intermediate People's Court, Criminal Second Instance, Final No. 5, 2006.

plaintiff's technical information through legal means and in a reasonable way. As regards the further argument by the defendant (appellant) that the plaintiff had not taken sufficient steps to keep their technical information secret, the court confirmed the facts after investigating that the defendants were responsible for keeping secrets and had knowledge of the plaintiff company's confidentiality agreement and internal IPR protection measures that had been issued to each of them beforehand. In this case, the People's Court also affirmed the method for calculation of fines based on the actual illegal income, the loss of profit (the average selling profit rate and the yearly unit prices for goods) to calculate the loss. The case is regarded as a typical violation of Article 10 AUCL. Both defendants were charged under the AUCL. Also, they were charged under Articles 19, 53, and 200 of the Chinese Criminal Law 1997 (as amended), including the Regulations of the Supreme People's Court on Several Questions Concerning the Application of Property Orientated Penalty 2000.[8]

In another case, *Zhang Tongzhou violation of trade secrets,* [9] the defendant, Mr Zhang, infringed the business secrets of his former employer, Jinwang, in the city of Qingdao (site of the recent water Olympics, 2008), Shan Dong Province. The case was first tried as a criminal case involving the Chinese Procuratorate.[10] There is some controversy in Chinese academic circles as to whether trade secret offenses should be charged under the criminal law, whereas in most countries (other than for espionage for example), similar cases would be heard in the civil courts. The *Zhang Tongzhou* case is about the infringement of operational business secrets. The main issue before the court was how to define the scope of the business secrets involved. Two criteria mentioned as important were (a) that the information should be classed as secret and not generally be available to the public; and (b) the information should be specific and practical (in terms of functional use).

The difference between criminal and civil trials is that they adopt different standards of proof. In criminal cases, the Procuratorate bears the

---

[8] The regulations cited are a guide to the lower courts on how to enforce criminal law on property-related penalties.

[9] Qin Dao Intermediate People's Court, Shan Dong Province, Criminal, 2nd Instance, Final No. 4, 2006.

[10] In criminal cases, the Procuratorate is responsible for bringing the plaintiff's prosecution to court (the level of the Procuratorate is dependent upon the level of the Court). Under Article 129 of the Chinese Constitution Law, the People's Procuratorate are the State's organs for legal supervision. Its functions are defined by the Organic Law of the People's Procuratorates (1983). For further details, see: http://en.wikipedia.org/wiki/Law_of_the_People's_Republic_of_China#People.27s_procuratorates, accessed July 2010.

liability to clearly and accurately describe the scope of business secrets involved.[11] Specific to the case, the court confirmed the plaintiff's operational secret as a commercial order from the US retailer Wal-Mart, and the resulting additional information, including manufacturers, supply and price, information that was known neither to the plaintiff's internal staff nor to external suppliers. In defining 'secrecy', the court emphasized that the information must not be in the public domain, and that any person who obtains the information must make reasonable efforts to obtain the information lawfully and to pay a cost to do so. In defining how information should be kept secret, the court considered a number of 'objective' tests: (a) the formation process of the information; (b) possession of business information is not 'publishing' the information; and (c) the way in which the defendant obtains the information will not be the same means by which other similar industries and enterprises obtain similar information. With regard to the criteria of practicality, the court held that commercial secrets must be specific, certain, can be immediately applied rather than being abstract and vague. For a specific transaction, the kind of information that would be regarded as 'practical' would include: product specifications; model; price; the number of transactions; quality; suppliers; buyers and other similar types of information.

5.4. BUSINESS DEFAMATION

Business defamation refers to any act of a business operator who fabricates, spreads false facts to defame or devalue the goodwill of a competitor and the reputation of his/her goods in order to weaken his/her competitive standing. Article 14 of the AUCL sets out the relevant law.

The act of business defamation refers mainly to fabrication of false facts and the spreading of false facts. Fabrication of false facts refers to an act where a business operator describes a competitor's information inconsistently with the truth. The spreading of false facts includes the act of spreading false facts among non-specific people and among specific clients or business operators in the same industry. Infringers often use *comparative advertising* to devalue the goodwill of competitors, or pay third parties to file complaints against other competitors in order to ruin their goodwill, or

[11] In civil cases, both defence and prosecution will present their own interpretations as to what is or what is not a trade secret depending on the circumstances of the case. As a result, the interpretation used by the court may be quite wide (as compared with criminal cases).

release business information in order to slander the quality of competitor's goods.

The purpose of business defamation is to damage the business goodwill of other competitors. Goodwill is the positive social evaluation accumulated by a business operator over a long period and is a form of intangible property. In order to obtain a competitive advantage in the market, some business operators try to damage the goodwill of others through fabricating false facts.

Business operators who conduct business defamation and cause damage to those infringed are liable to pay compensation for damages. The amount of compensation will be equivalent to the profit made by the infringer during its period of infringement if damages are difficult to quantify and further, the infringer will be liable to pay the reasonable costs incurred by the infringed party, in investigating the acts of unfair competition by the infringer. The infringed party may bring an action against the infringer in the People's Court for breach of Article 14 AUCL.

5.5. COMMERCIAL BRIBERY

Commercial bribery is an act of unfair competition in which a business operator offers or promises to offer property or benefit to the adversary party to the transaction and his employee or agent for the purpose of gaining a benefit from the transaction.

Article 8.1 of the AUCL provides:

> Business operators shall not use money or properties or other means to practice bribery in order to sell or purchase commodities. It shall be guilty of offering a bribe if business operators give a secret commission to other entity or individual without normal accounting records. It shall be guilty of taking bribe, if the entity or individual accept the secret discount without normal accounting records.

First, it is clear from this provision that the subject of commercial bribery is the business operator. Anyone who is not engaged in production and operation cannot be the subject of commercial bribery; second, the purpose of commercial bribery is to obtain a transaction opportunity and to crowd out competitors; third, the business operator bribes in competition, mainly in the form of a 'commission'.

The act of commercial bribery undermines the interests of other competitors and the normal market order, and violates the principles of honesty, good faith and fair competition. Article 22 of the AUCL sets out the liability for the act of commercial bribery, which states that 'a business operator bribe by giving money or properties or using any other means in order to sell or purchase commodities and violate the Criminal Law, shall be investigated in accordance with the Criminal Law; if the acts as first mentioned do not violate the Criminal Law, the supervisor may fine an amount from more than 10,000 to less than 200,000 yuan in light of the circumstances, and confiscate the illegal income'. In addition to criminal liability and administrative liability, the infringer who commits commercial bribery shall be liable for the damages.

5.6. UNLAWFUL LOTTERY TICKET SALES

Lottery ticket sales refer to the act by which the business operator sells his commodity by means of offering items or money for promotion. If the sale is done in accordance with law, it is a lawful lottery ticket sale; otherwise, it is an unlawful lottery ticket sale.

According to Article 13 of the AUCL, unlawful lottery ticket sales include the following acts: (1) selling a commodity by way of making a fake award or arranging for an inside person to win the lottery; (2) selling unqualified or high-priced commodities by way of awarding selling; (3) selling a commodity with a lottery award where the top award is more than 5,000 yuan.

Unlawful lottery ticket sales are prohibited and punished because this form of anti-competitive conduct cheats customers, damages the interests of other competitors and disturbs the market order. Consequently, Article 26 of the AUCL provides that supervising authorities shall order to cease illegal acts, and may fine business operators between 10,000 to 100,000 Yuan for infringing Article 13.

5.7. ADDITIONAL FORCED PURCHASE OR SALES WITH UNREASONABLE CONDITION

The act of additional forced purchase or selling with unreasonable conditions refers to an act for its own economic advantage, and against the customer's wishes. Here the business operator requires the customer to buy additional commodities or requires the customer to accept additional services, or attaches other unreasonable conditions to the price, when s/he sells a commodity or provides service to the customer.

With these acts, the business operator is using his advantageous position in product selling or providing services, forcing the consumer to accept unreasonable conditions in order to promote the sales of inferior goods or services. This act can seriously damage the interests of the consumer.

Article 23 of the AUCL provides that if the business operator of a public facility enterprise or other enterprise with a legal monopoly forces others to purchase particular commodities that the business operator manages for the purpose of pushing other business operators out of competition, the provincial or municipal supervising authority shall order the cessation of illegal acts, and may impose a fine of not less than 50,000 Yuan but not more than 200,000 Yuan in light of the circumstances. The supervising authority may confiscate illegal income, and may fine an amount from one to three times of illegal income, if the operator sells low-quality but high-price commodities or overcharges.

5.8. DUMPING

Dumping is the act of charging at a price below cost for a good or service with the purpose of crowding out other competitors from the market. On the surface, this act of selling at less than 'fair value' seems to be more favorable to consumers; however, the real purpose is to crowd out other competitors. If other competitors exit the market, the dumping operator would monopolize the market and raise prices, which will ultimately damage the interests of customers. Dumping is an act infringing both other competitors and customers.

It should be noted that Article 11 of the AUCL provides some exceptions for the dumping offense. Article 11 states that none of the following acts constitute acts of unfair competition: (1) selling fresh or live goods; (2) disposing of goods the useful life of which is about to expire or other overstocked goods; (3) reducing prices seasonably; (4) selling goods at reduced prices to pay off debts, change the line of production or close the business.

In accordance with Article 20 AUCL, other competitors who are infringed by the act of dumping are entitled to claim for damages against the business operator who conducts the dumping.

5.9. BID RIGGING

Bid rigging is a form of fraud in which bidders collude with each other in a bidding process, or bidders and tenders collude with each other on the bid, for the purpose of crowding out other bidders from the market.

According to Article 27 AUCL, the undertaking will be required to pay damages to the infringed bidders. Moreover, the People's Court may render a judgment declaring that the winning bidder is valid. The supervising authorities may impose a fine on the infringer of an amount not less than 10,000 Yuan but not more than 200,000 Yuan.

5.10. COMPETITION RESTRICTION OF PUBLIC-FACILITY OR OTHER MONOPOLIZED ENTERPRISES

The act of restricting competition conducted by public-facility enterprises or other enterprises which legally monopolize the special market covers those business operators who limit the customers on their purchase, requiring customers to buy designated goods which they produce or manage, for the purpose of crowding out competition.

This act of restricting competition not only infringes the interests of customers but also damages the interests of other lawful competitors. Article 23 AUCL provides that if the business operator of a public facility enterprise or another enterprise with a legal monopoly position forces others to purchase designated commodities which the operator manages, or pushes other operators out of competition, the provincial or municipal supervising authorities shall order the cessation of illegal acts, and may fine not less than 50,000 Yuan and not more than 200,000 Yuan in light of the circumstances. The supervisor may confiscate illegal income, and may fine an amount between one to three times of illegal income if the business operator takes the chance to sell low-quality but high-price commodities or overcharges. Other operators who are infringed by this act are entitled to claim for damages against the infringer.

5.11. COMPETITION RESTRICTION OF GOVERNMENT ORGANS

The act of restricting competition conducted by government organs is referred to as the act in which government and its organs misuse their power to force others to purchase designated commodities from the designated business operator, or to limit the fair competition of other competitors, or make restrictions on outside commodities entering the home market or domestic commodities flowing to outside markets. This type of unfair competition act damages the legal interests of other competitors.

Article 30 of the AUCL states that,

> If the government or its departments violate Article 7 of this Law to force the others to purchase the commodities from the designated business operator,

limit the others fair competition, or limit commodities to transfer between regions, the higher level government shall order to correct these mistakes. If the fact is serious, the same level government organ or the higher level government organ shall render administrative punishment to the person who bears the direct responsibility. The designated business operator takes the chance to sell the low-quality but high-price commodities, the supervising authorities shall confiscate the illegal income, and may fine amount from more than one to less than three times of illegal income.

5.12. PROBLEMS OF IMPLEMENTING THE ANTI-UNFAIR COMPETITION LAW OF PRC

The AUCL is the first Chinese legislation on fair competition. Since its implementation, the AUCL has played an important role in encouraging and protecting fair competition, prohibiting unfair competition, maintaining the legal rights and interests of business operators and customers, and safeguarding the healthy development of a socialist market economy. However, with the development of the market economy, the current law has revealed several problems, and many new problems are appearing in the process of implementation or law enforcement. It is clear, now that the law has been in force for several years, that the law needs revision in light of developments in China's market economy. There are several problems that need to be considered:

5.12.1. The Term 'Unfair Competition Act'

The term 'unfair competition act' is not precisely defined. Article 1 of the AUCL states, 'Unfair competition, in this Law, means acts made by business operators who damage the others' legal rights and interests, disturb the order of social economy and violate the provisions of this Law'. 'Violate the provisions of this Law' is referred to as violation of the AUCL, which covers only eleven acts provided for in the Law. This provision seriously restricts the scope of unfair competition activities. In fact, besides these eleven acts, there exist many other acts which actually disturb the order of market competition and have the nature of unfair competition. It is necessary therefore to redefine the term for 'unfair competition activities' and widen its scope.

5.12.2. The Scope of Unfair Competition Acts in the AUCL

As mentioned, the scope of unfair competition acts provided in the AUCL is too narrow. Many new unfair competition activities are not regulated. For instance: the counterfeiting of *unregistered* trademarks; the counterfeiting of the title of the work or name of a book or journal; cybersquatting, all of which have the essence of unfair competition and would seriously influence the healthy development of the Chinese market economy. However, these new acts are not covered in the AUCL. The types of infringing activity should therefore be expanded.

5.12.3. Provisions regarding Unfair Competition in the AUCL

Some provisions regarding unfair competition provided in the AUCL are not complete or are too abstract. In terms of the eleven unfair competition activities provided for, the relevant provisions are too abstract, incomplete in scope or lack practical operability, including: (1) some acts of counterfeiting are not covered in the definition of counterfeiting, such as acts of 'passing off', 'selling, storing, displaying, transporting, exporting' counterfeit goods etc. Moreover, this Law does not provide any liability in respect of acts of fraudulent use of certification marks, famous marks etc.; (2) the scope of the subjects of infringing business secrets provided in the AUCL is too narrow, and non-business operators are not included; (3) the AUCL does not make a definite provision on comparative advertising.

5.12.4. The Supervising Power of the Administrative Law Enforcement Organs in the AUCL

The supervising power of the administrative law enforcement organs provided in the AUCL is very weak and not equipped to meet the need to crack down on unfair competition. Due to these weak powers, many problems occur in terms of supervision. For example, the supervising authorities are not authorized to take some administrative coercive measures, such as sealing up, seizure of assets, freezing etc., and consequently they can do nothing when the infringer transfers his property, destroys relevant evidence, or refuses to allow checks or provide relevant materials, for the purpose of avoiding punishment.

5.12.5. The Liability Provisions in AUCL

The liability provisions provided in AUCL are not sufficiently high to deter unfair competition effectively. Although the Law provides for civil liability, administrative liability and criminal liability for some unfair competition activities, there exist several flaws, including: (1) administrative liability is not applied to or imposed on the following three activities (making these activities difficult to prohibit) selling goods at a price lower than cost, additional forced purchases and business defamation; (2) no liabilities are imposed on acts in which the infringing business operator refuses to accept legal inspection, or to truthfully provide relevant information, etc. Due to the vague provisions of the AUCL, the infringer often refuses to fulfill statutory obligations and therefore some case facts are difficult to identify; (3) the AUCL only provides for fines on selected unfair competition activities; however, it does not state the type of punishment or whether illegal income should be confiscated. Moreover, the amount of the fine is too low, which allows the infringing business operator to continue to make a profit from his/her unfair competition even after being prosecuted, effectively diluting the deterrent effects of the Law; (4) the standard for calculating the fine is difficult to follow in practice. The AUCL provides that the amount of the fine imposed for some illegal acts should be calculated on the basis of the actual amount of illegal income; however, it is difficult to obtain evidence to prove or determine the level of illegal income.

5.13. IDEAS FOR IMPROVING THE ANTI-UNFAIR COMPETITION LAW OF THE PRC

In order to deal with the problems mentioned above, the AUCL should be revised in accordance with international convention or best practice from foreign law. In particular, the AUCL can be improved or perfected in the following ways:

5.13.1. Redefining the Term 'Unfair Competition Act'

For example, under the relevant provisions of the Paris Convention for the Protection of Industrial Property, the Model Law for Developing Countries on Trademarks, Trade Names and Acts of Unfair Competition drafted by WIPO, or German law, unfair competition can be defined as 'any act of competition in violation of the principles of voluntariness, impartiality, equality, honesty and good faith, contrary to honest practices in industrial or commercial matters, infringing the legal rights and interests of other competitors and customers, and disturbing the order of market competition'. According to this definition, some new acts of unfair competition can be identified as unfair competition acts under the Law.

5.13.2. Expanding the Types of Unfair Competition Activities

Some prominent and serious acts of unfair competition that need to be prohibited could be included as follows:

5.13.2.1. Abuse of a dominant market position

For example, refusal of a transaction without good reasons; differential treatment of trading partners without good reason; forced transactions; forcing competitors to avoid or to give up on a transaction; improperly luring the customers of competitors; using improper means to impede or restrict the business activities of competitors, etc. Such a provision would need to be carefully coordinated with the Anti Monopoly Law.

5.13.2.2. Joint actions

The AUCL only stipulates provisions on bid rigging. However, some other joint actions are not included in this Law, such as jointly refusing sales, jointly restricting sales price, etc. Therefore, this Law should expand the examples of joint actions that seriously infringe the interests of other competitors and customers and destroy the fair competition order and infringe social public interests. For instance, prohibiting business operators from jointly making agreements, determining or using other methods regarding the price, quantity of production or sales, market division, or jointly boycotting transactions.

5.13.2.3. Other acts of unfair competition

Due to increased market competition, some business operators are using new acts of unfair competition to distort competition or seize the market. Therefore, as mentioned above, the term for unfair competition should be defined more broadly as meaning 'any act in violation of competition, specifically the principles of voluntariness, impartiality, equality, honesty and good faith, contrary to honest practices in industrial or commercial matters, infringing the legal rights and interests of other competitors and customers, and disturbing the order of market competition, constitutes an act of unfair competition'.

The case of *P&G Inc. v Shanghai Chen-Hyun Intelligent Technology Development Co.*[12] is the first judgment made by the People's Court on the conflict of domain names and trademarks. This case established the standard that using others' trademark registration as a domain name constitutes an act of unfair competition. There are two views. The first view is that China's Anti-Unfair Competition Law does not provide for use of another's trademark registration as a domain name as an act of unfair competition. The second view holds that acts of unfair competition are constantly changing and new methods, such as cybersquatting, are

---

[12] Filed at No. 2 Intermediate People's Court of Shanghai Municipality, (2000) Hu Er Zhong Zhi Chu Zi No. 23.

being used by some business operators to distort competition. The court confirmed four factors that could be used to determine if using another's trademark registration as a domain name constitutes an act of unfair competition: (1) the registered user of disputed domain name has a fault; (2) the registration and use of a disputed domain name damages the interests of the trademark owner; (3) there is a causal relationship between the damage and registration behavior; (4) the registered trademark user does not enjoy the legal rights or interests of the domain name. The court finally adopted the second view above and confirmed that the act of defendant, Chen-Hyun Intelligent Technology Development Co., constituted an act of unfair competition.

5.13.3. Improving the Operability of the Provisions of the Law

5.13.3.1. Adding types of counterfeiting

The following could be added to the AUCL as examples of counterfeiting:

- Unauthorized use of the trademarks, domain names, titles of works which are identical to or similar with those already known to the public and have been used first by other people, resulting in causing or likely to cause market confusion and mislead customers;
- unauthorized use of the same or similar well-known names, packing, decoration, shape and other unique business logo, with the result of causing confusion between well-known goods and other goods and therefore causing the purchase of other goods by mistake;
- unauthorized replacement of other people's registered trademarks, names, unique packaging and decoration and putting goods bearing false trademarks on the market;
- improper use of its own registered trademark, appearance of patent or name, with the result of causing or being likely to cause market confusion and leading to the purchase of commodities through misunderstanding;
- the use of a business name which contains the same or similar trademark, unique name or title of goods, or domain name which has first been used by others, causing or being likely to cause market confusion and leading to the purchase of commodities through misunderstanding;
- use of the domain name which contains the same or similar trademark, unique name or title of goods which has first been used by other people, causing or being likely to cause market confusion and leading to the purchase of commodities through misunderstanding;

- use of the trademark containing the same or similar unique name of goods, or domain name and which has first been used by other people, causing or being likely to cause market confusion and leading to the purchase of commodities through misunderstanding;
- the use of a business name containing a well-known trademark or the name of enterprises which have been registered in other countries or regions, causing or being likely to cause market confusion and leading to the purchase of commodities through misunderstanding.

5.13.3.2. Infringement of business secrets

In practice, the subject who infringes business secrets includes not only the business operator, but also non-business operators, or the government organ. Therefore, the AUCL should extend the category of those who infringe business secrets to cover all entities and individuals.

5.13.3.3. Unfair lottery ticket sales

Currently, one form of prize-winning sales – 'tickets return' – is becoming increasingly common, with the prize amount also increasing, leading to a form of 'consumption trap'. The AUCL should provide restrictions on this form of selling, for instance, the business operator should not sell goods with the offer of 'gifts with a value exceeding 10% of the price of goods, or the maximum amount of gifts exceeding 5000 Yuan'.

5.13.3.4. Comparative advertising

Genuine comparative advertising may play a positive role in helping customers understand the differences between different commodities; however, it can also be used to defame other competitors. The AUCL should provide that if comparative advertising is used to infringe a competitor's goodwill or commodity reputation, such advertising constitutes an act of unfair competition.

5.13.4. Authorizing Administrative Organs with the Necessary Power of Supervision

In order to effectively prohibit acts of unfair competition, during its revision, the AUCL should include the following provision: 'during its supervision, the supervising authorities are entitled to make on-site inspections of the venues or properties suspected of being used for acts of unfair competition; to inquire into the bank accounts of suspected business operators and require the bank to suspend the payment of deposits'.

5.13.5. Improving the Provisions on Liability

In order to timely and effectively prohibit unfair competition acts, punish the infringing business operator and protect the interests of customers, the provisions of liability need to be improved in the following respects. First, all administrative liability should be applied to all acts of unfair competition. Second, administrative liability should be imposed for acts of refusing to accept lawful inspection or providing truthful information. Third, the maximum amount of fines should be increased. Fourth, the standard of calculating fines should be made on the basis of the illegal income earned from unfair competition acts.

5.14. CONCLUSION

The AUCL plays an important role in encouraging and protecting the order of fair market competition, prohibiting acts of unfair competition and safeguarding the interests of competitors and customers. However, the time has now come to revise this Law in order to deal with new forms of anti-competitive conduct, often based on new technology, such as cybersquatting. Although China has made progress in reforming its law on unfair competition, further opportunities exist for revision that can draw on the best practice of other countries to improve China's domestic legislation.

6. Unfair competition/trade secrets/ know-how (2)

Liu Xiaohai[1]

The previous chapter focused on trade secrets. This chapter opens with a summary of the fundamental components of Chinese trade secrets law introduced in Chapter 5, before looking at the overlap between trade secrets and other IP rights, such as copyright and the law of trademark, and then going on to discuss the licensing of know-how and confidentiality in Chinese employment contracts.

6.1. OVERVIEW OF TRADE SECRETS

6.1.1. Definition of Trade Secret

According to Article 10(3) of the Anti-Unfair Competition Law of the People's Republic of China and Article 219(3) of the Criminal Law of the People's Republic of China (2007), a trade secret refers to technical and management information which is: (1) unknown to the public; (2) capable of bringing economic benefits to the owners of rights in the information; (3) has practical applicability; (4) is kept secret through various measures taken by the owners. However, under Article 39 of the TRIPS Agreement, Chinese legal doctrine and judicial practice usually combine elements 2 and 3 in accordance with TRIPS. Management information includes customer lists, management plans, financial documents, sources of supply, bid prices, bid documents and so on. Technical information includes

1 Professor of Law at Tongji University. For English versions of the provisions of laws and regulations cited or referred to in this chapter, except those that have official English versions, refer to Chinalawinfor.com, <http://www.chinalawinfo.com/>. The editor is grateful for the help of Miss Li Jia (LLM International Commercial Law student, Cardiff University and graduate of East China University of Political Science and Law) for help with translation, and Mr Robert James (LLM International Commercial Law student, Cardiff University).

formulas, process flows, design drawings, product models, source codes and documentation of programs, core data and so on.

6.1.2. Concrete Terms of Trade Secret

In order to clarify the specific standard used in the application of the law and to maintain consistency among the criteria followed by people's courts in trials, the Supreme People's Court has set out guidelines on trade secrets in the Interpretation of the Supreme People's Court on Some Issues Concerning the Application of Law in the Trial of Civil Cases Involving Unfair Competition 2006 ('Judicial Interpretation').[2]

6.1.2.1. 'Unknown to the public'

The term 'unknown to the public' means that the relevant information will not generally be known or readily accessed by persons in the field which normally deals with this kind of information. For example, if the information is not the common sense or trade usage of persons in the relevant technical or economic field, and it cannot be obtained directly by the public through knowledge of the products, the information could be classed as being unknown to the public. In contrast, the following kinds of information are deemed as 'known to the public': (1) information that has been publicly disclosed in any publication or any other media; (2) information that has been disclosed through reports or exhibits; (3) information that could easily be accessed without any price.[3] The customer lists that may be recognized as a trade secret generally refer to specific client information. This includes such things as names, addresses, contact information, trading habits, trading intent of customers that differ from public information, and includes lists of both a large number of general customers, as well as specific customers with whom the company holding the information has a long-term and stable trading relationship.[4]

---

[2] The Judicial interpretation of the Supreme People's Court has several characteristics. According to Article 33 of the Organic Law of the People's Court of the People's Republic of China (1983), the Supreme People's Court may give an interpretation on issues of how to apply laws and regulations in trial situations. Judicial interpretation by the Supreme People's Court has universal legal force and will be followed in the lower courts. See www.court.gov.cn/lawdata/explain/. . ./200701180013.htm, for further information (accessed September 2010).

[3] See Article 9 of Judicial Interpretation, translated from the original using <http://vip.chinalawinfo.com/newlaw2002/SLC/SLC.asp?Db=chl&Gid=83311> (accessed September 2010).

[4] See Article 13 of Judicial Interpretation.

6.1.2.2. 'Capable of bringing economic benefit to the owners whilst having practical applicability'

Bringing economic benefits to the owner generally means that the confidential information has actual or potential commercial value and could provide a competitive edge to the owners.[5] Therefore, confidential information can only be protected as a trade secret when it has commercial value. Such commercial value may be actual (e.g. new products or new technology could be developed based on the information), or potential (e.g. laboratory results or interim breakthroughs and so on). Notwithstanding, the information must be capable of bringing a competitive edge to the owners. In other words, if the confidential information cannot bring a competitive edge to the owners, it will not be a trade secret, which is important for deciding whether negative information could be a trade secret. Negative information generally refers to information about what not to do, for example, relevant information about records of failures during development. Some negative information or broken negative information cannot bring any competitive edge to the owners. Negative information with commercial value that is capable of bringing a competitive edge is information from which positive and useful information can be derived.

6.1.2.3. 'Rights owners have taken security measures'

It is important for rights owners to take proper protective measures based on the information's commercial value and other specific circumstances to prevent information leakage. Generally speaking, the People's Court will decide whether or not rights owners have employed security measures according to the relevant information carrier, the effort to protect information by rights owners, the identifiable level of secrecy used, and the difficulty for non-authorized individuals of obtaining the information. The following security measures will be deemed as sufficient: (1) limiting the scope of access to confidential information, and only informing relevant persons about the confidential information; (2) locking the carrier of the confidential information or taking any other security measure; (3) marking the carrier of confidential information as classified; (4) using passwords or codes to access confidential information; (5) concluding a confidentiality agreement; (6) limiting visitors to confidential machinery, factory, workshop or any other places or requiring them to keep a secret; or (7) taking any other proper measures to maintain the confidentiality of information.[6]

---

5 See Article 10 of the Judicial Interpretation.

6 See Article 11 of the Judicial Interpretation, ibid.

Any confidential information in accordance with the terms stated above will be recognized as a trade secret under Chinese law.[7]

6.1.3. The Relationship between Patent, Copyright and Trade Secret

6.1.3.1. The relationship between trade secrets and patents

Under Chinese law, the relationship between trade secrets and patents is (before the patent application becomes public), anything related to the patent application. Patents and trade secrets coexist in the technical solutions set out in the patent. The termination of the patent would not prevent the trade secret from continuing to exist in the patented technical solution. For example, according to Article 26 of the Patent Law of the People's Republic of China (as amended 2008) ('The New Patent Law'), the description of an application for a patent for invention or utility will include information on the technical points of the information, as claimed by the applicant, in such terms that a person having ordinary skill in the art can understand it and carry out the invention or utility model.[8] After applying for the patent, the applicant does not have to disclose any further improvement of the technical points, which could be protected as a trade secret. If further improvement of the technical points has not been disclosed until the expiration of the patent, these may continue to be protected as a trade secret.

6.1.3.2. The relationship between trade secrets and copyright

Under Chinese law, copyright work can be protected as a trade secret as long as it has not been partially or fully disclosed. For example, if the confidential part of the source code of computer software has not been disclosed, it may still be protected as a trade secret.[9] When applying for registration of software copyright, the applicant may request that the source code, file(s) or sample be sealed. No one other than the applicant or the judicial authority may break the seal.[10] In addition, according to Article 24(1)(3) of the Regulations for the Protection of Computer Software,

---

[7] Ibid, footnote 4.

[8] Article 26 New Patent Law (2008): 'The description shall clearly and completely describe the invention or utility model so as to enable a person skilled in the relevant field of technology to carry it out; where necessary, drawings are required. The abstract shall state briefly the main technical points of the invention or utility model.'

[9] See Article 12 of the Measures for the Registration of Computer Software Copyright (2002).

[10] See Article 13, ibid.

evading or damaging the technical measures taken by the copyright owner to protect his/her software copyright *intentionally* when applying for registration of software copyright may constitute infringement of copyright and trade secret simultaneously.

6.2. PROTECTION OF TRADE SECRETS OBTAINED LEGALLY IN EMPLOYMENT RELATIONSHIPS

As a result of an employment relationship, an employer may disclose a trade secret to employees, and employees may also produce non-public technical information and management information, which would become their employer's trade secret. According to Article 6(1) of the New Patent Law and Article 326 of the Contract Law of the People's Republic of China, any invention or technical achievement made by employees during the course of employment is termed a 'service invention', and the right to apply for a patent for the service invention vests in the employer, as long as it has not been made public and the employer has taken relevant security measures.[11] Under Chinese law, the regulatory provisions of employees' confidentiality obligations exist mainly in the Labour Law of the People's Republic of China 1995 and the Employment Contract Law of the People's Republic of China 2008.

6.2.1. Employees' Confidentiality Obligation

6.2.1.1. Confidentiality obligations of serving employees

Employers may conclude agreements with employees concerning confidential matters of trade secrets and intellectual property.[12] If there are confidentiality clauses in an employment contract, any employee who has signed the contract will be obliged to keep trade secrets. Employees who breach confidentiality clauses or confidentiality agreements (resulting in losses to the employer) shall be liable for compensation.[13] Employers may

---

[11] Article 6 New Patent Law (2008): 'An invention made by a person in the execution of the tasks of the entity for which he works or made by him by taking advantage of the material and technical means of this entity shall be a service invention. The right to apply for patenting a service invention shall remain with the entity. After the application is approved, the entity shall be the patentee.'

[12] See Article 22 of the Labour Law and Article 23(1) of the Employment Contract Law.

[13] See Article 102 of the Labour Law and Article 90 of the Employment Contract Law.

also establish rules and regulations to protect trade secrets.[14] The rules and regulations established by employers to protect trade secrets create confidentiality obligations that apply to all employees. Although violation of such rules or regulations has no specific consequences under the Labour Law, in practice it is generally deemed a breach of any agreement with the right owner entered into by employees. Such instances will be settled under Article 10(1)(3) of the Anti-Unfair Competition Law.

It should be noted that, according to Articles 23[15] and 25[16] of the Employment Contract Law, employers cannot conclude liquidated damages clauses with employees regarding confidentiality obligations. However, Article 26(2) of the Regulation on the Implementation of the Employment Contract Law of the People's Republic of China (No. 535) provides that an employer is entitled to terminate the employment contract and claim for liquidated damages if (1) an employee *seriously* violates the rules and regulations established by their employer; or (2) the employee has neglected their duties, or engaged in malpractice for personal gain, resulting in significant damage to the employer. Therefore, even though generally an

---

14 Article 3(2) of the Labour Law provides that employees shall comply with labour disciplines and professional ethics; Article 4 provides that employers shall establish and improve rules and regulations to ensure employees enjoy rights and perform obligations. Article 28(1) of the Law of the People's Republic of China on Promoting the Transformation of Scientific and Technological Achievements provides that enterprises and institutions shall establish rules and regulations to protect their know-how. Employees shall comply with such rules and regulations. Translated from the original using <http://vip.chinalawinfo.com/newlaw2002/SLC/SLC.asp?Db=chl&Gid=14408> (accessed July 2010).

15 Article 23(1) of the Employment Contract Law provides that 'employers may conclude agreements with employees concerning confidential matters of trade secrets and intellectual property'; Article 23(2) provides that 'an employer and an employee who are subject to confidentiality obligations may conclude a competition restriction clause in the employment contract or confidentiality agreement. The employer shall pay financial compensation to the employee on a monthly basis during the term of the competition restriction. If the employee breaches the competition restriction provisions, he shall pay liquidated damages to the employer.' It could be assumed that there is no provision of liquidated damages concerning breach of confidentiality; however, there is provision of liquidated damages concerning breach of a competition restriction. Translated from the original using <http://vip.chinalawinfo.com/newlaw2002/SLC/SLC.asp?Db=chl&Gid=94833> (accessed July 2010). See Section 6.2.2.1 below.

16 Article 25 of the Employment Contract Law provides that 'except for the circumstances otherwise provided by Article 22 and 23 of this law, employers and employees cannot conclude liquidated damages paid by employees.' Thus, liquidated damages cannot be concluded under the circumstances provided in Article 23(1).

employer cannot conclude liquidated damages clauses with an employee, they may do so under the circumstances noted above. Additionally, as long as the rules and regulations established by an employee include provisions regarding the keeping of trade secrets, that employer may conclude liquidated damages clauses in employment contracts. Thus, in sum, in order to protect trade secrets an employer must establish rules and regulations for the protection of trade secrets, specify the consequences of violating those rules and regulations and conclude any corresponding liquidated damages clauses that exist in the employment contract.

6.2.1.2. Confidentiality obligations of former employees

There are no specific laws obliging employees to keep trade secrets for their former employers.[17] However, judicial practice obliges employees to *respect* the confidentiality of the trade secrets of their former employers. Therefore, they cannot use or disclose the trade secret without authorization, regardless of whether or not they were party to special confidentiality agreements. This is because Chinese law recognizes trade secrets as an employer's intangible asset. With regard to confidentiality obligations contained in employment contracts, an employee is obliged to keep trade secrets belonging to former employers without being entitled to payment. However, the stipulation of a confidentiality obligation clause cannot result in a competition restriction obligation to the former employee. If a confidentiality obligation clause is equal to a competition restriction clause, it will be invalidated if no financial compensation is supplied. Therefore in order for an employer to effectively protect trade secrets and prevent confidentiality obligations from becoming competition restriction obligations they must first, specify the scope of a trade secret and second, specify any legal consequences of leaking those trade secrets, effectively mandating former employees to comply with the obligation of keeping trade secrets.[18]

---

[17] Only Article 28(2) of the Law of the People's Republic of China on Promoting the Transformation of Scientific and Technological Achievements provides that enterprises and institutions may conclude agreements with persons who participate in the transformation of technological achievements regarding keeping trade secrets during employment or for a certain term after they quit or retire. Such persons shall not breach stipulations regarding disclosure of an employer's know-how, or engage in the same activities as their employer's transformation of technological achievements. Employees shall not transfer, or transfer in disguise, the technological achievements of employment without authorization. Translated from the original using <http://vip.chinalawinfo.com/newlaw2002/SLC/SLC.asp?Db=chl&Gid=14408> (accessed July 2010).

[18] In general, an employer cannot conclude liquidated damages with a former employee for breach of confidentiality. Articles 23 and 25 of the Employment

6.2.2. Competition Restriction Obligations of Employees

6.2.2.1. Competition restriction obligation of serving employees

An employer may establish rules and regulations on the *competition* restriction obligations of serving employees. An employer may terminate the employment contract with an employee if (1) an employee substantially violates such rules and regulations; (2) has established an employment relationship with another employer, materially affecting their standard of work with their original employer; or (3) the employee refuses to rectify the matter following notification by their original employer.[19] If any of the above are present, the employer may claim for liquidated damages under the employment contract.[20]

6.2.2.2. Competition restriction obligations of former employees

According to the Chinese Employment Contract Law, an employer and an employee who are party to a confidentiality obligation may also include a competition restriction clause in the employment contract or confidentiality agreement. A valid competition restriction clause shall meet the following conditions;[21] (1) competition restrictions shall only be applied to members of the employer's senior management, senior technicians and other personnel that are party to confidentiality obligations; (2) the scope, territory and terms of the competition restriction shall be agreed upon by both the employer and the employee, and such an agreement shall not violate laws and regulations on the subject; (3) the employer shall pay financial compensation to the employee on a monthly

---

Contract Law provide that concluding liquidated damages clauses in relation to a former employee's confidentiality obligations is prohibited. However, see the next section (6.2.2.1).

[19] See Articles 39(1)(2) and 39(1)(4) of the Employment Contract Law, translated from the original using <http://vip.chinalawinfo.com/newlaw2002/SLC/SLC.asp?Db=chl&Gid=94833> (accessed July 2010).

[20] According to Article 26(2)(3) of the Regulation on the Implementation of the Employment Contract Law, if an employee has additionally established an employment relationship with another employer which materially affects their work with their original employer, or the employee refuses to correct the matter after being given notice by their original employer, the original employer may terminate the employment contract and claim for liquidated damages in accordance with the employment contract. Translated from the original using http://vip.chinalawinfo.com/newlaw2002/SLC/SLC.asp?Db=chl&Gid=108577> (accessed July 2010).

[21] See Articles 23(2) and 24(1) of the Employment Contract Law, translated from the original using <http://vip.chinalawinfo.com/newlaw2002/SLC/SLC.asp?Db=chl&Gid=94833> (accessed July 2010).

basis for the duration of the term of the competition restriction; (4) if the employee breaches the competition restriction clause, he shall pay liquidated damages to the employer.

A competition restriction implies that an employee shall not work for a competing employer producing similar products or engaging in the same type of business as his current employer. Similarly, an employee shall not establish his own business in order to produce similar products or engage in the same type of business.[22]

There are no specific laws regarding liquidated damages, as the people's courts have offered differing opinions. The High People's Court of Shanghai is partial to the view that if the amount of liquidated damages is unclear, the two parties should continue negotiations regarding the standard of liquidated damages being used. However, if the parties cannot reach an agreement, the employer will be required to pay an amount equal to 20–50% of the employee's normal salary as liquidated damages.[23] In contrast, the High People's Court of Zhejiang is of the opinion that if an employer concludes a competition restriction clause with an employee that results in no financial compensation being awarded, or the agreed amount of financial compensation is apparently too low to maintain the employee's local minimum living standard, the competition restriction clause will be invalid.[24]

A former employee that breaches a competition restriction clause must pay liquidated damages to his former employer, as agreed in the employment contract;[25] and if the breach results in financial loss on the part of the employer, the former employee shall be liable for compensation.[26]

---

[22] See Article 24(2) of the Employment Contract Law, translated from the original using <http://vip.chinalawinfo.com/newlaw2002/SLC/SLC.asp?Db=chl&Gid=94833> (accessed July 2010).

[23] See Article 13 of the Opinions of Several Issues Concerning the Application of the Labor Contract Law (2009) of the Higher People's Court of Shanghai, translated from the original using <http://www.giprs.org/ch/node/496> (accessed July 2010).

[24] See Article 40 of the Opinions of Some Issues Concerning the Trial of Cases on Employment Dispute (Trial Implementation) (2009) of the High People's Court of Zhejiang, translated from the original using <http://lawyergujing.fyfz.cn/blog/lawyergujing/index.aspx?blogid=481590> (accessed July 2010).

[25] See the second sentence of Article 23(2) of the Employment Contract Law, translated from the original using http://vip.chinalawinfo.com/newlaw2002/SLC/SLC.asp?Db=chl&Gid=94833> (accessed July 2010).

[26] See Article 90 of the Employment Contract Law, translated from the original using <http://vip.chinalawinfo.com/newlaw2002/SLC/SLC.asp?Db=chl&Gid=94833> (accessed July 2010).

6.2.2.3. Principles followed by People's Courts in competition restriction cases

According to the opinion of the Supreme People's Court, all people's courts shall take into account the actual level of economy and technology in China, as well as the public interests, when considering competition restriction cases. All the people's courts shall not only maintain fair competition in the socialist market economy, but also balance the interests of different market players. This not only limits the effect that the inappropriate expansion of the scope of competition restriction has on the freedom of career choice, but also protects the rights of employers, such as the right of trade secrets. Additionally, it fulfills the legislative intent and purpose of establishing rules and regulations concerning competition restriction.[27]

6.3. THE PROTECTION OF TRADE SECRETS OBTAINED THROUGH TRANSACTIONS

6.3.1. General Rules

6.3.1.1. Contract law

The Contract Law provides principal rules regarding confidentiality obligations in concluding, performing and following the termination of a contract. A trade secret learned by the parties in concluding a contract shall not be disclosed or improperly used, regardless of whether the contract is established or not. If the party discloses or improperly uses such a trade secret, thus incurring losses to the other party, the disclosing party shall be liable for damages.[28] During the course of performing a contract, the parties shall follow principles of good faith, and perform obligations of notification, assistance and confidentiality in accordance with the nature and purpose of the contract and the transaction practice.[29] After the termination of the rights and obligations under the contract, the parties shall

---

[27] See Article 10 of the Guidance of Trial of Cases on Employment Dispute under Current Situation (2009) of the Supreme People's Court, translated from the original using <http://vip.chinalawinfo.com/newlaw2002/SLC/SLC.asp?Db=chl&Gid=119160> (accessed July 2010).

[28] See Article 43 of the Contract Law, translated from the original using <http://vip.chinalawinfo.com/newlaw2002/SLC/SLC.asp?Db=chl&Gid=21651> (accessed July 2010).

[29] See Article 60(2) of the Contract Law, translated from the original using <http://vip.chinalawinfo.com/newlaw2002/SLC/SLC.asp?Db=chl&Gid=21651> (accessed July 2010).

follow principles of honesty and good faith and perform the obligations of notification, assistance and confidentiality in accordance with relevant transaction practices.[30] These provisions reflect the positive attitude of Chinese Contract Law towards the protection of trade secrets. As long as there are trade secrets involved in the transaction, the parties shall follow principles of honesty and good faith and perform their confidentiality obligations in accordance with transaction practices. These obligations are statutory. Even if the rights owner of the trade secret has not expressly included a confidentiality requirement, the counter-party shall have a statutory confidentiality obligation if s/he knows that the information is a trade secret, based on the nature and objective of the contract and transaction practices. For example, in a know-how licensing agreement, some information will not be marked as 'classified' in the technical materials that are handed over by the rights owner to the counter-party. As long as it is probable that such information is not public information, based on the nature and objective of the contract and relevant transaction practices, the counter-party cannot claim that s/he is not subject to a confidentiality obligation purely because there is a no 'classified' mark on the documents.

6.3.1.2. Tort law

According to Article 10(3) of the Anti-Unfair Competition Law, disclosing, using or allowing others to use trade secrets duly obtained by either (1) breaking an agreement, or (2) disregarding the right owner's requirements of keeping trade secrets may be actionable under the law of tort. The protection of trade secrets by tort law may be implied as a result of the agreements between the parties or as the result of a unilateral request on behalf of the right owner of a trade secret. For example, during the negotiation stage of a contract, if one party gives materials that are marked as 'classified' to the other party, the receiving party shall not disclose or use these materials for other purposes on the basis of an absence of a confidentiality agreement between the parties.

Breach of confidentiality can fall under contract law or the law of tort. According to Article 122 of the Contract Law, the aggrieved party is entitled to choose whether to bring the claim under the Contract Law, or to claim under other laws (including tort). Under Article 266 of the Contract Law, the contractor is obliged to keep relevant information confidential if instructed to do so by the ordering party, and shall not retain any replica

---

30 See Article 90 of the Contract Law, translated from the original using <http://vip.chinalawinfo.com/newlaw2002/SLC/SLC.asp?Db=chl&Gid=21651> (accessed July 2010).

or technical material without the permission of the ordering party. The retaining of any replica or technical material by the contractor may constitute a tort as well as a breach of contract. This provision is very important for the protection of know-how in OEM transactions.

6.3.2. Trade Secret Licensing Agreements

In China, trade secrets are recognized as a kind of intellectual property and intangible asset that can be the object of an intellectual property transaction. In practice, trade secrets are usually traded with patents, trademarks and copyright, constituting part of a mixed licensing agreement. Trade secret licensing pertains mainly to know-how licensing, while management secret licensing generally exists in commercial franchises. According to Chinese law, 'Commercial Franchises' (hereinafter referred to as 'franchises') are defined as an enterprise that possesses the following: (1) a registered trademark; (2) an enterprise mark; (3) a patent; (4) know-how; or (5) any other business resource for any other business operator (hereinafter referred as 'franchisee') through contract. The franchisee conducts business under a uniform business model, as stipulated in the contract, and pays franchising fees to the franchiser.[31] The mixed license of trademarks, patents and trade secrets is an important part of franchises. According to Article 18(2) of the Regulation on the Administration of Commercial Franchises, a franchisee may not disclose the franchiser's trade secrets to which it has access to anyone else, or allow anyone else to use it. According to Chinese Contract Law, the term 'know-how licensing' is generally referred to as 'technology transfer'. Know-how licensing agreements contain stipulations relating to the special equipment or raw materials provided by the licensor to the licensee for the exploitation of the technology, or for the provision of relevant technical consulting or technical services. Therefore disputes arising out of such matters shall be settled in a way applicable to know-how licensing agreements.[32] The validity of clauses in know-how licensing agreements is discussed below.

---

[31] See Article 3 of the Regulation on the Administration of Commercial Franchises (2007), translated from the original using <http://vip.chinalawinfo.com/newlaw2002/SLC/SLC.asp?Db=chl&Gid=88185> (accessed July 2010).

[32] See Article 22(2) of the Interpretation of the Supreme People's Court concerning Some Issues on Application of Law for the Trial of Cases on Disputes over Technology Contracts (2004) of the Supreme People's Court, translated from the original using <http://vip.chinalawinfo.com/newlaw2002/SLC/SLC.asp?Db=chl&Gid=56393> (accessed July 2010).

6.3.2.1. Valid clauses in know-how licensing agreements

(1) *Licensing*: Licensing know-how is similar to licensing patents, and includes sole licenses for exploitation, licenses for exclusive exploitation and common licenses for exploitation.[33] A sole license for exploitation is a license where the licensor licenses the exploitation of know-how, within a stipulated license scope, to only one licensee, and the licensor may not exploit this know-how pursuant to the contract. Licenses for exclusive exploitation are identical to sole licenses for exploitation, except that the transferor himself may exploit this know-how pursuant to the contract. Licenses for exclusive exploitation are distinguished from sole licenses for exploitation by the fact that the transferor himself is not excluded from exploiting the know-how. Common licenses for exploitation are again similar to the above methods of licensing, except that the know-how is transferred to multiple transferees for exploitation. The licensor is able to exploit this know-how herself/himself. Where there are no stipulations between the parties on the method of licensing to be used for the exploitation of know-how, or such stipulations are not clear, the default method of licensing shall be deemed a common license for exploitation.[34]

(2) *The scope of exploitation of know-how*: Stipulation of the scope of exploitation of know-how can be given. It should include the duration, territory and method of exploitation, as well as the identities of the persons with access to the technical secrets, and so on. However, technical competition and technical development shall not be limited.[35] Where there are no stipulations between the parties on the duration of the exploitation of know-how, or such stipulations are

---

[33] See Article 25(3) of the Interpretation of the Supreme People's Court concerning Some Issues on Application of Law for the Trial of Cases on Disputes over Technology Contracts (2004) of the Supreme People's Court, translated from the original using <http://vip.chinalawinfo.com/newlaw2002/SLC/SLC.asp?Db=chl&Gid=56393> (accessed July 2010).

[34] See Article 25(2) of the Interpretation of the Supreme People's Court concerning Some Issues on Application of Law for the Trial of Cases on Disputes over Technology Contracts (2004) of the Supreme People's Court, translated from the original using <http://vip.chinalawinfo.com/newlaw2002/SLC/SLC.asp?Db=chl&Gid=56393> (accessed July 2010).

[35] See Article 28(1) of the Interpretation of the Supreme People's Court concerning Some Issues on Application of Law for the Trial of Cases on Disputes over Technology Contracts (2004) of the Supreme People's Court, translated from the original using <http://vip.chinalawinfo.com/newlaw2002/SLC/SLC.asp?Db=chl&Gid=56393> (accessed July 2010).

unclear, the licensee shall not be restricted by duration from exploiting the know-how.[36] It is worth noting that in terms of importing technology by Chinese-Foreign joint venture enterprises, the duration for a technology transfer agreement is generally no longer than ten years, according to Article 43(2) of the Regulations for the Implementation of the Law of the People's Republic of China on Joint Ventures Using Chinese and Foreign Investment. After the expiration of a technology transfer agreement, the technology importing party shall have the right to use the technology continuously.

(3) *Methods of sharing any subsequent improvements resulting from the exploitation of know-how*: The parties may, on the basis of mutual benefit, provide in the technology transfer agreement the method of sharing any subsequent improvement resulting from the exploitation of the know-how. If this method is not stipulated, the agreement is unclear, or it is found not to fall within the ambit of Article 61,[37] neither party is entitled to share any subsequent improvement made by the other party.[38]

(4) *The parties' confidentiality obligations*: The licensor and licensee of know-how licensing agreements may agree to confidentiality obligations. However, the licensor shall not be prevented from applying for patent protection, unless otherwise stipulated between the parties.[39] After the know-how is patented, the original know-how licensing

---

[36] See Article 28(2) of the Interpretation of the Supreme People's Court concerning Some Issues on Application of Law for the Trial of Cases on Disputes over Technology Contracts (2004) of the Supreme People's Court, translated from the original using <http://vip.chinalawinfo.com/newlaw2002/SLC/SLC.asp?Db=chl&Gid=56393> (accessed July 2010).

[37] Article 61 of the Contract Law provides that: 'where, after the contract becomes effective, there is no stipulation in the contract between the parties on such contents as quality, price or remuneration, or place of performance etc., or such stipulation is not clear, the parties may agree upon supplementary terms through consultation. If a supplementary agreement cannot be reached, such terms shall be determined in accordance with the relevant provisions of the contract or the transaction practices', translated from the original using <http://vip.chinalawinfo.com/newlaw2002/SLC/SLC.asp?Db=chl&Gid=21651> (accessed July 2010).

[38] See Article 354 of the Contract Law, translated from the original using <http://vip.chinalawinfo.com/newlaw2002/SLC/SLC.asp?Db=chl&Gid=21651> (accessed July 2010).

[39] See Article 29(1) of the Interpretation of the Supreme People's Court concerning Some Issues on Application of Law for the Trial of Cases on Disputes over Technology Contracts (2004) of the Supreme People's Court, translated from the original using <http://vip.chinalawinfo.com/newlaw2002/SLC/SLC.asp?Db=chl&Gid=56393> (accessed July 2010).

agreement shall be changed to a license for the exploitation of the patent.[40] Duration of confidentiality is not subject to limitations. As long as the know-how has not been made public, the parties shall be subject to confidentiality obligations.

(5) *Warranties of the licensor*: The licensor in a know-how licensing agreement is required to warrant that he is the lawful owner of the technology and that the technology provided is practicable, complete, credible, effective, and capable of achieving the prescribed goals.[41] Where the exploitation of the know-how by the licensee, in accordance with the agreement, infringes the lawful interests of any other person, the licensor shall be liable, unless otherwise agreed by the parties.[42]

6.3.2.2. Invalid clauses of know-how licensing agreements

According to Article 329 of the Contract Law, a technology contract that illegally monopolizes technology, impairs technology progress or infringes on the technology of a third party is invalid. In the view of the the Supreme People's Court, and in accordance with Article 329,[43] the following circumstances shall be deemed to illegally monopolize technology and impair technology progress:

(1) (i) Restricting one of the parties from either carrying out new research and development based on the technology, which is the subject matter of the contract, or using the improved technology; or (ii) where the conditions for the exchange of the improved technologies between the parties are not reciprocal, for example, requiring one party to provide improved technology to the other without price, or transferring the improved technology to the other party

---

40 See Article 29(2) of the Interpretation of the Supreme People's Court concerning Some Issues on Application of Law for the Trial of Cases on Disputes over Technology Contracts (2004) of the Supreme People's Court, translated from the original using <http://vip.chinalawinfo.com/newlaw2002/SLC/SLC.asp?Db=chl&Gid=56393> (accessed July 2010).

41 See Articles 347 and 349 of the Contract Law, translated from the original using <http://vip.chinalawinfo.com/newlaw2002/SLC/SLC.asp?Db=chl&Gid=21651> (accessed July 2010).

42 See Article 353 of the Contract Law, translated from the original using <http://vip.chinalawinfo.com/newlaw2002/SLC/SLC.asp?Db=chl&Gid=21651> (accessed July 2010).

43 See Article 40 of the Interpretation of the Supreme People's Court concerning Some Issues on Application of Law for the Trial of Cases on Disputes over Technology Contracts (2004) of the Supreme People's Court.

non-reciprocally; or (iii) to solely occupy, or jointly own the intellectual property rights to the improved technology;

(2) Restricting one party from obtaining technology from other resources, which are similar to, or that compete against, the technology of the technology provider;
(3) Restricting one party from fully exploiting the technology in a reasonable way pursuant to market demands. This includes providing for the quantity, variety, price, sales channel or export market of the products or services produced by the licensee by exploiting the technology in an obviously unreasonable way;
(4) Imposing additional conditions on the licensee, before allowing the licensee to fully exploit the technology. This includes purchasing dispensable technologies, raw materials, products, equipment, services or accepting dispensable personnel;
(5) Unreasonably restricting the channels or resources for the licensee to purchase raw materials, parts and components, products or equipment, etc; and
(6) Prohibiting the licensee from challenging the validity of the intellectual property rights of the technology, or the setting up of additional conditions to the challenge.[44]

6.3.2.3. Consequences of exploiting know-how by breaching know-how licensing agreements subject to Contract Law

(1) Where an agreement exists and the licensor fails to transfer technology pursuant to the terms of it, repayment of a licensing fee shall be made in part or in whole, and the licensor will be liable for breach of contract. Where the licensor exploits the know-how beyond the predetermined scope of the agreement, or unilaterally allows a third party to exploit the know-how as a result of a breach of contract, the breach must cease and the licensor will be liable for breach of contract. Additionally, where the licensor breaches any stipulated confidentiality obligations, he will be liable for breach of contract.[45]
(2) In the event that the licensee fails to pay the agreed licensing fee on time, the licensee shall be liable to pay the overdue fee as well as liquidated damages pursuant to the agreement. If the licensee fails

[44] Translated from the original using <http://vip.chinalawinfo.com/newlaw2002/SLC/SLC.asp?Db=chl&Gid=56393> (accessed July 2010).

[45] See Article 351 of the Contract Law, translated from the original using <http://vip.chinalawinfo.com/newlaw2002/SLC/SLC.asp?Db=chl&Gid=21651> (accessed July 2010).

to pay both the overdue licensing fee and liquidated damages, the licensee is required to cease any exploitation of the know-how, return the technical materials, and will be liable for breach of contract. If it transpires that the licensee is exploiting the know-how beyond the agreed scope, or allows a third party to exploit the know-how without authorization of the transferor by breaching the agreement, the licensee must cease the breach and will be liable for breach of contract. Additionally, if the licensee breaches any stipulated confidentiality obligations, the licensee will be liable for breach of contract.[46]

6.3.3. Protection of Trade Secrets in Technology Development Contracts

6.3.3.1. Introduction to technology development contracts

According to Article 330 of the Contract Law, a technology development contract is a contract concerning the development of a new technology, product, technique or material and the associated system. Technology development contracts include commissioned development and cooperative development contracts. Contracts that deal with the conversion of scientific achievements that may have possible industrial applications also fall within the ambit of technology development contracts. In addition, contracts concluded for the purpose of realizing a scientific or technological achievement with industrial application are considered technology development contracts; a contract that concerns a scientific and technological achievement (including a technological achievement that has reached a certain stage) that has practical value, but where industrial application has not yet been realized, and in which such content as follow-up experiments, development and application are included, are considered to be technology development contracts.[47]

6.3.3.2. Owner of know-how resulting from technology development contracts and relevant confidentiality obligations of the parties

Technological achievement forms the subject matter of a technology development contract. Where the technology is made public by a third

---

[46] See Article 352 of the Contract Law, translated from the original using <http://vip.chinalawinfo.com/newlaw2002/SLC/SLC.asp?Db=chl&Gid=21651> (accessed July 2010).

[47] See Article 18 of the Interpretation of the Supreme People's Court concerning Some Issues on Application of Law for the Trial of Cases on Disputes over Technology Contracts (2004) of the Supreme People's Court, translated from the original using <http://vip.chinalawinfo.com/newlaw2002/SLC/SLC.asp?Db=chl&Gid=56393> (accessed July 2010).

party, thereby rendering performance of the technology development contract meaningless, the parties may terminate the contract.[48] Therefore, as long as the technological achievement has not been made public, the parties shall be subject to confidentiality obligations. In respect of to whom the right over the technological achievement shall belong, and to whom and how to allocate the profits, the parties may expressly stipulate relevant clauses in the contract. If the parties have not stipulated clauses regarding such matters, the following provisions of the Contract Law shall be applied.

(1) Unless otherwise agreed upon by the parties, the right to apply for patent protection over the invention or innovation resulting from a commissioned development belongs to the developer. When the developer is granted a patent, the commissioning party may exploit that patent for free. Where the developer transfers the right to apply for a patent, the commissioning party shall have priority in acquiring the right under the same conditions.[49] Therefore the commissioning party is subject to confidentiality obligations before the invention or innovation is made public.
(2) The right to apply for patent protection over an invention or innovation resulting from a cooperative development is shared jointly by the parties, unless otherwise agreed. When a party wishes to transfer its joint patent application right, the other parties shall have priority in acquiring that right under the same conditions. Where a party in the cooperative development waives its joint patent application right, the other party may apply by itself, or the other parties may jointly apply, depending on how many parties are subject to the cooperative development. In the event that the invention or innovation is patented, the party waiving its patent application right may exploit the patent for free. If any party in the cooperative development does not consent to an application for patent protection, the other party, or parties, may not apply.[50] Therefore, if a party to a cooperative

---

[48] See Article 337 of the Contract Law, translated from the original using <http://vip.chinalawinfo.com/newlaw2002/SLC/SLC.asp?Db=chl&Gid=21651> (accessed July 2010).

[49] See Article 339 of the Contract Law, translated from the original using <http://vip.chinalawinfo.com/newlaw2002/SLC/SLC.asp?Db=chl&Gid=21651> (accessed July 2010).

[50] See Article 340 of the Contract Law, translated from the original using <http://vip.chinalawinfo.com/newlaw2002/SLC/SLC.asp?Db=chl&Gid=21651> (accessed July 2010).

development does not consent to applying for patent protection, the invention or innovation shall be protected as a trade secret.

(3) All of the parties are entitled to use and transfer the technological achievement, whether they are under a commissioned development contract or a cooperative development contract. However, the developer in a commissioned development contract may not transfer the know-how to a third party before it delivers the technology to the commissioning party.[51] Either party has the right to use or license know-how to a third party by means of a common license, without the consent of the other party, and will be entitled to any profits gained by doing so. If one party chooses to either assign the right to transfer the technological achievement to others, or licenses the know-how to others by means of a sole or an exclusive license, without the other party's consent or confirmation, the assignment or license shall be deemed invalid.[52] If a party to a technology development contract cannot meet the conditions to independently exploit the patent or know-how, that party may instead license the patent or know-how by using a common license for exploitation.[53]

6.4. INFRINGEMENT OF TRADE SECRETS AND CORRESPONDING LEGAL LIABILITY

6.4.1. Infringement of Trade Secrets

6.4.1.1. The Anti-Unfair Competition Law

Article 10(1) and (2) of the Anti-Unfair Competition Law lists acts which are deemed to be infringements of trade secrets: (1) obtaining a trade secret from its owner by stealing, luring by promising financial gain,

[51] See Article 341 of the Contract Law, translated from the original using <http://vip.chinalawinfo.com/newlaw2002/SLC/SLC.asp?Db=chl&Gid=21651> (accessed July 2010).

[52] See Article 20 of the Interpretation of the Supreme People's Court concerning Some Issues on Application of Law for the Trial of Cases on Disputes over Technology Contracts (2004) of the Supreme People's Court, translated from the original using <http://vip.chinalawinfo.com/newlaw2002/SLC/SLC.asp?Db=chl&Gid=56393> (accessed July 2010).

[53] See Article 21 of the Interpretation of the Supreme People's Court concerning Some Issues on Application of Law for the Trial of Cases on Disputes over Technology Contracts (2004) of the Supreme People's Court, translated from the original using <http://vip.chinalawinfo.com/newlaw2002/SLC/SLC.asp?Db=chl&Gid=56393> (accessed July 2010).

intimidating or by other illegitimate means; (2) disclosing, using or allowing others to use a trade secret obtained by the aforementioned means; (3) disclosing, using or allowing others to use a legally obtained trade secret by breaking an agreement or disregarding the owners' requirement to preserve the trade secret; (4) where a third party obtains, uses or discloses the trade secret of another when the third party has or should have full knowledge of the aforementioned illegal acts, or the third party is deemed to have infringed on the trade secret of the lawful owner. In respect of point 3, above, unless the act involves the unauthorized disclosing and using of a trade secret which is legally obtained, all the other illegal acts involve obtaining trade secrets by illegitimate means. As the second illegal act is a continuation of the first, there exists no substantial definition for establishing a tort, or a violation of administrative law, under which the second act would fall.

6.4.1.2. Obtaining trade secrets by illegitimate means

Problems arise when attempting to define illegitimate means of obtaining trade secrets other than stealing, luring by promising financial gain and intimidating. There is no express answer to the problem in Article 10 of the Anti-Unfair Competition Law. However, Article 2(1) provides that when carrying out transactions in the market, operators must follow the principles of voluntariness, equality, fairness, honesty and credibility, whilst observing generally recognized business ethics. Unfair competition in this context refers to acts of operators that violate provisions of these regulations, resulting in damage to the legal rights and interests of other operators and thus disturbing the socio-economic order. Therefore, in terms of competition law, an operator that obtains a trade secret by violating the principles of honesty and credibility or generally recognized business ethics will be considered as having done so by using illegitimate means, and this conduct will be an infringement of the trade secret.

Reverse engineering does not constitute an illegitimate means. In the opinion of the Supreme People's Court, obtaining a trade secret through reverse engineering is lawful. Reverse engineering refers to dismantling, mapping or analyzing products acquired through public channels in order to obtain the relevant technical information.[54] In accordance with this definition, the products subjected to reverse engineering must be obtained

---

[54] See the first sentence of Article 12(2) of the Interpretation of the Supreme People's Court on Some Issues Concerning the Application of Law in the Trial of Civil Cases Involving Unfair Competition, translated from the original using <http://vip.chinalawinfo.com/newlaw2002/SLC/SLC.asp?Db=chl&Gid=83311> (accessed July 2010).

through public channels. However, the term 'public channels' remains undefined by the Supreme People's Court, except that direct transactions fall within the ambit of a public channel. Claiming that products have been obtained through public channels has significant implications. If a competitor legally purchases or obtains a product that is subject to trade secret protection from a third party, with the intention to dismantle and analyze it, but cannot successfully claim that they have done so through public channels, it will be deemed as obtaining the trade secret by illegitimate means. This constitutes an infringement of a trade secret. In relation to *acquiring a product*, this is generally defined as owning the product that is to be subjected to reverse engineering. Therefore, if an operator that only has the right of use or custody dismantles, maps or analyzes a product in order to obtain a trade secret, that operator will infringe the trade secret. If a party gains knowledge of a trade secret by illegitimate means and then claims it acquired it through reverse engineering, it shall still be deemed unlawful.[55] Therefore, the act of obtaining a trade secret by illegitimate means in itself will render the party liable for infringement; and reverse engineering will not be accepted as a valid excuse.

Disclosing, using or allowing others to use a legally obtained trade secret by breaking an agreement or disregarding the requirements of the rights owner will constitute an infringement (in tort). If the tortfeasor obtains the trade secret by complying with stipulations or requirements given by the rights owner in order to preserve a trade secret, the tortfeasor shall be subject to a confidentiality obligation. Generally, a person who has obtained a trade secret based on complying with the right owner's requirements and who is subject to a confidentiality obligation has a special relationship with the rights owner, for example, they are in the course of concluding a contract, or they have a pre-existing business or employment relationship. If a trade secret rights owner discloses the trade secret to a person with whom no special relationship exists, that person will not be subject to a confidentiality obligation, for example, if the rights owner discloses confidential information to a potential client, without any advance contact or negotiation, the potential client will not be subject to a confidentiality obligation.

[55] See second sentence of Article 12(2) of the Interpretation of the Supreme People's Court on Some Issues Concerning the Application of Law in the Trial of Civil Cases Involving Unfair Competition, translated from the original using <http://vip.chinalawinfo.com/newlaw2002/SLC/SLC.asp?Db=chl&Gid=83311> (July 2010).

6.4.1.3. Infringing of trade secrets by malicious third parties

According to Article 10(2) of the Anti-Unfair Competition Law and Article 219(2) of the Criminal Law, if a third party obtains, uses or discloses a trade secret, when that third party has or should have full knowledge that the trade secret has been obtained, used or disclosed illegally by others, it will be deemed to have infringed the trade secret. This provision is influenced by Article 39 of the TRIPS Agreement, but is much stricter. According to this provision, a malicious third party is a party that has or should have full knowledge. 'Has full knowledge' in this context corresponds to the third party knowing; and 'should have full knowledge' is taken as being grossly negligent in failing to know; as is the case in Article 39 of the TRIPS Agreement.[56] It should be noted that according to Article 39 of the TRIPS Agreement, the period when the party is understood to have knowledge or was grossly negligent in failing to have knowledge is taken to be when the third party acquires the trade secret of others. However, according to Chinese law, this period is not limited to when a third party acquires a trade secret, but also includes when the third party uses or discloses the trade secret. To clarify, even if a third party acts in good faith when it acquires a trade secret, it may still become a malicious third party, and thus infringe the trade secret, if it later has or should have full knowledge of the trade secret being obtained or disclosed illegally by others when it chooses to use or disclose the trade secret itself. If a third party has no knowledge that the trade secret was disclosed or licensed by others illegally until it starts to use the trade secret, the third party's liability shall be decided according to regulatory provisions regarding the liability of third parties acting in good faith (see Section 6.1.2.3 above).

6.4.1.4. Restraint of trade (restrictions on former employees)

In the view of the Supreme People's Court, situations arise where a customer relies on a particular employee and thus conducts transactions with the employer of that employee. If it can be proved that if the employee were to leave their position, the customer would subsequently and voluntarily choose to continue to conduct transactions with the employee or his new employer, it shall be affirmed that no illegitimate means have been adopted, unless otherwise stipulated between the employee and their previous employer.[57] This provision takes into consideration specialized

---

[56] Compare to Article 39 of the TRIPS Agreement: '. . . the acquisition of undisclosed information by third parties who knew, or were grossly negligent in failing to know, that such practices were involved in the acquisition'.

[57] See Article 13(2) of the Interpretation of the Supreme People's Court on Some Issues Concerning the Application of Law in the Trial of Civil Cases

professions, including solicitors, physicians and other similar professions, because of the relationship that is built between professional and client, and the fact that it is not uncommon for those in these professions to often change their employers. Clients rely on the ability and morality of the particular person and it would be unfair to prohibit clients from engaging in transactions with them after they leave their original position.[58] However, future transactions must meet the following conditions: (1) the former employee has no prohibiting stipulation with his former employer; (2) clients of the former employer are voluntary, choosing to continue to deal with the former employee, and the employee has not lured, bribed or intimidated the clients.

6.4.2. Civil Liability for Infringing Trade Secrets

According to Article 134 of the General Principles of the Civil Law of the People's Republic of China, the main methods of bearing civil liability are: (1) cessation of infringements; (2) removal of obstacles; (3) allocating risk and prevention or reduction of harm; (4) return of property; (5) restoration of original condition; (6) repair, reworking or replacement; (7) compensation for losses; (8) payment of liquidated damages; (9) elimination of ill effects and rehabilitation of reputation; and (10) extension of apology. In addition to applying the above stipulations, a people's court may serve admonitions, order the offender to sign a pledge of repentance, and confiscate the property used in carrying out illegal activities and any illegal income obtained. It may also impose fines or detentions as stipulated by law. The main methods of bearing civil liability for infringing trade secrets are cessation of infringements and compensation for losses.

6.4.2.1. Cessation of infringements

In the view of the Supreme People's Court, when the people's court rules upon the civil liability of stopping the infringement of a trade secret, the period for stopping the infringement shall generally be understood to begin when the trade secret was first made known to the public. If the period for stopping the infringement is determined according to the

---

Involving Unfair Competition, translated from the original using http://vip.chinalawinfo.com/newlaw2002/SLC/SLC.asp?Db=chl&Gid=83311> (accessed July 2010).

[58] See Jiang, Z, Kong, X, and Wang, Y, '*The Understanding and Application of the "Interpretation of Several Issues of Application of Laws in Deciding Civil Cases Concerning Unfair Competition"', Guidance of Trial of Cases on Intellectual Property*, 104 (2007) 2.

preceding provision, but is clearly inappropriate, the tortfeasor may be ordered to stop the use of the trade secret within a certain term, or scope, under the premise that the competitive edge of the right owner of the trade secret is protected.[59] For example, if the tortfeasor is capable of obtaining the trade secret through reverse engineering, or he illegally uses customer lists, the period of stopping the infringement may be limited to the period of time it has taken for the tortfeasor to conduct reverse engineering or to legally develop similar customer lists, rather than from the moment the trade secret had been made known to the public.

6.4.2.2. Compensation for losses

According to Article 20 of the Anti-Unfair Competition Law, where a tortfeasor causes damage to the owner of a trade secret, they shall be liable for compensation. Where the losses suffered by the rights owner are difficult to calculate, the amount of damages shall be considered equal to the profits earned by the tortfeasor during the period of infringement. The tortfeasor shall also bear all reasonable costs paid by the rights owner in investigating the acts of unfair competition committed by the tortfeasor suspected of infringing their lawful rights and interests.

In accordance with judicial interpretation by the Supreme People's Court, the determination of compensation for infringing trade secrets (as listed in Article 10 of the Anti-Unfair Competition Law) may use the same methods of determining compensation for patent infringements.[60] Article 65(1) of the New Patent Law of the People's Republic of China (2008 as amended) provides that the amount of compensation for a patent infringement shall be determined by the value of the actual loss suffered by the patentee as a result of an infringement. If the actual loss proves difficult to calculate, it may be determined by the value of the gains obtained by the infringer as a result of the infringement. If it is difficult to determine the value of the losses suffered by the patentee, as well the profits obtained by the infringer, it may be determined by reference to the multiple royalties that may exist for the patent, as long as this calculated value is reason-

---

[59] See Article 16 of the Interpretation of the Supreme People's Court on Some Issues Concerning the Application of Law in the Trial of Civil Cases Involving Unfair Competition, translated from the original using <http://vip.chinalawinfo.com/newlaw2002/SLC/SLC.asp?Db=chl&Gid=83311> (accessed July 2010).

[60] See the first sentence of Article 17(1) of the Interpretation of the Supreme People's Court on Some Issues Concerning the Application of Law in the Trial of Civil Cases Involving Unfair Competition, translated from the original using <http://vip.chinalawinfo.com/newlaw2002/SLC/SLC.asp?Db=chl&Gid=83311> (accessed July 2010).

able. In addition, compensation shall include any reasonable expenses that the patentee has paid for in seeking to stop the infringement. Article 65(2) provides that if it is difficult to determine the actual loss, profits and royalty, the people's court may, by taking into account factors such as the nature of the patent, and the nature and particulars of the infringement, etc., decide upon the amount of compensation, within a range of no less than 10,000 Yuan but not more than 1 million Yuan. Thus, the range of methods available for calculating the value of compensation (including statutory compensation) for infringing trade secrets has increased, making the task of protecting trade secrets less problematic.

Issues arise when determining the amount of compensation when a trade secret has been made known to the public as a result of an infringement. If an infringement results in a trade secret being publicized, damages will be determined according to the commercial value of the trade secret. The commercial value of the trade secret will be determined by calculating the total value of the research and development costs, the proceeds from using the trade secret, any possible benefits, and the time consumed maintaining the competitive edge of the trade secret, etc.[61] The objective of these provisions is to strengthen the protection of trade secrets.

6.4.2.3. Liability of third parties who obtain trade secrets in good faith

(1) *A third party who obtains a trade secret in good faith*: This kind of third party is without knowledge and is not expected to have any knowledge of the fact that the person who disclosed the trade secret used illegal means to obtain or disclose the trade secret. If a third party acting in good faith becomes aware during the course of using a trade secret that the trade secret has been disclosed illegally, whether the third party can continue using the trade secret without being found liable depends on interpretation and is likely to be decided on a case-by-case basis. The definition of 'using' in particular requires clarification. Using the trade secret directly, investing human, material and financial resources for the purpose of using the trade secret and having the conditions to use the trade secret all fall within the definition of 'using' in this context.

---

[61] See Article 17(2) of the Interpretation of the Supreme People's Court on Some Issues Concerning the Application of Law in the Trial of Civil Cases Involving Unfair Competition, translated from the original using <http://vip.chinalawinfo.com/newlaw2002/SLC/SLC.asp?Db=chl&Gid=83311> (accessed July 2010).

(2) *Continuing use of know-how*: In the view of the Supreme People's Court, a party that obtains know-how in good faith may, unless otherwise provided for in law or administrative regulation, continue using the know-how within the same scope as when the party first obtained it. However, the party must then pay the rights owner reasonable royalties and be subject to confidentiality obligations.[62] Where a person who is in a position to continue using know-how is in dispute with the rights owner over the payment of royalties, either party may ask the people's court for settlement. The people's court must determine royalties reasonably and on the basis of the normal royalties paid to a rights owner of this type of know-how, or the royalties paid by a user to obtain this type of know-how, as well as by taking into consideration such factors as research and development costs, the extent of conversion and application of the achievement, the user's scale of use and financial profits, etc.[63] If a person continues using know-how without making royalty payments, the people's court may, upon the rights owner's request, rule that the person must cease using it.[64] Although, in pursuance of the judicial interpretation, the continuing user (of the know-how) is not subject to a confidentiality obligation, according to Article 10(2) of the Anti-Unfair Competition Law, a user disclosing a trade secret illegally is also deemed to have infringed the trade secret.

(3) *Party's liability for using a trade secret before notice, and liability when a party should have known it is obtained or disclosed illegally*: According to the judicial interpretation of the Supreme People's Court, no matter whether the user continues using the know-how or not, the people's court must rule that the user pays the rights

---

[62] See Article 12 of the Interpretation of the Supreme People's Court concerning Some Issues on Application of Law for the Trial of Cases on Disputes over Technology Contracts (2004), translated from the original using <http://vip.chinalawinfo.com/newlaw2002/SLC/SLC.asp?Db=chl&Gid=56393> (accessed July 2010).

[63] See the first sentence of Article 13(1) and Article 13(2) of the Interpretation of the Supreme People's Court concerning Some Issues on Application of Law for the Trial of Cases on Disputes over Technology Contracts (2004), translated from the original using <http://vip.chinalawinfo.com/newlaw2002/SLC/SLC.asp?Db=chl&Gid=56393> (accessed July 2010).

[64] See second sentence of Article 13(1) of the Interpretation of the Supreme People's Court concerning Some Issues on Application of Law for the Trial of Cases on Disputes over Technology Contracts(2004), translated from the original using <http://vip.chinalawinfo.com/newlaw2002/SLC/SLC.asp?Db=chl&Gid=56393> (accessed July 2010).

owner royalties for the duration of the know-how's period of use. Additionally, the licensor must refund any royalties received from the know-how user under an invalid contract.[65]

(4) *Use of management secrets*: There are no clear provisions contained in relative laws and judicial interpretation regarding whether or not a third party acting in good faith may continue to use management secrets. However, it cannot be concluded that a third party acting in good faith is prohibited from doing so. It seems to the author that from the perspective of a balance of interests, a third party acting in good faith may continue using a management secret if: (1) prohibiting the continuing use of the management secret may cause great loss to the human, material and financial resources invested in using the management secret and; (2) use of the management secret has no significant influence on the rights owner's competitive edge.

6.4.2.4. Problems with tort litigation

(1) *Bringing litigation for infringement of trade secrets*: According to the judicial interpretation of the Supreme People's Court, the following are permitted: (1) In cases concerning infringement of any trade secret, if the licensee of a sole license for exploitation of the trade secret brings litigation, the people's court must accept it; (2) In situations where the licensee of an exclusive license for exploitation brings and the rights owner jointly brings, or the licensee brings litigation alone under the circumstance that the rights owner does not wish to do so, the people's court must accept it; (3) In cases where the licensee of a common license for exploitation brings litigation jointly with the rights owner, or the licensee brings litigation alone upon written authorization of the rights owner, the people's court must accept it.[66]

(2) *Plaintiff's burden of proof*: In the opinion of the Supreme People's Court, if a party claims that someone else has infringed its trade

---

[65] See Article 13 of the Interpretation of the Supreme People's Court concerning Some Issues on Application of Law for the Trial of Cases on Disputes over Technology Contracts (2004), translated from the original using <http://vip.chinalawinfo.com/newlaw2002/SLC/SLC.asp?Db=chl&Gid=56393> (accessed July 2010).

[66] See Article 15 of the Interpretation of the Supreme People's Court on Some Issues Concerning the Application of Law in the Trial of Civil Cases Involving Unfair Competition (2006), translated from the original using <http://vip.chinalawinfo.com/newlaw2002/SLC/SLC.asp?Db=chl&Gid=83311> (accessed July 2010).

secret, the complaining party shall assume the burden of proof to prove that the trade secret meets the statutory requirements; the other party's use is similar or substantially similar to their own trade secret; and the other party has employed illegitimate means. Additionally, the evidence relied upon to prove that the complaining party's trade secret meets statutory requirements must include the following: carrier, specific contents, commercial value of the trade secret as well as any specific confidentiality measures adopted to protect the trade secret.[67] Difficulties arise when seeking to prove that a defendant has used illegitimate means to obtain the plaintiff's trade secret. This is rarely ever proven. For example, if the defendant employs a former employee of the plaintiff, they are likely to obtain information which is either the same, or substantially the same, as the plaintiff's trade secret. However, it is difficult for a plaintiff to prove that the former employee has made any disclosures by violating confidentiality obligations. Therefore, in cases lacking direct evidence, the people's court will consider indirect evidence and general rules of thumb to determine whether a plaintiff has met the burden of proof.

(3) *Interim measures in civil procedure*: The Civil Procedure Law of the People's Republic of China does not provide pre-litigation interim injunctions; however, it provides for advance enforcement. According to Article 97 of the Civil Procedure Law 1991,[68] the people's court may, at the request of a party (petitioner), order measures for cases which need enforcement in advance because of the need to act urgently. Furthermore, Article 98 provides that the people's court shall make sure the following conditions are met before making an enforcement order in advance: (1) the relationship between the rights and obligations of the parties is definite, and refusal of advance enforcement would seriously affect the life or business operation of the petitioners; and (2) the defending party is capable of fulfilling any obligations given by the advance enforcement. The people's court may order the petitioners to provide securities and if a petitioner

---

67 See Article 14 of the Interpretation of the Supreme People's Court on Some Issues Concerning the Application of Law in the Trial of Civil Cases Involving Unfair Competition (2006), translated from the original using <http://vip.chinalawinfo.com/newlaw2002/SLC/SLC.asp?Db=chl&Gid=83311> (accessed July 2010).

68 Adopted by the Fourth Session of the Seventh National People's Congress on 9 April, 1991, promulgated by Order No. 44 of the President of the People's Republic of China.

fails to do so, his petition may be rejected. If the petitioner loses the case, s/he is required to compensate the defending party for any loss caused by the advance enforcement. In relation to cases involving trade secrets, if a party applies for advance enforcement, it usually asks the people's court to order cessation of the infringement, a decision that will be supported by the people's court.

6.4.3. Criminal Liability for Infringing Trade Secrets

6.4.3.1. Encroachment upon trade secrets

Not all acts that infringe trade secrets can constitute a criminal offense under Chinese law. As mentioned in Chapter 5, there is considerable discussion amongst scholars and practioners as to whether infringement of trade secrets should fall under the criminal or civil law in China. Under Article 219(1) Criminal Law of the People's Republic of China 1979 (as amended),[69] the following acts, which cause significant loss to the rights owner of a trade secret, are considered to be an encroachment upon a trade secret (and therefore subject to the criminal law): (1) obtaining a trade secret via theft, luring by promising gain, intimidation, or other illegitimate means; (2) disclosing, using, or allowing others to use a trade secret which is obtained through using aforementioned means; (3) disclosing, using, or allowing others to use a legally obtained trade secret, in violation of an agreement with the rights owner or the right owner's request to keep the trade secret. In addition, Article 219(2) provides that a person who obtains, uses or discloses another's trade secret when he has knowledge or should have knowledge of the above acts, shall be deemed to have encroached upon the trade secret. Note that the four acts listed above are almost identical to the four acts provided in relation to the Anti-Unfair Competition Law, the only difference being that the presence of the above acts constitutes a criminal offence.

6.4.3.2. Subjective elements of encroachment upon trade secrets

(1) According to Article 219 of the Criminal Law, the following acts will constitute criminal offences: (1) obtaining a trade secret by illegitimate means; (2) disclosing, using or allowing others to use a trade secret by breaking an agreement with the rights owner; or

---

[69] Adopted by the Second Session of the Fifth National People's Congress on 1 July 1979 and amended by the Fifth Session of the Eighth National People's Congress on 14 March 1997.

(3) disregarding a request from the rights owner to keep the trade secret.[70] Criminal liability arises from negligent crimes only when stipulated by the law in pursuance with Article 15(2) of the Criminal Law. With regard to motive, no motive is required by Article 219(1); it is unnecessary to consider motive when determining whether or not an infringer's acts constitute an encroachment upon a trade secret.

(2) Encroachment upon a trade secret by a third party, as provided by Article 219(2), requires that the third party has knowledge or should have knowledge that the acts listed above are involved. This provision corresponds with the relevant provision of the Anti-Unfair Competition Law. Having knowledge falls under the ambit of an intentional crime, as according to Article 14(1) of the Criminal Law, an intentional crime is one that results from clear knowledge that one's acts will result in a socially dangerous outcome, with intention to commit or being indifferent, to that outcome. According to Article 15(1) of the Criminal Law, a negligent crime occurs when a party should foresee that his/her actions may cause socially dangerous consequences, but fails to do so because of carelessness or, having foreseen the consequences, readily assumes s/he can prevent them, with the result that these consequences occur. However, it

---

[70] Article 219: 'Any of the following categories of persons who infringe upon commercial secrets shall, if the offense causes another person who enjoys the rights of the commercial secrets to suffer heavy losses, be sentenced to fixed-term imprisonment of not more than three years or criminal detention, and concurrently or independently be sentenced to a fine. If the offense causes especially serious consequences, the offender shall be sentenced to fixed-term imprisonment of not less than three years and not more than seven years, and concurrently be sentenced to a fine: (1) acquiring commercial secrets of another person who enjoys the rights by stealing, lure, force or other improper means; (2) revealing, using or permitting other persons to use the commercial secrets of another person who enjoys the rights of the secrets by means specified in the preceding paragraph; or (3) revealing, using or permitting other persons to use another person's commercial secrets which are held by him contrary to his promise or to the demands by the person who enjoys the rights involving protection of the commercial secrets. Whoever acquires, uses or reveals another person's commercial secrets knowing well or who ought to know the acts listed in the preceding paragraph shall be punished as an act of infringement upon commercial secrets. "Commercial secrets" mentioned in this Article refers to the practical technical information and management information which is unknown by the public, can bring economic profits to the person who enjoys the rights, and the person who enjoys the rights has taken classified measures. "The person who enjoys the rights" mentioned in this Article refers to the owner of a commercial secret or user of a commercial secret who is permitted by the owner of the commercial secret.' See IPR Global Research Centre at: http://www.giprs.org/node/359, accessed July 2010.

should be noted that the Supreme People's Court and the Supreme People's Procuratorate are of the opinion that the threshold for knowledge must be to *clearly know*. This is pursuant to the interpretation of the meaning of 'clearly know' which is used in Article 241 of the Criminal Law.[71] Such an interpretation is inconsistent with the definition of negligent crimes under Criminal Law. However, regardless of the meaning of 'should have known', the subjective element required by Article 219(1) is stricter than that contained in Article 219(2).

6.4.3.3. Objective elements of encroachment upon trade secrets

An encroachment upon a trade secret is a consequential offence, meaning only an infringement of the trade secret that results in significant loss to the rights owner may constitute a criminal offence. What is the meaning of 'significant loss'? According to the interpretation of the Supreme People's Court and Supreme People's Procuratorate, a significant loss is defined as an amount of loss totaling over 500,000 Yuan. An act which infringes a trade secret, by using illegitimate means, that does not cause significant loss to the rights owner cannot constitute a criminal offense, thus rendering provisions contained in Article 219(1)(1) unnecessary. A special characteristic of Chinese law is that encroachments upon trade secrets are considered consequential offenses.

6.4.3.4. Punishment

According to Article 219 of the Criminal Law, whoever engages in acts which infringe upon a trade secret and bring significant loss to the rights owner shall be sentenced to not more than three years of fixed-term imprisonment or criminal detention. They may, additionally or exclusively be sentenced to a fine; or be sentenced to a fixed term of imprisonment lasting between three and seven years and a fine, if the infringement results in particularly serious consequences. If the amount of loss caused to the rights owner is no less than 2,500,000 Yuan, the infringing party shall be

---

[71] Compare to Article 9(2) of the Interpretation of the Supreme People's Court and the Supreme People's Procuratorate Concerning Some Issues on the Specific Application of Law for Handling Criminal Cases of Infringement upon Intellectual Property Rights (2004): 'In any of the following circumstances, the violator shall be determined to clearly know the fact as prescribed Article 214 of the Criminal Law: . . . (4) Other circumstances in which he/it knows or should have known the merchandise under the counterfeited registered trademark', translated from the original using <http://vip.chinalawinfo.com/newlaw2002/SLC/SLC.asp?Db=chl&Gid=56358> (accessed July 2010).

deemed to have caused particularly serious consequences, as prescribed in Article 219 of the Criminal Law.[72]

According to Article 220, a *unit* may also encroach upon a trade secret.[73] When a unit commits an encroachment upon a trade secret, it will be liable to pay a fine; those in charge, and other personnel with direct responsibility, shall be punished in accordance with the provisions respectively stated in the relevant Articles.

6.4.4. Administrative Liability for Infringing Trade Secrets

6.4.4.1. Administrative punishment

According to Article 25 of the Anti-Unfair Competition Law, where a party infringes a trade secret by violating the provisions of Article 10 of this Law, the relevant control and inspection authority shall order it to stop the infringement,[74] and in light of any relevant circumstances, impose a fine of between RMB 10,000 Yuan and RMB 200,000 Yuan. If the infringer refuses to comply and continues to infringe the trade secret, it shall be deemed to have committed a new violation and shall be given a more severe punishment.[75]

---

[72] Compare to Article 7(2) of the Interpretation of the Supreme People's Court and the Supreme People's Procuratorate Concerning Some Issues on the Specific Application of Law for Handling Criminal Cases of Infringement upon Intellectual Property Rights (2004): 'If the amount of loss caused to the trade secret [rights owner] is no less than 2,500,000 Yuan, it shall be deemed to have caused "particularly serious consequences", as prescribed in Article 219 of the Criminal Law, and shall be sentenced to a fixed-term imprisonment of between three and seven years for the crime of infringing the trade secret, and shall also be liable for payment of a pecuniary fine', translated from the original using http://vip.chinalawinfo.com/newlaw2002/SLC/SLC.asp?Db=chl&Gid=56358> (accessed July 2010).

[73] The term 'unit' is peculiar to Chinese law in that it encompasses state-owned facilities, such as a factory, workplace etc.

[74] The state organ responsible for enforcing the Anti-Unfair Competition Act is the State Administration for Industry and Commerce (SAIC). The SAIC devolves its powers to provincial and town-level Administrations for Industry and Commerce. It is these bodies that have the power to enforce specific fines against specific infringers (as opposed to making abstract administrative acts, such as issuing laws, regulations, decrees, order etc., that have no specific target). Specific Administrative Acts will include the granting of fines, seizure of assets etc. Specific administrative acts are open to judicial review through the courts.

[75] See Article 8 of the Provisions on Prohibiting Infringements of Trade Secrets (1998) by the State Administration for industry and commerce, translated from the original using http://vip.chinalawinfo.com/newlaw2002/SLC/SLC.asp?Db=chl&Gid=23598> (accessed July 2010).

6.4.4.2. Burden of proof of the rights owner

According to the regulation of the State Administration for Industry and Commerce, when a rights owner of a trade secret believes that any of its trade secrets have been infringed, the rights owner will need to provide evidence to prove the existence of the trade secret and infringement when applying to the industry and commerce administrative authorities for investigation and subsequent punishment of the infringer.[76] If the rights owner can prove that the information used by the respondents is identical with or similar to its trade secret, and that the respondent could have access to its trade secret, while the respondent is unable, or refuses, to provide evidence to the contrary, the industry and commerce administrative authorities shall determine that the respondent has infringed the trade secret on the basis of the relevant evidence.[77] The threshold for the rights owner's burden of proof in administrative procedures is lighter than that in civil procedures. The rights owner must only prove that the respondent could gain *access* to its trade secret.

6.4.4.3. Interim measures in administrative procedures

Upon receiving a right owner's request, and upon receiving a written promise that they will voluntarily bear liability for any consequences of taking mandatory measures, the State Administration for Industry and Commerce may order a respondent to stop selling products that employ a right owner's trade secret. This can occur when a respondent illegally discloses, uses or allows others to use a trade secret that results in irrecoverable loss to the rights owner.[78]

---

[76] See Article 5(1), ibid., translated from the original using <http://vip.chinalawinfo.com/newlaw2002/SLC/SLC.asp?Db=chl&Gid=23598> (accessed July 2010).

[77] See Article 5(3) of the Provisions on Prohibiting Infringements of Trade Secrets (1998) by the State Administration for industry and commerce, translated from the original using <http://vip.chinalawinfo.com/newlaw2002/SLC/SLC.asp?Db=chl&Gid=23598> (accessed July 2010).

[78] See Article 6 of the Provisions on Prohibiting Infringements of Trade Secrets (1998) by the State Administration for industry and commerce, translated from the original using <http://vip.chinalawinfo.com/newlaw2002/SLC/SLC.asp?Db=chl&Gid=23598> (accessed July 2010).

6.5. LEGISLATIVE TRENDS FOR PROTECTING TRADE SECRETS

On the whole, the legislative protection of trade secrets in China complies with the requirements of the TRIPS Agreement and meets the standards of protection of trade secrets present in developed countries. The Anti-Unfair Competition Law is undergoing revision at present, and the provisions regarding protection of trade secrets will be improved further. The government issued new draft regulations to revise the current Anti-Unfair Competition Law in May 2010. Public consultation on the draft regulations closed in June 2010. The draft regulations are intended to supplement Chapter 5 of the Chinese Anti Monopoly Law.[79] For example, The revised draft of the Anti-Unfair Competition Law provides that an employee that discloses, uses or allows others to use the trade secret of a rights owner by breaking an agreement with the rights owner, or disregarding the rights owner's requirement to keep the trade secret, shall constitute infringement. In terms of the rights owner's burden of proof, if the rights owner can prove that the information used by others is identical to, or similar to, its trade secret and that others could gain access to the trade secret, unless the defending party can provide evidence to the contrary, infringement shall be established. In order to strengthen the administrative liability of an operator for infringing trade secrets, the draft provides that illegal products shall be confiscated and a fine no greater than 1,000,000 Yuan shall be imposed. If any illegal gains are made, the gains shall also be confiscated. In serious cases, business licenses can be revoked. In addition, the draft provides that government departments must not disclose confidential test data or other data submitted by the rights owner, except if disclosing the data protects the public interest. They may also adopt other confidential measures to protect the data from illegitimate commercial use. Where a department violates such a provision, it shall be ordered by the authority at the next higher level to correct this violation. The person who is directly responsible for the matter shall be subject to administrative sanctions; or if the actions constitute a crime, criminal liability shall be imposed according to the law.

The infringement of trade secrets are regarded with seriousness in China, and due to this fact, both scholars and practitioners are lobbying for the level of protection of trade secrets under criminal law to be strengthened. To do so, criminal sanctions must be enhanced, the required amount of losses reduced, and boundaries between crime and non-crime clarified.

---

[79] See Chapters 11 and 12.

Some suggest establishing a new crime for negligent encroachment of trade secrets. However, the practicalities involved with revising the relevant provisions of the Criminal Law and with large-scale implementation of criminal sanctions are inconsistent with the purpose of legislation that aims at protecting trade secrets. Infringing trade secrets is usually considered a behavioral offense, as opposed to a consequential one, in developed countries. However, there are not many cases that involve affixing criminal liability for infringing trade secrets in the developed world.

In the opinion of the author, if the Supreme People's Court and the Supreme People's Procuratorate could put forward a judicial interpretation to provide further guidance on the standard of criminal punishment and the determination of crimes involving the infringing of trade secrets, current provisions regarding criminal sanctions imposed for the infringement of trade secrets will provide sufficient regulation in this area.

Scholars and practitioners also suggest establishing a special law for the protection of trade secrets; however, no such official legislative plan exists at present. Only a few countries have a specific law that offers protection over trade secrets. As China is a civil law system, the protection offered by the Anti-Unfair Competition Law, accompanied by supplemental protection provided by other substantive laws (e.g. the Criminal Law) and adjective laws, is feasible. Additional protection is supplied by judicial interpretation offered by the Supreme People's Court and the Supreme People's Procuratorate. Therefore, there is little need to establish a further specific Law of Protecting Trade Secrets.

7. Protection of intellectual property in Hong Kong

Michael Pendleton[1]

7.1. INTRODUCTION

Hong Kong is a Special Administrative Region (SAR) of the People's Republic of China. Much of China's entire legal system was created in the early 1980s, the Trademark Law 1982 for example. However, Hong Kong has as long a history and immersion in intellectual property as many countries of Western Europe or the United States. This, of course, is due to the influence of the United Kingdom during the period in which it colonized Hong Kong. As a result, Hong Kong's intellectual property laws are rich and diverse. For at least a century, these laws have also been heavily biased in favour of the rights holder, the colonial power having taken the view that this is essential to enticing foreign capital. Indeed Hong Kong, which is a member of the World Trade Organization (WTO), was the first member of the WTO to seek TRIPS compliance for its intellectual property laws. Hong Kong is a member of the WTO independently of China and in its own right. In fact, it is the only non-sovereign member state of the WTO.

In addition to the complexity of Hong Kong's intellectual property law, the judge-made law, that is the common law, is equally rich and diverse. For a long time, and even to an extent today, members of the Hong Kong judiciary were appointed from the ranks of experienced barristers (advocates) from foreign jurisdictions such as England, Australia, New Zealand and other Commonwealth countries. Today, large numbers of its judges are selected from the best and most experienced counsel appearing before the Hong Kong courts, many of whom were locally educated (the

[1] Michael Pendleton, Professor of Law at the Chinese University of Hong Kong. For a full treatment of this area see Michael Pendleton, Jared Margolis and Alice Lee, *Intellectual Property Rights – Hong Kong and People's Republic of China*, Lexis Nexis Butterworths (2009). The editor is grateful for the help of Miss Katie Richards (LLB student with French, Cardiff Law School), Cardiff University with this chapter.

University of Hong Kong was established in the 19th century, though the law school only began in the 1970s). This mix of judges has resulted in a very comparative approach to intellectual property law and one that is conducted in the English language.

Hong Kong has a strong regime to enforce and protect intellectual property. Civil remedies include the *ex parte* Anton Piller order, Mareva and interlocutory injunctions. For over half a century, the criminal enforcement regime has been a pioneer, instigating criminal enforcement of copyright from the 1960s. In the recent case *Chan Nai Ming v Hong Kong SAR*, a man was jailed for uploading a genuine VCD to a P2P server. He was held to have distributed an infringing copy, ie the copy of the genuine VCD he made on his PC to facilitate uploading.[2]

7.2. TRADE MARKS

7.2.1. Common law unregistered trade marks – the action for passing off

The common law tort of passing off is the original source from which the registered trade mark system drew its inspiration, its criteria of protection and even its scheme of organisation.

The law of passing off involves establishing three major elements:

(1) the plaintiff's reputation or goodwill via a badge of consumer recognition;
(2) a misrepresentation by the defendant involving this badge of recognition; and
(3) damage, or likelihood of damage, to the plaintiff's goodwill caused by the misrepresentation.

These three elements of the action are not watertight categories. On the contrary, each must be considered in relation to the others. What is required to satisfy each of these elements will now be discussed.

7.2.1.1. Plaintiff's reputation or goodwill

Reputation and goodwill (referred to as 'reputation') is itself a rather amorphous concept. The plaintiff must prove a sufficient reputation in the minds of the public as a logically necessary prerequisite to establishing the necessary degree of deception or confusion.

---

2 *HKSAR v Chan Nai Ming* [2007] 1 HKLRD 95.

The plaintiff 's badge of recognition with the relevant public The plaintiff's reputation or goodwill may be known to the public via various badges of recognition.

Names and logos The badge of recognition might be either an English or a Chinese name or a name in any or no language.[3]

Utilitarian get-up Some authorities have expressed the view that get-up which is purely functional or utilitarian may be objectionable as a badge of recognition of the plaintiff's reputation. However, in *Reckitt & Colman Products v Borden Inc*,[4] the House of Lords held that a plastic replica of a lemon containing lemon juice could serve as a badge of recognition of the plaintiff's reputation.

Non-utilitarian get-up In *Kjeldsen & Co v Hong Kong Peggy Foods*,[5] the badge of recognition included the get-up of the goods. Liu J found the plaintiff's 'get-up' of the butter cookies had been consistent throughout some ten years and went on to say that there was no magic in the word get-up; they were merely an available badge of recognition through which reputation might or might not be proved to exist in the minds of the relevant public.

Reputation as a purchaser rather than as a retailer It is the plaintiff's connection with the goods and services that is in issue in relation to the question of reputation. This connection may take the form of various indications of a manufacturer's, wholesaler's, retailer's, selector's or distributor's reputation.

Descriptive trade names and acquisition of secondary meaning One of the leading Hong Kong cases in this area is *Commercial Trade Mark Services SA v Liscaroll Co Ltd t/a Commercial Investigation Services & Ors*,[6] where the plaintiff was found to have acquired a protectable badge or recognition in the name Commercial Trademark Services.

Personal names Personal, family or geographical names are a special category of descriptive names and the general rule of establishing secondary meaning applies subject to the prima facie right of an individual to trade

---

3 HCA No 165 of 1981.
4 [1990] 1 WLR 491, [1990] 1 All ER 873, [1990] UKHL 12, [1990] RPC 341.
5 [1982] 11 EIPR D250.
6 [1983] 2 HKC 474.

under his own name, provided it is sufficiently distinguished from that of a well-known trader of the same name.

Character merchandising, personality rights and sponsorship The ambit of character merchandising covers:

(1) human, non-fictitious persons – included here are sports celebrities, actors, musicians, singers, entertainers, and artists – indeed, potentially any person with a public reputation;
(2) human, fictitious characters – this category typically concerns the characters portrayed in a motion picture or television performance; and
(3) non-human, fictitious characters – this category includes cartoon characters.

The 1972 Hong Kong High Court decision in *Shaw Brothers v Golden Harvest*[7] was one of the first instances of judicial recognition of rights in a fictional character in Commonwealth jurisprudence. In response to the defendant's argument that there is no property right in a fictional character under English law, Huggins J held that such absence of authority was not a decisive factor. Accordingly, he held that the plaintiffs had goodwill worthy of protection by the court.

Transnational reputation and goodwill This is concerned with those cases where a plaintiff's reputation may be well established overseas, even worldwide, yet its reputation in Hong Kong is less evident or non-existent. The related question of local defendants committing or assisting in passing off in foreign jurisdictions is considered below. The major question is in what circumstances the Hong Kong courts will lend such a foreign trader a remedy in passing off. The courts have generally laid down the approach that provided there is goodwill in Hong Kong, there will be a remedy even if there is no trading presence.

7.2.1.2. Defendant's representation – the test of deception or confusion

The defendant's state of mind In general, a defendant who is unaware that his conduct is causing deception is liable even though his innocence may be relevant when the measure of damages is assessed. However, a

---

[7] *Shaw Brothers (Hong Kong) Ltd (No 2) v Golden Harvest (HK) Ltd* [1972] HKLR 147, 28 April 1972 FC.

defendant who deliberately seeks to imitate, copy or pass his goods or services off as those of the plaintiff's is not liable unless and until he succeeds in causing the requisite degree of confusion. Even so, the condition precedent is that the plaintiff has a sufficient reputation and real damage occurs or is likely to occur.

Explicit or implicit disclaimers of connection with the plaintiff The most difficult cases in passing off occur where there is no arguable misrepresentation yet there is a blatant misappropriation. For example, an unauthorised or counterfeit Rolex watch might bear a prominent notice to the effect that this is a counterfeit Rolex watch, and this notice is displayed at the point of sale and on the watch in large English letters and Chinese characters. It is difficult to argue misrepresentation in this context even though it is naked misappropriation. This is the paradigm example of why passing off is hamstrung by its reliance on the test of misrepresentation. To seek to argue that the notice might be removable is to focus on misrepresentation post purchase and by the members of the public who observe the purchaser of the fake. This is a substantial departure from the existing passing off doctrine but no doubt might be employed by a court eager to prevent this type of misappropriation.

Proof of likely deception, or assisting in the deception of a foreign populace The law of Hong Kong sets out a general principle that acts done in a foreign country cannot come before its courts if they are not unlawful in the country in which they took place.

7.2.1.3. Damage or likelihood of damage

Difficulties arise where the defendant's goods or services are not of the same description as the plaintiff's (to borrow from the jargon of registered trade mark law). It is submitted that the preferable test in such cases is whether the plaintiff is likely to suffer real damage.

Parallel imports and passing off 'Parallel import' means the import into Hong Kong of a brand of goods for resale (i.e. under a badge of recognition and other intellectual property rights) which has been manufactured elsewhere, by or with the authority of the owner of the relevant intellectual property rights in that place, with a view to competing with the authorised Hong Kong distributor of the same brand of goods. In order for parallel imports to be actionable in passing off, it is necessary to show some misrepresentation rather than a mere unauthorised import. The availability of the intellectual property causes of action in the parallel import context (in this case passing off) itself forms the basis of whether or not there is power to authorise the import. The misrepresentation most frequently complained of in the area of parallel imports and passing off is that the defendant is representing the sale of his goods as having been authorised by the plaintiff when that is not the case.

Remedies The plaintiff may claim injunction and/or damages or an account of profits. Damages may reflect the nature of the damage to property in terms of loss of profits, dilution in value of reputation or opportunity to charge a licence fee. Exemplary damages may also be available.

7.2.2. Registered Trade Marks

Historical background Hong Kong has a long history of trade mark protection. A registered trade mark scheme was first introduced in Hong Kong in 1873 to alleviate the time and expense trade mark owners in Hong Kong might have to spend in obtaining proof of their reputation and exclusive right in their places of origin. It was only two years later that the United Kingdom adopted its own trade mark legislation, the Trade Marks Registration Act 1875. The current Trade Marks Ordinance (Cap 559) ('TMO'), which came into force on 4 April 2003, largely retains the spirit of its predecessors. The Ordinance follows the United Kingdom Trade Marks Act 1994 closely, with necessary modifications to accommodate the unique situation in Hong Kong. Hence, relevant United Kingdom cases still provide guidance on the interpretation of Hong Kong trade mark laws, even though they are only of persuasive authority to the Hong Kong courts. Judgments from the ECJ are also relevant, in particular those which are made in relation to the EC Directive which is the basis of the new trade mark terminology in the United Kingdom.

7.2.2.1. Definition of trade marks

What is a mark? There are essentially three requirements for a mark: (1) a sign, (2) visual perceptibility, and (3) graphic representation. There is no further definition of a sign, but a non-exhaustive list of examples of 'sign' is provided in the second part of the definition. 'Visual perceptibility' simply means that a mark must be visible, thereby excluding intangible indicia such as smells and sounds, whereas 'graphic representation' refers to the requirement that a mark be capable of specific and accurate description.

In short, the purpose of a trade mark is to indicate the origin of goods. Signs which cannot be represented graphically must be rejected under section 3(1) of the TMO. This requirement is, however, not difficult to fulfil as there are many ways in which a mark can be represented graphically.

Sound, smell and colour marks Under the broadened definition of trade mark in the TMO, sound marks and smell marks may now be registered. Note that section 3(2) also refers to colours, thus there is the possibility of a single colour or a combination of colours being registered as a trade mark, though this will require evidence of capability to distinguish.

A sound mark may be graphically represented in conventional musical notation or onomatopoeic words. An example from the United States is the registration of a mark that consists of the famous Tarzan yell for toy action figures. Also, the 'famous Tarzan yodel' has been registered in Hong Kong, where the mark is described as 'a yell consisting of a series of approximately ten seconds, alternating between the chest and falsetto registers of the voice', followed by details of the ten different sounds.

Shape marks A shape mark is registrable provided that it falls within the definition of a mark under section 3(1) and (2) of the TMO and that there are no grounds of objection under section 11 (Absolute Grounds) or section 12 (Relative Grounds). Indeed, shapes have been registrable under the old TMO, subject to the restrictions in section 12(3), which provides that a sign is not registrable if it consists exclusively of:

(a) the shape that results from the nature of the goods themselves;
(b) the shape of goods that is necessary to obtain a technical result; or
(c) the shape that gives substantial value to goods.

7.2.2.2. Registrability of trade marks

Absolute grounds for refusal under the TMO Under the TMO, a mark is registrable unless it falls foul of the Absolute Grounds or Relative Grounds for refusal of registration. A presumption is created that a trade mark is registrable, unless it can be shown to be contrary to one of the grounds of objection. This relieves the applicant of the onus of establishing that his trade mark qualifies for registration.

The 'Absolute Grounds' for refusal of registration are set out in section 11 of the TMO. Generally speaking, they are targeted at marks which are not distinctive in some way. The word 'Absolute' connotes that these grounds are not dependent on a prior registered trade mark or earlier right.

In Hong Kong, the *BABYDRY* case[8] was considered in *MGA Entertainment Inc v Yokon International Ltd & Ors*,[9] where the validity

---

8 *Procter & Gamble v OHIM* (BABYDRY case: C-383/99 P) [2001] ETMR 829.
9 HCA No 4380 of 2003.

of the plaintiff's mark 'BRATZ', registered in respect of dolls and doll accessories, was challenged. It was contended on behalf of the defendants that 'BRATZ' was 'a play on the word "BRATS" which, in its ordinary English meaning, meant "a child" and especially "an ill-behaved child"'. Such contention did not find favour with Yam J, who emphasised that the objection under section 11(1)(c) was that the mark was descriptive of *the goods* in respect of which it was registered. Even if 'BRATZ' could be said to be descriptive of children or girls, it was clearly not descriptive of dolls or doll accessories.

Under section 11(2), an objection under section 11(1)(b), (c) and/or (d) can be overcome if it can be shown that, before the date of application for registration, the trade mark has in fact acquired a distinctive character as a result of its particular use (section 11(2)). Thus, subsection (2) has come to be regarded as a proviso to subsection (1).

Under section 11(4)(b), the phrase 'likely to deceive the public' targets those marks which raise an expectation that cannot be fulfilled, such as the classic example of 'Orwoola' for clothes which do not contain wool. Widely phrased as it is, this limb can also cover deception arising from similarity between marks, which is specifically dealt with elsewhere, viz, the 'Relative Grounds' set out in section 12 of the current TMO and its predecessor, section 20 of the old TMO.

Section 11(5) and (6), other 'Absolute Grounds', include section 11(5)(a) which forbids the registration of a mark the use of which is prohibited in Hong Kong under or by virtue of any law; section 11(5)(b) which prohibits an application for registration that is made in bad faith; and section 11(6) which prohibits marks comprising national or regional flags or emblems.

Relative grounds for refusal under the TMO Section 12 of the TMO sets out the 'Relative Grounds' on which a trade mark could be refused registration. These are very similar to, but more extensive than, the provisions in section 20 of the old TMO.

Basically, section 12 prohibits registration in the following situations:

- Subsection (1): Identical marks for identical goods or services. Confusion is presumed.
- Subsection (2): Identical marks for similar goods or services. Confusion must be proved.
- Subsection (3): Similar marks for identical or similar goods or services. Again, confusion is required.
- Subsection (4): Identical or similar marks for goods or services which are not identical or similar, provided that the earlier mark is a well-known trade mark and that the use of the proposed mark

> without due cause would take unfair advantage of, or be detrimental to, the distinctive character or repute of the earlier trade mark.

Note also subsections (5) and (6). The former refers to marks which are prohibited under the law of passing off, copyright or registered designs,[10] whereas the latter provides that the grounds mentioned in subsections (4) and (5) can only be raised in opposition proceedings.[11]

Section 12(4) – protection of well-known trade marks Section 12(4) is revolutionary in that it does not require the applicant's and the opponent's goods or services to be identical or similar. The only prerequisites are that the earlier trade mark[12] must be one 'entitled to protection under the Paris Convention as a well-known trade mark'[13] and that the use of the proposed mark 'would take unfair advantage of, or be detrimental to, the distinctive character or repute of the earlier trade mark'. The omission of any reference to any likelihood of confusion is deliberate as it was felt necessary to extend the protection for well-known marks to goods and services unrelated or dissimilar to those for which such marks have been used. Section 12(4) actually reflects the requirements under Article 16(3) of the TRIPS Agreement:

> Article 6*bis* of the Paris Convention (1967) shall apply, mutatis mutandis,to goods or services which are not similar to those in respect of which a trademark is registered, provided that use of that trade mark in relation to those goods or

---

[10] The law of passing off has always co-existed with the statutory protection for registered trade marks; see old TMO, s 36. See also old TMO, s 12(1), which prohibits, inter alia, the registration of a mark that would be 'disentitled to protection in a court of justice', such expression having been held to refer to protection which would be given by a passing off action (*'Excello' Trade Mark* [1972] HKDCLR 67); see also *Re Daiwa Associate (HK) Ltd* [2003] 3 HKC 283. As to the current s 12(5), see *Re Ping An Securities Ltd* [2006] 4 HKC 355.

[11] For opposition proceedings, see TMO, s 44.

[12] As seen in the body text, an 'earlier trade mark' can be either a registered trade mark with an earlier date of application or a trade mark that is entitled to protection under the Paris Convention as a well-known trade mark: TMO, s 5(1).

[13] That means a trade mark which is well-known in Hong Kong and which is the trade mark of a person who (a) is a national of, or is domiciled or ordinarily resident in, a Paris Convention country or WTO member; (b) has a right of abode in Hong Kong; or (c) has a real and effective industrial or commercial establishment in a Paris Convention country, a WTO member or Hong Kong, whether or not that person carries on business in Hong Kong or owns any goodwill in a business in Hong Kong: TMO, s 4(1). Section 4(2) also refers to Sch 2, see below.

services would indicate a connection between those goods or services and the owner of the registered trademark and provided that the interests of the owner of the registered trademark are likely to be damaged by such use.

Section 12(4) differs from its United Kingdom counterpart, section 5(3) of the Trade Marks Act 1994, in that the latter refers solely to a trade mark that has a reputation in the United Kingdom.

Honest concurrent use and Registrar's discretion Under the old TMO, even if the marks and goods in question are found to be identical or similar, registration may still be allowed provided 'honest and concurrent use' can be established under section 22. The United Kingdom equivalent to this provision is found in section 12(2) of the 1938 Act.

Term and scope of registration Under the old TMO, a trade mark shall be registered for an initial period of seven years and thereafter for 14 years upon renewal (sections 17(2) and 45). Now, under section 49 of the TMO, the initial term shall be ten years beginning on the date of registration and may be renewed in accordance with section 50 for further periods of ten years.

Collective and certification trade marks The concept of collective trade marks is introduced for the first time by section 61 of the TMO.

Defensive and well-known trade marks Unlike the 1994 Act, the TMO retains the registration for defensive trade marks, for which the requirements of section 60(1) must be satisfied, namely, that the mark must have been registered and 'used so much in relation to all or any of the goods or services for which it is registered that it has become exceptionally well-known in Hong Kong and, as a result, its use in relation to other goods or services would be likely to detract from its distinctive character in relation to the goods or services for which it has been so used.'

Such a mark may be registered as a defensive trade mark in respect of any or all of those *other* goods or services, even if the owner of the mark does not use or intend to use the mark in relation to such goods or services.

7.2.2.3. Ownership and use of registered trade marks

All previous legal restrictions have been removed and the only requirement is that an assignment of, or an assent relating to, a registered trade mark must be in writing and signed by or on behalf of the assignor or his personal representative (section 27(4) of the TMO).

7.2.2.4. Infringement of registered trade marks

> 18. Infringement of registered trade mark
> (1) A person infringes a registered trade mark if he uses in the course of trade or business a sign which is identical to the trade mark in relation to goods or services which are identical to those for which it is registered.
> (2) A person infringes a registered trade mark if –
> (a) he uses in the course of trade or business a sign which is identical to the trade mark in relation to goods or services which are similar to those for which it is registered; and
> (b) the use of the sign in relation to those goods or services is likely to cause confusion on the part of the public.
> (3) A person infringes a registered trade mark if –
> (a) he uses in the course of trade or business a sign which is similar to the trade mark in relation to goods or services which are identical or similar to those for which it is registered; and
> (b) the use of the sign in relation to those goods or services is likely to cause confusion on the part of the public.
> (4) A person infringes a registered trade mark if –
> (a) he uses in the course of trade or business a sign which is identical or similar to the trade mark in relation to goods or services which are not identical or similar to those for which it is registered;
> (b) the trade mark is entitled to protection under the Paris Convention as a well-known trade mark; and
> (c) the use of the sign, being without due cause, takes unfair advantage of, or is detrimental to, the distinctive character or repute of the trade mark.

Furthermore, section 18(5) expressly provides that a person uses a sign if he:

(a) applies it to goods or their packaging;
(b) offers or exposes goods for sale under the sign;
(c) puts goods on the market under the sign;
(d) stocks goods under the sign for the purpose of offering or exposing them for sale or of putting them on the market;
(e) offers or supplies services under the sign;
(f) imports or exports goods under the sign; or
(g) uses the sign on business papers or in advertising.

Comparative advertising Section 21 of the TMO clarifies the previously ambiguous legal position and makes it possible for a trader to use a competitor's trade marks for the purpose of identifying the latter's goods or services provided that such use is 'in accordance with honest practices in industrial or commercial matters'. Although 'use' is not further defined, the explicit heading 'Use in advertising etc' confirms that comparative advertising is within the ambit of the section.

Exceptions to infringement Section 19(2) of the TMO provides that a registered trade mark is not infringed by the use of another registered trade mark in relation to goods or services for which the latter is registered. This corresponds to section 11(1) of the 1994 Act, which is inserted to reinforce the protection offered by the honest concurrent use provisions.

Parallel imports and exhaustion of rights While subsection (1) permits the use of registered trade marks in relation to goods which have been put on the market anywhere in the world by or with the consent of the owners, thereby incorporating the notion of international exhaustion, subsection (2) provides an exception whereby a trade mark owner can prevent parallel imports when the condition of those parallel-imported goods has been changed or impaired after they have been put on the market, and when the reputation or distinctiveness of the mark in question will be adversely affected through the circulation of such goods in Hong Kong. This is to protect the reputation of established trade marks in Hong Kong as well as to safeguard consumers against deception.

Groundless threats Groundless threats of infringement proceedings, whether made to a trader or his customers, can be pernicious to the business concerned. Hence, Article 8(2) of the TRIPS Agreement recognises the need for appropriate measures to safeguard against the abuse of intellectual property rights by right holders[14] and section 26 of the TMO provides a new cause of action against those who make groundless threats of trade mark infringement proceedings.

7.2.2.5. Criminal sanctions

In addition to infringement proceedings under the Trade Marks Ordinance, criminal sanctions are also available against forgery of trade marks.

7.2.2.6. Revocation and declaration of invalidity

Section 52(2) of the TMO sets out the grounds upon which the registration of a trade mark may be revoked:

(a) that the trade mark has not been genuinely used in Hong Kong by the owner or with his consent, in relation to the goods or services for which it is registered, for a continuous period of at least 3 years, and there are no

---

[14] 'Appropriate measures, provided that they are consistent with the provisions of this Agreement, may be needed to prevent the abuse of intellectual property rights by right holders or the resort to practices which unreasonably restrain trade or adversely affect the international transfer of technology.'

valid reasons for non-use (such as import restrictions on, or other governmental requirements for, goods or services protected by the trade mark);

(b) that the trade mark consists of a sign that, in consequence of the acts or the inactivity of the owner –

   (i) has become the common name in the trade for goods or services for which the trade mark is registered; or
   (ii) has become generally accepted within the trade as the sign that describes goods or services for which the trade mark is registered;

(c) that in consequence of the use made of it by the owner or with his consent, in relation to the goods or services for which it is registered, the trade mark is liable to mislead the public, particularly as to the nature, quality or geographical origin of those goods or services; or

(d) that there has been a contravention of or a failure to observe any condition entered in the register in relation to its registration.

The most important ground is the first one, namely, that the registered mark has not been genuinely used in Hong Kong, in relation to the goods or services for which it is registered, for a continuous period of at least three years.

7.3. COPYRIGHT

The Copyright Ordinance[15] defines the nine categories of copyright works individually in their respective sections:

- Literary works (Section 4)
- Dramatic works (Section 4)
- Musical works (Section 4)
- Artistic works (Section 5)
- Sound recordings (Section 6)
- Films (Section 7)
- Broadcasts (Section 8)
- Cable programmes (Section 9)
- Published editions (Section 10)

Furthermore, moral rights are introduced for the first time in Hong Kong and dealt with in Division IV of Part II of the Ordinance:

---

15 Cap 528.

- Right to be identified as author or director (Sections 89 to 91)
- Right to object to derogatory treatment of work (Sections 92 to 95)
- False attribution of work (Section 96)

Finally, artists' performances, first introduced in Hong Kong in 1996 by virtue of the Intellectual Property (World Trade Organization Amendments) Ordinance,[16] are now protected under Part III of the Copyright Ordinance.

In addition to the Copyright Ordinance, there is also a short Ordinance specifically for the protection of layout-designs (typographies) designed for incorporation into an integrated circuit which can be incorporated into any type of material, whether semi-conducting material or not.

7.3.1. Subsistence of Copyright

Copyright may protect a diverse array of things, provided that certain conditions are met. Such protected works might include a work of great literature, a translation, a drawing, a football coupon, a screenplay, the words of a song, the music of a symphony, a sculpture, a video recording, a building, a photograph, a film, a sound recording, a broadcast or even the design for the exhaust pipe of a car. The relevant conditions can be discussed under the three following headings.

Original work of one of the specified categories Essentially, the Copyright Ordinance requires three related criteria to be satisfied before something can qualify for copyright protection: first, the subject matter must be a 'work'; secondly, it must fall within one of the nine categories of work specified in section 2(1); and thirdly, if the subject matter is a literary, dramatic, musical or artistic work, it must satisfy the additional requirement of being original.

Original in a copyright sense A literary work must be original in the sense that it originated in the author independently or at least this must be substantially so.

Thus, two identical works may both be original, provided they were independently created. Such original, identical works may well be rare, but given the current explosion of knowledge and the move towards an information technology-based society, it may well be that this phenomenon will become more commonplace.

---

16 Ord No 11 of 1996.

Artistic works Provided that a work may be described as falling within the category of a painting,[17] drawing,[18] sculpture,[19] engraving[20] or photograph,[21] there is no artistic element required. A simple line sketch of a hand putting a cross on a ballot paper,[22] a design for a confectionary tin[23] and three concentric rings as part of the design for a technical device[24] have all been held to be protected by artistic copyright. It seems clear that the courts have been particularly anxious not to become involved in any dispute as to questions relating to what constitutes art.

Fixation A fundamental point about copyright law in Hong Kong and other jurisdictions which adhere to the Berne Convention is that copyright

---

17 In *Merchandising Corp of America v Harpbond* [1983] FSR 32 (CA), it was said that 'painting', not being defined in the statute, was a word in the ordinary usage of the English language. It was a question of fact in any particular case whether what was being considered was or was not a painting. On the facts of the case, facial make-up was not a painting.

18 For example, in *Easey Garment Factory Ltd & Anor v Hoo Wah Garment Factory*, HCA No 6418 of 1981, the plaintiff alleged copyright, inter alia, in the design of its jeans, the name 'Commando' and a crossed swords device on an application for an interlocutory injunction. The court held artistic copyright to be unlikely in the word 'Commando' in black edging, but arguable in the crossed swords device and the design of the jeans. The decision was reversed on appeal as damages would be adequate. In *Swatch AG v Captoon Industries Ltd* [1995] 2 HKC 444, another interlocutory injunction application, the Court of Appeal confirmed that the drawings of the plaintiff's 'Scuba 200' series were original and entitled to copyright protection.

19 See, for instance, *Novex Electronics Co Ltd v Wave-Sonic Electronics Ltd* [1980] HKC 708, where the plaintiff alleged breach of copyright in a clock/radio manufactured by the defendant under a contract with it. An imitation of the work, sold by a third party, appeared in Italy. The plaintiff alleged that the defendant had begun to manufacture a clock/radio substantially similar to the plaintiff's, and one clock/radio was provided by the plaintiff's agent, allegedly as a sample. A mock-up clock/radio was held to be a 'sculpture' and thus an artistic work under s 3(1)(a) of the Copyright Act 1956. For a more restrictive view, see *Metix v Maughan* [1997] FSR 718.

20 In *Hi Tech Autoparts Ltd v Towergate Two Ltd* [2002] FSR 15 (p 254), an engraved metal plate which was used to produce rubber mats for use in cars was held to be an 'engraving' within the meaning of the 1988 Act. See also *Wham-O Manufacturing Co v Lincoln Industries Ltd* [1985] RPC 127 (CA (NZ)) and *Greenfield Products Pty Ltd v Rover-Scott Bonnar Ltd* (1990) 17 IPR 417 (Fed Ct (Aust)), both cited in the *Hi Tech* case.

21 Even a snapshot taken 'surreptitiously from a discreet distance' is entitled to copyright protection; see *Oriental Press Group Ltd v Apple Daily Ltd* [1997] 2 HKC 515 (CA); [1998] 4 HKC 131 (CFA).

22 *Kenrick v Lawrence* (1890) 25 QBD 99.

23 *Tavener Rutledge Ltd v Specters Ltd* [1959] RPC 355.

24 *Solar Thomson Engineering Co Ltd & Anor v Barton* [1977] RPC 537.

subsists in a work as soon as the work is created, without needing to satisfy any formalities; for example no registration is required or is even possible. The only requirement is that, in the case of a literary, dramatic or musical work, there must be some form of recording. This is stipulated in section 4(2) of the Copyright Ordinance: 'Copyright does not subsist in a literary, dramatic or musical work unless and until it is recorded, in writing or otherwise.'

The recording, also called fixation, may be done by the author or by someone else, and it is immaterial whether it is with or without the author's permission.[25]

No qualifying factors Division X of Part II of the current Copyright Ordinance has adopted an 'open qualification system'[26] under which all entities, wherever domiciled, resident or incorporated, can own Hong Kong copyright unless the Chief Executive expressly denies protection to their jurisdiction of origin on the basis that such jurisdiction does not adequately protect Hong Kong copyright works.

7.3.2. Duration of Copyright

Sections 17 to 21 of the Copyright Ordinance govern the duration of copyright works. For literary, dramatic, musical and artistic works, the general provisions are in section 17(1) to (5), which make the duration of copyright dependent upon whether the identity of the author is known: if so, the duration of copyright is the life of the author plus 50 years;[27] if not, the duration is 50 years from the end of the year in which the work was first made, or if it is made available to the public during that period, 50 years from the year in which it is first so made available.[28] Computer-generated works and works of joint authorship are covered in section 17(6) and (7), whereas government copyright is expressly excluded from these general provisions[29] and specifically dealt with in sections 182 to 184 of the Copyright Ordinance.

---

25 Copyright Ordinance, s 4(3).

26 M Pendleton, 'The Danger of Protecting Too Much: A Comparative Analysis of Aspects of Intellectual Property in Hong Kong, Britain and the United States' [2000] EIPR 69 at p 71.

27 Section 17(2). Note that the duration is different in the UK (s 12(2) of the 1988 Act).

28 Section 17(3). See also s 17(5) for the meaning of 'making available to the public'.

29 Section 17(8).

The duration of copyright in other works, except published editions, is also 50 years from certain specified events. A sound recording enjoys copyright protection for 50 years from the year in which it is made or released, whichever is the longer.[30] A film normally[31] enjoys copyright for 50 years from the year in which the last of the following designated persons dies:

(1) the principal director;
(2) the author of the screenplay;
(3) the author of the dialogue; or
(4) the composer of music specially created for and used in the film.[32]

If the identity of such persons is unknown, then copyright will last for 50 years from the end of the year in which the film is made, or if it is made available to the public during that period, 50 years from the year when it is so made available.[33] Broadcasts and cable programmes are protected for 50 years from the year in which the broadcast was made or the programme was included in a cable programme service.[34]

Finally, for published editions, the copyright in the typographical arrangements lasts for 25 years from the first year of publication.[35]

7.3.3. Copyright and Industrial Designs

Before the Registered Designs Ordinance (Cap 522) came into force on 27 June 1997, designs which were registered in the United Kingdom under the Registered Designs Act 1949 were protected in Hong Kong pursuant to the now repealed United Kingdom Designs (Protection) Ordinance (Cap 44). Artistic works made before 1 June 1957 which were capable of registration under the 1949 Act and were intended at the time of creation to be multiplied by an industrial process would be excluded from the Copyright Act 1956.[36] Additionally, section 10 meant that any design which could not be registered under the 1949 Act would also be beyond the protection offered by the 1956 Act. However, registrable designs not used or intended

---

[30] Provided that the sound recording is released within 50 years of its making; see s 18(2).

[31] That is, a film with a known director, author or composer; see s 19(2) and (3). Note that the duration in the UK is different (s 13B of the 1988 Act).

[32] Section 19(2).

[33] Section 19(4). See also sub-ss (5) to (8).

[34] Section 20(2).

[35] Section 21.

[36] This was the effect of the interaction of Copyright Act, s 10 and Sch 7.

to be used as models or patterns to be multiplied by an industrial process were protected under the 1956 Act provided they were not registered under the 1949 Act.

This situation continued until 25 October 1968 when the Copyright Act 1956 was amended by the Design Copyright Act 1968, under which any registrable design, regardless of whether or not it had been registered, obtained 15 years' protection from the date of first industrial application. The decisions in *Dorling v Honnor Marine*[37] and *Amp v Utilux*,[38] however, held that the effect of the amendment was to make any industrial design which did not appeal solely to the eye, such as a non-aesthetic functional design, unregistrable, and thus it would always possess full copyright protection, that is, for the life of the author plus 50 years. This result was bizarre and fortuitously generous to certain industrial design holders. The later case of *Interlego AG v Tyco Industries Inc & Ors*,[39] decided by the Judicial Committee of the Privy Council, shed light on the law of artistic copyright and industrial designs. In that case, Interlego had originally registered some of its toy bricks under the Registered Designs Act 1949. Those registrations then expired, ostensibly bringing the brick designs into the public domain. Interlego then argued that its bricks had never been registrable in the first place because of the functionality inherent in the interlocking mechanism of the bricks. The Privy Council held that the brick designs were indeed now in the public domain and found against Interlego in respect of its claim for infringement of copyright in two sets of more recent manufacturing drawings of Lego bricks. It was held that copyright did not subsist in the recent drawings because they merely reproduced earlier drawings without any additional original input. Specifically, the case establishes that the addition of new literary matter to a work of artistic copyright does not assist in establishing originality of the drawings so revised.

7.3.4. Authorship and Ownership of Copyright

Authorship and ownership are two different concepts in copyright law. The author of a work is the one who creates it[40] and by whose life the duration of copyright is measured, whereas its owner is the one who has the exclusive

---

37 [1965] Ch 1.

38 [1972] RPC 103. Quaere: the effect of *Hoover v Hulme* [1982] FSR 565.

39 [1989] 1 AC 217.

40 Copyright Ordinance, s 11(1). In the case of a computer-generated work, the author is taken to be the person by whom the arrangements necessary for the creation of the work are undertaken (s 11(3)); see, for instance, *Nova Productions Ltd v Mazooma Games Ltd* [2006] RPC 14 (p 379).

right to make, issue or otherwise deal with copies of the work. Thus, in relation to a work of joint authorship,[41] the 50-year period would begin when the last of the joint authors dies,[42] whereas the co-owners of a work (who may or may not be joint authors) would share the exclusive right to deal with the work.[43] In the case of a literary, dramatic, musical or artistic work, any person who is named as the author on the surface of the work or its copies is presumed to be the author until the contrary is proved.[44] For sound recordings and films, both of which are entrepreneurial works, there is a similar presumption in favour of persons who are named as owners.[45] Both authorship and ownership could be proved by evidence in an affidavit.

First ownership The author of a work is the first owner of any copyright in it,[46] subject to the exceptions in sections 14 to 16. Section 14 is the most important and most frequently invoked of the statutory exceptions. It provides that the copyright in a work made by an employee in the course of his employment belongs to his employer unless there is a contrary agreement.

Assignment and licensing Copyright is assignable and can be the subject matter of a licence. To be effective at law, an assignment of copyright must be in writing and signed by or on behalf of the assignor.[47] There are no formal requirements for a licence,[48] but an exclusive licence must also be in writing and signed by or on behalf of the copyright owner.[49]

---

[41] Copyright Ordinance, s 12(1): a 'work of joint authorship' means a work made by the collaboration of two or more authors in which the contribution of each author is not distinct from that of the other author or authors. See, for instance, *Cala Homes (South) Ltd v Alfred McAlpine Homes East Ltd* [1995] FSR 818; *Robin Ray v Classic FM Plc* [1998] FSR 622; *Beckingham v Hodgens* [2003] FSR 14 (p 238); *Barrett v Universal-Island Records Ltd* [2006] EMLR 21 (p 567).

[42] Copyright Ordinance, s 17(7).

[43] Copyright Ordinance, s 194(2).

[44] Copyright Ordinance, s 115.

[45] Copyright Ordinance, s 116.

[46] Copyright Ordinance, s 13. See also s 12(4), which provides that, in relation to a work of joint authorship, references to the author of a work are construed as references to all the authors of the work.

[47] Copyright Ordinance, s 101(3). Cf 1956 Act, s 36, considered in *Novello & Co Ltd v Keith Prowse Music Publishing Co Ltd* [2005] RPC 23 (p 578) (CA), and locally in *Star TV Filmed Entertainment (HK) Ltd & Anor v Golden Princess Amusement Co Ltd & Anor*, HCMP No 1556 of 2006.

[48] Copyright Ordinance, s 101(4) simply deals with the enforceability of a licence without stipulating any formality.

[49] Copyright Ordinance, s 103(1), considered in *Swing Studio Entertainment Ltd v Excel Media Technologies Ltd*, HCA No 8932 of 2000. For an example of an

7.3.5. Infringement of Copyright

Part II, Division II of the Copyright Ordinance lays down the copyright owner's rights, with reference to which infringing acts are to be defined. Section 22 sets out a list of acts restricted by copyright, the doing of which without the copyright owner's consent constitutes what is generally referred to as primary infringement of copyright. Detailed definitions of those acts are to be found in sections 23 to 29, followed by the description of five acts of secondary infringement in sections 30 to 34.

Primary infringement According to section 22(1) and (2), any person who does or authorises another to do any of the following acts in relation to a work without the licence of the copyright owner, who has the exclusive right to do those acts, infringes the copyright in the work:

(1) to copy the work (section 23);
(2) to issue copies of the work to the public (section 24);
(3) to rent copies of the work to the public (section 25);[50]
(4) to make copies of the work available to the public (section 26);
(5) to perform, show or play the work in public (section 27);
(6) to broadcast the work or include it in a cable programme service (section 28); and
(7) to make an adaptation of the work or do any of the above in relation to an adaptation (section 29).

Section 22(3) further requires that the doing of any of the restricted acts must be in relation to at least a substantial part of the work. What is substantial in this context? What amounts to substantial copying? These concepts and the meaning of 'authorising' will be considered in turn.

Copying – the concept Copying, the most fundamental of the copyright owner's rights, is also the most common instance of copyright infringement. It is defined in section 23(2) as reproducing the work in any

---

exclusive licence, see *Tong Hok Tak Daffy & Ors v Beverly Consultants Ltd & Ors* [2004] 2 HKLRD 394 (CA).

50 The rental right, which, under the Copyright Ordinance as enacted, applied only to computer programs and sound recordings, has been extended to films, typographical arrangement of published editions of comic books, literary or artistic works included in comic books, as well as literary, dramatic or musical works included in sound recordings; see Copyright (Amendment) Ordinance 2007 (Ord No 15 of 2007), s 6.

material form, including storing the work in any medium by electronic means.[51]

In Hong Kong, in *Wu Luk-fuk (t/a Wu Luk Lee) v BG Lighting Co Ltd*,[52] a case involving an allegation of copyright infringement in drawings for a lighting arrangement, the trial judge granted summary judgment in favour of the plaintiff on the basis that the defendant had adduced no evidence to explain the strong similarities between the products. The Court of Appeal, in upholding the defendant's appeal, held, however, that 'such an overwhelming inference of substantial reproduction of the plaintiff's drawings could not be drawn on a comparison of the products so as to lead to the conclusion that there was clearly no defence to the claim'. The defendant, having an arguable defence, should be given leave to defend.

In another important Hong Kong case, *Lam Tai Hing v Koo Chih Ling Linda & Anor*,[53] the Court of Appeal confirmed Bokhary J's findings[54] that the defendant had infringed the plaintiff's copyright in a questionnaire. Despite substantial differences in the questionnaires and the defendant's denial of copying, expert evidence pointed to striking and exceptional similarities, in a qualitative sense, in the defendant's questionnaire that could not have arisen by chance.

A similar result was reached in *Elanco Products v Mandops*.[55] In this case, the plaintiff owned the literary copyright in instructions for a weed killer. The defendant, who also manufactured weed killer, originally copied the plaintiff's material verbatim, but subsequently composed a version of the necessary instructions for the use of its weed killer which did not reproduce the plaintiff's wording but did convey the same information. An interlocutory injunction was granted to prohibit the use of the defendant's instructions.

Another important decision on the question of what constitutes copying is *Solar Thomson Engineering Co Ltd v Barton*.[56] This decision illustrates the extent to which the courts are prepared to go in preventing the defendant from appropriating what the court considers to be the plaintiff's work and effort. The defendant had commissioned an independent designer to

---

[51] For an example of an infringing act of storing, see *Ocular Sciences Ltd & Anor v Aspect Vision Care & Ors* [1997] RPC 289 at p 418.

[52] [1993] 1 HKLR 36, also reported at [1993] AIPR 436.

[53] [1993] 2 HKC 1, [1993] AIPR 410 (CA).

[54] *Koo Chih Ling Linda & Anor v Lam Tai Hing* [1992] 1 HKC 193, also reported at (1991–92) 23 IPR 607. As to the breach of confidence claim, see its own chapter.

[55] [1980] RPC 213. Even though only an interlocutory decision, this case is frequently cited. See, for instance, *Lam Tai Hing v Koo Chih Ling Linda & Anor* [1993] 2 HKC 1, [1993] AIPR 410 (CA).

[56] [1977] RPC 537.

produce a particular industrial component specifically in order to avoid infringing copyright. Irrespective of the independent creation of the designer, the court held that copyright was infringed because the instructions and parameters given to the independent designer were such that, in the court's view, he would inevitably come up with a design that infringed the plaintiff's copyright. In these circumstances, the work of the independent designer could not meaningfully be described as an independent work.

Taking a substantial part of a copyright work Even if copying is found to have occurred, it will not amount to infringement unless a substantial part of the copyright work has been taken. Professor Cornish has described this requirement of substantial taking as a 'major tool for giving expression to the court's sense of fair play'.[57]One may go on to say that the court's 'substantiality' varies according to the degree of originality of the work being protected, or of the particular feature of work with which the court is concerned. For instance, in *Chow Wai Man, Vivian & Polygram Records Ltd v Easy Finder Ltd*,[58] the issue was whether there was substantial reproduction of the photographs of the first plaintiff, a singer and actress. In this case, only the first plaintiff's face from the original photographs was reproduced, but Findlay J rejected the argument that this did not amount to substantial reproduction of the photographs. In fact, that particular feature of the photograph was, he held, of itself 'substantial in relation to the creative process'.

Reproduction in a material form This heading raises the troubling question of trans-dimensional reproduction, particularly in relation to artistic works, for which section 23(3) provides that reproduction includes reproducing a two-dimensional work in three dimensions or vice versa.[59]

In another Hong Kong case, *Canon Kabushiki Kaisha v Green Cartridge Co (HK) Ltd & Anor*,[60] the High Court considered whether the right to repair defence, recognised in the *British Leyland*[61] case, applied to the alleged infringement of copyright in drawings of cartridges, and parts thereof, for printers and copiers by the manufacture and dealings in the cartridges and parts. The trial judge indicated that the *British Leyland*

[57] *Intellectual Property*, 4th ed (W Cornish, London: Sweet & Maxwell 1999), para 11-06.

[58] HCA No 4042 of 1995.

[59] See the discussion in *Autospin (Oil Seals) Ltd v Beehive Spinning (a firm)* [1995] RPC 683 at pp 697–701, per Laddie J.

[60] [1995] 1 HKC 729, [1995] AIPR 124, [1995] FSR 877 (HC); [1996] 2 HKC 180 (CA); [1997] 2 HKC 1 (Privy Council).

[61] [1986] AC 577.

defence could only apply where the individual parts were repaired by the narrowest means; in this case, the cartridges, as a whole, did not require repair. The plaintiff, therefore, succeeded at first instance in his *allegations* that the defendant had infringed copyright because the defendants had manufactured *complete* cartridges for the purpose of replacing cartridges when the toner was depleted or when a component of the cartridge failed. This did not, according to the court, constitute repair as commonly understood. This was reversed on appeal as the majority of the court held that replacement of the cartridge as a whole was within the *British Leyland* repair defence, being the only practical means for the owner to repair its machine and keep it in working order. On appeal, the Privy Council restored the decision at first instance.

Authorising infringement of copyright Authorising any of the restricted acts mentioned in section 22(1) is also a type of primary infringement.[62] It has been judicially defined as including acts or omissions which have the effect of sanctioning or approving the infringing acts of others. So it seems, therefore, that in order to make out a case of authorising, proof of a specific intent or perhaps even affirmative action is required. The cases below consider what is meant by 'authorising', though at times it is extremely difficult to reconcile these decisions.

The exceptions to infringement

FAIR DEALING This defence, initially a common law defence at the time of the Copyright Act 1911, is now incorporated into Division III of Part II of the Copyright Ordinance, which in its original version[63] provides that fair dealing with a copyright work does not amount to infringement if it is for the purposes of:

(1) research or private study[64] (section 38) or
(2) criticism, review or news reporting[65] (section 39).

---

62 Copyright Ordinance, s 22(2).

63 New provisions for 'Fair dealing for purposes of giving or receiving instruction' (s 41A) and 'Fair dealing for purposes of public administration' (s 54A) have been inserted by virtue of the Copyright (Amendment) Ordinance 2007 (Ord No 15 of 2007), s 14. The former is considered under 'The education exception' below.

64 See *Sillitoe v McGraw Hill Book Co (UK) Ltd* [1983] FSR 545. See also the explanation in an Australian case, *De Garis v Neville Jeffress Pidler Pty Ltd* (1990) 18 IPR 292 at pp 298–99.

65 For criticism or review, see *Hubbard v Vosper* [1972] 2 QB 84 (CA), *Beloff*

For defences under section 39, there is an additional requirement of sufficient acknowledgment, except in the case of reporting of current events by means of a sound recording, film, broadcast or cable programme.

Another difficulty is the meaning and scope of 'fair dealing'. Three factors are suggested in the section 38(3) as enacted:

(a) the purpose and nature of the dealing;
(b) the nature of the work; and
(c) the amount and substantiality of the portion dealt with in relation to the work as a whole.

By virtue of the 2007 amendments, a fourth factor has been added to the list:[66]

(d) the effect of the dealing on the potential market for or value of the work.

THE EDUCATION EXCEPTION Copyright is not infringed by the reproduction, other than by a reprographic process, of a work, to a reasonable extent, in the course of instruction or for the purposes of examination (section 41). In relation to reprographic reproduction, section 45(1) provides that copying, to a reasonable extent, by or on behalf of an educational establishment[67] for the purposes of giving instruction, or by a pupil for the purposes of receiving instruction in a specified course of

---

v Pressdram Ltd & Anor [1973] RPC 765; *Pro Sieben Media AG v Carlton UK Television Ltd* [1999] FSR 610 (CA); *Fraser-Woodward Ltd v BBC* [2005] FSR 36 (p 762); and the Australian case *De Garis v Neville Jeffress Pidler Pty Ltd* (1990) 18 IPR 292. For news reporting, see *BBC v British Satellite Broadcasting Ltd* [1992] Ch 141, *Pro Sieben Media AG v Carlton UK Television Ltd* [1999] FSR 610 (CA); *Newspaper Licensing Agency Ltd v Marks & Spencer Plc* [2001] Ch 257, [2000] 3 WLR 1256, [2001] RPC 5 (p 76) (CA); *Hyde Park Residence Ltd v Yelland* [2001] Ch 143, [2000] 3 WLR 215, [2000] RPC 604 (CA); [2000] Ent LR 116 (Jeremy Philips); [2000] Ent LR N77 (Gavin Llewellyn). See also *Ashdown v Telegraph Group Ltd* [2002] Ch 149, [2002] RPC 5 (p 235) (CA).

66 Copyright (Amendment) Ordinance 2007 (Ord No 15 of 2007), s 12. With the fourth factor, the list is similar to that in the 'fair use' provisions of the US Copyright Act and the fair dealing provisions of the Australian and Singaporean copyright law; see the consultation document issued by the Commerce & Industry Branch, 'Review of Certain Provisions of Copyright Ordinance' (December 2004), para 1.14.

67 For the definition of 'education establishment', see Copyright Ordinance, s 195 and Sch 1.

study provided by the educational establishment[68] does not infringe any copyright in the work. This provision does not apply, however, if there is any licensing scheme in place, in which case copying is only authorised if it is made in compliance with the conditions stipulated under the scheme or the licence.[69]

Further, the performance of a literary, dramatic or musical work before an audience consisting of teachers and pupils as well as the pupils' parents or guardians[70] at an educational establishment is not regarded as a public performance under section 27 and is thus not an infringement.[71] In view of the changes in teaching methods and pedagogy, Hong Kong has also introduced a medium-neutral fair dealing exception for the purposes of giving or receiving instruction.

THE LIBRARY EXCEPTION Sections 46 to 53 of the Copyright Ordinance permit copying by librarians and archivists under the conditions set out in those sections. The Secretary for Commerce and Economic Development[72] is empowered to make regulations regarding copying by libraries.[73]

Secondary infringement Dealing with articles which one knows, or has reason to believe,[74] are infringing copies, for the purposes of commercial exploitation, constitutes secondary infringement of copyright, as stipu-

---

[68] The phrase 'by a pupil . . . provided by an educational establishment' was inserted by virtue of the Copyright (Amendment) Ordinance 2007, s 16.

[69] Copyright Ordinance, s 45(2). For licensing schemes, see below. For the aborted proposals to remove the restriction imposed by s 45(2), see Legislative Council, Report of the Bills Committee on Copyright (Amendment) Bill 2006, paras 95–9.

[70] The phrase 'parents or guardians' was inserted by virtue of the Copyright (Amendment) Ordinance 2007, s 15; see Legislative Council, Report of the Bills Committee on Copyright (Amendment) Bill 2006, paras 92–4.

[71] Copyright Ordinance, s 43. For the meaning of public performances, see 'Permitting performances in public' below.

[72] Formerly the Secretary for Commerce and Industry (amended by virtue of LN 130 of 2007).

[73] Copyright Ordinance, s 46.

[74] 'To prove secondary infringement of copyright (ie importing or dealing with infringing copies), the plaintiff has to prove actual knowledge or constructive knowledge (ie reason to believe) on the part of the defendant that the articles are infringing copies': *Liao Fu Pin & Anor v Ad-Magnetics Co Ltd & Anor*, HCA No 1778 of 2006 at para 21. For 'reason to believe', see *Golden Bright Manufacturer Ltd v Sunlight Electronic Toys Manufacturing Co Ltd & Anor* [2007] 2 HKLRD 589, [2007] 2 HKC 357, at paras 72–3; *Yuen Chuk v Muhammad Farooq & Ors* [1999] 3 HKC 692 (CFI), where *Sillitoe v McGraw Hill Book Co (UK) Ltd* [1983] FSR 545; *LA Gear Inc v Hi-Tec Sports Plc* [1992] FSR 121 (CA); and *ZYX Music*

lated in sections 30 to 34 of the Copyright Ordinance. The dealings include the import, export, sale, letting for hire, and offering or exposing for sale or hire, of copies which are infringing copies made in Hong Kong or which would be infringing copies if made in Hong Kong,[75] as well as the possession, distribution, and exhibition in public of such copies for the purpose of, or in the course of,[76] any trade or business.[77] Distribution otherwise than for the purpose of or in the course of any trade or business also constitutes secondary infringement if the distribution is to such an extent as to affect prejudicially the owner of the copyright.

Dealings with articles specifically designed or intended for making copies of a particular work,[78] the transmission of a copyright work via a telecommunications system,[79] the permission for a place of public entertainment to be used for the performance of a literary, dramatic or musical copyright work,[80] and the provision of apparatus for an infringing performance[81] are also now classified as secondary infringements.

INFRINGING COPIES It is important to remember that no question of secondary infringement can arise until it is established that the copies in question are produced in breach of copyright. On the first sale of goods legitimately manufactured within Hong Kong, the copyright owners' rights are exhausted, that is, any subsequent dealing with the copyright works will not constitute an infringement. A purchaser may resell or even destroy the goods with impunity.[82] For goods manufactured abroad, the

---

GmbH v King [1997] 2 All ER 129 were considered. See also *Vermaat and Powell v Boncrest Ltd* [2001] FSR 5 (p 43).

[75] See 'Infringing copies' below.

[76] The previous phrase 'in the course of, or in connection with', inserted by the Intellectual Property (Miscellaneous Amendments) Ordinance 2000 (Ord No 64 of 2000), s 2, is now replaced by the shorter phrase 'in the course of': Copyright (Amendment) Ordinance 2007 (Ord No 15 of 2007), s 7. See also s 31(2), which was added by virtue of Ord No 64 of 2000 to clarify the meaning of the inserted phrase.

[77] Copyright Ordinance, ss 30 and 31(1)(a), (b), (c). See also s 36 which stipulates defences for the purposes of these two sections. 'Business' is defined in s 198(1) as including any trade or profession, and has been held to include business activities carried on by a governmental body pursuant to its obligations: *Pensher Security Door Co Ltd v Sunderland City Council* [2000] RPC 249 (CA).

[78] Copyright Ordinance, s 32(1).

[79] Copyright Ordinance, s 32(2), as to which see *Cinepoly Records Co Ltd & Ors v Hong Kong Broadband Network Ltd & Ors*, HCMP No 943 of 2006.

[80] Copyright Ordinance, s 33. For the meaning of 'place of public entertainment', see s 33(2).

[81] Copyright Ordinance, s 34.

[82] Note that this may not be the situation under patent law.

test of whether they would constitute infringing copies was laid down in *CBS United Kingdom v Charmdale Record Distributors*.[83] If the person who actually manufactured the goods abroad would have infringed copyright had he manufactured them in Hong Kong, then the goods are infringing copies. It is not material to enquire whether the importer (or indeed anyone other than the actual manufacturer) would have infringed copyright by manufacturing the goods in Hong Kong.

7.3.6. Remedies

Both the copyright owner and the exclusive licensee may sue for copyright infringement[84] and their relief may be by way of damages, injunctions, accounts or otherwise.[85]

7.3.7. Criminal Sanctions

Copyright Ordinance Offences are listed in sections 118 to 120 of the current Ordinance, supplemented by provisions in relation to the admission of evidence (section 121), investigation and related powers (sections 122 to 124), disclosure of information and inspection of articles (sections 126 to 130), and forfeiture and disposal of seized articles (sections 131 to 133). Under section 118(1), it is a criminal offence to commit any of the following acts without the licence of the copyright owner:

(1) the making of an infringing copy for sale or hire;
(2) the import or export of an infringing copy other than for private and domestic use;
(3) the sale, offer, exhibition or distribution of an infringing copy for the purpose of, or in the course of[86] any trade or business;

---

83 [1980] 2 All ER 807.

84 For the copyright owner, see s 107(1); for the exclusive licensee, see s 112(1), considered in *Fédération Internationale de Football Association & Anor v Eatery Ltd*, HCA No 1532 of 2006. Note that their rights and remedies are concurrent (s 112(2)), and neither can, without the leave of the court, proceed with an action for copyright infringement unless the other is joined as a plaintiff (s 113). See, for instance, *Swing Studio Entertainment Ltd v Excel Media Technologies Ltd*, HCA No 8932 of 2000.

85 Copyright Ordinance, s 107(2).

86 Copyright (Amendment) Ordinance 2007 (Ord No 15 of 2007), s 31. Before that, a longer phrase 'in the course of, or in connection with' was inserted by the Intellectual Property (Miscellaneous Amendments) Ordinance 2000 with a view to deterring the commercial use and possession of infringing copies. It was thought

(4) the possession of an infringing copy with a view to (i) its being sold or let for hire by any person for the purpose of or in the course of any trade or business; or (ii) its being exhibited in public or distributed by any person for the purpose of or in the course of any trade or business which consists of dealing in infringing copies of copyright works;[87] and

(5) the distribution of an infringing copy (other than for the purpose of or in the course of any trade or business) to such an extent as to affect prejudicially the owner of the copyright.[88]

The final type of infringing act, which does not involve any trade or business, appears to be wider in scope than the others. In *HKSAR v Chan Nai Ming*,[89] the first prosecution of its kind, the defendant was charged with, inter alia, attempting to distribute infringing copies of three copyright films contrary to the original section 118(1)(f) (now section 118(1)(g)). The distribution was by means of a peer-to-peer system called BitTorrent, and the defendant was the 'seeder' who created the seed files for others to download.

The defendant was sentenced to three months' imprisonment on each

---

that the original expression 'for the purpose of trade or business' might have unnecessarily restricted the scope of criminal liability for copyright infringement to the sale of or dealing in infringing copies. Hence provisions were inserted to clarify that 'it is immaterial whether or not the trade or business consists of dealing in infringing copies of copyright works' (see for instance s 118(8A), added by the 2000 Ordinance). However, against all expectations, the new provisions aroused grave public concern in response to which the Copyright (Suspension of Amendments) Ordinance 2001 (Ord No 13 of 2001) was enacted to revert the criminal provisions under ss 118 and 120 back to the position before the implementation of the 2000 Ordinance in relation to (a) parallel-imported computer programs lawfully made overseas; (b) infringing copies in a printed form (such as photocopies of newspapers); and (c) infringing copies downloaded from the Internet and technically required for the viewing or listening of works other than computer programs. The Suspension Ordinance was enacted on 22 June 2001, with retroactive effect from 1 April 2001 (the commencement date of the 2000 Ordinance).

[87] The two limbs (i) and (ii) were inserted by virtue of the Copyright (Amendment) Ordinance 2007, s 31. The original phrase was 'with a view to committing any act infringing the copyright'. Cf 'with a view to its being used' in s 118(2A), discussed below.

[88] Copyright Ordinance, s 118(1). See also subsections (1A), (1B), (2A)–(2G), (3A) and (3B), all inserted by virtue of the Copyright (Amendment) Ordinance 2007, s 31.

[89] [2005] 4 HKLRD 142; [2007] 1 HKLRD 95 (CFI); [2007] 2 HKLRD 489 (CFA). The reasons for sentence were given separately on 7 November 2005 (TMCC No 1268 of 2005).

charge, the sentences to run concurrently. The case went all the way to the Court of Final Appeal and the decision and sentence were upheld. The fact that this was the first such conviction did not amount to exceptional circumstances which would justify a suspended sentence.

ANTI-CIRCUMVENTION OF TECHNOLOGICAL MEASURES FOR COPYRIGHT PROTECTION Copyright owners commonly employ technological measures to prevent or restrict unauthorised access to, or copying of, copyright works in electronic form that are issued or made available to the public.[90] The Copyright Ordinance has already provided civil liability for the circumvention of such measures.[91] To further combat such circumvention, the civil liability provisions have been expanded, and new criminal sanctions introduced following the 2007 amendments.[92]

Prevention of Copyright Piracy Ordinance (Cap 544) This Ordinance was enacted in 1998[93] to introduce a licensing scheme for the first time for the manufacture of optical discs in Hong Kong to be administered by the Commissioner of Customs and Excise. The ordinance requires that locally produced optical discs be embossed with a code indicating their source of manufacture. This also enables the Customs officers to differentiate between authentic and infringing copies and to identify and inspect factories suspected of producing pirated optical discs. The major criminal offences created by the Ordinance are:

(1) manufacturing optical discs in Hong Kong without a valid licence (sections 3 and 21(1));
(2) manufacturing optical discs in any place in Hong Kong other than a licensed premises (sections 4 and 21(2));
(3) failing to cause each optical disc to be marked with the manufacturer's code endorsed on the licence (sections 15 and 21(2));
(4) manufacturing optical discs in contravention of any conditions endorsed on the licence (section 21(3)); and
(5) failing to display the licence at all times in a conspicuous location at the licensed premises (sections 9 and 21(4)).

---

90 See the consultation document issued by the Commerce & Industry Branch, 'Review of Certain Provisions of Copyright Ordinance' (December 2004), para 6.1.

91 Copyright Ordinance, s 273, as enacted.

92 Copyright Ordinance, s 273A to s 273C, inserted by virtue of the Copyright (Amendment) Ordinance 2007, s 69. See also the exceptions in s 273D to s 273F.

93 LN 235 of 1988, taking effect on 29 August 1998.

Any person who commits an offence under section 21(1) is liable, on a first conviction, to a fine of $500,000 and to imprisonment for two years. The penalties for subsection (2) are a fine of $100,000 and two years' imprisonment, whereas those for subsections (3) and (4) are a fine of $5,000 and six months' imprisonment. There are also offences in relation to coding under section 22(1), such as forging a manufacturer's code, falsely applying a manufacturer's code to an optical disc and making any die, block, machine or other instrument for the purpose of forging a manufacturing code.

Under section 18(1), authorised officers are empowered to enter and search any place, and to stop, board and search any vessel, aircraft or vehicle, in which they reasonably suspect that there is any optical disc which has been manufactured in contravention of Part II of the Ordinance, or that there is any machinery, equipment or other thing.

Organised and Serious Crimes Ordinance (Cap 455) By virtue of the Organized and Serious Crimes Ordinance (Amendment of Schedule 1) Order 1999, which took effect on 14 January 2000, offences under sections 118(1), (4) and (8), and 120(1), (2), (3) and (4) of the Copyright Ordinance have been classified as offences under the Organised and Serious Crimes Ordinance. From now on the list will also include the recently added copyright offences.

Following this amendment, the extensive powers of search and investigation conferred by the Organised and Serious Crimes Ordinance on police and customs officers can also be used in relation to investigations of copyright infringement.

7.4. PATENTS

Hong Kong does not have a patent office with examination facilities. Instead it re-registers certain patents granted elsewhere – at the present time, China, the United Kingdom and the European Patent Office.

7.4.1. Summary of the Patents Ordinance

The types of patent which can be registered It is now possible to register two types of patent in Hong Kong, the usual 20-year patent (called a 'standard patent') and a new eight-year patent (called a 'short-term patent').

Application for and grant of a standard patent The Patents Ordinance provides for the registration as a standard patent of a patent which has been registered in a 'designated patent office'. The application has to be made in two stages known as a 'request to record' and a 'request for registration and grant'. The applicant must request the Registrar of Patents to record the application within six months of publication of a patent application in a designated patent office. Provided that the formal requirements are satisfied, the Registrar must record the application, publish the request to record and advertise the fact in the *Gazette*. The request for registration and grant can only be filed after the request to record has been published and the patent granted in the designated patent office. The applicant, within six months of the later of those two events, must request the Registrar to register the designated patent and grant a standard patent.

Application for and grant of a short-term patent An application for a short-term patent may be made by a person alone or jointly with another. It must be filed with the Registrar and has to comply with a number of formal requirements set out in section 113, including the provision of a specification with a description, one or more claims but no more than one independent claim, an abstract and a search report.

Terms of patents granted under the Ordinance The term of a standard patent is 20 years from the date the application is filed in a designated patent office, subject to payment of renewal fees from the third year after its grant.

Property in patents and applications; registration Patents and patent applications, both standard and short term, are personal property and can be assigned or mortgaged and vested by operation of law in the same way as any other personal property.

Employees' inventions An invention made by an employee in the course of his normal duties or duties specifically assigned to him belongs to the employer where an invention might reasonably be expected to result from such duties. Such an invention will also belong to the employer if the employee had a special obligation, by virtue of the nature of his duties, to further the employer's interest.

'Tie in Clauses' as to patented products Under section 62(1), any condition or term of a contract for the supply of a patented product or of a licence to work a patented invention, or of a contract relating to such supply or licence, shall be void insofar as it restricts the right of the person supplied or licensed to acquire non-patented products from persons other than the patentee or his nominee, or obliges him to buy such products

from the patentee or his nominee. This provision does not apply to contracts made or licences granted before section 62 came into force.

Compulsory licences for standard patents After three years from the granting of a standard patent, any person may apply to the court under section 62(1) and (2) for a compulsory licence on any one of a number of grounds relating mainly to insufficient exploitation of the invention in Hong Kong. The court has the power to grant such licences as it thinks fit, provided that it is satisfied that the applicant has made reasonable efforts to obtain a licence from the proprietor on reasonable commercial terms and conditions and that such efforts have not been successful within a reasonable time.

The court may also grant licences to customers of the applicant if it is satisfied that the manufacture, use or disposal of materials not protected by the patent is unfairly prejudiced as a result of conditions imposed by the proprietor on the grant of licences.

The proprietor or any other person wishing to oppose an application for a compulsory licence may give notice of opposition to the court and the court shall consider the opposition in deciding whether to grant the application. Any person aggrieved by a compulsory licence order may apply to the court for variation or cancellation of the licence if the court in all the circumstances should think fit.

Government use of patented inventions Government use of a patent or of an invention which is the subject of a patent application can be made without the consent of the proprietor or applicant during a period of declared extreme urgency without committing an infringement under sections 68, 69(1) and (3). The government use must be on terms agreed with the proprietor before or after use or as determined by the court in default of agreement. The proprietor or exclusive licensee may be compensated for any loss of profit suffered as a result of government use. Any disputes may be referred to the court for resolution which has broad powers in this area.

The rights conferred by patents and patent applications A patent (both standard and short term) confers on its proprietor the right to prevent third parties from doing a number of specified acts in Hong Kong without his consent. In relation to any product which is the subject matter of the patent, the specified acts under section 73(a) are: (1) making, putting on the market, using or importing the product, or (2) stocking the product, whether for the purpose of putting it on the market (in Hong Kong or elsewhere) or otherwise. In relation to any process which is the subject matter of the patent, the specified acts under section 73(b) are: (1) using the process, or (2) offering the process for use in Hong Kong when the third party knows, or it is obvious to a reasonable person in the circumstances, that the use of the process is prohibited without the consent of the proprietor. Where the invention is a process, the following acts are specified under section 73(c) in respect of any product obtained directly by means of that process: (1) putting on the market, using or importing the product, or (2) stocking the product, whether for the purpose of putting it on the market (in Hong Kong or elsewhere) or otherwise.

Infringement Under section 80(1), civil proceedings may be brought by the proprietor of a patent (both standard and short term) for an injunction, delivery up, damages or an account and a declaration that the patent is valid and has been infringed.

Neither damages nor an account can be made against persons who were not aware and did not have reasonable grounds for believing that the patent existed.

Where a patent is amended, no damages shall be awarded for pre-amendment acts, unless the specification as originally published was framed in good faith and with reasonable skill and knowledge.

Where there are co-owners of a patent, the right to prevent infringement belongs to those co-owners with the right to do the act in question and there will be an infringement unless the consent of all such co-owners is obtained under section 85(1). One co-owner can sue for infringement without the consent of the others, but all must be parties, and defendants if necessary pursuant to section 85(2). Under section 86, an exclusive licensee can sue for infringement but the proprietor must be joined, as plaintiff or defendant. Any person becoming an owner, co-owner or exclusive licensee of a patent is not entitled to damages or an account in respect of the period between the transaction and its registration, unless he applies to register it within six months of its date or the court is satisfied that this was not practical in the circumstances.

Revocation of patents Under section 90, the court may revoke a patent (standard or short term) on any of the following grounds:

(1) the invention is not a patentable invention;
(2) the patent was granted to a person not entitled to it;
(3) the specification does not describe the invention clearly and completely enough for it to be performed by a person skilled in the art;
(4) the matter disclosed in the specification extends beyond that disclosed in the application;

(5) the protection conferred by the patent has been extended by an invalid amendment of the application or specification;
(6) the patent is one of two standard patents for the same invention, the applications having the same deemed filing date and being made by the same person;
(7) the patent is one of two short-term patents having the characteristics in (6);
(8) the patent is one of two patents granted for the same invention, one standard and the other short term, the applications having the characteristics in (6) but the patents being owned by different persons; or
(9) in the case of a standard patent, the corresponding designated patent has been revoked by the designated patent office.

Novelty In order to be patentable under section 1(1)(a) of the Patents Ordinance, an invention must be new, that is to say, it must not form part of the state of the art as defined in section 2(1). The state of the art comprises all matter which has been made available to the public anywhere by written or oral description, use or in any other way.[94] Such sources, however, are not to be read in combination for novelty purposes. Briefly stated, if a prior publication contains clear and unmistakeable directions to do what the patentee claims to have invented, that claim will lack novelty. In *Merrell Dow Pharmaceuticals Ltd v NH Norton & Co Ltd*, the following statement of the law was cited with approval by the Court of Appeal:[95]

> If the prior inventor's publication contains a clear description of, or clear instructions to do or make, something that would infringe the patentee's claim if carried out after the grant of the patentee's patent, the patentee's claim will have been shown to lack the necessary novelty, that is to say, it will have been anticipated.

Obviousness or lack of inventive step In order to be patentable, an invention must possess an inventive step.[96] An inventive step is present where,

94 Patents (Transitional Arrangements) Rules, s 2(2). Availability to the public has been held to mean that the matter must have been available to at least one member of the public who was free in law and equity to use it: *PLG Research Ltd v Ardon International Ltd* [1993] FSR 197 at 226. This obviously does not include disclosures made in confidence. The articles by C Floyd,'Novelty under the Patents Act 1977: the state of the art after Merrell Dow', [1996] 9 EIPR 480 and R Doble, 'Novelty under the EPC and the Patents Act 1977', [1996] 9 EIPR 511 provide interesting reading on the subject.

95 [1995] RPC 233 at p 241(CA), upholding Aldous J at [1994] RPC 1.

96 Patents Act 1977, s 3.

having regard to the state of the art, the invention is not obvious to a man skilled in the particular art. The state of the art extends to all sources as defined for novelty purposes (apart from certain patent applications published on or after the priority date). The question of obviousness was canvassed by Rogers J in *Canon v GCC*,[97] where he adopted and applied the conventional approach expounded by the English Court of Appeal in *PLG Research Ltd v Ardon International Ltd*.[98] As to the meaning of obvious, the question is whether what is claimed is 'so obvious that it would at once occur to anyone acquainted with the subject, and desirous of accomplishing the end . . .'.[99] In applying the test, the court must be wary of *ex post facto* analysis giving a false impression of obviousness. Further, the burden lies on a defendant to establish obviousness.

Infringement Remedies include the availability of an injunction, damages or an account of profits. Section 62(1) of the 1977 Act (the effect of which was almost certainly felt in Hong Kong)[100] provides that a defendant will not be liable if he can prove that at the time of the infringement he was not aware of and did not have reasonable grounds to believe that the patent existed.

7.4.2. Registered Designs

Whilst patents protect new inventions, registered designs protect the appearance of new designs. Although their scope of protection is fundamentally different, patents and registered designs have certain features in common. They both have novelty as a basic requirement and, if valid, they both confer true monopolies, in that (unlike copyright) no copying or even knowledge of their existence need be proved in order to establish infringement. In some jurisdictions, such as China and the United States, registered designs are known as design patents. As of 27 June 1997, the Registered Designs Ordinance (Cap 522) repealed the United Kingdom Designs (Protection) Ordinance, which extended the privileges and rights which the owner of a United Kingdom registered design held in the United Kingdom to Hong Kong. However, the old law is still relevant. First, the validity of designs registered or applied for in the United Kingdom before 27 June 1997 is to be determined in accordance with the Registered

---

97 [1995] AIPR 124 at pp 152–4, [1995] 1 HKC 729 at pp 757–9.
98 [1993] FSR 197.
99 *Siddell v Vickers* (1890) 7 RPC 292 at p 304, per Lord Herschell.
100 *Canon v GCC* [1995] AIPR 124 at p 140, [1995] 1 HKC 729 at p 746.

Designs Act 1949 (as amended by the Copyright, Designs and Patents Act 1988). Secondly, acts of alleged infringement occurring before 27 June 1997 are determined according to the law of the United Kingdom existing at that time. Under the new Registered Design Ordinance, registered design applications are examined and processed in Hong Kong, unlike the patent regime, which is still essentially a re-registration system.

7.4.3. Meaning of Design under the Ordinance

Section 2(1) of the Ordinance provides that 'design' means features of shape, configuration, pattern or ornament applied to an article by any industrial process, being features which in the finished article appeal to and are judged by the eye, but does not include –

(1) a method or principle of construction; or
(2) features of shape or configuration of an article which –
    (i) are dictated solely by the function which the article has to perform; or
    (ii) are dependent upon the appearance of another article of which the article is intended by the designer to form an integral part.

This provision adds to the exclusionary part of the definition features of shape or configuration which 'are dependent upon the appearance of another article of which the article is intended by the author to form an integral part'. The effect of this amendment is that certain spare and replacement parts are not registrable. In *Ford Motor Co Ltd's Design Application*,[101] a case concerning applications for registration of vehicle parts, the Divisional Court held that in order to be an 'article' within the meaning of the Registered Designs Act, the thing in question had to have an independent life as an article of commerce and not merely be an adjunct of some larger article of which it formed a part. This interpretation was upheld by the House of Lords,[102] which distinguished between:

(1) an item designed for incorporation, either as a spare part or an original component, in a particular article or range of articles made by the manufacturer of the component; and
(2) an item designed for general use.

---

[101] [1994] RPC 545 (Div Ct), an unsuccessful application to review the decision of the Registered Designs Appeal Tribunal.

[102] [1995] RPC 167, [1995] 1 WLR 18.

The House of Lords upheld the Divisional Court and Tribunal's finding that items such as main body panels, doors, bonnet lids, boot lids and windscreens fell within category (1) and were not 'articles' within the meaning of the Act. The Divisional Court also held that such items fell foul of section 1(1)(b)(ii) of the Act in that the makers had no design freedom, given the appearance of the vehicle, which was the 'other article'. The position is different with items such as wing mirrors, seats, wheels and steering wheels which have a commercial life of their own and are subsidiary to the essential shape of the vehicle. There was no challenge to the Tribunal's finding that such items are, in principle, registrable.

7.4.4. Registrable Designs

7.4.4.1. Novelty

In order to be registrable, a design must be new. Any new design can be registered in respect of an article or a set of articles. Section 5(2) of the Ordinance is central to the question of novelty and provides that:

> A design for which an application for registration is made shall not be regarded as new if it is the same as:
> (a) a design that has been registered in pursuance of a prior application, whether or not that design has been registered in respect of the same article for which the application is made or in respect of any other article; or
> (b) a design that has been published in Hong Kong or elsewhere before the filing date of the application, whether or not that design has been published in respect of the same article for which the application is made or in respect of any other article, or if it differs from such a design only in immaterial details or in features which are variants commonly used in the trade.

This provision is similar to the amended United Kingdom Act, with one extremely important difference, namely that novelty under the Ordinance is assessed on a worldwide basis. The requirement of novelty can be defeated either by designs registered (in Hong Kong) pursuant to prior applications or designs published anywhere in the world before the filing of the application. Publication of a design takes place when there is disclosure to one person, free of obligations of confidence, in the form of clear and unmistakable directions as to how to make an article having the features of the design. Such disclosure can take the form of an actual article or a paper publication. Theoretically, it is also possible for a verbal description to amount to prior publication, provided that the reader can see the design in his mind's eye without the need for any originality on his part.

The prohibition is absolute and even a prior publication of a copy of a subsequently registered design will destroy novelty.

A design corresponding to an artistic work can be registered by or with the consent of the copyright owner, notwithstanding prior use of the artistic work, unless such use consisted of or included the sale of or any other dealing (by or with the consent of the copyright owner) with articles to which the design or a similar design had been applied industrially. A design is applied industrially if it has been applied to more than 50 articles which do not form a single set or to articles manufactured in lengths or pieces which are not hand-made. A registered proprietor of a design can validly register the same design in respect of other articles or a similar design in respect of the same or other articles.

7.4.4.2. Designs excluded from registration

A design is not registrable if the appearance of the article is not material, that is, if aesthetic considerations are not normally taken into account to a material extent by people acquiring or using such articles.

Neither designs contrary to public order or morality are registrable, nor are computer programs or protected layout designs (topographies) (section 8 of the Registered Designs Ordinance). Works of sculpture (except casts and models for multiplication), wall plaques, medals, medallions and printed matter of a literary or artistic character are also excluded from registration.

Term of design registered under the Ordinance The initial period of registration of a design is five years beginning on the date at which the application is filed; the period of registration is then renewable for four further five-year terms, giving a possible total term of 25 years. An owner wishing to renew must apply and pay the renewal fee during the three-month period before the expiry of the current term. If the renewal fee is not paid, the registration ceases to have effect at the end of the current term. However, if the owner pays the fee (including any additional fee) within a six-month period after the end of the current term, the registration is treated as having been renewed prior to expiry. If, at the time of registration, the design was a corresponding design in relation to an artistic work in which copyright subsisted or which was only registrable because of section 10(1), the period of registration expires at the same time as the copyright in the artistic work.

'Corresponding design' means a design which, if applied to an artistic work, would produce something which would be regarded as a copy of the work for the purposes of the Copyright, Designs and Patents Act 1988: Registered Designs Ordinance, section 2(1). Previous use had been made of the artistic work with the consent of the copyright owner but such use did not consist of or include the sale, letting for hire, or offer or exposure for sale or hire of articles to which the design (or a design differing only in immaterial details or common trade variants) had been applied.

7.4.5. Infringement under the Ordinance

Infringement under the Ordinance consists of doing one of the acts set out in section 31(2). These are:

(1) doing anything which by virtue of section 31(1) is the exclusive right of the registered owner;
(2) making anything for enabling an article referred to in section 31(1) to be made in Hong Kong or elsewhere;
(3) doing anything in relation to a kit which would constitute infringement if done in relation to the assembled article; or
(4) making anything for enabling a kit to be made or assembled, in Hong Kong or elsewhere, if the assembled article would be an article referred to in section 31(1).

The exclusive right of the registered owner is then defined in section 31(1) as the exclusive right:

(1) to make in Hong Kong or import into Hong Kong –

    (i) for sale or hire; or
    (ii) for use for the purpose of trade or business; or

(2) to sell, hire or offer or expose for sale or hire in Hong Kong any article in respect of which the design is registered and to which that design or a design not substantially different from it has been applied.

This definition is central to infringement and, except where the designs are the same, the question in almost every infringement action is whether the design of the alleged infringement is 'not substantially different' from the registered design. This is dealt with below. The other prohibited acts in section 31(2) are subsidiary to this central question: (b) covers items such as moulds, dies, etc, for making infringing articles, and (d) similar items for making kits; the kits themselves are covered by (c). Acts done privately for non-commercial purposes are excluded from infringement, as are acts done for the purpose of evaluation, analysis, research or teaching under section 31(3). There will be no infringement simply by reproducing the following features of a registered design, namely, those which are dictated solely by the function of the article and those which are dependent upon the appearance of another article of which the registered article is intended to be an integral part.

7.4.5.1. Not substantially different

Since registered designs protect features which appeal to the eye, it is the eye alone which is the judge of whether an alleged infringement is substantially different from the registered design.[103] The test is easier to state than to apply but certain principles are well established. First, it is through the eyes of the inexpert customers that the comparison has to be made. In *Sanury v Wai Fat*,[104] the judge considered the question through three notional sets of eyes: those of exporters, foreign buyers and ordinary purchasers in Hong Kong and abroad. For this reason, expert evidence as to similarities is of limited importance and the judge's initial impression is an important factor, being formed before he gains undue familiarity with the design during the course of the trial which could cloud his assessment. In making the comparison, the court is allowed to (and frequently does) look at the article manufactured according to the registered design, although strictly the alleged infringement should be compared with the certificate of registration. The two articles should be looked at and compared side by side and separately, and the concept of imperfect recollection as articulated in *Valor Heating Co Ltd v Main Gas Appliances Ltd*[105] should also be applied:

> . . . you must consider infringement not merely upon the basis of the side by side comparison but also upon the basis of having had a look at the registered design, then having gone away and come back and perhaps being put in a position of deciding whether some other article is the one you originally saw.

7.4.5.2. Nature of infringing article

The subject of the registered design can be crucial to the question of infringement. In order to commit an infringement, an article must be one in respect of which the design is registered. In *Sanury v Wai Fat*, the design was registered in respect of a combined unit of headphones for a stereo set and a radio receiver. The alleged infringement consisted of headphones which operated as a radio receiver but could not be used as headphones for a stereo set. The court held that, on a fair reading of the words, the

---

[103] The objective for which the article was made is irrelevant: *Hecla Foundry Co v Walker Hunter and Co* (1889) 14 App Cas 550, 59 LJPC 46, 61 LT 738, 6 RPC 554.

[104] HCA No 5089 of 1980.

[105] [1973] RPC 871 at p 878.

description of the registered article could cover the defendant's product. A different result was reached in the English case of *Bourjois v British Home Stores*.[106] In that case, the design was registered in respect of 'a container primarily for a perfume bottle', the container being in the shape of a champagne bottle in an ice bucket. The top of the bucket and the champagne bottle lifted up to give access to a space for the perfume bottle. The defendant's alleged infringement consisted of a bucket, a perfume bottle and some packing which simulated ice. Although the appearance of the defendant's item was very similar to the registration, the court, on an interlocutory application, upheld *Sanury v Wai Fat*.

Right of third party to continue use under section 35 A person who, in Hong Kong before the filing date of an application, does or makes in good faith effective and serious preparations to do an act which would infringe the design after registration, can continue or (as the case may be) do the act. If the acts or preparations were done by an individual in the course of a business, that person can assign the right to do the acts or transfer it on death and authorise any of his partners to do them in the course of that business. If the acts or preparations were by a corporate body in the course of a business, it can assign the right to do them or transfer the right on dissolution. The right to do the acts cannot, however, be licensed.

7.5. TRADE SECRETS – THE ACTION FOR BREACH OF CONFIDENCE

Under Anglo-Hong Kong law, there is no distinction as to industrial or non-industrial subject matter in the protection afforded by the action for breach of confidence. The action protects personal information and trade secrets alike. The action is, like passing off, entirely judge-made law untrammelled by statutory modification. In the majority of cases, the law of confidential information in Hong Kong might be said to coincide exactly with English law. However, in *Linda Chih Ling Koo v Lam Tai Hing*,[107] Bokhary J, sitting in the Supreme Court of Hong Kong, was prepared to hold that notwithstanding the House of Lords's reservation in the *Spycatcher* cases,[108] confidential information can be property.

---

[106] (1951) 68 RPC 280.

[107] (1991–1992) 23 IPR 607, at p 633. Subsequently, upheld on appeal to the Court of Appeal.

[108] *Attorney General v Guardian Newspapers (No 2)* [1990] AC 109.

> A man's confidential information is his property. The courts have jurisdiction to protect such property from misuse . . . The conclusion that the proprietary jurisdiction exists is one at which I am happy to arrive.

This is quite a revolutionary statement and one the courts have hitherto shied away from in virtually all common law jurisdictions.

7.5.1. Existing Law

The leading and most robust case throughout the Commonwealth on breach of confidence is *Coco v Clark*[109] (*Coco*'s case). In his judgment, Megarry J (as he then was) isolated three elements of the action. First, the information itself must have the necessary quality of confidence about it. Secondly, that information must have been imparted in circumstances importing an obligation of confidence. Thirdly, there must be an unauthorised use of that information to the detriment of the party communicating it.[110] The remaining part of this section is concerned with an examination of each of the three elements of the cause of action identified by Megarry J. It must be stressed that the elements of the action are not watertight compartments and are highly interrelated. Information must possess the necessary quality of confidence.

The first element of the action for breach of confidence may be summarised as requiring the information to possess the following attributes:

(1) production of the information may require a minimum intellectual effort;
(2) the information must not be common knowledge; and
(3) the information must not constitute an 'inequity'[111] or information for which protection will be refused in the public interest.

---

109 [1969] RPC 41.

110 See Cornish, *Intellectual Property*, at p 268, where he appears to assume that *Coco v Clark* represents an authoritative modern statement of the law of confidence. This assumption has been supported in a number of judgments. However, the Law Commission Report has cast doubt on this by characterising the reasonable man test for determining whether an obligation of confidence exists as an *obiter dictum*, ie the second element in Megarry's formulation. See 'Information imported under circumstances importing an obligation of confidence', below.

111 This early narrow formulation of what confidence will not protect has evolved into a modern public interest defence.

In *Naomi Campbell v Mirror Newspapers*,[112] the plaintiff's attendance at Narcotics Anonymous was sufficient to make out quality of confidence. Morland J stated:

> In my judgment, to succeed in her claim for breach of confidentiality Miss Naomi Campbell must establish three things. First, that the details given by the publications complained of about her attendance at Narcotics Anonymous meetings have the necessary quality of confidence about them. Secondly, that those details must have been imparted in circumstances importing an obligation of confidence. Thirdly, that the publication of the details must be to her detriment. In my judgment the details of Miss Naomi Campbell's attendance at Narcotics Anonymous do have the necessary quality of confidence about them. They bear the badge or mark of confidentiality . . . To echo the words of Gleeson CJ in *Australian Broadcasting Corporation v Lenah Game Meats Pty Ltd* [2001] HCA 63 at paragraph 42 information relating to Miss Naomi Campbell's therapy for drug addiction giving details that it was by regular attendance at Narcotics Anonymous meetings is in my judgment easily identifiable as private and disclosure of that information would be highly offensive to a reasonable person of ordinary sensibilities. Or to use the guideline test given by Lord Woolf CJ in *A v B* (CA 11th March 2002) at paragraph 11(vii), it is obvious in my judgment that there existed a private interest worthy of protection. In my judgment the information giving details of her regular attendance at Narcotics Anonymous meetings for therapy must have been imparted in circumstances importing an obligation of confidence. The undisclosed source whether a fellow sufferer of drug addiction attending Narcotics Anonymous meetings or a member of Miss Naomi Campbell's staff or entourage owed her an obligation of confidence in relation to the information; whether or not that information was supplemented by a Mirror reporter attending a Narcotics Anonymous meeting or by covert photography. The information clearly bore the badge of confidentiality and when received by the defendants they, Mr Morgan and the Mirror journalists were clothed in conscience with the duty of confidentiality . . . In my judgment clearly the publication of information about details of her therapy in regularly attending meetings of Narcotics Anonymous was to Miss Naomi Campbell's detriment. It was, viewed objectively, likely to effect adversely her attendance and participation in therapy meetings.

In the context of an oral idea for a television series, *Fraser v Thames Television* is authority for a perhaps more specific formulation of the necessary quality of confidence:[113]

> To succeed in his claim, the plaintiff must establish not only that the occasion of communication was confidential, but also that the content of the idea was clearly identifiable, original, of potential commercial attractiveness and capable of being realised in actuality.

---

112 [2002] 2 All ER 120.
113 At p 936.

A detailed consideration of the three components of necessary quality of confidence follows.

7.5.2. Minimum Intellectual Effort

In this context, it may well be that some distinction might exist or be in the process of formation as between information on the nature of trade secrets, and personal or other information. Megarry J stated in *Coco*'s case that mere 'trivial tittle tattle' would not be protected.[114] Cornish suggests that the courts might well be reluctant to protect material that has only involved minimal intellectual effort, for instance, where the material would not qualify for copyright protection.[115] However, if such a distinction exists, it is clear the test is very lenient.[116] In *Nicrotherm v Percy*,[117] a disclosure that a mechanical feeding device was required for pig keeping was apparently regarded by the court as having the necessary quality of confidence. It seems clear, however, that a trade secret which falls short of patent law requirements of inventiveness or obviousness will still be protected.[118]

7.5.3. Information must Not be Public Knowledge

There is a point at which the purportedly secret information becomes so self-evident or obvious (somewhat akin to the patent law sense of want of novelty and obviousness) that it enters the public domain and loses its requisite secret quality. In Working Paper No 58, the English Law Commission characterised lack of secrecy in information as a defence to an action for breach of confidence. In Report No 110, they modified their view and stated secrecy to be a positive element of the action. It appears to be of no great consequence, save in respect of which party bears the onus of proof. The same question arises as to whether certain types of information are able to be protected because they are alleged as having overriding public interest and thus do not have the requisite quality of confidence or because a defence of public interest may be argued.

---

[114] At p 48.

[115] W.R. Cornish, *Intellectual Property*, 4th ed (London: Sweet & Maxwell, 1999), at p 131.

[116] See *GTV v Talbot*, where an idea for a television program about Australian millionaires was held to have the necessary quality of confidence.

[117] [1957] RPC 207, at p 209.

[118] *Saltman Engineering Co Ltd v Campbell Engineering Co Ltd* (1948) 65 RPC 203, at p 215 (Lord Greene MR) and *Underwater Welders & Repairers v Street* [1968] RPC 498.

It is interesting to note that the Law Commission's recommendation is for an action to protect confidence based solely on tort. It recommends, inter alia, a strict application of the public domain test and a liberal public interest defence. This would appear consonant with what has been identified by some writers as a trend in the 1970s, which peaked in the mid-1980s, away from exclusionary property rights towards a recognition of the contemporary demand for access to property both public and private.[119] It seems that the latter trend appears to be in the process of slowing, if not in the midst of a reversal.[120]

Confidential information may be imparted by permitted observation as well as by direct disclosure. It may also lose its secret character through uncontrollable observation by a sufficient number of persons. In *Woodward v Hutchins*,[121] an incident, which the plaintiff said was confidential information, took place on board a jumbo jet and was subsequently disclosed by the defendant in a book. However, the information was held to fall into the public domain as all other passengers had been able to view the incident.

This matter of relative secrecy was raised, but not pursued, by the Court of Appeal in Hong Kong in *Re Application by John Leroy Mitchell & Ors*[122] (*Mitchell* case). The case involved an application for certiorari by a number of members of the Department of Journalism at a well known university in Hong Kong. They sought to quash a resolution of the Senate. The Senate had censured them for disclosing, in a student newspaper under their supervision, a report by a committee which made recommendations to the Vice-Chancellor on the recruitment of administrative officers to the Hong Kong government.

The judgment does not state whether the committee was internal or external to the university, nor does it give any other indication of the committee's status.

Copies of the report in question originally came to the first applicant, the Head of the Department of Journalism, in his capacity as Secretary of the Board of Studies of that Department. It was marked 'Strictly Confidential' and 'Confidential'. Further copies were circulated to all Academic Board Secretaries and apparently were discussed at meetings of Academic Boards at which students, apparently student representative members, were present. No special instructions were issued as to the

---

119 *Seager v Copydex (No 2)* [1969] RPC 250.

120 See, for example, *Reckitt & Colman Products v Borden Inc* [1990] 1 All ER 873, [1990] 1 WLR 491, [1990] RPC 341.

121 [1977] 2 All ER 751, [1977] 1 WLR 760.

122 HCMP No 322 of 1976, unreported.

confidential nature of the report. In fact, it was a persistent complaint of the applicants that the university authorities did not complain of alleged breach of confidence, merely of criticising the university's shortcomings. The Court of Appeal observed:[123]

> It might however have been possible for him (the Head of Journalism) to persuade President Chuan or the Senate, had he been given a hearing, that the breach of confidentiality had to some extent been induced by the wide dissemination of such material to many Academic Board Secretaries and meetings at which students would occasionally be present, who would be unaware, without special instructions in that regard, that some of the matters issued were of a confidential nature.

As the university had apparently not, at the time, complained of breach of confidence, these representations may have been futile. Yet the crux of the matter of whether the information lost its requisite quality of confidence through widespread dissemination, or whether it remained relatively secret, was a matter for the court. The court persistently referred to the information as confidential and, in fact, based part of its judgment on this finding, yet it avoided any reference to its criteria of what constitutes confidential information.

Even relative secrecy, for example where some people know of the secret information, may still be sufficient to imbue the information with the requisite quality of confidence. It is a question of degree in every case.[124]

7.5.4. Springboards and Headstarts Doctrine

One problem evident in the public domain test is, as we have seen above, that information might be only relatively, or partially, in the public domain. In this context, a distinction may be said to have arisen between personal information and trade secrets. It is mainly in the latter area that the courts have devised a concept known as the 'springboard' or 'headstart' doctrine.[125] The essence of this concept was stated in *Ackroyds (London) Ltd v Islington Plastics*.[126]

---

123 At p 14.
124 *Franchi v Franchi* [1967] RPC 149.
125 The doctrine was originally enunciated in 1959 by Roxburgh J in *Terrapin v Builders Supply* [1967] RPC 375 and applied in a number of recent cases.
126 [1962] RPC 97.

> As I understand it, the essence of this branch of the law, whatever the origin of it may be, is that a person who has obtained information in confidence is not allowed to use it as a springboard for activities detrimental to the person who made the confidential communication, and springboard it remains even when all the features have been published or can be ascertained by actual inspection by any member of the public.

The effects of a springboard or a headstart apparently do not last forever. In the *Potters-Ballotini* case, Lord Denning said that in a situation where information had been made public, but the disclosee retained a headstart over other members of the public in exploiting the trade secret, it would be appropriate to grant an injunction limited in time rather than a perpetual prohibition.

Such an injunction, limited in time to correspond to the period of the headstart, was granted by Whitford J in *Fisher Karpark Industries Ltd v Nicols.*[127] This was believed to be the first case in the United Kingdom in which an injunction was awarded subject to a time limit. It appears that some of the information was held to have entered the public domain and Whitford J held the springboard or headstart doctrine was applicable to this information. He granted an injunction to last for one year.

The Supreme Court of South Africa also appeared prepared to grant relief subject to a time limit to correspond with the defendant's headstart. With some novelty, they characterised a suite of computer programs, the subject information of the litigation, as trade secrets only for the purpose of this headstart.[128]

The springboard doctrine received passing consideration in Hong Kong in *Sonca Industries Ltd v Tung Pak Kie.*[129] The plaintiff alleged that the defendant, who was a former employee of the plaintiff, had breached his obligation to keep the plaintiff's secret design for a lantern which featured an angled lamp confidential. The defendant had agreed to a covenant in his contract of employment whereby he undertook to keep his employer's trade secrets confidential. The defendant had been asked to leave the plaintiff's employment when it was suspected he was working for a rival company. The plaintiff admitted that it had based its design for the lamp in question on a telephone/walkie-talkie design which used an angled format. It was accepted that this design was public knowledge.

The defendant had apparently been employed to collect market

---

[127] [1982] FSR 351. See 'John Hill Headstarts and Interlocutory Injunctions: *Fisher Karpark Industries v Nicol*', (1982) EIPR 242.

[128] *Northern Office Microcomputers (Pty) Ltd v Rosenstein* [1982] FSR 124.

[129] HCA No 4322 of 1979.

intelligence for the plaintiff company. The plaintiff alleged that, while he was employed, the defendant had been shown sketches of the design for the lamp in question. At a later time, but while still employed by the plaintiff, the defendant had shown a sketch of the design of a lantern (which featured an angled lamp) to one of the plaintiff's mechanical engineers. The defendant asked him to comment on the merits of the design and the costs of manufacture. The plaintiff subsequently sought an interlocutory injunction to restrain the defendant from dealing in any way with the design in question, as they suspected he was going into commercial production of the lamp.

Counsel for the defendant referred to Megarry J's decision in *Coco v Clark*. The judgment refers to this submission as follows:[130] 'As I understand Mr Rogers, he is submitting the springboard doctrine so lucidly summarised by Megarry J.'

The report then continues to outline the three elements of the action for breach of confidence laid down by Megarry J. There is no specific reference to the springboard doctrine. Further, there is no mention in the judgment of any argument that the design for the lantern or any part of it was in the public domain apart, that is, from the telephone/walkie-talkie design, from which the lantern apparently derived its inspiration.

It appears that the relevance of the springboard doctrine, referred to by the judge, may have been in relation to the form of the injunction sought. His Lordship cited *Potters-Ballotini v Weston-Baker*,[131] where the plaintiffs had sought an injunction in the widest of terms. Lord Denning referred to the great difficulty of defining what are and what are not the items of confidential information which the plaintiffs would be entitled to protect, and to the need for an injunction to be certain. The judge in the instant case commented[132] that he would, with respect, echo those words in relation to the injunction sought in the present case. As a result, the injunction was denied.

7.5.5. Personal Knowledge, Skill or Experience Acquired at Work

It is established law that information having the necessary quality of confidence must be other than personal knowledge, skill or experience acquired at work. The latter cannot be protected by a former employer on public policy grounds.

---

130 At p 14 of the unreported judgment.
131 Cited at note 56, above.
132 Cited at note 61, above.

In *Gilman Engineering Ltd v Simon Ho Shek On*,[133] a former senior employee of the plaintiff was alleged to have canvassed its clients informing them of his plans to go into business independently and of memorising or taking away lists of customers. Liu J applied *Faccenda Chicken v Fowler*,[134] which provides the contemporary statement of what information acquired during his employment an ex-employee is entitled to retain. In *Faccenda Chicken*, the English Court of Appeal distinguished between two types of information an ex-employee may have had access to during the course of employment. On one hand, an ex-employee must continue to honour trade secrets after leaving the employment. On the other hand, there is information not falling into the first class but which the implied contractual term of fidelity requires the employee to honour during the course of the employment. However, after the employment ceases, if the information is inevitably carried away in the ex-employee's head along with general skill and knowledge acquired at work, he or she is entitled to use the information free of conditions of confidence. Liu J characterised the lists of customers[135] as falling into the second class and refused the injunction as such customers were commonly known to anyone in the industry.

Confidential information and the employment contract The common law rule that personal skill and knowledge acquired at work does not have the necessary quality of confidence to be protected at the suit of a past employer has already been considered above. It remains to be determined what information arising out of the employment contract is protected or protectable under the first limb of *Faccenda Chicken v Fowler*,[136] namely a trade secret. It seems this depends, at least initially, on whether there exists a covenant prohibiting disclosure or use of information upon leaving the covenantee's employment. It is established law that any such covenant must run the gauntlet of the restraint of trade doctrine and those covenants which offend it will be held void.

In the absence of a covenant, only confidential information belonging to the employer, if any, is protected. What information is confidential, in this context, can be determined by what a man of average intelligence and honesty would recognise as belonging to his employer. In *Printers & Finishers v Holloway*,[137] Cross J said:

---

133 (1987) 8 IPR 313.

134 [1985] 1 All ER 724.

135 A similar customer list case occurred in *Roger Bullivant v Ellis* [1987] FSR 172.

136 [1985] 1 All ER 724.

137 [1964] 3 All ER 54. See *Morrison v Moat* (1851) 9 Hare 241 and *Stephenson, Jordan & Harrison v McDonald & Evans* (1952) 69 RPC 10.

> I do not think that a man of average intelligence and honesty would think that there was anything improper (the first defendant) putting his memory of particular features of his late employer's plant at the disposal of his new employer. The law will defeat its own object if it seeks to enforce in this field standards which would be rejected by the ordinary man.

This appeal to objective reasonableness is the connecting factor between confidential information belonging to an employer under the general law, and confidential information belonging to an employer by virtue of an enforceable covenant in an employment contract. Protection is not granted under either head, unless such protection would be reasonable. In the absence of a covenant, it has been suggested that the test of reasonableness, as stated above, should depend on the man of average intelligence and honesty.

Covenants against disclosure Despite the fact that covenants in restraint of trade, including those which restrict the use of information connected with the conduct of one's trade or calling, are prima facie void unless shown to be reasonable as between the parties, and reasonable having regard to the public interest, there has been a constant volume of litigation in this area.

In *Sonca Industries v Tung Pak Kie*[138] *('Sonca')*, Silke J quoted from Whitford J's judgment in *Reinforced Plastics v Swansea Plastics*:[139]

> It is altogether too easy when employees leave, and are employed by a rival firm, to harass that rival firm upon the basis that the employees who have left the plaintiffs and joined them have taken away trade secrets of great value . . . It is not really to be considered that proceedings of this kind should be allowed to go forward on nothing more than a speculative basis.

It should be borne in mind that the courts have traditionally had recourse to the concept of reasonableness in the context of an economic system based on the assumed merits of competition. Invariably, the problem in this area is to determine what a trade secret is and what is the ordinary skill and knowledge of the particular employee. In *Sonca*, one of the factors which contributed to the court refusing an interlocutory injunction was the difficulty of framing an injunction in words sufficiently certain so that the defendant would be able to appreciate what he could and could not do. The burden on the plaintiff to define with great accuracy

138 HCA No 4322 of 1979.
139 [1979] FSR 182.

what is alleged to be confidential is established by the authorities[140] and is particularly onerous in an application for interlocutory relief.[141]

In *Susan Buchanan v Janesville Ltd*,[142] the Court of Appeal of Hong Kong had to consider a covenant in a hairdresser's contract of service, which forbade her working in competition with her employer anywhere in Hong Kong for one year after termination of employment. After finding the clause void as to the geographical operation of the clause, the Court of Appeal considered a prohibition in the covenant, against working 'in any capacity connected with hairdressing'.[143] The court said it had to consider whether the clause was reasonable as between the parties. The Court of Appeal held that the question of the clause's reasonableness as between the covenantor and the public did not arise in this particular dispute.

This was an unfortunate conclusion as the case law since *Esso Petroleum v Harper's Garage*[144] has demonstrated that the requirement of reasonableness turns on the public interest in competition. This is the underlying policy for holding covenants in restraint of trade as prima facie void. It is difficult to imagine what is reasonable as between the parties, considered in isolation from the public interest. The Court of Appeal's assumption might, however, be explained on the basis that no argument was put before the court on that point.

The Court of Appeal considered three aspects of the covenant's operation: first, its reasonableness at that point of time; secondly, its reasonable geographic or spatial operation; and thirdly, reasonableness as to the type of work the covenant seeks to restrain.

> Each clause has to be construed in the light of its own words and it is to be noted that the words in this clause are different from and wider than the words in the clause in *Marion White v Frances* [1972] 1 WLR 1423. In our judgment this clause is bad for the additional reason that it prevents the appellant from engaging in any sort of work in connection with hairdressing, for example, selling hairdressing lotion to hairdressing salons and matters of that kind such as hairdressing equipment. That is a far wider protection than the respondents' interests require.

The court held that the temporal limitation was valid, namely that the injunction would last for one year after termination of employment, although validity appeared to have been conceded by the covenantor.[145]

140 See *Diamond Stylus v Bauden* [1972] FSR 177.
141 See *Technograph v Chalwyn* [1967] FSR 307.
142 [1981] HKLR 700.
143 At p 702. See *Deacons v Robin M Bridge* (CA No 28 of 1983), discussed below.
144 [1968] AC 269.
145 At p 701.

The geographical limitation contained in the covenant, the whole of Hong Kong, was considered to be unreasonable. The Court of Appeal rejected a submission from counsel for the covenantee in the following terms.[146]

> He [counsel for the covenantee] says it must have been the intent of the parties that the likelihood was that any Salon which was in competition with La Coupe Salon would have been or would be in fairly close proximity to La Coupe Salon even though it might be on the other side of the Island. But this in effect is asking us to re-write the terms of Clause 7.

The court referred to a hypothetical salon being opened by the covenantor at Stanley. They said it was unreasonable, having regard to the local clientele living there, to protect the covenantee from competition from the covenantor, ie La Coupe Salon clients are unlikely to be drawn to the covenantor's hypothetical salon in Stanley. They expressed no view on the covenantor's present situation in Tsimshatsui – the covenantee having its salon in Central. Indeed, such a view was unnecessary, as having found the covenant unreasonable in relation to the geographical restriction, there was no suggestion of severing the offending part. In the result, the appeal against the grant of an injunction was upheld.

There have been very few cases on the operation of restrictive covenants as applied to partners. In *Deacons v Robin M Bridge*,[147] the Court of Appeal of Hong Kong had to consider the validity of a restrictive covenant pertaining to a partner of a firm of solicitors on an appeal against the grant of an interlocutory injunction. The judgment was upheld by the Judicial Committee of the Privy Council.[148] The covenant forbade any partner, who had retired for whatever reason, from practising for five years as a solicitor, notary, trade mark or patent agent, or in any similar capacity in Hong Kong for clients of the partnership, or for those who had been clients within three years of the partner's retirement. The covenantor alleged the covenant was void as unreasonable between the parties and against the public interest. Fuad JA, with whom Leonard VP and Cons JA concurred, referred to the House of Lords decision in *Esso Petroleum Co Ltd v Harper's Garage (Stourport) Ltd*,[149] where their Lordships endorsed Lord McNaughten's principle in *Nordenfelt v Maxim Nordenfelt*:[150]

---

146 At p 702.
147 CA No 28 of 1983.
148 [1984] 2 All ER 19.
149 [1968] AC 269.
150 [1894] AC 535, at p 565.

> All interference with individual liberty of action in trading, and restraints of trade of themselves, if there is nothing more, are contrary to public policy, and therefore void. That is the general rule. But there are exceptions: restraints of trade and interference with individual liberty of action may be justified by the special circumstances of a particular case. *It is a sufficient justification, and indeed it is the only justification, if the restriction is reasonable – reasonable, that is, in reference to the interests of the parties concerned and reasonable in reference to the interests of the public, so framed and so guarded as to afford adequate protection to the party in whose favour it is imposed, while at the same time is in no way injurious to the public.* (Emphasis added.)

There were suggestions in *Herbert Morris Ltd v Saxelby*[151] that the onus of establishing reasonableness vis-à-vis the parties and the public may sometimes differ, though in practice the distinction will rarely arise. Fuad JA cited a passage from Lord Pearce's judgment in the *Esso* case, which it is suggested removes a great deal of confusion from this area.[152] 'There is one broad question: is it in the interests of the community that this restraint should, as between the parties, be held to be reasonable and enforceable.' Fuad JA provided the following incisive comment:[153]

> The cases certainly show that most of the decisions reached in the Courts over the years in this area of the law were on the basis of reasonableness between the parties, and it seems to me that the House of Lords in the *Esso Petroleum* case must be understood to have stressed the importance of the public interest consideration and placed it in its proper context.

In the instant case, the appellant/covenantor argued that the only interest the respondent could legitimately protect are those clients of the intellectual property department which the appellant had formerly headed, and not clients of other departments of the partnership.

The court found, on the evidence, that the appellant had signed the covenant as an experienced professional man dealing with his future partners at arm's length. Thus, there was no room for suggestions of unreasonableness on the grounds of unequal bargaining positions. Certain arguments peculiar to the practice of solicitors were proffered. It was argued that having regard to the size of Deacons, a covenant restraining dealings with all clients must be more strictly construed. Fuad JA said:[154]

---

151 [1916] AC 688.
152 At p 324.
153 At p 7.
154 At p 14.

> All the facts and circumstances of the case must, of course, be taken into account, but I am bound to say I can see no justification for applying different criteria to covenants of this kind between solicitors, depending on their prestige and the number of their clients.

The appellant also relied on the judgments in *Oswald, Hickson, Collier & Co v Carter-Ruck*[155] and a decision by Walton J in *Edwards & Ors v Worboys*,[156] and the English Court of Appeal's review of Walton J's judgment.[157] These judgments appear to have been understood by the Court of Appeal of Hong Kong as authority for the following proposition only. An argument that it is contrary to public policy for a solicitor to be precluded by a covenant from acting for a client, when the client wants him to so act, constitutes a serious question to be tried in relation to an application for an interlocutory injunction.

Fuad JA acknowledged that it was open for the House of Lords or Privy Council to countenance this as a general principle, but if they did, it would be an exception only in the case of solicitors to a long line of authorities. Why, for instance, not exempt doctors and various others, his Lordship enquired rhetorically. It was argued that the respondent had not adduced any evidence of why it reasonably needed protection from the appellant seeking to deal with its non-intellectual property department clients. The court replied:[158]

> If there are special circumstances which are put forward to justify a particular reservation or its width, evidence is both admissible and necessary, but surely Deacon's case cannot fall to the ground because the affidavit evidence filed on their behalf does not expressly say that they were interested in keeping their clients, and explain why.

However, the appellant's argument had been addressed to the position concerning non-intellectual property department clients, not clients per se. The court held that the respondent's general concern for losing its clients to the appellant did not require articulation as they could rely on a wider self-evident interest.

The Court of Appeal concluded that the restraints imposed in the covenant went no further than affording adequate protection to the legitimate interest of the respondents in keeping all their clients, not just those who had dealt with the appellant's department.

---

155 English Court of Appeal, 20 January 1982, unreported.
156 18 March 1983, unreported.
157 25 March 1983, unreported.
158 At p 13.

7.5.6. Information Imparted under Circumstances Importing an Obligation of Confidence

Prior to the English Law Commission Report, the English courts and those of various Commonwealth jurisdictions appeared content to follow *Coco*'s case in adopting the reasonable man test to determine when information has been imparted under circumstances importing an obligation of confidence. In *Coco*, Megarry J said:[159]

> It may be that that hard worked creature, the reasonable man, may be pressed into service once more; for I do not see why he should not labour in equity as well as at law. It seems to me that if the circumstances are such that any reasonable man standing in the shoes of the recipient of the information would have realised that upon reasonable grounds the information was being given to him, in confidence, then this should suffice to impose upon him the equitable obligation of confidence.

The Law Commission has tried, ultimately unsuccessfully, to place a dampner on the apparent eagerness of the courts to embrace what the Law Commission called the 'wide reaching and obiter test in *Coco v Clark*'.[160] Although recognising that the result may often be the same, the Law Commission recommended a test of express or implied acceptance of the information, rather than the test of how a reasonable man in the position of the recipient would view it.

No doubt, this was in some measure due to concern about unsolicited, valuable information being placed in the hands of a recipient who did not want the information in the first place, and certainly did not wish to be bound by any confidence. One could imagine two rival firms working on, say, a drug to cure cancer. Firm A knows that research at firm B must be proceeding along similar lines, and it may suspect firm B's research to be more advanced. Firm A then sends to firm B a confidential letter detailing all its research findings to date. Unless firm B can disclaim this confidential information, firm A may be able to threaten to sue for any breakthrough drug firm B seeks to market. It is settled law that if firm B could prove autonomous research and development, then it would have a defence to any action framed in breach of confidence, but given firm A's letter, this would be difficult to prove.

What perhaps worried the Law Commission was that Megarry J's test does not specifically allow for information to be disclaimed in the above

---

159 At p 47.
160 Para 4.4.

type of situation. One merit of the Law Commission's recommendation is that it would rationalise a later decision of Megarry VC in *Malone v Commissioner of Police*.[161] In that case, the defendant alleged breach of confidence in consequence of alleged illegal wire tapping. Megarry VC essentially disposed of the case on the basis that people using the telephone do not necessarily expect their conversations to be private. He drew an analogy to people shouting over the back fence. The decision was undoubtedly difficult and is now viewed as a test case for the legality of wire tapping without statutory authorisation and would seem to bear out the adage, 'hard cases make bad law'.

This case is difficult to reconcile with the decision in the Supreme Court of Queensland in *Franklin v Giddins*.[162] In that case, information inherent in stolen goods was held to give rise to an action for breach of confidence against the third party recipient of the goods. This case is now frequently cited in cases of covert interception of communications.

Following *Malone*, the Law Commission concluded that it is very doubtful, under present law, whether information can be impressed with obligations of confidence simply if it is obtained by reprehensible means. This conclusion is now highly doubtful. See sub-heading 'Confidential information as property', below. The Supreme Court of Victoria has recently reformulated Megarry's VC reasonable man test to take specific account of a recipient's desire to disclaim confidential material. Fullagher H (as he then was) held:[163]

> The ultimate question . . . can be expressed by asking whether a reasonable man in all the circumstances would recognise the information as being the property of the plaintiff. That of course is not an unhelpful way of putting it, but it should not however be used in any sense which conjures up the familiar if bewildered man from the seat of the Clapham omnibus, dragged this time out of his seat to give a judgment in the Court of Chancery. If the question conjures up that picture, then it is better to ask instead whether an equity lawyer, observing the analogies so far drawn from the product of labour, would in all the circumstances recognise the information in question as being the property of the plaintiff.

It is suggested this test is preferable to the Law Commission's formulation of express or implied acceptance. Implied acceptance inevitably requires some notional test of reasonableness. Fullagher J's test of the reasonable equity lawyer is really the reasonable man, mindful of what

---

161 [1979] Ch 344.

162 [1978] Qd R 72.

163 *Delta Nominees v Viscount Plastics* [1979] VR 167, at p 191.

information has been produced by labour, skill and effort and mindful of where it is reasonable to disclaim confidential information by reference to analogous situations. In this guise, the test may lead to results which perhaps tally with most people's considered concepts of commercial honesty. However, in the absence of the development of a body of case law depicting real situations where disclaiming is, or is not, said to be reasonable, the dispute may deteriorate to a mere exercise in semantics.

In this context, it is useful to consider the facts of the *Mitchell* case[164] discussed above. Would the reasonable man, or the reasonable equity lawyer, recognise that the information was communicated in confidence? Could the Head of the Department of Journalism effectively disclaim any obligations of confidence attached to the information? Could he then have authorised the newspaper story solely on the basis of what the student reporters were able to uncover? This latter question is also bound up with the public interest defence and the obligations of a third party disclosee and will be considered below.

The former question is an apt illustration of the difficulty in this area. The judgment of the Court of Appeal refers to the attitude of the recipients of the alleged confidential report:

> Indeed Mr Lee, the person previously responsible for the production of the newspaper, would appear to have taken the line that the publication of this material was not detrimental to the interests of the University and that, on the contrary, it showed a laudable ingenuity on the part of the student reporters in uncovering factual material of interest within the University and to the public at large. He said he did not recall President Chuen bringing up the question of breach of confidentiality at all, and that the confidential nature of the material was only drawn to his attention when he was later apprised of the censure.[165]

And:

> There was some measure of contest on the affidavits as to whether the issue of confidentiality was raised at the meeting and Mr Mitchell even seems to be disposed to suggest that the matter published, admittedly based upon the report, was not truly of a confidential nature.[166]

It is unfortunate that the court assumed throughout that the report was confidential and what they were called upon to decide was merely whether those concerned had a right to have the censure motion quashed on the

164 Cited at note 122, above.
165 At p 4.
166 Ibid.

basis of the *audi alteram partem* rule of administrative law. There appeared to be questions of whether the information retained its confidential nature despite wide dissemination, whether the information was imparted under circumstances importing an obligation of confidence, and even assuming an affirmative response to the foregoing, whether a public interest defence was available. It may have been that, on the basis of the Law Commission's suggested text of express or implied acceptance, there was no obligation of confidence as it was in dispute whether the confidential nature of the report was ever communicated to the disclosees. If the reasonable man test propounded by Megarry VC is applied, it seems clear the court thought it was only reasonable that the report should be regarded as confidential.

Confidential information as property As mentoned above, in *Linda Chih Ling Koo v Lam Tai Hing*,[167] Bokhary J held that, notwithstanding the Privy Council's reservation in the *Spycatcher* cases,[168] confidential information can be property:

> A man's confidential information is his property. The courts have jurisdiction to protect such property from misuse . . . The conclusion that the proprietary jurisdiction exists is one at which I am happy to arrive.

The first plaintiff, Ms Linda Koo, was a lecturer at the University of Hong Kong's Department of Community Medicine. Assisted by the second plaintiff, who was not employed by the university, she drafted a questionnaire for monitoring the incidence and circumstances of lung cancer in Hong Kong Chinese women. The questionnaire was used as part of a retrospective case control study. It was first drafted between 1980 and 1981. The defendant, a senior lecturer in the same department, was also engaged in a parallel retrospective case control study of the same phenomenon. He first drafted a questionnaire for use in the study in April 1983. The plaintiffs alleged the defendant obtained surreptitious access to their questionnaire and reproduced it in such a manner as to infringe their copyright and give rise to an action for breach of confidence. The plaintiffs claimed damages.

Bokhary J held that the plaintiffs were entitled to damages and conversion damages for infringement of their copyright, and damages for misuse of their confidential information.[169] It was found that the defendant had

[167] (1991–92) 23 IPR 607, at p 633. Upheld by the Court of Appeal.

[168] *Attorney General v Guardian Newspapers (No 2)* [1990] AC 109.

[169] Costs were awarded against the defendant on a common fund basis, evincing some evidence of how blatant the court regarded the defendant's conduct.

obtained surreptitious access to the questionnaire (it was not disclosed to the defendant by the plaintiffs) and he had reproduced substantial parts of it in his own questionnaire.

The questionnaire was held to be confidential subject matter, relying on the Supreme Court of New South Wales decision in *Interfirm Comparison (Aust) Pty Ltd v Law Society of NSW*.[170]

Bokhary J held, for the first time in any Commonwealth jurisdiction, that the jurisdiction to restrain surreptitious use of confidential information is proprietary – there is no need for a confidential disclosure.[171]

Bokhary J's dicta is to be welcomed for there are strong policy reasons for freeing the protection of information, surreptitiously obtained, from the need for a specific disclosure between plaintiff and defendant. However, property is a very blunt instrument for performing the fine balancing of interests often required in this area.

7.5.7. Third Party Disclosees of Confidential Information

The Law Commission was of the view that on the then state of the law in this area, a person was not liable for breach of confidence in disclosing or using information which was in fact subjected to an obligation of confidence, as long as he had no actual or constructive knowledge of its confidential character.[172] Once he acquired such knowledge, he became liable, from that time onwards, for any subsequent disclosure or use of the information.

This is, presumably, subject to a right to disclaim the obligations of confidence in conformity with the Law Commission's recommendations in relation to direct disclosees of information. How a third party disclosee disclaims, and who he must disclaim to, were not considered by the Law Commission. The answers are far from self-evident.

It is established law that the original discloser of the information alone has standing to sue a third party disclosee.[173]

---

170 [1977] RPC 137.

171 His Lordship cited *Prince Albert v Strange* (1849) 64 ER 293, *Exchange Telegraph Co Ltd v Howard* (1906) 22 TLR 375, *Coco v Clark* [1969] RPC 41, *Saltman Engineering Co Ltd v Campbell Engineering Co Ltd* (1948) 65 RPC 203 and *Attorney General v Guardian Newspapers (No 2)* [1990] AC 109. The reality is that none of these cases contains any authority for the revolutionary pronouncement his Lordship articulated.

172 As stated above, this is questionable in the light of the *Linda Koo* case, cited at note 54, above.

173 See *Fraser v Evans* [1969] 1 QB 349.

There is some suggestion that a bona fide purchaser for value of confidential information may be exempt from the duty of confidence.[174] This is discussed under 'Defences' (see sub-heading 'Bona fide purchaser in good faith of confidential information') below.

An unauthorised disclosure of the information causing detriment to the discloser. This is the third element of Megarry J's formulation for an action for breach of confidence. There does not appear to be any precise rule which defines all unauthorised uses of confidential information other than to say the disclosure may take place outside the limited purposes for which it was revealed. In *AB Consolidates v Europe Strength Food Co*,[175] the New Zealand High Court held that once obligations of confidence are established, the recipient is under a duty of good faith which requires him to use the information for the purpose for which it was disclosed to him and not for any purpose detrimental to the discloser. The latter requirement of detriment to the plaintiff is a matter Megarry J left open in *Coco*'s case.[176] Cornish has drawn attention to the differing public policy requirement in this respect as regards personal information and trade secrets.[177] In the case of personal information, he argues that the requirement of a detriment may well be desirable in order to justify encroachment upon the public interest in freedom of information. The public interest concerning trade secrets, however, may not be so dire.

In *Li v Genesis Films*,[178] the defendant was a production company for Cantonese films. It persuaded the plaintiff, a life insurance salesman, to allow his photograph to be taken on the understanding that he would be considered for casting in a film. No contract was claimed to exist. The defendant used the photograph of the plaintiff without his permission in a bawdy film comedy, *Seven Angels*. The plaintiff's photograph was shown hanging above an ancestral shrine in the leading lady's living room. At one point in the film, the leading lady reflected on her lack of sexual activity in the previous ten years, while the camera zoomed in on the photograph of the plaintiff. Although the plaintiff's photograph featured in the film for only 12 seconds, his mother blamed the film for the death of his father some six months after the film was released. The plaintiff suffered considerable embarrassment among friends and family, and claimed that

174 See *Morrison v Moat* (1851) 9 Hare 241 and *Stephenson, Jordan & Harrison v McDonald & Evans* (1952) 69 RPC 10.

175 [1978] 2 NZLR 515, applied in *House of Spring Gardens v Point Blank Ltd* [1983] FSR 213.

176 [1969] RPC 41.

177 Cornish, *Intellectual Property*, at p 285.

178 Noted in (1987) HKLJ 362. HCA 7610 of 1985, unreported.

the film had affected his rapport with his customers. The plaintiff sued for defamation.

Rhind J awarded damages of $25,000 to the plaintiff and granted an injunction preventing the film being shown with the scenes featuring the plaintiff's photograph, and the defendant was liable to the plaintiff on two causes of action, namely, breach of confidence and defamation. Interestingly, his Lordship stated that although breach of confidence was not mentioned in the statement of claim, the facts pleaded were sufficient to support such an action. His Lordship referred to *Coco v Clark*[179] for a convenient summary of the elements of an action for breach of confidence. The first element requires that the information possess the necessary quality of confidence. His Lordship said that although nobody can prevent himself from being photographed, where a person makes himself available to be photographed by another in circumstances where one would expect confidentiality to be respected, a duty of confidence on the part of the person taking the photograph arises. In support of this, his Lordship cited *Pollard v Photographic Co.*[180]

The second element of the action for breach of confidence was held satisfied by the circumstances in which the plaintiff agreed that the photograph be taken. He allowed the photograph to be taken for the limited purpose of ascertaining whether he might be invited to play a part in a new film. His Lordship said:

> The circumstances are a far cry from showing that Mr Li had agreed that Genesis could make him a public figure. The law will protect activities occurring in a confidential situation because it recognises, 'A man may employ himself in private in a manner very harmless, but which, disclosed to society, may destroy the comfort in his life or even his success in it': *Prince Albert v Strange* . . .[181]

Additionally, his Lordship stated that any officious bystander would agree that the defendant knew or ought to have known the circumstances under which Mr Li's photograph was taken, that is, for the sole purpose of future casting.

As regards the third element in *Coco v Clark*, his Lordship found there was clearly an unauthorised use and a detriment to the plaintiff in the distress and embarrassment caused to him. On the facts, he held the detriment requirement was satisfied by the injury to feelings, having dismissed

---

179 [1969] RPC 41.

180 (1888) 40 Ch D 345.

181 (1849) 64 ER 293, at p 312.

as unfounded a claim of pecuniary injury in alleged damaged relations with life insurance clients.

It is not clear from the judgment what part of the damages award related to the claim for breach of confidence. His Lordship merely stated: 'Whether on the basis of breach of confidence (*Seager v Copydex (No 2)*)[182] or libel, Mr Li is entitled to compensation for the injury to his proper feelings of dignity and pride.'

As far as the writer is aware, breach of confidence has never been extended, within the non-American common law world, quite as far as in the present case (save perhaps the *Linda Koo* case). The judge had no difficulty in holding that a photograph has the necessary quality of confidence (secrecy) and, in so doing, no comment was addressed as to whether the photograph was in the public domain. Whether there is a necessity to prove sufficient detriment in an action for breach of confidence is perhaps still an open question,[183] though in those cases where it has been insisted upon, it was not enough to prove an injury to feelings as distinct from economic loss.[184] This insistence upon economic loss explains why the action for breach of confidence has never developed as a full blown protection for privacy in the United Kingdom or the Commonwealth, though it has done so in the United States, initially on the basis of the early English case *Prince Albert v Strange*.[185] The judge in the present case specifically discounted the plaintiff's claim of economic loss due to the exhibition of his photograph in the film. It follows that the sole detriment suffered by the plaintiff was an injury to his feelings or, by extension, an invasion of his privacy. A further problem not addressed in the judgment is that, assuming the defendant owned the film in its camera, copyright in the photograph would belong to the defendant, not the plaintiff, unless the photograph could be said to have been commissioned.[186]

One gains the impression that the judge was very much impressed by the character and dignity of the plaintiff and was outraged by the manner in which the defendant had invaded the plaintiff's privacy. It would be going too far to say that this decision must be regarded as wrongly decided for there can be little doubt that the present law of confidence is in a very fluid state, but the decision certainly does constitute a very significant extension to the present law. Whether it was realised that it constituted such an extension is, however, doubtful.

---

182 [1969] RPC 250.

183 See *Coco v Clark* [1969] RPC 41.

184 *Williams v Settle* [1960] 1 WLR 1072.

185 (1849) 47 ER 302.

186 Cf Copyright Act 1956, s 4.

It seems special criteria on sufficient detriment apply to government secrets. In the *Commonwealth of Australia v John Fairfax Pty Ltd*,[187] Mason J in the High Court of Australia said:

> It may be a sufficient detriment to the citizen that disclosure of information relating to his affairs will expose his actions to public discussion and criticism. But it can scarcely be a relevant detriment to the Government that publication of material concerning its actions will merely expose it to public discussion and criticism.

7.5.8. Defences

The public interest in confidential information The House of Lords in *British Steel v Granada*[188] affirmed that the public interest can only justify disclosure of confidential information where the information concerns an 'iniquity'. The term iniquity derives from the decision in *Gartside v Outram*,[189] and probably extends to serious criminal, tortuous or other legally wrongful conduct.[190] In *British Steel v Granada*, the alleged inefficiency of a nationalised industry was held, on the basis of the above test, not to constitute a matter of public interest. The Law Commission has, however, suggested that iniquity extends to misconduct.[191] This has been confirmed by the English Court of Appeal in recent years in *Francome v Mirror Group Newspapers*,[192] cited with approval in *Attorney General v Observer Newspapers (No 2)*[193] and *Lion Laboratories v Evans*.[194] These cases have now established a true public interest defence and are canvassed below.

The Law Commission has reported:[195]

> In our view the courts, in considering whether the balance of public interest lies in favour of the disclosure of information, should not be restricted to considering only information which concerns misconduct. We think there are important

---

187 (1980) 55 ALJR 45.
188 [1980] 3 WLR 774.
189 (1856) 26 LJ Ch 133.
190 Cornish suggests this interpretation, at p 272 and footnotes 54 and 55.
191 See *Hubbard v Vosper* [1972] 1 All ER 1023, *Woodward v Hutchins* [1977] 2 All ER 751, *Schering Chemicals v Falkman* [1981] 2 WLR 848 and *Dunford v Johnson* [1977] 1 Lloyd's Rep 50, at p 59.
192 [1984] 2 All ER 408.
193 [1990] 1 AC 109.
194 [1984] 2 All ER 417, applied by a similarly constituted Court of Appeal to that in the *Francome* case.
195 Para 6.78.

areas of information, not necessarily involving misconduct, where the public claim to be informed should be weighed by the courts against the interest in protecting confidentiality.

Lord Denning has been a persistent advocate of a wide public interest defence. In *Sun Printers v Westminster Press Ltd*,[196] the plaintiff attempted to restrain publication of a newspaper report on its financial plight that had been distributed to its various managers and certain union officials. Lord Denning held that, even if the information was confidential, which was doubtful due to the wide dissemination of the report, the public interest in access to the information outweighed any confidentiality.[197]

As stated above, the public interest defence appears to be established by the English Court of Appeal decisions in *Francome v Mirror Group Newspapers*[198] and *Lion Laboratories v Evans*.[199] In *Francome*, a journalist's source provided a tape to a newspaper of conversations between a husband and wife which suggested their involvement in horse race fixing. The husband sued the newspaper for an injunction to restrain publication. The newspaper claimed that publication was in the public interest and this defeated any claim of confidentiality. The Court of Appeal agreed that the public interest defence existed and extended to misconduct but the disclosure of confidential information pertaining to such misconduct had to be to the appropriate body. The appropriate body was the best placed to ameliorate the misconduct and depended on the peculiar facts of the case. In this case, the appropriate body was the police not the public via the newspaper's primary interest of boosting its circulation.

The *Lion Laboratories v Evans* case illustrates when a newspaper will be the appropriate channel for the disclosure of confidential information. In this case, the plaintiff sought an injunction to restrain disclosure of confidential information by an ex-employee who had worked on an intoximeter or breathalyser for measuring alcohol in the body via the breath. This instrument was to be used to secure criminal driving convictions. The defendant claimed to have data which showed that the intoximeter's accuracy was severely impaired. Complaints to the responsible minister, the Home Secretary, were to no avail. In these circumstances, the Court of Appeal held the defendant had no choice but to go to the newspapers, as approaches to the appropriate body had been fruitless.

---

196 [1982] IRLR 292.
197 At p 310.
198 [1984] 2 All ER 408.
199 [1984] 2 All ER 417.

No doubt an argument could be constructed to suggest a public interest defence in the information arising on the facts of the *Mitchell* case.[200]

7.5.9. Bona Fide Purchaser in Good Faith of Confidential Information

According to the English Law Commission, it is doubtful whether a bona fide purchaser for value of confidential information, in good faith, is entitled to disclose the information. This is supported by the decision of the Supreme Court of New South Wales in *Wheatley v Bell*,[201] where the court rejected the defence as inappropriate to confidence. See, however, the decision in *International Tools Ltd v Koller*,[202] where the Court of Appeal of Ontario held the defence was available in a breach of confidence action.

7.6. CONCLUSION

With a Trademark law beginning in 1873, Hong Kong is not a recent convert to intellectual property. Though weaned at the breast of the United Kingdom through its first century as a colony, Hong Kong in China is increasingly likely to influence China as much as it is to be influenced. Only a decade ago it was impolitic to refer in the mainland to Hong Kong's lead in intellectual property and legal system in general. This is no longer the case as Hong Kong is increasingly cited in the mainland as a precedent for change. Change looms large across the world in regard to digital subject matter and copyright and not least in Hong Kong which was the first jurisdiction to imprison a person for uploading a film to a P2P server, beginning with a lawful copy. In trademark law, the increasingly Germanic black and white approach of the European Court of Justice and its binding effect on British courts may cause Hong Kong courts to canvass a different and more nuanced precedent like the pre-EU British approach. Irrespective of this, the intellectual property law of the Hong Kong SAR of the People's Republic of China remains as dynamic as it ever was.

---

[200] Cited at note 122, above.

[201] For a full discussion, see '*Wheatley v Bell*: Confidential Information – Property or Not? Robyn Durie', [1983] 7 EIPR 194.

[202] (1968) 67 DLR (2d) 386.

8. Copyright protection under the network environment

Liu Chuntian[1]

Along with the appearance and widespread use of the computer as the core of network technology, there is a new economic era arriving with the use of web technology. The network is becoming part of our lives and our way of life, and an important element in the environment in which we live. Internet technology has greatly changed people's way of life. The human being's way of behavior, living and his/her way of thinking have changed dramatically. Behavior is one of the issues that most concerns us since behavior is not only primary to human social activity, but also at the core of standardization and research in law and legal science. However, the law is selective in terms of human behavior. There is an ancient but always well-used principle about the law that 'the law ignores the little things'. Under a network environment, what concerns the 'law' is human behavior that gives rise to innovation, change and elimination of the economic and social order, studying these new behaviorial forms and giving appropriate titles to these behaviors, and integrating these behaviors into the existing system to achieve systemization. There is also a need to regulate behavior in order to achieve a balance of norms and to promote the harmony and progress of the economy and society. Based on the above logic, this chapter proposes two aspects that need to be examined more deeply: (1) What is the network? What are the differences and similarities compared with other technological advances in history? What has network technology changed? (2) From the legal point of view, how can we face the challenges that network technology brings us?

[1] Professor of Law and Executive Director of the IP Teaching and Research Center, Renmin University of China.

8.1. NETWORK TECHNOLOGY: A NEW WAY OF HUMAN LIFE

The network is a concept linked with computer technology with a specific connotation and usually refers to a system that connects computers distributed in different geographical regions to specialized external devices so that a large number of computers can easily transfer information to each other and share knowledge resources simultaneously.

The development of the network is based on computer technology. Digital technology-based computer technology has only six or seven decades of history from its initial invention, but it has developed and popularized rapidly with its unique advantage since the development of the Internet. With the advent of communication, news, e-commerce and video, the network shows unparalleled superiority as Pandora's black box in the fields of intelligence, academia, education, personal communication, market transactions, entertainment, telephone and television etc. Today, the digital network exists everywhere regardless of political, economic, military or cultural aspects. From the state to the individual, from production to life, the network has become indispensable and can collect all the knowledge of the history of mankind with a 'clean sweep'. The network has become one of the most important ways of life of the human being, so much so, that in modern society, people cannot live normal lives without the network. Therefore, in China, the network is often called the fourth medium, following newspapers, radio and television and is superior to the others since it is not only a synthesis of the previous three kinds of media, but also constitutes a non-reversable threat to the traditional media with its technological advantages of unique interactivity, hypertext links and a global reach.

8.2. KNOWLEDGE PATTERNS: THE NETWORK AS A TECHNICAL PATTERN (NOT A NEW FORM OF WORK)

Human beings are animals with knowledge. Knowledge is the description of a human's achievement. In the history of knowledge creation, there have been a variety of landmark technology forms, such as technical writing, modelling techniques of painting, sculpture and architecture, performance technology, printing technology, recording technology, photography technology, radio broadcasting technology, film technology, TV technology, reproduction technology, cable TV technology, the technology of computer memory storage and retrieval of works, and the creative use of computer technology. All of these technologies produced a tremendous effect respectively on innovation in knowledge categories and knowledge of expression, storage, transmission, extraction and display means. However, the function and nature of different technologies are different. The invention of writing technologies brought human beings a basic means of description, which is not only the method of creation, storage, transmission and display, but also a unique form of expression – an independent form of literary art. Similarly, modeling techniques, performance techniques, recording techniques, photography techniques, movie technology, TV technologies etc., are different means of describing knowledge, also became special art forms of their own; the remaining technologies, such as printing, radio, and copying techniques, cable television and computer technology, are only the creation, storage, transmission, extraction of the inherent knowledge and innovation of the display means, but they do not constitute a new form of work. It should be specifically pointed out that although human beings' existing knowledge is enormous and diverse, its essence is the same – all knowledge is expressive and descriptive. All knowledge has recourse to a kind of 'form', symbols that exist; any form and symbol can be transformed into a proportional relationship, and any proportion can be described by numbers. Therefore, all knowledge can be converted into digital form. Digital expression is the common language of knowledge, not a new form of work. In short, the digital technology-based network technology is purely a technical issue. Although it greatly enriches the creation, storage, transmission, extraction and display methods of knowledge, it never becomes a new form of work. So the common terms in media, such 'network works', 'network copyright' or 'network infringement' are imprecise and misleading.

8.3. NETWORK TECHNOLOGY AND THE LAW OF PROPERTY

Our lives have experienced great change with the application and continuous development of network technology. The network language, in contrast to traditional print media, is 'rushing towards us like snowflakes'. It is concise, vivid, developing rapidly, and as a result, a so-called Internet language and culture have emerged, together with new 'behaviors' under the network environment. Through trade-offs, change and adjustment of the law, what should concern us most is the law of property. As mentioned above, the emergence and extensive application of network technology provides brand new ways and means of knowledge creation, storage, transmission and display, and also creates a series of unprecedented new behaviors in human life. Simultaneously, network technology creates the need to adjust the way in which social wealth is transferred, leading us to a reform of the law of property. As a new medium, the network can store all kinds of traditional works in the digital format free from the limitations of geography and political boundaries. Once a work is uploaded to the network, it can be accessed anywhere in the world so long as the work is 'connected' to the Internet. This reform of the concept of (intangible) property is the real reason for the interest of the international community in both protecting and accessing such works. Also because of this reason, the World Intellectual Property Organization (WIPO) concluded two important conventions: the WIPO Copyright Treaty and the WIPO Performances and Phonograms Treaty in 1996. The greatest value of these two conventions is that they reflect the legal issues in the fields of copyright and neighboring rights due to the emergence of digital technology and the Internet.

8.4. THE INTERACTION OF CHINESE LEGISLATION AND JUDICIAL PRACTICE: COPYRIGHT LAW AND NETWORK TECHNOLOGY

Each time, the reason why the emergence of new technology attracts society's attention is not novelty and the progress of technology itself, but rather the flow of material and knowledge caused by the application of the technology, as well as changes in the ownership of property affected by this flow pattern. Network technology has swept the world with its superiority. In particular, this network technology has been quickly and widely adopted by China. During China's industrialization, the country also faced copyright protection issues, alongside Western developed countries, as a result of the emergence of network technology. There is a causal and interactive relationship between legislation and practice. Law is the summary and enhancement of practice, and any legal requirements should come from the social economy and life, and the general requirements of social life. Practice is the objective criteria to test legal theory and legislation. As such, all theories and laws that are divorced from the ordinary requirements of social life will face difficulties in practice. China has experience in both areas.

On the one hand, the practice calls for canonical experience if there is no legal regulation. This is essentially the same as judge-made law, which is a test of both the judges' ability and quality. In 1999, there was a case in China that concerned Internet companies who loaded Wang Meng and five other writers' works online without the writers' consent.[2] The writers' private negotiations for settlement with the Internet Service Provider (ISP) proved unsuccessful and they subsequently filed a lawsuit in the courts. According to China's contemporary Copyright Law provision, the law did not explicitly state that the authors enjoyed the Network Information Transmission Right, in their works. The ISP argued that copyright in the works could only apply to paper works, but when the works were transmitted online, the copyright's ownership and existence were questionable, and so the company refused to accept the court's decision that copyright in the works had been infringed. In the hearing of the Beijing First Intermediate People's Court, the judges captured the essence of the case in that the ISP had transmitted copyright works online without the rights' owner's consent, and the nature of this activity in using others' copyright works commercially was an infringement despite the fact that no such specific offence was recorded in the statute books at the time. The court held that the ISP had infringed the copyright in the works and this established a precedent in China for intangible works, and subsequently brought a measure of legal certainty and good social effect. The court's decision also provided a solid foundation for the subsequent legislative and judicial amendments to China's copyright law. When China revised its Copyright Law in 2001, regarding the issue of network transmission of works protected by copyright law, the court had already made several more mature judicial decisions to support an amendment to the law by adding an Information Network Transmission Right to the law, which was an appropriate legislative amendment to meet the general requirements of social life, and which then provided a legal basis for the subsequent release of China's Information Network Transmission Right Protection Ordinance 2006.[3]

On the other hand, it is difficult to apply new legislation in practice. The practical application of new legislation makes higher demands on the judiciary and the ability of the judge. For example, the issue of how to understand and apply 'rental rights' in China has proved particularly challenging. In 2001, the right to lease copyright works was added to Article 10 of China's Copyright Law. Article 10(7) states: 'the right of lease, that is, the right to nongratuitously permit others to temporarily exploit a cinematographic work, a work created in a way similar to cinematography or

---

[2] *Wang Meng and others v Cenpok Telecommunication Technology Ltd.*, Bejing Haidian District Court, 18 September 1999.

[3] Also translated as 'Regulations for the Protection of the Right of Communication through Information Network 2006', available at: http://www.ipr2.org/ipsearch/list.php?id=16, accessed September 2010.

computer software, unless the computer software is not the main object under the lease'. Before the law changed, China had experience of leasing films in practice, but had not encountered the legal use of rental rights with computer software. 'Rental rights' reflects the copyright expansion requirements of developed countries, and in a way, China amended its copyright law by adding this provision as a result of migration and adoption of developed countries' laws. If the law is to provide a service to the life of a society, the norms of provision of the law need to be easily understood. On the surface, the concept of 'rental rights' in computer software is not difficult to understand. But in terms of actual practice, due to a lack of precedent in the area, the application of the new 'rental rights' provision was very difficult. The case of *Shenzhen Tencent Inc. v Taobao for QQ number sales*, completed in 2009, reflects this situation.[4] Tencent's customers sold QQ numbers provided free of charge at Taobao websites without Tencent's prior authorization. Tencent QQ software is an instant messaging software developed by the Tencent company. The software provides free services to Tencent users on condition that users need to register with the Tencent network with their real name and sign an end-user agreement, Tencent QQ User Terms of Service, online. Following this, the user is then able to obtain a QQ number and password provided by Tencent to log on and use Tencent's software free of charge. Under the terms of the Tencent QQ customer service agreement, QQ accounts are owned by Tencent, and the user only has a usage right, and this usage right only belongs to the person who initially registered. Tencent specifically prohibited the transfer and sale of accounts, the transfer of the QQ number and password to others, and the transfer of the account privately with or without payment. Later, Tencent found that QQ numbers were being sold online through the Taobao website platform. Tencent believed that its interests were being harmed, but was unsure of its specific rights and how these rights were being infringed under Chinese law. In order to stop the online trade in QQ numbers and accounts, Tencent sued a user who sold QQ numbers through Taobao in the Shenzhen Nanshan district court on three grounds of property rights violation, unfair competition, and copyright infringement of computer software. The court requested that Tencent give up two grounds and required Tencent to pursue a claim only on the ground of 'violation of copyright of computer software'. Eventually, the court supported Tencent's request and it won the first trial. However, during two years of litigation from the commencement of Tencent becoming aware

---

[4] *Shenzhen Tencent Inc. v Taobao (Tencent Computer Inc. v Wang Youjin and Zhejiang Taobao Network Ltd)*, Shennan Fa Zhi Chu Zi Decision No. 7 (2007).

that its rights had been infringed to the end of the first instance proceedings, neither Tencent nor the first instance court knew the exact subject of litigation. This was similar, for example, to an injured person coming to a doctor for medical treatment, where the patient only knew that he was in pain, but did not know the location of the injury. Later in the second instance trial, the judge asked Tencent to make clear exactly which right under copyright was being infringed, otherwise the court would not be able to support Tencent's general claim of 'copyright infringement'. After a careful study of copyright law, Tencent clarified that its rental right in its computer software was being infringed. The second instance court supported this claim and maintained the first instance court's decision and dismissed the defendant's appeal.

Rent is a familiar concept in the Chinese people's daily life, but the idea of a rental right in the field of copyright is an alien term for the ordinary man. Rental is a behavior of reproduction and distribution. In Western Society, it is reasonably common for private individuals to copy (in the past, perhaps 'videotape') copyrighted programs, such as television broadcast material, for private use only. This of course leads to questions about exhaustion of the right to reproduction and distribution. Each country will have its own domestic rules on exhaustion of rights which will vary country by country. Rental rights were conceived to regulate private copying of copyrighted material. However, due to a divergence of adoption in different Western countries, the main consensus was reflected in the TRIPS Agreement, where the scope of rental rights was limited to three types of works, including computer programs, cinematographic works and sound recordings according to the domestic laws of WTO member states. Due to this lack of uniformity, there is no overall consensus on the scope of rental rights. Moreover, neither the TRIPS agreement nor the subsequent conclusion of the WCT and WPPT defined 'rent' and 'commercial rent'. An earlier draft of the WPPT defined 'rent' as follows: 'sound recordings rent is a transfer of possession of copies of sound recordings in any form in a limited period of time to get payment'.[5] The version of the WPPT adopted no longer has a definition of rent. The rental right is set out in Article 13 (WPPT). Therefore, we can see that the formation of 'rental rights' has incorporated different conditions in different domestic laws and social backgrounds, but (within international law) also has its own specific meaning. In the absence of similar experience with the development of both a cultural and legal history of rental rights in

[5] Mihalyfi Archer, *Copyright and the Internet*, Guo Shoukang, Wan Yong and Xiang Jin, trans., China Encyclopedia Press, 2009, p. 715.

China, China has copied the multilateral treaties and international treaty provisions, which given the West's own historical problems in dealing with rental rights, will give rise to challenges and practical problems (legally and socially) in enforcing international provisions in domestic law in China. China simply does not have the same level of experience in dealing with rental rights as the West. For the Chinese, therefore, it is worth considering the following question for lawmakers: should Chinese practice follow the arrangement of the law or should the law conform to practical life in China?

8.5. IMPROVEMENTS OF COPYRIGHT LAW UNDER THE NETWORK ENVIRONMENT

The application of Internet technology not only provides unprecedented new tools for knowledge creation, storage and delivery, but has also contributed to a new flow and distribution of property. In response to the challenges of network technology, China's copyright law was amended in 2001 to include 'rental rights' and the 'Information Network Transmission Right'. These new rights were added in the copyright section with the adoption of the Regulations for the Protections of Computer Software (CSPR) 2001; Regulations for the Implementation of the Copyright Law of 2002; Regulations for the Collective Management of Copyrights 2005, and regulations for the Protection of the Right of Communication through Information Networks 2006, together with a series of regulations related to computer networks. Also, the Supreme People's Court and Supreme People's Procuratorate made corresponding judicial interpretations.[6] This series of measures provided an effective legal means for the emergence of new social networking applications (such as QQ, which is the equivalent of MSN in China), economic relations and legal issues arising from new network technology. This new law would then cover mainstream applications, but is of course only one side of the picture. As in the West, new applications such as peer-to-peer (P2P) have gained prominence in more specialist markets and so China needs to consider how the law can be perfected to cover these as well. There are several issues to consider here.

---

[6] Judicial Interpretations of the Supreme People's Court Concerning the Application of Laws to the Trial of Copyright Cases involving the Disputes over Computer Network (CNJI, effective from 22 November 2000, and revised in 2003 and 2006 respectively). For further details, see Chapter 4 on copyright.

8.5.1. Private Rights and State Regulations

The effect of any functioning intellectual property system is to conditionally restrict competition, creating limited monopoly rights to protect an undertaking's exclusive right in intellectual property. From the macro point of view, the state's intervention is a necessary condition for an Intellectual Property (IP) system's establishment and survival. However, despite the intervention of the state, Intellectual Property Rights (IPRs) have always been a matter of negotiation between undertakings, and dictated by economic and cultural needs and the free movement of the market. IPRs are essentially private rights. And yet new networking technology is making available content protected by private IPRs in a very 'public way'. The Internet has allowed for mass distribution of material. Some would argue therefore that IPRs are no longer 'private' in nature, but should in fact be regulated as 'public' rights. However, the idea that 'private rights of intellectual property should be viewed as public rights' as a consequence of new technologies is absurd in theory, and dangerous in practice. China is a socialist country and has developed through a long-term 'planned' economy. In China, the concept of 'collective ownership' is deeply ingrained and so the idea of 'private' IPRs being viewed as 'public rights' is not so strange. However, with China's membership of the WTO and therefore the necessary adoption of the TRIPS as a requirement of membership, China's view on IPRs has most certainly been guided by TRIPS, in particular the preamble to TRIPS that 'All members should recognize intellectual property rights are private rights'. This declaration is an important reference point for guiding the Chinese people and in helping them to understand how to improve China's legal system.

8.5.2. The Principle of Systematization of Law and Integration with China's Civil Law System

The idea of ensuring that the law is effectively harmonized and systemized is an inherent quality of law which depends neither on state authority nor on an individual's likes or dislikes. We can look to the natural systems of nature for examples to guide our own 'human systems'. Consider, for example, a tree: the foliage of a tree is a broad, subtle, and complex, orderly life system built by countless systems at different levels, from root to tree trunk, branches and leaves, all forming a trouble-free system with production, distribution, storage, consumption, and metabolism. The nature of intellectual property is private; however, in China, the regulation and enforcement of IP comes under civil law. Civil law has its own inherent spirit, ideas, characteristics and principles, which must be followed.

Historically, intellectual property laws have been made independently (or outside) the traditional Chinese civil law system, but follow in practice the principles of civil law. China lacks a civil law tradition and has no comprehensive civil code (unlike Germany and France), but instead has many different 'regulations'. And so, in China, the regulation of intellectual property is undertaken under the auspices of functional departments. This can give rise to a lack of coordination between different departments and therefore lead to a deviation from the normal principles of civil law to be found outside of China for example. Legislation has designed rules for economic activity, and efficiency is the highest principle of economic activity. Legislation should respect traditions, but also develop with the times. European countries and America have well-developed civil legal systems, but their intellectual property laws do not have long histories (as compared with their civil law systems for example) and they have failed to be effectively incorporated into their civil law systems. However, in recent years, a number of less advanced countries have successfully integrated IPR laws into their existing civil codes. This is an important revelation for China's policymakers in IPR and Civil Code codification. It will be a step forward for Chinese legislators to find a way of integrating IPR law into Chinese traditional civil law.

8.6. THE UNITY OF GLOBALIZATION AND CHALLENGES FROM NETWORK TECHNOLOGY

Network technology has derived new tools from its original application to date. Technology itself is very complex and trying to devise legal frameworks from the 'inside' that are dependent on technology can be confusing and misleading. But looking 'externally', and analysing the effect and impact of technology on society, might be a better way to help achieve effective regulation. Facing these new technical challenges, the key for China is to find a development model for its intellectual property system – not only to conform with the trend of globalization, but also to be in line with China's national conditions. To achieve this, the following issues need to be considered.

8.6.1. China as a Developing Country

China has greatly improved over the last 30 years, basically as a result of the freedom to manufacture, but it is still at the early stages of industrialization. Although China has stepped onto the express train of new technologies, China's development is far from complete. China is still in the difficult process of evolving from a 'subsistence' society to one that has moderate prosperity throughout the whole community. China's intellectual property system has achieved significant progress in the past 20 years on the basis of starting from scratch with regard to intellectual property rights.[7] As we all know, Rome was not built in a day. There is no one country that has developed so rapidly in 20 years compared with the many other countries that have developed their IPR systems over 200 years. We cannot delude ourselves; China has to develop on a step-by-step basis on all issues, including IP, so that the result is true, reliable, and conforms to the wishes of the international community.

8.6.2. Legislating for Problems of New Technology and Local Conditions

Legislation in this area is a complicated project. China is not a case law country, nor can it be simply classified as a constitutional law country. Currently, as mentioned, China's technological level throughout the country (as opposed to the large cities) is relatively low, and countrywide skill in dealing with intellectual property legislation is still not mature. In this respect, China has to be careful not to rush to follow the examples of developed countries or international organizations' new approach to legislation, when lack of knowledge could possibly damage China's self-interest. China needs a flexible IPR policy that leaves sufficient room for maneuver. In the construction of an intellectual property legal system, China has formed its own unique three-stage model. The first stage is to focus on the trial of a case and the establishment of any new principles. The second stage is to collate experience to support the formation of a court's 'judicial interpretation' and to guide the judiciary in delivering their judgments. The final (third) stage is to adopt the 'judicial interpretation' into legislation when it is mature enough. Jurisprudence has proved that this model is practical, feasible and effective, and should therefore be followed.

8.6.3. Building Innovation

With the rapid development of a private economy, China's society has shown tremendous variety: the market is growing exponentially. For the coming 30 years, however, innovation will be the only means to obtain

---

[7] However, see for example the development of early systems of 'copyright' under the Qing Dynasty, as highlighted in Chapter 4 on copyright.

substantial progress, and for this, the system of intellectual property protection is key in China. In the future, the main application of intellectual property will be by private undertakings engaged in enterprise. The development of China's IPR legal system will depend mainly on these enterprises, and government and private industry must be prepared to switch roles. The government will need to convert its role, changing from current leader to advisor, and converting from one who has many different and simultaneous roles on the pitch, such as formulating the rules of the game, being a player in his or own right, and a coach, to one who functions instead as sole referee.

9. Computer software, information technology and e-commerce (1)

Zhang Ping[1] and Meng Zhaoping

9.1. INTRODUCTION

The application of computer software, information technology and e-commerce in China developed contemporaneously with changes in technology worldwide. The relevant Chinese legislation has also taken note of the laws of the developed countries as well as relevant international treaties.

In China, computer software is primarily protected by copyright law. With the development of expectations by rights owners of software for substantive protection of the technology, as well as increasing competition in the market, patent protection has also been sought. However, software-related patents are mainly filed by foreign companies through the Patent Cooperation Treaty.[2] Importantly, the provisions on computer software-related patent applications have been incorporated into the Chinese Patent Examination Guidelines in order to clarify the requirements of software-related patents, as provided by China's Patent Law for granting patent rights to computer software, and which is in line with other modern developed patent systems throughout the world.[3]

The protection of software under contract law has always been applied by enterprises in software trade activities. Since Chinese enterprises, in

---

1 Zhang Ping, Professor of Law, Administrative Vice President, School of Intellectual Property, Peking University; Meng Zhaoping, Peking University. The authors are grateful to He Huaiwen for help with translation.

2 The Patent Cooperation Treaty (PCT) allows for patent protection for an invention simultaneously in each of a large number of countries by filing an 'international' patent application. The application can be filed by anyone who is a national or resident of a PCT contracting State. It may generally be filed with the national patent office of the contracting State of which the applicant is a national or resident or, if the applicant chooses, with the International Bureau of WIPO in Geneva. See the WIPO website at: http://www.wipo.int/treaties/en/registration/pct/summary_pct.html. China is a member of the PCT.

3 See Chapter 2 for a more complete discussion of Chinese patent law.

most cases, are licensees, they usually use contracts provided by rights owners from developed countries, which sometimes contain unfair clauses. However, they usually have to accept these unfair license conditions owing to their weaker status in negotiations. The forms of shrink-wrap contracts and click-wrap contracts are both accepted in China, yet whether all the clauses in these contracts are regarded as valid depends on whether the conclusion of the contracts is complied with under the basic principles of Chinese contract law as well as whether there are any clauses that have been prohibited explicitly by the law. *Open source* software has been widely used in China in recent years. Yet research on license agreements concerning open source software is inadequate and the business community in China has seldom conducted research on such license clauses and the legal risks in the application of open source.

With the wide use of the internet, legislation regarding network security, computer crime and electronic signatures have also been taken into account. The Electronic Signature Law of the PRC was adopted in 2004, which can be regarded as the first specific law related to e-commerce in China. In view of the new copyright issues in the digital industry, the Chinese copyright law was amended in 2001, when the 'right of information network dissemination' and the 'right of lease concerning a work' created in a way similar to cinematography and computer software were introduced in accordance with the WIPO Copyright Treaty and WIPO Performances and Phonograms Treaty.[4] Currently, there are still several gaps in Chinese legislation with regard to information technology. For instance, the legitimacy and enforceability of 'virtual property' calls for specific provision in the law.[5]

In the information technology legislation, we also need to look at the regulation of intellectual property rights and the abuse of monopoly rights. The Anti-monopoly Law of the PRC was adopted on 1 August 2008 and administrative organs have been established in three related areas.[6] The issue of balancing the legitimate monopoly rights of those who hold IPRs and the (potential) abuse of such rights is within the scope of the anti-monopoly law; however, specific regulations are still pending.[7]

---

[4] Copyright Law, Art. 10.

[5] See Chapter 4 on copyright.

[6] The three administrative organs include the Anti-monopoly Bureau of the Ministry of Commerce, Department of Price Supervision of National Development and Reform Commission, and Enforcement Bureau of Anti-monopoly and Anti-Unfair Competition of the State Administration for Industry and Commerce. They are jointly led by the Anti-monopoly Commission of the State Council.

[7] See Chapters 11 and 12.

After China's accession to the World Trade Organization (WTO), the WTO rules have had a significant impact on Chinese intellectual property legislation. The second amendment of the Patent Law and Trademark Law, as well as the first amendment of the Copyright Law,[8] have been made to meet the requirements of the TRIPS Agreement. However, although domestic Chinese law has been amended, knowledge and application of WTO rules within Chinese society is still inadequate, and the preparation of domestic enterprises for the application of such rules also inadequate. This leads to the result that when Chinese enterprises export large quantities of products overseas, they quite often encounter barriers which hinder them from international markets, including intellectual property barriers, customs seizure, patent hold-up, abuse of litigation rights, etc. These problems can only be solved with the development and maturity of Chinese enterprises and their working knowledge of IPR. For this reason, the Chinese government needs to pursue active strategies[9] rather than taking passive countermeasures.

9.2. MAIN CHINESE LAWS PROTECTING COMPUTER SOFTWARE

Legal protection of computer software is a complicated issue which requires cooperation on many levels. The rights owner usually has several options in deciding which legal methods or measures to use to provide more complete and more effective protection of its computer software. In China, after a computer software-related product has been completed, the inventor or the designer may protect the product via copyright law, patent law, trademark law, anti-unfair competition law as well as contract law as mentioned above and discussed further below.

9.2.1. Copyright Law

Computer software in China is primarily protected by China's Copyright Law, which was adopted on 7 September 1990.[10] Further, the Regulations

---

[8] In 2000, in order to meet the requirements for entry into the WTO, China completely reviewed and amended the Patent Law, the Trademark Law and the Copyright Law in line with the WTO agreements.

[9] See Outline of the National Intellectual Property Strategy, issued by the State Council in June 2008, available at: http://www.sipo.gov.cn/sipo2008/yw/2008/200806/t20080611_406125.html.

[10] See Copyright Law, Art. 3. The copyright law was revised in 2007, and again in 2010. See Chapter 4 for further details.

for the Protection of Computer Software[11] (hereinafter referred to as 'RPCS'), which were adopted in June 1991, are specific on implementing copyright protection for computer software. The amendment to the RPCS, which was adopted on 20 December 2001, has kept the original basic principles. The RPCS is discussed in the next section.

9.2.1.1. Definition of computer software

Article 2 RPCS, provides that the term 'computer software' shall mean computer programs and their relevant files. 'Computer program' shall mean a coded command sequence, or a symbolic command sequence or symbolic statement sequence automatically convertible to a coded command sequence that can be executed by a device capable of processing information, such as a computer or other such devices, where the purpose of such a sequence is to achieve a certain result. The source program and the target program of the same computer program shall be the same work. 'Files' means written information and diagrams used to describe the contents, composition, design, function specifications, development details, test results and method of use of a program, such as program design explanations, flow charts and user's manuals.

Owing to the special features of computer software, whether other aspects of software that have not been defined by the law, such as character databases, menu and user interfaces, are protected by copyright law is still under discussion.

9.2.1.2. Copyright in computer software

Like copyright in literary or artistic works, copyright in computer software includes moral rights and property rights. The former includes the right of publication, the right of authorship and the right of revision, whilst the latter includes the right of reproduction, the right of distribution, the right of lease, the right of information network dissemination, the right of translation. Specifically, copyright owners of computer software have the following rights:[12]

1. The right of publication refers to the right to decide whether to make the software available to the public. 'Available to the public' means presenting, exhibiting, displaying or using the said software to unspecified members of the public. Available to the public does not

---

[11] Also translated as the Regulations for the Protections of Computer Software (CSPR).

[12] RPCS, Art. 8.

necessarily mean publishing. Software copyright owners are entitled to exercise fully the right of publication, namely, they are entitled to determine where, when and how to publish, the means of publication as well as not to publish at all.

2. The right of authorship refers to the right to be identified as the developer and to affix one's name to the software developed, including one's genuine name, fake name as well as the right not to affix the name.
3. The right of revision refers to the right to make additions and supplements to, or abridgement of the software, or change the order of commands and statements.
4. The right of reproduction refers to the right to make one or more copies of the software.
5. The right of distribution refers to the right to provide originals or copies of software to the public by sale or gift.
6. The right of lease refers to the right to permit others to temporarily use software for charge, unless the software itself is not the essential object of the lease.
7. The right of information network dissemination refers to the right to make Software available to the public by wire or by wireless means, enabling members of the public to access the software at a time and from a place individually chosen by them.
8. The right of translation refers to the right to convert original software from one natural language to another natural language.

In addition, a software copyright owner may license or assign others to exercise all or part of his/her software copyright, and has the right to receive remuneration.

9.2.1.3. Limitations of copyright in computer software

Like traditional copyright, copyright in software is not absolute. There are quite a few limitations on the exercise of copyright provided in laws and regulations. However, the amendment of the RPCS in 2001 raised the level of protection and deleted the provisions regarding statutory and compulsory licenses.

Article 17 RPCS provides that where software is used for installing, displaying, transmitting or saving for the purpose of learning and studying design concepts and principles, permission from and payment of remuneration to the software copyright owner is not required. This is regarded as a limitation on the right of reproduction of the software right owners.

Article 16 RPCS provides that an owner of a lawful copy of Software shall enjoy the following rights:

1. To install the software in a computer and other device that has the capacity for information processing as required for use;
2. To make a back-up in order to prevent damage to the lawful copy. Such back-up copy may not be made available to others by any means. The owner of that copy is then responsible for destroying the back-up copy when he ceases to be the rightful owner of the lawful copy; and
3. To make necessary modifications to the software in order to use it in the actual computer application environment or to improve its functions and performance. Unless agreed otherwise in a contract, the modified software may not be provided to any third party without permission of the software copyright owner.

9.2.1.4. Term of protection

The copyright in software shall arise when the software is completed.[13] A natural person's copyright in software shall be protected for a period consisting of the natural person's lifetime and 50 years after his death, with the end date being on 31 December of the 50th year after the natural person's death. Where the software is jointly developed, such period shall end on 31 December of the 50th year after the death of the last surviving natural person.[14]

The copyright in software of a legal person or other organization shall be protected for a period of 50 years, ending on 31 December of the 50th year after the first publication of the software. If such software is not published within 50 years from the date of completion, it shall no longer be protected.[15]

Where copyright in software is owned by a natural person, the successor to the software copyright may, after the death of the natural person, succeed to the rights except the right of attribution in accordance with the relevant provisions of the Chinese Inheritance Law within the period of protection of the software copyright.[16]

Where copyright in software is owned by a legal person or other organization, the copyright shall, after such legal person or other organization is changed or terminated, be transferred to the legal person or other organization that succeeds to the former's rights and obligations or, if no legal

---

13 RPCS, Art. 14.

14 *Id.*

15 *Id.*

16 RPCS, Art. 15.

person or other organization succeeds to such rights and obligations, to the State, for the remaining period of protection.[17]

9.2.1.5. Registration of computer software

Copyright in a work vests on the date when the work is completed. It does not depend on any legal procedure. The same rule applies to software. Copyright in software shall begin when the software is completed. Registration of software is for the purpose of the administration by relevant organs and providing a certificate for the software rights owner.[18] Registration is not a prerequisite for copyright protection for software, that is, software, even if not registered, is still entitled to enjoy copyright protection.

9.2.1.6. Infringement and liabilities

The doctrine for determining copyright infringement of computer software is access plus substantial similarity. Generally, liabilities for infringement of computer software include (i) civil liabilities for publication or registration of or affixing one's name to software without permission from the owner of the copyright therein; and (ii) civil, administrative or even criminal liabilities for reproduction, distribution or lease without permission from the owner of the copyright therein.[19]

The infringer must provide compensation on the basis of the right owner's actual loss. Where actual loss is difficult to calculate, compensation may be made on the basis of the infringer's illegal gains. The amount of compensation also includes reasonable expenses incurred by the rights owner for stopping the infringement. Where the rights owner's actual losses or the infringer's illegal gains cannot be determined, the courts shall consider the circumstances of the infringement and may award compensation of RMB 500,000 or less.[20]

If a publisher or producer of software reproductions is unable to give evidence that his/her publication or production was lawfully authorized, or if a distributor of a software copy or a person who leases software copies is unable to produce evidence of the lawful origin of that copy leased, he/she shall be liable.[21] Where software developed by a software developer is similar to existing software because there are only limited forms of expression that may be used, there will be no infringement for such similarity.

---

17 *Id.*
18 See RPCS, Art. 7.
19 See RPCS, Art. 23–4.
20 *Id.*
21 See RPCS, Art. 28.

If the holder of a software copy does not know or there are no reasonable grounds for him to know that the software is an infringing copy, s/he shall not be liable for compensation, but s/he should cease to use and destroy the illegal copy. If the cessation of use and destruction of the infringing copy will result in major losses to the user of the copy, s/he may continue to use it on condition of paying the software copyright owner a reasonable fee.[22]

9.2.2. Patent Law

The Chinese Patent Law 2008 has explicitly excluded abstract ideas from being protected. As a result, pure computer programs are not patentable. However, the Patent Examination Guidelines 2010 (hereinafter referred to as 'PEG') provide that computer software involving technical solutions can be eligible for the grant of a patent. In practice, it is common to file a patent application based on a combination of computer software and equipment or device.

It is not clearly provided in the Chinese patent law whether an invention relating to computer software is ineligible for patent protection. However, Article 25 of the Patent Law provides that to be eligible, a subject matter for patent protection should (i) be a new technical solution; and (ii) rules and methods for mental activities are not eligible subject matter.

Article 2 of the Patent Law can serve as a further legal ground and limitation for granting a patent in respect of computer software. Article 2 defines 'inventions-creations', the subject matter of patent protection, as inventions, utility models and designs. 'Invention' means any new technical solution relating to a product, a process or improvement thereof. 'Utility model' means any new technical solution relating to the shape, the structure, or their combination, of a product, which is fit for practical use. 'Design' means any new design of the shape, the pattern or their combination, or the combination of the color with shape or pattern, of a product, which creates an aesthetic feeling and is fit for industrial application.

Article 25 Patent Law provides that for any of the following, no patent right shall be granted: (1) scientific discoveries; (2) rules and methods for mental activities; (3) methods for the diagnosis or for the treatment of diseases; (4) animal and plant varieties; (5) substances obtained by means of nuclear transformation; (6) two dimensional designs of images, colors or combinations of the two that mainly serve as indicators.

It is clear from the above that pure computer programs will be excluded

22 See RPCS, Art. 30.

from patent protection if the program constitutes rules and methods for mental activities. Yet, computer software is usually applied in technical areas. A patent can be granted if the invention comprising of software is applied in certain technical solutions and achieves certain technical results, satisfying the subject matter eligibility criteria under patent law. Therefore, the guidelines to the Patent Law provide that in determining whether or not a claimed subject matter in a patent application involving rules and methods for mental activities is eligible, the following principles shall apply:

1. If a claim concerns only rules and methods for mental activities, it shall not be granted a patent right.
2. Besides 1, if a claim as a whole contains not only subject matter of rule or method for mental activities but also technical features, then the claim, viewed as a whole, is not a rule or method for mental activities, and shall not be excluded from patentability under Article 25.

There are also specific provisions in the PEG for examining computer software-related patent applications:[23]

1. If a claim merely relates to an algorithm, or mathematical computing rules, or computer programs as such, or computer programs recorded in mediums (such as tapes, discs, optical discs, magnetic optical discs, ROM, PROM, VCD, DVD, or other computer-readable mediums), or rules or methods for games, etc., it falls within 'rules and methods for mental activities' and is not eligible subject matter for patent protection.

   If all the elements of a claim, except its title of the subject matter, merely relate to an algorithm, or mathematical computing rule or program as such, or rules or methods for games, etc., the claim essentially merely relates to rules and methods for mental activities, and does not constitute eligible subject matter for patent protection.
2. Besides 1, if all the elements of a claim include not only rules and methods for mental activities but also technical features, for example, the elements defining the above-mentioned devices for computer

[23] See Patent Examination Guidelines 2010 (PEG), Chapter 9, Examination of Computer Program Related Invention. After the third amendment to the Chinese Patent Law came into effect on 1 October 2009, the Implementing Regulations of the Chinese Patent Law (2009) and the PEG came into force together on 1 February 2010. The PEG 2010 revised the earlier Patent Examination Guidelines 2006.

> games include rules for games and technical features as well, then the claim as a whole is not rules and methods for mental activities, and shall not be excluded from patentability in accordance with Article 25.

In accordance with Rule 2.1 Patent Examination Guidelines (2010), 'invention' under Article 2.2 Patent Law means 'any new technical solution relating to a product, a process or improvement thereof. An invention application relating to computer programs is eligible subject matter for patent protection only if it constitutes a technical solution.'

If the solution of an invention application relating to computer programs involves the execution of computer programs in order to solve technical problems, and reflects technical means in conformity with the laws of nature by computers running programs to control and process external or internal objects, and thus technical effects in conformity with the laws of nature are obtained, the solution is a technical solution as provided for in Article 2.2 Patent Law and is eligible subject matter for patent protection.

If the solution of an invention application relating to computer programs involves the execution of computer programs the purpose of which is not to solve technical problems, or does not reflect technical means in conformity with the laws of nature by computers running programs to control and process external or internal objects, or the effect obtained is not restrained by the laws of nature, the solution is not a technical solution as provided for in Article 2.2 Patent Law, and is not eligible subject matter for patent protection.

If the solution of an invention application relating to computer programs involves execution of computer programs the purpose of which is to process external technical data, completes a series of technical processes on the technical data in accordance with the laws of nature through execution of a technical data process program by a computer, and thus technical data process effects in conformity with the laws of nature are obtained, the solution is a technical solution as provided for in Article 2.2 Patent Law and is eligible subject matter for patent protection.

Again, the PEG states at Rule 2.1: 'If the solution of an invention application relating to computer programs involves execution of computer programs the purpose of which is to improve the internal performance of a computer system, completes a series of setting or configuration to parts of a computer system in accordance with the laws of nature through execution of a kind of system internal performance improvement program by a computer, and thus internal performance improvement effects of the computer system in conformity with the laws of nature are obtained, the solution is a technical solution as provided for in Article 2.2 and is eligible subject matter for patent protection.'

Under Chinese law, databases can also be protected. A database comprises of data and a system for managing the data. The system management software may be eligible for patent protection. For example, the invention 'System and method for executing search in a relational database' was granted a patent on 14 January 2009.[24]

The development of e-commerce has generated a large number of business method-related inventions. As early as 1996, CitiBank filed business method applications with the Chinese State Intellectual Property Office (SIPO) and was granted patents.[25] The essential issue lies in the patentability of computer software. It should be noted that pure business methods under the Patent Law are not patentable.

9.2.3. Anti-Unfair Competition Law

Aside from copyright protection and patent protection, computer software can be protected as a trade secret under the Anti-Unfair Competition Law. The Anti-Unfair Competition Law of the PRC (hereafter referred as AUCL) was adopted on 2 September 1993. The AUCL entitles the rights owner of a trade secret to prevent others from misappropriating his/her trade secret as embodied in computer software. 'Trade secret' refers to technical information and business information unknown to the public which may create business interests or profit for its legal owners and has practical utility and which is maintained as confidential.[26] When computer software meets these legal requirements for a trade secret, it can be protected accordingly. Although in most countries computer software is protected by copyright law, in China, the protection of software under the AUCL, as a supplementary measure, is still feasible.[27]

9.2.4. Trademark Law

Trademark protection is crucial for marketing computer software products. Some trademarks are used to identify the enterprises of the software products, such as Ufida, Huawei, Founder, etc., while some are used to indicate specific software products, such as QQ as an instant messaging service, Kingsoft dictionary and Sohu Chinese input methods and so

[24] Patent Application No. 200610064263.4; Issuance No. 100452047C.

[25] For instance, patent application No. 92113147.X was granted on 18 December 2002.

[26] AUCL, Art. 10.

[27] For a more detailed discussion of China's anti-unfair competition law, see Chapters 6 and 7.

on, which are symbols of the functions and features of specific software products.

If users are sufficiently familiar with the functions of certain software, they no longer care about the copyright or the patent right of the said software, but would rather make a choice on the basis of brand. In this case, a good trademark will be beneficial as regards competition in the market. At the same time, the expansion of the reputation of the trademark is great promotion for the copyright and patent right of the said software. For a more detailed discussion of Chinese trademark law, including domain names, see Chapters 3 (Trademarks) and 10 (E-Commerce 2).

9.2.5. Contract Law

The software developer may, by means of confidentiality provisions in contract, protect computer software as a form of a trade secret. The contract could further specify the rights of the software owners beyond protection provided by law and thus give better protection. The protection provided by contract law requires familiarity with the regulations concerning protection of computer software in various countries. A complete system covered by contract law will include contracts between enterprises and employees, enterprises and users, as well as enterprises and cooperators in the same area, in order to fully protect the rights in the software.

The Contract Law of the PRC was issued on 15 March 1999 and came into force on 1 October 1999. Computer software contracts are protected by the Contract Law. As provided by Article 137 of the Contract Law, when an object such as computer software in which intellectual property rights consist is sold, the intellectual property rights of such an object shall not be transferred to the buyer unless otherwise stipulated by law or agreed upon by the parties. There are no specific regulations regarding software contracts. Software contracts may be subsumed under contracts for technology[28] or contracts for sale[29] and are regulated accordingly.

According to Article 53 of the Copyright Law, when a party to a contract does not perform his contractual obligations or his performance does not comply with any contract terms and conditions, he shall be liable in accordance with the General Principles of the Civil Law of the People's Republic of China, the Contract Law of the People's Republic of China and other laws.

The Chinese Regulation for Computer Software Protection 2002

---

28 See Chapter 18, Contract Law.

29 See Chapter 9, Contract Law

(CPRS) contains several provisions that are relevant for protecting the rights of software owners.[30] Article 18 CPRS provides that to license others to exercise software copyrights, a licensing contract needs to be concluded. The licensee may not exercise any right that the software copyright owner has not explicitly licensed in the licensing contract.

Article 19 CPRS provides that to license others for exclusive exercise of software copyright, the parties shall conclude a written contract. Where there is no written contract or where there are no explicit terms defining the license as exclusive, the right to license shall be non-exclusive.

Article 20 CPRS provides that a written contract is required for the assignment of a software copyright.

Article 21 CPRS provides that licensing contracts that provide for exclusive license of software copyright or contracts for assignment of software copyright may be registered with the software registration authority verified by the copyright administration of the China State Council.

Article 31 CPRS provides that a dispute over infringement of software copyright may be submitted to arbitration. Likewise, a dispute over a software copyright contract may be submitted to an arbitration institution pursuant to an arbitration clause of the contract or a written agreement subsequently being concluded. If the parties have neither included an arbitration clause in their contract nor subsequently concluded a written arbitration agreement, then in the absence of arbitration they may proceed to litigation.

As is seen from the discussion above, the CPRS provides some general rules on contract protection of computer software which are common and useful. The next section discusses some specific contracts in relation to computer software.

9.2.6. Shrink-wrap and Click-wrap Contracts

Shrink-wrap contracts met with diametrically opposed reactions from the very date of their birth: the cheers of software sellers and the hostility of users. For software sellers, drafting a complete shrink-wrap contract aimed at different users means finding a new way to protect their interests, while for the users, it is painful to read through a lengthy and complicated contract full of legal terms when purchasing and using software. Moreover, at a time when users need to be kept happy, if they have to carefully use the software in accordance with the provisions in the shrink-wrap contract,

30 Promulgated on 20 December 2001 by Decree No. 339 of the State Council, and entering into force on 1 January 2002.

which most users would tend to consider as a requirement, the unsealing of the software is somehow similar to the timing fuse of a bomb. Therefore, from the very introduction of shrink-wrap contracts in China, there has been on-going debate concerning their legal status and legal effects.

The nature of a network click-wrap contract is similar to that of the shrink-wrap contract. When users seek online services, they usually have to 'sign' a lengthy service agreement. Where they are anxious to get the services and not patient enough to read through all the provisions, they are likely to skip to the bottom and directly click on the agree button when an effective agreement will then be concluded. As a result, the user will have to comply with provisions they may not necessarily be aware of. Such provisions often burden them with several obligations.

There were many disputes over clauses provided in e-mail services agreements. Users may have doubts over the legal effects of click-wrap contracts. However, the Contract Law of PRC recognizes the standard form contract. Shrink-wrap and click-wrap contracts are similar to standard form contracts. But the party who provides the standard terms should also provide for rights and obligations in accordance with the principle of fairness, and to remind the other party to pay attention to the clauses related to exemptions and restriction of liabilities by reasonable means, as well as give explanations upon reasonable request by the other party.[31] If a dispute occurs over the terms and conditions of a standard form contract, the disputed provision should be interpreted according to ordinary meaning.[32] Where there are two or more possible interpretations, the interpretation unfavourable to the party supplying the standard terms shall be preferred.[33] Where the standard terms are inconsistent with non-standard terms, the latter shall be adopted.[34]

With respect to click-wrap contracts related to free services such as e-mail or other contracts with small amounts at stake, users are usually capable of absorbing the risks of breach of the agreement by either party. Therefore, although there are quite a few disputes as to click-wrap contracts, few of them have ever been brought before the courts. Also, it should be noted that the rights specified in a shrink-wrap contract or a

---

[31] See Contract Law, Art. 39.

[32] See Contract Law, Art. 41.

Cf. Contract Law, Art. 125 (where the parties to a contract dispute terms and conditions in the contract, the meaning of such terms and conditions should be determined by the words used, related clauses, the purpose of the contract, custom of the trade and good faith).

[33] See Contract Law, Art. 41.

[34] *Id.*

click-wrap contract can be regarded as rights against the world, rather than rights relative to specific persons. It is possible for a rights owner of copyright to seek legal protection going far beyond that under existing statute, to the extent that even pure data is protected as property and fair use is eliminated. Even works in the public domain can be converted in this way into a form of quasi-personal property.

9.2.7. Open Licenses

Open source licensing, particularly the General Public License (GPL) as the key representative of this form, has deeply influenced the software industry in China. Nowadays, the essential idea in open source has gone beyond the software industry and has begun to influence traditional works. Free documentation licenses (FDL), Creative Commons (CC) and Wiki Encyclopedia are good examples. The zhidao.baidu.com is now the largest free Chinese online encyclopedia. All these new models focus on 'open', meaning that prior authorization from copyright owners is not required. The covered works can be used freely and safely on condition that the user follows the already published license agreements. These models can generally be categorized as 'open licensing'.

Open licensing has shifted from the early idea of anti-copyright[35] to a form of business model. With developing commercialization of open source software, open source activity has also shifted from confrontation against intellectual property systems to be compatible with the formal IP system. Open source software is not at all software in the public domain. In the abstract, there are some points in Open source software that conflict with intellectual property law; however, open source actually seeks comprehensive IP protection including under the general Copyright Law, Trademark (Domain Name) Law and Patent Law, which are combined with the licensing agreement (Contract Law). Thus, it is a comprehensive form of intellectual property protection that enables the establishment of open source software as an alternative form of legal protection for IP.

Open source software is both powerful competition for as well as effective supplementation of commercial software. For example, the free and open source Linux and Open Office forms a balance with costly software, such as Windows. In this respect, it can be argued that open source maintains and promotes a kind of 'biodiversity' within the protection

[35] See Richard Stallman, Free Software Definition, at http://www.fsf.org, http://www.fsf.org/fsf/fsf.html.

framework of the current international intellectual property and copyright regime.[36]

The above-mentioned open licenses are based on royalty-free arrangements, namely, the rights owners have agreed to relinquish their economic rights. It is true that open licenses have somehow solved the difficulties of gaining authorization in online environments. However, open source (such as the Creative Commons (CC) licenses) may not necessarily meet the demands of copyright owners interested in commercial benefits. With respect to copyrighted works, rights owners will continue to enjoy their economic rights, and due to a lack of such rights through open source licenses, it is unlikely that open source will become the main mode of licensing in China. The internet is likely to continue to be a forum by which traditional copyright and royalty provisions are enjoyed and so there is a need to create effective methods for creators of works to collect reasonable royalties from the commercial exploitation of digital copyright.

However, inspired by CC, the National Research Base for Digital Copyright at Peking University issued a Copyright Self-Service Agreement in June 2009.[37] Informed by the CC agreement, a solution to copyright authorization (taking copyright protection and effectively providing authorization to use works as well as enabling users to use such works for free without being burdened by heavy moral rights obligations) was established.[38] In this solution, the risks of infringement of copyright by internet service providers has also been incorporated. The Peking license is a commercial mode of paid and voluntary self-service license, which means that rights owners may identify the conditions for authorization for each work based on its different nature so that the conditions of licensing will be clear to users. If accepted by the user, the authorization agreement is concluded online and royalties for exploitation of the relevant work will be paid via an e-commerce platform. Taking the reality of gaining information for free or at a lower cost into consideration, the reasonable price for exploitation of works will make the Peking license much more acceptable

---

[36] See Zhang, Ping and Ma Xiao, *Sharing of Knowledge: Analysis on Intellectual Property Issues related to Open Source Software*, (Peking University Press, December 2005), pp. 3–4.

[37] See Internet Law Center at Peking University Law School, at: http://www.pkunetlaw.cn/; http://www.pkunetlaw.cn/News/Display.asp?NewsId=2600&ClassId=12; http://www.pkunetlaw.cn/News/Display.asp?NewsId=2601&ClassId=12.

[38] P2P and other forms of decentralized server access to copyrighted content is a problem worldwide. Some jurisdictions have provided for safe harbor provisions for ISPs, but even these safe harbor provisions are threatened when the ISP is put on notice of infringing behaviour.

than conventional licensing forms (for both rights owners and end-users) and will therefore greatly reduce disputes related to works distributed online. As for *Dōjin* work and articles published in blogs and open BBS platforms,[39] the Peking license encourages authors to use the mode of royalty-free licensing for non-profit-making and to obtain income from service providers for advertisements.

Proper solutions to issues related to digital copyright are crucial to the survival and development of the creative industry and the internet service industry. Within current legal structures, it can only be achieved by simplifying the authorization procedures and reducing the costs by all means so as to achieve a fair and reasonable standard of royalties. In this respect, the interests of the copyright owners and users, as well as the traditional cultural industry and internet industry, are maintained. The purpose of copyright protection is promoting the harmonious development of all parties in society.

9.3. INFORMATION TECHNOLOGY

9.3.1. Main Chinese Laws Protecting Internet Security

With the rapid development of the Chinese internet, the relevant administrations have been taking measures to safeguard internet security, both legislatively and technically. In 1994, the Regulations on Protection of Security of Computer Information System was issued, the earliest regulation for the security of computer information system. Thereafter, China gradually issued a series of laws and regulations for the security of the network and information system, the security of information content, the information security system and administration of products, confidentiality and password, prevention and control of computer virus and harmful programs, information security in specific areas, including finance, information security-related crimes. A legal system related to network security has been established. The following are the representative regulations:

1. Decision on Maintenance of Internet Security issued by the Standing Committee of National People's Congress in 2000;

---

[39] *Dōjin* is a general Japanese term for a group of people or friends who share an interest, activity, hobbies, or achievement. This term is used to refer to amateur self-published works, including but not limited to, Japanese manga, novels, fan guides, art collections, music and video games.

2. Regulations on Protection for Computer Information System Security of the PRC in 1994;
3. Provisional Measures for Managing the International Computer Information Network of the PRC in 1997;
4. Measures for Security Protection of International Computer Information Networking in 1997;
5. Measures for Administering Internet Information Services in 2000;
6. Measures for Licensing and Inspecting Products Exclusively Used for the Security of Computer Information System in 1997;
7. Regulations for Commercial Cipher Codes in 1999;
8. Provisional Regulations for Maintenance of Computer Information Systems Confidentiality in 1998;
9. Regulations for Maintenance of Confidentiality in the International Networking of Computer Information Systems in 2000;
10. Measures for Prevention and Control of Computer Virus in 2000;
11. Criminal Law of the PRC in 1997 and its amendments. Specifically, the Seventh Amendment, which was promulgated and effective as of 28 February 2009, provides for punishment for hacking and protection for personal data.[40]

9.3.2. Legal protection for databases

In China, databases can be protected via copyright and unfair competition laws.

9.3.2.1. Protection under the Copyright Law as a work created by compiling

A work created by compilation, as provided in the Copyright Law, refers to a work which is compiled from several works, fragments of works, or the data or other materials not constituting a work, where the choice or arrangement of the contents of which embodies an original creation.[41] The compiler has copyright in the work so compiled, provided that s/he does not infringe upon the copyright in the pre-existing works underlying the compilation. A database is viewed as a compilation work, and is protected by Chinese copyright law to the extent that it is an original selection and compilation of data. If there is no originality in selection and compilation, there is no copyright in the work compiled. For instance, it is difficult for a

40 See Seventh Amendment to Criminal Act, available at: http://www.gov.cn/flfg/2009-02/28/content_1246438.htm.

41 Copyright Law, Art. 16.

simple list of phone numbers to have the required originality for copyright protection.

9.3.2.2. Protection under the Anti-Unfair Competition Law

Article 2(1) of the Anti-Unfair Competition Law provides that in business transactions, undertakings shall abide by the principles of free will, fairness, good faith, and also adhere to generally recognized commercial morals.[42] This could serve as the legal grounds for protecting databases that do not meet the required originality for copyright discussed above: copyright vests only in databases that are original in the selection and compilation of data. However, for rights owners, in order to gain some form of competitive position in the market for their database products, they have expended considerable costs in developing their databases. For those competitors who directly copy such databases and gain competitive power without paying similar costs, the act of copying could be a violation of common commercial moralities under the Anti-Unfair Competition Act 1993 and will thus constitute unfair competition.[43]

9.3.3. DRM in China

Compared with the US, European countries and Japan, the application of Digital Rights Management technology (DRM) in China comes quite late. It was not until 2005 that there was any legislation applicable to DRM. The application areas of DRM are wide, and mainly include applications in internet and wireless areas. However, currently, these two markets in China are not yet mature enough, although the wireless market in China has great potential given the penetration of mobile phones in all parts of China, including both rural and urban sectors. China Mobile, perhaps the biggest of the state mobile phone operators in China, has the largest market share of the DRM market at present given its superior user subscriber base. In addition, the mobile handset system is more closed, with better encryption of mobile phone content that makes piracy more difficult. In general, the standardization of DRM over mobile phone networks has been more uniform given the number of operators and penetration of wireless technology in China. By contrast, the application of DRM for internet services in China has been more piecemeal, and driven more by specific media companies. In this respect, two cases in 2006 and 2007

42 AUCL, Art. 2.
43 See Chapters 5 (Unfair competition) and 6 ((Know-How/trade secrets).

are influential. They are *IFPI v Baidu.com*[44] and *IFPI v Yahoo China.*[45] In *IFPI v Baidu.com*, IFPI (International Federation of the Phonographic Industry)[46] claimed that Baidu provided a downloading service of musical works from seven companies for free without prior permission. IFPI required Baidu to desist from online playing and downloading the music works, and to make a public apology and compensate for economic losses. Baidu argued that the liabilities should be with the websites that provided pirated music work rather than Baidu who provided only a search engine service. In the first instance, the First Intermediate Court of Beijing City found that Baidu, as a search engine company, only provided search services for users to get the needed information quickly. The court argued that it was the websites that provided services for online listening and the downloading of musical works in the MP3 format. Consequently, Baidu could not identify, predict or control these MP3 files and were not liable. IFIP appealed, and the High Court of Beijing upheld the ruling.

Another case is *IFIP v Yahoo China*. On 10 April and 4 July 2006, IFIP sent two communications to Yahoo China, requesting that Yahoo China delete all links related to content infringing the albums in question. The communications informed Yahoo China that infringement existed, and provided information regarding the internet address of the IFIP's sound recordings and the names of the albums and singers of the songs in question, along with 33 specific Uniform Resource Locators (URL) as examples of each of the 33 songs at issue. Yahoo China took down only the 33 specific URLs. Dissatisfied with Yahoo China's response, IFPI brought the case before the Second Intermediate Court of Beijing City in January 2007.

The court delivered its judgment in 2008. The court held that upon receiving the communications from IFPI, Yahoo China was put on notice of the plaintiff's copyrights and the alleged infringing songs. Yahoo China should have known that its music search service had links to content infringing the plaintiff's copyright. However, Yahoo China took down only the specific 33URLs and was inactive in performing its obligation to delete other links related to content infringing the songs in question, thus condoning infringement. The court concluded that Yahoo China was at fault, constituting aiding another person in infringing activities through

---

44 See the Beijing High Court, 2007 No. 1190, 2007 Gao Min Zhong Zi Di No. 1990.

45 The first instance judgments filed at the Beijing No. 2 Intermediate People's Court (April 2007), and the appeal filed at the Beijing Higher People's Court (December 2007).

46 IFPI refers to EMI, Universal Music, Sony, BMG, Warner Music, Go East Entertainment, Gold Typhoon Entertainment and Cinepoly Record.

the internet, and thus was liable. Yahoo China appealed. The High Court of Beijing City upheld the ruling in December 2008.

These two cases, like other infringement disputes concerning digital copyright in various countries, reflect the tension between the traditional copyright industry and the internet industry. The traditional media industry, represented by record and film companies, has dominated the authorization of copyright in the cultural and entertainment market. They have been slower to exploit commercialization of their rights over the internet, whereas ISPs have been much faster in updating technology and their business models have greatly affected the interests of traditional copyright agents. Seen from the perspective of development, the interests of ISPs and end-users in gaining access to cheap digital content has generally led to a change in the structure of the market. Digital content, controlled by the grant of rights owners, has become the mainstay of providers of equipment, service providers of search engines and e-commerce websites. Taking Apple Mac as an example as the provider of the iTunes music network store, Apple controlled almost 80% of the music downloading market of legitimate digital music. Through the advent of platforms, such as iTunes, rights owners have moved away from traditional DRM techniques in favour of pay-per-use platforms. Online products, such as software, characters, pictures, e-books, music, videos, have various features, which make it hard to unify the DRM standard, which is one of the difficulties that rights owners have had in promoting DRM.

Recently, in the United States, two of the leading on-demand streaming music sites, iMeem and LaLa, have decided to drop DRM on their audio streams.[47] This seems to put an end to US legislation to mandate DRM for non-interactive webcasters and also undermines the argument that DRM for music is necessary for subscription services. The reason for major copyright holders to abolish DRM is to realize their market positions. Additionally, for the internet, digital products take various forms, such as software, characters, pictures, e-books, music, videos and so on. They possess different qualities, which makes it hard to unify a DRM standard.

It has been argued that the era of free digital content is coming to an end. However, it is too early to be definitive. The prospects for commercial cooperation between the rights holders and the providers of infrastructure, search engine providers and e-commerce websites are good. On 16 January 2007, EMI made an announcement to jointly expand the digital music

---

[47] Fred Von Lohmann, 'DRM for Streaming Music Dies a Quiet Death' (15 August 2008), at http://www.eff.org/deeplinks/2008/08/drm-quietly-dies-streaming-music.

market in China with Baidu, which will provide Chinese internet users with online Chinese music services.[48] On 15 March 2007, the Sina Music database, jointly created by Sina, Universal Music, Sony, BMG, Warner Music and Rock Records and Tapes, was put online.[49] Tudou.com, as a well-known video sharing website, has concluded agreements with Sony and BMG, launching a strategic cooperation including promotion of Chinese actors and actresses.[50]

Many rights owners appreciate the essence of the 'attention economy' on the internet, and have moved away from expecting profits from a (mechanical mode) of one-to-one authorization. These rights owners have begun to seek agreements with service providers whereby the users are allowed to use and download for free, allowing rights owners to earn their royalties via added business and advertisements from licensed works.

Scholars are also contributing to an effective commercial authorization model for digital copyright. As mentioned earlier, faculty at Peking University Law School have put forward the Copyright Self-Service Agreement,[51] which introduces a commercial authorization model inspired by the Creative Commons. According to this model, the options of the rights owners are respected, which will give rights owners the necessary confidence and protection to allow their work to be shared collectively. The model also takes into account the needs of end-users by allowing for easy access to information. End-users do not have to pay for every individual work directly. Rather, it is the service providers who directly pay for copyright authorization via gains from advertisements and other services.

9.4. E-COMMERCE LEGISLATION AND PRACTICE

For e-commerce, China has established a legal system led by the Contract Law and the Electronic Signature Law (hereafter referred as 'ESL') as the primary rules of law, and supplemented by a series of regulations, judicial interpretations, administrative regulations and rules and local regulations and rules. This e-commerce legal system has been greatly influenced by the UNCITRAL Model Law on Electronic Commerce, the UNCITRAL Model Law on Electronic Signatures and the United Nations Convention on the Use of Electronic Communications in International Contracts. The

48 See http://news.xinhuanet.com/internet/2007-01/23/content_5640991.htm.

49 See http://tech.sina.com.cn/i/2007-04-13/14021464658.shtml.

50 See http://p2p.lmtw.com/pnews/200803/49180.html.

51 See *supra* note 37.

principles established in these three international e-commerce instruments, including principles of non-discrimination, technological neutrality and functional equivalence, are also the cornerstones of Chinese regulation in this area and this will be further discussed below.

9.4.1. Relevant Rules in the Contract Law

The Chinese Contract Law of 1999 makes specific provisions for contracts concluded by means of data messages. Article 11 of the Contract Law makes clear that a data message is regarded as one kind of written form compliant with the law, and equivalent to written contractual agreements and letters. The effect is that the written form in Chinese law now encompasses any forms in which information is fixed in a tangible medium, such as a written contractual agreement, letters, and data messages. Moreover, the scope of the data message has also been interpreted to include telegrams, telexes, faxes, EDI and e-mails. There are specific provisions for the normal contractual rules of offer and acceptance, where a contract is concluded via a data message. When a contract is to be concluded via a data message, if the recipient appoints a specific system to receive the data message, the time when the data message enters the system is the time when the message is received; if no specific system is appointed, the time when the data message first enters any of the recipient's systems shall be regarded as the time when the message is received.[52] Such provisions are significant because, according to the Contract Law, an offer becomes effective when it reaches the offeree. After an offer becomes effective, if the offeree wants to make a contract, he should accept the offer within the time limit provided in the offer or within a reasonable time if there is no time requirement stipulated in the offer. An acceptance becomes effective when it reaches the offeror. This is also the time when a contract is concluded.

The Chinese Contract Law also provides for the place of a contract when a contract is concluded via a data message. If the contract is concluded via a data message, the principal business place of the recipient shall be the place where the contract is concluded.[53] If there is no principal business place, its habitual residence shall be considered to be the place where the contract is concluded.[54] Moreover, the parties can determine the place of the contract by mutual consent.[55]

---

[52] See Contract Law, Art. 16.
[53] See Contract Law, Art. 34.
[54] *Id.*
[55] *Id.*

However, there is no explicit provision for the definition of a data message and its legal effects in the Contract Law; neither does the law adopt the principle of function equivalence as provided in the aforesaid international treaties to solve the problem as to how a data message can meet the formality requirements of a traditional contract, namely, the written form requirement, signature, original copy, preservation and forms of evidence and so on. Those problems are solved in the Electronic Signature Law of PRC of 2004.

9.4.2. Electronic Signature Law

The Electronic Signature Law (ESL), which is the first specific law in the field of e-commerce in China, was adopted at the 11th Meeting of the Standing Committee of the Tenth National People's Congress on 28 August 2004. It consists of five chapters and 36 articles. The ESL confirms the legal effect of electronic signatures and data messages based on the principle of functional equivalence and technological neutrality, and provides for the legal status of electronic signature certification organizations, the certification procedure, access to markets as well as administrative licenses.

The ESL first recognizes the legal effect of data based on the principle of non-discrimination. Article 31 ESL provides that parties may agree to use or not to use electronic signature or data messages in such documentation as contracts and other documents, receipts and vouchers in civil activities. Where the parties concerned have agreed to use electronic signature or data messages, the legal effect of a document shall not be denied merely because of the form of electronic signature or data message used.

Also, the ESL makes clear the relation between data messages and traditional written forms on the basis of functional equivalence. This principle was first established in the UNCITRAL Model Law on Electronic Commerce. It means that when applying the requirements for the written form in traditional law to a network legal surrounding, the function that electronic communication tries to realize should be first analysed, and then compared with that of written documents. If they are identical, the law shall recognize electronic communications as having the same legal effect as that of written documents. These legal functions refer mainly to the legal requirements for a written form, signature, original copy, preservation and form of evidence. All of these are specified in Chapter 2 of the ESL.

9.4.3. Other E-commerce Legislation

Apart from the ESL, e-commerce legislation includes laws and regulations, such as Measures for Electronic Certification Services, Guiding Opinions on Online Transaction (for Interim Implementation), and Guidance on E-payment (Order No. 1).

The Measures for Electronic Certification Services were promulgated by the former Ministry of Information Industry on 8 February 2005, and were put into effect on 1 April 2005. The Measures, which focus on electronic certification service agencies, provide specifically for the establishment of electronic certification service agencies; norms for services and supervision and administration of suppliers of electronic certification services; the supervision and administration of electronic certification service agencies, all of which are required for the proper implementation of the ESL.

The Guidance on E-payment (Order No. 1) was issued by the People's Bank of China on 30 October 2005. This Guidance provides specifically for electronic payments, the sending and receiving of electronic orders for payment, security control and error solutions. E-payment refers to the activities of making instructions to electronic terminals so as to effect monetary payment and capital transfers. These activities can be done by institutions or individuals directly, or by others with their authorization.

The Guidelines for Online Transaction (Interim Implementation) were issued by the Ministry of Commerce on 6 March 2007, on the principles established in Several Opinions concerning Promotion of the Development of E-commerce issued by the General Office of the State Council. The Guideline's function is to support the legal interests of the participants of online transactions and promote the development of online transactions. According to the Guidelines, online transactions refer to transactions of products or services conducted by sellers and purchasers via the internet.

9.4.4. E-commerce Practice

According to the 27th Statistical Report on Internet Development in China[56] issued by the China Internet Network Information Centre (CNNIC) in January 2011, e-commerce is an important application of the network, which is extremely close to the everyday life of internet users. In 2010, there was a significant increase in online shopping (the fastest growing sub-sector). At year-end 2010, the number of Chinese internet users of online shopping is 161 million, with an annual increase rate of 48.6%.

Besides online shopping, online payment and E-Banking have also

---

[56] See Statistical Report on the Internet Development in China, available at: http://research.cnnic.cn/html/1295343518d2558.html, accessed July 2011.

Table 9.1 Comparison of users of e-commerce between 2009 and 2010

	End of 2009		End of 2010		Increase	
	Rate of use	Scope of internet users (million)	Rate of use	Scope of internet users (million)	Increase (million)	Increase rate
Online shopping	28.1%	108	35.1%	160.51	52.51	48.6%
Online banking	24.5%	94.12	30.5%	139.48	45.36	48.2%
Online payment	24.5%	94.06	30.0%	137.19	43.13	45.9%
Travel booking	7.9%	30.24	7.9%	36.13	5.89	19.5%

Source: CNNIC Report 2011

developed significantly. The number of internet users of online banking has reached 139.48 million.

Online payment, which is closely related to online shopping, has been developing rapidly in China. At year-end 2010, the number of internet users reached 137.19 million, with an annual increase rate of 45.9%.

Besides the figures mentioned above, which give a snapshot of e-commerce across the country, other industry-specific reports have also been published, for example, the China Mobile E-Commerce Market Report (2008–2009) published by IResearch Group. According to this report, business income from mobile e-commerce reached RMB 24 million in 2008. With the coming of 3G, traditional e-commerce enterprises such as Alibaba, the three major Chinese mobile operators China Mobile, China Telecom and China Unicom, as well as new entrants, such as Ufida Mobile, are entering the field of mobile business. It is predicted that business income will reach RMB 170 million in 2011.[57]

9.5. THE ANTI-MONOPOLY LAW OF PRC

The Anti-Monopoly Law of PRC came into force on 1 August 2008. This law, by taking the national conditions and practice into consideration and

57 See http://research.cnnic.cn/html/1249452528d1098.html.

taking the practice of antitrust provisions in other countries as a point of reference, has established a legal system for dealing with monopolies and the promotion of fair competition.

The purpose of the Anti-Monopoly Law is to prevent and stop monopolistic acts. There are 57 articles in the law. The monopolistic acts regulated by the law include monopoly agreements concluded by undertakings, abuse of dominant position in the market and the concentration of undertakings that may exclude or limit competition. The Anti-Monopoly Law has identified the limitation of monopolistic acts, established corresponding prohibited regulations and measures for review and supervision and provided the legal liabilities for infringement in order to achieve the aim of preventing and stopping abuse of a dominant position. As to whether dominant positions that arise through holding of intellectual property rights can be exempted, is provided in the law that with regard to the acts of the undertakings to exercise intellectual property rights according to law and regulations, the Anti-Monopoly Law will not be applied; however, for undertakings who abuse their dominance by way of holding intellectual property rights and who exclude and restrict competition, the Law will apply.

The feature of policy and specialization of the Anti-Monopoly Law is quite severe. The establishment of enforcement organs is crucial to the effective implementation of the Law. For the purpose of coordinating enforcement of Anti-Monopoly Law and to guarantee its unification, justice and authority, on the same date that the Anti-Monopoly Law came into force, the National Anti-Monopoly Commission was also established. On 24 May 2009, the first formal document, the Guidelines on the Definition of the Relevant Market by the National Anti-Monopoly Commission was issued, which provides guidance for the definition of a relevant market. In the Guidelines, it is clarified that under several circumstances, the definition of a relevant market should take full consideration of factors including intellectual property (see Chapter 11).

There are three administrative organs in charge of different areas of anti-monopoly affairs. The Ministry of Commerce is in charge of the anti-monopoly examination of the acts of concentration of undertakings according to law. On 28 March 2009, the Ministry of Commerce published the first anti-monopoly examination case, namely, the merger and acquisition by Coca-Cola of Chinese Huiyuan Group, and ruled that such concentration of undertakings should be prohibited. The National Development and Reform Commission is responsible for acts of illegal prices and price-related monopolistic acts. The State Administration for Industry and Commerce (SAIC) is responsible for monopolistic agreements, abuse of a dominant position in the market and exclusion and restriction of competition by abusing administrative powers (excluding price-related monopolistic acts). Two anti-monopoly regulations were issued simultaneously on 26 May 2009 by SAIC, namely, *Provisions on Procedures for the Administration for Industry and Commerce to Investigate and Tackle Cases in Relation to Monopoly Agreements* and *Abuse of Dominant Position in the Market and Provisions on Procedures for the Administration for Industry and Commerce to Prevent from Abusing Administrative Power to Exclude or Restrict Competition*, in which specific regulations concerning the investigation and handling of cases related to monopoly agreements and the abuse of a dominant position in the market, as well as preventing the abuse of administrative powers to exclude or restrict competition, are set out.[58] These provide specifically for monopoly agreements and abuse of a dominant position in the market, as well as abuse of administrative power to exclude or restrict competition.[59]

9.6. CONCLUSION

The intellectual property issues related to computer applications and the internet are new and unclear both in China and in the world. The current intellectual property system in China was initiated as a result of industrial and electronic revolution. The exclusive possession of intellectual property has become a powerful monopoly in the market and the interests of rights owners are generally realized via licenses. The information society and globalization have greatly impacted upon systems of intellectual property both in China and worldwide. On the one hand, there is no barrier to the communication of information protected by IP, and the regionalism of intellectual property rights is weakening. The difficulty arising from secondary innovation and IP has been felt in many sectors. The emerging economies and enterprises cannot escape the rights of those, mainly from the developed markets, who hold IP. On the other hand, the use and sharing of free content in a fast and convenient way over digital networks is inevitable. The whole society, including rights owners, are enjoying the benefits brought about by the information society. But rights owners and end-users also have completely different claims when it comes to content and sometimes their interests cannot be so easily reconciled. Therefore, legislation related to computer software, information technology and

58 See http://www.saic.gov.cn/zwgk/zyfb/qt/fld/200906/t20090605_61125.html.
59 See Chapters 11 and 12 on the Anti-Monopoly Law.

e-commerce sectors and their relationship with IP will need to follow both the developing rules of society and technology.

The protection of intellectual property is only the interim mission in the design of an effective intellectual property system and its practice. The final aim has to be the promotion of innovation and the expansion of the knowledge-based society.

10. Chinese e-commerce (2) and legal environment

Cong Lixian[1]

Chapter 9 provided an overview of IT, computer software and e-commerce. This chapter extends the discussion of e-commerce. In defining e-commerce, governments and international organizations worldwide have arrived at different conclusions. For example, the US government in its 'global framework for electronic commerce' has restricted the definition to the use of the internet to conduct various business activities such as advertising, buying and selling of goods and services, and other similar transactions taking place globally. Likewise, the European Parliament and the United Nations Economic Co-operation and Development Organisation upholds a similar but broader definition of e-commerce, characterizing it as a range of business activities conducted electronically. However, the World Trade Organization (WTO) work program on e-commerce includes e-commerce by encompassing not only cross-border and consumption abroad activities which are performed by way of the internet but also the transactions which are conducted using telecommunication networks or any other electronic information technology for production, marketing, sales and distribution.[2] As information technology and business networks undergo maturation, e-commerce has also been associated with great potential for development. The rise of electronic commercial transactions as a popular means of trade has required regulators to focus on the adoption of relevant policies and laws to regulate this emerging business activity, to ensure greater security on the internet, to promote fair trade, and finally to attain a more sustainable economy.[3]

---

1 Cong Lixian, Professor of Law, Beijing Foreign Studies University, and Research Fellow of Zhongnan University of Economics and Law.

2 Si Linsheng (ed.), *E-Commerce Case Analysis*, Chongqing University Press, September 2007, p. 1.

3 Qin Chengde (ed.), *E-Commerce Law and Practice*, Posts & Telecom Press, December 2008, p. 2.

10.1. EVOLUTION OF E-COMMERCE IN CHINA: AN OVERVIEW

The number of internet users in China increased 73.3 million from 2009, giving an annual growth rate of 19.1%. By the end of December 2010, the online population in China had reached approximately 457 million 'netizens', comprising 34.3% of the total Chinese population. China has already exceeded the global average internet penetration level and likewise the size of its internet user base (23.2% of world internet users and 55.4% of Asian internet users) continues to expand at a rapid pace. The total number of Broadband internet users in China reached 450 million, accounting for 98.3% of all internet users. Moreover, network business group users increased rapidly, using more 'hard core' e-commerce applications, such as online payment, E-bankings and the like in contrast to search engines, instant messaging, e-mail and other basic applications. Further, online shopping, online payments and other business transactions have increased dramatically.[4] Even though the share of the e-commerce group in China is not very high in comparison to the whole Chinese internet user market, its success is spectacular.

According to Nielsen's *Chinese Takeway Report* 2010[5], the number of internet users worldwide in 2009 was over 1.3 billion. Online retail sales have grown from $5 billion in the fourth quarter of 2009 to $30 billion in the first quarter of 2010 (US Census[6]). Traffic to social networking sites, such as Facebook was up almost 200% over 2009, and Twitter has seen an increase of almost 1500%. According to Nielsen, compared to a year ago, 'not only are more people visiting these sites, but they are also spending more time there – time spent per person is up 67%' over 2009[7].

As regards China, research data published by a research report, *Chinese Netizen's behaviour in E-commerce* (Q2 2011), shows China's online shopping user base reaching 495 million by the end of June 2011[8], primarily due to the vigorous development of e-commerce in China. In the second quarter of 2011, the shopping network is estimated to be worth 179.2 billion Yuan of which 90% of transactions in the market of C2C comes

---

4 China Internet Network Information Center (CNNIC), 'China Internet Development Statistics Report (January 2010)', http://research.cnnic.cn/html/1295343518d2558.html, accessed July 2011.

5 See http://cn.en.nielsen.com/documents/chinesetakeawayfinal.pdf, accessed July 2011.

6 Ibid., p. 101.

7 Ibid.

8 http://ch.gongchang.com/zt/ec_r_11Q2/, accessed July 2011.

from the Chinese online trader, Taobao, while in the B2C market, Taobao and 360 have shares of 48.5% and 18.1% respectively[9].

According to the research report of iResearch in 2011 (Quarter 2), Chinese online payment business transactions reached 456.6 billion Yuan, and Alipay is still leading the online payment market with a 49.62% share[10]. Also China's B2B e-commerce market turnover reached 3.42 billion Yuan. Alibaba controlled 54.8% market share by the second quarter of 2011[11].

In summary, the macro Chinese e-commerce market has been following five major trends: first, the market evolved from a domestic to an international one. As China's economy has become fully integrated into the international business community, e-commerce has taken the first step, with a high degree of internationalization. Second, the market went from partial adoption in the industry sector to full and deep adoption. As China's e-commerce policy and legal environment continue to develop, and large, medium and small enterprise development provide better conditions for the security of e-commerce transactions, e-commerce will expand into all sectors of the community. Third, the market has evolved from an amateur to a professional one. E-commerce in China has developed from a pilot business model into a mature business model, with consumer-oriented websites and vertical specialization sites. Fourth, the market went from being relatively independent to being a market characterized by integration and merger. Fifth, the market went from free development to scientific planning. In January 2005, the State Council published 'Advice on Accelerating the Development of E-commerce' to face the various challenges of the international financial crisis. In February 2009, Chinese Premier Wen Jiabao chaired the State Council executive meeting, which considered and adopted the 'Adjust and Revitalization Plan for Electronic Information Industry' and 'Adjust and Revitalization Plan for the Logistics Industry'. These plans point to the specific measures of scientific development in e-commerce that China wishes to achieve.

10.2. E-COMMERCE LEGAL SYSTEM AND PRACTICE IN CHINA

The Chinese legal framework for e-commerce is still in its nascent stage and has already experienced several problems. First, there is an absence of

---

9 http://ec.iresearch.cn/17/20110721/145234.shtml, acccssed July 2011.
10 http://ec.iresearch.cn/54/20110721/145122.shtml, accessed July 2011.
11 http://ec.iresearch.cn/53/20110720/145037.shtml, accessed July 2011.

explicit laws, rules and regulations. To date, the Electronic Signature Law is the only explicit code that addresses e-commerce directly.[12] However, a number of other codes also have relevance for e-commerce, including the Contract Law, the relevant provisions and other relevant laws and regulations as supported by 'The Ministry of Industry and Information Technology Service Management Approach to Electronic Authentication', 'The Chinese People Bank Electronic Payment Guidelines (No. 1)', 'The Ministry of Commerce On-line Trading Guidance (Interim)' and other departmental regulations, supplied by 'the State Council on Accelerating the Development of E-commerce Opinions'[13] and state provincial policies and regulations (for example, in Beijing and Shanghai on the registration requirements for e-commerce companies). Chapter 15 also discusses rules with regard to telecom networks and internet infrastructure and content regulation.

10.2.1. Present Situation of Chinese E-commerce Law

10.2.1.1. Electronic signatures

Electronic signatures were introduced in Chapter 9. As stated there, the electronic signature aimed to achieve the equivalent of traditional written signatures; generally the signatory's electronic signature indicates the relationship between the signature of the person and the information content, but also that it will be as reliable as paper-based signatures.[14] Electronic signatures have the following characteristics: (1) to confirm identity. In the electronic signature process, the private key can only be held by the issuer, so the identity of the issuer can be confirmed; (2) to confirm the authenticity of any data transmitted. The original data with electronic signatures cannot be changed after encryption and decryption, and both public and private keys must lock exactly. (3) The verification process of sender and recipient of documents is open; both sender and receiver will use their public keys provided by the sender in document verification, so that the verification process is a public process.[15] When using the term 'electronic signatures' (or

[12] Gao Huiyun (ed.), *Electronic Commerce Law Tutorial*, HuaWen Press, May 2005, p. 12. However, see Chapter 9, where Professors Zhang Ping and Meng Zhaoping detail various orders on network security and electronic payments that are relevant to e-commerce transactions.

[13] GUO FA [2007] No. 7, 8 January 2005, China.

[14] Yang Jianzheng (ed.), *Economic Law and E-commerce Law*, Higher Education Press, August 2004, p. 376.

[15] Gao Jun, Hu Haoyuan and Song Yongquan, *Network Transactions Legal Practice (Next)*, Law Press, November 2006, p. 77.

'electronic signature'), scholars have often preferred the use of 'electronic authentication' instead of 'electronic signature'. Although the suggestion has not been accepted so far, it may well be that 'electronic authentication' may one day replace the term electronic signature in China.[16]

In August 2004, China officially formulated and passed the Electronic Signature Law. The Law consists of five chapters, 36 rules, including: general provisions (comprising three articles), the data message (comprising nine articles), electronic signatures and certification (comprising a total of 14 articles), legal liability (comprising a total of seven articles), by-laws (comprising three articles). The Law confirmed that electronic signatures and data are equivalent in law to handwritten signatures and are sealed under 'functional equivalence' and 'technology neutrality' principles. The enactment of the law solved a number of key problems in the development process of e-commerce in China, which greatly improved the legal environment surrounding it. The Law was also known as China's Electronic Commerce Act.[17] Of course, there were scholars taking a cautious attitude towards the implementation of the effects of the code: the introduction of the Electronic Signature Law and confirmation of the validity of electronic signatures could increase confidence in using electronic signatures, but not necessarily lead to greater take-up of electronic signatures. Therefore, it was still necessary to establish the rule of written evidence of the effectiveness of electronic records without necessarily using electronic signatures.[18]

10.2.1.2. Trademarks and domain names

Trademarks and domain names have both links and differences. Both can identify the source of products or services and promote the holder's brands (good will). Normally, an organization registers the same domain name with its registered trademark or business name. Therefore, non-trademark owners who register domain names (cybersquat) can either confuse or deliberately mislead consumers.[19] There are, however, substantial differences between the two: domain names are not as good as trademarks in identifying goods. Domain names have a unique and proprietary character, while trademarks can be used for different types

---

[16] Wan Yixian (ed.), *Study of the Electronic Signature Law*, People's Court Press, October 2001, p. 193.

[17] Shang Ming (ed.), *International E-commerce Treaty and China E-commerce Legislation*, Law Press, May 2009, p. 303.

[18] Gao Fuping (ed.), *Electronic Contracts and Electronic Signature Law Study*, Beijing University Press, April 2005, p. 244.

[19] Zhang Liying and Li Juqian (eds), *Analysis on Electronic Commerce Law Typical Cases*, People's Court Press, February 2003, p. 79.

of goods simultaneously and can be employed and registered by different trademark owners. Further, trademarks are regional in scope, whilst a domain name is international and lacks regional characteristics (although second level domain names can be country specific and therefore can have a regional character). Given these differences, an argument exists for clarifying domain names not as a form of trademark but as a new type of commercial label to work in parallel with trademarks under the protection of intellectual property law.[20] The World Intellectual Property Organization (WIPO) stressed that domain names and trademarks could not be completely separated and that the existing national domain name registration process was basically out of touch with the traditional intellectual property protection system, which has to an extent led to cyber squatting and malicious registrations becoming commonplace. WIPO encouraged those seeking domain name registration to first enquire about any trademark registration in place and then apply for domain name registration in order to avoid any conflicts between the rights of domain name holders and trademark owners. Also, WIPO suggested that all domain name registration agreements require a warranty from the domain name holder so that any third party IP rights are not violated.[21] In case of domain name and trademark disputes in China, the Court will often consider the case under both the Trademark Law as well as the Anti-Unfair Competition Law. For example, China's first foreign-related domain name dispute – the *Ikea* case[22] – was a classic example of a dispute resolution applying the Anti-Unfair Competition Law.

In 1998, the YingTeAiJi Company set up a large home store using 'IKEA' as their trademark in Shanghai and Beijing in China. But when the company decided to register the domain name in China, they found that Beijing Country Network Information Co., Ltd. (BCNIC) had already registered it in 1997 at the China Internet Network Information Center (CNNIC) under the domain name, www.ikea.com.cn. In June 2000, the Beijing Second Intermediate People's Court passed a judgment in favor of YingTeAiJi, stating that BCNIC should cease to use the same English alphabet and pronunciation as YingTeAiJi's company logo 'ikea.com.cn', and apply for a revocation of this domain name to the China Internet

[20] Li Juqian and Yang Fan (eds), *Intellectual Property In Internet and E-commerce*, Beijing University of Posts and Telecommunications Press, August 2002, p. 127.

[21] Guo Weihua, Jin Chaowu and Wang Jing (eds), *Network Legal Problems and The Countermeasures*, Law Press, January 2001, p. 89.

[22] *IKEA Inter-systems Inc. v Beijing Cinet Co. Ltd*, Beijing High People's Court, Gao Zhi Zong Zi Civil Judgment No. 76 (2000).

Network Information Center. The Supreme Court official said that the ruling set three Chinese judicial precedents. First, the case established a precedent for the domain name registration of foreign companies to be respected, and was also the first to be settled in a Chinese court, applying the relevant provisions of international treaties dealing with networks and indicating enforcement of international standards in intellectual property protection in China. Second, the case was the first judgment delivered by the People's Court where the litigation involved well-known trademarks. Generally trademark litigation in China was handled by administrative authorities (under administrative law) through Chinese industrial and commercial administrative departments, but the *Ikea* case confirmed the significance of judicial power over executive power. Third, *Ikea* was the first apparent verdict given by the judiciary on the well-known trademarks and domain names conflict, showing that with both traditional intellectual property protection and with new cases, China's judicial protection of intellectual property rights had reached a higher level. In this case, the court held that 'IKEA' was a well-known trademark and its use by BCNIC as its domain name would mislead others, as they might confuse it with the well-known trademark 'IKEA' for the Swedish company, *Ingvar Kamprad Elmtaryd Agunnaryd.*

By using the good reputation of a well-known trademark such as IKEA, BCNIC could improve their site ranking and might also impede IKEA in using its own well-known trademark on the internet. BCNIC also registered a large number of domain names, which coincided with other well-known trademarks and were not being actively used. Furthermore, the registration for sale of these domains indicated bad faith on the part of BCNIC. The Court therefore concluded that the acts committed by BCNIC had constituted unfair competition, which was contrary to the principle and spirit of China's Anti-Unfair Competition Act 1993,[23] as well as running counter to the Paris Convention for the Protection of Industrial Property. The court therefore ruled that BCNIC should immediately stop using the 'IKEA' domain and revoked its registration.[24]

10.2.1.3. Copyright

The WIPO Copyright Treaty (WCT) and the WIPO Performances and Phonograms Treaty (WPPT) clearly state that authors of literary

---

[23] Discussed in more detail in Chapters 5 (anti-unfair competition) and 6 (trade secrets/know-how).

[24] http://www.cnnic.cn/zcfg/xgzt/201008/w020101108505082809156.doc, accessed July 2011.

and artistic works, performers and phonogram producers shall enjoy the exclusive right of authorizing any transmission to the public of their works, by way of the internet or otherwise, under the 'Right of Communication to the Public' and the 'Right of Distribution'.[25] China has several legal provisions relating to the 'Right of Communication to the Public' constituting both specific legislation and other laws and regulations for ancillary support. They are mainly reflected in three areas: (1) under the General Principles of Civil Law, Civil Rights, Copyright Law, Regulations for the Implementation of the Copyright Law, provisions provided in the Judicial Interpretation of the Supreme People's Court on a Number of Issues Concerning Application of Law in the Trial Cases Involving the Copyright Dispute over Computer Network, Information Network Transmission Right Protection Ordinance; (2) under administrative protection of Copyright Law: Regulations for the Implementation of Copyright Law; Measures for the Administrative Protection of Internet Copyright; Copyright Administrative Punishment Implementation Rules; Information Network Transmission Right Protection Ordinance; (3) under the Criminal Law, Copyright Law, Interpretation by the Supreme People's Court and the Supreme People's Procuratorate on a Number of Issues of Concrete Application of Laws in Handling Criminal Cases of Infringing Intellectual Property.

In 1999, China observed its first internet copyright infringement case where a group of six well-known authors, including writer and former culture minister, Wang Meng, indicted a Beijing website, owned and operated by *Beijing* Cenpok Intercom Technology Co Ltd, for copyright violations.[26] We saw in Chapter 8 of this book, that the judges of the Beijing First Intermediate People's Court determined that the ISP had transmitted copyright works online without the rights' owner's consent and that this was an infringement despite no specific offence being recorded in the statute books at the time. However, it was only after judgment was passed in the case of *Shanghai Busheng Music Culture Media Co. Ltd. v Beijing Baidu Reuters Technology Co. Ltd*[27] that the attitude of the Chinese judiciary changed for the better towards the internet search engine business. In the *Baidu.com Inc.* case, the Court (of first instance) judged that the

[25] Bao Yongzheng (ed.), *Legal System of E-Commerce Intellectual Property Rights Research*, Intellectual Property Press, October 2003, p. 12.

[26] Beijing Haidian District People's Court in civil judgments (1999), Hai Zhi Chu Zi No. 57. This case has also been discussed in Chapter 8.

[27] *Shanghai Push Sound Music & Entertainment v Baidu.com Inc,* Beijing Haidian District People's Court in civil judgments (2005), Hai Min Chu Zi No. 14665.

accused, Baidu.com, China's largest search engine, should immediately cease to illegally provide direct links to free digital music downloads, and in addition, should compensate the plaintiff's economic losses and litigation expenses.[28] However, on the second-instance appeal, the court presided over the defendant and plaintiff while both the parties agreed to a settlement, and eventually Baidu.com Inc. had to pay only a reasonable fine to the Shanghai Busheng Music Culture Media Company.[29] Baidu's case gave rise to a view that general copyright infringement could be divided into two kinds: direct and indirect. *Direct* infringement referred to copying of work from one network to another for others to download or share, reproducing copyrighted material by uploading or downloading it via the internet. *Indirect* infringement, on the other hand, is the facilitation of direct infringement and thus can be referred to in the sale of copied goods, renting of copyrighted goods, or simply instructing, guiding or suggesting to others how to carry out a direct infringement. Surprisingly, no direct or indirect infringement could be established in this case. Under Chinese copyright law (then, the Copyright Act 2001 – recently amended by the Copyright Act 2010), an indirect infringement must satisfy the following elements – 'knowingly', and 'having a commercial purpose'. Clearly, Baidu did have a commercial purpose, but none that obviously meant breaking the law. Alhough Baidu did not intend to deliberately gain any profits through the infringement, Baidu did adopt a laissez-faire attitude towards the results of the violation and could, therefore, satisfy the subjective and qualitative requirements for indirect infringement. Eventually, the internet search engine service providers could not avoid infringement liability for storing illegal content or sharing direct links. A very vivid metaphor used in this case was that if a commercial building is providing rental space to any store, and if any of its tenants sold fake brand-name goods, the commercial building owners would be jointly and severally liable for such infringing activities.[30] Similarly, the search engine service provider's search platform could be compared to a commercial building;

---

[28] *Beijing Haidian District People's Court in civil judgments* (2005), Hai Zhi Chu Zi No. 14665.

[29] *The Beijing First Intermediate People's Court civil mediation document* (2006), Yi Zhong Ming Zhong Zi No. 2491.

[30] Recently, in Beijing, a commercial building was sentenced to be jointly liable by the court for its tenant's activities of selling fake brand-name France Louis Vuitton LV bags. See Song Guang, 'Famous "LV" Only Sell for Hundred Yuan: A Beijing Commercial Building Suffered 15 Million Penalty for Selling of Fake Products', http://www.chinacourt.org/public/detail.php?id=202079, accessed 22 April 2010.

however, it would have to depend mainly on web traffic to earn interest. A search platform and network service provider should assume different responsibilities based on different situations for presenting search results, also known as 'hits'. It is to be noted that if the search engine returns only some basic network information, it does not need to bear responsibility for these checks, but if it presents detailed network content or other goods and services, it should bear the obligation of due diligence.[31]

10.2.1.4. Electronic contracts and their corresponding laws

Electronic contracts can broadly be defined as those contracts that are formed by electronic means through Electronic Data Interchange (EDI), e-mail, telegram, telex or fax. E-contracts refer to those contracts that are created over the internet using EDI or e-mail, where performance is entirely electronic and execution is through computer networks. Thus, the narrow concept of an electronic contract refers only to those contracts that are created, stored and performed in digital form, excluding telegram, fax and other electronic forms, which are mentioned in the United Nations Model Law on Electronic Commerce.[32] It can be said that most electronic contracts for e-commerce should be considered in terms of the narrowly defined concept, as the majority of courts already consider contracts formed through the telegraph or facsimile as common written contracts, instead of special e-commerce contracts.

China's Electronic Contract Law basically regulates the electronic contracts following its general legal norms, including that both the conclusion and performance of the contract can primarily be addressed through the electronic medium. However, the Electronic Contract Law is not suitable for the following three situations: first, where the agreement relates to personal relationships. Second, the Electronic Contract Law is a part of China's Electronic Signature Law; therefore, in case of conflict, the E-contract Law should step aside and the Signature Law should prevail. Third, electronic contracts between consumers and businesses must be regulated by the Consumer Protection Law, trumping the Electronic Contract Law since the former offers greater rights and interests to the consumer under normal circumstances. However, B2B (business to business) electronic contracts are regulated under the Electronic Contract Law.[33] In

[31] Cong Lixian, *Internet Copyright Issues Research*, Wuhan University Press, January 2007, p. 337.

[32] Gao Fuping (ed.), *Electronic Contracts and Electronic Signature Law Study*, Beijing University Press, April 2005, pp. 61–2.

[33] Qi Aimin, *E-Commerce Law*, Dongbei University of Finance & Economics Press, April 2009, pp. 45–6.

1999 in China, the then prevailing Contract Law, drawing on the relevant provisions of the United Nations Commission International Trade Law Model Law on Electronic Commerce, prescribed six provisions related to electronic contract for the purposes of electronic commerce and also legalized data messages. However, since the earlier Contract Law had certain shortcomings, such as that it was not very detailed, it did not meet the actual needs of the e-commerce industry and even though there were many provisions, they lacked effectiveness and operability. Consequently, all these issues paved the way for enhancement of the Electronic Signatures Law. In another case between *Hotmail Corporation v Van Money Pie Inc.*,[34] the plaintiff Hotmail was a free e-mail service provider. When users applied to use Hotmail's free e-mail service, they consented to terms and conditions under which the applicant was restricted from using the Hotmail account for dissemination of electronic commercial advertisements, also known as Spam. Only then could the user receive a free e-mail account. However, the defendant, Van Money Pie, used Hotmail's free e-mail service to send commercial advertisements to others, and since all the messages sent from the Hotmail account were checked for Spam, the plaintiff sued Van Money Pie for breach of contract. The court agreed that Hotmail's agreement was a valid contract, and that the defendant company, by sending out commercial advertisements, was in breach of the service agreement.[35]

10.2.1.5. Electronic payment system and governing laws

The convenience of making payment through an electronic system was an important factor in the development of electronic commerce. Broadly, e-payments refer to the transmission of money using secure means of electronic transmission over a digital network between trading parties, which include consumers, merchants and financial institutions.[36] In 1989, the Uniform Commercial Laws and Regulations, approved by the American Law Institute, defined 'electronic payment' as follows: 'E-payment involves a series of electronic transactions of currency between the sender who gives an order to the commercial bank where his funds are deposited to pay a certain sum of amount into the beneficiary's bank account through an assigned network.' Parties using online payment methods had to ensure the reliability of payment platforms, and when making online payments had to be careful when selecting options like 'cash on delivery' and/or

---

[34] 47U.S.P.Q. 2d (BNA) 1020, 1998 U.S. Dist. LEXIS 10729 (N.D.Cal.4/201/98)

[35] See E-commerce Law Teaching Cases http://210.33.28.152/wfxy/upload/20061018104156613.doc, accessed 28 September 2010.

[36] Zhao Bingzhi and Yu Zhigang: *A Comparative Study of Computer-related Crime*, Law Press, June 2004, pp. 340–41.

'pay in advance' to ensure the safety of their funds. In China, due to the promulgation and implementation of the Electronic Signatures Law and the People's Bank's Guidelines on Electronic Payments, the e-commerce electronic payment business was gradually moving towards a more regulated environment.

In the case of *Hao Brothers*,[37] in Yangzhou City, two Chinese computer hackers illegally hacked into the bank's computer system and transferred 720,000 yuan to their false bank accounts. The Chinese Criminal Law, academia[38] and China's highest judicial body[39] held that the illegal transfer of bank deposits by the two hackers to their own accounts or to third party should be considered an act of theft, although some scholars were of the opinion that the crime should not be judged as theft, but that fraud was more appropriate. In addition, even if the Court judged it as a case of theft, it did not mean that the defendant's crime was accomplished immediately upon transfer of the money through an electronic medium into his/her own account. Only when the bank loses control of the money electronically, and the defendant is actually liable to have taken the money, can the crime be established. As new types of computer-related fraud crimes constantly arise, the criminal courts would be better advised to expand the scope of interpretation of criminal or wrongful acts, as opposed to amending the Penal Code with each new crime.[40]

10.2.1.6. E-commerce transactions: safety and privacy issues

Whenever a system stores a customer's personal information, concern for the security, use and accuracy of personal content emerges.[41] Do businesses have the right to collect consumers' personal information? How

---

37 Hao Jing-long, a staff member of the Zhejiang branch of China Industrial and Commercial Bank, and his brother Hao Jing-wen were found guilty of hacking into the bank's database from their home. They transferred funds amounting to 720,000 RMB to 16 accounts which had been opened in false names. Hao Jing-wen was sentenced to death and Hao Jing-long was sentenced to life imprisonment. The first instance judgment was filed at Jiang Su Yangzhou Intermediate People's Court in December 1998 and the appeal was upheld by Jiang Su Yangzhou Higher People's Court.

38 Zhao Bingzhi and Yu Zhigang, *A Comparative Study of Computer-related Crime*, Law Press, June 2004, pp.340–41.

39 Supreme People's Court Criminal Trial No. 1 Court, No. 2 court, *Criminal Justice Cases*, Law Press, November 2002, p. 445.

40 Guo Yimei and Cai Qinghui (eds), *The Classic Case of Electronic Commerce Law Studies*, CITIC Press, September 2006, pp. 298–99.

41 Chen Jian, *Study of Electronic Payment*, China University of Political Science and Law Press, September 2006, p. 308.

do businesses use the consumer's personal information? Should businesses give consumers a right to choose when collecting personal data? The answer to all these questions can be found under China's Tort Law.[42] Protection of privacy is guaranteed under e-commerce transactions as one of the basic conditions and if it cannot be guaranteed, then e-commerce will lose its reliability. E-commerce transaction security and privacy protection mainly includes the security of bank card details, transaction data security, and other similar privacy issues. At present, China's e-commerce legal system on the privacy protection provisions is far from perfect and desperately needs strengthening. Under China's Civil Law system, privacy has not been defined as an independent civil right but has been given protection as part of the 'right to reputation', according to the applicable judicial interpretations issued by the Supreme People's Court. The protection of privacy becomes all the more important and should be strengthened when any crucial information is accessed and disseminated over a network environment. In 2008, China observed the first 'human flesh search' case,[43] which involved Jiang Yan, who committed suicide by jumping off a high building. A few months prior to her death, she discovered that her husband, Wang Fei (a high level government official at the time), was cheating on her. She filed for divorce. However, just before Jiang committed suicide, she published her 'death blog', in which she described her husband's infidelity as the cause of her suicide, and she also posted pictures of her husband and his mistress on the blog. After the content was made public through the internet, it was constantly reproduced, and Mr Wang became the target of a 'human flesh search' by internet users as they posted his personal information across China's information networks. In addition, Mr Wang received constant verbal abuse and threats over the internet as well as in real life. Wang was also dismissed by his employer as a result of the controversy. Also, his parents were repeatedly harassed and their house was covered with threat posters. Mr Wang claimed that three particular sites had infringed his privacy and sued them, seeking compensation for economic loss and mental harassment. After the court hearing, it was adjudged that two of the sites had a prima facie case of infringement to answer (for publishing the subject's real name, photos, contact details etc.) and they were accordingly ordered to cease further dissemination of Wang's details and pay 5,000 yuan in compensation for moral damage, along with an apology. However, the court decided that the second web-

---

[42] Yang Lixin (ed.), *E-Commerce Tort Law*, Intellectual Property Press, June 2005, pp. 32–5.

[43] Beijing 2nd Intermediate People's Court in civil judgment (2009).

site's postings did not constitute infringement. In the absence of a statute on privacy, the Wang case was one of the first cases in China to act as a form of precedent for guidelines on abuse of personal data.

10.2.1.7. Anti-counterfeit and the eBay-EachNet and Alibaba tale

As the internet and e-commerce have created an almost unlimited virtual space that has all but removed the physical barriers in world trade, the flow of business, logistics, capital and information have all helped to bring about the success of e-commerce. Through the combination of these four constituent elements, a variety of different types of e-business models have emerged.[44] However, along with the growth of such business models has also come growth in the trade in counterfeit products, as seen by e-commerce retailers such as eBay-EachNet and Alibaba in China.

eBay Inc. was founded in the United States in 1995 and EachNet was founded in 1999 in China, and later the two formed a joint venture in China, the eBay-EachNet company. eBay-EachNet launched mainly three e-commerce-related transactions: online auctions, online direct selling and business monopoly. eBay-EachNet became a professional 'product release and access information' website and its information services did not put any restriction on its content. The quality of information being shared on its website was very high level as compared with other sites. It had some obvious characteristics for obtaining and issuing business information, such as requiring a real name for information dissemination, information release fees, access to information had to be confirmed before purchase and breach of contract penalties etc. Although the eBay-EachNet e-commerce model achieved great success in China, as a people-based e-commerce system, the online auction system faced several hurdles. The first hurdle was imperfection in the social credit system, the second was an imperfect means of electronic payment, and the third was imperfection in the online auction rules.

Another interesting case relates to the largest B2B e-commerce brand in China, Alibaba, which successfully created an amalgamation of B2B, consumer-to-consumer (C2C), search engines and portals. Alibaba's services focused on the following aspects: first, China's supplier services. It earned more valuable international orders by promoting suppliers for China's outstanding export commodities. By December 2006, it had nearly 2 million registered members. Second, in promoting credibility, it introduced e-business credit services to help enterprises establish an online

44 Liu Shangzhi and Chen Jialin, *The E-Commerce and Computer Software Patent Protection*, March 2004, p. 272.

credit file and improve the efficiency and success of online businesses. Its third main focus was on Taobao, which was a C2C transaction site whose goal was to become China's biggest personal online trading portal. Fourth was Yahoo China, focused on the search engine business. Fifth was Ali software, which integrated e-commerce and online software services and accelerated the development of the software industry utilizing the World Wide Web.[45]

However, eBay-EachNet and Alibaba's greatest business risk was their operation and management model, which inadvertently had inputs of a large number of counterfeit products, eventually creating problems as eBay-EachNet were repeatedly forced to take liability for the sale of counterfeit products. In 2008, the French courts ordered eBay to pay 40 million euros (about 61 million US dollars) to Louis Vuitton and producers of other branded luxury goods to compensate for the counterfeited goods sold through the site and also forced eBay to take additional measures to investigate and stop the sale of counterfeit products.[46] As a principle for the development of e-commerce, the transacting parties involved had to respect IP laws and not engage in any activity that infringed the IP of rights holders. An e-commerce network service provider has to ensure that the products and services being made available through their portals do not violate local IP laws.

10.2.2. Regional Differences in the Laws Governing E-commerce: The Beijing and Shanghai example

China's local e-commerce legislation existed prior to national legal frameworks coming into existence. The more economically developed areas developed their own rules for e-commerce before the State enacted laws on electronic signatures and contract. For example, Guangdong Province promulgated the Guangdong Province Provisional Regulations on the Implementation of Electronic Data Interchange in Foreign Trade in the form of provincial government rules and regulations as early as 1996, and later developed local laws and regulations in the form of Electronic Transactions Ordinance in Guangdong Province in 2002. These legislative documents proved to be the cornerstone for national and other areas' legislation. This was mainly because e-commerce companies in

[45] Si Linsheng, *E-Commerce Case Analysis*, Chongqing University Press, September 2007, pp. 36–54.

[46] See http://tech.sina.com.cn/i/2008-07-01/00062293890.shtml, accessed 3 October 2010. eBay v Louis Vuitton, filed in Paris Commercial Court, 1st Chamber, Division B (30 June 2008).

China were mostly located in economically developed regions, where e-commerce was fast growing. Beijing and Shanghai were the most active areas in e-commerce in China. Beijing announced the *Beijing Municipal Administration for Industry and Commerce on the Registration and Filing of Online Business Operations and Standardized Online Advertising Business Qualifications* in 2000. Later, a supplementary notice (comments) related to these announcements was issued, the Beijing Information Promotion Regulations strengthening the supervision and management of e-commerce, issued in 2008, which was Beijing's most detailed framework for e-commerce and known as the Beijing 'Net Shop New Regulations'. The main points of the Regulations are as follows: (1) The principal body that uses the internet for e-commerce business activities had to register in accordance with the law and could only start business after applying for a business licence. Net shops of enterprises or the self-employed that already held business licenses had to re-apply for an upgrade related to the registration if they exceeded the original business registration scope. (2) These regulations applied only to e-shops in the Beijing area. If a legal person sold on the internet, replaced items for personal use and no profit purpose was involved, then no registration was required. Taobao, eBay and other net shops in the areas outside Beijing were not affected. (3) E-businesses were required to establish an *information disclosure* system. The 'E-Business Information Publicity' link had to be set at the bottom of a trader's website home page, and information needed to include the business name, registration number, and information of the website's (shop) principal. In addition, the service provider that provided the online shop should manage the website and check the business license and proof of merchants, and build electronic records of trade taking place with the consumers, and keep records for at least two years.

In 1999, Shanghai issued the Shanghai International Trade Electronic Data Interchange Administrative Regulations and the Shanghai E-business Price Management Interim Measures. Later, in November 2008, Shanghai formally developed and adopted the Shanghai Advancing e-business Development Regulation (Regulation). This Regulation provided a clear definition of e-commerce as selling of goods over the internet and stated that the relevant licenses based on the relevant State provisions should be obtained when an enterprise engages in e-commerce. The Regulation listed the priority items that the region supported to promote e-business development, including construction of e-commerce platforms for advance manufacturing and modern service industry and other key areas; construction of e-commerce service systems for electronic payments, secure authentication, credit services, logistics information systems, and development and promotion of key technologies for e-commerce. The Regulation defined clearly the responsibilities of the administrative departments, the relevant industry associations, e-commerce companies, and methods to improve facilities for e-commerce-related platforms and establishments concerned.

Shanghai's Regulation was very different to the Beijing Shop new regulation. Considering the legal framework aspect, Shanghai's Regulation was formally authorized by the People's Congress as the first Chinese local regulation to promote e-business development, while the Beijing Shop new regulation was a local normative document under the government sector. As regards legal impact, Shanghai's Regulation had a higher legal efficacy and the court could invoke its provisions as required, while the Beijing Shop new regulation had a lower effect legally and could only serve as an administrative guidance document. Considering the content's aspect, Shanghai's Regulation has the effect of monitoring with greater flexibility by distinguishing between an individual and an enterprise. Shanghai's Regulation monitored B2B and B2C website operators, while the C2C form of general sales required a voluntary license. For large-scale C2C sites, the Regulation took an incremental approach with the aim of ensuring uniformity in operational standards.

10.2.3. E-commerce Litigation and Dispute Resolution

The alternative dispute resolution mechanism for e-commerce can be divided into public and private solution mechanisms. The private solution uses self-determination, compromise and mutual concessions. The public solution can be divided into three kinds: arbitration, mediation and litigation, where litigation is the means of last resort.[47] In addition, due to the special nature of e-commerce, the industry is also actively searching for new forms of dispute resolution methods, such as online dispute resolution (Alternative Dispute Resolution). The ADR method refers to all methods or techniques of dispute resolution, including traditional arbitration, court-annexed arbitration, proposed arbitration, mediation arbitration, mediation, mini trial, summary jury trial, neutral experts determining facts and so on, except for litigation.[48]

Another interesting case involves the popular internet portal Yahoo Inc., from which the perspective of the French courts towards internet

---

[47] Qi Aimin, *E-Commerce Law*, Dongbei University of Finance & Economics Press, April 2009, pp. 192–5.

[48] Guo Yujun and Gan Yong, 'The U.S. Selective Dispute Resolution (ADR)–Mediated Assessment', *Chinese Law*, 2000, No. 5.

jurisdiction in civil and commercial cases is clearly given. When the Yahoo (France) site set out to auction Nazi memorabilia on the internet, the judiciary in France ordered Yahoo to censor its site for users in France and also to remove Nazi paraphernalia from its auction site within a period of 90 days; otherwise it would have to face a penalty of 100,000 francs (approximately 13,000 US dollars) per day. Subsequently, Yahoo appealed in the United States District Court in San Jose, California, where Yahoo was registered to limit the decision of the French court. The judgment issued by the French court faced criticism and raised questions as to whether its decision could obtain recognition and enforcement by the US courts. If the decision was confirmed, would it mean that all Nazi-impacted countries could exercise jurisdiction? Yahoo argued that this was unfair as they could not know beforehand the laws and history of all of the victimized countries. In fact, once an e-commerce company carried out business activities within a country, then its behavior would inevitably affect the country's trade and the ideology and culture of the country's customers. The case demonstrates the extra territoriality impact of protective jurisdiction in e-commerce.[49]

Electronic writs can be used as evidence in e-commerce litigation, but should be strictly examined for relevance as well as authenticity. Lawyers who use electronic evidence should fulfill the obligation to prove the integrity, authenticity, relevance (which can be certified), and dependability of such evidence.[50] To obtain notarization for electronic evidence, features like an application similar to the one used in cases of evidence under traditional legal rules and new network rules should also be established, based on the features of e-commerce. For the application of law in e-commerce, the most important factor is the link to choice of applicable law. Similar to the problem of finding an amenable jurisdiction, there arises the problem of finding the link for applicable law for tort and contract performance. Specifying or determining the nationality becomes complicated and confusing because of the virtual nature of the network. The principle of autonomy turns out to be the most suitable applicable law for a network environment, but it is still not the perfect policy. Therefore, in the current situation, Chinese national courts have generally adopted the 'old wine in new bottles' approach, which indicates the use of relevant traditional law for e-commerce cases, taking into account the 'network characteristics' of

[49] Li Shuangyuan and Wang Hailang, *A Number of Issues Research on Electronic Commerce Law*, Beijing University Press, December 2003, p. 380.

[50] Gao Fuping (ed.), *E-Commerce Legal Guide*, Law Press, March 2003, p. 768.

the transaction.[51] The convenience of the identification of foreign laws as a result of internet transactions has provided an even greater number of options for the judge to decide an e-commerce case. After considering the facts, the judge can identify interrelated national laws through the internet and identify the applicable law after a comparative analysis based on a fair and impartial examination. Thereby, the 'chosen result' could probably be converted from a theoretical analysis into a more practical choice of law.[52]

10.3. INFLUENCE OF INTERNATIONAL LAW ON THE LEGAL ENVIRONMENT OF E-COMMERCE IN CHINA

E-commerce legislation in different countries follows different models: the first is a modification of the 'application' model. This either modifies existing legal provisions or adds corresponding supplementary provisions to existing law, so that on the one hand the existing legal system maintains its basic form and structure, whilst on the other hand, the need for legal regulation is better adapted by initial access to e-commerce activities. The second approach is the model of 'special' legislation. This concentrates on solving new situations and problems of e-commerce and is (generally) more efficient. Also, it can coordinate well with existing laws, while maintaining the relative independence of e-commerce law. The third approach is the policy-oriented, 'put legislation on hold' mode. This is applied where the economy is lagging behind and e-commerce has just got going. This situation requires a more flexible policy in the beginning to guide the development of e-commerce until the situation is suitable for the development of a framework for e-commerce law and regulation.[53]

The rapid development of internet technology is not adequately reflected in private international law treaties. For example, the United Nations convention relating to a Uniform Law on International Sale of Goods and the UN convention on the International Sale of Goods Contract on Forming Unified Law in 1964, and the United Nations convention on the International Sale of Goods Contracts in 1980 do not reflect the e-commerce model in the internet age. An interesting

---

[51] GaoFuping and Zhang Chu, *E-Commerce Law*, Beijing University Press, first edition, January 2002, p. 301.

[52] He Qisheng: *Private International Law of E-Commerce Issues*, Law Press, January 2004, p. 270.

[53] Guan Yonghong (ed.), *E-Commerce Law*, South China University of Technology Press, September 2003, pp. 17–18.

question is whether the United Nations conventions should apply to international e-commerce? In this regard, a simple answer 'yes or no' is not easy. E-commerce has its own characteristics, whereas the international treaties established earlier with a common mode of sale of goods are appropriate for the conventional sale of physical goods. Some scholars have suggested establishing new international organizations, and signing a new special treaty to regulate and manage the internet, as well as the related issues of international treaties or other forms of uniform substantive law.[54]

In fact, the international community gave a high degree of attention to the legal issues arising from electronic commerce. The United Nations Commission on International Trade began to draft the legal rules on electronic commerce as early as 1992, and eventually adopted the UNCITRAL Model Law on Electronic Commerce in 1996. The Model Law not only regulated but also facilitated e-commerce. The Model Law is not legally binding on all countries. However, the enactment of the Model Law proved to be a good legal reference text for countries (in fact, all countries largely refer to its legislative outcomes for developing their own e-commerce law). In 2001, the United Nations Commission on International Trade completed and adopted the UNCITRAL Model Law on Electronic Signatures, containing comprehensive provisions on electronic signatures. The Model Law expanded and refined the principle content in Article VII of the Model Law on Electronic Commerce. In 2005, the United Nations Commission on International Trade Law adopted the United Nations Convention on the use of Electronic Communications in International Contracts.[55] The Convention's purpose was to solve the existing legal obstacles that block the development of electronic commerce in present conventions, and to provide a viable legal solution for the use of electronic communication means in contracts.

China showed a positive attitude by supporting and actively participating in e-commerce-related areas of international legislation and has participated in most of the international treaties in this area. In regard to the implementation of international treaties in China, on the one hand, Chinese courts can directly invoke specific provisions of international treaties to decide cases and the content of international treaties can also be amended and adopted by the legislature in domestic law. E-commerce

[54] Zhan Liyuan, 'Private International Law Problems and Solutions in Network Age', in *China's Private International Law and Comparative Law Annual 2002*, Law Press, October 2002, pp. 383–4.

[55] At present, there are 18 countries in the world that have signed the Convention on Electronic Communications. China signed on 6 July 2006.

as a new form of trade, has made low-cost cross-border trade possible and changed traditional shopping methods and trade patterns. It was greatly affected by the WTO. E-commerce-related WTO agreements include the GATS, the ITA agreement, basic telecommunications agreement, TRIPS etc. With the WTO's impact on China's e-commerce, most attention was obviously paid to the opening question of the telecommunications industry.[56] It became an inevitable choice of China's legislative and policy-making bodies to modify relevant laws, regulations, and policies to conform to the requirements of the WTO. In fact, the legislative bodies amended the relevant laws and regulations and basically met WTO requirements before and after China's accession to the WTO. As a large developing country, China chose to first meet the minimum requirements of the WTO relating to the issues of market regulation and intellectual property protection, and in the future, to adopt the higher level of protection in accordance with its gradually maturing market.

However, some specific provisions of the relevant Chinese laws and regulations went beyond the WTO's minimum requirements and achieved a higher level of protection. For example, in computer software protection, China reached a 'super-World Conservation level'. This was mainly reflected in the revised provision in section 17 of the Regulation on Protection of Computer Software shortly after China's accession to the WTO. According to section 22 of the Regulation, the scope of fair use of copyrighted material is severely restricted. In fact, TRIPS and the WCT did not require signatory countries to protect computer programs any differently from written work, but in the normal way of protection given to a literary work. At the same time, these two treaties did not prescribe that the protection to computer programs should be extended to all end-users regardless of object and purpose. In fact, the promises that China needed to undertake were only to give rental rights to the software copyright owner in accordance with the requirements of TRIPS and the WCT when amending the Computer Software Protection Regulations to enter the WTO.[57]

---

[56] Jiang Zhipei (ed.), *Internet and Electronic Commerce Law* (revised), Law Press, April 2002, pp. 551–3.

[57] Shou Bu, *Information Network and High-tech Legal Frontier*, Law Press, August 2003, pp. 99–112.

10.4. SUGGESTIONS FOR IMPROVING THE LEGAL ENVIRONMENT OF E-COMMERCE IN CHINA

While China has made great progress in the construction of policy and a legal environment for e-commerce, compared with the Western developed countries, due to the limitations of traditional legal constraints and the lack of necessary innovative policies, laws and the establishment of regulations, China is still lagging behind and the existing legal framework still has many gaps. The main problems are as follows: first, the Law conjoined with the Electronic Signature Law needs to be established as soon as possible. The Electronic Signature Law is a basic law, and it is necessary to establish a separate Electronic Transactions Act, Personal Privacy Protection Law and other related auxiliary laws. The existing relevant laws and regulations, such as the Negotiable Instruments Law, Accounting Law, Maritime Law, also need to be revised. In addition, the legality of electronic invoices needs to be confirmed by relevant laws. Second, the effectiveness of the existing provisions are inadequate for modern e-commerce. E-commerce laws and regulations are mostly departmental regulations and local laws, and their low-level effectiveness has a direct impact on limiting their scope and power. Third, coordination of the ministries concerned is too expensive and has resulted in low efficiencies. The regulations lack the necessary inter-departmental coordination. Also, the rules and regulations lack the necessary coordination at a local level. Fourth, there is still a gap in the technical operation on e-commerce legislation. A number of specific legislative provisions are not necessarily fully consistent with the characteristics and requirements of e-commerce. Fifth, the administration model is old-fashioned, and the e-government model does not satisfactorily compare with the e-commerce model for innovation. Management of e-commerce activities such as registration and licensing relates to an essentially fragmented management system, and is not well adapted to e-commerce features and requirements. Sixth, too much reliance on administration has resulted in excessive pressure on the executive authorities. There are widespread problems of overreliance on administrative measures (registration, filing, licensing, annual inspection, monitoring, etc.), whilst neglecting social forces and intermediary service organizations.[58]

China's legislators must not only explore the dynamics of world e-commerce legislation, but also understand their own national conditions, including national levels of development of electronic commerce,

[58] Allah Musi (ed.), *Network Transactions Legal Practice (book one)*, Law Press, November 2006, pp. 22–5.

the traditional characteristics of the legal system, as well as the people engaged in e-commerce. On the one hand, it should be recognized that China's e-commerce business has fluctuated and the majority of the legal issues have been discovered through trial and error. These legal difficulties have restricted the development of electronic commerce to a certain extent. On the other hand, it should also be noted that Chinese e-commerce legal issues are closely related to contract law, privacy law, consumer protection law, criminal law, procedural law, evidence law, private international law, tax law and advertising law. And also, nationally, the problems mentioned above are no different in relation to traditional legal departments.[59] Some scholars suggest that the Chinese e-commerce laws or regulations that need to be promulgated through the NPC or the State Council are new laws on telecommunications, the Electronic Transactions Act, management regulations for internet content, an electronic funds transfer law, specific laws of contract to protect the consumer online etc., and those that need to be revised are the Copyright Law, Trademark Law, Patent Law, Corporate Law, Maritime Law, Negotiable Instruments Law, Contract Law, Criminal Law, Civil Law, Criminal Procedure Law, Administrative Procedure Law etc.[60] Other scholars believe that China should practice a dual-track system by adopting a 'two-pronged approach' to create a safe and effective e-business legal environment. 'Dual track' does not mean that there are two different 'norms', but it allows industry and enterprise to develop norms within the basic framework and principles of legislation. Both legal systems have the same direction in essence, but with a different nature; they are complementary.[61]

The scope of e-commerce law is similar to commercial law: the basic need for commercial law is to ensure transaction security. Similarly, the main purpose of e-commerce legislation should also be ensuring transaction security. Specifically, the purpose of e-commerce legislation is to provide transparent, stable and effective rules of conduct in order to make online operators protect fair competition, protect consumer rights, protect intellectual property, and protect personal privacy. The development of peremptory norms should also encourage autonomy in the e-commerce industry and party autonomy, and encourage businesses to explore new rules and restrictive regulations established on a reasonable basis of the maintenance of transaction security. Proceeding from the above guiding

---

59 Wang Liming (ed.), *E-Commerce Legal System: Impact and Response*, People's Court Press, January 2005, pp. 15–16.

60 Guo Yimei, *E-Commerce Law and Practice*, Science Press, April 2004, p. 215.

61 Gao Fuping (ed.), *E-Commerce Legislative Study*, Law Press, March 2004, pp. 309–14.

ideology, Chinese e-commerce legislation should adopt the following five principles:

- convergence with international e-commerce standards;
- technological neutrality;
- the promotion of trade principles;
- the safety principles; and
- consumer protection.[62]

In the supporting policy measures, it is necessary to

- enhance planning and coordination;
- study and formulate taxation policies to encourage the development of electronic commerce;
- improve the e-commerce financing investment mechanism through acceleration of the construction of a credit system;
- establish and improve a safety certification system;
- establish and perfect national standards for e-commerce;
- promote online payment systems;
- develop a modern logistics system;
- continue to promote an entrepreneurial system;
- promote the backbone of enterprise e-business applications;
- promote industry e-commerce applications to support medium and small enterprises;
- promote consumer-oriented e-commerce applications;
- to develop e-commerce-related technology equipment and software;
- promote the construction of e-commerce service systems;
- increase e-business propaganda; and
- enhance role of intermediary organizations.

10.5. CONCLUSION

The rapid development of e-business has generated two unique outcomes: super-regional (transborder) commerce and super-industry (transsector) commercial structures and sectors. The transnational characteristics of e-commerce has generated a conflict at times between different national jurisdictions and their legal application. Also, geographical and physical

---

[62] Zhang Chu (ed.), *Electronic Commerce Law*, The Chinese People's University Press, September 2007, pp. 23–6.

limitations in e-commerce have completely broken down. Super-industry e-commerce has led markets from segmentation to integration. This has led to a number of conflicts and the original set of rights needs now to be adjusted.[63] In the future world of e-commerce, consumers and individual participants will find an unprecedented convenience in transacting online. E-commerce operators, as well as ancillary service providers, will gain ever-larger market shares and commercial space in the 'virtual world'. Being managers, government institutions will experience both the pressure to regulate effectively as well as power in influencing cross-border and domestic trade. Technology and legal systems, which have supported and guaranteed e-commerce, will continue to develop and improve.

In China, e-commerce has been an important part of the national economy and social information. The e-commerce government management departments or the parties involved have recognized that the development of e-commerce is an important measure to stimulate information technology for industrialization, to change the mode of economic growth, to improve the quality and efficiency of the national economy, and to take a new road to industrialization. In recent years, with the development and popularization of information technology, e-commerce in China has developed rapidly and promoted the development of information technology in the national economy. However, compared with developed countries, Chinese e-commerce is still in the early stages, and the problems of a limited range of applications still exist. The policy environment to promote e-business development urgently needs to be improved. Although Chinese e-commerce is taking the same steps as the rest of the developed world, it still lags behind in some specific key areas and cannot adapt to the rapid development of the global e-commerce industry. At present, China's top priority is to accelerate the construction of e-commerce laws and regulations, because the development of all industries is inseparable from a sound legal system. As mentioned above, China should accelerate research on laws and regulation problems relating to electronic transactions, credit management, security authentication, online payment, taxation, market access, privacy protection, and information resource management. The management practices of carrying out relevant business on the internet should also be accelerated. The services and protection system for promoting a network of arbitration and notarization should also be accelerated. The normal order of e-commerce should be protected by fighting illegal and criminal activity in e-commerce and the infringement of intellectual

---

[63] Xue Hong (ed.), *Intellectual Property and E-commerce*, Law Press, May 2003, p. 14.

property rights, which is endangering national security and damaging the people's vital interests. In addition, China could attempt to uphold the useful approach of reforming and being open to developing legal measures in pilot areas, which, once tried out in practice, could be fully developed on a national scale. Moreover, developed areas in eastern China should be brought into play, and given a more 'economically first-mover' advantage, with a good legal environment for e-commerce to promote industrial upgrading and continuous development, as well as to create a progressive legal experience. This could then be gradually expanded nationwide.

11. Anti Monopoly Law

Huang Young and Zhang Zhe[1]

11.1. INTRODUCTION

It is high time to look back on the formation process of the Chinese anti-trust legal system and particularly the Chinese Anti Monopoly Law (hereinafter referred to as the AML), which was promulgated on 30 August 2007 and came into effect on 1 August 2008 in the People's Republic of China.

11.1.1. History of China's Approach in the Area of Competition Policy

1978 is commonly recognized as a turning point in the contemporary history of China, when the Chinese central government made a strategic shift to adopt a 'reform and opening-up' policy. In 1980, the State Council issued the Provisional Regulation on Conducting and Protecting Socialist Competition (known as the 'Ten Clauses of Competition'),[2] which was the first-ever official document in this domain. Slowly but surely, the State Council then promulgated the Notice on Seriously Resolving the Problem of Tie-in Sale in 1986,[3] the Regulation on Pricing Administration in 1987[4] and the Notice on Breaking Local Market Blockade and further

1 Both of the University of International Business and Economics (UIBE).

2 For the full text, please refer to the website of the Legislative Affairs Office of the State Council of the People's Republic of China: http://fgk.chinalaw.gov.cn/article/xzfg/198010/19801000125495.shtml, accessed July 2010. The Regulation was valid from 17 October 1980 until 6 October 2001.

3 See the website of the Legislative Affairs Office of the State Council of the People's Republic of China: http://fgk.chinalaw.gov.cn/article/fgxwj/198605/19860500121981.shtml, accessed July 2010. The Notice was valid from 25 May 1986 until the present.

4 See the website of the Legislative Affairs Office of the State Council of the People's Republic of China: http://fgk.chinalaw.gov.cn/article/xzfg/198709/19870900125528.shtml, accessed July 2010. The Regulation was valid from 11 September 1987 until the present.

Activating Commodity Circulation in 1990.[5] The introduction of the Anti Unfair Competition Law on 2 September 1993[6] was a symbolic event, since it was the first time that some typical monopoly behaviors were prohibited by law under the term 'improper competition'. In 1994, the establishment of the AML was formally included in the legislation plan of the National People's Congress (NPC). At that time, even the boldest legal expert was not able to predict that the process would last for almost 14 years. Additionally, another important law in this regard was the Pricing Law adopted in 1997.

When China entered the 21st century, two events swayed its legislative reform process: the first was China's accession into the World Trade Organization (WTO) in 2001; and the second was the Decision Made by the Central Committee of the Communist Party of China (CPC) on Issues Concerning the Consummation of Socialist Market Economy System, passed at the Third Plenary Meeting of the Sixteenth Session of CPC's Conference.[7] These two events respectively represented the external and internal movements in China, which changed the mindset of the Chinese people. Afterwards, a series of documents with competition elements came into being, including: the Provisional Regulation on Merger with and Acquisition of Domestic Enterprises by Foreign Investors, issued by the Ministry of Commerce (MOFCOM) in 2003; the Provisional Regulation on Prohibiting Pricing Monopoly Behaviors and Notice on Guiding and Standardizing Market Pricing Activities, both issued by the National Development and Reform Commission (NDRC) in the same year; as well as Regulation on Merger with and Acquisition of Domestic Enterprises by Foreign Investors issued by MOFCOM in 2007.

In February 2004, MOFCOM submitted the draft text of the AML to

---

[5] See the website of the Legislative Affairs Office of the State Council of the People's Republic of China: http://fgk.chinalaw.gov.cn/article/fgxwj/199011/19901100121475.shtml, accessed July 2010. The Notice was valid from 10 November 1990 until the present.

[6] See the website of the Legislative Affairs Office of the State Council of the People's Republic of China: http://fgk.chinalaw.gov.cn/article/flk/199309/19930900124988.shtml, accessed July 2010. The Law was adopted at the third meeting of the Standing Committee of the Eighth Session of the National People's Congress (NPC) on 2 September 1993 and has been effective from 1 December 1993 until the present.

[7] See the website of the Legislative Affairs Office of the State Council of the People's Republic of China: http://fgk.chinalaw.gov.cn/article/fgxwj/200310/20031000120503.shtml, accessed July 2010. The Decision was adopted at the Third Plenary Meeting of the 16 Session of the Central Committee of the Communist Party of China (CPC) on 14 October 2003 and has been enforced since then.

the State Council for examination. Then the draft was put on the table of the Standing Committee of the NPC and the first round of legislation review was initiated in June 2006. The second and third rounds were carried out respectively in June and August 2007, ending in the adoption of the AML that we see today.

11.1.2. A Milestone on the Road of China's Economic Transition Period

Antitrust law has been internationally labeled as the 'great charter of the market economy', 'an economic constitution', or 'the core of economic law'. While China has transformed from a planning economy heavily influenced by the previous Soviet Union towards a fully functioning market economy, there are so many economic activities existing to be regulated by the newly released law. That is why, when the AML was introduced into Chinese society, it was soon regarded as a symbol or flag for achieving economic democracy and freedom in China. In that sense, the AML has gone far beyond the obligations or liabilities of its legal provisions – the AML now stands for the people's confidence, determination and sense of value.

It is fair to say that the long-lasting process of legislating the AML awakened people's consciousness about safeguarding fair competition when looking at the various surrounding activities in their daily lives. There are many case examples of anti competitive practices that have attracted a great deal of attention and public comment in China. For example, the pricing authority in Lanzhou City imposed a ceiling price on stretched noodles topped with beef with the excuse of 'caring about people's lives';[8] some Chinese dairy companies released the so-called 'Nanjing Declaration of Self-discipline' to abandon bundling and tying sales so as to maintain profit margins;[9] under the auspices of the China Branch of the International Instant Noodles Association, local instant

---

[8] For details, please refer to the press article published in Beijing Business News on 6 July 2007 from the website of Xinhua News Agency: http://news.xinhuanet.com/local/2007-07/06/content_6335899.htm. On 26 June 2007, the Lanzhou Pricing Administration joined forces with the Lanzhou Administration of Industry and Commerce as well as other three relevant authorities and released a decree to set a ceiling price on stretched noodles divided into four categories.

[9] The Self-discipline Declaration and its implementation plan were published on the website of the Dairy Association of China (DAC): http://www.dac.com.cn/view.php?articleid=246177&sortid=67, accessed July 2010. On 21 June 2007, 14 leading Chinese dairy companies endorsed the Declaration and agreed not to adopt any bundling or tying promotion activities nor to apply a dumping price, but to encourage a strategy of 'good price for good quality'.

noodle manufacturers struck a bargain to build up an alliance to collude in pricing;[10] the five biggest Chinese airlines unanimously reduced the supply of discount tickets for the route between Beijing and Shanghai.[11]

Now, armed with the AML, it is very natural that people have pinned high expectations on this law, although this is coupled with a great deal of worry and concern. But most importantly, the culture of competition has gradually become rooted in both companies and individuals. Similar to the West, people are beginning to think about whether they can enjoy the benefits arising from maintaining the pattern of sufficient competition, safeguarding the welfare of consumers, eradicating anti-competitive barriers or hindrances, etc.

11.1.3. Chinese Characteristics

The Chinese central government always advocates building 'a socialist market economy with Chinese characteristics'. A similar approach was taken with the drafting and adoption of the AML, which also contains 'Chinese flavors'.

The first Chinese characteristic concerns the concept of an administrative monopoly. Generally, administrative monopolies never reflect the rules of market economies. Instead, an administrative monopoly is caused by abuse of administrative power and improper intervention in economic activities. It is a long-existing phenomenon that some monopoly activities are authorized by administrative bodies. In this sense, Chapter V of the AML, which was once deleted from the draft law, is indeed a significant advance in this regard. However, it is worth noting that Article 51 provides that the AML enforcement authorities (referring to the Ministry of Commerce, the National Development and Reform Commission and the State Administration of Industry and Commerce within the current government) only possess the right to make suggestions when confronting the

---

10 See http://news.xinhuanet.com/life/2007-08/17/content_6548082.htm, accessed July 2010. The National Development and Reform Commission (NDRC) decided on 16 August 2007 that the agreed minutes and other activities carried out by the China Branch of the International Instant Noodle Association constituted the collusive inflation of prices.

11 See http://www.china.com.cn/city/txt/2007-08/06/content_8633012.htm, accessed July 2010 and http://www.gov.cn/fwxx/ly/2007-08/06/content_707557.htm. On 6 August 2007, under the auspices of the Civil Aviation Administration of China (CAAC), Air China and four other domestic airlines agreed to jointly operate the air route between Beijing and Shanghai. As a result, prices for tickets were observed to have increased by 10–30%. However, an official from the CAAC then denied the existence of a pricing cartel through the Xinhua News Agency.

question of how to handle a specific administrative monopoly behavior. It is for the superior authority above the administrative body concerned to decide whether to accept or give due consideration to such a suggestion.[12] Given the powers of the (superior authority) it is quite doubtful whether the powers of the AML enforcement authorities can function efficiently and whether efforts to eradicate administrative monopolies will be in vain, which could eventually turn Chapter V into 'a tiger without teeth'.

The second Chinese characteristic is to give special treatment to 'industries where state-owned companies occupy a controlling position, and national economic lifelines as well as national security are involved', or 'industries where the right of franchised business or sales is authorized by law' (Article 7, AML). Examples of such industries in these two categories include banking, telecommunications, electricity, petroleum and tobacco. This does not mean that these industries are exempted by the AML. We should not neglect the wording of this law that states the government only protects the 'legitimate operational activities' of undertakings in these areas, which means that large-scale state-owned enterprises (SOEs) have no choice but to respect the principles of the AML, coupled with other competition-based provisions, such as are found in the Pricing Law, the Anti Unfair Competition Law etc., under the supervision of the executive and legislature.

The third Chinese characteristic is the installation of enforcement authorities that can be described as 'two tiers and three institutions'. The first tier is the Anti Monopoly Committee, established within the State Council, which at the time of writing is chaired by Vice Premier Wang Qishan, a political appointment. The Committee is mainly responsible for working out competition policy in China, releasing assessment reports and guidelines, as well as coordinating significant issues in implementing the AML. However, the Committee is not equivalent to the Competition Commission in the United Kingdom, for example, as it is not involved in any phase II investigations or any decision-making in a specific case. Under the Anti Monopoly Committee, the second tier comprises three parallel ministries: the Ministry of Commerce (MOFCOM), the National Development and Reform Commission (NDRC) and the State Administration for Industry and Commerce (SAIC). Ministers from these

---

12 In China, almost all local administration is supervised by higher administrative organs respectively in a vertical way. For example, when an authority at the municipal level does something violating the AML, the nature of such a violation will trigger the intervention of one of three enforcement bodies. The latter will 'suggest' that the supervising authority at the provincial level handles the case by law. The same principle applies when the violation is conducted at the provincial level: the 'suggestion' then goes to the state administrative body.

three ministries (at the time of writing, namely Mr Chen Deming, Mr Zhang Ping, and Mr Zhou Bohua), plus a deputy secretary general of the State Council (Mr Bi Jingquan), are appointed to be the Vice Directors of the Anti Monopoly Committee, with 14 vice-ministers from different line ministries filling the positions of committee members.[13] The scenario has been described by journalists as the 'three dragons taming the water'. The work of enforcement is shared among these three ministries, among which MOFCOM mainly deals with investigations and the review of mergers and acquisitions; NDRC takes care of the pricing of monopoly activities, while the SAIC covers non-pricing monopoly agreements and abuse of market dominance. This two-tier structure has been used more for the sake of maintaining the current division of labor, rather than to follow international common practice of having an independent and unified enforcement body. As none of the above-mentioned ministries are willing to give up their competence in the area of anti monopoly law, it is unlikely that we will see a unified enforcement body in the near future, unless central government can gain acceptance for such a change in the next round of government restructuring due in early 2013.

There is one point worth mentioning here. Although the sovereignties of Hong Kong and Macau were handed over to the central government of the People's Republic of China by the British and Portuguese governments on 1 July 1997 and on 20 December 1999, respectively, in conformity with the theory of 'one country, two systems' proposed by Mr Deng Xiaoping, the Chinese leader in the 1980s, Hong Kong and Macau are able to maintain their separate legal systems so long as they are not in contradiction with the Basic Law of the Hong Kong Special Administrative Region and the Basic Law of the Macau Special Administrative Region. In this sense, the Chinese Anti Monopoly Law is *not* applicable in Hong Kong or Macau. In fact, on 6 May 2008, the local government of Hong Kong launched a second public consultation on its own competition law. However, the attempt encountered a major setback when, on 27 February, in the House Committee of the Legislative Council, the administration confirmed that the competition law would be postponed due to 'technical issues'. On the other hand, as provided by Article 2 of the Chinese AML, the exclusion of Hong Kong, Macau and Taiwan does not prevent the enforcement authorities from investigating any anti-competitive activities

---

13 For the main functions and manning of the Committee, please refer to http://www.lawinfochina.com/law/displayModeTwo.asp?id=7190&keyword, accessed July 2010. On 28 July 2008, the General Office of the State Council released Notice (2008) No. 104 with regard to the Committee.

with an impact on the Chinese domestic market. The case of *Arcelor Mittal v Oriental Steel*[14] is a good example, although Oriental Steel is a listed company on the Hong Kong Stock Exchange Market, but with assets and operations in the mainland of China.

11.2. THE AML AND RELEVANT LAWS AND REGULATIONS

11.2.1. Overview

To some extent, even though the Chinese AML is quite extensive, including eight chapters, 57 articles and over 6,000 Chinese characters, it sets out very general regulatory guidelines. The legal drafting is quite general in nature and there is great scope for further detail to be added in the future. Whether it is going to play a 'due role' in the elimination of legal loopholes and gaps in the law and whether the changes are going to be implemented in a smooth way depends on the further introduction of supporting laws and regulations, and on these being implemented and enforced by the competition authorities in a professional and efficient way.

Just like many other countries with antitrust laws, the Chinese AML targets three main monopoly behaviors: monopoly agreements; the abuse of market dominance; and the concentration of undertakings.

11.2.2. Monopoly Agreements

A monopoly agreement is defined in this Law as an agreement, a decision or other concerted activity that excludes or restricts competition. Articles 13 and 14 deal with horizontal and vertical agreements respectively.

A horizontal agreement refers to a monopoly agreement reached by undertakings in direct competition. Such behavior includes: (1) price fixing

---

[14] At the end of 2007, Arcelor Mittal announced its agreement with Oriental Steel to acquire 73.13% of the latter's shares. The Ministry of Commerce then launched an investigation into its influence in the domestic steel industry on the basis of Chapter V of the Regulation on Foreign Investors Merger with Domestic Enterprises (No. (2006) 10) issued by the Ministry of Commerce and five other line ministries (for the full text, please refer to http://www.fdi.gov.cn/pub/FDI/zcfg/law_ch_info.jsp?docid=56103, accessed July 2010). By the deadline of the Shareholders' Agreement, Oriental Steel decided to pull out of the agreement. Thus, it was not necessary for the Ministry of Commerce to make known the results of its investigation and its decision.

or altering; (2) restriction of production or sales quantity; (3) segmentation of sales markets or raw materials purchasing markets; (4) restrictions on purchasing new technology and new equipment or on developing new technology and new products; (5) joint refusal to deal; and (6) other forms of monopoly agreement identified by the anti monopoly enforcement authorities under the State Council.

A vertical agreement is an arrangement or concerted practice between two or more contract parties operating at different levels of the production, distribution or supply chain. Price fixing or minimum price setting for resale to a third party is prohibited, as well as other forms of monopoly agreement identified by the anti monopoly enforcement authorities under the State Council.

Article 15 provides some reasons that can be used to justify a behavior to be exempted from the application of Articles 13 and 14, such as: (1) for the purpose of improving technology and R&D of new products; (2) for the purpose of improving product quality, reducing cost, increasing efficiency, unifying product specifications and norms, or carrying out professional allocation of work; (3) for the purpose of increasing the operational efficiency of small and medium-sized undertakings, or enhancing their competitiveness; (4) for the purpose of realizing social and public interests such as energy saving, environmental protection, disaster salvation, etc.; (5) for the purpose of mitigating a substantial drop in sales volume or obviously excessive production due to an economic downturn; (6) for the purpose of safeguarding legitimate interests in foreign trade and external economic cooperation; (7) other circumstances as stipulated by law or by the State Council. Generally speaking, the party involved has to prove that such an agreement is in favor of either economic development or consumer benefits.

11.2.3. Abuse of Market Dominance

Article 17 defines market dominance as a market position where an under taking is capable of controlling price, quantity or other trading terms within a relevant market, or deterring or affecting other undertakings' ability to enter into a relevant market.

The relevant factors include: (1) the market share of the undertaking in the relevant market, and the competitive situation thereof; (2) the undertaking's ability to control the sales market or the raw materials purchasing market; (3) the financial strength and technological condition of the undertaking; (4) the degree of dependence of other undertakings on the undertaking in deal-making; (5) other factors related to the identification of market dominance held by the undertaking.

Article 19 further provides that in the circumstances of an undertaking occupying a market share of one-half and above, two undertakings holding a market share of two-thirds and above, or three undertakings reaching three-quarters and above, such a scenario will lead to the undertaking or undertakings being recognized as having market dominance or joint market dominance in a relevant market. The same article also provides that when an undertaking has a market share of less than one-tenth, it shall not be identified as being in a dominant market position.

When an undertaking is in a dominant market position, it might be a very natural consequence of winning over other competitors in the market by means of cost control, quality assurance or technical progress. In this sense, market dominance may be quite natural and not a consequence of abuse. However, where there is abuse, for example as mentioned above, where an undertaking has the ability or power to severely change the competitive structure of a market, the undertakings holding a dominant market position are prohibited by Article 17 from carrying out the following activities: (1) selling at an unfairly high price or buying at an unfairly low price; (2) selling at a price lower than cost without legitimate reasons; (3) refusing to deal with a counterpart without legitimate reasons; (4) binding a counterpart to strike deals only with the relevant undertaking that holds dominance itself or only with another undertaking designated by this undertaking without legitimate reasons; (5) doing tie-in sales without legitimate reasons, or attaching other unreasonable conditions to a deal; (6) discriminating between deal counterparts that offer the same conditions by means of pricing or other trading terms without legitimate reasons; (7) other abusing activities to be identified by the anti monopoly enforcement authorities under the State Council. In other words, it is all right for an undertaking to hold a dominant position in the market. However, it has to behave in a more cautious way so as not to touch upon the seven categories of activities mentioned above.

There have been further very recent developments. As from 1 July 2009, SAIC and its nationwide affiliates have applied two newly announced procedural regulations, respectively: the Regulation on Procedures Concerning Investigation and Punishment of Cases Involving Monopoly Agreement and Abuse of Market Dominance by Administrative Authorities for Industry and Commerce[15] and the Regulation on Procedures Concerning Prevention of Activities Involving Abuse of Administrative

[15] Also translated as Provisions on Procedures for Disposing Monopoly Agreement and Abuse of Dominant Position in the Market by the State Administration for Industry and Commerce.

Power to Exclude or Restrict Competition.[16] As procedural matters are absent in the AML, both these regulations have increased transparency by helping both the plaintiff and the accused to have greater legal certainties and predictabilities in the procedures that the enforcement authority will follow in handling a case. Furthermore, several new rules providing further guidance as to the AML's implementation were published in January 2011 (following a period of public consultation from the publication of draft rules in May 2010), such as the *Rules of Administrative Authority for Industry and Commerce on Prohibition of Abuse of Dominant Market Position* 'Dominance Rules' and coming into effect on 1 February 2011.[17]

11.2.4. Concentration of Undertakings

A more common term for the concentration of undertakings is merger and acquisition (M&A). The regulation of such activities is known as 'merger control'. Article 20 AML lists the scenarios for the concentration of undertakings, which include: (1) combination between undertakings; (2) an undertaking obtaining control over other undertakings by means of acquiring equity or assets; (3) an undertaking obtaining control over other undertakings or possessing the ability to apply decisive influence on other undertakings by means of contract, etc.

11.2.4.1. Filing

As in most legal systems in the world (with the exception of the United Kingdom which adopts voluntary filing), the Chinese AML adopts a compulsory filing system for concentrations (Article 21).

Detailed thresholds for such a filing are provided in a separate document, the Regulations of the State Council on Thresholds for Prior Notification of Concentrations of Undertakings. It provides that, in the following circumstances, the undertaking(s) concerned shall file a prior notification with MOFCOM: (1) the combined worldwide turnover of all the undertakings concerned in the preceding financial year is more than RMB 10 billion yuan, and the nationwide turnover within China of each of at least two of

---

[16] Also translated as Provisions on Procedures for Disposing Abuse of Administrative Power to Exclude or Restrict Competition by the State Administration for Industry and Commerce.

[17] Also published on the Anti Monopoly and Anti Unfair Competition Bureau of the State Administration for Industry and Commerce website were the *Rules on Monopoly Agreements* (2010) and *Rules on Prohibition of Abuse of Administrative Powers to Eliminate and Restrict Competition* (2010), both coming into effect on 1 February 2011.

the undertakings concerned in the preceding financial year was more than RMB 400 million yuan; or (2) the combined nationwide turnover within China of all the undertakings concerned in the preceding financial year was more than RMB 2 billion yuan, and the nationwide turnover within China of each of at least two of the undertakings concerned in the preceding financial year was more than RMB 400 million yuan.

However, the above thresholds do not apply to the financial industry, such as companies dealing in banking, insurance, securities and futures, for which one has to refer to Methods Concerning Turnover Calculation of Concentrations of Undertakings in the Financial Industry, jointly announced by five ministries, including MOFCOM, the People's Bank of China (PBC), the China Banking Regulatory Committee (CBRC), the China Securities Regulatory Committee (CSRC) and the China Insurance Regulatory Committee (CIRC) on 15 July 2009, which came into effect 30 days later than the proclamation date of the Method.

11.2.4.2. Factors to be considered in review

Article 27 provides the factors that MOFCOM considers when reviewing a concentration, which include: (1) the market share of the undertaking(s) involved in a concentration in a relevant market and their controlling power to the market; (2) the degree of concentration in the relevant market; (3) the impact of the concentration of undertakings on market access and technological progress; (4) the impact of the concentration of undertakings on consumers and other undertakings concerned; (5) the impact of the concentration of undertakings on national economic development; (6) other factors that affect market competition and are considered by anti monopoly enforcement authorities under the State Council. It is very common in Chinese legislation to include the last point, as the purpose is to leave more space for MOFCOM to interpret when they try to include something they have not yet figured out in future assessment processes. By weighing all these factors, MOFCOM will decide whether to approve or prohibit a concentration of undertakings, or whether to attach restrictive conditions that could mitigate the negative impact on market competition due to such a concentration.

11.2.4.3. National security

The concept of 'national security' is one of the biggest concerns raised by the public, especially by foreign-invested enterprises (FIEs) in China. There are problems with the clarity of the definition of this term in the current law and a clearer scope or definition of 'national security' is required to greatly increase certainty and predictability in a legal sense before foreign companies acquire local target companies.

Up to now, there is nothing more than what is provided in Article 31 of AML, which says 'in case the acquisition of domestic enterprises or participation in concentration of undertakings in other manners by foreign investors involves national security, besides being reviewed from the perspective of concentration of undertakings according to this law, such a case shall be put under national security review according to relevant national regulations'. However, there are no clear explanations in the current laws and regulations, including the AML itself, on the definition of 'national security', factors affecting national security, sectors where national security is concerned, procedures and institutions for national security review, etc. Therefore, although it is in line with the international tendency to carry out national security reviews on foreign-investor mergers and acquisitions, the uncertainties have been highlighted by foreign invested enterprises (FIEs), Chambers of Commerce and foreign governments through various channels.

11.2.4.4. Exemptions

Article 22 lists the exceptional circumstances where undertakings are to be exempted from filing with MOFCOM. For instance, if one undertaking which is a party to the concentration has already owned more than one-half of the equities or assets with voting rights of each of the other undertakings, or more than half of the equities or assets with voting rights of each of the undertakings involved in a concentration has already belonged to an undertaking that was not involved, such a case need not be filed with MOFCOM. The logic is that since these undertakings have already been either in a relationship of parent-and-child or under the umbrella of the same group, such a combination would not dramatically change the competitive situation in the market.

11.2.4.5. Procedural provisions

Figure 11.1 overleaf shows visually the stages of procedure for an Anti Monopoly review of a concentration of undertakings.

11.2.5. Facts and Figures

Minister Zhou Bohua of SAIC recently declared that in 2008 the nationwide affiliates for industry and commerce investigated and punished around 40,000 cases involving improper competition, while in the first half of 2009 the number of cases reached 21,700, with a value of RMB 1.567 billion yuan.[18]

---

18 See press coverage at: http://news.xinhuanet.com/fortune//2009-07/10/

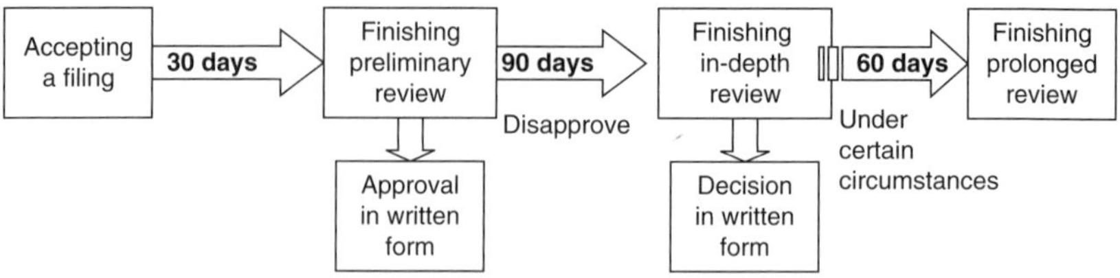

Statutory circumstances for prolonging the period of review (60 days maximum):

- the undertaking agrees to prolong the period of review;
- the documents and materials submitted by the undertaking are not correct and thus need to be further certified;
- significant changes occur to related circumstances after the undertaking submits the filing.

Figure 11.1 Anti monopoly review procedures for concentration of undertakings

We understand this figure also includes the application of the Anti Unfair Competition Law 1993.

Under MOFCOM, during the period from 1 August 2008 to 30 June 2009, 58 filings of concentrations of undertakings were accepted, on 46 of which the decisions have already been made. Among the 46 concluded cases, 43 were approved with no conditions, two were approved with attached conditions (InBev's acquisition of Anheuser-Busch;[19] Mitsubishi Rayon's acquisition of Lucite[20]), and only one case was prohibited (Coca-Cola's acquisition of Huiyuan Juice[21]). Like the case of *Carlyle v Xugong Engineering Machinery Co,*[22] in the pre-AML era, the *Coca-Cola*

content_11688315.htm, accessed July 2010. Minister Zhou Bohua announced these statistics at an internal conference attended by all the directors from the local Administration of Industry and Commerce nationwide.

[19] MOFCOM Notice (2008) No. 95 can be found at: http://fldj.mofcom.gov.cn/aarticle/ztxx/200811/20081105899216.html, accessed July 2010.

[20] MOFCOM Notice (2009) No. 28 can be found at: http://fldj.mofcom.gov.cn/aarticle/ztxx/200904/20090406198805.html, accessed July 2010.

[21] MOFCOM Notice (2009) No. 22 can be found at: http://fldj.mofcom.gov.cn/aarticle/ztxx/200903/20090306108494.html, accessed July 2010.

[22] The case of Carlyle purchasing the equity of Xugong Engineering Machinery Co., initiated in October 2005, attracted tremendous attention from the media for around three years as it is regarded as a symbolic event reflecting the conflict of two different attitudes towards foreign capital in China. The curtain closed when both Carlyle and Xugong jointly announced that they would not be continuing any further cooperation on 23 July 2008.

v Huiyuan Juice case soon turned into a political event with one camp advocating protection of traditional domestic brands of long standing, such as 'Huiyuan' from being ruined by foreign invaders; while the other accused China of adopting 'double standards' when treating inflows and outflows of capital, as the Chinese government is pushing its 'going global' strategy, making use of foreign capital reserves with a gross value of 2,000 billion US dollars and encouraging more investment by Chinese companies in other economies, for instance investing in mines and other strategic assets. This is why the Coca-Cola case received great media exposure in both China and overseas. Following the decision, the Chinese government came in for even greater criticism. Some politicians in Australia and Canada even proposed suspending China's overseas investments in oil, gas, iron ore and other energy and raw materials.

The NDRC also received a great deal of complaints or whistleblowing regarding the pricing of monopoly activities. According to the latest statistics released by NDRC, during the first half of 2009, 21,000 illegal cases involving pricing were discovered and punished nationwide, with total illegal income from such activities reaching RMB 780 million and economic sanctions of RMB 580 million (consisting of a refund to the users of RMB 170 million, forfeiture of illegal income of RMB 380 million, and a penalty of RMB 30 million). In the same period, there were 1,857 cases of improper pricing activities, attracting an economic sanction equivalent to RMB 12.51 million for the whole country. The top five categories of illegal cases involving pricing were: (1) pricing of pharmaceuticals and medical services (6,849 cases); (2) educational charges (5,044 cases); (3) pricing of transportation and shipping (2,507 cases); (4) charges levied by national administrative bodies (1,469 cases); (5) charges levied by property management companies (634 cases). However, no companies were actually named.

It is interesting to note that, although the Chinese system of people's courts (normally comprising criminal tribunals, civil tribunals and administrative tribunals) has quickly responded to the need to try a case involving competition concerns, it did not set any precedent for the future. In September 2008, the People's Court of Chaoyang District of Beijing accepted a lawsuit launched by a lawyer named Li Fangping against the Beijing Branch of CNC Group for abusing its market dominance in pricing terms and discriminating against prepayments of clients without registered permanent residency documents ('*hukou*' in Chinese) in Beijing. The case was later handed over to the Second Middle People's Court of Beijing and went to first trial in June 2009. It was unfortunate that the trial was not open to the public since the Court accepted CNC's application for the protection of commercial secrets.

The plaintiff (Li Fangping) in the case of *Li Fangping v China Netcom* was a lawyer by profession who brought proceedings against the Beijing branch of China Netcom (Group) Co. Ltd (CNC Beijing), a telecommunication services provider, arguing that CNC Beijing had abused its dominance in fixed-line telephony services by discriminating against him on grounds of his residency status (Li was not a 'formal resident' of Beijing, lacking the '*hukou*' mentioned above). As such, Li could not gain access to particular 'post-pay payment plans' that were available to Beijing residents. In its decision handed down on 9 June 2010, the Beijing Higher People's Court (on appeal from the first instance judgment of 18 December 2009 in the Beijing First People's Intermediate Court) affirmed the first instance decision, arguing that the plaintiff (Li) bore the burden of proof in relation to the market definition and proving that the defendant (CNC Beijing) had abused its dominance on that market. Li had argued that CNC Beijing was in breach of Article 17(6) AML in that it had abused its dominance by discriminating (through differential treatment) in the fixed-line telephony market. CNC Beijing argued that there were alternative 'post-pay payment plans' available to non-Beijing residents, but that non-residents were required to hold real estate in Beijing. CNC Beijing further argued that to open up its post-pay payment plan for Beijing residents to non-residents would expose the company to significant 'operational risks'. The court accepted both the defendant's arguments and dismissed Li's claim.[23]

The case is an important one (although being only a first instance judgment) in that it establishes the grounds for 'significant commercial reasons' as a defense to an abuse of dominance (as evidenced in cases in sectors other than telecoms) and also leaves open the evidence that is required to (1) define the relevant market and (2) define dominance in the relevant market. Li had referred to internet web-based data as pointing towards CNC Beijing's market share and dominance. The court found this data insufficient. The presumption is that more statistical evidence would be needed in terms of market share analysis through formal market research studies, but the point remains open. In other jurisdictions, such as the UK, the regulator, for example, is charged with having to complete regular market studies to determine whether 'effective competition' exists in a relevant market or not. In the European Union, effective competition will

---

[23] 23 *Li Fangping v Beijing Branch of China Netcom Group co*. (Beijing Higher People's Court), 9 June 2010. For further details of the case, see 'China Law Insight, Li Fangping v China Netcom', 19 September 2010, at: file:///Volumes/NO%20NAME/MISC/China%20Law%20Book/LAW/Li%20Fangping%20vs%20China%20Netcom%20-%20Abuse%20of%20Dominance%20Case%20Dismissed%20:%20China%20Law%20Insight.webarchive, accessed September 2010.

not exist where there is at least one undertaking with significant market power (SMP) in the relevant market in question. This is in conformity with the European Commission's Framework Directive for Electronic Networks and Services (Directive 2002/21/EC). A rebuttable presumption exists that an undertaking will have significant market power where the market share is in excess of 40%, but lower market shares have also been held to constitute SMP where the relevant market is narrow.

11.2.6. Delineation of Relevant Markets

In China, since the concept of a 'relevant market' is a horizontal issue, on 24 May 2009, the Anti Monopoly Committee of the State Council released the Guidelines on Delineation of Relevant Markets, which is a strong support to the application of the AML and has greatly increased the transparency of the methodology and technical analysis adopted by the enforcement authorities.

Like many mature antitrust jurisdictions, the Guidelines in China provide that the definition of relevant markets includes relevant product and relevant geographic markets plus a rarely used concept of the 'relevant technology market'. Analysis of demand-side substitutability and/or supply-side substitutability paves the way for delineating a relevant market, while the well-known SSNIP test (small but significant and non-transitory increase in price)[24] is also introduced as the most common tool when the scope of a market where undertakings compete with each other is not clear or not easy to define. The Guidelines provide a whole chapter explaining the methodology of the SSNIP test, but there is no difference from what prevails in Europe or the United States. A good example to demonstrate such influence is that the formulation of the test also takes the range of 5% to 10% to indicate 'significance' within the SSNIP formula as in the European Communities,[25] although in the United Kingdom, the Competition Commission has provided that it will postulate a price rise of 5% when applying the hypothetical monopolist test.[26]

---

[24] The SSNIP test was first deployed by the US Department of Justice and the Federal Trade Commission under the Horizontal Merger Guidelines of the United States (issued in 1992 and revised in 1997) when analysing horizontal mergers. The SSNIP test is not used in the US for the purpose of market definition in cartel and monopolization cases under ss 1 and 2 of Sherman Act 1890.

[25] Please see paragraph 17 of the Commission Notice on the Definition of the Relevant Market for the Purposes of Community Competition Law (OJ [1997] C 372/5).

[26] Please see paragraph 2.8 Merger References: Competition Commission Guidelines (June 2003, CC2).

11.3. PROBLEMS EXPOSED IN INTERPRETATION AND ENFORCEMENT

11.3.1. Coordination among Enforcement Authorities

Unlike most other sectors, MOFCOM, NDRC and the SAIC individually take on a specific part of the enforcement work, which makes the already intricate provisions of the AML even more complicated. We understand the situation is created as a compromise within the framework of current government installations and competences, simply because it is the only solution acceptable to all the parties involved.

When looking more closely at the allocation of work among the three authorities, it can be seen that the scope of responsibility intersects and overlaps. For example, NDRC undertakes the duty of handling pricing monopoly activities, but the concept of a pricing monopoly is, by itself, quite vague. Since pricing is a basic manifestation of both monopoly agreements and abusive behaviors, it may include any monopoly activities with an element of pricing and could occur everywhere. It is very difficult to distinguish a monopoly from a non-pricing monopoly. Therefore, there is a high probability of a situation of dispersed enforcement or duplicated enforcement arising.

In the case where a certain market strategy adopted by a company triggers both a pricing monopoly and a non-pricing monopoly, more than one enforcement authority could claim competence, or even worse, one authority might argue that it is less relevant to their enforcement activity, trying to leave the burden of processing the case to another authority.

Under the current pattern of enforcement, cost and efficiency are the two aspects to be negatively influenced. For instance, if two enforcement authorities carry out an investigation of the same activity of an undertaking, the question arises as to whether the enforcement authorities will conduct the investigation separately or in a combined way. Another problem is judging whether the red line stipulated by the AML has been crossed or not, as it may be difficult to reach a consensus of opinion across the three ministries, making the additional cost of coordination very high. It is clear therefore that it will become increasingly necessary to establish an independent, unified and professional quasi-judicial anti monopoly enforcement agency as antitrust enforcement matures in China.

11.3.2. Lack of Supportive Rules and Regulations

The process of legislation is always under the constraint of political, economic and social factors, and is driven forward by the combined force from groups representing these different interests. The enactment of the AML also involves many compromises among the major camps from liberal economy believers to nationalists, from enforcement authorities to sectoral regulators, and from state-owned enterprises (SOEs) to private companies as potential entrants in a currently monopolized market. It is not feasible for the AML to address all concerns relating to regulation of monopolies alone or 'to accomplish the task at one stroke'. In this sense, the need for construction and perfection of supportive rules and regulations to the AML is highly necessary in terms of both substance and procedure.

'Due process of law' is the best way for China to achieve the goals pursued by the AML, which means the need for 'visible justice'. This is why procedural rules for implementing the AML need to be continually improved and perfected. SAIC has made a great deal of progress with regard to procedures for handling cases involving monopoly agreements, abuse of market dominance or administrative monopolies. But this is only the starting point of the journey, not the end. Consumers and market players need clear guidance about channels and procedures in the implementation process of the whole competition system surrounding the AML.

Litigation is another area where supportive rules need to be strengthened. Due to the demanding requirements in terms of technicality and professionalism, civil lawsuits for anti monopoly actions will not only be time-consuming but also will incur tremendous expense. According to the experience in Western countries, it takes around four to five years on average for a complicated anti monopoly civil lawsuit to be completed. To find the necessary resources to cover lawsuit costs (including attorney fees) is an important factor that should not be underestimated in anti monopoly cases. For large corporations, it may be feasible to allocate the necessary funds and a dedicated team of external legal counsel to deal with the potential challenges arising from lawsuits; while for the small and medium-sized enterprises (SMEs) and individual consumers, this will not be the case. Based on this consideration, other countries have created many solutions in both theory and practice, such as punitive compensation for damages (such as triple compensation for damages in the United States), transfer of attorney's fees, aid for lawsuit fees, class actions, etc. All these measures are still absent from the Chinese anti monopoly civil procedures. Therefore, significant reform is needed if greater access to justice is to occur in China. However, when carrying out reform of supporting rules for AML litigation, the Chinese government is also facing a dilemma between reducing the costs of lawsuits against protection of SMEs and consumers and the social cost. If China is to encourage a radical system for civil anti monopoly lawsuits, it might raise costs and lead to a waste of social resources, and thus create a negative impact on the authority of civil adjudication. On the contrary, if China places too many restraints on the conditions for launching an action, this might also lead to making the AML redundant or unreachable for small and medium-sized market players and individual consumers.

11.3.3. Coordination with Previous Laws and Regulations with Anti Monopoly Contents

Before the promulgation of the AML, the Standing Committee of the NPC enacted a number of laws with anti monopoly content, among which the most important are the Pricing Law of December 1997, and the Anti Unfair Competition Law of September 1993. The relevant provisions are shown in Table 11.1.

The Law of Bid Invitation and Submission passed in August 1999 also contains the provision of prohibiting bid rigging. Also the Regulation Regarding Mergers and Acquisitions of Domestic Enterprises by Foreign

Table 11.1 Other selected Chinese laws with anti monopoly provisions

Pricing Law of the People's Republic of China	Article XIV	The operators shall not 'collude with each other, manipulate market price, or impair legitimate interests of other operators or consumers'.
Anti Unfair Competition Law of the People's Republic of China	Article VI	'Public enterprises or other operators in an exclusive position provided by law shall not oblige other people to purchase commodities from designated operators, so as to exclude other operators from fair competition.'
	Article VII	'The government and its affiliates shall not abuse their administrative power to restrain commodities produced elsewhere from entering into local market, or locally-produced commodities from flowing towards external markets.'
	Article XV	'The tenderers shall not do bid-rigging and increase or decrease the bidding price accordingly. The tenderers and the tenderees shall not collude with each other so as to exclude other competitors from fair competition.'

Investors published in 2006 has anti monopoly contents. Additionally, the State Council and its subordinate ministries issued several administrative regulations in the spirit of anti monopoly, particularly with regard to opposing local protectionism.

Further clarification is now necessary on how to coordinate and harmonize between the AML and the above-mentioned laws and regulations containing anti monopoly contents, and in fact since the coming into force of the AML, previous legal statutes encompassing antitrust provisions are still valid.

11.3.4. Coordination with Sectoral Regulators

How to coordinate the enforcement of the AML and sectoral regulation in a realistic and feasible way is a further issue worthy of serious attention. Authorities like the Ministry of Transport (MOT), Ministry of Railways (MOR), Ministry of Industry and Information Technology (MIIT), CBRC, CSRC, CIRC, China Electricity Regulatory Commission (CERC), State Post Office, and State Administration of Civil Aviation are also responsible for maintaining effective competition in the corresponding sectors under their control, and whether or not the sectors are simultaneously supervised by MOFCOM, NDRC and SAIC. Such a pattern of dual regulation might lead to enforcement work in each of the above sectors being conducted in a piecemeal way.

As the biggest developing country in the world, China certainly cares a great deal about the effects of its economic policy, including supporting, revitalizing and strengthening the competitiveness of its industries, as well as protecting its vulnerable industries. A conflict might arise when a sectoral regulator is not in favor of fair competition. If we look at the legal text, we may find that on the one hand, Article 7 of the AML requires the State to 'protect the lawful business activities' of state-owned enterprises in industries 'that implicate national economic vitality and national security' or 'in which there are legal monopolies'; on the other hand, the AML also prohibits such SOEs from impairing consumers' interests. Technically speaking, the Law does not exempt the SOEs from the jurisdiction of the AML. However, both the scope of sectors covered and the precise nature of the special treatment outlined are still ambiguous. Therefore, whether such a conflict could be addressed by weighing the overall economic efficiency and social welfare with potential economic harms has become a pressing issue for the AML. In our view, when sectoral interests contradict the objectives advocated by the AML, sectoral interests should give way to the latter and can only be protected with the precondition that they conform to competition policy and create minimum damage to market competition.

Another potential challenge is that all of these authorities are very powerful or at least at the same level as other line ministries, and were also established and authorized by a specific law, as were the anti monopoly enforcement authorities. The question arises as to how the sectoral regulators can concurrently share power with the AML enforcement authorities within the same sector. This is why the mechanism of concurrency to act between AML enforcement authorities and sectoral regulators needs to be established and perfected in time.

11.3.5. Unresolved Issues in Judicial Practice

The Supreme People's Court has attached great importance to the implementation of the AML since it came into effect, and at the time of writing, is considering the possibility of issuing judicial interpretations regarding AML-related civil lawsuits within the year, so as to pave the way for private actions. The Supreme People's Court has already set up a specific panel in the Intellectual Property Rights (IPR) Tribunal to deal with all kinds of anti monopoly civil cases beyond abuse of IPR. In Shanghai, an independent anti monopoly tribunal was introduced by several judicial institutions on an experimental basis. For example, the Shanghai Second Middle People's Court set up an ad hoc panel for anti monopoly cases.

Although efforts have been made in the area of judicial interpretation and institutional setup,[27] there are not too many cases referred by the lower court and reviewed by the upper court as yet. Furthermore, in the current few cases, none were won by the camp of consumers or small competitors (SMEs). Besides the above-mentioned *Li Fangping v Beijing Branch of CNC* case, there was another case brought by a private company. The Beijing Zhaoxin Information Technology Company and three other anti-counterfeiting technology companies launched a case against the Administration of Quality Supervision, Inspection and Quarantine (AQSIQ) for forcing the expansion of the Product Quality Electronic Supervision Network.[28] However, the Beijing First Middle People's Court

---

[27] China is not a nation in favor of the principle of case law. However, the judicial interpretation issued by the Supreme People's Court has become part of an official legal document. Although it is not clear for the moment how the judicial interpretation will apply in regard to competition, it is expected that the court will rely on the economic analysis of the administrative enforcement bodies but will adjudicate on its own reasoning and interpretation of law independently of the administrative decisions. Or in an administrative lawsuit case, one might use the platform of a court to challenge the decision of an administrative review.

[28] *Beijing Zhaoxin Information Technology Ltd., Eastern Huike Anti-*

finally used the excuse of 'exceeding the time limit for launching a suit' to adjudicate not to accept the case.

It is for certain that the Supreme People's Court will come across many difficult and complicated questions in the process of implementing the AML. Answers to these questions need to be determined as soon as possible. The main outstanding questions include:

BOX 11.1 FURTHER QUESTIONS ON THE AML FOR THE SPC TO SETTLE

Question 1: How to Ascertain the Jurisdiction?

As for AML civil cases, will we adopt general rules of jurisdiction or apply designated jurisdiction as in patent cases? If it is to be designated jurisdiction, are we referring to all AML civil cases? Or will we treat different types of monopoly activities with different approaches?

Question 2: How to Decide on the Qualifications of a Plaintiff?

To decide on whether a plaintiff is qualified to lodge an AML civil lawsuit, we have to consider what requirements need to be satisfied and to distinguish between a consumer and an undertaking.

Question 3: How to Apply an Injunction Remedy?

In terms of the forms of civil liabilities for monopoly activities, besides calculating the financial compensation for damages to the victim, the Supreme People's Court may also have to decide on how to apply injunction remedies and other civil remedies in detail.

Counterfeiting Technology Ltd., Zhongshe Wang Meng Information Security Technology Ltd., and Heng Xin Digital Technology Ltd. v State General Administration of Quality Supervision, Inspection and Quarantine (AQSIQ), filed 1 August 2008 in Beijing No. 1 Intermediate People's Court, assigned file number (2008) Yi Zhong Hang Chu Zi No. 1340.

Question 4: Is it Possible to Identify a Monopoly Activity Not Listed in the AML?

Is the Supreme People's court eligible to identify other monopoly activities not listed in the AML in civil cases?

Question 5: How to Link the AML Enforcement and Civil Lawsuits?

One major issue is how to coordinate between administrative enforcement of AML and civil lawsuits, particularly as regards the transfer of facts and judgments confirmed in administrative procedure to civil procedure or vice versa.

Question 6: How to Allocate the Burden of Proof?

To make clear the facts of a monopoly behavior, it becomes necessary to allocate the burden of proof and how to select a reliable analysis methodology, which relates to delineation of relevant markets, calculation of market share, investigation of the relationship among the parties involved, and many other practical issues.

Question 7: How to Distinguish IPR Protection from the AML?

How to cut a clear line between IPR protection and AML mainly relates to the enforcement of Article 55 of AML Law and also relates to coordination between applications of IPR monopoly provisions in Contract Law and the AML.[29]

11.4. IMPACT BY INTERNATIONAL FACTORS

11.4.1. Overview

The Chinese AML is well-connected with international norms and is very similar to the competition law seen in other countries, with the main

[29] See Chapter 12 for a further discussion of Article 55 and the IP–competition interface

contents being the prohibition of monopoly agreements, prohibition of abuse of market dominance and restriction of excessive concentration of economic power. During the process of legislation, the Chinese AML actually absorbed much from the legal code and experience of the European Union, the United States, etc. Differences only exist in ways of expression and some Chinese-featured provisions regarding administrative monopoly and state-owned enterprises.

As a latecomer to the family of nations who have formally adopted antitrust or competition laws, one advantage for China is that it may learn both from the success and from the lessons that developed countries have experienced in past decades, so that China can avoid some unnecessary problems.

International factors related to Chinese competition policy are discussed in the following two sub-sections.

11.4.2. Foreign Governments

With the backdrop of the current globalized market, it is important to trace the policy and law adjustments of foreign governments. A good example is the extraterritorial application by the United States of its Antitrust Law since the *Alcoa* case. The governments of other countries have accordingly adopted counter-measures to offset the United States' approach, including discovery-blocking provisions, judgment-blocking statues, claw-back clauses and diplomatic protest.

As for China, since it is still in the initial stage of implementing the AML and competition policy as a whole and the overall tone of China's diplomatic policy is in favor of 'mutual benefits and win-win', it is not possible for China to forcefully pursue unilateral implementation of its AML abroad. However, due to the global strategic pattern and existence of groups of interest, even a domestic ruling might attract concern or even hostility from other countries. It will become necessary therefore for the Chinese government to consider the possible consequences arising from the decisions of its courts and enforcement authorities, including for example, potential boycotts by foreign governments during the process of enforcing the AML. In this sense, retaliatory action taken by foreign governments is a related international factor. This happened in *Coca-Cola v Huiyuan Juice* (both are listed companies on overseas stock markets). The recent merger between two Australian companies, Rio Tinto and BHP Billiton, is another good example that displays interaction among the governments of different countries.

11.4.3. International Organizations

Since World War II, international organizations have played an increasingly important role in global affairs. International organizations may influence a government's potential to acquire information and opportunities. Failure to honor a commitment to an international treaty may severely jeopardize a government's reputation. The attitude and approach taken by organizations such as the United Nations Conference on Trade and Development (UNCTAD), the Organisation for Economic Co-operation and Development (OECD), the World Trade Organization (WTO), and the International Competition Network (ICN) toward China's implementation of its laws are important. China will need to consider international opinion to secure its own standing.

China has been deeply involved in the activities of various international organizations. It also takes an active participation in multilateral discussions in the framework of international competition cooperation, including rounds of negotiations on competition policy in the recent WTO Doha Round process. Actually, China undertook effective cooperation with the OECD and UNCTAD in its legislation of the AML. As a newcomer to the international competition club (on the platform of the WTO Doha Round, OECD and UNCTAD), China has shown great enthusiasm for learning and discussing best practice issues, joint fighting against international cartels, as well as how to deal with transnational mergers and acquisitions. Bilaterally, China has also started to include a competition chapter in its bilateral trade and investment agreements or even free trade agreements with other economies.[30] Now China is considering when to become a member of the ICN. With its size and economic status, China will be an important actor within the ICN.

11.5. FUTURE LEGISLATION

As mentioned above, the provisions of the AML are very general. More detailed supportive guidelines and legal opinions will pave the foundation for the smooth implementation of the AML, so as to avoid regulatory overload and unnecessary duplication of resources in regulating monopoly activities.

---

30 For example, there is a chapter on competition in China's negotiation with the European Communities to conclude a new bilateral agreement to upgrade their trade and economic cooperation agreement in 1985.

Table 11.2 AML provisions currently issued or in development (at time of writing)[1]

Anti Monopoly Committee, State Council	Regulations on Threshold Concentrations of Undertakings, August 2008 Working Rules of Anti Monopoly Committee of the State Council, September 2008 Guidelines on the Definition of the Relevant Market, May 2009
Division of Anti Pricing Monopoly and Market Supervision, Department of Pricing Supervision and Inspection, National Development and Reform Commission	Anti Pricing Monopoly Regulation (1 February 2011) Regulation on Enforcement Procedures of Anti Pricing Monopoly (1 February 2011)
Enforcement Bureau for Anti Monopoly and Anti Improper Competition, State Administration for Industry and Commerce	Regulation on Procedures Concerning Investigation and Punishment of Cases Involving Monopoly Agreement and Abuse of Market Dominance by Administrative Authorities for Industry and Commerce (valid from 1 July 2009) Regulation on Procedures Concerning Prevention of Activities Involving Abuse of Administrative Power to Exclude or Restrict Competition (valid from 1 July 2009) Regulations on Prohibiting Abuse of Market Dominance (valid from 1 February 2011) Regulations on Prohibiting Monopoly Agreement (valid from 1 February 2011) Guidelines for Anti Monopoly (Law Enforcement in the Area of IPR (Draft))
Anti Monopoly Bureau, Ministry of Commerce	Guiding Opinions on Filing of Concentration of Undertakings (valid from 7 January 2009) Guiding Opinions on Filing Documents and Materials Related to Concentration of Undertakings (valid from 7 January 2009) Provisional Measures on the Investigating and Handling of Concentrations of Undertakings Not Notified in Accordance with the Law (Draft) Provisional Measures on the Collection of Evidence for Suspected Monopolistic Concentrations of Undertakings Not Reaching the Notification Thresholds (Draft)

Table 11.2 (continued)

	Measures on the Notification of Concentration of Undertakings (1 January 2010) Measures on the Review of Concentrations of Undertakings (1 January 2010)
Supreme People's Court	Provisions on a Number of Issues Applicable to the Trial of Monopoly Civil Dispute (Draft for Comment) (25 April 2011)

Note: [1] The list displayed here may well have changed by the time of publication. For example, at the time of writing, Guidelines for Abusing IPR and Antimonopoly were actively being consulted upon.

11.6. RELATIONSHIP BETWEEN THE AML AND IPR PROTECTION

11.6.1. Monopoly: Same Word but with Two Meanings

Some scholars argue that there exists a certain degree of tension and conflict in the relationship between IPRs and the AML, since IPRs are a legitimate right of monopoly which restricts competition, while on the contrary the AML is aimed at promoting competition. The reasoning seems to be quite logical, but is perhaps misguided.

Before elaborating on such a relationship, it is perhaps better to first distinguish between the concept of 'monopoly' used in the AML and an IPR monopoly. The 'monopoly' used in the AML refers to stipulated behaviors: monopoly agreements, abuse of market dominance and excessive concentration of undertakings. Thus the AML is focused on tackling these behaviors rather than caring about whether a competitor has the status of a monopoly or not. In the domain of IPR, monopoly reflects a right or a state of exclusivity that the owner of an intellectual property has, which is by nature no different to other kinds of property rights, such as ownership.

11.6.2. Different Ways of Treatment

The AML is not concerned with whether a specific right is exclusive or not. It is aimed at whether a particular behavior will cause harm or threat to market competition so as to reduce the efficiency of the market and impair the overall consumers' welfare. Even in the case of an abuse of IPR, for instance, tagging a ridiculously high price to a product with IPR, or refusing to give licenses to other parties, although such behavior might impair the benefits of the counterpart of the deal, as long as it does not ruin the market mechanism, it will not necessarily trigger enforcement of the AML. IPRs are basically private rights. Where no competition issues are involved, abuse of IPRs can be handled by IPR and civil laws; but if abuse of an IPR causes substantial damage to market competition, the AML will be triggered.

In 1995, the US Department of Justice and the Federal Trade Committee jointly released an Antitrust Guidance for IP Licensing. This highlighted the uniqueness of IPRs and legal protection as monopoly rights as well as IPRs as tangible assets from the perspective of antitrust enforcement. Furthermore, it elaborated IPR's role in identifying a company's market power.

In 2004, the DG Competition of the European Commission also published Commission Regulation (EC) No. 772/2004 on the Application of Article 81(3) of the Treaty to Categories of Technology Transfer Agreements and the Guidelines on the Application of Article 81 (now Article 101 TFEU) of the EC Treaty to Technology Transfer Agreements (2004/C101/02). These documents repealed the so-called 'white clause' and 'grey clauses' and encouraged the undertakings involved to make a self-judgment of whether exemption applies.

In China, Article 55 of the AML explains the relationship between IPR and anti monopoly, which says, 'This law is not applicable to conducts by undertakings to implement their intellectual property rights in accordance with relevant IP laws and administrative regulations; however, this law is applicable to conduct by undertakings to eliminate or restrict market competition by abusing intellectual property rights'. But obviously, the same detailed regulations or guidelines as in the United States and the EU are still needed in China for the sake of handling specific cases.

11.6.3. Goals in Common But Not Reality as Yet?

The objective of the AML is to benefit consumers by means of safeguarding the market competition mechanism, which is consistent with IPR laws because the latter will finally benefit consumers by encouraging innovation and improving efficiency. It is not possible to stipulate all types of anti-competitive behaviors under the heading of 'prohibition of abuse of IPR', which is more in the domain of civil law. It is clear, however, that in China, anti-competitive behaviors involving abuse of IPRs will be handled within the framework of the AML.

As Article 55 of the AML does *not* clarify the distinction between the legitimate exercise of IP rights and abuse of them, there are reasonable concerns on the part of industry as to whether the AML will be enforced in a manner that undermines legitimate IP rights. It is not clear for the Chinese enforcement bodies when defining a market, whether an IP holder is dominant in a market due to its technology, and whether a unilateral refusal to license the technology to its competitors or charging royalties may be condemned as abusive. Therefore, detailed guidelines are definitely needed to define the relationship between the AML and the IP law and to solve concrete issues in practice.

Although no timelines are given, there are two positive signs in this direction. First, there is a vice minister representing the State Intellectual Property Office (SIPO) in the Anti Monopoly Committee of the State Council; second, Paragraph 4 of Article 3, 'definition of relevant market' in the Guidelines on Delineation of Relevant Markets issued by the Anti Monopoly Committee of the State Council on 24 May 2009 provides that, 'in the anti monopoly enforcement work concerning intellectual property such as trade in technology, licensing agreement, etc., it might be necessary to delineate the relevant technological market and consider the impact of such factors as intellectual rights and innovation'. Although at the time of writing, no details have been given, the cited comment demonstrates that the executive has noted the significance of such a need.

11.7. CONCLUSION

It will take time and energy for the culture of fair competition or 'competing on a level playing field' advocated by the AML to become deeply rooted within China, a developing country in transition toward a market economy. We have seen positive signs that consciousness of competition policy has started to grow in the hearts of Chinese consumers, market players and government officials, together with the new changes brought about by the law itself. It is fair to say that we still have to witness a long period of coexistence of progress and retrogress and of freedom and control in the process of consummating the anti monopoly legal system and its enforcement in China.

Although we are far from addressing the concerns arising from dispersed enforcement, lack of supportive rules and judicial remedial arrangements and inability to eradicate administrative monopolies, we still believe that as long as the advancement of economic democracy and freedom is not obstructed, it is certain that the spirit within the AML will demonstrate its far-reaching concurrency with the Chinese socialist market economy.

12. Intellectual property protection and competition law

Xu Shiying[1]

12.1. INTRODUCTION

With the conflict between the protection of Intellectual Property and the new Chinese Anti-Monopoly Law (AML), together with economic development and the advance of science and technology, there remains little doubt that intellectual property (IP) in China is playing an increasingly important role in global competition and is penetrating almost every level and field of international economic relations. Intellectual property rights (IPRs) comprise abstract property rights created by IP-based law. If we consider IP as a type of 'product', then IP laws not only stipulate how this 'product' is produced but also set the standard for both the import and export of IP across national borders. The World Trade Organization's (WTO's) Agreement on Trade-Related Aspects of IPRs (TRIPS) provides the highest degree of protection for IPRs at an international level. Also, other WTO agreements influence the manufacture, circulation and use of IP by affecting the flow of other relevant factors to the market. IPR rights holders may find themselves in a position in which they can abuse their position of dominance or engage in anti-competitive behaviour by virtue of their ownership of IP. This *potential* anti-competitive conduct is not only harmful to other competitors' legal rights and interests but can also interfere with the natural order of competition and social benefits. Since regulation by IP law may sometimes be inadequate to deal with anti-competitive practices, anti-monopoly law is also necessary to compensate for any shortfall created due to potential interference by the state.

China has established a legal system of IPR protection as well as a new competition framework following the adoption of the AML. China's

[1] Professor of Law, East China University of Political Science & Law. The editor is grateful for the help of Ms Katie Richards (LLB student with French, Cardiff Law School) for her help with this chapter.

national legislation aims to ensure that competition takes place in a fair and free manner.[2] Article 55 of the Anti-Monopoly Law of the People's Republic of China, which was adopted on 30 August 2007 and came into force on 1 August 2008, prescribes that 'business operators' conduct to eliminate or restrict market competition by abusing their IPRs shall be governed by this Law'. Several anti-monopoly cases involving IP have since emerged and are currently being heard by the Chinese courts. The following sections discuss the AML and its relationship with the regulation of IP in more detail.[3]

12.2. RELATIONSHIP BETWEEN ANTI-MONOPOLY LAW AND THE PROTECTION OF IPRs

12.2.1. The Changing Nature of the Relationship between the AML and the Protection of IPRs

Traditionally, IP law and competition law have been viewed as two independent legal branches. IP law, a special category of Chinese civil law, aims to promote innovation and economic growth by confirming ownership and granting proprietary and exclusive rights to patentees, trademark holders and copyright owners.

Comparatively, the objective of competition or anti-monopoly law, which is at the heart of modern economic law, is to restrict the exclusive rights of undertakings, eliminate anti-competitive behaviour in the market and ultimately to maintain a free market mechanism. Although embodying the public interest to some extent, IP law pays more attention to the protection of private interests and, therefore, is considered to be private law. In contrast, under the requirement for the 'public interest', competition law focuses on the realization of public welfare. Such comparison essentially reflects the potential conflicts between private rights and social interests in particular circumstances. In the very early stages, IP law (a private law) and competition law (a public law), especially anti-monopoly law, were as incompatible as oil and water. For rights owners, the enforcement of competition law brought about many negative impacts, such as the blocking of the exercise of their exclusive rights to freely use IP

[2] See Dong Tao, *Analysis of the Effect on IP, Intellectual Property, WTO Agreements (Except TRIPS)* No. 3, WTO Reports, 2003.

[3] For a further discussion of the AML in general (as opposed to the particular relationship of the AML with IP law, the subject of this chapter), please see Chapter 11.

(including licensing), and their expectant interests were correspondingly restricted. Moreover, it resulted in the lack of a driving force behind IP innovation. However, others in favour of anti-monopolization argued that while anti-monopoly law intends to maintain the vitality of a competitive economy, the protection given by IP law has hampered competition by prohibiting duplication or the use of another's creation without permission, and hence, that the objective of anti-monopoly law to create effective competition in the market is hindered.[4]

12.2.2. Anti-Competitive Practices in Abusing IPR

The IP legal system has established the doctrines of the term of protection (in respect of the period of exclusivity enjoyed by IP rights holders), the compulsory licence and fair use, which partially balance private rights and social benefits, to prevent the negative effects created by unlimited enjoyment of exclusive IP rights. However, under the general principles of private law, IP law is apt to protect private rights and oppose direct intervention by governments in markets at all levels, despite taking social benefits into account. Regulation by IP law is not macroscopic or wide but rather microscopic and narrow. Owing to the above reasons, IP law alone cannot overcome the market barriers of monopoly or anti-competitive behaviour. It is still possible for rights holders, therefore, to obtain an illegal monopoly position and to go beyond the scope of their legal rights.

12.2.2.1. Maintenance of monopoly

The maintenance of monopoly means conduct where rights holders do not themselves make use of their exclusive IP rights, but at the same time they do not allow others to use them, or they refuse to grant licences by setting conditions which are unreasonable or overly harsh. In most cases, refusal to license does not, of itself, constitute a violation of the law. However, in some particular cases, refusal to license may impede, restrict or even eliminate competition. This may include;

- Refusal to license, the purpose of which is to prevent competitors from entering the market. Where exclusivity is enjoyed by the rights holder, this may be permissible; however, as mentioned above, this may also restrict competition and create abuses such as an

---

[4] Willard K. Tom and Joshua A. Newberg, 'Antitrust and Intellectual Property: From Separate Spheres to Unified Field', *Antitrust Law Journal*, (1997), 66, 167 and 194–5.

uneconomical resource allocation, monopoly profits and damages to consumer interests. Furthermore, a refusal to license is likely to obstruct technology transfer.
- Hindering competition in relevant markets. Although common interests or implied relations between relevant undertakings in different markets exist, IP law generally protects and improves the interests of rights holders only and does not extend to related parties as this would fail to satisfy the aim of the law, namely to protect IP.

12.2.2.2. Anti-competitive practices concerning the exercise of IPRs

In pursuit of economic interests, rights holders may allow competitors to use their patents through licence agreements. However, it is possible for them to use such licences to restrict competition. These two possibilities make it difficult to distinguish legal licences from restrictive provisions, which is why careful analysis of the terms of use is necessary. Such anti-competitive practices can include:

- Cross-licensing, where two or more rights holders grant licences to each other through cross-licensing agreements.
- Pooling arrangements, where several rights holders agree to share technologies through a consortium. The consortium, such as the DVD6C patent pool, extends blanket non-exclusive licences with royalties allowed by rights holders.
- Grant-back requirements, where licensees are required to inform, release or grant back to the licensor improvements in the original technology or newly achieved patents.
- Territorial restrictions, where licensees are obliged to use authorized IP within a given territory.
- Restrictions on the range of usage, where licensors set limitations on the commercial use, scope and consumers of the authorized product.
- Quantitative limitations, where both the minimum and maximum output is limited to a certain amount.
- Resale price maintenance, where the resale price is still restricted by rights holders even where the patent for the product has been sold on.
- Non-challenge clauses, where licensees are deprived of the right to question the validity of the IPR involved in license agreements.
- Non-compete clauses, where licensees are prohibited from obtaining technologies that are the same as or similar to the licensed patents from other sources, or from competing against relevant companies in research, development or production with regard to competing products.

- Tying, where licensees are obliged to accept a second distinctive licence (the tied licence) when the licence they want is granted.
- Appointed technology source, where licensees are obliged to obtain technologies from appointed channels (usually the licensor or their affiliated enterprises) within the contract period, by means of which licensors can keep control over licensees.

12.2.2.3. IPRs and excessive concentration of market power merger

IP is an important asset and is often transferred through a merger. The merged company, which now has overlapping or complementary IP, will be in a stronger position to innovate more efficiently post-merger.[5] Hence, in analysing barriers to entry into a particular market, the position of IP in this particular market should be considered as an important factor from the start, since post-merger, new entrants may often be handicapped by the newly merged company. This would be the case where either or both parties involved in the merger hold a certain IP or an exclusive licence.[6] In the Ciba-Geigy/Sandoz merger,[7] the FTC (Federal Trade Commission) in the US held that potential development would be hindered following the merger as both parties to the merger controlled key IP regarding gene therapy products. Thus, the FTC withheld the consent order until the parties agreed to grant a package of gene therapy technology know-how and patent rights to a third party. The purpose of this was to ensure that the merger would not slow down R&D or raise prices for gene therapy products, thus allowing other firms to compete against the merged firm.[8] Sometimes, the acquisition of IP is important to gain market power and can significantly influence competition if undertakings are not sufficiently controlled.

12.2.3. New Challenges

Since the late 20th century, mankind has experienced a period of rapid technological change and today, breakthroughs in the so-called new technologies are easier to achieve and much more common than those in traditional industries. It seems by analogy that the exploration of new fields

---

[5] See Robert Pitofsky, 'Antitrust and Intellectual Property: Unresolved Issues at the Heart of the New Economy', www.ftc.gov.

[6] See Wang Xianlin, *Intellectual Property and Anti-Monopoly Law*, Law Press China, (No. 1 October 2001), p. 203.

[7] *Ciba-Geigy Limited, Ciba-Geigy Corporation, Chiron Corporation, Sandoz Ltd., Sandoz Corporation, and Novartis AG*, Docket No. C-3725 FTC File No. 961 0055, April 1997.

[8] See *supra* note 17.

is only a keystroke away, and a current monopoly position can easily be squashed, thus enabling the market to remain competitive. Accordingly, it is suggested that it is no longer necessary for anti-monopoly law to remain in force today. However, even in a changing market, a company can still avail itself of the accumulated advantages to achieve exclusive control over a particular product and as such maintain a monopoly position generation after generation. In some cases, to introduce new technologies too swiftly may actually enhance monopoly power. Microsoft is one example of a corporation which has managed to amass monopoly power in a fast-changing industry and continues to strengthen its position, which constitutes a threat to the development of the whole industry. The harm which such a monopoly may cause has a strong impact on the entire industry and equally at an individual level, and is much more serious than that caused by monopolies arising in traditional industries. As such, both the EU[9] and the earlier US[10] Microsoft cases demonstrate that anti-monopoly law has a vital role to play in the field of IP.

12.2.3.1. Regulations on acts of 'non-use'

The IP rights holders' option to decide *not* to use their exclusive IP has been challenged recently. Examples of IP non-use include sleeping patents.[11] In the United States, the legislator has adjusted the scope of rights holders' behaviour to conform to the doctrine of US competition law and has rejected those applications pursuant to a monopoly, thus helping to eliminate the possibilities of monopolies and the consequent abuse which

---

[9] *Microsoft Corp (The Computing Technology Industry Association Inc and Others Intervening) v Commission of the European Communities (Software & Information Industry Association and Others, Intervening)*, Case T-201/04, [2007] 5CMLR 11, September 2007.

[10] *United States of America v Microsoft Corporation*, Nos. 00-5212 and 00-5213, United States Court of Appeals, District of Columbia Circuit, argued 26 and 27 February 2001, June 2001.

[11] A *sleeping patent* refers to a patent, which is not (seemingly) exploited commercially. Often, it is a strategic move by a dominant operator to deter entry by competitors. One example is Xerox, which was alleged to have taken out patents over inferior technologies in order to block entry and protect its dominant position. For example, in *re Independent Service Organizations Antitrust Litigation*, 203 F.3d 1322 (Fed. Cir. 2000), *cert. denied*, 69 USLW 3552 (20 February 2001), CSU alleged that Xerox had changed its policies regarding pricing and availability of its patented parts in an effort to eliminate competition. Xerox argued that CSU's claims relied on injury solely caused by Xerox's lawful refusal to sell or license patented parts (including copyrighted software). The district court granted Xerox's motion for summary judgment, finding no violation of antitrust laws or misuse from Xerox's reliance on legitimate patents.

may occur. Usually, such 'non-use' intentions are invariably revealed as a consequence of the rights holder exerting their rights as opposed (for example) during the application process for a patent. Hence, it is only through withdrawing authorized patents that we realize the restriction on such abuses. However, the refusal by the rights holder to use his own patents does not necessarily constitute a monopoly. Theoretically, it would be a monopoly until the rights holder took further action, which could then be regulated by anti-monopoly law. In the interests of wider society, anti-monopoly law should only step in if such acts are harmful to the public or aid a monopoly.

12.2.3.2. Regulations on acts of 'wrongful acquisition'

Besides 'non-use', rights holders can also create or hold a monopoly or reduce competition by obtaining an exclusive right over potential competitive technologies. Specifically, this is done by refusing to use the technology him/herself or to grant licences to others, or by 'effectively' impeding others from making use of or developing the technology or product while he/she uses it. By this token, the fundamental standards to judge whether an act of 'acquisition' constitutes a violation of anti-monopoly law are: (1) if the acquired technology or product is competitive; and (2) whether such an act is going to reduce or even eliminate competition in the particular competitive technology.

12.2.3.3. Regulations on 'wrongful acts concerning licensing'

These kinds of wrongful acts comprise such behaviours as tying arrangements, blanket licences, price fixing, contractual constraints (e.g. licensees shall not deal in competitive products or challenge the validity of the licensed patent, exclusive grant backs), and the requirement for licensees to pay for an expired or invalid patent. In the United States, such behaviours are '*per se* illegal', namely they have been recognized as illegal through legal precedents, which identify clear boundaries between legal and illegal conduct and identify illegal behaviour that nevertheless avoids serious offences.

12.2.3.4. Regulations on other abuses of IP

Rights holders may do all they can to monopolize and this is why new kinds of abuses endlessly emerge. Two common examples of abusive behaviour are as follows:

1. artificial control over the time for formal products to be brought to market, thus causing competitors to drag their feet in developing or selling competitive products;

2. abuse of standard-setting procedures. A good trade standard is vital for improving innovation and efficiency in the whole industry, but anti-competitive consequences result if such procedures are misused by companies wishing to preserve their monopoly.

12.2.3.5. Summary

Anti-competitive behaviour involving IP is not only harmful to other competitors' legal rights and interests, but also interferes with competition order and social benefits. Due to the notion of the 'Autonomy of Private Law', protection by IP law is indirect, and the standard to judge whether a practice is impeding competition and violates the law is closely related to the economic policy and economic environment of the country concerned. The mere presence of IP law, however, makes it more likely that such a practice embodying anti-competitive practices could exist. Since IPRs affect competition, and regulation by IP law has shown its limitations when faced with anti-competitive practices, anti-monopoly law is therefore necessary to compensate for any shortfall created due to interference by the state.

12.3. MEASURES PREVENTING ABUSE AND EXCESSIVE MONOPOLY BY IP LAW ITSELF

IP law is a legal system that confirms ownership of IP and confers upon rights holders limited monopoly power to ensure the realization of IP benefits. However, another important aspect of this legal system is to realize the rational and efficient use of IP, thus accruing maximum social profits. In order to establish a system that is able to balance the individual against the public need, and to carry out the efficient development of a social economy on the basis of technological progress, IP law itself proposes several measures to restrict monopoly power involving IP.

12.3.1. Doctrine of 'Time Limit'

'Without a legal monopoly, not enough information will be produced but with the legal monopoly too little of the information will be used.'[12] IP is not an isolated or single term but an achievement that has evolved from study and research based on previous knowledge, which in this sense bears the characteristics of 'eternity'. If a legal system provides permanent

---

[12] See Robert Cooter and Thomas Ulen, *Law and Economics*, Shanghai People Press and Shanghai SanLian Press (1994), p. 185.

protection in consideration of such 'eternity', the inevitable consequences are expensive licence fees and huge amounts of repeated effort and resources for latecomers to create or upgrade technologies. Accordingly, excessively long-term protection can only lead the rights holder to acquire a monopoly position and simply increase the cost of using patents or other monopoly IP rights, which will ultimately damage fair competition.

Therefore, taking into account historical continuity and the cost-efficiency of later use, IP law specifies the duration of IPRs in order to limit any monopoly acquired Almost all countries have adopted such a regime so that protection of a patent, trademark or copyright is limited in time and upon expiry, the original rights holder will lose his exclusive rights unless the trademark can be renewed. This means that expired IP enters the public domain, enabling others to use or improve upon the original subject of the IPR without the original rights holder's permission. This doctrine serves to lower the expectant interests of rights holders and to oblige them to engage in further research and improvements to create more advanced technology and increase productivity.

12.3.2. Doctrine of 'compulsory licence'

In the context of patent law, this doctrine, widely accepted by most countries, refers to patent offices granting compulsory licences to other firms or individuals to exploit patents without the permission of rights holders, under certain conditions set out by law.[13] Analogously, to prevent trademark holders' malicious registration, trademark offices may revoke

---

[13] According to the Patent Law of the People's Republic of China (Patent Law of the PRC (as amended in 2008) 'New Patent Law'), a compulsory licence can be divided into three kinds: (1) Article 54: a general compulsory license, 'where any entity which is qualified to exploit the invention or utility model has made requests for authorization from the patentee of an invention or utility model to exploit its or his patent on reasonable terms and conditions and such efforts have not been successful within a reasonable period of time, the Patent Administration Department of the State Council may, upon the request of that entity, grant a compulsory license to exploit the patent for an invention or utility model'. (2) Article 49: a compulsory license, 'where a national emergency or any extraordinary state of affairs occurs, or where the public interest so requires, the Patent Administration Department of the State Council may grant a compulsory license to exploit the patent for invention or utility model'. (3) Article 51: a compulsory license for derivative rights, 'where the invention or utility model for which the patent right was granted involves major technical progress of considerable economic significance in relation to another invention or utility model for which the patent right has been granted earlier, and the exploitation of the later invention or utility model depends on the exploitation of the earlier one, the Patent Administration Department of

a registered trademark if it has not been used for three consecutive years. Such systematized arrangements are established to prevent rights holders' irrational non-use by encouraging the development of IP, which is also reflected in an annual fee payment.

12.3.3. Doctrine of 'Fair Use'

'Fair Use' is a doctrine that allows a third party to use IP without the permission of rights holders and free from prosecution. This doctrine, widely adopted all over the world, is introduced to exclude rights holders monopoly rights as a special exception and helps to fully realize the social value of IP, maximize public interests by resolving the conflicts between public and private interests and aims to achieve optimal allocation of resources without damaging public or private interests.

This doctrine applies to patent law essentially in the following sectors: (a) 'Exhaustion of exclusive rights'. The Patent Law of the People's Republic of China (2008) (New Patent Law) prescribes that after a patented product which is produced by the patentee or with the permission of the patentee has been sold on, other firms or individuals are entitled to use or sell it; (b) 'Prior use right of patent'. In China, anyone who has made an identical product or used an identical process or has made the necessary preparations for making such a product or using such a process prior to the date of filing is allowed to continue making such a product or using such a process within the original scope. Some of the above regulations are still under discussion. For example, Article 69 of the New Patent Law provides that there is no infringement of a patent if someone 'uses or sells a patented product without knowing that the product was made and sold without permission of the patentee', or 'uses the patent concerned solely for the purposes of scientific research and experimentation'.[14] Some believe that such provisions will offer an unreasonable defence against infringement and therefore should be amended.[15]

---

the State Council may, upon the request of the later patentee, grant a compulsory license to exploit the earlier invention or utility model'.

[14] See the Patent Law of the People's Republic of China, Article 63: 'None of the following shall be deemed an infringement of the patent right: (1) . . . (4) Any person uses the patent concerned solely for the purposes of scientific research and experimentation. Whoever uses or sells a patented product without knowing that the product was made and sold without permission of the patentee or a product directly obtained from a patented process for the purpose of production and business operation need not bear liabilities for compensation provided that it/he can prove that the product is obtained through legal avenues.'

[15] See Liu Maolin, *Economics Analysis of IPRs Law*, Law Press (1997), pp. 248–9.

We can also find this doctrine in copyright and trademark laws. In relation to copyright law, where work is exploited without the permission of and payment to the copyright holder, the fair use doctrine requires that the author and the provenance of the work be clearly acknowledged. Permission in these circumstances is authorized by law and there is no requirement that the copyright holder gives his consent.

12.4. CORRECTION OF ABUSES OF IP BY ANTI-MONOPOLY LAW

12.4.1. The Negative Effects of IPRs Monopoly

Sometimes IPRs do restrict competition, but this is thought to be sustainable since such restrictions are considered to be the costs of protecting an individual's intellectual property and encouraging technology, culture and innovation. The negative effects of intellectual monopoly were not evident in the past simply because there were fewer types and quantities of IPRs and competition in the market and the concentration of capital were significantly less fierce than today. Nowadays, however, due to the speed at which science and technology develop and to increasing competition, IPRs can easily be used in an improper manner, namely, beyond their legal and reasonable scope. In this way, IPRs can be used as tools to restrict competition. Hence, conflicts between IP protection and the competition order become apparent. The world-renowned Microsoft Corporation case provides an example. Microsoft was indicted on a number of charges such as 'abuse of the IP involving computer software', 'maintaining a monopoly position in the market for PC operating systems by anti-competitive measures', and 'tying its Internet Explorer web browser to Windows'. Although this case has now concluded, it forces us to reflect on such conflicts. The *Magill* case in the EU is another earlier example.[16] The European Court of

[16] *Magill*, Joined cases C-241/91P and C-242/91P [1995] ECR 1-743 [1995] 4 CMLR 718. In this case, three TV broadcasters in Ireland and Northern Ireland granted licences to several newspapers to publicize their daily programme schedules, but they did not allow a weekly guide for a specific channel or a comprehensive weekly guide covering all the channels. Instead, each broadcaster published a weekly guide for its programmes. They argued that they were entitled to reserve their copyrights in the programme listings, and the act of refusing to grant licences was one of the ways in which they exerted their exclusive rights. But the ECJ held that such conduct constituted an abuse of a dominant position, and requested them to grant licences so that a third party could, on the premise of non-discrimination, publicize or edit the weekly guide of all the broadcasts and TV programmes.

Justice states that, in principle, an author has the right to refuse freely to grant a licence. It is also possible that the right could be abused, thereby conflicting with competition law, which protects the public economic order.[17]

To coordinate the conflicts between these two different legal branches (IP and competition law) judicial practice is such that if the protected exclusive right is not going to be a threat to the public benefit in the context of public law, IP law should take precedence; otherwise, anti-monopoly law will be used to control any proven abusive conduct. Hence, we may deduce that the legal protection of IP moves between anti-monopoly law and IP law, that is, the monopoly advantage will be fully protected and developed if monopoly rights are exercised within the limits of the law, or will be restricted if not.

12.5. IMPACT OF INTERNATIONAL LAW ON THE CHINESE DOMESTIC MARKET IN THE SECTOR

Transnational IP-related trade brings about worldwide economic competition. There has been extensive concern in the international community that developed countries restrict competition in international trade by using the advantage of IP monopolies. In order to regulate economic competition and to safeguard the international competitive order, international competition rules with legal effect need to be adopted in the field of IP, which would promote the coordination and development of economic interests among countries.

12.5.1. Paris Convention for the Protection of Industrial Property (PCPIP)

Administered by the World Intellectual Property Organization (WIPO), the PCPIP was negotiated mainly for the protection of industrial property, but it also covers anti-competitive behaviour with industrial property protection and prescribes prohibitive provisions against anti-competitive behaviour. In effect, protection actually extends far beyond industrial property. Article 10bis provides that 'Any act of competition contrary to honest practices in industrial or commercial matters constitutes an act of

---

[17] For the original text, see J. Corbet, 'Copyright and Competition Law: Difficult Neighbours', in Jan J.G. Kabel, ed., *Intellectual Property and Information Law: Essays an Honour of Herman Cohen Jehoram*, The Hague, The Netherlands: Kluwer Law International (1998).

unfair competition'.[18] The PCPIP demonstrates an early example of the use of anti-competitive rules as a method of protecting industrial property. The PCPIP plays a guideline role that gives protection to unregistered but well-known trademarks, know-how, business secrets and other intangible property that can give rise to competitive advantages. At the same time, the PCPIP emphasizes that abuses of patent rights such as improper monopoly of the implementation of creations will violate the rules of international law and, accordingly, it provides the use of compulsory licenses to abolish such abuses.[19] At the 1981 Paris Convention, the parties reached a consensus to amend the rules regarding compulsory licences and to strengthen anti-monopoly measures in the field of industrial property.

12.5.2. Agreement on Trade-Related Aspects of IPRs (TRIPS)

TRIPS is a very important treaty under the framework of the WTO in strengthening the protection of IP and regulating anti-competitive behaviour. The basic principles of TRIPS state that:

> the protection and enforcement of intellectual property should contribute to the promotion of technological innovation and to the transfer and dissemination of technology, to the mutual advantage of producers and users of technological knowledge and in a manner conducive to social and economic welfare, and to a balance of rights and obligations.

The TRIPS also contains the requirement that contracting parties should take proper action to 'prevent the abuse of IPRs by rights holders'.[20] Continuing to be one of the most authoritative and comprehensive treaties on IP in the world, TRIPS' main characteristics and content are as follows:

(1) TRIPS builds a legal system of IP protection in the context of trade:
  - whereas the objective of the WTO is to govern international trade and promote global economic development, the adjust-

---

18 See Kong Xiangjun, *the Principles of Anti-Monopoly Law*, China Legal Publishing House (2001), p. 131.

19 See PCIPP: Article 5(A/2), 'Each country of the Union shall have the right to take legislative measures providing for the grant of compulsory licenses to prevent the abuses which might result from the exercise of the exclusive rights conferred by the patent, for example, failure to work'.

20 See TRIPS: Article 8(2): 'Appropriate measures, provided that they are consistent with the provisions of this Agreement, may be needed to prevent the abuse of IPRs by right holders or the resort to practices which unreasonably restrain trade or adversely affect the international transfer of technology'.

ment made by the WTO is necessarily bound up with international trade;[21]
- provides guidance on intellectual property as a whole including basic principles, rule of application and obtaining remedies;[22]
- with the multilateral trade system, the scope of protection is extended to all kinds of IP;[23]
- in accordance with the different development stages of parties, TRIPS sets down different timetables.[24]

(2) TRIPS itself has a particular way of dealing with the relationship between IP and competition policy:
- the compulsory licence legal system is prescribed as a remedy against anti-competitive behaviour;

---

21 See Part III of TRIPS: 'The judicial authorities shall have the authority to order prompt and effective provisional measures: (a) to prevent an infringement of any intellectual property right from occurring, and in particular to prevent the entry into the channels of commerce in their jurisdiction of goods, including imported goods', which involves the infringement of intellectual property, disposition of infringing goods, board measures, etc., and consequently introduces international protection of IP into the WTO multilateral trade system.

22 One of the deficiencies that former treaties have is the lack of provisions related to measures that members and rights holders can take when an infringement occurs, or else the provisions are too general. Besides general provisions and basic principles, TRIPS provides in Part III definite enforcement measures such as civil and administrative procedures and remedies, criminal procedures, provisional measures and border measures, thereby enhancing the exercise of enforcement measures.

23 Some important treaties on IP, such as that of the Committee on Patents, Copyrights & other Intellectual Property (PCPIP) and the Berne Convention for the Protection of Literary and Artistic Works, only protect particular forms of IP, specifically, the PCPIP for industrial property and the Berne Convention for copyright, while TRIPS is a comprehensive document for copyright and related rights, trademarks, geographical indications, industrial designs, patents, layout-designs (topographies) of integrated circuits and undisclosed information, where the scope of protection is extensively broadened.

24 Different from previous treaties, for the purpose of winning wider recognition from the international community, TRIPS provides different latest dates of application: 1996 for developed countries; 1 January 2000 for developing countries (including members that are in the process of transformation); and 1 January 2006 for least-developed countries. But for all the members, the doctrines of 'National Treatment' and 'Most-Favoured-Nation Treatment' apply from 1 January 1996. However in 2005 (IP/C/40), the TRIPS Council decided to extend the period to 2013. Also, the Doha Declaration on TRIPS and Public Health has extended the period for Least Developed Countries to comply with provisions on pharmaceuticals to 2016.

- parties are allowed to adopt appropriate measures so as to restrain anti-competitive behaviour in relation to licensing.[25]
- Moreover, TRIPS restricts three kinds of behaviour: exclusive grant backs, preventing challenges to IP validity and coercive package licensing. Also, the TRIPS sets the standard for judging whether anti-competitive behaviour such as these three examples are legal, based upon the doctrine of the 'Rule of Reason'. Since TRIPS regulations are very general and lack detailed control measures, conflicts between IP and competition provisions will always need to be settled by the domestic regulations of WTO member states. Some scholars consider that the sharp contrast between the detailed articles specifying how to protect IP and the generality of those defining how to prevent abuses reflects TRIPS' desire to favour developed members.[26]

(3) TRIPS is, in essence, a legal document for IP protection,[27] but it takes rights holders social responsibilities and obligations into consideration,[28] while safeguarding the protection of IP. Simply, its purpose is to confine abuse of rights[29] while protecting the exercise of IPRs. Additionally, the protection of IP under the framework of TRIPS is also to some extent balanced by competitive policies.

In most WTO member states, TRIPS as an international treaty applies by being transformed into domestic law. Determining what effect TRIPS

---

25 See Luo Changfa, 'The Relationship Between IPRs and Antitrust Law in WTO – A Case Study of Licensing Behaviors', *Development Direction of WTO and Economic and Trade Relations between Xianggang and Taiwan New Times Law Firm*, Taibei Shi (1997), pp. 323–6.

26 See Yin Xintian, 'TRIPS agreement and Prohibiting Abusing IPRs', *Patent Work Dynamic*, No. 11 (2000).

27 See TRIPS, Article 3(1), remark (3): 'For the purposes of Articles 3 and 4, 'protection' shall include matters affecting the availability, acquisition, scope, maintenance and enforcement of IPRs as well as those matters affecting the use of IPRs specifically addressed in this Agreement'.

28 See TRIPS, Article 7: 'The protection and enforcement of IPRs should contribute to the promotion of technological innovation and to the transfer and dissemination of technology, to the mutual advantage of producers and users of technological knowledge and in a manner conducive to social and economic welfare, and to a balance of rights and obligations.'

29 See TRIPS, Article 8(2): 'Appropriate measures, provided that they are consistent with the provisions of this Agreement, may be needed to prevent the abuse of IPRs by right holders or the resort to practices which unreasonably restrain trade or adversely affect the international transfer of technology'.

has on competition is beneficial not only in perfecting competition law but also in protecting IP.

12.6. IMPROVEMENT IN CHINA'S LEGAL SYSTEM OF ANTI-MONOPOLY LAW IN THE FIELD OF IP

In the age of the 'knowledge-based economy', economic competition manifests itself mainly in competition between technologies. Legal systems, especially IP law, play an important role in protecting the development of science and technology. China is faced with the important task of strengthening and improving its IP legal system because (1) the establishment of this legal system began fairly late, and the ability to develop independent IP still lags behind many developed nations, and (2) competition is becoming fierce and the contributions from scientific progress to economic growth is steadily increasing, making it possible for anti-competitive behaviour related to IP to emerge or even to spread. What cannot be neglected is that in China, the protection of IP is of less concern, while concern over anti-monopoly control of IP abuses is totally lacking. Further guidance is needed in this area.

Since China's accession to the WTO, more transnational enterprises have entered the Chinese market with the aim of exploiting their IP asset base. The increased protection and enforcement of IP through globalization may result in transnational enterprises gaining monopolies over IP, which will be of concern to Chinese regulatory agencies. To meet both the requirement of a market economy and the challenges of a knowledge-based economy and economic globalization, it will become increasingly necessary for China to regulate anti-competitive behaviour through its anti-monopoly law. In recent years, Chinese companies have been confronted with a series of disputes such as those concerning DVD patent licensing, digital television systems and the 3G communications standard, which attracted attention to monopoly issues concerning IP and standardization. Furthermore, cases such as *Cisco Systems v Huawei*,[30] *Intel v Shenzhen Dongjin Communication Tech Co., Ltd.*,[31] and *Sony v TSUM*[32]

---

[30] *Cisco Systems, Inc. v Huawei Technologies, Co., Ltd.*, 266 F.Supp.2d 551 (2003), No. CIV.QA.2:03-CV-027.United States District Court, E.D. Texas, Marshall Division.

[31] *Intel Corp. v Dongjin Co.*, filed in Shenzhen Middle People's Court (December 2004) and *Dongjin Co. v Intel Corp*, filed in Beijing People's No. 1 Intermediate Court (March 2005).

[32] Filed in Shanghai Municipality No. 1 People's Intermediate Court (November 2004) (not yet reported).

(about battery cells for DV (Digital Video)) added to the discussion on the relationship between IP protection and anti-monopoly.

12.6.1. The History and Current State of Chinese Law on Anti-Monopoly Involving IP

12.6.1.1. Competition rules concerning IP are contained within several laws

The Regulations for the Implementation of the Law on Joint Ventures Using Chinese and Foreign Investment, for example, provide that:

> Technology transfer agreements shall comply with the following stipulations: (1) Expenses for the use of technology shall be fair and reasonable. (2) Unless otherwise agreed upon by both parties, the technology exporting party shall not put any restrictions on the quantity, price or region of sale of the products that are to be imported by the technology importing party. (3) The term for a technology transfer agreement is generally no longer than ten years. (4) After the expiration of a technology transfer agreement, the technology importing party shall have the right to use the technology continuously. (5) The technology importing party shall have the right to buy the equipment, parts and raw materials needed from sources they deem suitable.

The Contract Law of the People's Republic of China, which came into force on 1 October 1999, retains the regulation established by the 1987 Technology Contract Law of the People's Republic of China, which prohibits restrictions on competition and development of technologies by contract clauses. Article 329 of the Contract Law prescribes that: 'A technology contract which illegally monopolizes technology, impairs technological advancement or infringes the technology of a third party is invalid'. Article 343 prescribes that 'A technology transfer contract may set forth the scope of exploitation of the patent or the use of the technical secret by the transferor and the transferee, provided that it may not restrict technological competition and technological development'. Article 33 of the Foreign Trade Law is a regulation forbidding acts squeezing out competitors as a result of unfair competition, which could be interpreted to include infringements of IP. Furthermore, the Anti Unfair Competition Law of the People's Republic of China, which came into force on 1 December 1993, is an incorporated law prohibiting unfair competition and monopoly behaviour. Article 12 of this law prescribes that '. . . An operator shall not, in sales of goods, make a tie-in sale against the wish of the buyer or attach other unreasonable conditions', which theoretically shall apply to IP-related transactions and tying arrangements, although it does not cover all kinds of anti-competitive behaviour.

Most of the above laws and regulations govern the clauses restricting competition in technology transfer agreements, but not specifically from an anti-monopoly viewpoint, and they do not regulate possible monopolies based on IP and unilateral abusive behaviour. Although some of these regulations are general enough such that they can be used to govern anti-competitive behaviour, judges find it hard to make decisions according to these regulations in practice and many provisions instead become examples of 'soft law'.

12.6.1.2. Anti-Monopoly Law

The Anti-monopoly Law of the People's Republic of China was promulgated on 30 August 2007 and became effective on 1 August 2008.[33] Article 55 prescribes that:

> This Law does not govern the conduct of business operators to exercise their IPRs under laws and relevant administrative regulations on IPRs; however, business operators' conduct to eliminate or restrict market competition by abusing their IPRs shall be governed by this Law.

Although the Anti-monopoly Law has been officially adopted and promulgated, whether it can play its part in full depends on further implementation.

> Judging by the experiences of anti-monopoly [law] in Europe and America, first, the perfect legislation would contain both procedural rules and substantive rules; second, whereas the anti-monopoly work is very professional, it is necessary to set up a specialized executing agency; Last, the EU and the United States have technical rules (rules for implementation or guidelines) to govern the procedure, . . . In our country's [China's] anti-monopoly law, only Article 55 mentions the relationship between IP and anti-monopoly in a general manner, which puts forward new tasks and requirement for further legislation.[34]

12.6.2. A Case Study: Legal Definition of 'Technical Measures'

Beijing Jingdiao Co., Ltd. ('Jingdiao') brought a suit in 2006 alleging that Naiky Electronic Technology Company ('Naiky')[35] had committed

---

[33] For a more general discussion of the Anti Monopoly Law, see Chapter 11 by Professor Huang Young and Dr Zhang Zhe.

[34] http://www.ccopyright.com.cn.

[35] *Beijing Jingdiao Co., Ltd. v Shanghai Naiky Electronic Technology Co., Ltd.*, First Instance Case filed in Shanghai Municipality No. 1 Intermediate People's Court (September 2006), Second Instance Case filed in Shanghai Municipality Higher People's Court (December 2006).

an infringement of its copyright, in that Naiky had developed software named NCStudio which aimed at reading the output format (Eng) of JDPaint. The latter software belonged to Jingdiao, but NCStudio made JDPaint available to other CNC (Computer Numerical Control) engraving machines ('machine'), which led to a falling off in usage of the Jingdiao machine and consequently caused damage to Jingdiao. Jingdiao's demands were that Naiky cease developing or selling the CNC system that could read the Eng data, that it should make a public apology, pay compensation for damages and stop other acts of infringement. Naiky argued that NCStudio was a control program for the mechanical industry that had been registered on 6 December 2001, while JDPaint was graphics software for the arts and crafts manufacturing industry. They were quite different in many respects, such as in terms of interface, function set and operating environment. In defence, Naiky argued that although it was true that NCStudio was able to read the Eng data output by JDPaint, the Eng data and the format of Eng were beyond the scope of computer software copyright protected by law and, therefore, Naiky had not committed an infringement, or that Naiky's conduct did not constitute an infringement. The Court of First Instance held that the documents in Eng format were data files, and not a part of the JDPaint program, and thus did not constitute an article of 'works' in the context of copyright law. Therefore, the court entered a judgment in favour of Naiky. Jingdiao then lodged an appeal, claiming that the document output by JDPaint, namely, the Eng format document, was the data exchange file (DXF) of Jingdiao NC engraving machines and was used to solve the problem of the communication between programs; the reason why Jingdiao chose to adopt the customized format of Eng rather that the standard NC format was to ensure that JDPaint was used only in the system developed by Jingdiao itself and to prevent JDPaint being used in other CNC systems. Jingdiao argued that Naiky's conduct unlocked the output documents of JDPaint and disrupted the technical measures adopted by Jingdiao to protect JDPaint. The higher court found that Naiky's conduct did not belong to acts undertaken 'intentionally to escape from or disrupt the technical measures adopted by the copyright owner for protecting his software copyright'.[36] The reasons given by the court were that: (1) Naiky's conduct would not directly lead to such conduct as illegal copying or distribution; (2) the Eng format was not developed for the purpose of protecting the copyright of JDPaint as a technical measure, but rather to limit JDPaint to being used solely in Jingdiao NC engraving machines, in other words, to establish and

[36] See Regulations on Computer Software Protection, Article 24.

consolidate the tying relationship between JDPaint and the NC engraving machines. This limitation would exclude opportunities for those who had legally acquired JDPaint to use this software in other CNC systems and therefore was beyond the scope of protection under copyright law. Hence, the court rejected the appeal and affirmed the original judgment. The judgment in this case attempts to define two particular problems which will now be considered.

12.6.2.1. Legal elements of technical measures

Since entering the digital and network era, information dissemination has become more and more accessible, followed by a huge number of infringements of illegal copying and transformation through digital technology and networks. Considering the limits of judicial support, such as its hysteretic quality and high cost, copyright owners always prefer to prevent others from using their works without permission by taking preventive measures themselves, which explains the basis for technical measures. Roughly speaking, technical measures can be divided into: (1) contact-controlling measures that restrict or prevent consumers from accessing the content of works by setting codes or passwords; (2) using controlling measures, which restrict consumers using the works by technical means. However, due to a cyclical effect, the above measures also expedite the emergence of new technical means to avoid or attack these measures, which has led to litigation and anti-circumvention legislation, for example the Digital Millennium Copyright Act (DMCA) 1998 in the United States.

Article 11 of the World Intellectual Property Organization (WIPO) Copyright Treaty (WCT 1996) prescribes that:

> Contracting Parties shall provide adequate legal protection and effective legal remedies against the circumvention of effective technological measures that are used by authors in connection with the exercise of their rights under this Treaty or the Berne Convention and that restrict acts, in respect of their works, which are not authorized by the authors concerned or permitted by law.

Article 18 of the WIPO Performances and Phonograms Treaty (WPPT, adopted in the same year)[37] is basically in agreement with the above-

---

[37] See Article 18 (*Obligations Concerning Technological Measures*): 'Contracting Parties shall provide adequate legal protection and effective legal remedies against the circumvention of effective technological measures that are used by performers or producers of phonograms in connection with the exercise of their rights under this Treaty and that restrict acts, in respect of their performances or phonograms, which are not authorized by the performers or the producers of phonograms concerned or permitted by law'.

mentioned Article 11. In China, the now revised Copyright Law prescribes that any act 'without the permission from the copyright owner or obligee related to the copyright, intentionally deleting or altering the electronic information on the management of the rights on the works, sound recordings or video recordings, except where otherwise provided in laws or administrative regulations' will constitute an infringement. Likewise, the Regulations for the Protection of Computer Software, the Regulation on the Protection of the Right to Network Dissemination of Information, and Interpretations of the Supreme People's Court on Several Issues Concerning the Application of Law in the Trial of Cases Involving Copyright Disputes over Computer Network have all been promulgated successively with similar regulations.

From the two WIPO treaties and the legislation of other countries (such as the US DMCA), we can conclude that technical measures that are protected by copyright law shall at least satisfy the following two elements: (1) to protect copyright and (2) to efficiently restrict or prevent infringements of copyright. The two elements are complementary where the purpose decides the technological function and the technological function in turn serves the purpose. It seems that the 'efficiency' of the technological function is a logical paradox and it might be thought that if such measures are able to discourage infringement, how could violations occur? In fact, 'efficiency' is an important standard to ensure the obligations of copyright owners and consumers. In particular, if a particular measure cannot prevent infringement, then this kind of measure is not a 'technical measure' in the context of copyright law. In addition, if a particular measure can prevent infringement but is so weak that even ordinary consumers without professional skills are able to breach it, then this kind of measure will also not be protected by law; otherwise, the interests of copyright owners will be overprotected and thus technological progress will be impeded. In this case, Naiky's conduct belongs to the former category.

Since copyright owners' rights mainly manifest themselves in the right of reproduction and distribution, technical measures in practice are designed primarily for protecting software from being illegally reproduced or distributed. Jingdiao's conduct in this case can neither prevent software from being copied or distributed nor control other infringements such as illegal modification. In other words, it cannot play a role in protecting copyright, so it cannot be recognized as coming under the remit of technical measures.

12.6.2.2. Borderline protection of 'technical measures'

As long as the law confirms the legal status of technical measures and holds the actor responsible for their acts in evading or disrupting technical measures, a change occurs to the objective and regulation paradigm of copyright law: (1) the object has been extended from applying to those infringers who directly commit an infringement to those (secondary infringers) who help to evade or disrupt technical measures by producing equipment or providing technical assistance, which essentially means to protect 'technical measures' as a 'work' and treat 'indirect infringement' as 'direct infringement'; (2) the principle of 'technological neutrality' has been abandoned, and there are no decisive boundaries between secondary infringers' technical measures and those of the primary infringers. These two changes undoubtedly make the legal balance incline in favour of copyright owners.

A degree of regulation is, therefore, needed to maintain the balance, namely to define the scope of interests that shall be protected by technical measures to prevent secondary infringers from abusing technical measures and equally to prescribe some exemptions in order to promote technological progress and to help maintain a competitive market and spread culture.

It is true that China still has no relevant laws or regulations about restrictions on abuses of technical measures or exemptions based on 'reasonable evading and infringement', but this does not hinder us from reasonably defining the protection scope of interests safeguarded by technical measures from the standpoint of the fundamental principles of law, the legislative spirit of copyright law, and the balancing of interests. The example of 'technical measures' tells us that copyright owners' property rights and personal rights are protected by multiple laws and regulations, and that each law or regulation has its own limits. The scope of technical measures enforced by copyright law should not exceed the scope of rights owners' interests protected by copyright law. Consequently, if a technical measure is designed for tying, it cannot be regarded as a technical measure, and legitimate third parties may seek remedies under contract law (namely, to ask the infringing party to assume liability for breach of contract as he has gone beyond the authorized scope of usage), but that he/she cannot invoke copyright law. The significance of this case is to determine the limits of a 'technical measure'.

12.6.3. Application of Anti-Monopoly Law to the Communications Industry

12.6.3.1. Case study of QQ Tencent

In the field of Chinese electronic communications, there has been the recent and well-known case of Tencent Inc.'s abuse of IPRs to restrict competition. In the Chinese instant messaging (IM) market, QQ, owned by Tencent, has held the dominant market share for many years. According to a survey conducted by Analysys International, the Chinese IM market breakdown for 2008 is given in Figure 12.1.

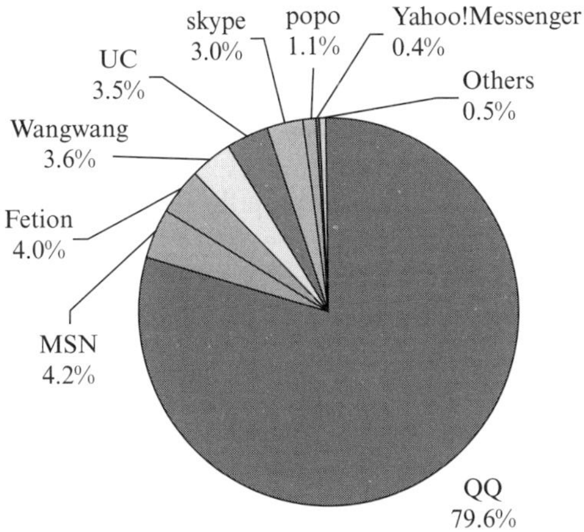

Source: Statistics from Analysis International. Available at: http://english.analysys.com.cn/3class/detail2008.php?id=956&name=news&FocusAreaTitleGB=&daohang=News&title=China%20IM%20Account%20Number%20Reached%20396%20mln%20in%20Q1%20 2008.

Figure 12.1 China IM market breakdown in Q1 2008

From Figure 12.1 it can be seen that although there are a few participants in the Chinese IM market, the market follows an oligopolistic structure. Tencent QQ dominates with a 79.6% market share, while seven other IMs only have 20% between them. With a limited market share, Tencent QQ's competitors are unable to threaten Tencent and it is clear that Tencent has a dominant market position in the relevant market for IM services under China's Anti-Monopoly Law. Over the years, Tencent has used IPR protection as an excuse to refuse to open QQ Application Program Interface (API) (similar to Windows MSN), which would allow for interoperability with other IM software, failing which other IM platforms can not interconnect with the QQ platform. The absence of interconnection has seriously hindered the development of China's IM market and has greatly inconvenienced subscribers. The early 2005 Beijing PICA Co. (hereinafter PICA) brought a lawsuit against Tencent.[38] The plaintiff

[38] *Tencent v Beijing PICA Co Ltd.*, filed in Beijing No. 1 Intermediate Court (February 2007). The Intermediate Court's decision ruled in favour of Tencent but found that only the claim based on unfair competition was justified. The court held that PICA was in breach of the 'good faith/honesty' principle set out in Article 2 of Law of the PRC Against Unfair Competition (http://wenku.baidu.

requested that Tencent cease its monopoly and unfair competition and disclose its restrictions on interconnection to the QQ instant messaging system. The defendant Tencent argued that PICA software was not given authorization rights to interconnect with the QQ system and therefore any interconnection should be deemed illegal. The Tencent case was the first case to be heard under the Anti-monopoly Law and different viewpoints on the case have since emerged.

12.6.3.2. Difference of opinion

It has been suggested that Tencent's actions are 'the conduct of business operators to eliminate or restrict market competition by abusing their IPRs'. In accordance with Article 55 of China's Anti-monopoly Law, Tencent's monopoly position would fall within the scope of the AML. Tencent's conduct demonstrates two types of abusive behaviour: first, refusing to allow interconnection with other IM platforms. 'Interconnection' means the establishment of an effective communications connection between telecommunication networks to enable the subscribers of one telecommunications carrier to communicate with the subscribers of another telecommunications carrier or to access the various telecommunications services of another telecommunications carrier.[39] In order to keep its market share, Tencent refused to interconnect with its competitors, such as MSN and Yahoo Messenger. Thus, subscribers had to give up the products of other competitors, including PICA, which had to withdraw from the market, which had a negative impact on the IM market's development and innovation. The second example of abusive behaviour is bundling. In order to extend its monopoly advantage in other markets, Tencent intentionally bundled other proprietary software with QQ, including QQ game, QQ music, QQ pet and so on. The bundling was

---

com/view/7a1d970ef12d2af90242e6e6.html, English version of the Act) by illegally inserting Tencent's access agreement into PICA's programme so as to get access to Mobile QQ's server. The court also rejected PICA's argument that it was their fundamental right to get access, based on the fact that the Mobile QQ system is a value added product and service viz-a-viz a basic telecommunications service. Following PICA's appeal to the High Court, the High Court upheld the decision of the Intermediate Court and held that PICA's anti-competitive practice in breach of 'good faith/honesty' principle set out in Article 2 of China's Anti Unfair Competition Law (AUCL – see chapters 5 and 6 of this book) had caused Tencent to loose potential paid users and market share, and ordered PICA to pay RMB 450 000 in compensation to Tencent.

[39] Provided in 'Administration of the Interconnection of Public Telecommunications Networks Provisions', promulgated by the Ministry of Information Industry in 2001.

mandatory, which greatly reduced the availability of other similar software or services to subscribers. As a consequence of this strategy, Tencent achieved remarkable expansion in casual games, e-commerce, and portal information within just a few years.

While experts expressed concern about the results of this case (see footnote 38 which describes Tencent's success in the High Court appeal), since the entry barriers to the instant messaging market are relatively low and more and more post-entrants have been challenging the dominant operators, Beijing PICA Co.'s failure in its action against Tencent, may result in the domestic instant messaging interoperability market becoming less competitive. Tencent's advantage however, derived from its user resources, will be greatly threatened by the post-entrants. As for the industry, Tencent's success could block development and innovation.

12.7. CONCLUSION

Competition laws are the basic rules for promoting and maintaining a competitive market and the system for protection of intellectual property plays an equally important role in generating innovation in modern society.

The relationship between competition law and intellectual property rights has veered towards greater harmony and unification. But what is the foundation of such harmony and unification? The answer is: the congruence of their fundamental goals, that is, to promote and defend efficiency. As Professor Ward Bergman has pointed out, the either/or aspect of these laws (patent law and anti-monopoly law) has disappeared. Both antitrust law and patent law have a common central economic goal: to maximize wealth by producing what consumers want at the lowest cost. Due to numerous factors related to law making, such as time, regime and international background, the legislative patterns of competition law vary widely across the globe. These can be loosely grouped into two kinds: (1) the two laws are enacted independently; (2) integration of both general and specific rules in that the intention and extension of the above-mentioned practices are not clearly prescribed. On the whole, such laws are quite distinct.

As we have seen in discussing network-based industries, such as instant messaging in China, we are able to explore the relationship between antimonopoly law and IPRs law. Due to the fact that IP legislation preceded the adoption of the Anti-monopoly Law, at least in China, there is now a great need in China to rationalize the relationship between the enforcement of IP and the Anti-monopoly Law, with further guidelines on the application of Article 55 of the AML.

13. China in the WTO: enforcement of the TRIPS Agreement and the Doha Agenda

Kong Qingjiang[1]

China's accession to the World Trade Organization (WTO) on 11 December 2001 was an historic event. For the rest of the world, admitting China into the world trading system was a great experiment. Indeed, as the most populated country, China's rapidly expanding economy reflected its significant role in decision-making concerning the world's resource allocation. There was no certainty at the time of accession that China's economic system would mesh well with WTO rules and other trading partners' market-oriented economies. Moreover, in the history of the world trading system, never had a country of such trading importance, and with a system that had been identified to be incompatible with WTO norms, been admitted.

It is no exaggeration that, at the time of the accession, given China's trade weight, its anticipated gigantic trade surge would disrupt the markets of its trading partners, and the rule-based multilateral trading system would be endangered if China opted to ignore WTO rules. With this apprehension in mind, even before admitting China into the world trading system, the leading trading partners, particularly the United States and the European Union (EU), had successfully forced China to accept a more comprehensive protocol on the accession, one in which China committed itself to ever more far-reaching obligations beyond the WTO. Moreover, China's leading trading partners kept a close watch on China's behavior in the WTO and formed task forces to monitor China's compliance with WTO commitments. It was the first time in the history of the world trading system that existing members formed monitoring task forces. Furthermore, China's trading partners have never been shy

1 Professor of International Economic Law, Zhejiang Gongshang University. The author wishes to thank Professor Rohan Kariyawasam for his insightful comments.

of taking full advantage of the built-in mechanisms in the WTO, i.e. the Trade Policy Review Mechanism and the Dispute Settlement Mechanism, to achieve this end.

When China joined, the WTO launched its new round of trade talks known as the Doha Development Agenda (Doha Round). After seven years of ordeals, the Doha Round disappointingly ended in failure due (mainly) to splits between wealthy and developing nations. The failure of the Doha Round talks just represents, in the short run, a missed opportunity for some additional steps in the direction of a more competitive and productive system of global economic activity and trade. Along with this, the dominance of the EU and the US in the global trading system will be weakened as China becomes more assertive in defending its perceived national interests. More alarming, however, is that China's refusal to cooperate in global trade talks would displace the world trade pattern, given the world's dependence on Chinese-manufactured products over the years.[2] Other global undertakings, from slashing greenhouse-gas emissions to ending food-export restrictions, will also face hurdles if China flexes its muscles and fails to cooperate.[3]

With these questions in mind, we examine China's international behavior in relation to the Agreement on Trade-Related Aspects of Intellectual Property Rights (TRIPS Agreement) since its accession to the WTO and investigate its implications. In the context of global integration, the increasingly important role of intellectual property rights (IPR) for economic development motivated related countries to put trade-related aspects of intellectual property rights (TRIPS) on the negotiating table of the Uruguay Round. Incorporation of IPRs in the negotiating agenda of the Uruguay Round and the conclusion of the TRIPS are generally viewed as a compromise on the part of developing countries in exchange for greater access to the markets of developed countries. The TRIPS Agreement sets forth an international minimum standard for IPR

---

2 It has been argued that as China continues to grow, the demand for its products in the US and EU will just be replaced by demand from Chinese consumers. What will be critical in the long run, however, is Chinese access to primary products from other countries: food, minerals, energy resources. In this context, a quasi-colonial system may even be envisaged with China ('the world's workshop') at the center, exporting its manufactured goods to resource-rich countries in exchange for their primary products.

3 Even the official news agency of China worries that '[i]f the Doha Round repeatedly fails, this will cast doubt on the ability of all parties to find solutions to complex problems, such as climate change, high oil prices and food prices within a global framework', though it naturally makes no reference to China. See Xinhua News Agency, 31 July 2008.

protection. Nevertheless, the developing countries have harbored the hope that the TRIPS Agreement could be flexible enough to accommodate the wide range of needs of WTO members. Since the launch of the Doha Development Agenda, the developing members have been eager to see that the new round will take due account of the interests and the needs of developing countries. However, since the Cancun conference, successive WTO Ministerial Conferences have failed to live up to the expectations of the developing world.

13.1. THE TRIPS AND THE DOHA AGENDA

At the Ministerial Conference in Doha, a number of key declarations and decisions were made that would have a direct impact on the operation of TRIPS.[4] In addition to setting out a negotiating agenda, these declarations and decisions also perform the multi-dimensional function of clarifying and reiterating existing rights and obligations and highlighting certain particular issues in the course of implementation. Providing clarity on a number of critical issues, the Ministerial Conference was an attempt to clear the way for future work on TRIPS. However, it is still the subject of an ongoing debate as to what exactly this future work should be and in which areas agreement (and therefore a mandate) has already been established.

Overall, the Doha declarations with respect to TRIPS are seen as a major victory for developing (and particularly the least developed) countries in securing flexibility in the use of IPRs, especially in the area of public health. Specifically, the Declaration on the TRIPS Agreement and Public Health[5] (the 'Declaration') lays down that in situations where action needs to be taken to deal with a national emergency, the set of options is not limited by the architecture of international IPRs. More generally, it reiterates the ability of countries to interpret the TRIPS in a way that is beneficial to or reflective of their needs. It thus makes it possible that in situations where TRIPS is open to interpretation, more than one interpretation might be feasible. While the TRIPS Agreement certainly puts many restrictions upon a member, efforts have been made

---

4 These Declarations and Decisions include the Ministerial Declaration, WT/MIN(01)/DEC/1; Decision on implementation-related issues and concerns, WT/MIN(01)/17; Declaration on the TRIPS Agreement and Public Health, WT/MIN(01)/DEC/2; Procedures for extensions under Article 27.4 for certain developing country members, g/scm/39.

5 WT/MIN(01)/DEC/2.

to emphasize the scope for discretion a country has in designing its own IPR system. The results of the Doha Ministerial Conference can be seen as an attempt to further stress the flexibility that is allowed within TRIPS.

Public health was not the only issue covered by the Doha declarations in relation to the TRIPS Agreement. The declarations also included issues ranging from how traditional knowledge relates to the TRIPS Agreement to geographical indications, which have also been the subject of ongoing negotiations.

13.1.1. Declaration on the TRIPS Agreement and Public Health

The importance of the issue of public health in relation to the TRIPS Agreement is underscored by the separate declaration made at the Ministerial Conference in Doha. The Declaration was a response to the need to clarify certain rules within the TRIPS Agreement, as well as being a response to the difficulties that many countries had met in exploiting the flexibility contained within it. High-profile examples with respect to HIV drugs in both South Africa and Brazil pointed to a future where even TRIPS-consistent laws would be challenged. In light of these cases, it has become necessary to reiterate the rights and to resolve the uncertainties within the framework of the TRIPS, especially in relation to the issue of public health.

13.1.1.1. Reiteration of TRIPS rights

The primary objective of the Declaration is to reiterate certain rights that are already contained within TRIPS. In particular, the Declaration indicates that:

- Each member has the right to grant compulsory licenses[6] and the freedom to determine the grounds upon which such licenses are granted.
- Each member has the right to determine what constitutes a national emergency or other circumstances of extreme urgency, it being understood that public health crises, including those relating to HIV/AIDS, tuberculosis, malaria and other epidemics, can represent a national emergency or other circumstances of extreme urgency.

---

[6] A compulsory license (for a patent for example) is a license granted by the government for the working of a patent by an entity other than the patent holder. The circumstances when a government can grant a compulsory license are set out in Article 31 of the TRIPS.

- The effect of the provisions in the TRIPS Agreement that are relevant to the exhaustion of IPR[7] is to leave each member free to establish its own regime for such exhaustion without challenge, subject to the MFN and national treatment obligations.[8]

By clarifying these points, the Declaration emphasizes the flexibility that is contained within TRIPS. One effect of this Declaration is that it may assist countries to exploit this flexibility more readily and in a manner that has not been utilized to date.

Even though Article 31 TRIPS allows grounds for the grant of compulsory licenses, by and large this provision has not been included in the patent laws of many developing countries. The effective implementation of the Doha Declaration in these members, therefore, would call for an amendment to national laws to incorporate the exceptions and safeguards indispensable for the protection of public health.

13.1.1.2. Clarification of uncertainties

The Declaration indicates that if a WTO member has the capacity to produce patented products, it can grant compulsory licenses to deal with national emergencies or other situations of extreme urgency. However, if this member does not have adequate domestic production capacity to deal with the emergency, the right to grant a compulsory license does not deliver any effective material assistance. This issue is particularly relevant in countries where the interest of public health demands unimpeded access to essential medicines.

However, only a small number of WTO members have the capacity to produce the active ingredients required for medicines. This means that when confronted with a national health emergency, most members may not be able to make effective use of the right to grant compulsory licenses, revealing a shortcoming of the TRIPS Agreement.

Furthermore, the TRIPS Agreement imposes a significant constraint on this type of behavior by stipulating that production under a compulsory license should be predominantly for use in the domestic market.[9]

---

[7] IPRs are typically exhausted once the goods or services have been sold. This means that further sale or distribution cannot be controlled by the IPR owner. As IPRs only operate within the country granting them, an exhaustion regime can be distinguished by whether it recognizes exhaustion for the first sale anywhere in the world by the IPR owner (international exhaustion) or first sale within the country granting the right (national exhaustion).

[8] See paragraph 5 of the Declaration.

[9] Article 31(f) of the TRIPS Agreement.

The Declaration recognized that 'WTO members with insufficient or no manufacturing capacities in the pharmaceutical sector could face difficulties in making effective use of compulsory licensing under the TRIPS Agreement' and instructed the Council for TRIPS 'to find an expeditious solution to this problem and to report to the General Council before the end of 2002'.[10]

Despite this possible solution, a further complication still exists that can potentially frustrate the intent of such a proposed solution. Since a compulsory license can only be granted when a patent exists, the wording of paragraph 6 seems to restrict attention only to cases where a pharmaceutical patent is already in force in the importing member. So for members that do not provide patent protection for pharmaceuticals, or where for whatever reason the required pharmaceutical is off-patent in that country but on-patent in others, there is no basis for a compulsory license.

Given that many of the least developed countries (LDCs) are not currently required to comply with the TRIPS Agreement and that these are also the members facing the most serious public health problems, this raises the possibility that a solution that the Council for TRIPS suggests may not be relevant to the WTO members most in need.

At first blush, the Declaration appears to be a victory for the developing and LDCs (this may still be the case for developing countries, once they fully comply with the TRIPS Agreement). However, a closer look reveals a number of potential problems. In particular, most of the benefits that the declaration purported to offer go disproportionately to countries that already provide patent protection. The extension of the transition period to 2016 is not associated with the increase of actual benefits in the area of public health in and of itself because the benefits implied by the Declaration may only be realized after patent protection is provided.

13.1.2. The Doha Declaration and Enforcement of the TRIPS Agreement

The Declaration is not only a strong political declaration, but also a ministerial decision with legal effects on the members and on the WTO bodies, particularly the Dispute Settlement Body and the Council for TRIPS. The Declaration provides an unambiguous road map to all the key flexibilities the TRIPS offers, including compulsory licensing, countries' freedom to determine the grounds for compulsory licensing, and parallel imports, and establishes a specific rule of interpretation that gives content to the general

10 See paragraph 6 of the Declaration.

interpretive provisions of the Vienna Convention on the Law of the Treaties on which GATT/WTO jurisprudence has been built. Moreover, in establishing that public health is a clearly stated purpose of the TRIPS Agreement, the Declaration amounts to an amendment of the TRIPS. Therefore, in cases of ambiguity, panels and the Appellate Body should opt for interpretations that are effectively 'supportive of WTO members' right to protect public health'.

However, the Doha Declaration risks becoming a useless piece of paper if countries and the international community do not step up efforts to operationalize it, because the changes in the TRIPS Agreement, or new interpretations, do not translate automatically into changes in national laws. Furthermore, any solution found at the Council for TRIPS is likely to call for amendments to national laws in potential exporting countries in order to become operative. All potential exporting countries, including developed countries, should appropriately amend national law to overcome the legal barriers of the patent system and facilitate effective implementation of the Council for TRIPS solution to the paragraph 6 problem.

The implementation of an effective solution under paragraph 6 may also depend on the conditions under which compulsory licenses are granted in the importing country. The remuneration to be paid to the patent holder should be such that it does not nullify the aim of the license, to ensure the supply of *low-cost* pharmaceuticals. In addition, national governments should carefully implement Article 31 (g)[11] of the TRIPS Agreement, in a manner that does not undermine the incentives to apply for and execute a compulsory license.[12]

The TRIPS Agreement has left room for flexibility at the national level and this has important political and legal implications. It indicates that the pressures to impede the use of available flexibilities runs counter to the spirit and purpose of the TRIPS Agreement. In legal terms, it means that panels and the Appellate Body must interpret the Agreement and the laws and regulations adopted to implement it in light of the public health needs of individual WTO members.

---

11 TRIPS Article 31 (g): '[The] authorization for such use shall be liable, subject to adequate protection of the legitimate interests of the persons so authorized, to be terminated if and when the circumstances which led to it cease to exist and are unlikely to recur. The competent authority shall have the authority to review, upon motivated request, the continued existence of these circumstances.' This language requires the authority that grants the compulsory licensing to terminate the license when it finds by reviewing that the public health crisis ceases to exist.

12 This also applies, of course, to a possible solution under Article 31 (f).

13.1.3. Other Doha Issues

Aside from the Declaration, the Ministerial Conference outlined a number of other areas with regard to which a review of the TRIPS Agreement is required. Some of the issues in this list have been the subject of negotiations as part of the built-in agenda contained within the TRIPS, such as the issues of geographical indications, patenting of plant and animal varieties and non-violation complaints. Besides, the list also identifies a number of new issues, including those of traditional knowledge, technology transfer, and the relationship between the TRIPS Agreement and the Convention on Biological Diversity (CBD).

Despite the prolonged and intense negotiations, WTO members were not able to reach consensus on an expeditious solution by the deadlines, due chiefly to the fact that the direction given for negotiations in these areas is not as specific as it is in that of public health. As a result, much of the work in these areas to date has been focused on the exploration of the extent to which the mandate applies.

Nevertheless, it should be pointed out that the Doha Agenda and beyond have ambivalent implications for China and for other developing countries as well in terms of enforcement of the TRIPS Agreement. On the one hand, in international negotiations or in the design of national laws, policymakers in China have to consider how to adapt existing IPR mechanisms to promote local innovation and to identify new alternatives that could better address their development needs. Several such mechanisms have been identified in academic literature and new ones are starting to arise in national legislation. Existing alternatives include the use of utility models or petty patents, industrial design law, trade secrets, and trademarks and geographical indications. Some of the emerging options include hybrid exclusive rights,[13] new *sui generis* systems[14] in food and agriculture, compensatory liability regimes, preservation of scientific/technological data for follow-on research, and low cost collective management of rights

[13] For example, the innovator of a utility model is generally awarded the exclusive right under the Chinese Patent Law. However, the Copyright Law can be accommodated to accord the exclusive right to the utility model as well.

[14] Generally speaking, protection for IP is extended to matter depending upon its characteristics. The main types of IPR law – copyrights, patents, and trademarks – define characteristics and any matter that meets such criteria are extended protection. However, there exist statutes in many countries that extend IPR-type protection to matter that do not meet traditional definitions of protected intellectual property. For example, there are rights which are known as being *sui generis* to owners of a small class of works, such IPRs in mask works, ship hull designs, databases, as well as plant varieties.

for small-scale innovators and creators. On the other hand, China needs to be aware of a new phenomenon called TRIPS-plus, which was derived after the Cancun Ministerial Conference when developed countries pressed the developing world to accept standards for the protection of IPR in excess of what the TRIPS Agreement requires (so called TRIPS-plus provisions), particularly in digital rights areas. TRIPS-plus not only refers to the negotiation of agreements that tend to introduce commitments beyond those already included or consolidated in the minimum standards of the TRIPS Agreement,[15] but also to any enforcement requirement to provide stronger IPR protection than the TRIPS Agreement dictates.

13.2. CHINA'S ENFORCEMENT OF THE TRIPS AGREEMENT IN THE DOHA ROUND

13.2.1. China and the Doha Agenda in General

With China now the world's second largest economy and trader (by purchasing power parity), Members look to China to assume greater leadership in shaping the multilateral trading system. China was urged to continue its active participation in the current negotiations and to continue to work towards a successful conclusion of the Doha Round. That is why whenever the talks were suspended during the Doha Round, either the WTO Director General or United States Trade Representative (USTR) or EU Trade Commissioner flew to Beijing to bring Chinese leaders on board. For example, not long after the talks were suspended in July 2006, Pascal Lamy and Susan Schwab visited Beijing to urge China to play a bigger role in reviving the Doha Round. In fact, China had the potential to become a leading player in the Doha Round and was in a position to contribute more than other developing countries to the final Doha Round accord. First, China is both a developing country and a trade giant. It has a perfect understanding of how other developing countries and developed countries feel in the talks. Due to this unique status, China has the potential to emerge as a mediator, helping to bridge the gaps between the developed and developing worlds. Secondly, the thrust of the Doha Round was, amongst other things, in agricultural products. China, unlike its peers among developing countries, is not reliant on agriculture for its economic growth and export revenue. Therefore, it has a smaller

[15] One of the processes where TRIPS-plus commitments could be developed is the negotiation of the Free Trade Area of the Americas (FTAA).

stake in the agricultural negotiations of the Doha Round. Thirdly, China's trade barriers are already low compared with other developing countries such as India and Brazil. If China offered improved access to its markets by cutting its tariffs on non-agricultural goods by, for example, a half compared with the current applied rates and liberalizing trade and investment in the financial and other service sectors, such action could yield important dividends, although as a matter of fact, this would not be as onerous as it sounds and large percentage cuts in base tariff rates would translate into small changes in China's applied tariffs. It would allow China to respond positively to protectionist pressures in Europe and the United States, and would reinforce Chinese economic and political relations with other developing countries in the WTO.

Importantly, China has already aligned itself with free trade not only rhetorically but also in practice. *A New York Times* article exclaimed, 'Since joining the WTO, China has been an outspoken defender of free-trade principles'. China also actively participated in WTO mini-ministerial meetings and other bilateral or multilateral consultations. China made more than 100 proposals altogether in the Doha Round, either alone or through cooperation with other developing countries. China did make major compromises and concessions on issues such as the OTDS (overall trade-distorting domestic support) reduction for developed members, sensitive products, SSG (Special Safeguard) and the ACC (anti-concentration clause). Also it indicated further market opening in some key sectors.[16]

However, there is a huge perception gap. In this regard, it is interesting to make a comparison between China's perception of its behavior in the Doha Round and that of other members. Indeed, both China and the other members recognize China's status in the world trading system. Up to the last moment of the Doha Round, China had been a constructive but low-key participant in the Doha Round. In particular, China played a useful role in advancing the negotiating process through its membership in the Group of 20 (G-20) coalition of developing countries. In the eyes of China, it certainly played an active role as a talk facilitator, in spite of the ups and downs during the talks. Throughout the Doha Round, China was from time to time found to echo the US and EU's call for greater free trade. China called on members to stand up to trade protectionism. When the Doha Round was suspended in July 2006, China helped the talks to resume by exchanging views with key players through various diplomatic channels.

---

[16] China's Commerce Minister Chen Deming made the remarks. See Chinese minister expresses 'deep regret' over trade talks failure, Xinhua News Agency, 29 July 2008.

In the eyes of WTO members, however, China has not offered additional reforms beyond the extensive commitments undertaken in its 2001 protocol of accession. And, moreover, it has somewhat routinely urged the US and EU to show sufficient political will to advance the Doha Round. Moreover, even China's low profile in the WTO talks was not benefiting its status as one of the world's largest economies and trading nations. More unacceptable to its major trade partners is that China's last-minute emergence as a swing factor was a surprise – and not only because it departed from its usual low-key negotiating style. Therefore, China deserved blame – along with India and other major trading nations – for the collapse of the talks.

13.2.2. China's Attitude towards IPR in the Doha Agenda

A growing assertiveness on the part of the developing countries is discernible in the Doha Agenda. While supporting the launch of the Doha Agenda, developing countries have been hoping that the new round will take fully into account their interests and reasonable needs in the capacity of developing countries. In line with the general attitudes of developing countries towards the Doha Agenda, China states that 'the objectives of the new multilateral negotiation should be, firstly, facilitate the establishment of a new international economic order which is fair, just and reasonable, secondly, promote the economic development and trade and investment facilitation worldwide, and thirdly, achieve a balance of interests between developed countries and developing countries, especially conducive to the development of developing countries' and that '[t]he new round should ensure full and effective participation of developing members and achieve overall balance regarding the final results of negotiation so as to reflect interests of all parties'.[17]

During the Cancun Conference, China joined other developing countries in taking a common stand on various issues including IPR. Noticeably, just before the Cancun Conference, China collaborated with the Group of 77 (G-77) in issuing a declaration on the upcoming conference.[18] In the declaration, China and the G-77 affirmed 'the right of WTO members to use in full the provisions of the TRIPS Agreement which provide flexibility for members to protect public health and promote access to medicines for

---

[17] See Speech by Mr Long Yongtu, Chief Negotiator and Vice-Minister of Foreign Trade and Economic Cooperation of the People's Republic of China, at the General Council Meeting of WTO (19 December 2001, Geneva).

[18] Declaration by the G-77 and China at the Fifth WTO Ministerial Conference (Cancun, Mexico, 10–14 September 2003), Geneva, 22 August 2003.

all'. In addition to underscoring the importance of the implementation of the mechanism in enforcing paragraph 6 of the Declaration on the TRIPS Agreement and Public Health to enabling developing countries, including LDCs, with insufficient or no manufacturing capacity in the pharmaceutical sector, to make effective use of compulsory licensing, they reiterated that 'any proposed solution in this regard should be multilateral in nature and should be agreed upon in the context of the WTO'.

Not only with regard to the evolving multilateral trading system in general, but also on specific issues in the negotiations, China united with other developing members, adopting a common stance or shared goals. For example, for developing countries to make use of the compulsory licensing authorized in the Declaration on the TRIPS Agreement and Public Health, an amendment to the TRIPS Agreement was required to provide the necessary legal mechanism. As an interim measure, WTO members agreed to place a moratorium on disputes regarding any measure taken in conformity with the provisions of a possible waiver, which would remain in force until the anticipated amendment to the TRIPS Agreement was accepted by all members. Work on the preparation of such an amendment was planned to start by the end of 2003 with a view to its adoption within six months. In this connection, China, together with Cuba, the Dominican Republic, Ecuador, India, Indonesia, Pakistan, Peru, Sri Lanka, Thailand and Venezuela, argued that the legal mechanism was so important to developing members that it would be advisable not to fix a deadline for the conclusion of the negotiations. Their proposal was accepted and negotiation on the critical issue was able to continue without arousing too much frustration after the deadline set previously.

Also, with regard to additional protection for geographical indications, China joined 19 other members, most of them developing or transition economy countries, and called for the extension of high geographical indications protection enjoyed by wines and spirits to other products.[19]

As for the TRIPS Agreement and biodiversity and traditional knowledge, China, in concert with Brazil, Cuba, the Dominican Republic, Ecuador, India, Pakistan, Thailand, Venezuela, Zambia and Zimbabwe, submitted a communication to the Council on TRIPS, stressing the need to modify the TRIPS Agreement and arguing that it contained no provisions to prevent biopiracy (illegal access and use) or ensure prior informed consent and the fair and equitable sharing of benefits. The communication proposed several conditions for the acquisition of patent rights related to biological materials of traditional knowledge, including requirements for

19 IP/C/W/353.

patent applicants to disclose the source of origin of the biological resource and associated traditional knowledge and evidence of prior informed consent and benefit-sharing.[20]

Against the backdrop that the Quad countries of the USA, Japan, Canada and the EU have been pushing for TRIPS-plus provisions in several bilateral and free trade agreements, China too is now adopting a similar position on the use of regional trade agreements to secure specific IPR provisions with its own bilateral and regional trade partners.[21]

13.2.3. China's Expectation of International Rule-Making within the WTO Framework

Needless to say, China's attitude toward international rule-making underlined its behavior relating to the TRIPS in the context of the Doha Agenda. China's attitude toward TRIPS in the new round of multilateral trade negotiation and its corresponding behavior in the Cancun Conference should be examined in the broader context of China's strategy with regard to international rule-making within the WTO.

In an interdependent world, international economic rules are crucial to the national interests of any country within the increasingly integrated global economic system. It is no exaggeration to say that rules predetermine the structure of international economic relations. This also holds true in the case of IPRs. The TRIPS Agreement, which combines major international rules in the field of IPRs, represents an international IPR scene that is dominated by the developed countries.

As a WTO member, China has to act within the boundary of the TRIPS Agreement whether it intends to promote its own trade interests or to fulfill its obligations towards other WTO members. Then the question arises: Is China satisfied with the TRIPS?

In China's eyes, although WTO rules are a result of conflict and compromises between developed and developing countries, there is no denying that the developed world led in the making of the WTO framework. For

---

20 IP/C/W/356.

21 At the time of writing, China and Peru are preparing for the negotiation of a free trade agreement. From the Joint Feasibility Report released by the Ministry of Foreign Trade and Tourism of Peru and the Ministry of Commerce of the People's Republic of China, both parties agreed that '[a]ccording to the characteristics of bilateral trade between China and Peru, the intellectual property protection can be fulfilled under the frame of TRIPS'. They seemed not go beyond the minimum requirements of the TRIPS Agreement. Available at http://www.mincetur.gob.pe/newweb/Portals/0/Peru-China%20JFS%20Final.pdf, accessed July 2010.

example, WTO rules to a large extent are based on the 'comparative advantage' theory and 'game' theory, which reflect the interests of the developed countries in their theorizing. Therefore, not all WTO rules are reasonable.[22] In name, the TRIPS Agreement is equally binding on both developed and developing countries. However, the developing world holds a much smaller pool of IPR than developed countries. Moreover, developing countries lack the necessary powers and means to enforce WTO rules against the developed countries. The binding force of the TRIPS is real for developing countries, but discounted with regard to developed countries.

China is destined to become a more powerful and responsible member of the world community. The late Chinese leader Deng Xiaoping pointed out long ago that China had to make its contribution to the international community. He was referring to a role in world affairs corresponding to China's status as an emerging power. After its entry into the WTO, to expand its influence over the making of international economic rules, in the long run, China cannot but ask for the cooperation of other members in various areas. In this context, one has reason to assume that by allying itself with other developing countries, China expects them to lend support to its initiatives in rule-making in the IPR domain. In other words, developing countries are expected to enhance China's balancing power in the reshaping of the IPR rules in the WTO context.

After all, as a developing country, China shares much in common with other developing countries when it comes to the making of international economic rules. With a formal or informal mechanism in place, shared interests between China and other developing countries would make plenty of room for the two sides to cooperate in the process of formation of international economic rules.[23]

Indeed, China is fully aware of its limited national strength vis-à-vis the United States, the European Union and Japan. It is not so unrealistic as to attempt to overhaul the existing rules on IPR. In fact, it does not have the ambition to do so. It is aware that, in the foreseeable future, the developed world will continue to dominate the process of rule-making in the field of IPR. Although it is clear that the Chinese government expects to lead in future rule-making, a China-initiated refurbishing of IPR rules is something that lies only in the distant future.[24]

---

22 See Yang Jingyu, Minister of the Legislative Office of the State Council, 'Accession to the WTO and the Legal Institution-Building in China', *Qiu Shi* (in Chinese) (2000), 3, p. 171.

23 The creation of the G-21 Group is an example of coordination among China and other major developing countries at the Cancun Conference.

24 Liu Guangxi, a member of China's WTO negotiation team, shared this view.

But China is equally aware of the fact that if it refrains from playing an active role in rule-making until its economy becomes fully developed, then it will have no choice but to follow the rules decided by other countries. From the perspective of *realpolitik*, it is understandable that China sometimes tries to pre-empt the right to participate in rule-making by taking the initiative.

13.2.4. Implementation of the Doha Declaration in Light of the Patent Law Revision

China revised the Patent Law for the third time on 27 December 2008 ('New Patent Law').[25] Since it was enacted in 1984, the Patent Law has been amended twice in 1992 and 2000.[26] The previous two amendments focused on importing advanced technologies and intensifying IPR protection for foreign investors,[27] while the third revision has concentrated on enhancing the capability of independent innovation and building an innovative country.

Among the major changes in the latest revision of the Patent Law are the absolute novelty requirement; prohibition against double patenting; permission for patent application abroad before filing in China; mandatory disclosure requirement on genetic resources; statutory exemption from patent infringement for activities associated with regulatory marketing approval; prior art defense and pre-trial evidence preservation in patent litigation; increased penalties and more reasonable remedies and statutory damages for patent infringement, as well as the grant of compulsory licenses in cases of public health crises abroad.[28]

The New Patent Law stipulates in Chapter VI that there is an obliga-

---

See Liu, 'Xing sheng jie yao ru shi', *Guoji Maoyi* (International Trade), 02/2002, p. 14.

[25] The third amendment to the Patent Law follows its introduction in 1984 and first and second amendments in 1992 and 2000 respectively.

[26] For a systematic analysis of the evolution of the patent regime since its enactment, see Kong Qingjiang, 'The Political Economy of the Intellectual Property Rights Regime-Building: The Evolution of the Chinese Patent Regime', *Pacific McGeorge Global Business& Development Law Journal* (2008), pp. 111 et seq.

[27] Specifically, the first amendment added pharmaceutical compositions to the list of patentable subject matter and inaugurated China's membership in the Patent Cooperation Treaty, and the second brought the Patent Law into compliance with the TRIPS Agreement.

[28] For an account of the changes to the Patent Law in the third amendment, see, for example, 'What Does the Third Amendment to China's Patent Law Mean to You?' *Jones Day Commentaries*, January 2009.

tion to use the patent, and if not fulfilled, the Patent Office (later the State Intellectual Property Office, SIPO) may grant a compulsory license to a qualified entity to exploit the patent.[29] However, no compulsory license has ever been granted in China by the authorities.[30]

China implemented the Doha Declaration through domestic legislation. On 29 November 2005, the SIPO issued the Measures Governing the Compulsory License of Patent Implementation Related to Public Health ('Pharmaceutical Compulsory Licensing Measures'), which came into effect on 1 January 2006. The promulgation of the Pharmaceutical Compulsory Licensing Measures made China one of the first WTO members to adopt a revision of the TRIPS Agreement into its national legislature in the spirit of the Doha Declaration.

On 28 October 2007, the Standing Committee of the National People's Congress approved the Protocol on Revising the Agreement on Trade-Related Aspects of Intellectual Property Rights. These two pieces of legislation further strengthened the legal grounds for compulsory licensing in case of public health crisis.

Aimed at implementing the Doha Declaration into the Patent Law, the third amendment to the Patent Law provides a more definitive statutory basis to compel compulsory licenses, and contains new rules that restrict the general scope of compulsory licensing, while making it more feasible and likely for compulsory licenses to be granted in the area of pharmaceuticals[31] and semiconductor technology.[32]

Moreover, the New Patent Law adopts a broader standard than that of the Pharmaceutical Compulsory Licensing Measures for issuing compulsory licensing of pharmaceuticals for any public health purposes. That is, the compulsory licensing provided under the New Patent Law is no longer limited to just 'for the treatment of contagious diseases' as under the Pharmaceutical Compulsory Licensing Measures. This in principle leaves potential scope for pharmaceutical therapies to be subject to compulsory licensing. As such, in the event of a public health crisis, such as SARS or bird flu, the Chinese government is likely to grant a compulsory license to manufacture and export the required patented drugs.

In addition to health-related compulsory licensing, the amendment also

---

[29] According to Article 51 of the pre-third amendment Patent Law, compulsory licensing may be granted where an entity is unable to obtain a license on reasonable terms and conditions within a reasonable period of time.

[30] See Chapter 2 of this book on Patents.

[31] Article 50 of the New Patent Law.

[32] Article 52 of the New Patent Law.

provides that the Chinese government may grant a compulsory license on a patent involving semiconductor technology if the license for exploitation is limited to use for the purposes of the public interest.

In this regard, it should be pointed out that the New Patent Law is now inextricably intertwined with the Anti-Monopoly Law in China. For example, the Anti-Monopoly Law provides that '[t]his Law is not applicable to conduct by business operators to exercise their legitimate intellectual property rights in accordance with intellectual property laws and relevant administrative regulations; however, this Law is applicable to the conduct of business operators to eliminate or restrict market competition by abusing intellectual property rights'.[33] It dictates that, for example, a patent holder would not be permitted to seek to leverage its lawful monopoly to extend it beyond the proper scope of the patent. Meanwhile, the New Patent Law stipulates that compulsory licensing may be granted to remove or reduce the negative effects of competition due to monopoly acts caused by the patentee exploiting the patent.[34] In other words, the issuance of a compulsory license is now a remedy for patent misuse. It remains to be seen whether the statutory role of the competition policy in the domain of compulsory licensing signifies a change in China's approach to IPR issues.

13.3. CONCLUDING REMARKS

The Ministerial Conference in Doha can be seen as an important illustration of the flexibility of the TRIPS Agreement. Nevertheless, the unfolding of the Doha Agenda – especially in relation to public health – exhibited the conflict between the national interest and IPRs. For China and the developing countries collectively, the goal should be, among others, to ensure that the TRIPS is modified so that IPRs are *not* obstacles to the management of public health emergencies.

With regard to the Doha Agenda, China's approach has been the following: honoring its own commitments, using the TRIPS Agreement to its own advantage and actively participating in the making of new rules. Although China was aware that aside from the area of public health, the prospects for future changes to the TRIPS Agreement appear to be relatively limited, this did not prevent China from taking a historically new posture in international rule-making. For a long time China had been

---

33 Article 55 of the Anti-Monopoly Law.

34 Article 48 of the New Patent Law.

accustomed to follow international rules formulated by other countries; now, in the field of IPR, for the first time, China has decided to take the initiative in propounding a set of new yet vaguely defined rules. This was a highly significant geopolitical event, for China, as well as for the world at large. Furthermore, by coming down squarely on the side of developing countries, China has, for the first time in a decade, put its cards on the table.

China's main reason for taking such a stance is its own self-interest, not a self-proclaimed leadership responsibility in the developing world. The latter was the case nearly half a century ago in Bandung when the country was in a state of revolutionary euphoria and Zhou Enlai inspired delegates from the Asian and African countries.[35] Today, its motives should be economic rather than political. Nevertheless, it did throw a curveball into the calculations in the United States, European Union, and Japan, who had long been second-guessing where China might stand after entering the WTO. Even if it were politically passive, China's sheer economic weight and market scale are going to give critical mass to the voice of developing countries, previously outgunned by the G-8 nations.

China finds itself accommodated on most occasions where it can act in the role of a bridge between developing countries and developed countries. If this is what the WTO expects to see,[36] it will be a blessing to the international trading community.

What is more important is that the lessons are learned from the Doha Round and beyond, posing both challenges and opportunities to a new member like China. The issue at stake is how to balance compliance and reform, and how to prioritize between adaptation and exploration. While participation invites sophisticated knowledge and skills, China, as the first step, should learn how to assess and calculate its interests and costs. It must not risk miscalculating its interests, and particularly whilst changing

---

[35] The famous Bandung Conference – also known as the Asian-African Conference – was a meeting of Asian and African states, most of which were newly independent, which took place between 18 and 24 April 1955 in Bandung, Indonesia. The conference was organized by Indonesia, Burma, Pakistan, Ceylon (Sri Lanka), and India. The conference's stated aims were to promote Afro-Asian economic and cultural cooperation and to oppose colonialism or neocolonialism. During the conference, the Chinese delegation, headed by Premier Zhou Enlai, diplomatically advocated the principle of seeking common ground while putting aside differences, which not only won the support of an overwhelming number of delegates but also laid the ground for the success of the Conference, which was characterized by the promotion of the national independence movement. See the Ministry of Foreign Affairs website: http://www.fmprc.gov.cn, accessed July 2010.

[36] *People's Daily*, 11 November 2003.

the course of its behavior. For example, a successful conclusion of the Doha Round would imply more responsibilities for China. If the cost of expectations were included in the calculations, it would have been in the interests of China to have had the Doha Round concluded.

14. Practical enforcement of IP in China: suggestions and comments from the Quality Brands Protection Committee (QBPC)

Jack Chang[1]

14.1. THE BACKGROUND AND HISTORY OF THE QBPC

The open policy adopted by China and her switch from a planned economy to a market economy system in 1978 attracted foreign investors from all over the world to set up manufacturing operations and develop businesses. Foreign Invested Enterprises (FIEs) soon realized that in this new world of opportunities, they were facing unprecedented challenges with the counterfeiting of trademarks. Some brand owners set up local brand protection offices in the 1990s, striving for ways to tackle counterfeiting problems, while many brand owners did not have the internal resources but hoped that the Chinese government would help them resolve the problem if they were more proactive with complaints. However, these complaints were often made without enough supporting facts or (even worse) led to negative press for China, where foreign brand owners had made investments.

In early 1998, representatives from British American Tobacco, Coca-Cola, Gillette, Johnson & Johnson, Nike, S.C. Johnson, Unilever and Procter & Gamble started meeting on an ad hoc basis to find ways to effectively fight the counterfeiters. The consensus was that no silver bullets existed and that no one company could fight the battle against

[1] Chairman of the Quality Brands Protection Committee and Senior IP Counsel, GE Asia. The QBPC is a subcommittee of the China Association of Enterprises with Foreign Investment (CAEFI), and represents the interests of foreign multinationals working in China. See the QBPC's website at: http://www.qbpc.org.cn/, accessed July 2010.

the counterfeit industry alone. Brand owners had to engage the Chinese government as a collective group. The first brand-owner-sponsored exchange meeting (known as the Guangdong Action Group) with Chinese law enforcement agencies at national and local levels was organized by Unilever, Mars, and Johnson & Johnson in November 1998 in Guangzhou City, the capital city of Guangdong Province in south China.[2] At this meeting, Chinese officials asked brand owners to be patient, as it took time to improve the legal framework and enforcement. However, foreign brand owners were also running out of patience as their sales revenue and profit margins were being affected by the loss of sales caused by counterfeiting. This first exchange meeting in Guangzhou City (even though lacking in specific deliverables) did lead to second and further meetings between Chinese law enforcement officials and foreign brand owners. The continuous dialog led to a form of understanding, which helped build mutual trust and friendship and that paved the way for effective cooperation between the government and industry. The ad hoc brand owners' gathering became more frequent and the membership continued to grow.

Finally, a business executive from a German brand owner asked whether this type of gathering, even though on an ad hoc basis and well organized, was itself illegal under Chinese law. The participants were reminded that, on the one hand, foreign brand owners were asking the Chinese government to enforce Chinese laws to protect their legitimate interests, but on the other, the foreign brand owners had set up an organization that operated in China without being legally registered. As a result, the foreign brand owners decided to set up a formal coalition and tried to get the coalition registered with the Chinese government. The coalition was named the China Anti-counterfeiting Coalition (CACC). The first issue of the CACC newsletter was issued to members on 12 October 1999 and the CACC, the first industry coalition dedicated to fighting trademark counterfeiting in China, was officially registered in Hong Kong on 24 December 1999, as it could not be registered in mainland China.[3] Even

---

[2] The idea to organize the exchange meeting between the brand owners with relevant department heads of the China Trademark Office of the State Administration for Industry & Commerce, General Administration of Customs, State Technical Supervision Bureau and the newly set up Economic Crime Investigation Department of the Ministry of Public Security came from Ms Linda Wong, A/P Legal Counsel, Unilever.

[3] The name CACC was itself viewed as confrontational. In addition, the coalition set up by foreign brand owners in the early days with the objective of fighting counterfeiting trademarks in mainland China could be viewed as a form

so, it was the first time that foreign brand owners started fighting the counterfeit trade in China in an organized fashion by engaging with Chinese policy makers and law enforcement and providing them with written comments to improve the legal framework and to enhance enforcement. The operation of CACC caught the attention of the former Chinese Ministry of Foreign Trade and Economic Cooperation (MOFTEC) and the China Association of Enterprises with Foreign Investment (CAEFI), which is a highly influential business association closely associated with MOFTEC. Leaders of MOFTEC and CAEFI encouraged the CACC leadership team and members to join CAEFI and offered to help CACC members set up a sub-working committee under CAEFI. After balancing the advantages and disadvantages, CACC leaders and members finally made the decision to join CAEFI. On 5 March 2000, the Quality Brands Protection Committee (QBPC) was officially set up under CAEFI by 28 member companies and was finally registered with both the MOFTEC and the Chinese Ministry of Civil Affairs. With this new platform (in China), which had a positive name and wore the hat of the CAEFI subcommittee, the QBPC was able to interact with Chinese law enforcement agencies on a regular basis and to jointly host IP workshops. Leaders of MOFTEC (later this name changed to the Ministry of Commerce or MOFCOM) and CAEFI not only constantly listened to QBPC briefings on issues and recommended solutions, but also provided guidance to QBPC members on how to engage Chinese government agencies in appropriate ways. QBPC members finally realized that confrontation and complaints would not take them anywhere, but that cooperation based on continuous dialog, mutual understanding, respect and trust would be the most productive way to make positive changes to the IP framework in China.[4]

of 'trouble maker'. Setting up NGOs in China still comes under strict legal restrictions. However, the setting up and development of the QBPC has demonstrated that foreign industry and the Chinese government can work closely hand-in-hand to tackle sensitive issues, as long as the stakeholders can ignore their differences and strive for 'win-win' solutions based on the approach of cooperation.

4 The success of the QBPC could not have been achieved without the contribution of Minister Ma Xiuhong of MOFCOM; Chairman Shi Guangsheng, Executive Vice Chairman Liu Zhiben, Vice Chairman Hu Guocai, former Vice Chairman Liu Wanzhong of CAEFI; Francisco F. Guerra of S.C. Johnson; Daniel Chow, Bill Dobson and John Yam of P&G (QBPC Chairman, 2002); Joe Johnson of Best Food, Unilever (QBPC Chairman, 2000–01), Phil Yang of MeadWestvaco, Patrick Wang of Nike and the APCO team led by Chris Murck.

14.2. THE MOST IMPORTANT QBPC OBJECTIVE: 'STRENGTHENING CRIMINAL ENFORCEMENT ACTIONS'

Initially, under the QBPC, there were five working committees: the Best Practice and Enforcement Committee (BPEC), the Communication Committee (CC), the Government Cooperation Committee (GCC), the Legal Committee (LC) and the Membership Service(s) Committee (MSC). At this early stage, the most important objective of the QBPC was to enhance criminal enforcement against trademark counterfeiters. Fortunately for the QBPC, the Development Research Center (DRC) of the State Council initiated a research project in 1999 with the objective of identifying through an industry survey the economic impact caused by counterfeiting. Four hundred and twenty copies of questionnaires were sent to state-owned enterprises, Chinese private and public companies as well as foreign invested enterprises, including the members of the CACC and later the QBPC via the QBPC's GCC. The geographic span of field investigations carried out by the DRC covered Beijing, Shanghai, Hangzhou, Wenzhou, Guangzhou, Shenzhen and other key cities. One hundred and fifty-two questionnaires with in-depth answers were collected. The survey results showed that the estimated value of counterfeit goods in the Chinese market was about RMB 132.927 billion in 1998, which was close to the estimated total value of goods smuggled into China in 1998 (RMB 154 billion). The estimated value of counterfeit goods was calculated according to the same formula for the calculation of the value of smuggled goods. The actual value of smuggled goods (RMB 154 billion) was ten times the figure of the value of seizures (RMB 15.4 billion), based on the assumption that only 10% of the smuggled goods could have been seized.[5]

The DRC research report immediately caught the attention of the leaders of the State Council. The question was how to effectively crack down on counterfeiting. Confirming the ancient Chinese proverb 'hit the iron when it is still hot', the QBPC immediately submitted a position paper to the State Council analysing the serious damage caused to China's investment environment, to brand owners, and to Chinese consumers. The paper emphasized the importance of effective criminal enforcement and

[5] 'The Report of the Research on Impact on the National Economy Caused by Manufacture and Sale of Counterfeiting Goods' by the Development Research Center of State Council, February 2000 pp. 2–4. The definition of 'counterfeiting goods in the survey' was broad, and might have covered copyright pirated goods and even fake and shoddy quality goods.

provided concrete recommendations on how to improve the legal framework for criminal enforcement. From reliable sources, the QBPC learned that former Premier Zhu Rongji had made a comment requesting the Supreme People's Court (SPC) and the Supreme People's Procuratorate (SPP)[6] to explore the feasibility of issuing a judicial interpretation to strengthen criminal enforcement against counterfeiting. The SPC and SPP invited QBPC members to provide comments on the draft judicial interpretation on 'Several Issues Concerning the Specific Application of Law to Criminal Cases of Producing and/or Selling Fake and/or Inferior Goods' (JI on F&I Goods). Interestingly, the notion of fighting fakes perceived by the general public and law enforcement in those days was related to the fight against fake and bad quality goods. The SPC and SPP were eager to improve the legal framework for fighting fake quality goods in order to better protect consumers. Even though the JI on F&I Goods was not related to fighting counterfeit trademarks, the major breakthrough was that those sellers – who used to argue that possession of a large quality of fake and shoddy quality goods (even with the intention to sell them) was not punishable under Art. 140 of the China Criminal Law,[7] since often no sales record could be found by the police and prosecutor – could finally be prosecuted and convicted for an 'attempted crime' under Art. 140, if the volume of the fake and shoddy quality goods seized had a value three times the sales amount threshold, according to the JI on F&I Goods.[8]

[6] According to Art. 127 of the Constitution Law of the People's Republic of China, the SPC is the highest court that supervises case trials by the courts at various lower levels. The SPC renders judicial interpretations and opinions for guidance to the lower courts. According to Art. 129 of the Constitution Law, the People's Procuratorates at various levels are responsible for supervising the enforcement of law by government agencies and courts. The SPP is the highest procuratorate in China. The SPP, together with the SPC, jointly drafts and issues judicial interpretations related to criminal prosecution and conviction. Both the SPC and SPP are responsible to the National People's Congress (NPC) and the Standing Committee of the NPC. It is said that the NPC has concerns about the SPC and SPP issuing judicial interpretations, as sometimes the judicial interpretations may have overlapped with the territory of the NPC, which is the highest authority and legislative body in China according to Art. 57 and 58 of the China Constitution Law.

[7] Under which a defendant could be sentenced to a fine, jail term or life sentence depending on the amount of proven sales ranging from not less than RMB 50,000 to not less than RMB 2 million.

[8] Art. 140 of China Criminal Law stipulates that 'Any producer or seller, who mixes up or adulterates products, passes fake imitations for genuine, sells seconds at best quality price, or passes unqualified products as qualified ones, with a sale amount of not less than RMB 50,000 and not more than RMB 200,000, is to be

Those QBPC members who participated in the process knew that the new JI on F&I Goods would be coming soon and therefore adjusted their strategy and action plans, which led to more criminal prosecution cases against counterfeiters based on Art. 140 of the Criminal Law and the new JI on F&I Goods (which came into effect on 10 April 2001). The JI on F&S Goods opened another door for brand owners to initiate criminal prosecution against trademark counterfeiters.

However, the JI on F&I Goods could not satisfy QBPC members, as it did not target IP crimes. The QBPC later sponsored some research on criminal IP crimes from the most prestigious academic criminal IP research center in China, the Criminal Law Research Center of Renmin

---

sentenced to not more than two years of fixed-term imprisonment or criminal detention and may in addition or exclusively be sentenced to a fine of not less than 50 percent and not more than 200 percent of the sale amount; when the sale amount is not less than RMB 200,000 and not more than RMB 500,000, is to be sentenced to not less than two years and not more than seven years of fixed-term imprisonment and may in addition be sentenced to a fine of not less than 50 percent and not more than 200 percent of the sale amount; when the sale amount is not less than RMB 500,000 and not more than RMB 2 million, is to be sentenced to not less than seven years and may in addition be sentenced to a fine of not less than 50 percent and not more than 200 percent of the sale amount; when the sale amount is not less than RMB 2 million, is to be sentenced to 15 years of fixed-term imprisonment or life imprisonment and may in addition be sentenced to a fine of not less than 50 percent and not more than 200 percent of the sale amount or confiscation of property.'

Art. 2 of the JI on F&I Goods stipulates that 'the term "sales amount" under Articles 140 and 149 of the Criminal Law means all illegal income received and receivable by a producer and/or seller after the sale of a fake and/or shoddy product.

If the merchandise value of unsold fake and/or shoddy products is not less than three times the sales amount stipulated in Article 140 of the Criminal Law, the perpetrator shall be convicted of and punished for the (attempted) crime of producing and/or selling fake and/or shoddy products. The merchandise value shall be calculated according to the *labeled price* of the illegally produced and/or sold fake and/or shoddy product. If there is no labeled price, the merchandise value shall be calculated according to the *median of the market price for the same type of product that meets relevant standards*. If the merchandise value is difficult to be determined, a *pricing appraisal* institution shall be entrusted with determining such price in accordance with *the Measures for the Administration of the Estimation of the Price of Articles Which Have Been Impounded, Recovered and/or Confiscated* jointly issued by the State Planning Commission, the Supreme People's Court, Supreme People's Procuratorate and the Ministry of Public Security on 22 April 1997. If multiple instances of producing and/or selling fake and/or shoddy goods have been committed but not handled, the sales amount or merchandise value of the fake and/or shoddy products shall be added together.'

(People's) University, which partnered the Second Criminal Tribunal of the SPC, with the aim of determining the feasibility of the SPC releasing a further judicial interpretation on IP crimes. When the QBPC members approached the Second Criminal Tribunal of the SPC to explore the necessity of issuing a judicial interpretation on IP crimes, the answer from the court was that it did not seem to be necessary as only a few cases had been referred from the provincial high courts to the SPC for guidance. The QBPC responded by arguing that there was no clear guidance on what constituted a 'serious case', nor was there guidance on what a 'relatively large sale amount' meant (the thresholds required for the crime of 'constituting trademark counterfeiting' and the crime of 'knowingly selling counterfeit goods respectively').[9] Criminal IP protection had become a question of the 'chicken and the egg', i.e. without being able to prove that the criminal thresholds had been met, the police could not and would not start a criminal investigation. At the same time, it was not possible for the brand owners to collect the required evidence themselves without the police first carrying out a criminal investigation. The Renmin research results showed that IP crimes took place in several Chinese provinces, but as there was no clear guidance on what constituted an IP crime, most of the criminal offences involving IP theft were handled through the administrative enforcement authorities, which 'put out the fire rather than hunting down the arsonists'. Only until the research results were released was the QBPC able to work with the Second Criminal Tribunal and the Research Office of the SPC on reviewing and commenting on the draft judicial interpretation on IP crimes, which was finally issued on 11 November 2004, and became effective on the 22 December 2004.[10]

---

[9] Manufacturing and/or selling counterfeit trademark goods violates the China Trademark Law and is subject to administrative punishment and civil remedies. It becomes a criminal offence, only if the situation of manufacturing counterfeit trademark goods is serious or the sale amount of the counterfeit goods is very large. Art. 213 of the China Criminal Law stipulates that 'Using an identical trademark on the same merchandise without permission of its registered owner shall, if the case is of a serious nature, be punished with imprisonment or criminal detention of less than three years, with a fine, or a separately imposed fine; for cases of a specially serious nature, with imprisonment of over three years and less than seven years, and with a fine'. Article 214 stipulates that 'Knowingly selling merchandise bearing a counterfeit trademark with a relatively large sale amount shall be punished with imprisonment or criminal detention of less than three years, with a fine or a separately imposed fine; in cases involving a huge sale amount, with imprisonment of more than three years but less than seven years, and with a fine'.

[10] The Judicial Interpretation on IP Crimes issued by the SPC and SPP in November 2004 and its English translation are available in the section on Policies, Laws and Regulations on the QBPC website: www.qbpc.org.cn.

14.3. THE SILVER BULLET DOES EXIST – A TRUE STORY OF SUCCESS

In early 1998, one of the Shanghai-based subsidiaries of Johnson & Johnson (J&J), a founding member of the QBPC, which had been enjoying considerable growth for years, spotted a small quantity of branded counterfeit Band-Aid® brand of adhesive bandages in the distribution channels of a few Chinese cities. J&J took the existence of counterfeit products seriously and engaged outside counsels and investigative firms to track down the sources in order to close them down. After several months' difficult work and significant investment in hiring outside firms, J&J obtained several reports on administrative raid actions, reporting a couple of large quality seizures of counterfeit goods, and resulting in a significant drop in the sales of the original goods. By late 1999, the J&J subsidiary in Shanghai had lost 70% of its sales and the production shifts were cut from 21 batches to five batches per week, leading eventually to production being completely shut down.

Some distributors challenged J&J by saying that if J&J could not quickly stop the counterfeiting, they would be forced to stop distributing the Band-Aid® brand of wound care products as they were making no profits competing against the counterfeiters. The J&J management was frustrated by China's lack of effective IP enforcement. Also there was tension between the management of the J&J subsidiary and its employees, who expected to be laid off if the subsidiary could not survive. Instead of giving up, however, J&J changed its strategy from depending on outside resources to setting up an internal brand protection team with dedicated manpower, a centralized budget and cross-functional resources.[11] Business leaders and supporting function department heads at the headquarters in New Brunswick, New Jersey, US and in Shanghai, China, including the corporate legal department, security, government affairs, public relations, quality assurance, the local sales force, and the newly set up China brand protection team, started bi-weekly conference calls to set objectives, to adjust tactics, and to monitor progress. Most importantly, the internal infrastructure, such as a computerized informant database and government contacts database, as well as the standard operating procedures of receiving and rewarding informants; analysing and processing intelligence; implementing safety guidelines, and training on how to initiate administrative enforcement and criminal prosecution, together with a compliance

---

11 The author was an Assistant General Counsel for J&J based in Shanghai and the J&J China brand protection team leader.

checking system, were gradually put in place. J&J's work to set up internal brand protection system and the effective criminal investigation cases completed by the Chinese police finally uncovered a counterfeit training group, which directly provided technology, production facilities and indirectly provided counterfeit packaging and raw materials to over 100 counterfeiters operating manufacturing sites across 17 provinces and two municipalities in China. In May 2000, J&J wrote a report to the Chinese State Council. The report was entitled 'Why China cannot stop counterfeiting; the counterfeiting trend and J&J's recommended actions' and was substantiated with statistics, case studies, photos taken during the enforcement action and other supporting evidence. No outside resources, law firms, or government relation consultants were engaged: the analysis and report were completed by J&J's in-house teams. No one knew what would happen. However, it took only five days for a response from former Vice Premier Wu Bangguo,[12] who gave instructions to the National Anti-counterfeiting Office, which was set up under the Chinese State Technical Supervision Bureau (STSB).[13] The STSB immediately initiated the 17 province and two municipality anti-counterfeiting Band-Aid® brand of wound care products campaign. In several key provinces and Shanghai City, the local Technical Supervision Bureau (TSB) and economic crime police set up a joint taskforce to track down the counterfeit ringleaders. Within a month after initiating the campaign, the sales of the J&J subsidiary increased 100% from the previously recorded lowest month. The subsidiary finally recovered completely in the next few months and expanded its China operation years later.

This success story has been widely discussed in both the public and private sectors in and outside of China. The most commonly asked questions were how did J&J turn this around? How did J&J manage to obtain the support of the Chinese national leader to help J&J, a US multinational, fight the counterfeit battle?

14.3.1. Counterfeit Threat is a Business Issue Rather Than simply a Legal Issue

To fight the battle, internal cross-functional resources must be mobilized and coordinated by business leaders

[12] At the time of writing, Mr Wu Bangguo is the current Chairman of the Standing Committee of China's National People's Congress.

[13] STSB is now called the General Administration of Quality Supervision, Inspection and Quarantine (QSIQ).

Many brand owners view the counterfeit threat as a legal issue and leave this problem to their lawyers, brand protection team and/or security. However, counterfeiters must be treated as the most dangerous and illegal competitors, as they use the same brand and packaging design that the brand owner uses; the greater the advertisement and promotion budget that the brand owner spends to support their brands, the more incentives for the counterfeiters to counterfeit the product, and as discussed above, counterfeiting may end up killing the brand and if the cancer is not cut out immediately, it will grow fast. In the competition against legitimate competitors in the market, brand owners have dedicated manpower and budgets for their marketing, sales, R&D, and business development departments etc. But when 'competing' against the most dangerous and illegal of 'competitors', brand owners normally have very limited resources and hope that their lawyers and brand protection teams will leverage government resources to stop the counterfeiting. This mindset cannot help brand owners win the battle and often complaints based on frustration damage the brand owners' relationship with the government. J&J's mobilizing of internal resources from business to supporting functions with dedicated manpower and funding, as well as effective standard operating procedures and database construction, not only saved its wound care business in China, which had suffered badly from counterfeiting and was close to the point of being shut down, but also built its brand protection team as one of the most effective and respected brand protection teams in China.

14.3.2. Recognizing and Promoting a Sense of Honor in Chinese Law Enforcement

Before the J&J campaign mentioned above was initiated, a drug administration officer and an economic crime police captain from Xin Jian County, Nangchang City of Jiangxi Province, were investigating a counterfeit ring Band-Aid® brand of wound care product. After several ringleaders were arrested by the county police, the counterfeit gang offered the police unit a bribe of half a million RMB. The offer was rejected. The counterfeit gang later increased the amount to RMB 1.2 million. Their attorneys suggested that the police accept the money as a legitimate bond to bail the ringleaders out. Knowing that the large number of counterfeiters throughout China trained by these ringleaders had tremendous resources and were well connected, instead of complaining about the problems of corruption and local protection perceived by quite a number of foreign brand owners, J&J managed to request a US Senator from New Jersey to write an appreciation letter to former Ambassador Li Zhaoxing of the Chinese Embassy in Washington, DC, commending the Chinese police for enforcing Chinese laws to protect J&J's legitimate interests. The letter proved of great value in terms of recognizing and promoting Chinese law enforcement's 'sense of honor'. Consequently, the county police and drug administration units did not yield to the ringleaders' corruption, despite all kinds of temptation and pressure and they finally obtained full support from the Public Order Department of the Ministry of Public Security and the provincial police to conduct an in-depth criminal investigation. The investigation findings of this single case, together with the intelligence gathered by the J&J internal team, finally unraveled the whole counterfeit network in China.

14.3.3. Firefighting; arsonist hunting and fire prevention are equally important

The Chinese intellectual property enforcement system can be largely classified as a combination of administrative enforcement and judicial enforcement. Administrative enforcement agencies include (in general) the following agencies:

- Administration for Industry and Commerce (AIC), which is responsible for enforcing the Trademark Law; Anti-unfair Competition Law; Consumer Interests Protection Law; Advertising Law and until recently the Anti-monopoly Law;[14]
- Quality Supervision Bureau, which is responsible for enforcing the Product Quality Law;[15]
- Copyright Administration, which is responsible for enforcing the Copyright Law;[16]

---

[14] The Trademark Law of China was promulgated by the Standing Committee of the National People's Congress (SCNPC) on 23 August 1982, effective 1 March 1983. It was amended for the first time in 1993 and then amended in 2001 for the second time. At the time of writing, it is currently going through its third amendment (see Chapter 3). The Anti-unfair Competition Law was passed by the SCNPC on 2 September 1993, effective 1 December 1993 and is also in the process of being revised (see Chapters 5 and 6). The Consumer Interests Protection Law was promulgated on 31 October 1993, effective 1 January 1994. It is also being revised. The Advertising Law was promulgated on 27 October 1994, effective 1 February 1995. The Anti-monopoly Law was promulgated on 30 August 2007, effective 1 August 2008 (see Chapters 11 and 12).

[15] The Product Quality Law was promulgated on 22 February 1993, effective 1 September 1993. It was amended in 2000. The amended Product Quality Law took effect on 1 September 2000.

[16] The Copyright Law was promulgated on 7 September 1990, effective 1 June 1991. It was amended in October 2001, and recently amended in 2009, becoming effective April 2010 (see Chapter 4).

- Intellectual Property Office, which is responsible for enforcing the Patent Law;[17] and
- Food and Drug Administration, which is responsible for enforcing the Drug Administration Law.[18]

Traditionally, brand owners depend on administrative agencies to conduct administration enforcement actions rather trying hard to pursue criminal judicial enforcement. The benefit of administrative enforcement lies in conducting timely enforcement raids and also in cost-effectiveness. For example, it takes only hours for a local Administration for Industry and Commerce (AIC) to organize and initiate a raid after receiving complaints from brand owners, if this particular agency accepts the brand owner's complaint and has manpower ready. No search warrant is needed for administrative raids. However, neither the AIC nor other administrative agencies are legally allowed to break into locked civilian premises, except that the police may search the residences of the suspects or of those whose residences may be used by the suspects as hideouts, or may conceal the evidence of a crime.[19] As a result, it is common for counterfeiters to simply lock the door and ignore the administrative enforcement officials waiting outside. The disadvantage of administrative enforcement is that it only seizes the counterfeit and infringing goods and leads to a later fine, which in many cases is difficult to enforce.[20] According to Chinese Criminal Procedure law, only the police may detain criminal suspects.[21] Administrative agencies such as the AIC, Quality Supervision,

---

[17] The China Patent Law was promulgated on 12 March 1984, effective 1 April 1985. The Patent Law was amended in September 1992, August 2000 and December 2008 respectively. The current Patent Law took effect on 1 October 2009 (see Chapter 2).

[18] The Drug Administration Law was promulgated on 20 September 1984, effective 1 July 1985. The Drug Administration Law was amended in February 2001, effective 1 December 2001.

[19] Art. 109–13 of the Criminal Procedure Law of China.

[20] Counterfeit manufacturing operations are commonly conducted at so-called 'underground plants', which have no licenses or registrations whatsoever. Often, the administrative enforcement agencies can hardly identify the ringleaders, who are the 'hands behind the operation', invisible to the administrative agencies, as the agencies have no criminal investigation skills or authority to track down these invisible hands. Even if the administrative agencies could do so in some cases, the counterfeiters simply ignore any administrative fines, as no fixed assets owned by the counterfeiters can be found by the agencies for enforcing the administrative fine. This is particularly problematic, when the counterfeiters are not locals.

[21] Articles 61, 64–65 and 69 of the China Criminal Procedure Law apply to the police detention of criminal suspects.

Copyright Administration and Drug Administration have no authority to detain suspects or to interrogate them. Accordingly, the administrative enforcement serves only the function of 'fire fighting', meaning temporarily shutting down the counterfeit operation. However, an effective police investigation, as proven by the above-mentioned J&J case and in many other cases, may hunt down those who start the fire, who create and run the supply chain of counterfeit goods, and put these 'invisible hands' operating the counterfeiting network in custody to face criminal charges. There have been debates on how far criminal IP protection in China should go and how many prisons need to be built, if foreign brand owners wish to put all the counterfeiters in jail. In fact, an effective police investigation is the key to finding the counterfeit network. By tracking down and putting the true ringleaders in jail, the whole counterfeit supply chain collapses. Getting the 'big fish' is the key.[22] Through the practice of filing complaints to the administrative agencies to initiate administrative enforcement, the brand owners' in-house brand protection teams gradually learn how to pick up information available during field operations and how to turn this information into valuable intelligence. Building up an intelligence database through participation in administrative enforcement action helps sharpen the skills of brand owners' in-house teams, which finally enables them to identify and lock on targets, as well as to work with the police to initiate criminal enforcement actions. The more administrative and criminal cases the brand owners work on, the more skillful they become in using the unique Chinese administrative and judicial intellectual property enforcement systems. Only when brand owners' in-house teams go through this process of training and enforcement, together with internal infrastructure, database and standard operating procedures being established, can the brand protection teams deliver valuable enforcement results, but also identify loopholes in their own companies' business processes from sourcing raw and packaging materials to selling products to end users. These lessons have taught QBPC members how to effectively combat the trade in counterfeit goods. The lessons prove that fire fighting (traditional administrative enforcement); arsonist hunting (effective criminal investigation) and fire prevention (fixing business process loopholes) are equally important.

---

22 Industry should emphasize that the objective of strengthening the effectiveness of police investigation at an early stage is to track down the ringleaders and their money chains in order to destroy their networks of operation. The objective is not to penalize heavily the migrant workers, who often work under poor conditions for the counterfeiters in order to scrape a living, but to target the network ringleaders.

14.3.4. Never Give Up: Constructive Recommendations get Chinese Top Leaders' Attention

Most brand owners, after discovering many of the difficulties illustrated above, and learning of the counterfeit network covering 17 provinces and two municipalities, would probably be too frustrated to remain confident of the Chinese government's political will and ability to crack down on such large networks in such a wide geographic area, let alone the counterfeiters throughout China who have already learned of the arrest of ringleaders and who would conceal their operations. Under the circumstances, initiating effective enforcement raids in all these provinces and municipalities to bring down the whole counterfeiting network seemed an impossible mission. J&J decided to send a report to the State Council. The report contained only facts: solid evidence and input based on in-depth analysis and constructive recommendation on actions, which not only attracted former Vice Premier Wu Bangguo's attention, but also triggered the large-scale enforcement campaign that eventually saved the J&J subsidiary. When former Vice Premier Wu received a J&J delegation led by former company Chairman, Mr Ralph Larsen, in October 2000, Mr Wu was glad to hear that his instructions had led to a successful enforcement action, which saved the J&J wound care business in China and many jobs. Through the action and the conversation with Mr Wu, J&J was convinced that Chinese leaders were truly serious about fighting trademark counterfeiting. The question was how to build on this success story and create a more universal mechanism for industry and the Chinese government to engage in constructive dialog to find a more permanent solution to tackling the trade in counterfeit goods.

14.4. THE ACHIEVEMENTS OF THE QBPC AND THE KEY FACTORS BOOSTING THE DEVELOPMENT OF QBPC

14.4.1. QBPC Ten-best-case Award

Local protection has been identified by both the Chinese central government and industry as one of the key obstacles in the effective fight against counterfeiting trademark and copyright piracy. The term has been commonly interpreted, by those who do not have on-the-ground enforcement experience, as protection for the counterfeiters and pirates by local government. In fact, QBPC members have not had hard evidence to prove that the Chinese local government protects counterfeiters or pirates. The situation in fact is that during a raid on a counterfeit goods manufacturing site, ringleaders are normally not on the spot, so the law enforcement agency apprehends only the workers and finished goods (as discussed above). The administrative enforcement agencies do not have the authority to detain the workers after the initial interview report has been completed. The workers will often never disclose the identity of their ringleaders, as they may often return to their jobs after their ringleaders have restarted the counterfeit operation, so long as they keep silent. With the lucrative profits ringleaders make from the counterfeiting business, they are able to mobilize their local networks to access specific law enforcers with the aim of removing the threat of legal action (often through bribery, personal relationships or even physical threat). In other words, local protection is more on a case-by-case basis and provided by individual officials rather than by local government's action, except for certain counties that have the reputation of being hot spots for manufacturing counterfeiting pharmaceuticals, auto parts, consumer goods and tobaccos, where local protection is provided in a more systematic fashion. But this is very likely attributed to a relatively large number of corrupt officials, which should not be characterized as local protection provided through local government. In October 2001, at one of the QBPC regular meetings, a member who had suffered seriously from local protection, where some local officials either failed to enforce the IP laws or even protected local counterfeiters, proposed the idea of compiling a blacklist of those notorious cities where local protection was often provided for counterfeiters and pirates. When asked how the QBPC were going to use the 'blacklist', the answer silenced the group. One comment made was that 'QBPC was set up only last year, if we come up with this blacklist and give it to the international media, we could be shut down next year'. In fact, QBPC members do conduct successful cases, which not only proves that Chinese law enforcement agencies aggressively protect QBPC members' trademarks but also demonstrates the integrity of those law enforcement officials who refuse to take bribes and resist pressure from counterfeiters (as evidenced in the J&J case discussed above). 'Why don't we come up with a transparent process and standard to select 10 model anti-counterfeit cases each year and invite the winning agencies to the QBPC anniversary in Beijing to recognize the agencies' achievements by inviting ministry level officials to grant awards to the winning agencies?'[23] The proposal was unanimously accepted by the QBPC leadership and was fully supported by CAEFI and the MOFTEC.

[23] The author was the QBPC Legal Committee Chairman, who made the proposal to initiate the QBPC ten-best-case award ceremony in October 2001.

The first QBPC ten-best-case award ceremony was conducted in March 2002, the first anniversary of the QBPC. Assistant Minister Madam Ma Xiuhong of MOFTEC attended the QBPC anniversary and presented the awards to the winning agencies. There were only seven winning cases. Several agencies that members approached were not interested in competing for this honor, as given their status as government agencies, these agencies felt uncomfortable receiving recognition from an industry group of foreign brand owners. The agencies realized thereafter that they were wrong in thinking this, as the honor had been recognized by (higher) central level government agencies. The QBPC quickly realized that good programs need good marketing. The whole process of the ceremony including Assistant Minister Ma's encouraging speech on the successful collaboration between the Chinese law enforcement agencies and the QBPC was widely reported by the Chinese press and was video-recorded and saved to DVD discs as evidence showing that the agencies' achievements in protecting the trademarks of foreign brand owners were recognized (at ministerial level) by both MOFTEC and the QBPC. The QBPC encouraged the winning agencies to share the discs with the Foreign Trade and Economic Cooperation Commissions of their cities and counties. The value of the QBPC ten-best-case award was further maximized, after the local city and county governments leveraged the MOFTEC and QBPC recognition when introducing the investment environment of their cities and counties to potential foreign investors. There was real competition in the selection process for the winning cases for the second QBPC ten-best-case award in 2003. The QBPC had now opened the competition to cases of criminal enforcement; border protection; trademark infringement and other types of intellectual property infringement cases. The ten-best-cases award has continued to grow more competitive each year. It is now a well-known brand of the QBPC! Not only does this recognition drive law enforcement to improve the protection of the IP of QBPC members, but the lessons learned from each individual successful case is shared among members, which helps other members to replicate the same models for success in other jurisdictions, and enables the QBPC to provide valuable and constructive proposals on how to further improve the legal framework and enforcement. This approach has helped to differentiate the QBPC from being characterized as a 'pressure group' and to be recognized more as a think tank and partner to the Chinese government, and its law enforcement agencies.

Among the winning cases in 2008–09, the following cases deserve special mention:

- The criminal case involving counterfeit car parts nominated by Honeywell International Inc. 92,800 pieces of counterfeit car parts bearing trademarks owned by ten different auto companies were seized by Xiapu County Administration for Industry and Commerce (AIC) based on Honeywell's complaint. The case was almost closed as an administrative violation until the QBPC sent reports to Fujian provincial government and the Supreme People's Procuratorate for help.[24] Xiapu County Procuratorate stepped in and assessed the value of the seized counterfeiting goods based on the price of genuine goods, which was in line with the formula stipulated in the Judicial Interpretation on IP Crimes released by the Supreme People's Court and the Supreme People's Procuratorate in 2004.[25] As a result, the counterfeiters were finally indicted and convicted.

- The criminal case involving a retailer selling pirated DVDs in Beijing, nominated by Time Warner and NBC Universal. This case was the first case in Beijing, where the pirated audio-visual products retailer was convicted under the crime of 'copyright piracy' and sentenced to jail for one year.[26]
- The criminal case involving the sale of pirated software handled by the economic crime police and procuratorate, of Pudong District, Shanghai, nominated by Microsoft. This case was the first criminal case convicting Microsoft's authorized distributor, who sold both

---

[24] The Investigation Supervision Department (ISD) of the Procuratorate has the authority to guide and supervise the police investigation. If the police fail to start a criminal investigation of an IP crime (after the AIC has transferred the case to the police), the ISD of Procuratorate may step in to instruct the police to start the investigation. The Department of Dereliction of Duty Investigation of Procuratorate may investigate on the administrative agencies' refusal to transfer an obvious criminal case to the police for investigation. The ISD of the Supreme People's Procuratorate has been very supportive of the QBPC.

[25] Id., note 6.

[26] A Mr Zhou operated The Beijing Wuzhou Friendship Audio-visual Center located inside the Friendship supermarket in the downtown area of Chaoyang District, Beijing. The Center had previously been reported for selling pirated DVDs. In October 2007, a complaint was filed by the copyright owners to Chaoyang District police. The police, through an initial investigation, identified Mr Zhou as the responsible person. After the Motion Picture Association and the Beijing Copyright Administration reached a consensus on how to conduct the copyright verification, the police raided the Center on 15 December 2007, seized 10,934 copies of pirated or illegally published DVDs and arrested Mr Zhou. Among the seized DVDs, 849 copies of DVDs were pirated movies infringing the copyright of Universal and Warner Brothers etc. Mr Zhou was indicted by Chaoyang District Procuratorate on 19 February 2008 and convicted by Chaoyang District Court of committing the crime of copyright infringement.

legitimate and pirated copies of software by changing the number of copies sold to an end user in the license agreement.[27]

- The administrative border IP protection case handled by the US Customs and Border Protection (CBP) and General Administration of Customs of China (GACC) nominated by Nike International Ltd. In July 2008, GACC received an informant report that 17 containers carrying counterfeit Nike shoes were heading to the US. After a quick investigation, which showed that the containers were already on the high seas, GACC immediately informed the CBP and the two agencies worked together to monitor the ship carrying these containers. CBP finally seized 133,408 pairs of counterfeit Nike and several other brands of shoes, valued at US$4,348,080. In addition, four additional containers containing 30,685 items of luxury French brands of handbags, valued at US$458,023 were also seized based on the intelligence shared by the GACC. This case demonstrated the close cooperation between the CBP and GACC.

As to trade secret protection, the winning case in 2007–08 nominated by General Electric was a model case demonstrating China's unique system of administrative and judicial protection. A former service engineer, after leaving the company, set up his own company to provide training courses for fees by using GE trade secrets, including an equipment maintenance manual. Hangzhou AIC accepted the complaint filed by GE and immediately conducted a raid to seize the infringer's laptop, which revealed critical evidence. A notary public was brought in to notarize the critical evidence seized, and this helped to have the evidence seized during the administrative enforcement proceeding later admitted through a quick process to the civil court. Xian Intermediate Court quickly issued a court order to freeze the bank accounts of the infringer and rendered a decision favorable to the brand owner by ordering the infringer to compensate GE.

---

[27] During the period July to August 2007, a Shanghai-based company purchased copies of certain Microsoft computer software worth over RMB 420,000 (US$60,000 approx.) through Microsoft's authorized dealer. The company was not aware that some of the software it purchased were pirated copies until it tried to upgrade the software by verifying the authorization records via the Microsoft website and reported the matter to Microsoft. In October, Microsoft reported the case to Pudong District police, Shanghai. The police immediately conducted an investigation and arrested the suspects and froze their illegal gains to the tune of RMB 290,000 (US$41,000 approx.). Pudong District Procuratorate indicted the two defendants and the Pudong District Court rendered the decision on 14 July 2008, convicting the defendants.

At the time of writing, the '2009–10' ten-best cases have been selected. The top five criminal cases are:

(1) The first case, *Min Yue No. 1*, relates to counterfeit tobacco, which was jointly nominated by British American Tobacco and Philip Morris. The case involves foreign buyers placing orders with Chinese manufacturers for counterfeit tobacco. The Chinese manufacturers had been supplying different brands of counterfeit tobacco since April 2005. During the period from February to June 2008, the total value of counterfeit tobacco exported to countries in Europe, Africa and the Middle East was around RMB 150 million. The case also involved the crime of production and sale of fake and shoddy quality goods due to the poor quality of the counterfeit tobacco. Two primary defendants were sentenced to 15 years in jail without probation, while other defendants were sentenced to between one and half to thirteen years without probation.
(2) The second case, *A Gang in Foshan Manufacturing and Distributing Counterfeit HP Packing Materials*, involved counterfeit packaging and trademark labeling materials for printing consumable goods, which was nominated by HP. More than 600,000 items of counterfeit packaging and labeling materials, as well as product specifications, were seized. Five defendants were sentenced to five, four and three years respectively without probation plus fines ranging from RMB 100 to 1 million respectively.
(3) The third case, the *Tomato Garden* case, involved copyright infringement, which was nominated by Microsoft. The defendants, who run a well-known website, provided pirated Microsoft software on their website for the public to download free of charge, while it made significant profits from the advertisement fees paid by those who placed advertisements on its website. Two defendants were sentenced to three and a half years without probation plus a fine (RMB 1 million) and two years without probation plus a fine (RMB 100,000) respectively. This was probably the first criminal case in China involving the illegal downloading of pirated software.
(4) The fourth case, *Wu & Lou Manufacturing and Selling Fake Band-Aid Benzalkonium Chloride Patches in Chengdu, Sichuan Province*, involved a counterfeit Band-Aid® brand of adhesive bandages, which was nominated by Johnson & Johnson. The counterfeiter and supplier of the production machine and raw materials were sentenced to one and a half years without probation plus a fine of RMB 180,000 and one year without probation plus a fine of RMB 180,000, respectively.

(5) The fifth case, *Zhejiang Dongyang Fujia Auto Glass Factory aka WU Fuping, JI Jianjun, LIU Jiayong*, involved counterfeit auto windshield glass, which was jointly nominated by Toyota, BMW, Daimler, Ford, General Motor, Nissan, PSA Peugeot Citroen and Volkswagen AG. The police tracked down and arrested the ring-leader before over a hundred police officers and officials of the Administration for Industry and Commerce raided the target plant. The raid uncovered 7,600 items of counterfeit auto windshield glass bearing more than 20 well-known foreign and domestic Chinese brands. The three ringleaders were sentenced to three and a half years without probation and one and a half years without probation, respectively.

14.4.2. Criminal enforcement: Strong partnership between the QBPC and the Chinese police, the Economic Crime Investigation Department (ECID) of the Ministry of Public Security (MPS)

The QBPC partnership with the Chinese police, particularly the ECID/MPS, is another well-known brand of the QBPC. The ECID was spun off from the Criminal Investigation Department of the MPS in 1998, after the Chinese Criminal Law and Criminal Procedure Law were revised in 1996. According to MPS procedures, the ECID is in charge of (among many other economic crimes) investigating the Counterfeiting Trademark Crimes (Art. 213–15 of China Criminal Law), Counterfeit Patent Crime (Art. 216) and Trade Secret Theft Crime (Art. 219). The Public Order Department (also referred as the 'Social Order Department' or 'SOD'), in addition to many other public order-related crimes, is in charge of investigations into Copyright Piracy Crime (Art. 217 and 218) and Fake and Shoddy Quality Goods Crimes (Art. 140–48).[28] As mentioned above, over ten years ago, the notion of 'fighting fakes' was related to 'fighting fake and shoddy quality goods'. Moreover, the industry – particularly foreign brand owners – was not familiar with the newly set up ECID at national and local levels. As a result, in 1998 the CACC, and later the QBPC, started approaching the SOD of the MPS, seeking support to fight counterfeiting trademark crimes via the route of fighting 'fake and shoddy quality goods'. The SOD/MPS support was very encouraging and the first QBPC criminal enforcement workshop hosted by the SOD/MPS and sponsored by the QBPC was conducted in January 2001 in Shenzhen City,

---

[28] See the revised China Criminal Law, promulgated 17 March, effective 1 October 1997.

Guangdong Province in south China, the frontier of China's journey to open policy. However, a long-term partnership and systematic approach to conduct cooperation programs with SOD/MPS had not yet been established.

In late 2001, Deputy Director General Gao Feng of ECID/MPS approached the QBPC. Mr Gao was concerned about intellectual property crimes threatening China's national economic security and therefore proposed to work with the QBPC to co-organize a workshop for both the ECID officials at provincial and city levels as well as for QBPC members. The objectives were to generate awareness by ECID officers of the importance of dealing with intellectual property crimes, and at the same time, helping QBPC members better understand the legal framework and practices of criminal intellectual property enforcement. Mr Gao's vision was highly commended and his proposal was fully supported by the QBPC. The first workshop was conducted in April 2002 in Qingdao City, Shandong Province, with the objective of generating awareness of ECID officers and to familiarize QBPC members with the Chinese legal framework and practice. In December 2002, the second meeting between ECID/MPS and QBPC was conducted in Sanya City, Hainan Province. A declaration to urge the participating ECID officers to put fighting intellectual property crimes on their priority list was passed at the meeting. A third meeting was held in Shantou City, Guangdong Province in August 2003, which was co-hosted by the ECID/MPS and the Inspection Supervision Department of the Supreme People's Procuratorate. The objective was to build up ECID officers' capacity. Selective provincial ECID heads were given assignments to research on issues, such as the trend in counterfeiting trademark and copyright piracy, jurisdiction, burden of proof, admissibility of evidence, investigation skills etc. The provincial ECID heads reported their findings at the third ECID/QBPC criminal enforcement meeting. Thereafter, based on the case studies related to and QBPC reports on cross-border trade of counterfeiting goods, the ECID/MPS decided to initiate a one-year nationwide operation called 'Operation Mountain Eagle' focused on cross-border trade of counterfeiting goods conducted by foreign traders, who collected samples of newly launched and/or best-selling goods either for consumer or industrial use from overseas markets and brought them to China looking for original equipment manufacturers (OEM) to manufacture the counterfeiting goods for export to the foreign traders' designated markets. In November 2004, the fourth gathering of ECID from national and local levels and QBPC members was held in Nanning City, Guangxi Province, with the objective of preparing for Operation Mountain Eagle, initiated immediately after the fourth meeting. Given the success of the operation (from November 2004 to

December 2005), Phase 2 of Operation Mountain Eagle was conducted from March to December 2006. According to MPS statistics, the Phase 1 operation successfully investigated 3,149 counterfeit cases and arrested 5,981 suspects, while the Phase 2 operation successfully investigated 3,775 intellectual property crime cases and arrested 5,698 suspects. The result of the QBPC annual anonymous membership survey conducted in 2006 indicated (for the first time) a positive improvement in counterfeiting and piracy problems in China.

Based on the lessons learned, the ECID/MPS and QBPC recognized that counterfeiting and piracy had become an international problem. To better deal with this problem, the ECID/MPS and QBPC decided to work together to organize the fifth program as an international forum. From 31 March to 1 April 2006, the international program was conducted in Shanghai. The host was elevated from the ECID to the MPS. Representatives from Interpol, law enforcement representatives from the US, Germany, France, Canada, Australia and Japan attended and spoke at the forum. Representatives from QBPC members and influential Chinese domestic companies spoke and exchanged views on counterfeiting and piracy. It was probably the first time that the voice of Chinese companies concerned about counterfeiting and piracy had been heard at a forum having international participants. Furthermore, an important document called the 'Shanghai Initiative' was passed at the forum advocating and urging Chinese police to start investigations based on suspicious leads (probable cause) rather than being restricted by amount/volume thresholds.[29] It had for years been the practice in China that the police initiated raid actions based on their intelligence or brand owners' complaints without officially initiating investigations to identify who the ringleaders were and where the money was coming from, or where the money was going. After the raid action, the second step was to evaluate the value of seized items to ascertain whether the extent of the illegal operation met the criminal thresholds. Finally, the official investigation started, if the thresholds were met. Such practices created a large obstacle to timely and effective investigation into counterfeiting and piracy rings. After the Shanghai Initiative was passed, a few local-level ECID units

---

[29] Counterfeiting trademark, patent, copyright piracy and trade secret theft, under Chinese Criminal Law, do not necessarily constitute criminal offences unless the situation is serious (depending on the amount of illegal products) or the sale amount is relatively large in value or causes serious economic damage. For example, in order to constitute a counterfeiting trademark crime under Art. 213 of the China Criminal Law, the prior sale amount and/or value of counterfeiting goods seized must be RMB 50,000 (US$7,300 approx.) or above.

started testing the new approach, i.e. starting investigations based on suspicious leads; researching the 'invisible hands' behind the operation, and then initiating raids and arresting the targeted ringleaders simultaneously. Unfortunately, however, this new approach has not been consistently adopted by the ECID at a local level. The sixth and seventh MPS/QBPC forums of criminal enforcement were conducted in June 2007 in Shenzhen City, Guangdong Province, and in April 2008, in Shanghai, respectively to further boost international collaboration. Due to the partnership built between the ECID/MPS and the QBPC, Shanghai and Sichuan Provincial ECIDs signed cooperation MOUs with the QBPC in July 2005 and November 2008, respectively, to cascade down the partnership to a local level. As a result, the ECID/MPS and the local ECID police have become the 'cornerstones' of China's criminal protection for intellectual property and have won most of the QBPC ten-best-case awards in the past eight years. Mr John Newton, IPR Program Manager of Interpol, commended the Chinese police at the QBPC eighth anniversary on 28 March 2008, saying that 'The winners of the best criminal cases awards are an example of what can be achieved in a difficult and challenging operational environment to IP crime investigators in other parts of the world. Each of the winning cases exemplifies the commitment of the Chinese police authorities and a determination to make a meaningful contribution to collective efforts to combat transnational organized crime.'[30]

Through these cooperation programs and many exchange meetings in the past eight years, the ECID at national and local levels has become one of QBPC's strongest partners. The relationship has been built on professionalism, mutual understanding, respect, trust and both parties' commitment to seek a 'win-win' solution.[31]

---

[30] The remarks of Mr John Newton, IPR Program Manager of Interpol, made at the QBPC's eighth anniversary are available at QBPC's Activities section of www.qbpc.org.cn, accessed July 2010.

[31] In addition to Deputy Director General Gao Feng of ECID/MPS, former Director General Hu Anfu of ECID/MPS, Deputy Director general level inspector Che Yaohua, former Director Li Jinfa, Wu Weihua, Zhao Bin, Cao Yingping, Li Ziyong of the Ninth Division (now called IP Division) of ECID/MPS and Director Wang Zhiguang of IP Division of ECID/MPS jointly contributed to the great partnership between ECID/MPS and QBPC. Director General Meng Qingfa of ECID/MPS is also a strong advocate of intellectual property protection and supporter of the QBPC. ECID was identified by the QBPC anonymous membership survey in 2007 and 2008 as the most effective criminal enforcement agency. In addition, in 2007, the ECID/MPS won a highly commended award as a government agency granted by the Global Anti-counterfeiting Group (www.gacg.org).

14.4.3. Strengthening border intellectual property protection: setting up the Customs Committee in 2001

Transformation of China's economy has created opportunities for China to emerge as the world's factory in the past 20 years. Unfortunately, IP infringement is a by-product arising from the rapid expansion of China's manufacturing industry. In view of the massive volumes of exports from China, both the Chinese government and IPR owners have to think across borders in tackling the challenges. In 1995, the General Administration of Customs of China (GACC) set up the Intellectual Property Division under the Policy and Law Department, with dedicated personnel, expertise and authority in cross-border intellectual property enforcement. Having witnessed the increasing problems of cross-border trade in counterfeit and pirated goods, the QBPC set up the Customs Committee in 2001 to build a partnership with the GACC and to educate members on how to utilize the Chinese border intellectual property protection system, such as online recording of intellectual property, particularly trademarks and applying for general bonds to avoid the trouble of posting bonds within three working days on a case-by-case basis, whenever there was a Customs seizure of infringing goods, and to promote international collaboration between Customs.[32]

With the support of the GACC, local Customs has been interacting with QBPC members and other foreign intellectual property owners to maximize synergies between the private sector and Chinese Customs. In particular, hundreds of training seminars have been organized by local

---

[32] In order to balance the needs for speedy Customs clearance to facilitate international trade and effective border IP protection, Chinese Customs requires the brand owners to post a monetary bond with Customs, which spots suspicious infringing goods. The bond is used to cover the damage suffered by the importer or exporter, request seizure and to cover the warehousing, storage and disposal fees. See Art. 14, 15 and 16 of Customs IP Protection Regulation 1995. The State Council has revised the regulation with effect from 1 April 2010. Art. 11 has been revised and now reads: 'In case of any change to the registration of an intellectual property right, the right holder shall go through a registration alteration or cancellation process at the General Administration of Customs'. Art. 23 (11) has also been revised as 'After applying to the Customs for protection, the right holder may, in accordance with the provisions in the Trademark Law, the Copyright Law, the Patent Law or other relevant laws, apply to the people's court for the stopping of the infringement act or taking property preservation measures with respect to the goods being detained for alleged infringement'. A new subsection 5 has been included within Art. 24: 'Where, before Customs confirms that the alleged infringement goods being detained are infringement goods, the right holder withdraws the application for detaining the alleged infringement goods'.

Customs in the past five to six years which have helped to enhance: (i) Customs officials' awareness and understanding of the corporate culture of QBPC members and the key enforcement concerns of members; (ii) QBPC members' understanding of Customs' practices and needs in relation to risk analysis, inspection and seizure of infringing goods across borders, which has over time, facilitated capacity building of border enforcement of both Customs and QBPC members. In order to strengthen communications with the QBPC, annually the GACC has invited QBPC members at the beginning of each year to brief members of their work done in the previous year and the key focused items in the coming year. Through this annual briefing, QBPC members have been able to prepare for engaging in the amendment process of the Customs Intellectual Property Protection Regulation and the promulgation of the Regulation Regarding the General Bond.[33]

As e-commerce is becoming popular, export of counterfeiting goods through postal channels has become a headache for many brand owners, especially those in the tobacco, luxury goods, pharmaceutical, personal care, and automobile industries.[34] In 2008, Chinese Customs seizures of intellectual property infringing goods through postal channels accounted for 89.8% of total Customs seizures, which is a quantum leap from 2007. GACC immediately launched a special project to focus on this issue in 2009.[35]

According to the GACC statistics, close to 99% of the Chinese Customs

---

33 The General Administration of Customs (GAC) announced on 31 May 2006 (GAC Announcement No. 31-2006, effective 1 July 2006) that brand owners may provide a bank guarantee letter to the GAC as the general bond for a validity term from the date when the bank issues the guarantee letter to 30 June of the following year, instead of having the brand owners post the bond within three working days on a case-by-case basis.

34 The cross-border trade of counterfeit goods is no longer limited to shipments by sea of large quantities of counterfeit goods from sourcing countries to destination markets where consumers buy them at stores, but over the internet through e-stores that show catalogs of hundreds of different items of counterfeit goods in all industries. Electronic order of counterfeit goods has built significant trade volumes across borders. The counterfeit sellers order specific counterfeit goods from their networks of suppliers based on the specific orders collected from consumers and/or retailers over the internet from all over the world and then ship the counterfeit goods in small quantities out of the country via courier and postal services. This trend has led to a change of traditional inspection patterns by Customs officials.

35 Part of the content in this section was written by Lawrence Wong from Diageo, the Chairman of the QBPC Customs Committee in 2009. In 2006, GACC won the highly commended award as a government agency granted by the Global Anti-counterfeiting Group (www.gacg.org).

seizures were initiated *ex officio* by personnel and related to exports. Chinese Customs is another strong government partner with the QBPC. The timely set up of the Customs Committee not only has helped QBPC members better utilize China's border intellectual property system but has also contributed jointly with the Chinese Customs to the improvement of border intellectual property protection.

14.4.4. 'QBPC is my capable right hand assistant' (recognition from former Vice Premier Madam Wuyi)

On 8 September 2003, QBPC members were invited by CAEFI to attend (for the first time) a forum chaired by former Vice Premier Madam Wuyi in Xiamen City, Fujian Province. More than 70 QBPC member representatives attended the meeting. Members' presentations and questions were focused on intellectual property protection. One proposal raised by the author of this chapter was to set up a quarterly exchange meeting mechanism between the QBPC members and the Market Order Rectification Office (MORO) under Madam Wuyi's leadership.[36] Members were extremely impressed by Madam Wuyi's straightforward and efficient handling of sensitive and difficult issues with regard to IP protection and enforcement. The QBPC proposal to set up quarterly exchange meetings was immediately accepted by Madam Wuyi. With Madam Wuyi's support, the first exchange meeting was conducted two weeks later. Until early 2008, the QBPC and MORO conducted 19 exchange meetings, which have helped to resolve many difficult cases involving local protection. On 7 September 2004, after the author's presentation on behalf of the QBPC directly illustrating the hot spots for counterfeiting and making further constructive recommendations, Madam Wuyi highly commended the QBPC by publicly describing QBPC as her 'capable right hand assistant'. Further, the misperception of some government agencies that QBPC was a foreign pressure group was clarified. Moreover, the professionalism and reputation of the QBPC, being an industry group dedicated to improving China's intellectual property and investment environment based on an approach of cooperation, was strongly recognized.[37] Figure 14.1 shows the author Jack Chang with Madam Wuyi.

---

[36] After the leadership change and government restructuring early in 2008, the MORO was abolished and the responsibility for coordinating intellectual property enforcement agencies was shifted to the Department of Protection Coordination under the State Intellectual Property Office set up in late 2008.

[37] The author reported on behalf of the QBPC to Madam Wuyi in 2003, 2004 and 2006.

Figure 14.1 *Jack Chang (author), Chairman of the QBPC with Madam Wuyi (ex-Vice Premier of China)*

14.4.5. From the Anti-counterfeiting of Trademarks to Covering all Intellectual Property

The QBPC started as an organization dedicated to fighting counterfeit trademarks. However, as China moves from 'made in China' to 'created in China', new intellectual property issues related to patent infringement, trade secret theft, standards and technology transfer etc., are evolving. Many of these issues cannot be resolved through traditional administrative enforcement or the gradually improving criminal enforcement systems. A transparent, consistent and effective judicial civil intellectual property protection system is needed, as Chinese markets and industrial structures evolve. QBPC members have a strong need to leverage the QBPC platform and resources to work with Chinese intellectual property policy makers, judiciary and the State Intellectual Property Office (SIPO), which was responsible for the design and implementation of the National IP Strategy Outline released in June 2008. [38]

[38] See the section of Policy, Laws & Reg. via www.qpbc.org.cn for the National IP Strategy Outline.

To cope with these increasing needs, the QBPC set up its Patent Committee in 2005.[39]

China's Patent Law was first promulgated in April 1985, following a period of serious debate on whether China really needed a patent law. In 1992, the Patent Law was revised for the first time after China and the United States signed an MOU on Intellectual Property. In 2000, the second amendment was completed in order to meet the TRIPS requirements, when China was ready to join the World Trade Organization. The third amendment completed in 2009 was a further step forward in trying to build China into an innovation-based country by 2020.

The process of amending China's Patent Law started with the State Intellectual Property Office (SIPO), which first commissioned research on identified subjects to academic institutes and outside patent firms.[40] Thereafter, SIPO drafted the first amendment and sought public comments. The second step involved SIPO submitting its final draft to the State Council Legislative Affairs Office (SCLAO) for review.[41] Thereafter,

---

[39] The Patent Committee was set up and led by Sam Li, who was the Chief IP Counsel for Rohm & Haas based in Shanghai. At the time of writing, Zhang Yan from IBM is the current Patent Committee Chairperson.

[40] In October 2004, the China State Intellectual Property Office (SIPO) officially initiated the preparation work for the third amendment to the Patent Law. To ensure the good quality of the amendment work, SIPO selected research groups through the process of competition via public bidding amongst academia, research institutes, government agencies, judiciary and patent-related service providers to research on subjects such as cross-protection for invention and utility models, international harmonization of patent laws, standards on substance examination of invention and utility models, design, disclosure of sources of biogenetic resources, invalidation, ownership of service inventions and inventor remuneration, patent and standards, legal remedies for patent abuse, compulsory licenses, unified IP courts, restrictions on patent rights, standards to determine patent infringement and contributory infringement etc. Forty research reports were submitted to SIPO, which were compiled and published by the Treaty & Law Department of SIPO (only Chinese version available) in April 2006 (ISBN 7-80011-915-7).

[41] SIPO released its first draft on 31 July 2006 on its website, seeking public comment. In early 2007, after reviewing comments received, SIPO submitted its final draft to the State Council Legislative Affairs Office (SCLAO) for review. In early 2008, the SCLAO released its draft, dated 28 February 2008, for public comment. After reviewing comments received, SCLAO submitted its final draft to the State Council. On behalf of the State Council, Premier Wen Jiabao on 5 August 2008 submitted the draft to the Standing Committee of National People's Congress (the legislative body) for review. The third amendment to the Patent Law was passed by the Standing Committee on 27 December 2008, effective 1 October 2009. The above-mentioned drafts and revised Patent Law, together with their English translations and the QBPC comments on various drafts, are available at the section of the Patent Committee via www.qbpc.org.cn.

the SCLAO sent its further revised draft to the National People's Congress (NPC) for final review. As soon as SIPO published for public comment its first draft in August 2006 on the SIPO website, the QBPC Patent Committee organized a taskforce to draft the QBPC position paper, focusing on the articles related to the definition of service invention; employee researcher remuneration; foreign filing license; patent examination; compulsory license; patent protection; prior art defense;[42] laches;[43] and several

---

42 Traditionally, when the defendant of a patent infringement lawsuit files an invalidation action against the plaintiff's patent based on lack of novelty, the court generally puts the case on hold pending the outcome of the invalidation action. Under the revised Patent Law, if the court is convinced that the evidence submitted by the defendant is enough to prove that prior art did exist before the filing of the patent, the court may go ahead to render the decision to dismiss the plaintiff's lawsuit without waiting for the outcome of the invalidation action. Article 62 of the revised Patent Law stipulates that 'in a patent infringement dispute, where the accused infringer has evidence demonstrating that the technology and design exploited by it or him were prior art or prior design, the said exploitation act shall not constitute an infringing act'.

43 'Laches' or *Vigilantibus et non dormientibus jura subveninut* means that the law 'aids those who are vigilant, not those who sleep upon their rights'. Article A13 of the first SIPO draft, dated 31 July 2006, stipulated that 'Where the patentee or any interested party initiates legal proceedings after the statutory limitation for initiating legal proceedings expires, it or he shall not request for compensation for damages caused by an infringement act occurring 2 years before the date of initiating the legal proceedings; where the infringing act still continues at the time of the initiation of the legal proceedings, it or he may request the people's court or the patent administration department to order the infringer to stop the infringing act. Where the infringing act has lasted for five years counted from the date on which the patentee or any interested party knew or should have known the infringing act, but the patentee or the interested party fails to claim its or his right without any justifiable reason, if the infringer is willing to pay an amount of exploitation fees agreed upon by both parties or determined by the people's court, the infringer may not stop its or his act of exploiting the said patent.' Industry groups were particularly concerned about the situation where by paying the court the determined exploitation fee, the infringer would be legally allowed to continue the infringing act, encouraging further infringement, as the infringer's only risk was to pay the exploitation fee, once caught and sued. The QBPC and other industry groups recommended that SIPO delete such wording. Article 72 of the SIPO final draft submitted to the SCLAO in early 2007 deleted this wording. Now, Article 72 stipulates that: 'Where the patentee or any interested party initiates legal proceedings before the people's court or requests the patent administrative department to handle the matter after the statutory limitation for initiating legal proceedings expires, it or he may be granted a compensation for damages caused by an infringement act occurring 2 years before the date of initiating the legal proceedings or requesting the handling; where the patentee or any interested party initiates legal proceedings before the people's court or requests the patent administrative department to handle the matter 3 years after the expiration

exceptions to patent infringement. The format of the QBPC position paper was in line with the standard format of amendments to many Chinese laws, which has four columns on each page focusing on (a) the articles of the current law; (b) the articles of the amended draft with changes highlighted;

---

of the statutory limitation for initiating legal proceedings without justifiable reason, it or he shall not be entitled to a compensation for damages caused by an infringement act occurred before the date of initiating the legal proceedings or requesting the handling; in the above situation, where the infringing act still continues at the time of the initiation of the legal proceedings or the request for handling, it or he may request the people's court or the patent administrative department to order the infringer to stop the infringing act immediately.' However, the SIPO final draft added a new Article 73, which stipulates that: 'Where the relevant act, indication of intention or silence of the patentee or any interested party makes the entity or the individual exploiting the patent thereof have reasons to believe that the patentee or the interested party will not claim its or his right over the exploitation, whereas it or he subsequently initiates legal proceedings before the people's court or requests the patent administrative department to handle the matter, its or his claiming of right is obviously contrary to the principle of good faith, and it or he shall not be entitled to a compensation for damages caused by an act exploited before the date of instituting the legal proceedings or requesting the handling, nor shall it or he be entitled to request the people's court or the patent administrative department to order the entity or the individual to stop the exploitation of the act.' However, the problematic wording in Article 72 of the first SIPO draft as discussed above, or the even more problematic wording, included in Article 72 of the SCLAO draft dated 28 February 2008, which stipulates that 'For the act of infringing a patent right, where the patentee or any interested party initiates legal proceedings before the people's court or requests the Patent Administrative Department to handle the matter 2 years after the date on which the patentee or any interested party knew or should have known the infringement act, the infringer is not liable for the compensation for the damages caused by the infringement act before the date of initiating the legal proceedings or requesting the handling by the patentee or the interested party. However, the infringer shall stop infringement act after the patentee or the interested party institutes the legal proceedings or requests the handling; Nevertheless, the infringer may continue exploiting the relevant patent subject to payment of reasonable amount of fee.' After relentless effort on both the part of the SCLAO and the QBPC discussing the advantages and disadvantages of including this wording regarding laches, the SCLAO was extremely open-minded and finally took out all of the problematic wording from its final draft submitted to the State Council for review on 5 August 2008. Now, the revised Patent Law does not have any provision for laches. However, Article 15 of the Supreme People's Court's Several Opinions on Several Issues relating to Intellectual Property Trial under Current Economy Situation (SPC Opinions), which was issued on 21 April 2009, adopts similar wording for laches as given above, namely that 'if the patentee failed to protect its or his rights for a long period of time but initiated legal actions thereafter, the court after prudently reviewing the situation may decide not to order the defendant to stop the infringing act, if the court order to stop infringement would cause relatively large unbalance in the interests between the parties'. The plaintiff's right to claim compensation shall not be negatively affected,

(c) the QBPC suggested language based on the amended draft; and (d) the rationale for the QBPC suggested changes. The reader-friendly format and the practical changes suggested by the QBPC based on valid rationale have enhanced the QBPC's reputation with both SIPO and the SCLAO. In February 2007, when the SCLAO received the QBPC delegation, both parties agreed to maximize the positive image of China being transparent in the IP legislative reform.[44] With the approval from the SCLAO, QBPC had the SIPO submission draft translated and circulated to almost 20 industry groups, including the International Chamber of Commerce; US Chamber

---

according to said article. The Chinese version of the SPC Opinions is available at the 'Policies, Laws and Regulations' section of the QBPC website (www.qbpc.org.cn).

[44] Many people outside of China have questioned the transparency of IP legislative reform in China. The experiences of many QBPC colleagues of working with the Legal Affairs Office of the National People's Congress, the State Council Legislative Affairs Office (SCLAO), Supreme People's Court, Supreme People's Procuratorate, Ministry of Public Security, Ministry of Commerce, General Administration of Customs, State Intellectual Property Office (SIPO), National Copyright Administration, China Trademark Office, Anti-monopoly and Anti-unfair Competition Office etc., during the past ten years has convinced many QBPC colleagues that China is getting more and more transparent in terms of listening to different opinions by sharing draft policies, laws and regulations for public comment. The third amendment of the Patent Law demonstrated China's unprecedented transparency by SIPO and the SCLAO. Not only was the process transparent but also the opinions of QBPC were acceptable and were fully discussed. In a recent meeting on 22 January 2010 between SIPO officials and the QBPC delegation, including the author and the chairpersons of the QBPC Patent and Legal Committees, SIPO recognized the QBPC's efforts to provide a position paper on China's innovation policy in early December 2009. The concerns expressed in the report on inventor remuneration clauses in the draft Implementation Rules of the Patent Law, pending the State Council's review, were further taken into consideration by SIPO and SCLAO, which triggered the last minute changes to rules on: agreement between the employer and the employee researchers; the company work rules and regulations stipulating reasonable remuneration mechanism. This change reduces the risks of triggering labor disputes between the employer and employee researchers over the remuneration system by challenging the validity of the agreement. Article 76 of the Implementation Rules of the Patent Law, promulgated on 9 January 2010 by the State Council, effective 1 February 2010, stipulates that: 'The entity to which a patent right is granted may agree with the inventor or creator on, or provide in its rules and regulations formulated according to law the method and amount of the reward and remuneration provided in Article 16 of the Patent Law. The reward and remuneration the enterprise or institution awards to the inventor or creator shall be handled in accordance with the provisions of the state relating to the financial and accounting systems.' It was very unusual for the State Council to agree last minutes changes to the draft laws or regulations. This once again proves that constructive recommendations substantiated by solid analysis are welcome in China.

of Commerce; AmCham China, AmCham Shanghai, Intellectual Property Owners Association; American BioIndustry Alliance; US Information Technology Office and EU Chamber of Commerce in China etc. All the industry groups provided valuable comments, which were channeled to the SCLAO through the QBPC. In order to have a face-to-face exchange of thoughts, the SCLAO further organized an International Seminar on the Chinese Patent Law Revision in Beijing in October 2007, sponsored by the QBPC. Experts from developed and developing countries including China, India, Brazil, the US, and Germany had the opportunity to discuss China's third amendment to the Patent Law. Many foreign experts involved in the amendment process commented that China's third amendment to the Patent Law was unprecedentedly transparent and that the Chinese officials' expertise and open-minded approach was impressive. For the QBPC, another lesson learned was to always consider the position of both sides (a 'win win approach') in order to bring value to members; to gain credit for China and the QBPC, and to help construct a bridge for China to the international community.[45]

The comments from the QBPC and other industry groups were well received by the SCLAO. The comments, particularly on the foreign filing license; inventor remuneration; laches; and patent protection, have made a positive impact on the revised Patent Law ('New Patent Law'), which came into effect on 1 October 2009. The QBPC position paper in particular was circulated by the Chinese government agencies to many domestic academic institutes for their reference and comment. Some of the academic IP opinion leaders further shared the QBPC papers with domestic Chinese companies, encouraging them to become actively involved in the IP legislative reform process in China.

During the meeting between QBPC leaders and SIPO officials on 22 January 2010, SIPO informed the QBPC that its position paper on China's Innovation Policy and the Inventor Remuneration[46] sent to various ministries on 23 December 2009 (one week before the revised draft Implementation Rules of the Patent Law were approved by the

---

[45] On 1 March 2010, the SCLAO once again forwarded the draft amendment of the Trademark Law, which was submitted by the State Administration for Industry and Commerce to the SCLAO for review, to the QBPC for comment and allowed the QBPC to have it translated and to forward it further for comment. This move by the SCLAO demonstrates the trust between the Chinese government agencies and the QBPC, which has helped to make the IP legislative reform process in China increasingly transparent.

[46] The position paper was drafted by the author of this chapter with inputs from members, primarily Intel.

State Council), had triggered a last minute change to the Patent Law. The change was made by the State Council to include wording allowing employers to stipulate an inventor remuneration scheme in company rules and regulations through a legal process instead of allowing the employers to stipulate it only in the agreement with employee researchers, and which could expose the employer to the risk of having the validity of the agreement challenged at a later date. This positive news greatly encouraged QBPC leaders and the example once again shows that the Chinese government is able to accept constructive recommendations presented appropriately via proper channels. A good portion of the credit goes to a group of Chinese high tech companies led by Hua Wei Technology Co., Ltd., a highly successful Chinese company. This group of Chinese companies has been actively involved in the revision process of the Patent Law and Implementation Rules. They encouraged the QBPC to further suggest to the Chinese government provisions on an inventor remuneration scheme right before the State Council was going to pass the revised draft of the Implementation Rules.

As in many other jurisdictions, patent infringement in China is not a criminal offence.[47] To better protect intellectual property, particularly patents, which is critical to the transformation of China into an innovation based country, the Intellectual Property Tribunal (IP Tribunal) of the Supreme People's Court and their counterparts at Provincial High Court level, and the Intermediate Courts of key cities, have been conducting capacity-building programs for IP judges over the past few years. From 2006, the QBPC Patent and Legal Committee started working with the IP Tribunal of the Supreme People's Court to organize an International Conference on Judicial Protection of IPR in China.

Until September 2009, there were three international conferences

---

47 Article 216 of the China Criminal Law stipulates that 'whoever counterfeits other people's patents, and when the circumstances are serious, is to be sentenced to not more than three years of fixed-term imprisonment, criminal detention, and may in addition or exclusively be sentenced to a fine'. However, the definition of counterfeit patents refers to forging or falsifying the patent certificate, patent documents or patent application documents of another person; or unauthorized use of another's patent number on the products, packaging, advertisement or in the contact, thereby causing people to mistakenly believe that the technology involved is the patented technology of another person (see Article 10 of the Judicial Interpretation on Intellectual Property Crimes, jointly issued by the Supreme People's Court and the Supreme People's Procuratorate, effective 22 December 2004). Unauthorized use of another's patented technology may be a patent infringement act and is a civil and administrative violation, but not the crime of counterfeiting a patent.

successfully conducted in Chongqing, Shanghai and Chengdu City of Sichuan Provinces respectively. The international conferences were probably the highest profile judicial IP conferences ever hosted by the Chinese Supreme People's Court. Former Executive Vice President Cao Jiaming, Vice President Xi Xiaoming,[48] and Vice President Wan E'xiang of the Supreme People's Court spoke at each of the three international conferences respectively. Internationally well-known judges from mainland China, Taipei City, the United Kingdom, Germany, France, Holland, United States, India and Japan[49] attended and spoke at the conferences. The key issues discussed at the third International Conference on 10 and 11 September 2009 included patent claims interpretation and the doctrine of equivalents, prior art defense and prior use, the scope of protection for patents, contributory patent infringement, the limitations to the patents included in the technical standards, the regulation of anti-monopoly, and the misuse of IPR protection on the internet, amongst others. The discussion of claims interpretation focused on whether the specifications could be used to interpret the claims (if yes, whether the specifications should be used in cases with inaccurate or unclear wording in claims). The interpretation for cases with claim contents that are not in accordance with specifications and drawings should be subject to the records of claims (records that are not favorable to the patentee). The discussion also covered the kind of rules that should be used to interpret claims; who has the right to interpret the claims; and the circumstances under which claims interpretation is a matter of fact or law.

Different countries have different standards for the doctrine of equivalents, which is widely used in patent infringement litigation. In China, if the following two conditions are met at the same time, it will be deemed equivalent to the patent: one is allegedly infringing device's means, func-

[48] Mr Cao Jianming became the Chief Prosecutor of the Supreme People's Procuratorate in 2008.

[49] The sharing of wisdom and experiences by Professor Jiang Zhipei, former Chief Judge of the IP Tribunal and Chief Judge Kong Xiangjun of the IP Tribunal of the China Supreme Court; Judge Wang Hanqing and Judge Zeng Qimou from the IP Court in Taipei; the Honorable Lord Justice Robin Jacob, Justice Christopher Floyd and Justice Robert Michael Fysh from the United Kingdom; Judge Joachim Bornkamm and Judge Klause Grabinski from the German Federal Supreme Court; Judge Alice Pezard from the French Supreme Court; Judge Rober van Peursem from Holland; Judge Randall R. Rader, Judge Kent A. Jordan, Judge Larry J. McKinney and Judge Marvin J. Garbis from the US; Justice Mukundakam Sharma from the Supreme Court of India; Judge Tatsubumi Sato, Judge Toshiaki Iimura and Judge Ken Asai from Japan, as well as many others, has made the three international conferences a great success.

tion and results are essentially identical; the other is that the technology character of the device is obvious to a person skilled in the art. In Germany, an allegedly infringing device is considered to be equivalent if there is commonality with respect to the problem to be solved and the effect, even if the manner in which the device operates is not the same. In the UK, the doctrine of equivalents approach has never been employed. In response to this, the UK courts developed the 'pith and marrow' approach, which tries to distinguish between the essential and non-essential features of a patent claim when deciding infringement cases. In the US, if the allegedly infringing device performs substantially the same function and yields substantially the same result in substantially the same way, it is deemed equivalent to the patent, and the doctrine of equivalents analysis is applied to individual claim limitations, not to the invention as a whole. The main aim of the patent law (with regard to patent trolls, the injunction, the compulsory license defense in patent infringement proceedings, the misuse of the IPR and the anti-monopoly regulation) is to encourage invention and innovation by empowering the patentee to exclude others from utilizing the patent without a proper license to enter the market. If the competitive conduct by the patentee excluding others from entering the market is punished, then the protection provided in the patent law would be rendered void. Such punishment would impair science and technology innovation and be unfavorable to the advancement of society. Therefore, most countries adopt a more cautious approach when dealing with these issues and allow the patentee to possess exclusive rights within the scope of its patent.

At this international conference, both the basic theory research and judicial practices related to IPR were discussed, giving participants a better understanding of the latest developments and trends in global IPR protection. In order to meet the special needs of IPR trials and to ensure that the laws and regulations related to IPR could be effectively and consistently implemented, participants suggested that a uniform IP court of appeals and a judicial system *combining* the civil, administrative and criminal IPR trials should be established in most countries, as most IP cases are complex and involve cutting-edge science and technology, as well as increasing volumes of newly emerging types of IP cases with international ramifications.[50] Through co-sponsorship of the conferences, the EU-China IP 2 Project Office and QBPC built up a strong partnership

[50] The summary of the 2009 International Conference on Judicial Protection of IPR hosted by the IP Tribunal of China Supreme People's Court, co-sponsored by EU–China IP 2 Office and the QBPC was prepared by the QBPC Patent Committee leaders and the QBPC Legal Staff.

to further collaborate on many other key IP projects. Although it is not practicable to expect that the new ideas and best practices discussed by the invited foreign judges and experts will be adopted by China overnight, the conferences did, however, lead to a candid exchange of thought. The exposure and learning from agreement and disagreement at the conferences have benefited the Chinese and foreign judiciary, as well as IP owners, in terms of building mutual understanding and capacity, and this (in the author's opinion) has the potential to lead to a mindset change in the long run.

As regards *copyright*, as early as 2004, members in the copyright industry leveraged the QBPC platform to provide valuable input to the Supreme People Court and Supreme People's Procuratorate on the draft judicial interpretation on IP crimes, of which the final version was issued on 11 November 2004, becoming effective on 22 December 2004.[51] One important breakthrough was that Paragraph 2 of Art. 11 of the judicial interpretation for the first time characterized 'reproduction of copyrighted work in the volume exceeding the authorized volume' as 'reproduction without authorization', which characterized over-reproduced works as copyright infringement goods. Trademark members, however, have not been able, even today, to resolve the disputes on whether over-run trademark goods by an authorized producer can be classed as trademark infringement goods or only giving rise to a breech of contract by the authorized producer. Since 2008, the QBPC has allocated more resources on copyright matters. Several copyright experts have been elected to the leadership team.[52] In November 2009, the Legal Committee on behalf of the QBPC co-sponsored a program with EU-China IP2 and US industry groups organized by Zhong Nan University of Economy and Law on researching potential amendments to the Copyright Law.[53] These efforts further boosted the evolution of QBPC into a comprehensive professional IP industry group tackling all kinds of IP issues.

---

[51] The judicial interpretation and its English translation is available at the section on Policies, Laws and Regulations at the QBPC website: www.qbpc.org.cn.

[52] In addition to two copyright lawyers from Microsoft and GE/NBCU respectively, who joined the Legal Committee leadership team, Mr Hugh Stephens, Senior Vice President for International Relations and Public Policy at Time Warner, was elected in 2008 as Vice Chairman of the QBPC and helped significantly to direct the QBPC focus and resources to copyright-related issues.

[53] The Zhongnan University of Economics and Law is one of the most prestigious universities in China. The university's President, Professor Wu Handong, has delivered IP lectures to many government agencies, including top-level national leaders.

14.5. ONGOING CHALLENGES AND QBPC ACTIONS

14.5.1. Global Financial Crisis and IP Enforcement

Due to the global financial crisis, many IP owners have been facing restrictions on increasing headcount and budget cuts, which has slowed IP enforcement actions and capacity building in China. At the same time, governments worldwide are faced with the task of maintaining economic growth and jobs in order to ensure social stability. While at the national level, the Chinese government continues to emphasize the strengthening of IP protection, as stated in China's National IP Strategy Outlines, there have been reports from QBPC members that some Chinese local level enforcement agencies are reluctant to take enforcement actions based on members' complaints. Members have learned that one of the reasons for this 'slowing down' of local IP enforcement is the local officials' mindset of keeping their jobs during the economic downturn. According to the QBPC membership annual survey published early in the second quarter 2009, the percentage of those members ranking the counterfeit problem in China as serious had increased from 35% (2007) to 44% (2008), a 9% increase.[54] In terms of the problem of counterfeit trade in the international market, the percentage of those stating that the 'situation had worsened' was 34%, a 5% increase compared with the previous year. The survey confirmed the top five sourcing countries for counterfeit goods as China, Vietnam, India, Korea and Thailand, while the top five destination markets were Europe, the Middle East, China, the USA and Latin America. The QBPC recognizes that cross-border trade of counterfeit and pirated goods is an international problem and obviously China is also a victim country like others, according to the survey results. Chinese Customs, however, continues to dedicate resources to strengthening border enforcement, particularly with export inspections and postal delivery of counterfeit goods. Chinese Customs and the Economic Crime police remain effective partners with the QBPC in dealing with counterfeit trade.

54 The public version of the QBPC 2008–09 membership survey results is available on the QBPC website (www.qbpc.org.cn).

14.5.2. The Abolishing of the Chinese Government's IP Enforcement Coordination Taskforce and the Newly Set up Department Responsible for IP Coordination

The Market Order Rectification Office (MORO) was an IP enforcement coordination taskforce set up by the Ministry of Commerce (MOFCOM) under the leadership of former Vice Premier, Madam Wuyi. MORO later wore another hat as the State Office of IP Protection (SOIPP), which also came under MOFCOM and Madam Wuyi's leadership. MORO/SOIPP started exchange meetings with the QBPC in September 2003, after former Vice Premier Wuyi accepted the recommendation made by Jack Chang, QBPC Chairman, at the meeting chaired by Madam Wuyi in Xiamen City on 8 September 2003 that MORO and the QBPC meet on a quarterly basis to allow the QBPC to report first-hand information on IP infringement and enforcement (discussed above). The aim of this dialogue was to strengthen cooperation between the Chinese government and the QBPC and that MORO/SOIPP could help follow up on difficult cases facing local protection experienced by QBPC members. Successful solutions to these difficult individual cases would contribute to legislative and enforcement reform in the future. MORO/SOIPP was abolished due to government function restructuring in early 2008 and the coordination function was shifted to the IP Protection Coordination Department (IPPCD) of the State Intellectual Property Office (SIPO), set up in late 2008. Even though SIPO traditionally handled primarily patent prosecution matters, in recent years, SIPO has evolved into a government agency driving and implementing the National IP Strategy Outline.[55] QBPC members expect SIPO's IPPCD to soon play an important role in IP enforcement coordination in a similar way to the past role of the MORO/SOIPP.

14.5.3. Innovation Policies Driving Changes in the Business Environment

In February 2006, the Chinese State Council issued the National Mid and Long Term Science and Technology Development and Planning Outline ('Outline').[56] The objective of the Outline is to build China into an innovative country by 2020 through various supporting policies and measures,

---

[55] The Chinese version of the China National IP Strategy Outline and relevant materials are available at the section of Policies, Laws & Regulations of the QBPC website (www.qbpc.org.cn).

[56] The Chinese version of the National Mid and Long Term Science and Technology Development & Planning Outline is available at the section of Policies, Laws & Regulations of the QBPC website (www.qbpc.org.cn).

including but not limited to leveraging the power of government procurement for National Indigenous and Independent Innovation Products (NIIP),[57] stimulating the demand and supply of Chinese-made products;[58] combining incentive programs to encourage more R&D investment by Chinese companies, and leveraging government support to allow innovative Chinese-made creations to be patented and adopted into domestic national standards, and even international standards. On the positive side, China is becoming increasingly transparent in publishing her innovation policies and implementation measures to the public. However the increased use of government procurement policies favoring products made by domestic Chinese companies causes concern among foreign entrants over potential unfair competition for foreign companies based in China, such as QBPC members, and which could also negatively impact China's efforts to become an innovative country, as it discourages foreign companies from investing in R&D in China. Recognizing China's need to build her innovation capacity, finding a 'win-win' solution to support China in achieving this objective without creating potential trade disputes, and at the same time, helping QBPC members compete fairly, as well as helping members strengthen Chinese IP protection, has become the most challenging work for the QBPC in the near future.

14.5.4. QBPC Actions and the Future

The QBPC Best Practice and Enforcement Committee continues to work with the Ministry of Public Security on the Draft Police Investigation Guidelines,[59] and also conducted the nationwide Criminal IP Enforcement

---

57 The process of accrediting NIIP is for the applicant to apply to the Provincial Science and Technology Commission, which will review the application together with the provincial level Development and Reform Commission and Finance Department. If accredited as a provincial level IIP, it is subject to the discretion of the Provincial Science and Technology Commission to select some of the Provincial IIPs to report to the Ministry of Science and Technology (MOST) for further review. The MOST will jointly review the report with the National Development and Reform Commission and Ministry of Finance.

58 The MOST identifies as Chinese companies those companies owned by majority Chinese shareholders, while the MOFCOM spokesperson stated at the press briefing on 16 December 2009 that 'This policy treats all companies set up in China equally as long as they pay tax, employ Chinese staff here and own intellectual properties created here'.

59 The objectives of issuing the Police Investigation Guidelines is to clarify confusion caused by several terms in the Criminal Law such as 'identical trademark', 'same goods', 'profit-making purpose' and to tackle new issues, such as how to apply the volume thresholds (for example, unauthorized reproduction or

Workshop in April 2009 for prosecutors, hosted by the Investigation Supervision Department of the Supreme People's Procuratorate. Also, the QBPC Communications Committee successfully strengthened QBPC's image by partnering with Chinese media. The Communications Committee promoted public IP awareness by expanding the circulation and revising the content of the QBPC brochure entitled 'Experience the Real China; Buy the Real Thing',[60] and enhanced both internal and external communications with members and the general public by continuously improving the QBPC website. The Customs Committee organized a forum between China Customs and the Ministry of Public Security on transfer of potential criminal cases involving cross-border IP infringement and two workshops with China Customs to discuss specific issues and best practices for border IP enforcement.[61] After MORO and SOIPP (under MOFCOM) were abolished and the function of coordinat-

---

distribution of others' copyrighted works for profit-making purpose constitutes the copyright infringement crime under Article 217 of the Criminal Law) to *on-line copyright piracy*, which has no physical copies. Also, how to determine the loss caused by trade secret theft, and to guide the police to conduct effective and timely investigations.

[60] The QBPC has witnessed many examples of foreign travelers purchasing counterfeit and pirated goods in China or from tour guides circulating at five-star hotels advising tourists where to buy counterfeit goods, or Chinese salespersons targeting foreign tourists at famous tourist places to promote the sale of counterfeit and pirated goods etc. Therefore, QBPC compiled a brochure named 'Experience The Real China; Buy The Real Thing', which contains comments on the harm to society caused unintentionally by those who purchase counterfeit and pirated goods for fun, as not only their demand stimulates more supply but also money from sales of counterfeit goods goes to organized criminal gangs, who operate the underground supply chain of counterfeit and pirated goods. The brochure also contains convincing photographs showing child labour employed by counterfeiters in developing countries. The silent message to the audience is 'if you are not a child labour supporter, don't buy counterfeit and pirated goods'. The brochure has been widely circulated with the help of Chinese government agencies and the US Embassy, Consulate General Offices in various cities in China, as well as the EU's IP delegation in China and the European Chamber of Commerce in China. For more information, see the Communication Committee activities at www.qbpc.org.cn.

[61] The forum was conducted on 14 October 2009 in Wuyishan City, Fujian Province (south east China). Forty seven officials from the General Administration of Customs, Customs from various ports, the Ministry of Public Security and State Intellectual Property Office, as well as representatives from 21 QBPC member companies, attended the forum. The group reached a consensus on the proper channels to share intelligence between Customs officials and police regarding counterfeit export cases involving different jurisdictions, where the production of counterfeit goods, the location of the export company, and the Customs seizing the

ing IP enforcement agencies was shifted to the IPPCD of SIPO (mentioned above), the QBPC Government Cooperation Committee (GCC) managed to establish an immediate partnership with the IPPCD.[62] On 18 November 2009, exactly one year after the first exchange meeting, the second exchange meeting for the QBPC with the IPPCD of SIPO chaired by Deputy Commissioner Gan Shaoning of SIPO was conducted with the support and coordination of the GCC (again in Chongqing City). This meeting helped foster mutual trust and established a platform for further cooperation.[63] During 2010, the GCC has continued to build strong partnerships with the IPPCD, MOFCOM and the national and key provincial and city governments to better serve QBPC members' needs. The Legal Committee provided the China Trademark Office in August 2006, November 2007 and July 2009 respectively with QBPC position papers on the various draft amendments to the Trademark Law[64] and provided the Anti-monopoly and Anti-unfair Competition Bureau of the State Administration for Industry and Commerce on 4 August 2009 with QBPC comments on the Regulation on Anti-monopolistic Conduct involving IP, and successfully cooperated with government agencies, judicial authorities, and/or influential law schools to organize a series of seminars on trademark and copyright amendments and the trial practice for criminal IPR cases, as well as judicial protection of IPR in Guangdong. Also, the Legal Committee co-organized the high level forum on judicial protection of IPR and a seminar on the drafting of the Anti-monopoly Law (judicial interpretation) jointly with the patent committee.[65]

---

counterfeit goods are in different jurisdictions. For more information, please check Customs Committee activities on www.qbpc.org.cn.

[62] The Government Cooperation Committee (GCC) approached the newly set up Intellectual Property Protection Coordination Department (IPPCD) of the State Intellectual Property Office immediately after the IPPCD was established in late 2008 to introduce the QBPC and to express the QBPC wish to resume the regular exchange meetings with IPPCD, and to seek its help to coordinate law enforcement agencies to work on tough IP enforcement cases. The GCC coordinated with the IPPCD to set up the first exchange meeting between IPPCD and QBPC on 18 November 2008 in Chongqing City (west China).

[63] After the meeting, the IPPCD in principle agreed to hold two meetings per year with the QBPC to learn from QBPC members about tough enforcement cases and to coordinate with relevant law enforcement agencies in order to move these cases forward.

[64] The various amendment drafts of the Trademark Law and the QBPC comments are available by checking the Legal Committee activities at www.qbpc.org.cn.

[65] The Anti-monopoly Law is discussed in detail in Chapters 11 and 12 respectively.

The QBPC Membership Service(s) Committee (MSC) managed to retain over 180 members, despite members facing serious budget cuts in the financial year. In addition, the MSC conducted training courses for members at membership meetings by inviting speakers from the Chinese public and private sectors and other countries to address members' needs.[66] The QBPC Patent Committee provided comments on several amendment drafts to the Implementation Regulations of the Patent Law, which was passed by the State Council on 30 December 2009; the draft Judicial Interpretation by the Supreme People's Court on Some Issues Concerning the Application of Laws to the Trial of Patent Infringement Disputes (JI), which was issued on 28 December 2009; and the draft Interim Provisions by the Standard Administration of China on the Formulation and Revision of Patent-related National Standards.[67] Also, the Patent Committee successfully organized a high profile seminar with SIPO on the Patent Practices under the Newly Amended Patent Law as well as working with the Supreme People's Court and Beijing First Intermediate Court on comprehensive research projects and conferences on the JI and patent defenses respectively. In addition, the QBPC launched its Ethical On-line Advertising Initiative with a Code of Conduct for members to voluntarily implement.[68] This Campaign has

---

[66] At the QBPC General Meeting on 8 September 2009, Madam Nancy Kremers, the new Senior IPR Attache of the United States based in Beijing and Mr Mark Cohen, former Senior IPR Attache of the United States spoke to the members on their vision to continue the collaboration. Thereafter, the panel with the theme of 'Problems and Solutions – Partnering with ISPs to Combat Internet Sales of Counterfeit & Pirated Goods' was moderated by Ms Lucy Nichols from Nokia, a Vice Chair of QBPC in 2009 and a QBPC Representative in North America. The panel consisted of Mr Steven Liew from eBay, Mr Tim Steinert and Ms Elsa Wong from Alibaba, and Mr Chris Cosgrove from Mattel. The goal of the panel discussion was to share information on policies and practices at eBay and Alibaba, which members could proactively utilize to promote a partnership to combat sales of infringing products listed on the two ISP websites. The QBPC taskforce on anti-internet sales of counterfeit goods was set up at the end of the panel.

[67] The Standardization Administration of China (SAC) released the Draft Regulation on National Standards Involving Patents in 2004 for public comments. On 2 November 2009, the SAC released a new draft named the 'Draft Interim Regulation on Formulation and Revision of National Standards Involving Patents' for public comments. A Chinese version and English translation are available by checking the section of Policies, Laws and Regulations on www.qbpc.org.cn.

[68] The QBPC realized that member companies could unintentionally place advertisements for their products on those websites that without permission provide copyrighted works for unauthorized downloading. To reduce funding

been successful not only in curbing online piracy by putting pressure on advertising revenue sources generated through infringing portals, but also in attracting the attention of the Chinese authorities, media, and many local rights holders/legitimate new media operators, all of which showed great support for the campaign. It also helps build QBPC and its members' image through putting into effect Corporate Social Responsibility (CSR) in supporting IPR protection and business ethics in China. The QBPC set up the taskforce dealing with internet sales and the postal delivery of counterfeit goods.[69] The QBPC keeps strengthening the partnership with the Confederation of Indian Industry and has built a partnership with the Brand Owners' Protection Group of the Gulf Cooperation Council countries and Yemen, based in Dubai.

14.6. CONCLUSION

In concluding, the QBPC has witnessed significant progress in China with China's adoption of an increasingly transparent intellectual property policy and legislative reform process. A true partnership between Chinese government agencies and the QBPC has been built through years of mutual trust and cooperation; a successful capacity-building programme initiated by the leaders of civil IP court judges, and Customs officials, prosecutors and police officers. The QBPC recognizes that it will take more effort to further improve IP enforcement in China and to find winning

---

to these sites, the QBPC initiated the ethical on-line advertisement initiative to regularly monitor the targeted sites and to send notices to members alerting them of their advertisements found on the sites providing copyright works without permission for unauthorized downloading. Once notified, members normally remove their advertisement from such sites. Members have realized that this initiative works more effectively on those ISPs than filing legal actions, as cutting advertisement funding causes bigger losses to the sites than a fine or civil compensation awarded by a court. The outcome of this campaign has led to other ISPs that provide only authorized copyrighted works for authorized downloading proactively approaching the QBPC to express their support for the QBPC's initiative.

[69] The QBPC taskforce on anti-internet sale of counterfeit goods was set up at the 8 September General Meeting in 2009. At the meeting, Mr Li Qunying, Director of the IP Division of Policy and Legal Affairs Department of the General Administration of Customs (GAC) gave a presentation with the theme of 'Strengthening Border IP Protection against Delivering Counterfeit Goods via the Postal Service'. Director Li disclosed that 80% of Customs seizures were conducted in the post and courier sectors and the unit prices of these seized goods were getting higher.

solutions to help China in achieving its goals of establishing a culture of innovation. Practical experience of doing business in China has taught the QBPC that it takes great wisdom to foresee changes; courage to face these changes, and knowledge to deal with the changes. And most importantly, and above all, to keep making positive changes![70]

[70] The views and comments of the author were formed and made through years of experience working in the public and private sectors in China and with QBPC members. The author has tried to be as objective as possible but given the diversified industries, focus areas and experiences of members, the views and comments of the author should not be taken as being those of the QBPC or of the General Electric Company.

15. Telecommunications and the internet

Rohan Kariyawasam[1]

15.1. INTRODUCTION

This chapter discusses the current regulation of telecommunications and internet networks in China. The chapter looks at the regulation of the network itself in China and attempts to provide a snapshot of the main regulations impacting the delivery of electronic material over digital networks, and therefore combines a discussion of both the regulations on networks and to some extent content, such as regarding broadcasting and electronic commerce. At the time of writing, China is yet to agree amendments to the PRC's Telecommunications Regulations 2000 (effective 25 September 2000). The Financial and Economic Committee of the National People's Congress (NPC) has already submitted the latest draft of a new telecoms law to the State Council, and therefore, the discussion of telecoms in this chapter is written bearing this in mind. There may be many changes ahead given the complex political and economic status of telecommunications in China. The focus of network infrastructure regulation is on aspects of the digital network that looks to deliver new content services, such as IPTV (TV over internet networks) and mobile TV, where there is overlap between infrastructure regulation and content regulation (viz. broadcasting).

Section 15.2 provides an overview of the Chinese telecoms market. Section 15.3 discusses the current Telecommunications Regulations with a focus on licensing, and particularly the Ministry of Industry and Information Technology's (MIIT's) Measures on the Administration of Licensing for Telecommunication Services Business (effective 10 April 2009),[2] and interconnection, and clarifying the status of the Telecommunications Regulations within the complex hierarchy of laws, regulations, measures,

---

1 Professor of Law, Cardiff Law School, Cardiff University.

2 This replaced the older Measures on the Administration of Licensing for Telecommunication Services Business (1 January 2002).

rules and notices within China. Section 15.4 reviews the regulation of internet infrastructure, and the convergence of audiovisual services delivered over internet networks, and new measures introduced on network security in 2009. Section 15.5 looks at the complex regulatory environment for foreign telecommunication enterprises in China under the Provisions for the Administration of Foreign-Investment Telecommunications Enterprises (Revised), State Council Decree No. 534 (promulgated and effective 10 September 2008) ('FITE Rules'). Section 15.6 reviews the interplay of the Anti Monopoly Law (AML) with the Telecommunications Regulations, including the 2010 revised dominance rules published by the State Administration for Industry and Commerce (SAIC) in January 2011 and coming into effect on 1 February 2011, while Section 15.7 concludes with a brief discussion of the new draft Telecommunications Law, currently, at the time of writing, before the State Council.

15.2. OVERVIEW

At the time of writing, the Chinese telecommunications market is dominated by three Chinese telecommunication operators (financed mainly in Hong Kong), two of which operate fixed-line networks with national licenses (China Telecommunications Corporation-China Telecom and China United Network Communications Group Co. Ltd-China Unicom), and three who operate wireless networks (China Telecom, China Mobile Communications Corporation-China Mobile, and China Unicom). Telecommunication services are regulated under the recently formed Ministry of Industry and Information Technology (MIIT), formerly the Ministry of Postage and Ministry of Information Industry. Under the PRC Telecommunications Regulations 2000 ('Telecommunications Regulations', promulgated by the State Council and coming into effect on 1 October 2000), services regulation is divided into two main categories, basic telecommunication services and value-added telecommunications services (VATs). In addition to the Telecommunications Regulations, there are a host of measures and circulars issued by both the State Council and MIIT that cover telecommunications and increasingly the overlap of infrastructure with the internet, following China's accession to the WTO. These are discussed further below.

15.3. REGULATION OF TELECOMMUNICATIONS

The regulatory regime for telecommunications in China is complex in that it involves a mix of both state and administrative provisions. It can be described as pyramidal, where at the very apex of the pyramid lies the Chinese Constitution, followed by a second layer of national laws, a third layer of administrative regulations (such as the Telecommunications Regulations 2000), and finally departmental rules, such as rules emanating from the Department of Industry, Transport and Commerce of the State Council (the department, for example, responsible for oversight of the drafting of the new telecoms law).[3] The current Telecommunications Regulations 2000 ('Regulations') therefore are *not* laws, but administrative regulations. The impact of this distinction lies in the hierarchy of legislative instruments used in Chinese legal practice. So, for example, the National People's Congress (NPC) is the highest authority and has responsibility for any amendments to the Chinese constitution. Both the NPC and its Standing Committee are responsible for the enactment and amendment of laws. The State Council formulates administrative regulations according to the Constitution and laws. The State Council will often enact administrative regulations, including Ordinances, measures, provisions, rules and decisions with a formal law (through the NPC) generally coming afterwards. Local law/regulations are enacted by local people's congresses; departmental regulations are enacted by the separate Ministries (e.g. MIIT, MOFCOM etc.) which fall under the jurisdiction of the State Council. Therefore, the general hierarchy of laws in China is the Constitution; NPC Laws; State Council Administrative regulations; local laws/regulations, and departmental regulations. If there is any conflict between local laws/regulations and departmental regulations, the State Council decides which law/regulation/measure etc., will apply.[4]

It is also highly significant that the NPC has the power to withdraw departmental or local administrative laws, regulations, measures etc., that contravene laws that the NPC has already issued. This power illustrates well the internal dynamics of China's legislative structure – it is one primarily of subordination, unification and supervision, and quite unlike the internal dynamics, for example, of Western structures, which tend rather to represent a relationship of restraint and legislative balance between the legislature, judiciary and executive.[5] Further, no Chinese administrative or local law, measure, regulation, rule or ordinance is allowed to

---

3 Zhao Xiaoguang, Department of Industry, Transport, and Commerce of the LAO (Legal Affairs Office, State Council), 'PRC: China's Telecommunications Law in the Future', October 2009.

4 For a more complete discussion of these issues (in Chinese) see: http://www.sypf.com/fzxw/pfcz01/074.htm, accessed November 2010.

5 See China's current legislation and structure (in English) at: http://www.china.org.cn/english/kuaixun/76212.htm, accessed November 2010.

contravene the state Constitution and state law. In exceptional cases, some laws and regulations of autonomous regions may differ from the Constitution and state law,[6] whilst drafting such laws, regional legislative institutions must abide by the Constitution, the Law of Self-government in Minority Autonomous Regions and the Law of the People's Republic of China on Legislation (Law on Legislation), and report to the NPC's Standing Committee for prior approval.[7]

The Telecommunication Regulations consist of 81 articles together with an annex, the Classification Catalogue (Classification of Telecommunications Services), which lists the services that can be considered as basic telecom services and those which are VATs. The Regulations are divided into four main sections: general provisions, telecommunications market, telecommunications services, telecommunications-related construction (construction of telecommunication facilities), security of telecommunications, penal provisions (criminal and civil sanctions), and finally supplementary provisions that refer mainly to a clause requiring the State Council to issue later procedures covering investment by foreign operators in the domestic Chinese sector. This has been duly done in the form of Provisions for the Administration of Foreign-Investment Telecommunications Enterprises (Revised), State Council Decree No. 534 (promulgated and effective 10 September 2008) (FITE Rules).[8] The FITE Rules are administrative regulations (as opposed to laws) and have proven to be contentious in China in that they have led inadvertently to foreign-owned corporate structures in telecoms that are not entirely recognized in law by the state (so-called China-China Foreign (CCF)[9] structures), but are more or less permitted (discussed further below). Whether this

---

[6] There are five autonomous regions in China: the Tibetans in Tibet, the Zhuangs in Guangxi, the Uyghurs in Xinjiang, the Mongols in Inner Mongolia, and the Huis in Ningxia. See Wikipedia at: http://en.wikipedia.org/wiki/Autonomous_regions_of_the_People's_Republic_of_China, accessed November 2010.

[7] China's current legislation and structure (in English) at: http://www.china.org.cn/english/kuaixun/76212.htm, accessed November 2010.

[8] The FITE Rules replaced the earlier rules, the Administration of Foreign-Invested Telecommunications Enterprises, State Council Decree No. 333 (promulgated 11 December 2001, effective 1 January 2002).

[9] In 1995, China Unicom developed the 'CCF' model as a means of circumventing the restrictions by foreign companies on foreign direct investment (FDI) into China. Under this model, China Unicom created subsidiaries which in turn contracted by means of joint ventures with strategic foreign investors. Tripartite contracts between China Unicom, its subsidiary and the joint venture company for equipment leasing, royalties, consulting, and license fees under network contracts effectively allowed the foreign investor to enjoy 'equity-like' returns. For further details, see: Scott Yunxiang Guan, '"China's Telecommunications Reforms":

position will be allowed to continue under the planned (new) draft law on telecommunications remains to be seen.

Article 2 Regulations defines 'telecommunications' as 'the activity of using wired or wireless electromagnetic or optoelectronic systems to transmit voice, text, data, images or any other form of information'. This definition is intended to cover internet and broadcast networks, thereby enabling the MIIT to regulate converged networks, although as we will see when discussing IPTV and mobile TV, the current Chinese regulatory framework is more complex, with different regulators and ministries being involved. As mentioned above, the Regulations (Article 8) distinguishes basic telecommunication services from VATs. Basic telecom services are defined as 'the business of providing network infrastructure, public data transmission and basic voice communications services'. By contrast, value-added telecommunications services means the 'telecommunications and information services provided through the public network infrastructure'.

As to whether internet services fall under either the basic or the VATs definition of services has proved a contentious point in China. Internet services also fall under the scope of a number of different *laws* (viz., Decision on Maintaining the Security of the Internet, adopted by the Standing Committee of the National People's Congress in December 2000) and administrative *regulations* formulated by the State Council (viz., Administrative Measures for Internet Administration Services 2000), and *rules* formulated by the MIIT itself (viz., Measures for the Administration of Domain Names of China's Interconnected Networks, December 2004). These are just a few of the measures that cover this sector and the regulation of internet services is further discussed below. US businesses have been pushing for some years for a clearer definition of basic and value added services and the draft New Telecoms Law seems to represent an improvement in this highly significant area as the Chinese executive begins to integrate the concept of convergence of broadcasting, telecommunications and information technology networks into its regulatory thinking. As mentioned, the Schedule of Classification of Telecommunications Services ('Classification Annex') attached to the current Regulations sets out the list of basic (including amongst other service categories for example: fixed domestic long distance, local telephone, international communications infrastructure and business, mobile telephone and data, satellite communications and mobile satellite, internet and other public

---

From Monopoly towards Competition', in *Asian Economic and Political Issues*, 9 (ed. Frank Columbus), Nova Science Publishers Inc., 2003.

data transmission, leasing and sale of bandwidth) and VATs (this includes services where the supplier adds value to customer information by enhancing its form of content or providing for storage and retrieval).[10] Under Article 9 Regulations, any new type of telecom service (not listed in the Classification Annex) to be supplied, perhaps on an experimental basis as an example of innovation in the sector, must be approved beforehand through a filing to the telecommunications administration authority of the relevant Chinese province.[11] The Regulations provide for the State Council's department in charge of the information industry to amend the list from time to time, which provides the room for some flexibility from the regulator's perspective. Also, this provision for amendment by the State Council highlights that the real power to structure the telecoms sector lies in the hands of the State Council, in turn controlled to some extent by China's political executive.

The newly formed MIIT (established in 2008) integrates the industrial management responsibilities of the National Development and Reform Commission, the function of the State Administration of Science and Technology and Industry for National Defence (except nuclear power management), the function of the previous Ministry of Information Industry (previously itself an amalgamation of two rival ministries, the Ministry of Electronic Industry and Ministry of Posts and Telecommunications in 1998), and the function of the Information Office of the State Council. Although the MIIT is the formally designated regulator of the communications sector in China, above the MIIT sits the political executive (Communist Party) and two powerful state institutions: the National Development and Reform Commission (NDRC) and the State-Owned Asset Supervision and Administration Commission (SASAC), the state organ that holds shares in China Telecom, China Mobile, and China Unicom. So although the MIIT is the de facto regulator of the communications sector (*jianguan jiegou*),[12] it is in fact a state-designated administrative agency, and therefore under the influence of both the political executive

---

[10] The Schedule of Classification of Telecommunication Services (sometimes known as the 'Catalogue of Telecommunication Services') and attached to the Telecommunication Regulations, was revised in February 2003.

[11] It could therefore be an option for cable and DSL operators to provide telecom services in China, although at the time of writing, the filing option under Article 9 has only been exercised in a very limited way (e.g. in Shanghai, with the technical convergence of telecommunications, internet and cable sectors: see Li, G., 'Moving towards Unsustainability: A Study of the Chinese Telecommunications Regulation', *International Journal of Private Law*, 1 (1/2), 2008, p. 59).

[12] Yeo, Y., Regulatory Politics in China's Telecommunications Service Industry: When Socialist Market Economy Meets Independent Regulator Model,

and the National People's Congress (NPC). All industrial policies and regulations drafted by the MIIT will be reviewed by the NDRC before approval by the State Council, and ultimately the NPC. In this respect, the MIIT is not the independent regulator envisaged by the WTO's Secretariat when negotiating China's accession protocol to the WTO,[13] and specially envisaged under the WTO's Basic Agreement on Telecommunications to the GATS (sometimes known as the Fourth Protocol), and under Article 5 of China's regulatory Reference Paper ('RP' – an additional commitment under China's schedule of Specific Commitments under the GATS). China incorporated the RP into its GATS schedule covering both value-added and basic telecommunications services, although the scope of the Reference Paper is limited to basic services only.[14] Section 5 of the RP states: 'The regulatory body is separate from, and not accountable to, any supplier of basic telecommunications services. The decisions of and the procedures used by regulators shall be impartial with respect to all market participants.'[15] The draft of the New Telecoms Law, discussed further below, makes no changes to the current structure of the MIIT, although further provisions have been added to give effect to the convergence of telecom and broadcasting networks (discussed below). Whether this will change or not following the passage of the New Telecoms Law through the State Council remains to be seen.

In terms of licensing, under the current Regulations, applications for basic operating telecommunication services (Basic Telecommunications Service Operating Permit) must be submitted to the MIIT for approval,[16] and the MITT must either approve or reject the application within 180 days of receipt.[17] Article 10 Regulations sets out the conditions that need to be met by the applicant for the award of a basic services permit and which include: a state shareholding of at least 51% in the applicant; the submission of feasibility and technical plans; the availability of relevant

June 2008, at http://regulation.upf.edu/utrecht-08-papers/yyeo.pdf, accessed October 2010.

13 WTO Ministerial Conference, Report of the Working Party on the Accession of China, WT/MIN(01)/3 (10 November 2001); WTO Ministerial Conference, Accession of the People's Republic of China: Decision of 10 November 2001, WT/L/432 (23 November 2001). China accepted the Protocol on the Accession of the People's Republic of China (annexed to the Decision of 10 November 2001) on 11 November 2001 and, in accordance with its terms, became a WTO Member on 11 December 2001.

14 China GATS Schedule 46.

15 China GATS Schedule 48.

16 Article 9, Telecommunications Regulations 2000 ('Regulations').

17 Ibid, Article 10.

funds and specialized personnel to carry out services; a relevant site and corresponding resources to carry out business activities; the applicant's reputation for providing long-term services, and 'other conditions' specified by the State which remain undefined in the Regulations. Under Article 12 Regulations, the issuance of a basic telecoms permit will be as a result of a tendering process. This aspect of the Regulations has been criticized for a lack of transparency (as required by China's WTO accession protocol for example).[18] VAT services covering two or more provinces, autonomous regions and/or municipalities directly under the control of the central government require approval by the State Council and the issue of a Cross-regional Value Added Telecommunications Service Operating Permit.[19] Licensing under the Telecommunications Regulations is more specifically covered by the MIIT's Measures on the Administration of Licensing for Telecommunication Services Business (effective 10 April 2009),[20] which repeats many of the provisions to be found in the Telecommunications Regulations, but with more detailed guidance on application procedures. Under Article 5.6 (Chapter II) of the new licensing rules, the registered capital threshold has now been lowered to RMB 100 million (down from RMB 200 million) for intra-regional operators and RMB 1 billion (down from RMB 2 billion) for national (or cross-regional) operators. This reduction in required capital is likely to allow for a greater number of players to enter the telecoms market and could, for example, lead to greater integration of telecommunication, cable TV and internet service providers. Under Article 34.33 (Chapter VI), the administrative procedures required to exit the telecommunications market have been strengthened (including the specification of a 30 day notice period). Under Article 37.39 (Chapter VII), the MIIT now has a wider range of powers to inspect both VATs and basic telecommunication licensees on an annual basis. The new licensing measures also create stronger obligations on licensees to monitor third party services (for example, if a basic telecoms licensee, monitoring the content of any contracted third party value-added service providers). Also, VATs licensees who provide access to websites are prohibited from sublicensing network access to other VATs licensees. This latter prohibition is likely to restrict the range of cooperative licensing arrangements that foreign service providers are able to enter into with domestic VATs licensees.

---

[18] Li G., 'Moving towards Unsustainability: A Study of the Chinese Telecommunications Regulation', *International Journal of Private Law*, 1 (1/2), 2008, p. 59.

[19] Article 9, Regulations.

[20] This replaced the older Measures on the Administration of Licensing for Telecommunication Services Business (1 January 2002).

The Interconnection provisions are set out in Articles 17–22 Regulations. Interconnection is vital to an operator and allows the subscribers of any one operator's network to connect with another. For new entrants, the viability of an undertaking's business will be dependent on the ability of the new entrant to interconnect with the incumbent's network on transparent and non-discriminatory terms.[21] Unlike the European Union's Access and Interconnection Directive, for example,[22] the Telecommunication Regulations do not make a distinction between interconnection obligations on the one hand (physical and logical interconnection of networks) and access on the other (often access to the incumbent's network at layers above the network's 'physical' infrastructure layer). Quite often the problem with lack of effective competition in value-added services has to do with restricted or diminished access rights, as opposed to physical interconnection of the underlying networks (although this too can be a problem).

Article 17 Regulations requires that interconnection shall be on the basis of technical feasibility, economic sense, fairness, impartiality and mutual 'complementation'. The Regulations create specific obligations for Leading Telecommunication Business Operators (LTOs), requiring LTOs not to refuse interconnection requests. LTOs are defined in Article 17 as 'operators that control vital telecommunications infrastructure, have a relatively large share of the telecommunications market and can materially influence the entry of other telecommunications business operators into the telecommunications business market'. The issue as to which operator can be designated as an LTO is determined by the relevant department within the State Council responsible for the information industry (MIIT). In a similar way to how the EC requires operators with significant market power (SMP) under the Interconnection and Access Directive mentioned above to publish Reference Interconnection Offers,[23] the Chinese Regulations require LTOs to formulate interconnection rules that include details on procedure and time for network interconnection and a list of unbundled network elements in accordance with the principle of

[21] For a detailed treatment of the general subject of interconnection, see Kariyawasam, R., 'Interconnection Law and Precedent', in *Telecommunications Law* (eds I. Walden and J. Angel), Blackstone Press, 1 edition, 1997.

[22] Directive 2002/19/EC. See, for example, Article 12 Directive, where the Commission sets out extensive rights for access to a network, involving, for example, access to user interfaces and program interfaces, and providing the National Regulatory Authority in European Member States with the right to impose mandatory access obligations in certain defined circumstances.

[23] Article 9(2) Directive 2002/19/EC.

non-discrimination.[24] Again the interconnection rules have to be approved by the MIIT. Disputes on interconnection are to be mediated by the MIIT and a decision reached within 45 days after the application for mediation.[25] If the disputing parties are unable to reach agreement within 45 days, the MIIT can consult externally with advisers and impose a network interconnection plan on the parties. [26] Further rules granting the MIIT the power to mediate interconnection disputes and issue binding administrative decisions were published in the form of the Telecommunications Network Connectivity Dispute Resolution Measures (effective 1 January 2002).

Since the publication of the Telecommunication Regulations, the MIIT has introduced new provisions on interconnection, including the Telecommunications Network Connectivity Rules (effective 10 May 2001). Under these rules, interconnection of public telecommunications networks is mandated for basic telecommunications services operators and the rules prohibit the limitation or delay of access to third party telecommunications providers. But to qualify for interconnection rights, an enterprise must have a basic telecommunications operating license in the first instance.

As regards the regulation of end-users' charges in the telecoms sector, Article 24 Regulations sets out the basis of regulation as being a combination of both market-led and government-regulated charges (either government guided or government fixed): by contrast, charges for VATs are either regulated by the market or only *guided* by government. For those charges that are to be fixed by government, the prices will be determined by the State Council's pricing department in conjunction with the MIIT and following final approval by the State Council.[27] In this respect, operators in China are able to provide differentiated charging, charging in accordance with the type of service being offered. Furthermore, both basic telecommunication and VATs licenses (including licenses for the delivery of internet content–discussed below) allow service providers to block content that violates China's constitution.

A good aspect of the Regulations is that under Article 26, any telecommunication tariffs that are to be fixed or guided by government shall only be confirmed following a period of open consultation with operators and subscribers in the sector. Again, since the publication of the Telecommunication Regulations, the MIIT has introduced further provi-

24 Article 18 Regulations.
25 Article 20 Regulations.
26 Ibid.
27 Articles 24 and 25 Regulations.

sions on charging, which are subject to periodic amendment, depending on the originating and receiving party under the Measures on the Settlement of Call Charges between Telecommunication Networks (effective 21 March 2001), and also the Public Telecommunication Interconnection Settlement and Cost-sharing Measures (effective 1 December 2003).[28]

15.4. REGULATION OF INTERNET SERVICES

As with telecommunications, the internet sector is regulated by several institutions with overlapping jurisdictions. These include MIIT, the Ministry of Commerce (MOFCOM), State Administration for Industry and Commerce (SAIC), the Ministry of Public Security (MPS), the State Administration of Radio, Film and Television (SARFT), and the General Administration of Press and Publication (GAPP). The MIIT and MOFCOM have the principle responsibility for assessing for qualification of permits, overseeing the market structure and the daily operation of internet businesses, whilst the other institutions are more concerned with the regulation of internet content. As with the complexity in regulatory control, one can expect that the ensuing laws, regulations, rules and notices emanating from these institutions are equally complex. The Administration of Internet Information Service Procedures ('Internet Procedures', 25 September 2000) provide for two types of category of internet services.[29] Under Article 3 of the Internet Procedures, for services provided for remuneration (fee based), these are categorized as *Commercial Internet Information Services*, defined as 'service activities such as compensated provision to online subscribers through the internet of information services or website production etc.' Under Article 4, the operator concerned must apply for a permit (Internet Content Provider – 'ICP' permit) to the telecommunication administration authority of the province, autonomous region or municipality directly under the central

---

[28] The original Chinese version of this measure can be accessed at: http://bbs.c114.net/uploadImages/200412231557139919.doc, accessed November 2010.

[29] Administration of Internet Information Services Procedures, Decree of State Council No. 292, effective date 25 September 2000 (hereafter, 'Internet Procedures'). There appear to be several different versions of the English translation of these administrative provisions (for example, one version refers at Article 3 to 'Operational internet information services', whereas the body text above refers to 'Commercial Internet Information Services'. However, both carry the same meaning. The official (Chinese) version can be found at The Ministry of Public Security PRC website at: http://www.mps.gov.cn/n16/n1282/n3493/n3778/n492863/493177.html, accessed November 2010.

government or the MIIT for a VATs Operating Permit (Article 7). The MIIT is then under an obligation to issue a permit or reject the application within 60 days of the application, and if rejecting, must explain its reasons in writing.[30] Free internet (or uncompensated) services are categorized as *non-commercial internet information services*, defined as 'the service activity of non-compensated provision to online subscribers through the internet of information that is in the public domain and openly accessible'. The supplying operator of a non-commercial internet information service need only register (record filing procedure) with the MIIT or the relevant telecommunications administration authority at a provincial level.[31] However, even for the provision of free internet services, the record-filing procedure is not a simple 'rubber stamping affair'. Under Article 8 Internet Procedures, several materials must be provided at the time of the filing, including: information on the work unit providing the services and the persons responsible for the website; the website's URL and the services to be provided. If the services fall under specific categories, such as news, publishing, education, medical treatment, health, pharmaceuticals or medical apparatus, they require specific examination and consent by the relevant competent authority in each of these areas before filing can take place with the MIIT. A letter of consent from this competent authority also needs to be submitted as part of the MIIT's record filing procedure. Even bulletin board services need to be registered[32] (there is a separate measure covering Electronic Messaging Services discussed further below). Under Article 12 Internet Procedures, all companies providing internet information services in China need to post their Operating Permit or registration numbers prominently on their websites.

One of the most interesting provisions, set out at Article 14 Internet Procedures, states that internet information service providers that 'engage in the provision of such services as news, publishing or electronic bulletin board services . . .' shall keep a record of the information they provide, the times of dissemination and the URLs or domain names. Internet access service providers shall keep a record of such information as the times online subscribers are online, the subscribers' account numbers, the URLs or domain names, the callers' telephone numbers, etc. These records need to be kept for at least 60 days and must be provided to the relevant state authorities when required. The data recording provisions under Article 14 work hand in hand with the public security provisions built into Article

---

[30] Article 7 Internet Procedures.
[31] Article 8 Internet Procedures.
[32] Article 9 Internet Procedures.

15 which set out the usual provisions for the protection of state interests vis-à-vis the Chinese Constitution, restricting internet information service providers from producing, reproducing, disseminating or broadcasting information with content that divulges state secrets, harms the dignity of the state, incitement to ethnic hatred, sabotages state religious policy, disseminates rumours, disturbs social order, propagates obscencity, pornography etc.

A significant area in telecommunications regulation is in the convergence of broadcasting, information technology and telecommunications services. This convergence raises complex issues of regulation of both infrastructure and content services, impacting on the use of both technology and IP laws, which is the central focus of this book. In China, a good example of this complex overlap is seen in the regulation of television programming over internet networks (IPTV) and over mobile networks (Mobile TV). Traditional telecommunications concern point-to-point communications (a single telephone accessing another telephone on a different network), whereas public broadcasting concerns point to multipoint communications. With both IPTC and Mobile TV, telecommunications and broadcasting functions merge. Also, IPTV networks are very often closed user groups in the sense that access to the network will depend on a subscription to an ISP, whereas Mobile TV requires a SIM card that provides access to a mobile network. In China, IPTV is provided mainly by China Telecom and China Netcom, with predictions for a subscriber base of over 21 million by year end 2011.[33] One of the greatest advantages offered by IPTV is the time-shifting function (pause and drawback on live TV programming), allowing subscribers to download the desired content on demand.[34] However, under current Chinese law, VATs licensees cannot offer IPTV services. In order to do so, the VATs licensee needs to have a collaborative relationship with a broadcast TV enterprise that already has an IPTV license. This is in contrast to the European market for example, where under the deregulated framework of the European Commission's new regulatory framework for electronic networks and services, converged services are permissible. In China, this regulatory restriction is likely to lead to gateway (and perhaps a bottleneck) access to content in the event that broadcast TV enterprises are reluctant to license content to VATs licensees rather than offering it to digital TV broadcasters.

---

[33] Holznagel, B., Xu, J., and Hart, T. (eds)., *Regulating Telecommunications in the EU and China: What Lessons to be Learned?* LIT Verlag, Germany, 2009, p. 149.

[34] Ibid, p. 153.

Mobile TV in China was used extensively for the recent Olympic Games in Beijing in 2008. One of the key restrictions on its proliferation across China is the standard of technology to be used. In China, two standards are common: DAB and CMMB. In terms of regulation, both the IPTV and Mobile TV sectors are regulated by the MIIT (regulating the telecommunication networks), and the State Administration of Radio, Film and Television (SARFT – regulating the broadcast television network and services). As we saw earlier, telecommunications are regulated both centrally by the State and at a provincial level. Broadcasting, however, is structured along a 'four level establishment and four level management' hierarchy. 'Each level, including central, province (autonomous region, municipality), city (prefecture) and county (county-level city), establishes its own broadcast TV station and manages its broadcast TV enterprise through its own broadcast TV administration departments'.[35] At present, the SARFT also regulates satellite, terrestrial and cable TV broadcasts. The joint regulation by both the MIIT and SARFT of this sector has proved contentious with telecoms operators challenging the restrictions in broadcasting law restricting their sole ownership of broadcast TV licenses. At the time of writing, current law includes the *Administrative Provisions on Internet Audio-Visual Programme Service (Decree No. 56)* issued jointly by SARFT and MIIT in January 2008, and the *Management Measures for Transmitting Audio and Video Programmes over Internet and Other Information Networks (Decree No. 39)* issued by SARFT in July 2004. Decree No. 56 contains several provisions on the protection of the national socialist culture and society and is an important aspect of the licensing process.[36] Under both Decrees No. 39 and 56, in order to provide Mobile or IPTV services in China, both a telecommunications Internet Content Provider (ICP) License[37] and a License for Information Network Communication Audio-Visual Programme (INCAVP License)[38] are required. All websites in China must carry an ICP number and a link to the MIIT website on the front page. Further, Decree No. 56 requires that all applicants who are intending to provide internet audiovisual programming services be wholly state-owned or state-controlled and have no record of illegal activities for a period of three years prior to the application

35 Ibid, p. 159.

36 See Articles 4–6 Decree No. 56.

37 Article 19 Decree No. 56 provides, 'Internet A/V[audiovisual] program service providers shall choose network operations work units that have a lawfully-obtained internet access services telecommunications management license or a radio/television programming transmission management license . . .'.

38 Article 7 Decree No. 56.

date.[39] The licensing scheme is further complicated by the fact that if the undertaking wishing to provide IPTV and Mobile TV services is also planning to offer *current affairs* (either audio or video) programming, a broadcast television license or Internet News Information Service license is required (besides the ICP and INCAVP licenses).[40] Both broadcast and Internet News Information licenses carry restrictions on the broadcasting of prohibited content, such as content challenging the Chinese Constitution, the unity of the nation, content to incite national hatred or discrimination, disturbing public order and endangering fine folk traditions etc. Restrictions of this type are common in all forms of media content licenses in China. Audiovisual program content needs to be kept for a minimum of 60 days.[41] Further, for those providers who use 'self made channels' (not defined in the law) to broadcast, audiovisual programs need to be submitted to radio and television stations at the local (municipal) level and above or central news work units.[42] Failure to follow the procedures and rules set out in Decree No. 56 could (ultimately) lead to fines (generally RMB 30,000)[43] and sanctions (e.g. restrictions on primary investors and managers investing in or providing internet A/V programming services for at least five years from the date of punishment),[44] or as set out in the Regulations for the Administration of Radio and Television 1997.[45]

Other internet services that involve a telecoms component and that fall to be regulated by the state include email services and private bulletin messaging boards. Under Article 4 Measures for the Administration of Internet Email Services 2006 ('Email Measures'), undertakings intending to provide internet email services (defined in the Email Measures as: 'activities of establishing internet email servers to provide conditions for internet users to send and receive emails . . .'[46]), must obtain a VATs license beforehand.[47] Both ISPs and telecommunication operators are prevented from providing an operator of email services with access to a network unless a VATs license is in place or the undertaking concerned has performed the

39 Article 8(1) Decree No. 56.
40 Article 9 Decree No. 56.
41 Article 15 Decree No. 56.
42 Article 9 Decree No. 56.
43 Article 24 Decree No. 56.
44 Article 27 Decree No. 56 (for internet A/V program service providers that engage in major illegal and unlawful activities).
45 Adopted at the 61 Executive Meeting of the State Council on 1 August 1997, promulgated by Decree No. 228 of the State Council of the Peoples Republic of China on 11 August 1997, and effective 1 September 1997.
46 Article 2 Email Measures 2006.
47 Article 4 Email Measures 2006.

procedures for the 'archival filing of non-operational internet information services'. Therefore, if the undertaking is not intending to offer commercial email services, the undertaking only need register its interest (with the MIIT or the communication administrative bureau of the relevant province, autonomous region, or municipality directly under the central government[48]). Further, the internet email service provider needs to record the time of sending or receiving internet emails via its email server, including the internet email and Internet IP addresses of *both* senders and recipients for at least a period of 60 days.[49]

Electronic messaging services (EMS) fall to be regulated under the Provisions on the Management of Internet BBS Service 2000 (BBS Measures). Electronic messaging is defined as: 'Acts enabling online subscribers to publish information on the internet in an interactive form, such as bulletin boards, whiteboards, discussion forums, chat rooms and message boards'.[50] In order to provide EMS services, an internet information service provider will need to have already applied for a VATs license from the relevant authority as set out in the Internet Procedures discussed above.[51] Further, the provider will need to either file a dedicated application for a permit (if providing commercial internet information services) or carry out a dedicated record-filing procedure (non-commercial services) with the same authority that granted its VATs license, before launching an EMS.[52]

On-line advertising is regulated by the State Administration for Industry and Commerce (SAIC) and its provincial departments. Currently, at the national level, the Administrative Measures for Advertising Operating Permits (effective November 2004) apply. Under these measures, only radio or television stations, newspaper, magazine publishers, non-profit institutions, and 'other entities' as required by PRC laws and regulations (not defined in the measure) to have a specific permit for online advertising. For general commercial businesses, the government has relaxed the conditions and these businesses only need file a registration with the MIIT's publicly accessible file management system. The position is slightly different in specific provinces/municipalities, such as Beijing, where the Beijing branch of the SAIC has issued its own Provisional Measures of

---

48 So, for example, under Article 6 Email Measures, an internet email service provider must, 20 days prior to the opening of its email server, register the IP address of the internet email server with the communications administrative bureau.

49 Article 10 Email Measures 2006.

50 Article 2 BBS Measures 2000.

51 Article 7 BBS Measures 2000.

52 Ibid.

Administration of Online Advertising Businesses of Beijing Municipality (effective May 2001), where commercial businesses advertising online had to have both an ICP license and an advertising permit. There is some conflict therefore in the law on this.[53] E-commerce has been discussed at greater length in Chapters 9 and 10, where it is clear that both Beijing and Shanghai municipalities have issued specific regulations on e-commerce, and that business permits with slightly differing conditions are required for trading online. Other regulatory instruments issued that touch on internet regulation include Provisions on the Administration of Internet Audio and Video Programming Services (effective 31 January 2008), discussed above; Notice issued by the Ministry of Culture Concerning Strengthening and Improving Network Music Content Examination Work (notified August 2009), which seeks to strengthen the regulatory oversight of imported musical content delivered over online networks in China (for example, under Article 7, a network cultural business permit to import online music is required from the Ministry of Culture); circular issued by the Ministry of Culture/MOFCOM on the use of virtual currency in online games (June 2009).

Also, a number of new provisions have been introduced to strengthen security on the internet, including: Mechanisms for Identifying and Resolving Trojan Horse and Botnet Activities (effective June 2009) and Measures for the Administration of Communication Network Protection (effective March 2010). Under Article 7 of the Communication Network Protection Measure, 'communications network operation units' (basic telecom operators, VATs and internet domain name holders etc.) are required to classify their network operations into five separate categories in the event that their networks come under attack (e.g. by a virus). The categories are classed in accordance with the level of threat perceived to national security, economic operation, social order and public interest that may be caused by damage to the relevant network. Under Article 22 of the same measure, operators who fail to abide by the measures can be ordered to remedy the situation by the telecom authorities according to its authority and, if the operator refuses, a fine of more than RMB 5,000 but less than RMB 30,000 can be imposed.

Such security measures reflect similar concerns in other jurisdictions over a potential attack of telecom networks by third parties causing breaches of both security and personal privacy. In Europe, for example,

---

[53] Sha, W., and Yu, D., 'Internet Content Provider Licenses in the People's Republic of China's Internet Industry: A Practical Perspective', available at: http://www.ipschool.net/CIIP/files/cht07.pdf, accessed November 2010.

the European Commission has recently introduced a new directive, the Citizenship Rights Directive,[54] to supplement existing privacy protection under its 2002 regulatory framework for electronic networks and services. Article 2(4(c)) 2009 Citizenship Rights Directive amends the 2002 E-Privacy Directive by inserting a new provision at Article 4(3) E-Privacy Directive, which reads:

> In the case of a personal data breach, the provider of publicly available electronic communications services shall, without undue delay, notify the personal data breach to the competent national authority.
>
> When the personal data breach is likely to adversely affect the personal data or privacy of a subscriber or individual, the provider shall also notify the subscriber or individual of the breach without undue delay.[55]

One of the differences therefore between the Chinese Communication Network Protection Measure discussed above and the amended EC E-Privacy Directive is that the latter requires (in addition) to the relevant regulator being notified in the EC Member State that a network breach has occurred, that also individual *subscribers* are notified of any network breach that directly affects the subscriber's privacy.

It can be readily seen from the above discussion that the classification of telecommunications services in China's GATS Schedule, and the interpretation of that schedule, are crucial in determining the breadth of market access opportunities that exist for foreign service providers in the internet sector in China. For example, in the Internet Protocol-Virtual Private Network (IP-VPN) sector, China currently classifies IP-VPN services as basic telecommunication services attracting higher regulatory restrictions under the Telecommunications Regulations and revised FITE Rules set out above (and presumably also in the new telecommunications law that is still in the drafting stage). Also, the MIIT has reclassified VoIP (Voice over Internet Protocol) as a *basic* telecommunications service in the Catalogue of Telecommunication Services that forms an annex to the Telecommunication Regulations (2000). This is at odds with developed markets in the West where similar services have either been classified as VATs or as information services to avoid the higher regulatory burdens imposed by classification as a public telecommunications service (Europe) or as a common carrier service (United States). At the time of writing, in

---

[54] Council Directive (EC) 2009/136/EC amending Directive 2002/58/EC [2009] OJ L 337, 18.12.2009.

[55] Council Directive (EC) 2002/58 on privacy and electronic communications [2002] OJ L 201, 31.07.2002 ('E-Privacy Directive').

order to provide VoIP services in China, therefore, an undertaking needs to have a basic telecommunications license, which requires a greater level of investment and regulatory conditions to be satisfied than the holder of a VATs license.

15.4.1. Next Generation Networks

The position on the future regulation of next generation networks (NGN) remains unclear. The Chinese NGN (*Zhōngguó Xià Yīdài Hùliánwǎng*) is a state inspired five-year plan that seeks to adopt Internet Protocol – Version 6 (IPv6) throughout China.[56] Currently, the two most important developments in internet architecture – and those that will have important implications for network connectivity between the developed and developing worlds – are the migration of existing internet networks to a breed of NGN and the exhaustion of IPv4 addresses and the rollout of new IPv6 addresses in 2010/2011.[57] The migration to NGN makes it possible for different underlying platforms (for example, fixed telecommunications and cable television) to offer equivalent services, which has both the potential to benefit competition, but simultaneously enables bundled offers of multiple services to the end-user (which could also give rise to new anti-competitive concerns). The NGN architecture is layered, with the physical infrastructure layer at the bottom and the higher-end service layers built on top. It is this layering concept that the new technology can deliver, making use of very high-speed communications through optical fiber and therefore delivery of high bandwidth applications, such as video over the internet.[58] China showcased IPv6 architecture at the 2008 Beijing Olympics. At the time of writing, over six nationwide backbone NGN networks exist, with a footprint extending to over 20 major cities and over 300 academic, industrial and government research campuses,[59] although at the time of writing no formal measures, regulations or rules governing NGNs have yet been published by the MIIT.

---

56 'China Next Generation Internet', Wikipedia, at: http://en.wikipedia.org/wiki/China_Next_Generation_Internet, accessed November 2010.

57 Kariyawasam, R., 'Next Generation Networks: A New Digital Divide?' *Journal of Innovation in the Digital Economy*, 3 (3), IGI Publishing, June–September 2010, p. 4.

58 Ibid., p. 5.

59 'China Next Generation Internet', Wikipedia, at: http://en.wikipedia.org/wiki/China_Next_Generation_Internet, accessed November 2010.

15.5. FOREIGN INVESTMENT

A foreign telecommunications supplier who wishes to provide telecommunications services in China must establish a Foreign-Investment Telecommunications Enterprise (FITE) by way of an equity joint venture (JV) with a Chinese partner.[60] The Chinese partner is required to apply for a telecommunications license on behalf of the FITE. At the time of writing, the three major basic telecommunication service suppliers do have limited foreign involvement, primarily through indirect investment. Under Article 5(1) FITE Rules, those operators providing basic telecommunication services nationwide or beyond a single province require registered share capital of RMB 1 billion (RMB 10 million for the VATs sector). Article 5(2) specifies that for operators providing basic telecommunication services within a province, autonomous region or municipality directly under the control of the central government, a lower registered capital of RMB 100 million is required (RMB 1 million for the VATs sector). In the VATs sector, according to the latest statistics available from the MIIT, there are currently 19 FITE JVs operating in the VATs sector in China.[61] For example, Microsoft's MSN service has been operating as a JV in China since 2005.[62] This compares with circa 20,000 Chinese VATs licensees.[63] As in many other service sectors in China, the proportion of foreign investment in an FITE must be a maximum of 49% (for fixed and mobile voice and data services) or 50% (for paging services and VATs).[64] According to Voon and Mitchell (2010), approximately half of the FITEs operating in the VATs sector in China have shareholders who are foreign investors based in Hong Kong, which benefits from limited preferential treatment in the VATs sector pursuant to the Closer Economic

---

[60] See Articles 2, 4, 11, 12 Provisions for the Administration of Foreign-Invested Telecommunications Enterprises (Revised), State Council Decree No. 534 (10 September 2008) (hereafter 'FITE' rules). These rules revised the earlier FITE rules circulated by the State Council in December 2001 (and which came into effect January 2002). The Chinese version of the revised FITE rules are at: http://www.edu.cn/20031105/3093883.shtml, accessed November 2010.

[61] MIIT at: http://bzxx.miit.gov.cn:8080/datainfo/miit/miit10063.jsp, accessed November 2010.

[62] Sha, W., and Yu, D., 'Internet Content Provider Licenses in the People's Republic of China's Internet Industry: A Practical Perspective', available at: http://www.ipschool.net/CIIP/files/cht07.pdf, accessed November 2010.

[63] Voon, T., and Mitchell, A., 'Open for Business? China's Telecommunications Service Market and the WTO', *Journal of International Economic Law*, 13(2), 2010, pp. 321–78.

[64] Article 6 FITE Rules.

Partnership Arrangement (CEPA) between the China Mainland and the Hong Kong Special Administrative Region.[65]

Under Chinese law, the main foreign investor in a FITE that provides basic telecommunications services (BTS) must have a permit or license to provide BTS in the country or region in which it is registered.[66] Also, the FITE must have 'the funds and professional personnel suitable for the business activities in keeping with the business activities to be engaged in' and have 'obtained good business results and operational experience in the provision of' BTS.[67] The FITE Rules make clear that similar conditions also apply to the main Chinese investor in a FITE providing basic telecommunication services.[68] Similarly, the main foreign investor in an FITE that provides VATs 'shall have obtained good business results and operational experience in the provision of value-added telecommunications services'.[69] The current FITE Rules and Telecommunications Regulations combined mean that a foreign investor will not be able to incorporate an FITE without having the necessary qualification of being a telecommunications supplier outside of China. Quite often, and because of such difficulties of directly investing in licenses in mainland China, foreign investors have resorted to more indirect means, known as 'CCF' structures to obtain licenses. These CCF structures generally involve three parties: (1) a wholly domestic-owned Chinese party with the necessary licenses and approvals; (2) a foreign-owned Chinese entity effectively controlling the first enterprise through a series of contracts; and (3) the foreign party which owns and controls the second enterprise.[70] 'CCF' structures are not wholly recognized by the state under Chinese law and in fact between 1995 and 1999, several were ordered to be closed by the Chinese government. Nevertheless, a number of FITEs do continue to use CCFs, particularly in the VATs sector. Whether this position will change under

---

65 Voon, T., and Mitchell, A., 'Open for Business? China's Telecommunications Service Market and the WTO', *Journal of International Economic Law*, 13(2), 2010, pp. 321–378, at p. 343.

66 Article 9(2) FITE.

67 Articles 9(3) and (4) FITE Rules.

68 Article 8(3) FITE Rules. The rules define the 'main Chinese investor' as an 'investor who makes the largest capital contribution among all the Chinese investors and whose capital contribution accounts for more than 30 percent of the total of the capital contributions of all the Chinese investors'.

69 Article 10 FITE Rules.

70 Aldrich, M. and Fernandez, G., *The International Comparative Legal Guide to Telecommunications Laws and Regulations* 2010, Chapter 13 (China), Global Legal Group, 2010, p. 90.

the new draft telecoms law currently going through the State Council remains to be seen.

15.6. APPLICABLE COMPETITION LAW IN TELECOMMUNICATIONS

Unlike the rules established in the EC new regulatory framework for electronic network services to regulate the behavior of undertakings with Significant Market Power (dominance) under the EC's Framework Directive,[71] and which look to defining dominance by reference to a relevant market (as established by a Recommendation on relevant markets),[72] at present, China has no telecoms specific dominance legislation, but it does have the Anti Monopoly Law 2008, which came into effect on 1 August 2008.[73] As Chapter 11 describes, on 24 May 2009, the Anti Monopoly Committee of the State Council released the Guidelines on Delineation of Relevant Markets ('relevant market guidelines'), which adds to the provisions of the AML and increases both the transparency of the methodology and technical analysis adopted by the enforcement authorities in antitrust procedure. Similar to mature antitrust jurisdictions, the Guidelines in China provide that the definition of relevant markets includes the relevant product and relevant geographic markets plus a rarely used concept of 'relevant technology market'. Also included is the concept of time. Article 12 AML defines a relevant market as:

> . . . the range of the commodities for which, and the regions where, undertakings compete each other during a given period of time for specific commodities or services (hereinafter referred to, in general, as 'commodities').

Under the 2009 relevant market guidelines, the analysis of demand-side substitutability and/or supply-side substitutability paves the basis for delineating a relevant market, while the well-known SSNIP test (small

---

71 Directive 2002/21/EC.

72 Commission Recommendation on relevant product and service markets within the electronic communications sector susceptible to ex ante regulation in accordance with Directive 2002/21/EC of the European Parliament and of the Council on a common regulatory framework for electronic communications networks and services, 2007/879/EC, 17 December 2007. The recommendation sets out seven services (including wholesale broadband access) that are susceptible to SMP regulation in the Annex to the Recommendation.

73 30 August 2007 of the Tenth National People's Congress Standing Commission. The AML is discussed in more detail in Chapters 11 and 12.

but significant and non-transitory increase in price)[74] is also introduced as the most common tool when the scope of a market where undertakings compete with each other is not clear or easy to define. The Guidelines provide a whole chapter explaining the methodology of the SSNIP test, illustrating little difference in the operation of the test as compared with its use in Europe or the United States. In addition, after a period of consultation, in April 2009, the Anti Monopoly and Anti Unfair Competition Bureau of SAIC published on its website three draft rules relating to the AML on Monopoly Agreements, Dominance, and Administrative Monopolies. In May 2010, the SAIC released revised draft versions (for comment) of these three rules.[75] The Public consultation ended in June 2010 and SAIC then published final versions of the rules in January 2011 with the rules coming into effect on 1 February 2011. The Dominance Rules are likely to have the most significant impact on the telecoms sector in that they outline rules prohibiting bundling,[76] and discrimination,[77] common antitrust complaints in vertically integrated markets such as converged broadcasting and telecommunications. Under Article 17 (Chapter III) AML, a 'dominant market position' is defined as:

> a market position held by undertakings that are capable of controlling the prices or quantities of commodities or other transaction terms in a relevant market, or preventing or exerting an influence on the access of other undertakings to the market.

This definition is very similar to the concept of SMP as set out in the EC's Framework Directive at Article 14(2), and which defines SMP as:

---

74 The SSNIP test was first deployed by the US Department of Justice and the Federal Trade Commission under the Horizontal Merger Guidelines of the United States (issued in 1992 and revised in 1997) when analysing horizontal mergers. The SSNIP test is not used in the US for the purpose of market definition in cartel and monopolization cases under ss 1 and 2 of Sherman Act 1890.

75 Relevant Provisions on the Prohibition of Abuse of a Dominant Position (2010) (hereafter 'Draft Dominance Rules'). The 2010 revised Draft Dominance Rules (Chinese) are available from the SAIC site at: http://www.saic.gov.cn/zwgk/zyfb/qt/fld/201005/t20100525_85718.html, accessed November 2010. An English version has been published by Baker & McKenzie at: http://www.bakermckenzie.com/files/Uploads/Documents/Asia%20Pacific/EyeOnChinaSession3/mm_eyeonchinasession3_relevantprovisionsdominantmarketposition.pdf, accessed November 2010. The final (2011) rules can be accessed on the SAIC website at: http://www.saic.gov.cn/zwgk/zyfb/zjl/fld/201101/t20110104_103266.html.

76 Article 6 Dominance Rules 2010 (coming into effect 1 February 2011).

77 Article 7 Dominance Rules 2010 (coming into effect 1 February 2011).

> An undertaking shall be deemed to have significant market power if, either individually or jointly with others, it enjoys a position equivalent to dominance, that is to say a position of economic strength affording it the power to behave to an appreciable extent independently of competitors, customers and ultimately consumers.

The AML definition does not provide for joint dominance, but does state in the interpretive guidelines to the AML (the 'Explanation')[78] that the term 'dominant market position' means an enterprise or group of enterprises being in a position to affect competition. Article 18 AML lists the factors for the identification of a dominant market position, which include the market share of the operator concerned; the operator's ability to control the sales market; the operator's financial ability and technical resources etc. Under Article 19 AML, an operator with a market share in excess of 50% can be presumed to have a dominant position, and joint dominance is assumed if two operators' market shares total at least 66% of the relevant market, and for three operators, at least 75% of the relevant market is the measure of dominance. This position remains unchanged by the 2010 Dominance Rules (the 2009 version of these rules did set out a different test for market share than that established in the AML, but this seems to have been dropped in the 2010 final version). The Telecommunications Regulations 2000 do not set out any specific tests for dominance, but they do allow under Article 18 Telecoms Regulations for Leading Telecommunications Business Operators (LTOs) to provide for interconnection rules that provide for procedure and time limits for network interconnection and a list of unbundled network elements in accordance with the principles of non-discrimination. This would compare, for example, with the imposition of various obligations on operators with SMP under the European Commission's Article 8(2) Framework Directive, which can include transparency, non-discrimination and accounting separation obligations for example.[79] Under Article 17 Chinese Telecoms Regulations, an LTO is defined as:

> Operators that control vital telecommunications infrastructure, have relatively large share of the telecommunications market and can materially influence the

---

[78] See Explanation of the Articles, Legislative Reasons, and Relevant Regulations of the Anti Monopoly Law, People's Republic of China (Chinese), Peking University Press, September 2007 at: http://product.dangdang.com/product.aspx?product_id=20024796, accessed November 2010.

[79] Articles 9, 10, 11 respectively Directive on Access to, and Interconnection of, Electronic Communications Networks and Associated Facilities, 2002/19/EC, 7 March 2002.

entry of other telecommunications business operators into the telecommunications business market.

It is clear therefore that the concept of defining an LTO requires the satisfaction of three elements: (1) that the operator has control of vital telecommunications infrastructure (this is not defined in the Telecoms Regulations, but presumably would mean infrastructure that would not be economic to duplicate, for example similar to the concept of an 'essential facility' in conventional antitrust terminology); and (2) that the operator has a large share of the relevant market (again this is not defined in the Telecoms Regulations, but the regulations do have a corresponding annex which lists the regulated services); and (3) the ability to materially influence other operators entering the market. The relevant authority for determining an LTO for the purposes of the Telecoms Regulations is the MIIT. However, under the AML, it is the SAIC that has the responsibility for determining abuse of a dominant position (other than for price monopolies).[80] There is a divergence therefore between the concept of an LTO as set out in the Telecoms Regulations and dominance as established by the AML. Presumably, the New Draft Telecoms Law, currently with the State Council, will address this issue.

15.7. CONCLUSION

It is clear from the discussion above that the regulation of telecommunications in China is a complex matter. A raft of rules, measures and regulations govern the sector and the position has been made more complex with the advent of the AML and the various notices and draft rules that help illustrate the workings of the AML. Nevertheless, China has done a remarkable job in a short space of time in developing a regulatory framework that is quickly adapting itself to a converged network environment. Clear challenges remain to integrate the concept of relevant market power and dominance under the AML with that of the Telecommunications Regulations, and perhaps this will be achieved by the draft New Telecommunications Law (it is rumored that this may be called the Communications Law – again a reflection of the convergence of broadcasting, telecommunications

80 Article 9 Dominance Rules 2010.

and the internet – when finally approved by the State Council and subsequently the National People's Congress).[81]

It is difficult to comment on the draft new Telecoms Law given that the version published at the time of writing is likely to change as it passes through the State Council and NPC.[82] One major concern perhaps with the new draft law remains the multiple regulators likely to have oversight of the sector, including the MIIT, SAIC, MOFCOM etc. In a review of the draft law by the US Telecommunications Industry Association and US Information Technology Office (USITO) and Information Technology Industry Council ('US Comments'),[83] the concern with overlapping regulators was highlighted, and also whether existing media regulators, such as the State Administration of Radio, Film and Television and SAIC, should continue to have oversight of new converged media services, or whether instead an independent regulator responsible for the converged services of telecoms, broadcasting and internet should be established (similar perhaps to OFCOM in the UK).[84] Further concerns are raised with regard to potential restrictions on the entry by telecom operators into the broadcasting sector. As we saw in Section 15.4 (regulating internet infrastructure) above, under both Decrees No. 39 and 56, in order to provide Mobile TV or IPTV services in China, both a telecommunications Internet Content Provider (ICP) License[85] and a License for Information Network Communication Audio-Visual Programme (INCAVP License)[86] are required. This involves a collaboration between telecom and broadcast TV operators.

At the time of writing, the New Draft Law provides for charge rates to be set by telecommunication operators directly, other than for basic

---

[81] See 'Rumour: Telecom Law to Take Effect from 2011', at: http://www.capitalvue.com/home/CE-news/inset/%4010063/post/1190391, accessed November 2010.

[82] See Unofficial Translation of the People's Republic of China draft Telecommunications Law (draft to solicit comments), available at: http://china.usc.edu/App_Images//Unofficial_Translation_China_Draft_Telecommunications_Law.pdf, accessed November 2010 ('New draft Telecoms Law').

[83] 'US Comments', available at: http://www.tiaonline.org/gov_affairs/fcc_filings/documents/comments_on_china%20_telecom_law_final.pdf, accessed November 2010.

[84] See comments under Articles 2 and 3 US Comments.

[85] Article 19 Decree No. 56 provides, 'Internet A/V[audiovisual] program service providers shall choose network operations work units that have a lawfully-obtained internet access services telecommunications management license or a radio/television programming transmission management license . . .'.

[86] Article 7 Decree No. 56.

telecommunication services that do not enjoy 'enough' market competition or that have close interests with telecommunications users, where the 'competent telecommunications department' jointly with the pricing department of the State Council shall set charges. It is not clear from the New Draft Law what the 'competent telecommunications department' is, but it does signal (perhaps) that the role of the MIIT as regulator will be made more arm's length from that of the State Council.[87]

Further concerns remain, such as: the foreign equity cap of 49%;[88] the requirement to preregister for prior approval of VATs services[89] and international telecommunication gateways with the MIIT;[90] the need to establish a dedicated right of access to a network that is distinct from the right of interconnection;[91] expanding the definition of 'Universal Service' to include 'Chinese citizens, Chinese legal persons, foreign legal persons and foreign individuals who have a legal operation in China';[92] and perhaps the mandatory obligation to share in the construction and use of facilities.[93] Despite these concerns with the draft new Telecoms Law, there

---

[87] Xiaoguang, Z., *China's Telecommunications Law in the Future*, Department of Industry, Transport and Commerce, State Council (LAO), October 2009.

[88] Article 9 New Draft Telecoms Law.

[89] Article 8 New Draft Telecoms Law.

[90] Article 15 New Draft Telecoms Law. Although one would expect that in most jurisdictions, an international facilities exchange that is likely either to be connected to a cable landing station or an uplink/downlink satellite earth station would require to be licensed and therefore require prior approval of the relevant state hosting the facility.

[91] See Articles 18, 19, 20 and 49 New Draft Telecoms Law, which set out interconnection rights (for all operators), but no specific access obligations. Also the interconnection obligations would indicate that both Leading Telecommunication Operators (equivalent perhaps to those who are 'major suppliers' under the WTO's regulatory reference paper) and new entrants are obliged to offer interconnection.

[92] See comments under Article 38 US Comments. The current version of Article 38 in the draft New Telecoms Law reads: 'Universal telecommunication service refers to the provision of basic telecommunication services complying with State regulations to all citizens in the People's Republic of China at a universally affordable rate'. By contrast, Recital 2 of the European Commission's Universal Services Directive 2002/22/EC defines universal service as: '. . . the provision of a defined minimum set of services to all end-users at an affordable price'.

[93] Article 59 draft New Telecoms Law, although similar provisions for mandatory sharing of facilities have recently been introduced by the European Commission in the Better Regulation Directive 2009/140/EC, where at Recital 43 it states: '. . . National regulatory authorities should in particular be able to impose the sharing of network elements and associated facilities, such as ducts, conduits, masts, manholes, cabinets, antennae, towers and other supporting constructions, buildings or entries into buildings, and a better coordination of civil works . . .'.

is no doubt that the Chinese government has come a remarkably long way in such a short period of time in creating a regulatory framework for converged services in China. More remains to be done and given the pace of new laws and measures passing through the State Council, we can expect much more in this area in the near future.

Index